T0207466

Lecture Notes in Computer Science 13041

More information about this subseries at https://link.springer.com/bookseries/7410

Min Yang · Chao Chen · Yang Liu (Eds.)

Network and System Security

15th International Conference, NSS 2021
Tianjin, China, October 23, 2021
Proceedings

 Springer

Editors
Min Yang
Fudan University
Shanghai, China

Yang Liu
Nanyang Technological University
Singapore, Singapore

Chao Chen
James Cook University
Townsville, QLD, Australia

ISSN 0302-9743   ISSN 1611-3349 (electronic)
Lecture Notes in Computer Science
ISBN 978-3-030-92707-3   ISBN 978-3-030-92708-0 (eBook)
https://doi.org/10.1007/978-3-030-92708-0

LNCS Sublibrary: SL4 – Security and Cryptology

Preface

This volume contains the papers selected for and presented at the 15th International Conference on Network and System Security (NSS 2021) held in Tianjin, China, on October 23, 2021.

The mission of NSS is to provide a forum for presenting novel contributions related to all theoretical and practical aspects related to network and system security, such as authentication, access control, availability, integrity, privacy, confidentiality, dependability, and sustainability of computer networks and systems. NSS provides a leading-edge forum to foster interaction between researchers and developers with the network and system security communities, and gives attendees an opportunity to interact with experts in academia, industry, and government.

There were 62 submissions for NSS 2021. Each submission was reviewed by at least 3, and on average 4.2, Program Committee members. The evaluation process was based on significance, novelty, and technical quality of the submissions. After a rigorous review process and thorough discussion of each submission, the Program Committee selected 16 full papers and 8 short papers to be presented during NSS 2021 and published in the LNCS volume 13041 proceedings. The submission and review processes were conducted using the EasyChair system.

The selected papers are devoted to topics such as secure operating system architectures, applications programming and security testing, intrusion and attack detection, cybersecurity intelligence, access control, cryptographic techniques, cryptocurrencies, ransomware, anonymity, trust, and recommendation systems, as well machine learning problems.

In addition to the contributed papers, NSS 2021 included invited keynote talks by Kui Ren and Yingying Chen.

We would like to thank our general chairs Keqiu Li, Elisa Bertino, and Mauro Conti; our publication chair Yu Wang; the local chair Xinyu Tong; our publicity co-chairs Guangquan Xu, Kaitai Liang, and Chunhua Su; our special issues co-chairs Weizhi Meng and Ding Wang; the local organization team; and all the Program Committee members for their support to this conference. Despite the disruptions brought by COVID-19, NSS 2021 was a great success. We owe this success to all our organization committee.

Finally, we also thank Tianjin University for their full support in organizing NSS 2021.

October 2021

Min Yang
Chao Chen
Yang Liu

Organization

General Co-chairs

Keqiu Li — Tianjin University, China
Elisa Bertino — Purdue University, USA
Mauro Conti — University of Padua, Italy

Program Co-chairs

Min Yang — Fudan University, China
Chao Chen — James Cook University, Australia
Yang Liu — Nanyang Technological University, Singapore

Publication Chair

Yu Wang — Guangzhou University, China

Local Chair

Xinyu Tong — Tianjin University, China

Publicity Co-chairs

Guangquan Xu — Tianjin University, China
Kaitai Liang — Delft University of Technology, The Netherlands
Chunhua Su — University of Aizu, Japan

Special Issues Co-chairs

Weizhi Meng — Technical University of Denmark, Denmark
Ding Wang — Nankai University, China

Registration Chair

Xiaojuan Liu — Tianjin University, China

Web Chair

Xiao Chen — Monash University, Australia

Program Committee

Arcangelo Castiglione	University of Salerno, Italy
Chaokun Zhang	Tianjin University, China
Chih Hung Wang	National Chiayi University, Taiwan, China
Chunhua Su	Osaka University, Japan
Chunpeng Ge	Nanjing University of Aeronautics and Astronautics, China
Cristina Alcaraz	University of Malaga, Spain
Daniele Antonioli	EURECOM, France
Ding Wang	Peking University, China
Fei Chen	Shenzhen University, China
Günther Pernul	Universität Regensburg, Germany
Guomin Yang	University of Wollongong, Australia
Haibo Zhang	University of Otago, New Zealand
Haisheng Yu	University of Electronic Science and Technology of China, China
Hongxin Hu	University at Buffalo, SUNY, USA
Hung-Min Sun	National Tsing Hua University, Taiwan, China
Hung-Yu Chien	National Chi Nan University, Taiwan, China
Jianfeng Wang	Xidian University, China
Jiangshan Yu	Monash University, Australia
Joonsang Baek	University of Wollongong, Australia
Jose Morales	Carnegie Mellon University, USA
Jun Shao	Zhejiang Gongshang University, China
Kaitai Liang	Delft University of Technology, The Netherlands
Kun Sun	George Mason University, USA
Kuo-Hui Yeh	National Dong Hwa University, Taiwan, China
Luca Caviglione	CNR-IMATI, Italy
Man Ho Au	University of Hong Kong, China
Mauro Conti	University of Padua, Italy
Mingwu Zhang	Hubei University of Technology, China
Minhui Xue	University of Adelaide, Australia
Pino Caballero-Gil	University of La Laguna, Spain
Qi Wang	University of Illinois at Urbana-Champaign, USA
Qianhong Wu	Beihang University, China
Ram Krishnan	University of Texas at San Antonio, USA
Ren Junn Hwang	Tamkang University, Taiwan, China
Rida Bazzi	Arizona State University, USA
Roberto Di Pietro	Hamad Bin Khalifa University, Qatar
Rongxing Lu	University of New Brunswick, Canada
Ruben Rios	University of Malaga, Spain
Shan Qu	Shanghai Jiao Tong University, China
Sheng Chen	Tianjin University, China
Shengli Liu	Shanghai Jiao Tong University, China
Shi-Feng Sun	Monash University, Australia
Shigang Liu	Swinburne University of Technology, Australia

Contents

An Architecture for Processing a Dynamic Heterogeneous Information
Network of Security Intelligence   185
    Marios Anagnostopoulos, Egon Kidmose, Amine Laghaout,
    Rasmus L. Olsen, Sajad Homayoun, Christian D. Jensen,
    and Jens M. Pedersen

The Complexity of Testing Cryptographic Devices on Input Faults   202
    Alisher Ikramov and Gayrat Juraev

A Malware Family Classification Method Based on the Point Cloud Model
DGCNN   210
    Yuxin Ding, Zihan Zhou, and Wen Qian

Collection of the Main Anti-Virus Detection and Bypass Techniques   222
    Jérémy Donadio, Guillaume Guerard, and Soufian Ben Amor

Profiled Attacks Against the Elliptic Curve Scalar Point Multiplication
Using Neural Networks   238
    Alessandro Barenghi, Diego Carrera, Silvia Mella, Andrea Pace,
    Gerardo Pelosi, and Ruggero Susella

Deep Cross-Modal Supervised Hashing Based on Joint Semantic Matrix   258
    Na Chen, Yuan Cao, and Chao Liu

Short Papers

Accurate Polar Harmonic Transform-Based Watermarking Using Blind
Statistical Detector   277
    Yu Sang, Yilin Bei, Zhiyang Yang, and Chen Zhao

Cloud Key Management Based on Verifiable Secret Sharing   289
    Mustapha Hedabou

A Scheme for Sensor Data Reconstruction in Smart Home   304
    Yegang Du

Privacy-Preserving and Auditable Federated Deep Reinforcement
Learning for Robotic Manipulation   314
    Xudong Zhu and Hui Li

HALNet: A Hybrid Deep Learning Model for Encrypted C&C Malware
Traffic Detection   326
    Ruiyuan Li, Zehui Song, Wei Xie, Chengwei Zhang, Guohui Zhong,
    and Xiaobing Pei

Full Papers

RLTree: Website Fingerprinting Through Resource Loading Tree

Changzhi Li[1,2], Lihai Nie[2], and Laiping Zhao[2(✉)]

[1] State Key Laboratory of Communication Content Cognition,
College of Intelligence and Computing (CIC), Tianjin University, Tianjin, China
kidultff@tju.edu.cn
[2] Tianjin Key Laboratory of Advanced Networking (TANKLab),
College of Intelligence & Computing (CIC), Tianjin University, Tianjin, China
{nlh3392,laiping}@tju.edu.cn

Abstract. Website fingerprinting (WF) attack is a type of traffic analysis technique that extracts the unique fingerprint from the traffic of each website demonstrating that the current privacy protection mechanism provided by HTTPS is still fragile. While prior WF attack methods that extract fingerprints only using the web traffic generated by the first TCP session can be easily compromised by the frequent website updates, we observe that it is still possible to identify a website accurately through fingerprinting the resource loading sequence generated by the multiple initial TCP sessions. We record the multiple TCP sessions by visiting a website and analyze its traffic structure. We find that despite the update of the website, the TCP establishment is always kept unchanged, and such TCP sequence can be used to fingerprint a website. Hence, we build a resource loading tree using the multiple TCP sessions and demonstrates its high precision in recognizing a website even under HTTPS protection. We collect data from 20 websites with a total of 7,326 traces, and show that the accuracy can achieve up to 95.9%.

Keywords: Website fingerprinting attack · Privacy and confidentiality · Traffic analysis.

1 Introduction

In order to defend against network sniff, HTTPS encrypts the network payload using Transport Layer Security (TLS) protocol. While TLS can protect the payload content, information like packet size, direction, timing can still be obtained easily. Website fingerprinting(WF) attacks enable a local and passive adversary to sniff the user's network behavior and identify the browsing activities using traffic analysis technique [12]. Typically, WF attacks collect the network traffic of the target websites and construct fingerprints for them. Here a fingerprint refers to an abstract of the corresponding network trace and is commonly extracted using substantial feature engineering [17]. Given a segment of traffic trace, the

© Springer Nature Switzerland AG 2021
M. Yang et al. (Eds.): NSS 2021, LNCS 13041, pp. 3–16, 2021.
https://doi.org/10.1007/978-3-030-92708-0_1

adversary can identify which website this is by measuring the similarity between the observed traffic and previously-stored fingerprints.

Website and webpage fingerprinting have been studied extensively [10]. Most existing solutions [17,18,21] extract fingerprint from the first TCP session traces for downloading a HTML webpage, and find the match from the fingerprint repository. We find that these WF attack methods are not robust, and they can be easily compromised through updating the webpage content.

We analyze the browsers' behaviors and find that the robustness of WF attacks can be improved through fingerprinting the multiple TCP connections established by the browser when visiting a webpage. Part of these connections are organized in a pre-defined dependence order, while the rest are established concurrently. Moreover, each session corresponds to a static resource (e.g., image) of the webpage. Despite most websites are updated frequently, their static resource like font files and images stay stable across updates. Thus it is a promising way to utilize the resource-based multiple flows to fingerprint a website robustly.

Therefore, we propose a novel WF attack, named *RLTree*, which can construct robust fingerprints for websites using the multiple TCP sessions established by the browser. Different from previous WF attacks, *RLTree* uses multiple flow-based features as fingerprints. Each node in the tree represents a TCP session (the TLS payload length sequence), and the sequence of TCP connections represents the tree structure. Since the multiple flow-based solution is easily affected by the background noise flows, we further design a greedy matching algorithm to filter the noises.

1.1   Related Work

In the early days, most of WF attack methods extract features from network traffic such as time and length, then employs classification methods [9,14,15,20] to identify which website belongs to. such as use cosine similarity [20], multinomial naive-bayes classifier [14], SVM [15] and FFT [9] to identify Tor websites. In recent years, *Jamie* and *George* [13] use some statistical features from the website traffic and use random forest to generate fingerprints. *Shen et al.* [17] use only packet length information to implement webpage fingerprinting. *Zhang et al.* [21] takes advantage of the priority of the browser to load resources and regards the order of data packets as an important feature, and use LRRS for WF attack. *Shen et al.* [18] proposed to use packet length accumulation to implement webpage fingerprinting attack. Some studies [19] focuses on DApps such as use GNN to identify DApps. *Dong et al.* [11] proposes the use of multiple TCP session for network flow analysis.

Tor network is a highly anonymized network, and there is no available plain text information, and the previous TLS 1.2 protocol used by HTTPS contains some plain text information such as website domain names, even using DPI can identify a website, which causes the Tor network WF attacks are more challenging than ordinary HTTPS WF attacks. However, in the lastest version of TLS, which is no available plain text information in its traffic, HTTPS WF attacks become very challenging. At present, most of the existing schemes are based on a single TCP session when accessing a webpage, which results in a WF attack with low accuracy and poor robustness. This article aims to solve this problem.

1.2 Contributions

We have verified through experiments that the single flow-based methods have low accuracy after the website content is updated, while the multiple flow-based scheme has high robustness and does not have this problem. We propose a resource loading tree-based WF method called RLTree and proposed a similarity measurement algorithm of RLTree. The main contributions of this paper are as follows:

1. We observe the multiple stable TCP connections in browsers when a webpage is loaded. We find that the resource loading sequence can help to improve the website fingerprinting robustness.
2. We propose a novel tree-based fingerprinting method to characterize the TCP connection trace during visiting a website. The website can be recognized easily through a similarity measure. We also propose a matrix data structure for storing fingerprint efficiently.
3. We collect the real traces by accessing the top websites during one-month and conduct extensive experiments over the collected traces. The evaluation results demonstrate that the accuracy of the our attack achieves up to 95.9%.

2   Preliminary

2.1   Encryption Protocols

HTTPS is a secure HTTP channel that uses SSL/TLS encryption protocol. It can encrypt the payload transmitted between clients and servers. A host that wants to establish a TLS connection needs to perform a TLS handshake first. During the handshake phase, the key and encryption parameters are negotiated. Server Name Indication (SNI) is an extension filed of TLS, which locates in the *Client Hello* packet transmit during the TLS handshake. It contains the domain name information of the website to visit. In versions before TLS 1.3, SNI is usually transmit in plain text. In this way, an attacker can quickly know which website the user has visited by parse the Client Hello packets. TLS 1.3 [6] provides both SNI and ESNI extensions. ESNI can encrypt SNI, and its principle is to use the DNS TXT record of the domain name to store the public key to encrypt the SNI. As a result, the attacker cannot get the website that the user visits from the traffic directly. Encrypt Client Hello (ECH) is the latest technology which makes up for the limitation that ESNI can only encrypt SNI. It encrypts the entire Client Hello packet to protects user privacy. Nowadays, most servers and clients are still using the compatible TLS 1.2 for communication since TLS 1.3 is still in the promotion period.

Traditional DNS transmits requests and responses in plain text via UDP, attackers can infer the websites that users is visiting from DNS information. While DoH transmits DNS data via HTTPS, making DNS information invisible.

Firefox Nightly, released in October 2018, begins to support ESNI. In February 2020, Mozilla enabled DoH by default for Firefox users in the United States. In Firefox 85, which released in January 2021, ECH was added to replace ESNI [5]. In October 2019, Google added DoH as an experimental feature in the newly released Chrome 78. In June 2020, Chrome 83 will make DoH an official feature [2].

2.2   Threat Model

We assume that there is an adversary that can passively observe the victim's traffic, including the victim's incoming and outgoing traffic. Passiveness means that encrypted traffic will not be decrypted and modified. Assume that the victim's browser has protected SNI through ESNI or ECH, and DoH is enabled to protect DNS queries from being discovered by the adversary. All monitored websites use HTTPS protocol. The adversary has a regularly updated fingerprint repository for similarity measurement with monitored traffic. A potential adversary can be an Internet Service Provider (ISP), a corporate network administrator or other hosts in the LAN without arp spoofing protection.

The attacker maintains a fingerprint repository containing all monitored websites. Fingerprints and corresponding website tags are stored in the fingerprint repository. The fingerprints are generated by the attacker actively visiting the website and using a certain fingerprinting method. For monitored user traffic, use the same method to generate traffic fingerprints and compare them with fingerprints in the fingerprint repository. If there are fingerprints with high similarity, it is considered that the user has visited the corresponding website (Fig. 1).

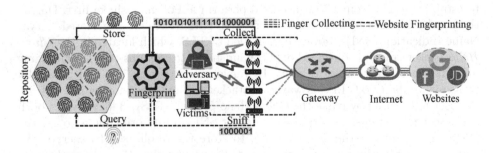

Fig. 1. Threat model

3   Motivation

3.1   Observation

Existing WF attacks commonly assume only one session is built when visiting the target website and thus utilize single flow-based feature to fingerprint the website. However, we observe that there are multiple related sessions while accessing only a webpage. Taking *Chrome* as an example, it develops a sophisticated algorithm [3] to assign priorities for different resources, like images and font files, and build individual sessions for loading each resource.

The browser downloads each resource by establishing a TCP connection. After the browser downloads a file, it will parse the file. If there are other reference files, they will be loaded according to the priority assigning algorithm. Resources with the same priority are loaded in the concurrent TCP connections, while resources with high priority are downloaded prior to the resources with low priority.

Based on the observation above, a tree can be used to represent the resource referencing structure of a webpage, where each node represents a TCP session, the depth indicates the priority of resource downloading. Since various webpages hold different resource referencing structures, then tree presenting file structures can be consider as the identification (fingerprinting) of a webpage (Fig. 2).

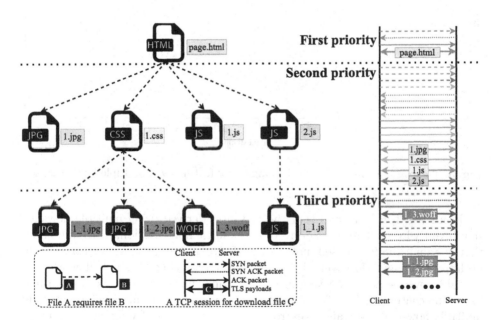

Fig. 2. The orders of requesting files and corresponding TCP sessions when loading a webpage.

3.2   Limitation of Existing Methods

Moreover, we observe their performances are highly sensitive to the contents of webpages. This greatly limits their practicality since the modern webpages constantly evolve and frequently update, e.g., *Sina News* updates the contents of homepage every 20 min on average.

We evaluate the robustness of the single flow-based WF solutions as follows. First, we collect the initial trace of visiting *Sina News* at the beginning time (6 p.m. on September 20, 2021). Subsequently, we continually collect a number of testing traces by visiting the identical website at a three-minute interval. Finally, we extract the TLS payload size as a feature vector and compute the distances between the initial and subsequent traces, where the small distance implies robust performance and vice versa. Moreover, we achieve an multiple flow-based distance computation solution under the same setting above. The performance of single flow-based and multiple flow-based solution are presented in Fig. 3.

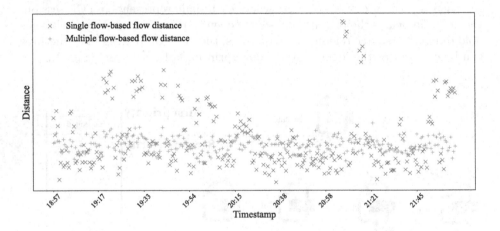

Fig. 3. Webpage distances derived by single flow features v.s. multiple flow features.

From Fig. 3, we can find that the distances derived using multiple flows are significantly lower than those derived by the single flow solution, which illustrates that the multiple flow-based method can derive a more accurate measure of the updated webpage. Moreover, the distances derived using the single flow are very unstable over time, while the ones of multiple flows are considerably stable. Since the content of *Sina News* is updated frequently, we can conclude that the multiple flow-based distances are robust to the variance of webpage content.

The reason accounting for the unstable performance of single flow-based distance measurements is presented as follows. When the contents of the webpage update, the first TCP session will changes. Then the single flow-based distances become larger. On the contrary, the static resources such as font file include by website hardly change. Therefore, the multi flow-based solution is more stable and can solve the problem of limitation of existing methods.

4   Resource Loading Tree-Base Website Fingerprint

This section proposes a novel and accurate WF attack scheme, which uses the Resource Loading tree (RLT) to represent a website. In Sect. 4.1, we describe and define the concurrent TCP flows when loading the resources of the identical priority. Section 4.2 presents the process of extracting features from multiple flows. We construct the RLTree structure based the extracted features in Sect. 4.3 measure the similarity between different RLTrees in Sect. 4.4.

4.1   Concurrent Connection Identification

According to RFC 793 [16], a TCP session is built using a three-way handshake mechanism, specifically client sends an SYN packet, receives an SYN+ACK packet, and sending an ACK packet sequentially. When a client wants to create concurrent TCP connections, it sends multiple SYN packets simultaneously. Ideally, the first packets (i.e., SYN packet) of concurrent TCP connections are successive. However, this commonly does not hold due to the influence of background traffic and network delay. To this end, we identify the TCP sessions, whose handshaking time overlays, as concurrent TCP connections. We describe the process of identifying concurrent TCP sessions as follows.

Given a sequence of monitored TCP packets $p_1, p_2, \cdots, p_n$, we firstly aggregate them into sessions $s_1, s_2, ...s_m$ by the four-tuple information (source IP, source port, destination IP, destination port). Denote $t_{start}^{s_k}$ and $t_{end}^{s_k}$ by the starting handshaking time and the ending handshaking time of session s_k, where $k \in [1, 2, \cdots, m]$. Then we say $s_{k'}$ and s_k are concurrent sessions once $t_{start}^{s_k} < t_{start}^{s_{k'}} < t_{start}^{s_k}$ or $t_{start}^{s_k'} < t_{start}^{s_k} < t_{start}^{s_{k'}}$. Moreover, we illustrate the three concurrent TCP sessions in Fig. 4.

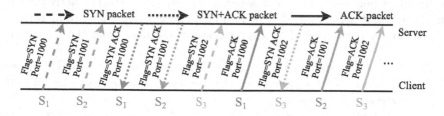

Fig. 4. Illustration of Concurrent TCP Parallel Connections: sessions S_1, S_2 and S_3 are established concurrently.

4.2   Feature Selection

Since we focus on encrypted WF attack, there only three types of features available: payload length, packet time and packet direction. We doesn't adopt the time feature because the TCP time interval are easily impacted by network condition. Then we use the directional payload length of the TLS application data as our feature. For session s with N packets, the feature of s is $[l_1, l_2, ...l_N]$, where $|l_i|$ is the length of the i-th application data in the TLS session. We define l_i is negative if it is a uploading packet and l_i is positive if it is downloading packet.

4.3   RLTree Construction

Given a sequence of TCP sessions, we categorize the concurrent sessions into a group and sort the sessions in the order of their beginning time. Moreover, the groups are sorted in the order of their first sessions' starting times. We construct RLTree as follows. We consider each session as a node and connect nodes of a group sequentially. Then each group is connected in the order of their beginning times.

In order to facilitate storage, we use a matrix to store the RLTree. Each row of the matrix represents a node of the tree. The first variable of a row is level representing the depth of current node, and the other variable is the features vector. When a new concurrent TCP connections is observed, we let level plus one and store the level and directional TLS payload length sequence in the matrix. In particular, we present four examples of webpage fingerprints in Fig. 5 and show the details of the algorithm in Algorithm 1.

4.4   Similarity Measurement

To measure the distance between two RLTree, we propose a tree similarity measurement as follows. For the convenience of computing, we unify the feature vector of session into the identical length k. When using multiple TCP sessions to extract features, a key problem is to remove the impact of background traffic. Specifically, when users browse a webpage, there may be other activities that visit the Internet services or download a file. Therefore, we need to identify the TCP session of requesting the target website's resources from the background traffic.

We use a greedy strategy to derive the distance between two RLTree T_1 and T_2. For each node n in T_2, we compute the its distances from the all nodes of T_1 and identify the node of the minimal distance as its matched node. It is noticeable that there is chance that two nodes of T_2 are matched with the one nodes of T_2. In this case, we match the node in T_2 with a sub-optimal node in T_1.

After matching the session, calculate the distances of all matching sessions, and sum them up, the result is the distance of T_1 and T_2.

Algorithm 1. RLTree Construction

Input: A series of packet $P = (p_1, p_2, ... p_N)$ resulting from a webpage loading process, The TLS payload length sequence dictionary contained in these packets $L = (l_1, l_2, ... l_N)$

Output: Webpage traffic tree T

1: Let $S = \emptyset, T = \emptyset, level = 0, last$
2: **for** all p $\in$ P **do**
3:    k $\leftarrow$ (p.src_ip+p.src_port+p.dst_ip+p.dst_port)
4:    **if** SYN $\in$ p.tcp_flag && $S_k = \emptyset$ **then**
5:       $S_k \leftarrow$ "establishing"
6:       last $\leftarrow$ k
7:    **else**
8:       **if** $S_k!=$"connected" **then**
9:          **if** $S_{last}=$"connected" **then**
10:             level+=1
11:          **end if**
12:          $S_k \leftarrow$ "connected"
13:          Append (level+L[key]) to T
14:       **end if**
15:    **end if**
16: **end for**
17: **return** T

---

level	TLS payload length							
1	-36	-3462	-281	-69	69	-282	-282	0
2	-36	-3462	-281	-69	69	87	448	-282
2	-36	-3464	-281	-69	69	-306	-306	-57
2	-36	-3464	-281	-69	69	-306	-306	-57
3	-36	-3464	-281	-69	69	-306	-306	-57
4	-36	-3464	-281	-69	69	-306	-306	-57
4	-42	-3462	-281	-69	69	87	427	-282
4	-42	-3462	-281	-69	69	87	366	-282

(a) item.jd.com-1

level	TLS payload length							
1	-36	-3462	-281	-69	69	-282	-282	-57
2	-36	-3462	-281	-69	69	87	448	-282
2	-36	-3464	-281	-69	69	-306	-306	-57
2	-36	-3464	-281	-69	69	-306	-306	-57
3	-36	-3464	-281	-69	69	-306	-306	-57
4	-42	-3462	-281	-69	69	87	427	-282
5	-36	-3464	-281	-69	69	87	558	-306
5	-42	-3464	-281	-69	69	87	366	-282

(b) item.jd.com-2

level	TLS payload length							
1	-42	-3464	-281	-69	69	637	306	-306
2	-42	-3464	-281	-69	69	-306	-306	-282
2	-36	-3464	-281	-69	69	87	448	-282
3	-36	-3464	-281	-69	69	-306	-306	-57
3	-36	-3464	-281	-69	69	-306	-306	-57
3	-94	425	103	104	104	104	103	-57
3	-36	-3464	-281	-69	69	12	3312	-73
4	-94	380	-64	33	-33	-2507	-1648	-1332

(c) www.jd.com-1

level	TLS payload length							
1	-42	-3464	-281	-69	69	637	306	-306
2	-36	-3464	-281	-69	69	87	448	-282
2	-42	-3464	-281	-69	69	-306	-306	-282
3	-36	-3464	-281	-69	69	-306	-306	-57
3	-36	-3464	-281	-69	69	-306	-306	-57
3	-42	-3462	-281	-69	69	12	3312	-73
3	-94	425	103	104	104	103	104	-57
4	-94	380	-64	33	-33	-2511	-1648	-1331

(d) www.jd.com-2

Fig. 5. 4 example of webpage fingerprints, all of this are visit the online mall platform JD.com. Both table A and B are visit a same product detail page, host is item.jd.com, both table C and D are visit the home page, host is www.jd.com. Each TCP session in the table only retains the first 8 sessions, and each session only retains the first 7 features

---

Algorithm 2. Distance of Traffic Tree

Input: 2 RLTrees $T_1 = (t_1, t_2, ...t_N)$ and $T_2 = (s_1, s_2, ...s_N)$. T_1 from repository, T_2 as
    a query fingerprint, both $t_i, s_i = \{position, l_1, l_2, ...l_k\}$
Output: Distance of traffic trees d
 1: Let $S \leftarrow \emptyset$, $S' \leftarrow \emptyset$, $D \leftarrow \emptyset$, $d \leftarrow 0$
 2: **while** $\exists$ session $i \in T_2 \Rightarrow S_{i_{pos}} \in \emptyset$ **do**
 3:     **for all** session $t \in \{x|x \in T_2, S_{x_{pos}} = \emptyset\}$ **do**
 4:         $D \leftarrow \emptyset$
 5:         **for all** $q \in T_1$ **do**
 6:             $D_q \leftarrow \|t[1:k] - q[1:k]\|$
 7:         **end for**
 8:         Sort D in ascending order
 9:         **for all** $q \in D$ **do**
10:             **if** $q \in S$ **then**
11:                 **if** $S'_{q_d} > D_q$ **then**
12:                     $previous \leftarrow S'_{q_p}$
13:                     delete $S_{previous}$
14:                 **else**
15:                     continue
16:                 **end if**
17:             **end if**
18:             $S'_{q_d} \leftarrow D_q$, $S'_{q_p} \leftarrow t$, $S_{t_d} \leftarrow D_q$, $S_{t_d} \leftarrow q$
19:             break
20:         **end for**
21:     **end for**
22: **end while**
23: **for** $i \in S$ **do**
24:     $d += min(100, |S_{i_d}|)$
25: **end for**
26: **return** d

---

5   Performance Evaluation

5.1   Dataset

Most of the datasets used in the previous works are the homepage traffic of the
monitored website. However, user commonly open the content page instead of
the homepage when they visit a website for the first time. Thus we mainly collect
the website content page traffic. We randomly select 20 websites from the Alexa
Top 100 website [1]. We randomly select 3 webpages from each website, finally
we select 60 websites as the monitor list. Selenium [7] is a tool that can directly
run the *Chrome* browser to access the target webpage. We write a script using
selenium to automatically collect traffic.

The dataset is divide into two parts: fingerprint repository and query traffic.
The fingerprint repository requires pure traffic without any background traffic.
When constructing the fingerprint repository, we use a computer which has no
software installed except Python and Chrome, but there is still some background

traffic such as Windows update and Google update. In order to eliminate noise, we removing traces whose IPs do not belong the target websites. Here the IP list can be obtained by resolving the domain names that target website registered through DNS.

In order to collect enough samples, we randomly browse a webpage from the monitor list every hour. When selenium starts Chrome to browse the webpage, the *tshark* [8] begins to capture packets. This computer runs daily applications such as QQ, WeChat, and NetEase Cloud Music to simulate real user scenarios. After a month of capture, a total of 7,326 pcap files were collected.

5.2 Traffic Preprocessing

In order to parse the pcap file, we wrote a script using Joy [4] to extract the fingerprints of the pcap sample one by one, taking $N = 20$ and $k = 10$, The selection of k is presented in Sect. 5.3, that is, each pcap preserves the first 20 sessions, and each session retains the first 10 payloads length as features. Add the level information, and get a 11 * 20 matrix. The same operation is used for all pcaps in the fingerprint repository.

5.3 Evaluation

When matching samples in the fingerprint repository, the distance between the sample and each fingerprint in the repository is derived, the obtained distances are sorted. We match all the captured pcaps with the fingerprints in the corresponding fingerprint repository, and finally get an accuracy of 95.8815%. The confusion matrix is shown in the Fig. 6.

In addition, we do further experiments, extracting only the first 10 payload lengths of the first session as features and constructing fingerprints, and the rest remain unchanged, and repeat the above experiments. The final accuracy drops to 69.8417%, and the confusion matrix is shown in the Fig. 7.

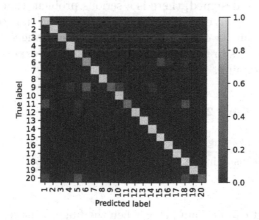

Fig. 6. Confusion matrix of Tree-WF attack

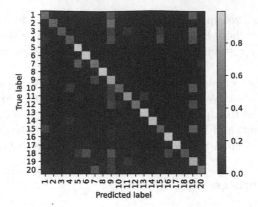

Fig. 7. Confusion matrix of use single TCP session WF attack

It can be seen that the effect of RLTree that uses the feature of multiple TCP sessions is better than that of the WF attack scheme that uses a single session, Tree-WF is more robust than using a single session for WF attack.

We also use different K for experiments, the accuracy are as Table 1. It can be seen that as K increases, the accuracy rate increases. When K is greater than 10, the increase in accuracy becomes small. The reason is that in the webpages we collect, 10 payload sizes are enough to distinguish a TCP session.

Table 1. The effect of different K values on accuracy

k	6	8	10	12	14
Accuracy	94.01%	95.42%	95.88%	95.88%	95.05%

In the scheme we designed, there is a serious problem that when the fingerprint repository is too large, it may cause the processing time of each traffic tree to be long. To this aim, we keep other conditions unchanged, add some fingerprints of other websites in the fingerprint repository, do experiments and record the total time-consuming.

Table 2. Predicting time vs. repository size

Number of fingerprints	300	600	900	1,200	1,500
Time-consuming(s)	22.85	42.56	64.18	85.62	102.83

From Table 2, it can be found that when the fingerprint repository increases, the time it takes to predict a fingerprint increases almost linearly. The reason is that the larger the fingerprint repository, the more similarity measurements are required. Therefore, when using RLTree, the fingerprint repository should not be too large.

6 Conclusion

In this paper, we propose a multiple flow-based and content-free WF attack method, which organizes the multiple flows as a *RLTree*. We consider the *RLTree* as the fingerprint of the visited website and propose a similarity measurement algorithm to recognize its real identity. Our evaluations show that *RLTree* achieves significant high precision. In the future, we would like to further improve the attack and defence considering more browser activities.

Acknowledgement. This work is supported in part by the National Key Research and Development Program of China No. 2019QY1302; the NSFC-General Technology Basic Research Joint Funds under Grant U1836214; NSFC-61872265; the New Generation of Artificial Intelligence Science and Technology Major Project of Tianjin under 19ZXZNGX00010.

References

1. Alexa website ranking. https://www.alexa.com/. Accessed 6 May 2021
2. Chrome release notes. https://chromereleases.googleblog.com/. Accessed 30 Sep 2021
3. Chrome resource priorities and scheduling. https://docs.google.com/document/d/1bCDuq9H1ih9iNjgzyAL0gpwNFiEP4TZS-YLRp_RuMlc/. Accessed 17 Aug 2021
4. Cisco joy. https://github.com/cisco/joy. Accessed 17 Aug 2021
5. Firefox release notes. https://www.mozilla.org/en-US/firefox/notes/ Accessed 30 Sep 2021
6. RFC 8446 - the transport layer security (TLS) protocol version 1.3. https://tools.ietf.org/html/rfc8446#section-4.1.2. Accessed 23 Dec 2020
7. Selenium, automating web applications for testing purposes tools. https://www.selenium.dev/. Accessed 17 Aug 2021
8. tshark - the wireshark network analyzer. https://www.wireshark.org/docs/man-pages/tshark.html. Accessed 23 Dec 2020
9. A novel passive website fingerprinting attack on tor using fast Fourier transform. Computer Communications Guildford Then Amsterdam Butterworth Scientific Limited Then Elsevier (2016)
10. Aminuddin, M.A.I.M., Zaaba, Z.F., Singh, M.K.M., Singh, D.S.M.: A survey on tor encrypted traffic monitoring. Int. J. Adv. Comput. Sci. Appl. **9**(8) (2018). https://doi.org/10.14569/IJACSA.2018.090815
11. Dong, C., Lu, Z., Cui, Z., Liu, B., Chen, K.: MBTree: detecting encryption rats communication using malicious behavior tree. IEEE Trans. Inf. Forensics Secur. **16**, 3589–3603 (2021)
12. Ghaleb, T.A.: Wireless/website traffic analysis amp; fingerprinting: a survey of attacking techniques and countermeasures. In: 2015 International Conference on Cloud Computing (ICCC), pp. 1–7 (2015). https://doi.org/10.1109/CLOUDCOMP.2015.7149665

13. Hayes, J., Danezis, G.: k-fingerprinting: a robust scalable website fingerprinting technique. In: 25th USENIX Security Symposium (USENIX Security 16), pp. 1187–1203 (2016)
14. Herrmann, D., Wendolsky, R., Federrath, H.: Website fingerprinting: attacking popular privacy enhancing technologies with the multinomial Nave-Bayes classifier. In: CCS 2009, Cloud Computing Security Workshop (2009)
15. Panchenko, A., Lanze, F., Zinnen, A., Henze, M., Engel, T.: Website fingerprinting at internet scale. In: Network & Distributed System Security Symposium (2016)
16. Postel, J.: Transmission control protocol. RFC 793, Internet Engineering Task Force, September 1981. http://www.rfc-editor.org/rfc/rfc793.txt
17. Shen, M., Liu, Y., Chen, S., Zhu, L., Zhang, Y.: Webpage fingerprinting using only packet length information. In: ICC 2019–2019 IEEE International Conference on Communications (ICC) (2019)
18. Shen, M., Liu, Y., Zhu, L., Du, X., Hu, J.: Fine-grained webpage fingerprinting using only packet length information of encrypted traffic. IEEE Trans. Inf. Forensics Secur. $16(99)$, 2046–2059 (2020)
19. Shen, M., Zhang, J., Zhu, L., Xu, K., Du, X.: Accurate decentralized application identification via encrypted traffic analysis using graph neural networks. IEEE Trans. Inf. Forensics Secur. $16(99)$, 2367–2380 (2021)
20. Shi, Y., Matsuura, K.: Fingerprinting attack on the tor anonymity system, pp. 425–438, December 2009
21. Zhang, Z., Kang, C., Xiong, G., Li, Z.: Deep forest with LRRS feature for fine-grained website fingerprinting with encrypted SSL/TLS. In: Proceedings of the 28th ACM International Conference on Information and Knowledge Management, pp. 851–860. CIKM 2019. Association for Computing Machinery (2019). https://doi.org/10.1145/3357384.3357993

Re-Check Your Certificates! Experiences and Lessons Learnt from Real-World HTTPS Certificate Deployments

Wenya Wang[1]([✉]), Yakang Li[1], Chao Wang[2], Yuan Yan[1], Juanru Li[1], and Dawu Gu[1]

[1] Shanghai Jiao Tong University, Shanghai, China
{ducky_97,liyakang_n,loccs,jarod,dwgu}@sjtu.edu.cn
[2] The Ohio State University, Columbus, USA
wang.15147@osu.edu

Abstract. HTTPS is the typical security best practice to protect data transmission. However, it is difficult to correctly deploy HTTPS even for administrators with technical expertise, and mis-configurations often lead to user-facing errors and potential vulnerabilities. One major reason is that administrators do not follow new features of HTTPS ecosystem evolution, and mistakes were unnoticed and existed for years.

In this paper, we conduct a large-scale and persistent study on HTTPS certificate deployment to investigate whether administrators follow the certificate management trend. We empirically evaluate HTTPS certificate deployment concerning five new issues of improper configurations, and discuss how four usability factors may influence the mistakes. We monitored domain names and their certificates in China Education and Research Network (CERNET). Using data collected from more than 30,000 domain names of 113 universities in 12 weeks, we gained a panorama of HTTPS deployment in academia and summarized typical mistakes that administrators tend to make. Our results demonstrated that incorrect deployments were common, and a stable ratio of administrators did not follow the latest HTTPS guidelines. We also observed that certain usability factors (e.g., certificate shared by multiple domain names) potentially correlate with insecure HTTPS websites.

Keywords: HTTPS · PKI · Digital certificate · CERNET

1 Introduction

Recent years have witnessed the significant growth of HTTPS among websites worldwide. By March 2021, 71% of the one million most visited websites worldwide have deployed HTTPS as their default [1]. To encourage web administrators and users to adopt HTTPS, many web browsers (e.g., Google Chrome) are enforcing HTTPS connections. However, the adoptions of HTTPS, especially the HTTPS certificate configuration part, is not easy for most websites

© Springer Nature Switzerland AG 2021
M. Yang et al. (Eds.): NSS 2021, LNCS 13041, pp. 17–37, 2021.
https://doi.org/10.1007/978-3-030-92708-0_2

administrators. Configuring a server to support HTTPS involves a wide variety of technical issues and is often error-prone. Efforts from both industry and academia have also been made to find insecurely deployed HTTPS websites. For instance, The Mozilla Observatory [2] has helped over 240,000 websites on how to configure their sites securely. Acer *et al.* [3] classified the top causes of HTTPS error warnings to implement actionable warnings for Chrome users. Unfortunately, the rapid evolution of HTTPS ecosystem (e.g., the use of TLS 1.3 protocol and Let's Encrypt Free Certificates) urges administrator to continuously upgrade security best practices. Therefore, a large potion of websites using HTTPS are still vulnerable due to recently emerged deployment issues, and this brings new challenges to administrators who are struggling for deploying HTTPS correctly.

We can blame certificate issuers for some deployment issues. Kumar *et al.* [4] systematically analyzed mechanical errors made by CAs when issuing certificates, and found that small CAs regularly made mistakes after analyzing 240 million browser-trust certificates. Schwittmann *et al.* [5] tested domain validation authorities and concluded that all major CAs were vulnerable in multiple ways because of insecure protocols they used. On the other hand, website administrators are also responsible for a variety of deployment problems. Recent researches have revealed that even for expert system administrators, the complexity of HTTPS certificates deployment often becomes a main obstacle for website security. Singanamalla *et al.* [6] measured HTTPS adoption of government websites around the world and found an overall lower https rate. Ukrop *et al.* [7] also found that self-signed certificates and name constrained certificates were over trusted by people in the IT industry, and notifications sometimes make no sense.

To better understand what are the most critical factors that lead to an incorrectly deployed HTTPS certificate in 2021, in this paper we conduct an empirical study of the HTTPS certificate deployment against more than 30,000 domain names and their corresponding certificate in China Education and Research Network (CERNET). We first surveyed a series of recent research papers on HTTPS certificate issuing, deployment, and revocation, summarized the trend of modern certificate management over the past five years. Then we evaluated the correctness of HTTPS deployment in CERNET by considering five new issues of HTTPS certificates deployment: subject alternative name (SAN) mismatching, long validity period, broken certificate chain, certificate opacity and obsolete crypto algorithms. In addition, we investigate four usability factors (certificate indicator, certificate issuer, certificate sharing and certificate revocation) and the potential correlation with above incorrect deployments. We conducted the study by consecutively monitoring how domain names of 113 universities configured their HTTPS certificates and relevant web/DNS parameters in 12 weeks (from November 4th, 2020 to January 20th, 2021), and summarizing the overall status of incorrect HTTPS certificate deployment in CERNET.

Our investigation shows that current deployment status of HTTPS certificates is not optimistic: even for administrators of CERNET (who are more likely to learn recently proposed guidelines and recommendations of HTTPS deployments), a stable portion of them (27%) did not adopt correct configurations. We found the top three deployment issues are **SAN mismatching, long validity, and broken certificate chain**. We also observed that certificate renewal would reproduce broken certificate chain issues and short lifespans would cause certificate expiration problems. Regarding the usability factors, we observed certain status of certificate (e.g., certificate sharing) strongly correlated with deployment issues.

Our contributions include:

- We summarized recent policies, guidelines, and recommendations of certificate management over the past five years, and evaluated how administrators followed those new changes at a large scale. The results showed that HTTPS certificate mis-configuration is widespread, and we found many popular web services (e.g., email services) were endangered.
- We analyzed the ratio of incorrectly deployed certificates/domain names in a certain period of time (12 weeks), and found the trend of improperly deploying certificates is not downwards: although many certificates were renewed and correctly configured, some updates introduced new mis-configurations.
- According to our study, we discussed whether typical usability factors (e.g., the selection of certificate issuer) correlate with incorrectly deployed certificates. Our analysis demonstrated that some factors did affect the certificate deployment and should be concerned by administrators.

2 Certificate Deployment in 2020s: Trends and Changes

In this section, we present a variety of details that reflect recent features and changes of HTTPS certificate management, and discuss best practices of certificate deployment.

HTTPS Certificates. HTTPS encrypts and authenticates data transmission to protect its integrity and confidentiality from attackers. During HTTPS handshake, the client examines the fields and chains of certificates delivered by the server for authentication. `Subject Alternative Name` (SAN) field consists of `DNS names`. The `DNS name` is the criterion for identifying whether a domain name could match the certificate. Based on SAN, HTTPS certificates are divided into three types. Single-domain type has only one `DNS name` and can only be used by a domain name (e.g., `domain.com`). Wildcard type containing two `DNS names` can match a domain name and its subdomain name (e.g., `domain.com` and `*.domain.com`). And multi-domain type with multiple `DNS Names` could match the domain names with different suffixes (e.g., `domain-A.com` and `domain-B.org`). Long life span certificates are gradually being deprecated, as they generally use outdated configurations and would increase the risks. For example, `SHA-1-to-SHA-2` transition takes 3 years due to the slow replacement of long-term certificates.

A complete certificate chain is composed with the leaf certificates up to the root certificates. While TLS handshaking, the server should also transmit the intermediate certificates. Only the client links them to a trusted root certificate stored in local, the client would trust the leaf certificate. Up to February 2021, about 1.7% of servers did not configure the proper certificate chain [8]. Existing technologies such as AIA Fetching technology, Intermediate Certificate Cache technology and Intermediate Certificate Preloading help fix the broken chains, some researchers argue that AIA Fetching and Intermediate Certificate Cache technology would compromise user privacy [9,10].

Certificate Authorities. Before 2015, applying for an HTTPS certificate costed much, and the installing process was sophisticated [11]. Let's Encrypt launched in late 2015 greatly improved this situation. Let's Encrypt issues the Domain Validation (DV) certificates free and automatically, and also helps maintain the certificates (e.g., renew the certificates). As of November 2020, 232 million websites install 144 million active certificates issued by Let's Encrypt [12]. CAs like Encryption Everywhere Program, cloud providers like Cloudflare also provide similar services for their customers.

And the other types, namely Extended Validation (EV), Individual Validation (IV) and Organization Validation (OV) provide more trust than DV certificates, especially EV certificates. As the certificates contain more details about the owners, and the verification process is more rigorous. CAs generally claim that EV would make phishing attacks harder and have higher warranties. However, attackers can still get an EV certificate with the same company name. And some EV certificates of well-known websites were not renewed in time. LinkedIn in 2017 forgot to renew its EV certificate [13], and Instagram in 2015 forgot to renew its EV certificate [13], Modern browsers have removed special indicators in the URL bar for EV certificates since 2019 [14–16].

Certificate Transparency and Revocation Records. Mis-issued certificates or the certificates with compromised private keys do great harm to the privacy of users. The revocation mechanism restrains the trust in malicious certificates, and certificate transparency provides an auditing and monitoring system for HTTPS ecosystem.

Online Certificate Status Protocol (OCSP) is the most widely adopted certificate revocation mechanism [17,18]. The client could perform an OCSP request about the certificate revocation status before the page finishes loading. This usually causes time delays. OCSP Stapling alleviates the latency problem to some extent, as servers can staple the OCSP response in the TLS handshakes. However, OCSP Stapling could be stripped by the attackers, and OCSP Must-Staple proposed in 2015 prevents this from happening [19]. Administrators could set OCSP Must-staple signal in the certificate extensions, and client like Firefox would block access to sites that set Must-staple but do not deliver OCSP Stapling [20]. But some browsers like Google Chrome consider that this would create new access-blocking issues and do not support OCSP Must-Staple [17].

In order to remedy incorrect or malicious certificates issuance by CAs, Certificate Transparency (CT) provides an auditing and monitoring system for HTTPS ecosystem. Certificate Transparency has been widely adopted [21]. Before a CA issues a certificate, it sends the pre-certificate of the certificate to CT logs first, and the logs respond with signed certificate timestamps (SCTs), which represents the promises of submission with the Maximum Merge Delay. And the CA embes the SCTs in the certificate before issuing. There are three ways to bind SCTs: certificate embedding, TLS extension and OCSP stapling. Certificate embedding is the most common and reliable way [22].

Certificate Sharing. The prevalence of wildcard and multi-domain certificates promotes certificate sharing between multiple domain names. CDN service, cloud service, and hosting service providers usually install one certificate for multiple customers. Although it is feasible and convenient for multiple domain names to share a certificate, security risks also increase, since copies of private keys are stored on different servers, and some of the servers may not securely protected [23]. Once one of the server is compromised, all domains that share the same certificate would be severely threatened. Actually, researchers have shown that sharing a certificate with low-profile domain names will reduce the security of the system [24, 25].

3   Investigating Certificate Deployment

To systematically study the deployment status of recent HTTPS certificate deployment and summarize experiences from real-world websites, in this paper we aim to answer the following research questions by conducting large-scale and lasting analysis against certificates in use.

RQ1: What is the overall trend of certificate deployment? Despite the fact that 71.0% of all the websites have deployed HTTPS as their default protocol [1] in 2021, there still exist several issues that affect the security of network communication. Specifically, we observed that many websites did not follow new features and recommendations that nowadays HTTPS certificate management should adopt. Therefore, although they did not affected by those well-known bad practices such as self-signed certificate, various new issues are still disturbing website administrators. In response, we aim to investigate the overall trend of how administrators handle new changes and corresponding issues. Furthermore, we concern about the ratio of domain names affected by new deployment issues, the distributions of each issues, and their variations in a certain period of time. With a long-term analysis rather than an analysis against a snapshot, we try to investigate whether a deployment issue a temporary mistake or is it a common situation.

RQ2: How user factors affect the deployment of certificates? To further understand the root cause of incorrect certificate deployments, we consider several user factors that may mislead administrators. For instance, we would like to examine whether the sharing of certificate between multiple domain names is a dependent factor of an ill-deployed certificate.

RQ3: How many users and what kinds of web services are affected? To evaluate the actual risks of those incorrectly deployed certificates, we would like to check if those popular web services (e.g., email service, identity authentication service) are suffering from certificate deployment issues (and how many users are threatened due to the problems), or only those less frequently accessed websites mis-configured their certificates.

4   Evaluation

We report in this section our investigation results on recently emerged HTTPS certificates deployment issues. We conducted a 12-week investigation against more than 30,000 domain names and their HTTPS certificates to examine to what extent website administrators have followed the latest trends of HTTPS certificate management, or if they made mistakes due to the unfamiliarity of those new changes. We first detail the built dataset of our investigation (Sect. 4.1), and then elaborate how recent certificates deployment issues affected the studied domain names/certificates (Sect. 4.2). Finally, we discuss four factors that may lead to incorrect certificates deployment (Sect. 4.3), and show the influence of incorrectly deployed certificates against popular web services (Sect. 4.4).

Ethical Statement. Our study did not tamper with any website with insecurely deployed certificate and executed a full responsible disclosure process by contacting the network administrators of relevant universities. In further, we only used port 80 and 443 to access the websites and did not perform any port scanning actions that might result in abuse of the hosts in the target.

4.1   Dataset and Experiment Setup

Our investigation utilized China Education and Research Network (CERNET) [26] as our research target. A typical feature of CERNET is that its members (i.e., universities), unlike enterprises or government departments, manage their belonging domain names and certificates in a de-centralized style. That is, even for the same university, all of its belonging web servers and certificates are often managed by different departments/institutes rather than a single bureau. Therefore, this network becomes a very typical example to study the diversification of HTTPS certificate managements (and how this diversity affects security).

To build a dataset for the certificate deployment analysis, we first collected all HTTPS-accessible domain names of CERNET. Our investigation monitored domain names of 113 major universities [27] of CERNET. More specifically, since in CERNET the domain and subdomain names of one specific university possess the same suffix in the form of name-abbreviation.edu.cn (e.g., pku.edu.cn is the common suffix for all domain names belonging to *Peking University* (PKU), and all subdomain names of PKU must follows the format of *.pku.edu.cn [28]). We started from generating an initial "seed" list of each university containing its common suffix, and then automatically collected their subdomain names of the domain in the list through utilizing both Sublist3r [29] subdomain name enumeration tool and ctr.sh [30] certificate transparency (CT) log search engine. After the collection, our dataset finally obtained 31,211 domain names, among which 19,493 (62.45%) domain names were accessible during our experiment period, and 11,718 (35.54%) domain names suffered from connection issues.

Table 1. The overall HTTP(S) connectivity.

HTTP	HTTPS	Number
✓	✗	7,820 (40.12%)
✓	✓	5,376 (27.58%)
✓[1]	✓	5,284 (27.11%)
✓	✓[2]	503 (2.58%)
✗	✓	420 (2.15%)
✓[1]	✓[2]	90 (0.46%)

[1]: redirected to HTTPS;
[2]: redirected to HTTP;

Next, we examined the HTTP(S) connectivity of the 19,493 accessible domain names. We utilized Requests [31] tool to access a domain name through both HTTP and HTTPS protocol to check its connectivity. Table 1 shows the overall status of HTTP/HTTPS connectivity in our first snapshot (Nov. 8th, 2020) of our dataset. In all 19,493 accessible domain names, we found 11,673 (59.88%) of them supported HTTPS connection. In detail, 420 domain names could only be connected through HTTPS. The HTTP connections of 5,284 domain names were directed HTTPS. 5,376 supported both HTTP and HTTPS, and 503 domain names redirected HTTPS connections to HTTP. Note that HTTP and HTTPS connections of 90 domain names were both redirected. This would not cause loop redirects, as at least one of them was finally redirected to other domain name.

The last step of our investigation checks the deployment correctness of each certificate (binding to one or multiple domain names). Particularly, we developed an analysis tool based on OpenSSL to first capture the certificate and then inspect whether its deployment suffered from five typical issues (Sect. 4.2) due to the evolution of HTTPS ecosystem. Note that in our investigation we did not only capture a snapshot of the entire analyzed domain names/certificates, but instead we kept monitoring their status and changes throughout a period of 12 weeks. That is, we captured a snapshot of all collected domain names once a week from November 4th, 2020 to January 20th, 2021. On average, for each snapshot a two-day analysis was required to obtain a 76 MB data that covers all those domain names.

4.2   Certificate Deployment Issues

In the following, we answered the proposed Research Questions 1 by elaborating our evaluation focusing on five new HTTPS certificate deployment issues over the past five years:

- **Subject Alternative Name (SAN) Mismatching.** If the tested domain name does not match anyone of the DNS Names listed in the SAN field of the HTTPS certificate, we consider the deployment as an SAN mismatching (which would be alerted by most web browsers). Note that if the domain name only matches the commonName field in the certificate, browsers nowadays would still reject the certificate because they only check SAN field [32,33] since 2016.
- **Long Validity Period.** Modern browsers require a certificate *issued on or after September 1st, 2020* should not possess a validity period longer than 398 days [34–36]. In our investigation, we consider a certificate with a long validity period (i.e., 398+ days) as an incorrectly deployed one. And in particular, for the certificates *issued before September 1st, 2020*, we consider an 825+ days period (as CA/Browser Forum [37] suggested) as potentially risky.
- **Broken Certificate Chain.** If the certificates provided by the domain names could not link the leaf certificate to the root certificate, we would think the deployment has the broken certificate chain issue. Browsers such as Firefox (lower than Version 75) [38] directly block HTTPS connections due to the lack of trust. Though in 2019 Intermediate Certificate Preloading adopted by Firefox (upper than Version 75) help fix this issue [38], technologies that are still in use (e.g., AIA Fetching technology and Intermediate Certificate Cache technology) are considered to violate user privacy [9,10].
- **Certificate Opacity.** To allow users to audit the reliability of the used certificate, a domain name must deliver the SCTs as well as the certificate during a TLS handshake. According to regulations of Chrome [39] and Safari [40], we consider a certificate *issued on or after April 2018* without delivering SCT as invalid.
- **Obsolete Crypto Algorithms.** As practical collision of MD5 and SHA-1 had already been found [41,42], both crypto algorithms have been abandoned by browsers since 2017 [43,44]. Therefore, we consider a certificate signed by them as invalid. Moreover, NIST have recommended that the public key length of RSA should be longer than 1024 bits [45], and crypto suites using RSA-1024 or lower are also considered as deprecated in our investigation.

To evaluate whether a domain name (and its HTTPS certificate) has suffered the above five issues, in our investigation we first fetched the certificate of the domain name. We used the 98 root certificates trusted by Chrome Root Store [46], Apple OS [47], Mozilla [48], and Windows Root Certificate Program [49] as our trusted root certificate list. To evaluate the broken certificate chain issue, we used the error message of OpenSSL to verify the certificate chain. For the other four issues, we simply used pyOpenSSL [50] to parse the certificate, extracted information of each field and then compared them with our pre-defined criterion. This helped us judge whether the certificate suffered from any deployment issues.

In particular, since the most common way to deliver the SCT is to attach it as an extension of the certificate [22], we directly check the SCT list in certificate extensions to obtain the SCT information.

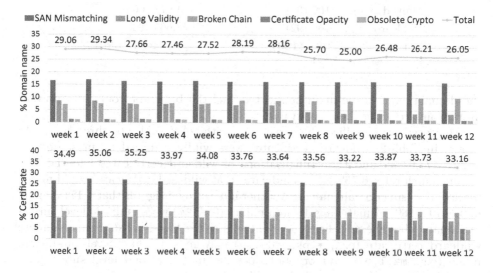

Fig. 1. Deployment issues

Overall Findings. In summary, we found during the entire 12-week investigation period, around 27% domain names with nearly 33% certificates suffered from at least one deployment issues. Figure 1 depicts the overall status during the 12 weeks. Our observation is that during our experiment, the ratio of incorrectly deployed certificates/domains is stable: it only slightly decreased between week 8 to week 9 due to the replacement of long-term certificates to short-term certificates of 306 domain names, and rebounded again in week 10 for 107 domain names emerged broken certificate chain issues. Among all issues, the most frequently occurred one is SAN mismatching, 16% domain names suffered from this issue. 9% certificates had excessively long validity duration. 8% domain names installed broken certificate chain. 5% of the evaluated certificates did not set SCTs, and 5% were signed by obsolete algorithms or had short public key. In the following, we discuss each issue of incorrectly deployed certificate, respectively.

SAN Mismatching. On average, we found nearly 16% domain names mismatched their certificates. Among the certificate mismatched by their domain names, we found 90 (8.40%) certificates of 252 domain names set CN field but not SAN field. Lack of SAN or SAN mismatching would cause the identity of

Table 2. SAN mismatching status of domain names and certificates (Nov. 8th).

Certificate type	Certificates (Mismatched)	Domains (Affected)
Single-domain	625 (64)	778 (182)
Multi-domain	100 (37)	1,978 (666)
Wildcard	256 (92)	8,665 (832)
Total	**981 (193)**	**11,421 (1,680)**

the domain name to be unauthenticated, and the browsers would also prevent users from accessing the domain name.

Moreover, we classified the certificates with SAN field into three types. As shown in Table 2, wildcard certificates were wildly installed by most domain names (77.62%), and the configurations of wildcard certificates had the lowest mismatch rate (8.76%). This indicates that wildcard certificates could match most of the using domain names. Another interesting insight is that 1,171 domain names of 1,680 mismatching domain names (69.70%) were multiple level subdomain names but the SAN field could only match the first-level subdomain names: wildcard certificate (e.g., `*.pku.edu.cn`) only matches first level subdomain name (e.g., `mail.pku.edu.cn`) but does not match second level subdomains (e.g., `its.lb.pku.edu.cn`). This implies that many administrators misunderstand the semantic of a wildcard certificate.

Long Validity Period. Among 12 weeks, we found 127 certificates with long validity period, which used by 1,067 domain names (i.e., more than 398 days or 825 days). Since the 398-day limit was enforced since *September 1st, 2020* [34–36], we further divided the certificates into two categories: issued before and after September 1, 2020. Figure 2 shows the distribution of certificate lifespans in 12 weeks, respectively. We found before September 1st, 2020, only 42.62% issued certificates adopted a validity period less than 398 days. In comparison, after that date, 99.47% certificates followed the new regulation. This indicates that most CAs have shortened the validity period of the certificate.

As Fig. 1 shows, the ratio of long-term certificates adoption kept decreasing. We observed especially in week 8 (Dec 23rd, 2020), the renewal of seven certificates significantly affected 306 domain names. However, certificates with short validity period introduced new issues. We observed that administrators often forgot to renew certificates, and thus a certificate with shorter lifespan has a larger chance to be used in real world after its expiration: the distribution of 125 expired certificates (230 domain names) in our first snapshot (Nov. 8th, 2020) demonstrates that nearly 70% expired but still-in-use certificates possessed a short validity period.

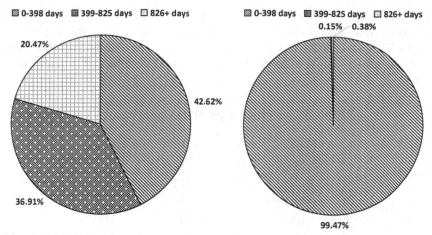

(a) Certificate Lifespans (Before Sep. 1st) (b) Certificate Lifespans (After Sep. 1st)

Fig. 2. Distribution of certificate lifespans

Broken Certificate Chain. We found around administrators of 8% domain names did not install intermediate certificates. In week 10 (Jan 6th, 2021), the number of domain names with the broken certificate chain issue increased from 1,042 to 1,211. For domain names that have newly generated the issue, we found 98.16% of them were caused by certificate updates.

We evaluated the cause of this issues. We found 89.00% domain names with this issue only provided the leaf certificates. This indicates that the main reason for this issue is that the administrators have no idea of installing a complete certificate chain. And the left 11.00% domain names offered wrong intermediate certificates. Among them, most domain names (90.23%) transferred their leaf certificates as intermediate certificates. 9.77% domain names provided the intermediate certificates of previously used certificates, which indicates that administrators forgot to change the certificate chain after updating. These suggest that administrators would not recheck the certificate chains after deployment.

Certificate Opacity. Most modern browsers require certificates *issued on or after April 2018* to provide Signed Certificate Timestamp (SCT), otherwise they fail to trust those certificates. Using certificate extension is the most common way to support certificate transparency (CT) policy. Among 1,789 certificates issued after the specified date, we observed 1,704 (95.25%) set SCT field in certificate extensions, and they were all issued by trustful CAs. This implies that most CAs support Certificate Transparency. The left 85 certificates without setting SCT field were all self-signed certificates. These certificates were unauditable: The users could not audit whether the certificates were issued incorrectly or the private keys of them were compromised. We also evaluated SCT deployment of the certificates issued before the specified date. We found 199 domain names installed four certificates without setting SCT. They were still considered correct by most browsers. And none of the domain names sent SCT through OCSP stapling or TLS extensions which are the other two ways to deliver SCT. This implies that unless CAs set the SCT, the administrators would not add it on their own.

Table 3. Adoption of signature algorithms.

Algorithm	Certificates	Domain names
SHA256-RSA	1,662	12,865
SHA384-ECDSA	171	88
SHA256-ECDSA	5	5
SHA384-RSA	3	2
SHA1-RSA	68	164
MD5-RSA	2	8

Table 4. Adoption of public keys.

Public key size	Certificates	Domain names
RSA 2048	1,191	12,298
RSA 4096	447	660
ECDSA 256	198	108
RSA 3072	20	13
ECDSA 384	11	8
RSA 1024	44	122

Obsolete Crypto Algorithms. Among the 1911 certificates collected, we found 70 certificates (3.66%) used obsolete signature algorithms and 44 certificates (2.30%) had insecure public key length. Table 3 shows signature hash algorithms used by 1,911 certificates. Among these certificates, crypto suites of 70 certificates (3.66%) were considered to be weak (MD5 with RSA of two certificates and SHA-1 with RSA of 68 certificates), which would cause certificates to be forged. The result shows that MD5 algorithm has been deprecated, but SHA-1 was still trusted over some administrator. In Table 4, we found the public key of 44 certificates (2.30%) is RSA 1024 which is in-approval by NIST [45]. We also observed that the above invalid certificates were all self-signed certificates, which indicates that the administrators choose the incorrect algorithms or public key sizes manually. This implies that certificates can be easily misconfigured by administrators.

4.3   Influence of Usability Factors

We answered the proposed Research Questions 2 in this section by analyzing the potential connection between four usability factors and certificate deployment correctness. In detail, we consider four usability factors: the type of certificate indicators, the selection of certificate issuers, the sharing of certificate between multiple domain names, and the revocation option made by certificate applicants.

Certificate Indicator. Excluding self-signed (or self-signed in certificate chain) certificates, we classified certificates collected in the dataset of November 8th into three types: EV, IV/OV, and DV. In detail, we identified EV certificates by checking whether `Certificate Policy` field of a certificate belonged to EV policy Object Identifier (OID) set [51]. And for the left certificates, we utilized `Subject` field for classification, as IV/OV certificates contain more information than DV certificates. As shown in Fig. 3, we found most of the certificates (75.94%) were DV, while IV/OV certificates were wildly installed on most domain names (65.48%).

We separately evaluated the deployment status of each type certificates. Though most CAs stated that EV certificates generally have the most quality warranty, followed by IV/OV, and finally DV. However in Fig. 3(a), we found the proportion of invalid deployment in EV certificates is the highest (83.70%) and DV certificates have the lowest invalid proportion (24.99%). For IV/OV certificates, we found 98.97% of the domain names share certificates with others, and 55.09% certificates are deployed incorrectly as shown in Fig. 3(b). This indicates that administrators usually deploy an IV/OV certificate on multiple domain names with deployment issues.

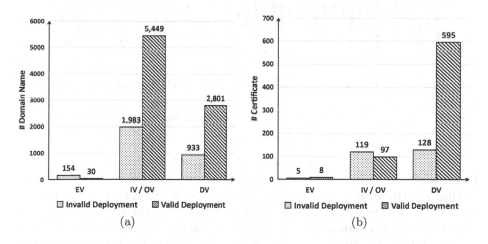

Fig. 3. Distribution of certificate types (Nov. 8th)

Certificate Issuer. We also checked the connections between certificate issuers and deployment conditions. We extracted the name of CA from `commonName` in `Issuer Name` field of the certificates. Figure 4(a) shows the distribution of involved certificate issuers in our evaluation. 1,750 (91.57%) certificates were issued by trustful CAs, 161 certificates were self-signed certificates and the issuers of three certificates were distrusted by most browsers. As Fig. 4(a) depicts, the most frequently used CAs is `Let's Encrypt` (55.68% are issued by this certificate authority).

Among 1,911 certificates, we found 1,441 free certificates (75.41%) used by 5,808 domains. As Sect. 2 introduced, free certificates usually provide automated deployment services. To further investigate whether this mechanism could reduce the probability of misconfigurations, we visualized the relationship between issuer mechanism and invalid deployment in Fig. 4(b). We notice that nearly 80% domain names with invalid deployment applied certificates from paid CAs. This indicates that the mechanism used by free-of-charge CA could help administrators deploy the certificates correctly.

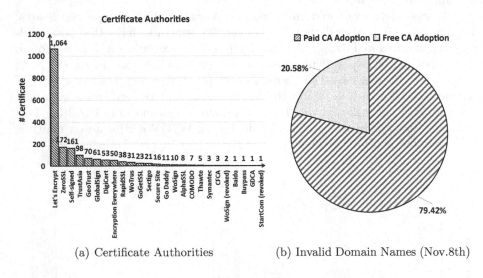

(a) Certificate Authorities   (b) Invalid Domain Names (Nov.8th)

Fig. 4. Certificate authorities

Certificate Sharing. We noted that the domain names tend to share the same certificates with other domain names. Overall, we observed that 11,676 domain names (89.03%) reused the same public key of 472 certificates (24.70%) with others. Among 472 certificates, the deployment of 311 certificates (65.89%) were invalid. Especially, we found 31 certificates are reused by 529 domain names crossing 82 universities, and all of the certificates had deployment issues.

Certificate sharing would connect to deployment inconsistencies in following three aspects. The first inconsistency is in the SAN matching. We found

2,695 domain names did not match the SAN field, and they reused 265 certificates with 10,427 domain names (89.30%). The second is certificate chain completeness inconsistency. 1,413 domain names sharing 203 certificates with 5,309 domain names (45.47%) had the broken certificate chain issue. The last one was the inconsistent renewal of expired certificates. We found the renewal status of 2,950 (25.27%) domain names sharing 48 certificates were not inconsistent. Take the 150 domain names of *Yunnan University* (ynu.edu.cn) as a example. When the sharing certificate was expired, 141 (94%) domain names renewed the certificate first, while nine of them updated later. The nine domain names included VPN service website and postgraduate management system. These inconsistencies indicate that certificate sharing would cause administrators to be unable to maintain the certificate deployment for all domain names correctly and simultaneously.

Certificate Revocation. We found 1,750 certificates issued by trustful CAs provided OCSP information, which allow browsers to check their revocation status. We used OCSP request to check revocation status of the certificates that were not expired. And for the expired ones, we extracted the issuers to evaluate whether their root certificates have been unrecognized by modern browsers. We found no certificates were revoked during their lifespans. The CAs of three expired certificates (i.e., StartCom and WoSign) were revoked by most browsers, and the certificates have been expired for a long time. This indicates that this passive revocation is imperceptible for the administrators.

We also evaluated the adoption of OCSP Stapling and OCSP Must-Staple. We extracted OCSP Stapling while TLS handshaking. For domain names with OCSP Stapling, we checked whether the certificate extensions set OID for OCSP Must-Staple [19]. Among the 11,673 domain names installing 1,750 certificates, we found only 1,828 domain names (15.66%) configured OCSP stapling on the server side, and none of them set OCSP Must-staple in their certificates. As both OCSP Must-staple and OCSP Stapling need to be added manually, no setting OCSP Must-staple and low adoption of OCSP Stapling infer that administrators did not actively support OCSP mechanisms.

4.4 Popular Web Services with Incorrectly Deployed Certificates

In this section, we discuss how widely used web services (e.g., email, identity authentication, VPN, software license authorization) are affected by insecurely deployed HTTPS.

Email Services. We found that it is common for universities to delegate their email services to third-party email service providers. However, such delegations often suffer from incorrect sharing. We found mail services of a university with 52,000+ users, a university with 18,000+ users and a university with 29,000+ users were delegated by eNetEase, and they installed the same certificates with mismatching errors. The same situation also occurs in the mail services of a university with 31,000+ users, a university with 40,000+ users and a university with 36,000+ users delegated by Tencent. Although these websites were managed by professional third-party email service providers, their used domain names and certificates were mismatched. For instance, one of the domain names adopted the certificate with SAN field `*.qiye.163.com`. We also found these domain names still supported HTTP access and thus the certificate mismatch issue may not be noticed by those third-party service providers. Denial of access through HTTPS would cause the users to connect the domain name with HTTP, and the attackers could eavesdrop the privacy of users through man-in-the-middle (MitM) attacks.

Software Distribution Services. We observed the licensed software (e.g., Microsoft Windows and Office) download website of a university with 42,000+ users, and the VPN software providers of 20 universities (with 661,000+ students and faculties in total), installed extremely insecure certificates with obsolete crypto suites and invalid lifespans. Therefore, a man-in-the-middle attack could be conducted easily against software downloading, and the users may download maliciously modified software. A further manual inspection showed that those certificates were all self-signed, which indicated why they adopted such dangerous settings.

Authenticating Services. We found a certificate of a university with 43,000+ users did not set SCT in the certificate extension, and the certificates was shared by 67 domain names related to 11 IP addresses. Most web services provided by these domain names involve the identity authentication of the users (students and faculties). Since this certificate was shared by so many servers, its private key data is very possible to be leaked due to insecure configurations of either the web servers or the web services. Unfortunately, we found this certificate was issued on January 4th, 2018 and its lifespan is 1,155 days, when the SCT has not yet been stipulated as required. Moreover, administrators of those 67 domains did not set SCT in their TLS extensions. Therefore, this certificate was hardly audited and less trustful.

We additionally observed a certificate of a university , issued on July 2015, was passively revoked due to its untrustful issuer (i.e., StartCom). Nevertheless, the website was still using this certificate. Considering that the website is providing Campus ID Card authentication service to 52,000+ users, and the untrustful CA would disclose the private key, the security and privacy of its users would severely threatened.

News Portal. We found news portal websites of a university with 25,000+ users, a university with 34,000+ users, and a university with 27,000+ users installed OV certificates. These domain names play an important role in the universities, as through them, schools advertise themselves, and students and faculties get notifications. However, the certificate chains of these domain names were broken. As a result, even though latest version of browsers adopt AIA fetching or intermediate certificate cache and may not report the certificate error against this case, some browsers or embedded web components would directly block such HTTPS connections, and users are not able to access these services.

5 Related Work

Certificate Ecosystem Measurement. Several work has provided large-scale measurements on certificate ecosystem, especially focusing on the vulnerabilities. Razaghpanah *et al.* [52] analyzed 7,258 Android apps and saw the adoption rate of certificate security measures, such as certificate pinning, was low. Alashwali *et al.* [53] analyzed the difference in TLS security configurations and certificates between two million plain-domains and their equivalent www-domains and they found www-domains tend to have stronger security configurations than their equivalent plain-domains. Singanamalla *et al.* [6] measured HTTPS deployment of government websites across the world and found that many of the domain names use misconfigured certificates, which is the most closest and recent work to our measurements. The difference is that we focused on the new policies and mechanisms of HTTPS certificate deployment in recent years. We analyzed the new polices with a large-scale, persistent measurement on CERNET and unearthed the causes and the consequences of the invalid deployments.

New Mechanism Measurement. Prior work also examined the new mechanisms from different perspectives. Some studies [11] found that Let's Encrypt and Certbot greatly facilitated the HTTPS certificate ecosystem. And [54] and [55] conducted control trials of HTTPS configuration to evaluate the usability of Let's Encrypt and Certbot in comparison to traditional ways. They found Let's Encrypt did improve the HTTPS deployment. We showed that the free-of-charge and auto-of-deployment mechanism used by Let's Encrypt and other CAs is indeed wildly adopted and improves HTTPS certificate deployments. Stark *et al.* [21] evaluated CT adoption on the web from many angles and found CT has been adopted widely and correctly. Nykvist *et al.* [22] analyzed SCT usage among one million domain names and found certificate extension is the major and simplest solution. We found that CA has attached SCT extensions for certificates after April 2018, which greatly reduce the tasks of certificate administrators. However, existing long-term certificates did not set SCT. Chung *et al.* [18] conducted extensive research on web PKI. They found that most certificates and clients support OCSP, while OCSP Must-Staple was not supported by major browsers and servers, and OCSP responders were still not available. We show that OCSP stapling still has low adoption and none of the certificate set OCSP Must-staple.

Study of Certificate Administrator. Some work has also been done on professionals and developers associated with certificate deployment and revealed that it is difficult to deploy certificates correctly. Ukrop *et al.* [7] did an empirical study with 75 IT professionals and found that they place too much confidence on self-signed certificates and name constrained certificates, and existing error notification mechanisms need be adjusted. Zeng *et al.* [56] tested the effectiveness of the notifications of HTTPS configurations.They sent secure notifications to the administrators of certificate misconfigured sites in two ways and found that notifications had moderate impact on error recoveries. Krombholz *et al.* [57] did a research of 28 knowledgeable participants related to HTTPS deployment on Apache and interviewed 7 experienced security auditors. And they revealed that making a correct TLS configurations on Apache including certificate installations was complicated. And our analysis show that there are still round 27% domain name administrators misconfigured the HTTPS certificates and this situation was maintained throughout our measurements.

6 Conclusion

In this paper, we first summarized the new trends of HTTPS certificate management over the past five years. We examined more than 30,000 domain names of CERNET belonging to 113 universities in 12 weeks. We found a stable ratio of domain names did not follow the latest guidelines. We also discussed the usability factors of misconfigurations, and observed some factors did relate to the deployment issues. We hope that our research efforts contribute to HTTPS deployment and fosters future work on network security.

References

1. Usage statistics of Default protocol https for websites. https://w3techs.com/technologies/details/ce-httpsdefault
2. The mozilla observatory. https://observatory.mozilla.org/
3. Acer, M.E., et al.: Where the wild warnings are: root causes of chrome https certificate errors. In: Proceedings of the 2017 ACM SIGSAC Conference on Computer and Communications Security 2017, pp. 1407–1420 (2017)
4. Kumar, D., et al.: Tracking certificate misissuance in the wild. In: IEEE Symposium on Security and Privacy (SP). IEEE 2018, pp. 785–798 (2018)
5. Schwittmann, L., Wander, M., Weis, T.: Domain impersonation is feasible: a study of ca domain validation vulnerabilities. In: IEEE European Symposium on Security and Privacy (EuroS&P). IEEE 2019, pp. 544–559 (2019)
6. Singanamalla, S., Jang, E.H.B., Anderson, R., Kohno, T., Heimerl, K.: Accept the risk and continue: measuring the long tail of government https adoption. In: Proceedings of the ACM Internet Measurement Conference 2020, pp. 577–597 (2020)
7. Ukrop, M., Kraus, L., Matyas, V., Wahsheh, H.A.M.: Will you trust this TLS certificate? Perceptions of people working in it. In: Proceedings of the 35th Annual Computer Security Applications Conference, 2019, pp. 718–731 (2019)
8. Ssl pulse. https://www.ssllabs.com/ssl-pulse/
9. All trusted web PKI certificate authority certificates known to Mozilla will be cached locally. https://lwn.net/Articles/817182/

10. Intermediate ca caching could be used to fingerprint firefox users. https://threatpost.com/intermediate-ca-caching-could-be-used-to-fingerprint-firefox-users/123834/

11. Aas, J., et al.: Let's encrypt: an automated certificate authority to encrypt the entire web. In: Proceedings of the 2019 ACM SIGSAC Conference on Computer and Communications Security 2019, pp. 2473–2487 (2019)

12. 2020 ISRG annual report. https://www.abetterinternet.org/documents/2020-ISRG-Annual-Report.pdf

13. Instagram forgets to renew its SSL certificate. https://news.netcraft.com/archives/2015/04/30/instagram-forgets-to-renew-its-ssl-certificate.html

14. EV UI Moving to Page Info. https://chromium.googlesource.com/chromium/src/+/HEAD/docs/security/ev-to-page-info.md

15. Improved security and privacy indicators in firefox 70. https://blog.mozilla.org/security/2019/10/15/improved-security-and-privacy-indicators-in-firefox-70/

16. Extended validation certificates are dead. https://www.troyhunt.com/extended-validation-certificates-are-dead/

17. Smith, T., Dickinson, L., Seamons, K.: Let's revoke: scalable global certificate revocation. In: 27th Annual Network and Distributed System Security Symposium, NDSS (2020)

18. Chung, T., et al.: Is the web ready for OCSP must-staple? In: Proceedings of the Internet Measurement Conference 2018, pp. 105–118 (2018)

19. Hallam-Baker, P.: X. 509v3 transport layer security (TLS) feature extension, RFC 7633 (2015)

20. CA/Revocation Checking in Firefox. https://wiki.mozilla.org/CA/Revocation_Checking_in_Firefox#OCSP_Must-staple

21. Stark, E., et al.: Does certificate transparency break the web? Measuring adoption and error rate. In: IEEE Symposium on Security and Privacy (SP) 2019, pp. 211–226. IEEE (2019)

22. Nykvist, C., Sjöström, L., Gustafsson, J., Carlsson, N.: Server-side adoption of certificate transparency. In: Beverly, R., Smaragdakis, G., Feldmann, A. (eds.) PAM 2018. LNCS, vol. 10771, pp. 186–199. Springer, Cham (2018). https://doi.org/10.1007/978-3-319-76481-8_14

23. Cangialosi, F., Chung, T., Choffnes, D., Levin, D., Maggs, B.M., Mislove, A., Wilson, C.: Measurement and analysis of private key sharing in the https ecosystem. In: Proceedings of the 2016 ACM SIGSAC Conference on Computer and Communications Security 2016, pp. 628–640 (2016)

24. Zhang, M., et al.: Talking with familiar strangers: an empirical study on https context confusion attacks. In: Proceedings of the 2020 ACM SIGSAC Conference on Computer and Communications Security, 2020, pp. 1939–1952 (2020)

25. Squarcina, M., Tempesta, M., Veronese, L., Calzavara, S., Maffei, M.: Can i take your subdomain? Exploring related-domain attacks in the modern web. arXiv preprint arXiv:2012.01946 (2020)

26. Cernet. http://www.edu.cn/english/

27. Project 211. https://en.wikipedia.org/wiki/Project_211

28. Network Service. https://its.pku.edu.cn/service_1_dns.jsp

29. Sublist3r. https://github.com/aboul3la/Sublist3r

30. ctr.sh. https://crt.sh/

31. Requests. https://requests.readthedocs.io/en/master/

32. Deprecations and Removals in Chrome 58. https://developers.google.com/web/updates/2017/03/chrome-58-deprecations

33. Requirements for trusted certificates in iOS 13 and macOS 10.15. https://support.apple.com/en-us/HT210176
34. About upcoming limits on trusted certificates. https://support.apple.com/en-us/HT211025
35. Certificate lifetimes. https://chromium.googlesource.com/chromium/src/+/master/net/docs/certificate_lifetimes.md
36. Reducing TLS certificate lifespans to 398 days. https://blog.mozilla.org/security/2020/07/09/reducing-tls-certificate-lifespans-to-398-days/
37. Ballot 193–825-day certificate lifetimes. https://cabforum.org/2017/03/17/ballot-193-825-day-certificate-lifetimes/
38. Preloading Intermediate CA Certificates into Firefox. https://blog.mozilla.org/security/2020/11/13/preloading-intermediate-ca-certificates-into-firefox/
39. Certificate transparency. https://chromium.googlesource.com/chromium/src/+/master/net/docs/certificate-transparency.md
40. Apple's certificate transparency policy. https://support.apple.com/en-us/HT205280
41. Wang, X., Yu, H.: How to break MD5 and other hash functions. In: Cramer, R. (ed.) EUROCRYPT 2005. LNCS, vol. 3494, pp. 19–35. Springer, Heidelberg (2005). https://doi.org/10.1007/11426639_2
42. Announcing the first sha1 collision. https://security.googleblog.com/2017/02/announcing-first-sha1-collision.html
43. Apple drops support for sha-1 certificates in macos catalina and ios 13. https://www.macrumors.com/2019/06/06/apple-deprecates-sha1-macos-catalina-ios-13/
44. A further update on SHA-1 certificates in chrome. https://www.chromium.org/Home/chromium-security/education/tls/sha-1
45. Barker, E., Roginsky, A.: Transitioning the use of cryptographic algorithms and key lengths. Technical report, National Institute of Standards and Technology (2018)
46. Chrome Root Store. https://www.chromium.org/Home/chromium-security/root-ca-policy
47. Available trusted root certificates for Apple operating systems. https://support.apple.com/en-us/HT209143
48. CA certificates extracted from Mozilla. https://curl.se/docs/caextract.html
49. Release notes - Microsoft Trusted Root Certificate Program. https://docs.microsoft.com/en-us/security/trusted-root/release-notes
50. pyOpenSSL's documentation. https://www.pyopenssl.org/en/stable/
51. ev_root_ca_metadata. https://chromium.googlesource.com/chromium/src/net/+/master/cert/ev_root_ca_metadata.cc
52. Razaghpanah, A., Niaki, A.A., Vallina-Rodriguez, N., Sundaresan, S., Amann, J., Gill, P.: Studying TLS usage in android apps. In: Proceedings of the 13th International Conference on Emerging Networking EXperiments and Technologies 2017, pp. 350–362 (2017)
53. Alashwali, E.S., Szalachowski, P., Martin, A.: Does www. mean better transport layer security?. In: Proceedings of the 14th International Conference on Availability, Reliability and Security 2019, pp. 1–7 (2019)
54. Tiefenau, C., von Zezschwitz, E., Häring, M., Krombholz, K., Smith, M.: A usability evaluation of let's encrypt and Certbot: usable security done right. In: Proceedings of the 2019 ACM SIGSAC Conference on Computer and Communications Security 2019, pp. 1971–1988 (2019)
55. Bernhard, M., Sharman, J., Acemyan, C.Z., Kortum, P., Wallach, D.S., Halderman, J.A.: On the usability of https deployment. In: Proceedings of the 2019 CHI Conference on Human Factors in Computing Systems 2019, pp. 1–10 (2019)

56. Zeng, E., Li, F., Stark, E., Felt, A.P., Tabriz, P.: Fixing https misconfigurations at scale: an experiment with security notifications (2019)

57. Krombholz, K., Mayer, W., Schmiedecker, M., Weippl, E.: "" i have no idea what i'm doing"-on the usability of deploying {HTTPS}". In: 26th {USENIX} Security Symposium ({USENIX} Security 17) 2017, pp. 1339–1356 (2017)

ZERMIA - A Fault Injector Framework for Testing Byzantine Fault Tolerant Protocols

João Soares[1,2]([envelope])[iD], Ricardo Fernandez[1], Miguel Silva[1], Tadeu Freitas[1][iD], and Rolando Martins[1,2][iD]

[1] Faculdade de Ciências, Universidade do Porto, 4169-007 Porto, Portugal
{joao.soares,rmartins}@fc.up.pt
[2] CRACS - INESC TEC, 4200-465 Porto, Portugal

Abstract. Byzantine fault tolerant (BFT) protocols are designed to increase system dependability and security. They guarantee *liveness* and *correctness* even in the presence of arbitrary faults. However, testing and validating BFT systems is not an easy task. As is the case for most concurrent and distributed applications, the correctness of these systems is not solely dependant on algorithm and protocol correctness. Ensuring the correct behaviour of BFT systems requires exhaustive testing under real-world scenarios. An approach is to use fault injection tools that deliberate introduce faults into a target system to observe its behaviour. However, existing tools tend to be designed for specific applications and systems, thus cannot be used generically.

We argue that more advanced and powerful tools and frameworks are needed for testing the security and safety of distributed applications in general, and BFT systems in particular. Specifically, a fault injection framework that can be integrated into both client and server side applications, for testing them exhaustively.

We present ZERMIA, a modular and extensible fault injection framework, designed for testing and validating concurrent and distributed applications. We validate ZERMIA's principles by conduction a series of experiments on a distributed applications and a state of the art BFT library, to show the benefits of ZERMIA for testing and validating applications.

Keywords: Fault injection · System validation · System testing · Testing · Fault · Byzantine fault tolerance · Fault tolerance systems · Distributed systems

This work was partially funded by POCI-01-0247-FEDER-041435 (SafeCities), POCI-01-0247-FEDER-047264 (Theia) and POCI-01-0247-FEDER-039598 (COP) financed by Fundo Europeu de Desenvolvimento Regional (FEDER), through COMPETE 2020 and Portugal 2020. Rolando Martins was partially supported by project EU H2020-SU-ICT-03-2018 No. 830929 CyberSec4Europe.

© Springer Nature Switzerland AG 2021
M. Yang et al. (Eds.): NSS 2021, LNCS 13041, pp. 38–60, 2021.
https://doi.org/10.1007/978-3-030-92708-0_3

1   Introduction

Byzantine fault tolerant (BFT) protocols [2,3,5,6,10,27,33] are designed to increase system dependability and security. They guarantee liveness and correctness even in the presence of arbitrary faults, including not only hardware/-software faults, but also malicious actors that try to compromise systems/applications by subverting their protocols.

BFT consensus protocols have also been adopted as the consensus mechanism used by different private blockchain systems [40,45]. These protocols replace the original and resource intensive proof-of-work based ones, with more efficient and high-performing ones. However, any compromises to their design and implementations can lead to a compromise of the underlying blockchain and application.

BFT systems are commonly theoretically proofed on their correction. Still, for these systems to be efficiently implemented in practice, some level of compromise is commonly needed. These compromises may invalidate the protocol correctness if not thoroughly tested and validated, and could be taken advantage of by highly skilled opponents. For example, many assumptions on liveness are based on predefined timeouts that, when misconfigured, can compromise the protocol's efficiency [31].

However, testing and validating BFT systems is not an easy task. As is the case for most concurrent and distributed applications, the correctness of these systems is not solely dependant on algorithm and protocol correctness but is also influenced by the reliability and latency of communications. This is aggravated when the protocol itself needs to deal with the possibility of agents trying to subvert the protocol. Thus, ensuring the correct behaviour of BFT systems requires exhaustive testing under real-world scenarios.

1.1   Fault Injection

An approach to test these systems in real-world scenarios is to use fault injection tools [4,20,22,41]. Fault injection is the deliberate introduction of faults into a system to observe its behaviour. This is a valuable approach to validate the dependability properties of systems and applications [1,30].

Fault injection tools typically fall into hardware-based, software-based, or hybrid hardware/software approaches. Software fault injection tools are typically designed to introduce faults either during pre-runtime (e.g., compile -time, executable image manipulation [20])or at runtime [22,41].

However, existing *Fault Injection* (FI) tools tend to be designed and implemented for specific applications and systems, thus cannot be used generically by any application. In fact, most FI tools are not designed for concurrent applications and systems, as such, are unable to deal with the requirements presented by these applications. Namely, inject faults on specific threads or processes, coordinate faults between threads and processes, and/or deal with non-deterministic execution flows that may occur in this class of applications. We argue that more advanced and powerful tools and frameworks need to be designed, for testing the security and safety of distributed applications in general, and BFT systems in particular.

To this end we present a brief study on one of the most influential BFT protocols, PBFT [5,6], to identify the requirements imposed by such protocols when designing a fault injector framework. Additionally, we present the design of a modular and extensible fault injection framework (called ZERMIA), that allows developers to use generic and/or design/implement tailor-made fault for testing their systems/application, without requiring modifications to the original systems.

The remainder of this paper is organized as follows: Sects. 2 and 3 presents relevant fault injection tools and frameworks, and PBFT's agreement protocol. Section 4, 5, and 6 present the design, implementation and evaluation of ZER-MIA; and, Sect. 7 concludes this paper by presenting some concluding remarks, lessons learned and future work.

2   Related Work

Software fault injection (SFI) [35] is a technique for testing and assessing the dependability of software systems. Ferrari [24] uses software traps to inject CPU, memory, and bus faults. It uses a parallel daemon process running on the host processor to control the application in which the faults need to be injected. It is capable of injecting faults in the address, data or the control lines of the processor.

In Ftape [42] bit-flip faults are injected into user-accessible registers in CPU modules, memory locations, and the disk subsystem. DOCTOR [20] allows injection of CPU faults, memory faults, and network communication faults. It uses three triggering methods to indicate the start of fault injection. These methods are time-out, trap, and code modification. Xception [4] takes advantage of advanced debugging and performance monitoring features present in modern processors to inject faults. In particular, it uses built-in hardware exception triggers to perform fault injections. This requires modification of the interrupt hardware vector. In FIAT [39] an approach to inject single bit flips in the instruction memory of the application was proposed.

The PROPANE (PROPagation ANalysis Environment) [21] tool injects faults in C code executing on desktop computers. The code is instrumented with fault injection mechanisms and probes for logging traces of data values and memory areas. PROPANE supports the injection of both software faults (by mutation of source code) and data errors (by manipulating variable and memory contents). Another tool that takes advantage of processor debugging facilities is MAFALDA [14]. This tool has aimed to evaluate the use of COTS micro-kernels in safety-critical systems.

Loki [7] is a fault injector for distributed systems that injects faults based on a partial view of the global system state. Loki allows the user to specify a state machine and a fault injection campaign in which faults are triggered by state changes.

FIRE [30] and JACA [29] use reflective programming to inject and monitor C++ and Java applications respectively can change the values of parameters, attributes and returned variables. J-SWFIT [36] is a framework for Java programs that provide two fault types.

PIN [23] dynamically inserts code at runtime allowing a fault to be injected at a specific code location which allows recreating faults that result from common coding errors. LLFI [28] and Relyzer [37] use compiler based techniques to inject code into the compiler for intermediate representation and to determine the equivalence of different fault sites in a target application.

Duraes et al. [12] study on bug fixing in open-source and commercial software systems has found that many software faults involve several program statements. More recently, study [11] on software bugs in OpenStack found that the fault model proposed by Duraes et al. [12] cannot cover some frequent bug types in distributed systems.

Gunawi et al. [19] describe a framework for systematically injecting sequences of faults in a system under test. The authors present Failure IDs as a means of identifying injection points and describe a method for systematically generating injection sequences. A take from this work is that relevant and efficient testing requires users to know the target application' specification for estimating relevant testing cases and if its behaviour is correct even under injection.

3   BFT Protocol Overview

Byzantine Fault Tolerant (BFT) protocols are designed to guarantee the correct system/application behaviour, even in the presence of arbitrary faults (i.e., Byzantine faults). Typically, BFT protocols use a state machine replication (SMR) approach [25,38], where multiples instances of the same state machine replicate the application's state. SMR guarantees that if all state machines (replicas) start in the same consistent state and execute the same set of operations in the same order, all correct machines will reach the same final state, ensuring state consistency among replicas (as long as state changes are deterministic).

BFT protocols are designed to ensure both *safety* and *liveness*. *Safety* ensures that correct replicas that execute the same set of operations in the same order reach the same final state and produce the same result, while *liveness* guarantees that correct replicas eventually execute all requests from correct clients.

Nodes (i.e., clients or replicas) communicate with each other by sending messages through a network that might drop, corrupt, or delay messages. No assumptions are made concerning the latency for delivering messages, as these systems are designed to ensure safety even in the absence of an upper bound on network and processing delays. However, to overcome the FLP impossibility [15] synchronous phases are required to guarantee liveness [8,13]. Nodes authenticate all messages they send either by using signatures (e.g., RSA [34]) or message authentication codes (MACs) [5,43].

A correct consensus protocol guarantees the following properties: *i*) Termination - correct replicas eventually learn about some decided value; *ii* Agreement - correct replicas must agree on the same value; *iii* Validity - if correct replicas propose a value, then all correct replicas eventually decide on that value;

iv Integrity - a correct replica can only decide on one value. If a correct replica decides on a value, then some other correct replicas must have proposed that value.

Faulty nodes (clients or replicas) are assumed to fail arbitrarily, possibly by: failing to send messages to each other; sending incorrect values; or, sending conflicting messages with diverging contents. Typically, no conjectures are made on the fault origins. Thus, there is no distinction between faulty replica behaviour caused by software bugs or replicas failing as the result of a successful malicious intrusion. In addition, nodes cannot determine whether a node is faulty or simply advances at a slower pace since they have no knowledge of the occurrence and duration of network synchrony. Finally, multiple compromised nodes are expected to potentially collude with each other. However, faulty nodes are assumed to not be able to break cryptographic primitives and consequently cannot impersonate correct nodes.

3.1   PBFT Protocol

PBFT [5,6] is the first practical BFT solution designed to work in asynchronous environments (i.e., the Internet). It is a leader-based SMR-BFT protocol that requires $N = 3f + 1$ replicas for guaranteeing *liveness* and *safety* in the presence of up to f faults. Assumes a partial synchronous network communication model and ensures node and message authentication based on either MACs or digital signatures.

Agreement Protocol. Figure 1 presents the PBFT's agreement protocol, consisting of the following steps[1]:

1. Clients send REQUEST messages to all replicas. These messages contain the operation to be executed, a timestamp (used for once-only semantics), and the client's identifier.
2. When a primary receives a REQUEST message, it authenticates the message. If valid, a PRE-PREPARE message is sent to all replicas. PRE-PREPARE messages include the current view number, a sequence number (assigned by the primary), and the client's message digest.
3. When replicas receive a PRE-PREPARE message, they validate it by checking if it has the expected view and sequence number. If valid, a PREPARE message is multicasted to all replicas. PREPARE messages include the current view number, the sequence number(formerly assigned by the primary), a digest of the client's request, and the replica's id.
4. When a replica receives at least $2f$ valid and matching PREPARE messages (i.e., with the same view, sequence number, and digest from different replicas), they multicast a COMMIT message to all replicas. COMMIT messages consist

---

[1] All messages exchanged during this protocol are signed by the respective sender for authentication purposes. Validating messages includes validating the message signature.

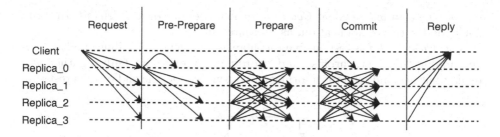

| Request | Pre-Prepare | Prepare | Commit | Reply |

Fig. 1. BFT-SMaRt agreement protocol

of the view and sequence number from the respective quorum of PREPARE messages and the replica's id.

5. When a replica receives $2f + 1$ valid and matching COMMIT (i.e., with the same view and sequence number, from different replicas) it can then execute the respective operation in the order defined by the view and sequence number (used for totally ordering REQUESTS), and send a REPLY message to the client. REPLY messages include the view number, the request's timestamp, the client's and replica's identifier, and the operation's result.

Clients that receive at least $2f + 1$ matching REPLY messages from different replicas have the guarantee that the operation executed successfully.

3.2 Faulty Behaviour

While PBFT has additional sub-protocols (including view-change, checkpoint, and recovery), their descriptions are outside of the article's scope. However, for the agreement protocol, it is possible to identify several ways in which a faulty node can behave, or how a malicious actor could try to subvert the protocol, by compromising one of the system's properties, namely: Termination, Agreement, Validity or Integrity.

Besides the typical communication-related faults (such as delaying, dropping, or corrupting messages), faulty nodes may send different messages to each replica, or a subset of replicas, to try and prevent termination from occurring. These include REQUEST messages with different operations and/or timestamps to each replica; PRE-PREPARE and PREPARE messages with different view and sequence numbers to each replica. All these faults prevent the agreement protocol from terminating. Note that these faults are in no way exhaustive. However, these allow to identify requirements for our fault injection tool, specifically for validation and evaluation purposes.

4   ZERMIA Design

ZERMIA is a fault injector designed for concurrent and distributed applications, with flexibility, extensibility, and efficiency in mind. It is based on a client-server model, where an independent *Coordinator* manages one or more *Agents* that run alongside the target application, as presented in Fig. 2.

The *Coordinator* is responsible for: managing Agents; distribute fault schedules among them; synchronise and coordinate Agents and faults; gather and display metrics and relevant information, during and at the end of each test run.

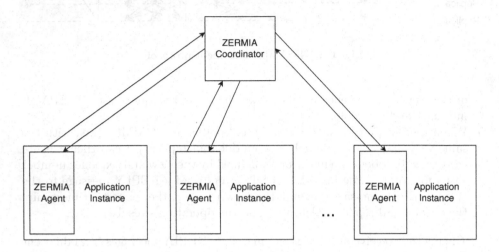

Fig. 2. Overview of the ZERMIA architecture

An *Agent* runs alongside the target application by sharing that process's runtime. When starting the target application, Agents execute their bootstrap, where they register with the Coordinator and request their respective fault scheduler. Then, they advance alongside the application triggering faults according to their fault schedule, gathering and sharing metrics with the Coordinator.

Agents attach to specific points of the target program, as defined in the fault schedule. They can alter the target's execution state and flow, by accessing method calls, arguments, return values and application state. Agents are also capable of maintaining additional state, independent of the application, such as the number of iterations of the application's main loop, or, in our case, the number of consensus rounds. This increases flexibility since ZERMIA can use this additional information for triggering faults.

4.1 Faults

In ZERMIA, faults are characterised by the following information: *what* is the fault (i.e., the code to be injected); *where* to inject the fault (i.e., the target function or method); *when* to inject the fault (i.e., the condition required to trigger the fault); and, *how* to trigger the fault (i.e., if the fault is to be triggered before, after, and if it prevents the target from executing). In addition, each fault may have additional parameters that allow users to customise or adjust their behaviour.

Since ZERMIA is designed for distributed applications in mind, it provides users with a set of predefined faults that can be parameterised and scheduled without modifications. These include communications and network-related faults (like message delay, message drop, message modifications, etc.) that are typical in these contexts. ZERMIA also defines a generic *Fault Interface* that offers users the means to design and build custom faults for testing their target applications.

4.2   Schedules

Schedules are a sequence of zero or more faults that will be injected into an application during a test run. These include information about the Agent that will apply the schedule, the set of faults that are to be injected by the Agent and the corresponding execution model.

ZERMIA provides scheduling flexibility, offering support for:

- independent fault schedules for each Agent, including fault free schedules (i.e., schedules with zero faults);
- fault dependencies within the same schedule, i.e., dependencies between faults triggered by a single Agent. For instance, prevent a fault from triggering if a previous (possibly different) fault has already been triggered;
- fault dependencies between schedules, i.e., dependencies between fault triggered by different Agents. For instance, only inject a fault after some other Agent has injected its own;
- a priority-based system, that orders faults according to their priority, for resolving possible fault scheduling conflicts deterministically. For example, when two or more faults can be triggered at the same instant.

Both the fault dependency and priority based mechanisms are designed for ZERMIA to deal with possible non-deterministic behaviour of concurrent and distributed applications.

Consider, for example, fault $f1$ that is scheduled based on a time instant (e.g., after application runs for 60 s), and fault $f2$ that is scheduled based on a message receive event (e.g., when receiving a message from another node). Depending on a node's performance or network latency, in some test runs, fault $f1$ may be scheduled before fault $f2$, or $f2$ may be scheduled before $f1$, or even in some cases, both faults can be scheduled at the same instant. Both mechanisms can be used to ensuring a deterministic behaviour (e.g., $f1$ is always triggered after $f2$ or vice-versa), and to allow testing applications with greater reliability, by testing all possible fault interleavings.

4.3   Triggers

While several frameworks and tools provide mechanisms for defining faults based on *What*, *Where* and *When* criteria [32], we consider these criteria to be insufficient for testing concurrent and distributed applications.

Typically, *What* allows users to specify the fault to be injected (i.e., the code of the fault), *Where* allows users to specify the location in which the fault is

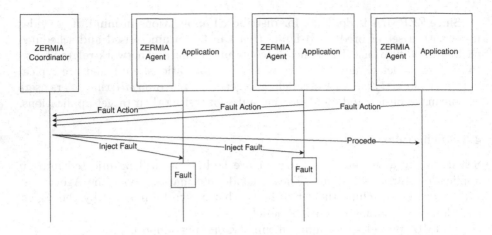

Fig. 3. Coordinator based triggering model

to be injected (i.e., method signature, memory address, et cetera.), and *When* allows users to specify an instance for injecting the fault (i.e., time or event dependency).

However, concurrent and distributed applications require faults to be triggered by specific threads, processes, or nodes. Additionally, the replicated nature of BFT protocols introduces additional problems, such as how to differentiate between primary and secondary replicas, since their codebase is the same.

For these reasons, ZERMIA uses a hybrid trigger approach, where faults are created and added to the target application's code at compile time and triggered *dynamically* at runtime.

For added flexibility, ZERMIA includes different trigger models, including: *i*) managed by the Coordinator; *ii*) managed by the Agent; and, *iii*) a hybrid approach managed by both the Agent and the Coordinator[2].

Furthermore, fault triggers can be state or event-based, i.e., dependant of target application's state or dependant on some event. For example, a fault can be triggered after a predefined number of consensus rounds, or whenever a message is received (independently of the message type, sender, contents, etc.).

Coordinator-Based Triggering Model. In the Coordinator-based approach, the Coordinator is responsible for managing and triggering faults. Agents query the Coordinator before each fault to determine if the fault is to be triggered or not, as presented in Fig. 3.

This allows the Coordinator to have a global view of the application execution history and state, and offers the possibility of synchronising and coordinating Agents before triggering faults.

---

[2] Note that Agents do not exchange information directly with each other, all synchronisation and coordination is managed by the Coordinator.

However, this synchronization may compromise testing, since it influences the target application's execution flow due to the added synchronization.

Agent-Based Triggering Model. The agent-based approach does not require the Agent to periodically contact the Coordinator, leaving the Agent responsible for triggering faults. This technique reduces overhead, compared with the previous model, as well as prevents the synchronization from compromising the target application's execution flows, since no communications are needed between Agents and the Coordinator.

However, this model requires Agents to maintain the application execution history and/or state, for validating if fault triggering conditions are satisfied, resulting in an increase of complexity for the Agent implementation. It also prevents external fault dependencies (i.e., fault dependencies between schedules) from triggering, since no synchronisation is performed with the Coordinator.

Hybrid Triggering Model. A Hybrid triggering model is also available, where Agents can trigger faults autonomously or synchronise with the Coordinator for triggering faults with external dependencies.

Like in the Agent-based model, this increases complexity in the Agent since it is responsible for managing target application history and/or state. However, it reduces overhead, compared with the Coordinator-based model, and increases flexibility, compared with the Agent-based model, since fault may have external dependencies and only these faults require synchronisation with the Coordinator.

Reducing the overhead is important, since an intrusive fault injector can compromise the target application's execution flow, which in turn compromises test run validity. ZERMIA tries to reach a balance between overhead and flexibility while being able to simulate a wide range of execution scenarios possible.

4.4   Dealing with Non-determinism

Concurrent and distributed applications typically suffer from non-deterministic execution traces due to different thread/process interleaving. This is known to result in concurrency errors, which are difficult to detect and reproduce [16,17, 26,44].

In order to reduce non-determinism and increase test coverage, ZERMIA provides different mechanisms, including the Coordinator-based and Hybrid triggering models, and the priority-based fault system.

Both triggering models reduce non-determinism and allows testing different fault interleavings by synchronising Agents with the Coordinator before triggering faults. This allows users to test all possible fault interleaving for their schedules based on these dependencies.

The fault priority system, that allows users to assign priorities to faults, can be used to order faults, when two or more faults can be triggered concurrently (i.e., at the same instant) [3]. Changing fault priorities allows users to test different fault orders.

4.5 Discussion

The client-server model of ZERMIA decouples the coordination and management from the Agents processes. This contributes to the extensibility of ZERMIA since Agents can be implemented in different programming languages without requiring any modifications to the Coordinator component. Furthermore, our

```
[
    Agent {
        id: 1,
        faults: [
            DelayFault_0 {
                what: zermia.fault.predefined.DelayFault,
                params: {
                    duration: 100,
                    unit: ms,
                },
                when: {
                    start: 5000,
                    end: 10000,
                    unit: round,
                },
                where: bftsmart.communication.
                    server.ServersCommunicationLayer.
                        send(..),
                how: before,
            },
            CrashFault_0 {
                fault: zermia.fault.predefined.Crash,
                when: {
                    start: 20000,
                    unit: round,
                },
                where: bftsmart.communication.
                    server.ServersConnection.
                        sendBytes(..)
                how: before,
            },
        ]
    },
    Agent {
        id: 2,
        faults: [
            CrashFault_1 {
                fault: zermia.fault.predefined.Crash,
                when: {
                    after: CrashFault_0,
                },
                where: bftsmart.communitation.
                    server.ServersConnection.
                        sendBytes(..)
                how: before,
            },
        ]
    }
]
```

Fig. 4. Example of a fault schedule

---

[3] Note that this can occur when fault triggering conditions are based on different factors, e.g., after a number of rounds and after receiving a specific message.

fault model allows users to design and develop custom faults by implementing the Fault interface, as discussed in Sect. 5.

The fault and schedule models provided by ZERMIA offer a flexible platform for testing different kinds of applications, independently of the concurrency model. For instance, in a non-concurrent application, ZERMIA can be used with a single Agent that is responsible for managing fault injection, while in a concurrent application, each process or thread can have its own Agent. This allows faults to be triggered independently on a per-process/thread basis, or to coordinate faults between processed/threads. The same principles apply to distributed and replicated applications, where each node/replica can have its own Agent.

Figure 4 represents an example of a fault schedule where Agent 1 executes a Delay fault (of 100 ms) between consensus rounds 5000 and 10000, before method *ServersCommunicationLayer.send*, and a Crash fault at round 20000 before method *ServersConnection.sendBytes*. Agent 2 executes a Crash fault before method *ServersConnection.sendBytes* only after Agent 1 has "crashed".

5 Implementation Details

ZERMIA is currently implemented in Java and uses AspectJ (an aspect-oriented programming extension) for integrating Agents with the target application. Communications between Coordinator and Agents use gRPC [18], decoupling both components and allowing users to extend the framework with support for additional programming languages without having to modify the Coordinator.

5.1 Coordinator

The Coordinator is responsible for managing and coordinating Agents and their respective fault schedulers. During startup, the fault schedule, defined by the users, is read from a file. Then the Coordinator initializes the gRPC communication channels and waits for Agents to connect.

gRPC Interface. Agents interact with the Coordinator using the gRPC interface presented in Fig. 5. This interface allows Agents to register, request their respective fault schedulers, validate fault triggering conditions, notify about fault execution, and update test metrics.

```
service ZermiaCoordinatorServices{
    rpc RegisterAgent {..}
    rpc RequestScheduller {..}
    rpc FaultTriggerValidation {..}
    rpc NotifyFaultExecution {..}
    rpc UpdateMetrics {..}
}
```

Fig. 5. Coordinator service interface (gRPC methods)

5.2   Agents

Agents are responsible for registering with the Coordinator and injecting faults into the target application. They integrate with the target application through the use of *advices*. *Advices* are blocks of code that are inserted into the target application's code at compile-time by the use of *join-points*. *Join-points* are the locations on the target application's code where the *advices* are inserted. These have an associated semantics for specifying if an advice executes before, after or around the respective join-point, referred to as *pointcuts*. The around semantics can also be used to prevent executing the corresponding join-point (i.e., target method). In our current implementation, an Agent is instantiated when a replica starts by using an advice associated with the replica's *main* function.

During bootstrap, the Agent registers with the Coordinator, requests its fault schedule (using the gRPC services presented in Fig. 5), and initialises the necessary data structures for maintaining its state. This includes the value of the current consensus round and the fault schedule (represented as a list of Fault objects). Figure 6 presents a simplified view of the Agent code.

During the application execution, whenever a join-point is called, the execution context is passed to the Agent that verifies if any fault in its schedule is to execute at that join-point, and if the fault's trigger conditions are met (using the *canTrigger* method). If both are true, then the fault is executed according to its semantics.

```
public class ZermiaAgent {
    // state variables
    List<Fault> schedule;
    int currentConsensusRound;
    (...)
    @Around ("execution method_signature1")
    public void execute(JointPoint jp) {
        for f in schedule {
            if ( f.canTrigger(jp, currentConsensusRound) ) {
                if (f.how() == Fault.AFTER)
                    jp.proceed();
                f.triggerFault();
                if (f.how() == Fault.INSTEAD)
                    return;
                else //Fault.BEFORE
                    jp.proceed();
            }
        }
    }
    @After ("execution main_app_loop")
    public void new_iteration() {
        currentConsensusRound += 1;
    }
    (...)
}
```

Fig. 6. Agent implementation example (JAVA)

Additional Join-points. Agents may use additional join-points for managing their state. In our case, we identified the application's main loop to be associated with the consensus round. When a new PRE-PREPARE message is received, a new consensus round starts, as presented in Fig. 1. When the join-point is called, the Agent updates its current consensus round (Fig. 6). This allows an Agent to decide to trigger faults based on this information.

```
public class DelayFault implements Fault {
    //parameter variables
    String methodName;
    int start;
    int end;
    int duration;
    int how;
    (...)
    public boolean canTrigger(JointPoint jp, int currentRound) {
        if (jp.getName().equals(methodName))
            return this.start <= currentRound && currentRound <= end;
        return false;
    }
    public FaultResult triggerFault() {
        try {
            Thread.currentThread().sleep(duration);
        } catch (...) {..}
    }
}
```

Fig. 7. Delay fault implementation example (JAVA)

5.3   Faults

Rather than being mapped as advices and inserted into joint-points at compile-time, faults are instantiated during an Agent bootstrap and base on the description received from the Coordinator. Each fault in the schedule is instantiated using the corresponding class loader, configured according to its parameters, and added to the respective schedule.

When an Agent calls the *canTrigger* method, it validates if its join-point is the same as the one passed by the Agent and if the associated conditions are met. Figure 7 presents an example of a delay fault that delays the execution of the respective joint-point for some period of time. Its preconditions are only related to the joint-point signature, and the value of consensus round passed as argument. If all conditions are true, the fault can execute, being bypassed otherwise.

Fault Interface. For custom building fault, ZERMIA provides users with a generic Fault interface, as presented in Fig. 8. This interface contains three methods: *canTrigger*, *triggerFault*, and *how*. The first two methods are used by the Agent to validate the preconditions of the fault (i.e., if it can be triggered) and to execute the fault if the preconditions are satisfied, while the last is used to determine the fault's semantics (i.e., fault's pointcuts)

```
public interface Fault {
    public boolean canTrigger(JointPoint jp);
    public FaultResult triggerFault();
    public int how();
}
```

Fig. 8. Generic fault interface (JAVA)

5.4   Predefined Faults and Extensibility

In its current implementation, ZERMIA includes a set of common faults for testing distributed systems. Although these are generic faults, they can be configured
according to the user's requirements. These include:

- **Delay Thread** - Delays execution flow through the use of *Thread.sleep()*
  method. The user can configure the delay in milliseconds.
- **Message Dropping** - Prevents messages from being sent by preventing the
  target method call.
- **Modify Message** - Replaces messages contents by modifying argument values passed to the target join-point. Message contents can be defined by the
  user and may be empty.
- **Message Flood** - Sends a variable number of messages by enclosing the
  target method in a loop. The user can define the number of loop iterations
  (i.e., messages to send).
- **Crash** - Crashes the application by calling the *System.exit()* method.

6   Evaluation

In this section we present the evaluation of ZERMIA by showing its flexibility and efficiency. To this end, we designed different fault schedules that target
BFT-SMaRt [3], a Byzantine Fault tolerant library based on PBFT's agreement
protocol, and applying these schedules when that library is used by an independent application, and under different configurations.

We used YCSB [9] as the application that used the BFT-SMaRt library,
as it presents metrics that allows us to view the influence in performance each
schedule has on the target library.

6.1   Experimental Setup

Each experiment consisted in running YCSB with 50 clients, for a total of 2.5
million operations (approximately 350000 consensus rounds) and measuring the
system throghput (in operations per second). Fault triggering started in consensus round number 50000 for $f = 1$, and rounds 100000 and 150000 for $f = 3$.
Period of fault injection lasted for a variable number of rounds (depending on
the type of fault). BFT-SMaRt was configured with $f = 1$ and $f = 3$, $N = 4$
and $N = 10$ replicas respectively. Specific fault schedules where designed for

each leader and non-leader replicas depending on the experiment, always taking into consideration the protocol's invariant of $f \leq \frac{N-1}{3}$.

A total of twelve virtual machines from Google Cloud services where used: 3–10 for the BFT-SMaRt replicas, 1 for the YCSB clients, and 1 for the Zermia Coordinator. Each machine ran Ubuntu 18.04.5 LTS operative system, with 16 GB of RAM, 4-core AMD EPYC 7B12 clocked at 2.25 GHz, and 10 GB of HDD. The presented results are the average from the results of 5 consecutive runs.

6.2   Baseline Results

Figs. 9a and 9b present the results obtained from fault-free schedules, for $f = 1$ and $f = 3$ respectively. Similar throughput is achieved despite the increase in the number of replicas. These serve as a baseline for comparison when injecting faults.

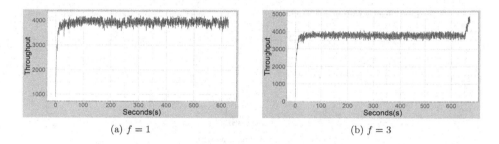

(a) $f = 1$ (b) $f = 3$

Fig. 9. Results from a fault-free schedule

6.3   Delaying Replicas

This experiment consisted in executing a schedule that delayed replicas before sending messages (independent of message type). Faults were triggered for 10000 consecutive consensus rounds, starting at consensus round 50000, 100000, and 150000, with delay intervals of 20 milliseconds, 50 milliseconds, and 100 milliseconds respectively.

Figure 10 presents the results when targeting different replicas with this schedule: the leader (Fig. 10a), the leader and 2 non-leader replicas (Fig. 10b), and 3 non-leader replicas (Fig. 10c).

It is possible to observe a degradation in performance whenever a delay fault targets the primary replica. Additionally, collusion between a primary and secondary replicas yields a similar outcome (Fig. 10b), as system performance is directly related to the rate of *PRE-PROPOSE*. Since these are only transmitted by the primary replicas, delaying secondary replicas does not influence the system performance since the remaining non-faulty replicas are sufficient to guarantee *liveness*. This is corroborated by the results obtained when targeting only secondary replicas (Fig. 10c).

6.4 Crashing Replicas

This experiment consisted in executing a schedule that crashes replicas, triggered at consensus round 50000 for $f = 1$, and 100000 and 150000 for $f = 3$. The schedules targeted both leader and non-leader replicas.

Figure 11 presents the results when targeting only leader replicas for $f = 1$ (Fig. 11a), $f = 3$ (Fig. 11b, and non-leader replicas (Fig. 11c). These schedules result in a performance drop when the fault is injected, i.e., when the leader fails.

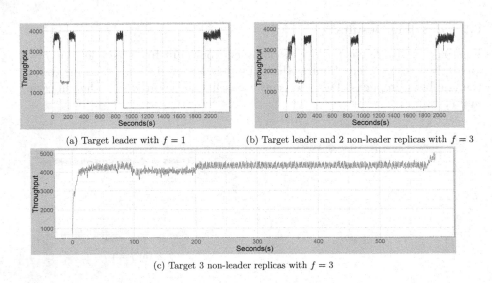

(a) Target leader with $f = 1$ (b) Target leader and 2 non-leader replicas with $f = 3$

(c) Target 3 non-leader replicas with $f = 3$

Fig. 10. Results from a the delay fault schedule

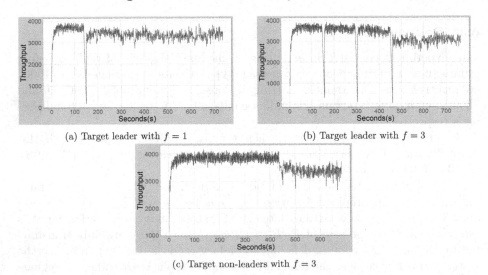

(a) Target leader with $f = 1$ (b) Target leader with $f = 3$

(c) Target non-leaders with $f = 3$

Fig. 11. Results for a crash fault schedule

This is consequence of the protocol adjusting to the crashing replica by electing a new primary. Additionally, it is possible to see a drop in system performance when the system reaches the minimum number of replicas needed to guarantee *safety*.

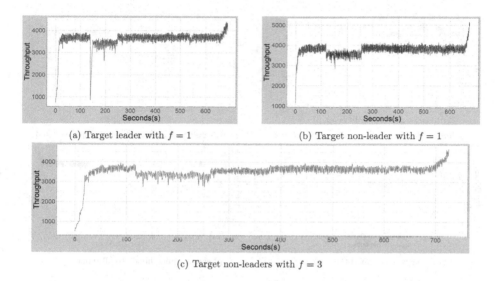

(a) Target leader with $f = 1$ (b) Target non-leader with $f = 1$

(c) Target non-leaders with $f = 3$

Fig. 12. Results for a message dropper schedule

6.5   Message Dropping

This experiment consisted in executing a schedule that drops messages, by bypassing message sending methods, triggering once replicas reached the consensus round 50000, for a duration of 50000 rounds.

Figure 12 presents the obtained results when targeting: the leader with $f = 1$ (Fig. 12a), a non-leader with $f = 1$ (Fig. 12b), and when targeting non-leader replicas with $f = 3$ (Fig. 12c).

These schedules result in a reduction of application performance during the fault period. This reduction in performance is similar to previous results when the number of non-faulty replicas reaches the minimum required for the system to guarantee safety.

6.6   Message Flooding

This experiment consisted in executing different schedules for flooding the system with messages. Faults were triggered at consensus round 50000, for a period 50000 rounds, unless stated otherwise. The flooding consisted in unicasting or multicasting 5000 additional messages for every legitimate message sent, depending on the schedule.

Four different schedules were used, including: a non-leader replica flooding all replicas; a non-leader replica flooding the leader replica; and the leader replica flooding all replicas. For the latter schedule, the period was reduced to 10000 rounds for experiment duration purposes.

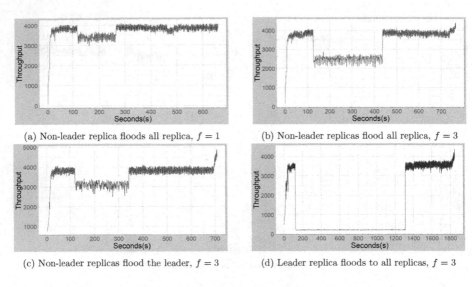

(a) Non-leader replica floods all replica, $f = 1$ (b) Non-leader replicas flood all replica, $f = 3$

(c) Non-leader replicas flood the leader, $f = 3$ (d) Leader replica floods to all replicas, $f = 3$

Fig. 13. Results for a flood schedule

Figure 13 presents the results from this experiment when a non-leader flood all replicas in a $f = 1$ and $f = 3$ configuration (Figs. 13a and 13b respectively), a non-leader floods the leader replica (Fig. 13c), and when the primary floods the system (Fig. 13d).

The presented results show that, increasing the number of replicas flooding the system directly influences the performance impact of the fault, as witnessed by the drop in performance of Fig. 13b compared to Fig. 13a, which result from the increase in the total number of messages that flood the system. And also, that flooding the entire system has greater impact in system performance than targeting solely the leader, as put in evidence by the reduction in performance when comparing Figs. 13c and 13b.

However, the greatest impact in system performance results from the a leader replica flooding the system, as observed in Fig. 13d. This results from the influence the leader has in performance due to its responsibilities within the system (proposing the order of operations). Finally, note that the number of flood messages is sufficiently high to impact system performance without triggering a leader election, since some client requests are still answered before their respective timeouts are triggered.

7 Conclusions and Future Work

In this work we presented ZERMIA. A software fault injector designed for testing and validating concurrent and distributed applications, with special focus on flexibility and extensibility. Its design allows users and developers to test their applications, without requiring any modifications to the target application code, and provides users with different fault and trigger models that allow them to test application is realistic scenarios, including monitoring and managing different thread/process interleaving for testing concurrency associated bugs.

We evaluated ZERMIA using a concurrent bench-marking tool, YCSB, and a state of the art Byzantine Fault Tolerance library, BFT-SMaRt. This combination allowed us to present and validate the capabilities of ZERMIA in testing concurrent and distributed applications, and its flexibility by designing different fault schedules that allowed us to run different experiments without any modifications to either the applications and the BFT library. These results also allowed us to show the performance impact communication related faults can have in these systems. We intend to further use ZERMIA to exhaustively test this and other BFT systems, specifically by studying the influence faulty clients may have in these systems.

Additionally, we are working on a generalization of the system so it can be easily ported to other programming languages, and used to test a wider variety of applications. Also, to abstract users from possibly complex Agent implementations, we are working on a Domain Specific Language (DSL) that will allow developers to design and build custom Agents based on fault and schedule descriptions.

References

1. Arlat, J., et al.: Fault injection for dependability validation: a methodology and some applications. IEEE Trans. Softw. Eng. 16(2), 166–182 (1990). https://doi.org/10.1109/32.44380
2. Aublin, P.L., Mokhtar, S.B., Quéma, V.: Rbft: redundant byzantine fault tolerance. In: 2013 IEEE 33rd International Conference on Distributed Computing Systems, pp. 297–306 (2013). https://doi.org/10.1109/ICDCS.2013.53
3. Bessani, A., Sousa, J., Alchieri, E.E.: State machine replication for the masses with bft-smart. In: 2014 44th Annual IEEE/IFIP International Conference on Dependable Systems and Networks, pp. 355–362 (2014). https://doi.org/10.1109/DSN.2014.43
4. Carreira, J., Madeira, H., Silva, J.: Xception: a technique for the experimental evaluation of dependability in modern computers. IEEE Trans. Softw. Eng. 24(2), 125–136 (1998). https://doi.org/10.1109/32.666826
5. Castro, M., Liskov, B.: Practical byzantine fault tolerance. In: Proceedings of the Third Symposium on Operating Systems Design and Implementation, pp. 173–186. OSDI 1999, USENIX Association, USA (1999)
6. Castro, M., Liskov, B.: Practical byzantine fault tolerance and proactive recovery. ACM Trans. Comput. Syst. 20(4), 398–461 (2002)

7. Chandra, R., Lefever, R., Cukier, M., Sanders, W.: Loki: a state-driven fault injector for distributed systems. In: Proceeding International Conference on Dependable Systems and Networks. DSN 2000, pp. 237–242 (2000). https://doi.org/10.1109/ICDSN.2000.857544

8. Chandra, T.D., Toueg, S.: Unreliable failure detectors for reliable distributed systems. J. ACM **43**(2), 225–267 (1996)

9. Cooper, B.F., Silberstein, A., Tam, E., Ramakrishnan, R., Sears, R.: Benchmarking cloud serving systems with ycsb. In: Proceedings of the 1st ACM Symposium on Cloud Computing, pp. 143–154. SoCC 2010, Association for Computing Machinery, New York, NY, USA (2010). https://doi.org/10.1145/1807128.1807152

10. Correia, M., Veronese, G.S., Neves, N.F., Verissimo, P.: Byzantine consensus in asynchronous message-passing systems: a survey. Int. J. Crit. Comput. Based Syst. **2**(2), 141–161 (2011)

11. Cotroneo, D., De Simone, L., Liguori, P., Natella, R., Bidokhti, N.: How bad can a bug get? An empirical analysis of software failures in the openstack cloud computing platform. In: Proceedings of the 2019 27th ACM Joint Meeting on European Software Engineering Conference and Symposium on the Foundations of Software Engineering, pp. 200–211. ESEC/FSE 2019, Association for Computing Machinery, New York, NY, USA (2019). https://doi.org/10.1145/3338906.3338916

12. Duraes, J.A., Madeira, H.S.: Emulation of software faults: a field data study and a practical approach. IEEE Trans. Softw. Eng. **32**(11), 849–867 (2006). https://doi.org/10.1109/TSE.2006.113

13. Dwork, C., Lynch, N., Stockmeyer, L.: Consensus in the presence of partial synchrony. J. ACM **35**(2), 288–323 (1988)

14. Fabre, J.C., Salles, F., Moreno, M., Arlat, J.: Assessment of cots microkernels by fault injection. In: Dependable Computing for Critical Applications, vol. 7, pp. 25–44 (1999). https://doi.org/10.1109/DCFTS.1999.814288

15. Fischer, M.J., Lynch, N.A., Paterson, M.S.: Impossibility of distributed consensus with one faulty process. J. ACM **32**(2), 374–382 (1985)

16. Fonseca, P., Li, C., Rodrigues, R.: Finding complex concurrency bugs in large multi-threaded applications. In: Proceedings of the Sixth Conference on Computer Systems, pp. 215–228. EuroSys 2011, Association for Computing Machinery, New York, NY, USA (2011). https://doi.org/10.1145/1966445.1966465

17. Fonseca, P., Li, C., Singhal, V., Rodrigues, R.: A study of the internal and external effects of concurrency bugs. In: 2010 IEEE/IFIP International Conference on Dependable Systems Networks (DSN), pp. 221–230 (2010). https://doi.org/10.1109/DSN.2010.5544315

18. Google: gRPC - A High-Performance Open-Source Universal RPC Framework (2015). http://www.grpc.io/. Accessed 01 July 2021

19. Gunawi, H.S., et al.: Fate and destini: a framework for cloud recovery testing. In: Proceedings of the 8th USENIX Conference on Networked Systems Design and Implementation, pp. 238–252. NSDI 2011, USENIX Association, USA (2011)

20. Han, S., Shin, K., Rosenberg, H.: Doctor: an integrated software fault injection environment for distributed real-time systems. In: Proceedings of 1995 IEEE International Computer Performance and Dependability Symposium, pp. 204–213 (1995). https://doi.org/10.1109/IPDS.1995.395831

21. Hiller, M., Jhumka, A., Suri, N.: Propane: an environment for examining the propagation of errors in software. In: Proceedings of the 2002 ACM SIGSOFT International Symposium on Software Testing and Analysis, pp. 81–85. ISSTA 2002, Association for Computing Machinery, New York, NY, USA (2002). https://doi.org/10.1145/566172.566184

22. Hsueh, M.C., Tsai, T., Iyer, R.: Fault injection techniques and tools. Computer **30**(4), 75–82 (1997). https://doi.org/10.1109/2.585157

23. Jin, A., Jiang, J., Hu, J., Lou, J.: A pin-based dynamic software fault injection system. In: 2008 The 9th International Conference for Young Computer Scientists, pp. 2160–2167 (2008). https://doi.org/10.1109/ICYCS.2008.329

24. Kanawati, G., Kanawati, N., Abraham, J.: Ferrari: a flexible software-based fault and error injection system. IEEE Trans. Comput. **44**(2), 248–260 (1995). https://doi.org/10.1109/12.364536

25. Lamport, L.: Time, clocks, and the ordering of events in a distributed system. Commun. ACM **21**(7), 558–565 (1978)

26. Li, G., Lu, S., Musuvathi, M., Nath, S., Padhye, R.: Efficient scalable thread-safety-violation detection: finding thousands of concurrency bugs during testing. In: Proceedings of the 27th ACM Symposium on Operating Systems Principles, pp. 162–180. SOSP 2019, Association for Computing Machinery, New York, NY, USA (2019). https://doi.org/10.1145/3341301.3359638

27. Liu, S., Viotti, P., Cachin, C., Quéma, V., Vukolic, M.: XFT: practical fault tolerance beyond crashes. In: Proceedings of the 12th USENIX Conference on Operating Systems Design and Implementation, pp. 485–500. OSDI 2016, USENIX Association, USA (2016)

28. Lu, Q., Farahani, M., Wei, J., Thomas, A., Pattabiraman, K.: Llfi: an intermediate code-level fault injection tool for hardware faults. In: 2015 IEEE International Conference on Software Quality, Reliability and Security, pp. 11–16 (2015). https://doi.org/10.1109/QRS.2015.13

29. Martins, E., Rubira, C., Leme, N.: Jaca: a reflective fault injection tool based on patterns. In: Proceedings International Conference on Dependable Systems and Networks, pp. 483–487 (2002). https://doi.org/10.1109/DSN.2002.1028934

30. Martins, M., Rosa, A.: A fault injection approach based on reflective programming. In: Proceeding International Conference on Dependable Systems and Networks. DSN 2000, pp. 407–416 (2000). https://doi.org/10.1109/ICDSN.2000.857569

31. Martins, R., et al.: Experiences with fault-injection in a byzantine fault-tolerant protocol. In: Eyers, D., Schwan, K. (eds.) Middleware 2013. LNCS, vol. 8275, pp. 41–61. Springer, Heidelberg (2013). https://doi.org/10.1007/978-3-642-45065-5_3

32. Natella, R., Cotroneo, D., Madeira, H.S.: Assessing dependability with software fault injection: a survey. ACM Comput. Surv. **48**(3) (2016). https://doi.org/10.1145/2841425

33. Platania, M., Obenshain, D., Tantillo, T., Amir, Y., Suri, N.: On choosing server- or client-side solutions for bft. ACM Comput. Surv. **48**(4) (2016). https://doi.org/10.1145/2886780

34. Rivest, R.L., Shamir, A., Adleman, L.: A method for obtaining digital signatures and public-key cryptosystems. Commun. ACM **21**(2), 120–126 (1978)

35. Rosenberg, H., Shin, K.: Software fault injection and its application in distributed systems. In: FTCS-23 The Twenty-Third International Symposium on Fault-Tolerant Computing, pp. 208–217 (1993). https://doi.org/10.1109/FTCS.1993.627324

36. Sanches, B.P., Basso, T., Moraes, R.: J-swfit: a java software fault injection tool. In: 2011 5th Latin-American Symposium on Dependable Computing, pp. 106–115 (2011). https://doi.org/10.1109/LADC.2011.20

37. Sastry Hari, S.K., Adve, S.V., Naeimi, H., Ramachandran, P.: Relyzer: application resiliency analyzer for transient faults. IEEE Micro **33**(3), 58–66 (2013). https://doi.org/10.1109/MM.2013.30

38. Schneider, F.B.: Implementing fault-tolerant services using the state machine approach: a tutorial. ACM Comput. Surv. **22**(4), 299–319 (1990)
39. Segall, Z., et al.: Fiat - fault injection based automated testing environment. In: Twenty-Fifth International Symposium on Fault-Tolerant Computing, 1995, Highlights from Twenty-Five Years, p. 394 (1995). https://doi.org/10.1109/FTCSH. 1995.532663
40. Sousa, J., Bessani, A., Vukolic, M.: A byzantine fault-tolerant ordering service for the hyperledger fabric blockchain platform. In: 2018 48th Annual IEEE/IFIP International Conference on Dependable Systems and Networks (DSN), pp. 51–58 (2018). https://doi.org/10.1109/DSN.2018.00018
41. Svenningsson, R., Vinter, J., Eriksson, H., Törngren, M.: MODIFI: a model-implemented fault injection tool. In: Schoitsch, E. (ed.) SAFECOMP 2010. LNCS, vol. 6351, pp. 210–222. Springer, Heidelberg (2010). https://doi.org/10.1007/978-3-642-15651-9_16
42. Tsai, T.K., Iyer, R.K.: Measuring fault tolerance with the FTAPE fault injection tool. In: Beilner, H., Bause, F. (eds.) TOOLS 1995. LNCS, vol. 977, pp. 26–40. Springer, Heidelberg (1995). https://doi.org/10.1007/BFb0024305
43. Tsudik, G.: Message authentication with one-way hash functions. SIGCOMM Comput. Commun. Rev. **22**(5), 29–38 (1992)
44. Wang, J., et al.: A comprehensive study on real world concurrency bugs in node.js. In: 2017 32nd IEEE/ACM International Conference on Automated Software Engineering (ASE), pp. 520–531 (2017). https://doi.org/10.1109/ASE.2017.8115663
45. Yin, M., Malkhi, D., Reiter, M.K., Gueta, G.G., Abraham, I.: Hotstuff: bft consensus with linearity and responsiveness. In: Proceedings of the 2019 ACM Symposium on Principles of Distributed Computing, pp. 347–356. PODC 2019, Association for Computing Machinery, New York, NY, USA (2019). https://doi.org/10.1145/3293611.3331591

Revocable Data Sharing Methodology Based on SGX and Blockchain

Liang Zhang[1,2], Haibin Kan[1,2(✉)] ⓘ, Yang Xu[3] ⓘ, and Jinhao Ran[1,2]

[1] Shanghai Key Laboratory of Intelligent Information Processing,
School of Computer Science, Fudan University, Shanghai 200433, China
{liangzhang19,hbkan,21210240095}@fudan.edu.cn
[2] Shanghai Engineering Research Center of Blockchain, Shanghai 200433, China
[3] College of Computer Science and Electronic Engineering, Hunan University,
Changsha 410082, Hunan, China
xuyangcs@hnu.edu.cn

Abstract. Data sharing methodology has recently been an active research area due to the development of information technology. As blockchain gets popular, decentralized storage mode becomes a favorable method for data sharing. Moreover, non-repudiation, confidentiality, revocability and fine-grained access are sometimes indispensable in practice. In light of these requirements, we propose a solution by combining decentralized ciphertext-policy attribute-based encryption (CP-ABE) and Software Guard eXtension (SGX) with blockchain. In our framework, the use of blockchain makes shared data publicly accessible and undeniable. To ensure confidentiality and fine-grained access control, we take advantage of decentralized CP-ABE to encrypt data. SGX is utilized as a key management service for the decentralized CP-ABE, making our data sharing methodology revocable without updating ciphertext. Overall, our methodology achieves privacy protection, revocability and decentralized fine-grained access. In addition, we perform experiments on Ethereum, and the results demonstrate that our approach is feasible.

Keywords: Revocability · Data sharing · Blockchain · CP-ABE · Ethereum · SGX

1 Introduction

Data fuels digital business. Data sharing is a valuable part of the scientific method that allows users to share data with each other. Data availability, authenticity and access control concerns emerge in conjunction with data sharing. Cloud platforms are often used to store data, and different kinds of public-key cryptography are explored for access control [1–3].

The massive generation of data and frequent storage failures have dramatically increased the popularity of distributed storage systems. They are instrumental in allowing data to be replicated in geographically dispersed storage

© Springer Nature Switzerland AG 2021
M. Yang et al. (Eds.): NSS 2021, LNCS 13041, pp. 61–78, 2021.
https://doi.org/10.1007/978-3-030-92708-0_4

devices. A significant issue that the distributed storage systems face is maintaining consistency. Blockchain has been a breakthrough technical achievement and solves consistency problems with consensus algorithm. More and more research on blockchain-based clouds is also in progress to mitigate the single-point bottleneck problem in the cloud. For example, to solve the problems of weakened networking control and the risk of majority attack of blockchain, Zhu et al. [4] propose a controllable blockchain data management model.

Ciphertext-policy attribute-based encryption (CP-ABE) enables one to encrypt a message with distributed parties' attributes. Thus it is natural to use it in data sharing where the single-point bottleneck problem is overcome. Some previous literature uses CP-ABE as the building block in a data-sharing system [1,7,8] to gain fine-grained access control management. A trusted execution environment, such as Intel's SGX, is a hardware-based infrastructure widely incorporated to enhance privacy and confidentiality. SGX [6] can work as a reliable proxy to protect data and code securely.

Some researches related to data sharing take advantage of blockchain or different cryptographic primitives. Zheng et al. [3] use homomorphic encryption and Paillier cryptosystem to realize threshold data sharing. Zyskind et al. [24] store encrypted personal privacy data on the blockchain to authenticate oneself, but their method could not share data or exchange value. Zhang et al. [21] propose a privacy protection and fast decryption ABE scheme for outsourced data security in the cloud with no much consideration about the revocation. He et al. [22] combine CP-ABE with the smart contract to share personal data. When considering practicality, each user has to initiate a smart contract to manage data sharing. Wang et al. [23] use multi-authority CP-ABE to build a decentralized data storage system. However, they ignore revocability when putting it into practice. Guo et al. [20] construct a revocable MA ABE scheme and use it in a telemedicine system along with blockchain technology. The scheme suffers the problem that ciphertexts and decryption keys both need to be updated when revoking attributes.

Some other pieces of literature use SGX to enhance the functionalities of blockchain. SDTE [25] constructs a blockchain-based ecosystem where SGX acts as a secure code execution container to protect data and analysis results from direct access. BITE [26] proposes a new approach to improve the privacy of light clients in Bitcoin. It uses SGX to provide private information retrieval and side-channel protection techniques that serve privacy-preserving requests from light clients. Kosba et al. [15] present a decentralized smart contract system to protect transactional privacy. They use zero-knowledge proofs to generate private smart contracts by its compiler, in which SGX is used to instantiate the manager.

It would be a good idea to combine blockchain, CP-ABE and SGX in a data-sharing methodology. This paper introduces a data sharing methodology by leveraging the techniques CP-ABE, SGX and blockchain. In this methodology, blockchain is used to store the CP-ABE ciphertext and SGX is used to manage the CP-ABE decryption keys. As a result, we obtain a decentralized many-to-many data sharing paradigm, in which the revocation is quite feasible.

Table 1. Comparison of different method on data sharing

Method	Privacy	Decentralized	Revocable	No CT update	Threshold
Zheng et al. [3]	Yes	No	No	–	Yes
Zhang et al. [21]	Yes	No	No	–	Yes
He et al. [22]	Yes	Yes	Yes	No	No
Wang et al. [23]	Yes	Yes	No	–	Yes
Guo et al. [20]	Yes	Yes	Yes	No	Yes
Ours	Yes	Yes	Yes	Yes	Yes

Table 1 gives a comparison with related literature. A method with a trusted authority or a cloud is centralized. When considering revocability, some methods need to update keys and ciphertext (CT) simultaneously. In Guo et al. [20], it has to update ciphertext ("ReEncryption" in their paper) and decryption key simultaneously when revocation, since the user can remember its previous decryption key privately. In SCDP [22], He et al. manages access control via smart contract. However, they do not provide details on how to manage the CP-ABE decryption keys. They also need to update the ciphertext when revocation, as far as we are concerned. Our method only updates the keys in SGX, and no information about the keys is leaked.

Our contributions are threefold:

1) We propose a new data-sharing methodology based on blockchain, which is publicly available and tamper-resistant. We integrate the decentralized CP-ABE scheme in the data sharing methodology to guarantee privacy and security. We acheive a many-to-many, fine-grained access data sharing paradigm.
2) We use SGX to manage the CP-ABE decryption keys so that keys can be updated privately in SGX. Thus, we do not need to update ciphertext when revocation. Moreover, the consensus of SGX data is under consideration.
3) We test our methodology by performing experiments on Ethereum and SGX. Further, we comprehensively analyze the efficiency and security of the proposed methodology.

2   Preliminaries

2.1   Blockchain and Ethereum

Blockchain was introduced in October 2008 [5] as part of the proposal for bitcoin. Bitcoin is a virtual currency system that eschewed a central authority for issuing currency, transferring ownership, and confirming transactions. A blockchain is essentially a distributed ledger with data signed and organized in a series of blocks. Unlike bitcoin, Ethereum [9] constructs a Turing-complete machine (the Ethereum virtual machine or EVM) where smart contracts could run. Just like bitcoin, Ethereum has a digital cryptocurrency called Ether (ETH). Storage and computation in transactions cost a certain amount of gas. Wei and ether are measurements unit of Ethereum gas, 1ether $= 10^{18}$ wei. While the EVM is executing the transaction, the gas is gradually depleted from a specified account. The smart contract enables developers to produce decentralized applications (DAPPs). Go-ethereum[1] is the implementations of Ethereum. "abigen" is the tool to compile solidity into bytecode so that EVM can run. With a simulated blockchain, a node could configure options of the blockchain; a node could connect to other nodes if it has peers; a node could share or fetch data as a full node; a node could mine if it acts as a miner; a node could help to manage accounts. In the test environment, developers could focus on smart contracts that construct complex DAPPs. Libraries are automated linked, and smart contracts are automated compiled.

2.2 Decentralized CP-ABE

In a CP-ABE scheme, an attribute set is included in the secret key, while the ciphertext is associated with an access structure. A multi-authority (MA) CP-ABE [10,11] system is comprised of the following 5 algorithms:

Global Setup$(\lambda) \to$ GP. It takes in the security parameter λ and outputs global parameters GP for the whole system.

Authority Setup(GP, θ) $\to$ SK$_\theta$, PK$_\theta$. Each authority θ takes GP as input to produce its secret key and public key pair, SK$_\theta$, PK$_\theta$.

Encrypt(M, A, GP, {PK$_\theta$}) $\to$ CT. The algorithm takes in a message M, an access structure A, a set of public keys, and the global parameters. It outputs a ciphertext CT.

KeyGen(GID, GP, u, SK$_\theta$) $\to$ K$_{u,\text{GID}}$. The algorithm takes in an identity GID, the global parameters, an attribute u belonging to the authority θ, and the secret key SK$_\theta$ for this authority. It produces a key K$_{u,\text{GID}}$ for this attribute and identity pair (GID, u).

Decrypt(CT, GP, {K$_{u,\text{GID}}$}) $\to$ M. The decryption algorithm takes in the global parameters, the ciphertext, and a collection of decryption keys that are generated for GID. Only if the attributes set in decryption keys satisfies the access structure corresponding to the ciphertext, it outputs the message M.

2.3 SGX

Softwares based on the current operating system have security, privacy, and integrity problems by cracks or attacks. Due to these problems, a trusted execution environment (TEE) [13] was proposed to enhance integrity and confidentiality by providing a secure area in a processor. Intel's Software Guard Extensions (SGX) [6] is one of the most popular TEE in personal computer and cloud server,

---

[1] https://github.com/ethereum/go-ethereum, Accessed: Nov 2020.

and its popularity roar with the rise of blockchain [14,16–18]. SGX is hardware-based instructions to the Intel architecture, which protect integrity and confidentiality for sensitive computation. It allocates private regions of memory, called enclaves, to run user-level code. Enclave is a secure and shielded container that is designed to protect data and code from the outside environment. An enclave can read/write data outside the enclave, but no other enclave or process can access the enclave memory. SGX provides an attestation service that a remote system can verify the running result of an enclave. Attestation in SGX could prove an enclave's identity and provides proof that a software is running inside an enclave. A client could prove to others that an enclave is doing a specific computation inside a specific machine with remote attestation.

3   Revocable Data Sharing Model

3.1   System Assumption

We assume that each blockchain participant has the SGX foundation, which securely protects the data and code. We only consider "small data" in our sharing scheme, such as big data hash or secret keys, since big data can be protected by secret keys. Moreover, (searchable) big file sharing [19] is another topic that is beyond our discussion in this paper. When t-out-of-n participants want to share data collectively, we assume that no more than t-1 of the participants are malicious. We follow the protocol, complexity assumption, and security proof of Rouselakis's scheme [11]. ABE toolkit is realized in python and requires a pairing-based cryptography library. In our methodology, the attacks or security limitation of SGX, such as cache timing attack or CPU bugs, is out of scope, which means we regard SGX as a secure tool. An enclave is securely created in SGX. We assume the code in the enclave is confidential. We also consider the remote attestation a reliable process.

3.2   Security Model

Entities are introduced and possible risks is presented below:

Ethereum: Data and smart contract in Ethereum can be sure of integrity, but they are not confidential.

Data Owner (DO): 1) A data owner may want to revoke his/her shared data to fraud. 2) his/her personal information is leaked against his/her wishes.

Data User (DU): A data user, as a malicious adversary, may try to steal the keys in SGX or collude to decrypt shared data on blockchain.

Attribute Authority (AA): There are two scenarios which attribute authorities may participate in. The first one is that an AA may issue fake keys to decrypt, and the other one is that he/she denies having issued a correct key.

Enclave/SGX: An enclave in SGX is a secure container that protects the keys, and the code runs on it.

Denial of Service (DoS): Any malicious one deviates from our protocol to exhaust the whole network resources.

3.3 Design Goals

We intend to achieve a revocable data sharing prototype in which data is encrypted using decentralized CP-ABE. We aim at achieving the following goals:

Decentralization. No single-point bottleneck problem or no trusted third party is responsible for the shared data.

Revocability. Any AA could revoke the keys associating with an attribute of a data user such that the data user is deprived of decrypting the ciphertext. Meanwhile, it is unnecessary to update the ciphertext.

Dynamicity. DU can decrypt shared data only if his/her attribute sets satisfy the access structures [12] in the ciphertext, whenever he/she joins in the system.

Non-repudiation. 1) No AA could deny generating keys for an honest user. 2) No data user can deny that an honest key has been issued to it.

Privacy. 1) Data are encrypted to protect illegal users from obtaining them. 2) Data owners could share data confidentially if they like. 3) Data in SGX are private and secure.

4 Overview

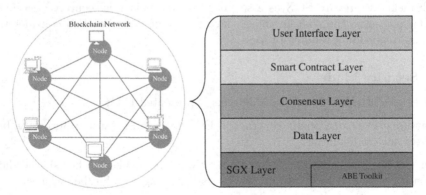

User Interface Layer: Entrance for users to share data or revoke attributes.

Smart Contract Layer: Transform user operation into standard transactions into smart contract.

Consensus Layer: Global algorithms to make blocks and SGX data consistency.

Data Layer: Store the encrypted data for sharing among nodes.

SGX Layer: Store private data, such as keys.

ABE Toolkit: Provide basic ABE algorithms.

Fig. 1. Architecture of the data sharing methodology

Figure 1 shows that we divide our methodology into five parts from the bottom up, namely SGX Layer, Data Layer, Consensus Layer, Smart Contract Layer, and User Interface Layer. Decryption keys in ABE Toolkit are kept in SGX so that they are unknown to anyone. SGX Layer records the relationship of decryption keys, attribute authorities, and decryptors. SGX also runs code that should be confidential, such as decryption algorithms. Data Layer stores encrypted data and maintains data consistency under Consensus Layer. Smart Contract Layer makes it possible for developers to combine ABE algorithms and blockchain operations. User Interface Layer allows anyone to share their data or revoke others' authority. From the horizontal perspective, Consensus Layer help to maintain the consistency of blockchain via P2P network. Data (keys) in SGX Layer reach consistency by remote attestation under a synchronized clock.

In our methodology, everyone is an attribute authority, an encryptor, and a decryptor. All participants have equal rights to share data or fetch data. We realize an ABE Toolkit, a standalone component that runs in SGX and traditional CPU. SGX is the qualified component of each node.

To reach an agreement on the data in SGX among different blockchain nodes, each SGX firstly authenticates itself through remote attestation, then constructs secure communication channels to counterparts and transfers the newest data. In Sect. 5.2, we will give a more detailed explanation.

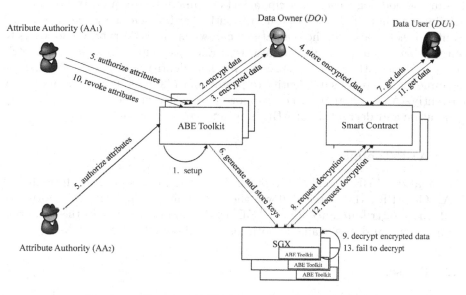

Fig. 2. Revocable data sharing model: each participant has access to its node, which contains smart contract, ABE Toolkit and SGX.

Our methodology not only provides one-to-one, one-to-many, many-to-one, and many-to-many data sharing protocol, but also makes data sharing practically revocable. Each node of a participant has all the features of Ethereum smart contract, ABE Toolkit and SGX. Figure 2 briefly shows an example of sharing data and revoking attributes. In this example, DU_1 could decrypt the data shared by DO_1 only with both AA_1's and AA_2's issued attributes. Here, we emphasize that DU_1 wants to use data owned by DO_1, AA_1 and AA_2 have the corresponding rights to issue decryption keys for DU_1. DU_1 can be AA or DO in other occasions, DO_1 can be AA or DU in other situations as well. When someone wants to share data, he/she encrypts it with ABE Toolkit and then stores the ciphertext in blockchain through a smart contract. Some attribute authorities assign attributes to a decryptor as desired, and the generated keys are stored in SGX. When someone else needs to decrypt the shared data, it requests SGX, and SGX acts as a reliable agent to do the decryption. Only if the decryptor's attributes satisfy the access structure in the ciphertext can the decryptor gain the plain text successfully. In another scenario where some attribute authority revokes its attribute for the decryptor, SGX will update the decryptor's corresponding keys. The decryptor may fail to decrypt when trying to start a new decryption if his/her new attribute set does not satisfy the access structure. The data in SGX is transparent to both users and to a smart contract.

5   Implementation Details

In our methodology, each participant acts as an encryptor, a decryptor, and an attribute authority. To describe it straightforward, when one is encryptor who wants to share data, he/she is a data owner; when one is decryptor who wants to obtain shared data, he/she is a data user. Each participant gets an asymmetric key pair from Ethereum to represent his/her identity. Each SGX also has an asymmetric key pair as its identity to protect data in different nodes. Since SGX currently (Aug. 2020) does not support pairing-based encryption, we do key generation and decryption of ABE in a sandbox environment.

5.1   ABE Toolkit

We realize ABE Toolkit according to the mathematical formula of MA CP-ABE [11] and follow the attribute string in the form of "data_user@attribute_authority". ABE Toolkit is independent of the execution environment, and it is available both inside and outside SGX.

5.2   Consensus of SGX

Encrypted data will be consistent under the blockchain consensus. In Fig. 3, we demonstrate how to reach an agreement of the keys managed in SGX. SGX should only transfer the keys to other enabled enclaves. We require each SGX to execute remote attestation to show its quality to request data from others.

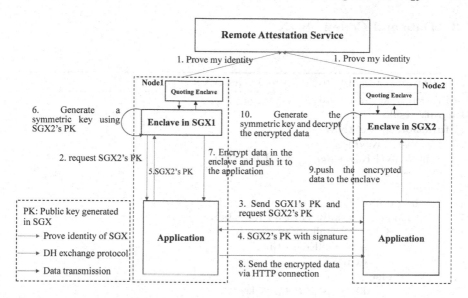

Fig. 3. Establishing secure channel for synchronizing data in SGX between two nodes

Remote attestation is a challenge and response protocol. When receiving a challenge, an enclave generates its computation proof with its internal private key. If the proof is verified, a secure channel could be established by the challenger with the counterpart's public key. Through the secure channel, enclaves in different SGX could synchronize data (i.e., the keys of decentralized CP-ABE). Figure 3 shows that we use the Diffie-Hellman (DH) exchange to establish a secure data transmission channel. Quoting Enclave [6] is a privileged component in SGX, which is essential in the remote attestation. The PKs in Node1 and Node2 are generated in respective enclaves privately and are only used for DH exchange protocol. The picture demonstrates how SGX1 synchronizes data with SGX2 in different nodes. Remote attestation is necessary here to prevent the man-in-the-middle attack. With a secure data transmission channel, authenticated SGX could exchange data confidentially to reach consistency. SGX, which provides private storage and computation, is a critical resource as part of the decentralized protocol. We could charge for SGX operations as Ethereum blockchain [9], which will prohibit the abuse of SGX as well. How to design the incentive and reputation model is out of scope.

5.3   Data and Code in SGX

Algorithm 1. Create/update/remove an AA's key

Input: PK_{do}, key, attribute, PK_{aa}, $sig_{SK_{aa}}$
Output: result
 1: **function** MANAGEKEY
 2:     global allKeyList
 3:     **if** Verify(PK_{aa}, $sig_{SK_{aa}}$) == False **then**
 4:         **return** 0
 5:     **end if**
 6:     **while** i in *allKeyList* **do**
 7:         **if** PK_{aa} == allKeyList[i].PK_{aa} **then**
 8:             **if** key == null **then**
 9:                 remove allKeyList[i]
10:                 **return** 1
11:             **else**
12:                 allKeyList[i].PK_{do} = key
13:                 allKeyList[i].attribute = attribute
14:                 **return** 2
15:             **end if**
16:         **end if**
17:     **end while**
18:     allKeyList.append([PK_{do}, key,[]])
19:     allKeyList.[allKeyList.length-1].append((attribute, PK_{aa}))
20:     **return** 3
21: **end function**

We have described how to synchronize data among SGXs in different nodes. Apart from the public and private key pairs generated for the DH exchange protocol, this subsection will give other details about the data structures related to ABE Toolkit in the enclave. After creating an enclave app, we start a standalone process to manage the enclave and provide interfaces to handle the data in the enclave. In our methodology, SGX in each node uses an enclave as a secure container to store the keys of ABE Toolkit. We demonstrate the data structure in the enclave memory as <key, PK_{do}, <attr, PK_{aa}>>, where "PK_{do}" is the public key of attribute receiver, "attr" and "PK_{aa}" are the attribute and public key of attribute authority, "key" is the generated key. Data in the enclave memory is destroyed once the computer shuts down. When SGX in a node starts, it initiates and stores a random private key sk, and dispatches the public key pk. It requests and synchronizes the main data from other nodes using key exchange and remote attestation techniques. SGX mainly maintains the keys of *DU*s. Algorithm 1 shows the program of managing keys in the enclave. Algorithm 2 shows the decryption process with ABE Toolkit.

Algorithm 2. Decrypt a ciphertext using ABE Toolkit

Input: ciphertext, pk$_{du}$, sig$_{SK_{du}}$
Output: result
1: **function** DECRYPT
2:     **if** Verify(PK$_{du}$, sig$_{SK_{du}}$) == False **then**
3:       **return** null
4:     **end if**
5:     **while** i in *allKeyList* **do**
6:       **if** PK$_{du}$ == allKeyList[i].*PK$_{du}$* **then**
7:         **return** ABE Toolkit.decrypt(ciphetext, allKeyList[i].key)
8:       **end if**
9:     **end while**
10: **end function**

5.4   Blockchain Operations

Smart contract is the interface between *DO*s and blockchain. Go-ethereum helps to deploy smart contracts and provides interface to start smart contract calls. In our methodology, we design a smart contract to allow users to write and read data. Here, "write" means a *DO* encrypts his/her data and store it on the blockchain; "read" means a *DU* loads a ciphertext from blockchain and decrypts it. Algorithm 3 and Algorithm 4 demonstrate how to utilize SGX and ABE Toolkit when smart contract interacts with blockchain.

Algorithm 3. Encrypt data and save to blockchain

Input: data, PK$_{do}$
Output: result
1: **function** ENCRYPTANDSTORE
2:     CT = ABE Toolkit.encrypt(data, PK$_{do}$)
3:     store(CT)
4:     **return** CT.ciphertextID
5: **end function**

Algorithm 4. Read ciphertext from blockchain and decrypt

Input: PK$_{du}$, SK_{du}, ciphertextID
Output: result
1: **function** LOADANDDECRYPT
2:     sig = sign(SK_{du})
3:     ct = load(ciphertextID)
4:     data = SGX.decrypt(ct, PK$_{du}$, sig)
5:     **return** data
6: **end function**

5.5   Data Sharing and Attribute Revoking

Many-to-Many Data Sharing. We realize decentralized data sharing and make many-to-many data sharing possible, which makes our methodology more applicable. We make an example to show the threshold data sharing. Suppose n DOs would like to share n piece of data to another m DUs if more than t of the n DOs agree. DO_i is the ith one in the n DOs, DU_j is the jth one in the m DUs. All the n DOs use the same access structure "(t-of-n $(DU_1@DO_i)_{for\,i\,in\,n}$) or (t-of-n $(DU_2@DO_i)_{for\,i\,in\,n}$) or ... or (t-of-n $(DU_m@DO_i)_{for\,i\,in\,n}$)" to encrypt the data and store the ciphertext in blockchain. Each DO_i could act as AA and has the right to assign attribute "$DU_j@DO_i$" to each DU_j. Thus, anyone in the m DUs, who has received t attributes from the n DOs, could successfully decrypt the ciphertext and gain the data.

Attribute Revoking. Since the must keys to decrypt a ciphertext are stored in SGX secure area, no one could back up the keys. An attribute authority could prove to SGX that he/she is the owner of some key by providing a specific ciphertext that only the corresponding key could be used to decrypt. If the keys are updated privately in the SGX, nothing will leak to anyone. Attribute authorities make good use of this to revoke old attributes or update new attributes of data users. Let's go further with the above example. Suppose t DOs, namely DO_1, DO_2,... DO_t, have assigned attributes to all the m DUs, all the m DUs could decrypt ciphertext currently. If DO_1 wants to revoke his/her attribute for DU_1, SGX will delete the corresponding key in its confidential space. DU_1 will fail to decrypt the ciphertext next time, and other DUs still succeed. Compared to other revocable ABE methods, keys are kept unknown to everyone, and ciphertext has no need to be updated or removed.

6   Analysis and Evaluation

6.1   Properties

In this section, we show that our methodology achieves the desirable properties of data sharing.

Lemma 1 (Non-repudiation). *1) An AA cannot deny having issued a key to an honest data user. 2) A data user could not deny that an honest key is generated for him/her.*

Proof. 1) If AA_j has issued a key to an honest DU_i, DU_i could prove this fact if necessary. Since the key is stored in SGX, DU_i cannot show the key to others directly. To prove it, DU_i could construct an extra ciphertext and ask for the SGX for decryption. Suppose the key is generated with attributes "$DU_i@AA_j$", the honest DU_i encrypts plaintext "1" with access structure of (1-of-1 $DU_i@AA_j$) to generate the extra ciphertext. Then the SGX could try to decrypt the extra ciphertext. If the result is "1", AA_j is believed to have generated the key to DU_i. 2) When an honest AA invokes Algorithm 1 to issue a key to a data user, SGX could conduct the above operations to prove that the data user has an honest key without disclosing it.

Lemma 2 (Decentralization). *No single-point bottleneck problem or no trusted third party is responsible for the shared data.*

Proof. Blockchain and SGX are basic infrastructures in our methodology. Decentralized CP-ABE is our cryptographic primitive to protect privacy. We will talk about them to show the property of decentralization. Blockchain is known to all as a distributed ledger and it is tamper-resistant by any third party under the consensus algorithm. Data on blockchain in our methodology are encrypted, which will not leak useful information to anyone. The decryption keys are generated by different attribute authorities which guarantees the decentralization. SGXs protect the decryption keys and invoke the decryption algorithm in an isolated environment. The keys are transferred from one SGX to another through a secure channel Sect. 5.2, thus preventing any third party from gaining useful information. Remote attestation is required to establish a secure channel between SGXs; however, Intel would not learn information about the keys in our protocol.

Lemma 3 (Privacy). *1) Data are encrypted to protect illegal users from obtaining them. 2) Data owners could share data confidentially if they like. 3) Data in SGX are private and secure.*

Proof. 1) Legal DUs are those with keys issued by the related AAs. Ethereum provides public accessible storage, and anyone could get all the data. Nevertheless, data are protected in encrypted mode by CP-ABE scheme, which is based on q-type assumption on prime order bilinear groups [11]. Thus, illegal users are not able to read the original data. 2) From the encryption algorithm construction in Sect. 5.1, a DO encrypts a message without any individual information. Identity in Ethereum is a public key which will not leak the encryptor's information either. This would satisfy some privacy-protection application scenarios, such as anonymous vote and survey systems. 3) SGX is considered a basic tool in our assumption, secure in protecting its storage and computation. Based on SGX remote attestation, we take advantage of key exchange protocol 3 to construct a secure communication channel. Decision Diffie-Hellman problem guarantees the data privacy outside SGX in our methodology.

Lemma 4 (Dynamicity). *A data user can decrypt a shared data only if his/her attribute sets satisfy the access structures in the ciphertext, no matter when he/she joins in the system.*

Proof. This property inherits the property of CP-ABE scheme. By 2) of lemma 3 and the encryption algorithm construction in Sect. 5.1, we could see that a DO encrypts data with a specified access structure and may not predict who the decryptors are. By the decryption algorithm construction in Sect. 5.1, we could see that a DU decrypts the ciphertext with his/her keys issued by AAs without any help of the DO. Since CP-ABE cryptosystems are not time-aware, data users even could decrypt ciphertext at any time in the absence of AAs and DOs.

Lemma 5 (Revocability). *An AA could revoke his/her keys for a data user without update the ciphertext.*

Proof. Smart contract in Ethereum could store arbitrary data, and all the data reach consistency under proof-of-work consensus protocol. The shared data stored on blockchain are considered tamper-resistant as a result. Thus, no one could update the shared data. By Lemma 4, a data owner does not care about who will be the decryptors and can be absent while decrypting. By Lemma 1 1), we can conclude that AAs determine who could decrypt a ciphertext. An AA could revoke his/her decryption key of a data user by telling SGX to remove or update a key as Algorithm 1 demonstrates. Since ciphertext is encrypted with fine-grained access structure, revoking a DU's key does not affect other users' privileges. By Lemma 1 1), a DU could further prove his/her key has indeed been revoked.

6.2 Performance Evaluation

We realized ABE Toolkit with Charm[2] in python. We simulated a blockchain with Go-ethereum, and deploy smart contract with "abigen". Codes that uses SGX as key management service. All our experiments were executed on 8 cores of an Intel(R) Core(TM) i5-8400 CPU @ 2.80 GHz with 8 GB RAM is running Linux Ubuntu 4.15.0-29-generic with Intel SGX Linux 2.7 release. Ganache 2.3.0[3] is used to simulate full Ethereum node.

It cost about 9 ms to execute "KeyGen" algorithm, 7 ms to encrypt a message and 6ms to decrypt a ciphertext when one attribute is associated. Our methodology supports fine-grained data sharing and threshold data sharing. SGX enclave can have the maximum memory of 128 MB, AA's generated key is about 900 bytes in our experiment. It means we could store 100000 keys in an enclave, which is sufficient for most data sharing groups or organizations. The experimental results show that the data transmission time between two SGXs is ~0.4 ms.

Figure 4 shows the encryption and decryption time cost of the decentralized CP-ABE. The experimental results show that both the CP-ABE "Encrypt" and "Decrypt" algorithms cost $O(n)$, where n is the number of attributes in the access structure. Figure 5 depicts the ciphertext size when n attributes is involved in the access control policy. We can conclude that the CP-ABE ciphertext size increases linearly with the attributes set size in access structure. The ciphertext is about 1 kB if only one attribute in the access structure, and it increases 800 B for each additional attribute. When there are 200 attributes, the ciphertext size is about 222 kb.

---

[2] https://jhuisi.github.io/charm/, Accessed: Sep. 2020.
[3] Ganache: https://www.trufflesuite.com/ganache.

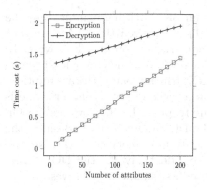

Fig. 4. Encryption and decryption time cost

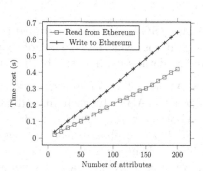

Fig. 5. Ciphertext size

Figure 6 gives the gas consumption of storing the ciphertexts on Ethereum when increasing the number of attributes in the access control policy. We can conclude that the gas consumption of storage also increases linearly with the size of the ciphertext. When the ciphertext is of size 222 kb (i.e., 200 attribtues in the access structure), the gas cost is about $0.98 \cdot 10^9$ wei. Figure 7 shows the time of reading and writing ciphertext from blockchain. The writing time cost is in a second, since the consensus is reached shortly in our experimental environment.

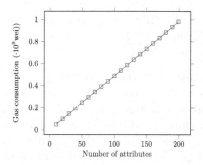

Fig. 6. Gas consumption of storage

Fig. 7. Reading and writing time

6.3   Security Analysis

In this section, we will analyze the risks to prove security in our system as described in Sect. 3.2.

Ethereum. Ethereum Blockchain is a public distributed ledger and it is tamper-resistant under the consensus algorithm. Everyone could get the data that are encrypted on Ethereuem. The encryption will guarantee confidentiality in our methodology.

Data Owner. 1) Since ciphertexts are written on Blockchain, indicating the ciphertexts could not be modified. Lemma 1 1) has proved that AA could not deny having issued a key for a DU. Any malicious revocation attack is overt. To maliciously revoke the shared data, the data owner has to delete at least t-out-of-n honest participants' decryption keys in SGX, which violates the assumption. 2) A DO has two possible ideas when sharing a piece of data. The first one is that he encrypts the data and signs the result to prove his/her ownership. On this occasion, once a DU decrypts the data, the DO cannot deny it. Besides, the DO couldn't revoke the ciphertext since it is written on blockchain. The second one is that DO submits the encrypted data confidentially. As the DO wishes, his/her personal information will not be exposed as Lemma 3 2) proves.

Data User. A malicious DU is always curious about the plaintext of ciphertext which he could easily get on blockchain. The probability of cracking decentralized CP-ABE is negligible. The malicious DU does not have the necessary keys from AAs. Suppose we have multiple malicious DUs and they collude to share their already owned keys. However, decentralized CP-ABE is collusion-resistant [11]. An alternative attack is to break SGX and get possible decryption keys of honest ones, Lemma 3 3) indicates this also will be impossible.

Attribute Authority. A malicious AA may try to generate a key for himself/herself when he/she is as a DU. From Sect. 5.1, we can see that each authority has a unique public/private key pair, and the public key is used in encrypting a ciphertext. The fake keys simulated by the malicious AA will fail to decrypt the ciphertext.

Enclave/SGX. We have assumed that SGX is a reliable component Sect. 3.1, though it has risks that are out of scope in this paper. By Lemma 3 3), we prove that the data is confidential both inside and outside SGX.

DoS Attack. By Lemma 2, we kept decentralization when combining decentralized CP-ABE, blockchain and SGX. The endless computation may block the whole network; continuous data may lead to full storage. As described in Sect. 5.2, we emphasize that storage and computation of SGX are also charging fees as Ethereum does. If anyone who would like to abuse the resources in Ethereum or SGX, he/she soon will get out of gas. In this design, there are limitations for data owners to store unused ciphertext; for attribute authorities to use SGX; for data users to abuse computation on Ethereum and SGX. Enclave has limited memory, SGX provides "Seal" operation [6] to store confidential data outside the enclave.

7   Conclusions

We propose an innovative methodology for data sharing in this paper. By storing ciphertext in a blockchain, tamper-resistant data sharing is accomplished. With decentralized multi-authority CP-ABE, we achieve flexible many-to-many data sharing, and fine-grained access is controlled by the data owner. SGX is introduced to protect the keys for decryption so that keys are unavailable to anyone. The data sharing methodology is revocable with SGX so that we don't need to update ciphertexts, which it's more reasonable in practice. We will put our methodology in a real production environment in the future.

References

1. Yu, S., Wang, C., Ren, K., Lou, W.: Achieving secure, scalable, and fine-grained data access control in cloud computing. In: 2010 Proceedings IEEE INFOCOM, pp. 1–9, March 2010
2. Xu, Y., Zeng, Q., Wang, G., Zhang, C., Ren, J., Zhang, Y.: An efficient privacy-enhanced attribute-based access control mechanism. Concurr. Comput. Pract. Exp. **32**, e5556 (2020). https://doi.org/10.1002/cpe.5556
3. Zheng, B.K., Zhu, L.H., Shen, M., et al.: Scalable and privacy preserving data sharing based on blockchain. J. Comput. Sci. Technol. **33**(3), 557–567 (2018)
4. Zhu, L., Wu, Y., Gai, K., Choo, K.K.R.: Controllable and trustworthy blockchain-based cloud data management. Future Gener. Comput. Syst. **91**, 527–535 (2019)
5. Nakamoto, S.: Bitcoin: a peer-to-peer electronic cash system. Technical report (2008). http://bitcoin.org/bitcoin.pdf. Accessed October 2019
6. Costan, V., Devadas, S.: Intel SGX explained. Technical report, Cryptology ePrint Archive, Report 2016/086 (2016). https://eprint.iacr.org/2016/086. Accessed October 2019
7. Li, J., Zhang, Y., Chen, X., Xiang, Y.: Secure attribute-based data sharing for resource-limited users in cloud computing. Comput. Secur. **72**, 1–12 (2018)
8. Wu, A., Zhang, Y., Zheng, X., et al.: Efficient and privacy-preserving traceable attribute-based encryption in blockchain. Ann. Telecommun. **74**, 401–411 (2019)
9. Wood, G.: Ethereum: a secure decentralized generalised transaction ledger. Ethereum Project Yellow Paper (2014). https://ethereum.github.io/yellowpaper/paper.pdf. Accessed October 2019
10. Lewko, A., Waters, B.: Decentralizing attribute-based encryption. In: Paterson, K.G. (ed.) EUROCRYPT 2011. LNCS, vol. 6632, pp. 568–588. Springer, Heidelberg (2011). https://doi.org/10.1007/978-3-642-20465-4_31
11. Rouselakis, Y., Waters, B.: Efficient statically-secure large-universe multi-authority attribute-based encryption. In: Böhme, R., Okamoto, T. (eds.) FC 2015. LNCS, vol. 8975, pp. 315–332. Springer, Heidelberg (2015). https://doi.org/10.1007/978-3-662-47854-7_19
12. Beimel, A.: Secure schemes for secret sharing and key distribution [Ph.D. thesis]. Israel Institute of Technology, Technion, Haifa, Israel (1996)
13. Sabt, M., Achemlal, M., Bouabdallah, A.: Trusted execution environment: what it is, and what it is not. In: Proceedings of 2015 IEEE Trustcom/BigDataSE/ISPA, Helsinki, Finland, pp. 57–64 (2015)
14. Lind, J., et al.: Teechan: payment channels using trusted execution environments. ArXiv arXiv:1612.07766 (2016). N. pag
15. Kosba, A., Miller, A., Shi, E., Wen, Z., Papamanthou, C.: Hawk: the blockchain model of cryptography and privacy-preserving smart contracts. In: Proceedings of IEEE Symposium on Security and Privacy (SP), San Jose, CA, USA, pp. 839–858 (2016)
16. Milutinovic, M., He, W., Wu, H., Kanwal, M.: Proof of luck: an efficient blockchain consensus protocol. In: Proceedings of 1st Workshop System Software, pp. 1–6 (2016)

17. Yuan, R., Xia, Y.-B., Chen, H.-B., Zang, B.-Y., Xie, J.: ShadowEth: private smart contract on public blockchain. J. Comput. Sci. Technol. **33**(3), 542–556 (2018). https://doi.org/10.1007/s11390-018-1839-y
18. Shetty, S., Liang, X., Bowden, D., Zhao, J., Zhang, L.: Blockchain-based decentralized accountability and self-sovereignty in healthcare systems. In: Treiblmaier, H., Beck, R. (eds.) Business Transformation through Blockchain, pp. 119–149. Springer, Cham (2019). https://doi.org/10.1007/978-3-319-99058-3_5
19. Wang, S., Zhang, D., Zhang, Y., Liu, L.: Efficiently revocable and searchable attribute-based encryption scheme for mobile cloud storage. IEEE Access **6**, 30444–30457 (2018)
20. Guo, R., Shi, H., Zheng, D., Jing, C., Zhuang, C., Wang, Z.: Flexible and efficient blockchain-based ABE scheme with multi-authority for medical on demand in telemedicine system. IEEE Access **7**, 88012–88025 (2019)
21. Zhang, Y., Chen, X., Li, J., Wong, D.S., Li, H., You, I.: Ensuring attribute privacy protection and fast decryption for outsourced data security in mobile cloud computing. Inf. Sci. **379**, 42–61 (2017)
22. He, Y., Chen, Y.C., Guo, Z.Y., Tso, R., Ye, S.Z.: Smart contract-based decentralized privacy system for securing data ownership management. Commun. CCISA **25**, 1–21 (2019)
23. Wang, S., Zhang, Y., Zhang, Y.: A blockchain-based framework for data sharing with fine-grained access control in decentralized storage systems. IEEE Access **6**, 38437–38450 (2008)
24. Zyskind, G., Nathan, O., Pentland, A.: Decentralizing privacy: using blockchain to protect personal data. In: 2015 IEEE Security and Privacy Workshops, pp. 180–184, May 2015
25. Dai, W., Dai, C., Choo, K.R., Cui, C., Zou, D., Jin, H.: SDTE: a secure blockchain-based data trading ecosystem. IEEE Trans. Inf. Forensics Secur. **15**, 725–737 (2020)
26. Matetic, S., Wust, K., Schneider, M., Kostiainen, K., Karame, G.O., Capkun, S.: BITE: bitcoin lightweight client privacy using trusted execution. IACR Cryptology ePrint Archive (2018)

On the Analysis of the Outsourced Revocable Identity-Based Encryption from Lattices

Yanhua Zhang[1(✉)], Ximeng Liu[2], Yupu Hu[3], and Huiwen Jia[4]

[1] Guangxi Key Laboratory of Cryptography and Information Security,
Guilin University of Electronic Technology, Guangxi 541004, China
yhzhang@email.zzuli.edu.cn
[2] Fuzhou University, Fuzhou 350108, China
[3] Xidian University, Xi'an 710071, China
yphu@mail.xidian.edu.cn
[4] Guangzhou University, Guangzhou 510006, China
hwjia@gzhu.edu.cn

Abstract. For identity-based encryption (IBE) with identity revocation, or simply revocable IBE (R-IBE), an indirect revocation method in which a trusted center (i.e., private key generator, PKG) initially generates all users' long-term private keys and periodically issues time update keys for non-revoked users seems to be a flexible choice, because it invites a sender to generate ciphertexts without caring about revoked (and non-revocked) users. However, these computation and communication overheads in frequent time keys update operations remain as a daunting task for PKG. In order to alleviate the offload of PKG and improve its scalability in the quantum computers attack environment, Dong et al. recently extended the concept of R-IBE to support outsourcing computation with a semi-trusted key update cloud service provider (KU-CSP), and proposed an outsourced revocable lattice-based IBE (OR-IBE) scheme.

In this work, we show that the OR-IBE scheme of Dong et al. does not satisfy the correctness property of OR-IBE, meanwhile, it is not decryption key exposure resistance (DKER), a default security requirement for R-IBE. In addition, we provide a modification of their construction to be a correct and secure OR-IBE scheme. In particular, the first lattice-based OR-IBE scheme with DKER is introduced.

Keywords: IBE · Lattices · Revocation · Outsourcing computation

1 Introduction

Identity-based encryption (IBE) [22] with identity (or key) revocation, or simply revocable IBE (R-IBE) [4], is an interesting extension of IBE in which the public-key infrastructure in conventional public-key cryptosystem is eliminated and a personal identity information string plays the role of a public key, in addition, it

© Springer Nature Switzerland AG 2021
M. Yang et al. (Eds.): NSS 2021, LNCS 13041, pp. 79–99, 2021.
https://doi.org/10.1007/978-3-030-92708-0_5

supports the identity (or key) revocation functionality. In R-IBE cryptosystem, compared with a direct revocation method in which the sender can specify the message receiver (a non-revoked user), an indirect revocation method in which a trusted center (in general, private key generator, PKG) initially generates all users' long-term private keys and periodically issues time update keys for non-revoked users seems to be a more flexible choice, because it invites the sender to generate ciphertexts without caring about revoked (and non-revoked) users.

Obviously, the computation and communication complexity in frequent time keys update operations remain as a daunting task for PKG. To date, cloud-based technology (including cloud computing service and cloud storage service, etc.) has already created a new generation of computing paradigm, and with a flexible assistance of cloud, many conventional costly computations and bulky storages can be performed with ease. Therefore, introducing the cloud computing service into R-IBE is an interesting idea to alleviate the load of PKG.

Lattice-based cryptography (LBC), believed to be secure in quantum computers attack environment and the most promising candidate for post-quantum cryptography, enjoys several competitive advantages over conventional number-theoretic problems: simpler arithmetic operations, rich cryptographic functionalities and proven secure based on the *worst-case* hardness assumptions. Since the creative works of Ajtai [2], Regev [20] and Gentry et al. [10], LBC has become an exciting cryptographic research field, and to design efficient and proven secure LBC schemes has attracted significant interest by the research community.

Recently, an outsourced revocable lattice-based IBE (OR-IBE) scheme was proposed by Dong et al. [9]. The basic idea of this OR-IBE scheme is inspired by the work of Li et al. [14] to extend the concept of R-IBE to support outsourcing computation with a semi-trusted key update cloud service provider (KU-CSP). In particular, Dong et al. adopted the (H)IBE scheme of Agrawal et al. [1] for under-lying lattice-based IBE scheme and complete subtree (CS) revocation scheme of Chen et al. [7] for lattice-based keys revocation and time keys update. Additionally, they added a user map which stores an identity hash and outsourcing key pair to improve the efficiency of KU-CSP's querying on outsourcing keys. In detail, previous offloads of PKG to issue time update keys for non-revoked users are now completely delegated to KU-CSP, which is only with an extra cost that PKG distributes a corresponding identity outsourcing key to KU-CSP.

OUR CONTRIBUTIONS. In this paper, we first show that there is a serious problem in the lattice-based OR-IBE scheme of Dong et al. That is, a ciphertext generated for a non-revoked user id at time t cannot be decrypted correctly by using a decryption key derived from id's long-term private key and a time update key with time t. The reason of this decryption failure problem is that the construction of ciphertext is not correct in which a public matrix of KU-CSP is missed, and the non-revoked user id adopts his decryption key at time t cannot get the original message which is now exactly masked by some noise (a vector) with a larger size (in lattice-based encryptions, in order to decrypt a ciphertext successfully, the ultimate noise must has a shorter size). Secondly, we show that their lattice-based OR-IBE scheme cannot be decryption key exposure resistance (DKER), a default security requirement since it was first introduced into R-IBE by Seo and Emura [21]. To be more clear, the detailed explanations of these two problems are given in the later part (see Sect. 3) of this paper. Furthermore, to remedy these problems, we redesign the ciphertext and the long-term private key of a user to modify the lattice-based OR-IBE scheme of Dong et al. to be secure without the decryption failure problem and with DKER, and thus, the first lattice-based OR-IBE with DKER that is quantum-resistance is introduced.

RELATED WORKS. As mentioned earlier, a relatively ideal identity revocation method for IBE is an indirect revocation in which the sender can generate ciphertexts as same as that of IBE without caring about the state of a receiver (a revoked or non-revoked user), and only the receiver needs to check his revocation state (i.e., only a non-revoked user could obtain his short-term decryption key) to decrypt these ciphertexts. The first IBE scheme with revocation capability was shown by Boneh and Franklin [4], whose scheme is not scalable and inefficient for large-scale system, as each user has to receive an updated private key from PKG via a *secure* channel, and the workload of PKG also grows linearly in the number of users N. The first scalable R-IBE scheme was designed by Boldyreva et al. [5], whose scheme is constructed by combining a fuzzy IBE scheme and the CS revocation scheme. After that, the fully secure R-IBE, R-IBE with DKER, and R-IBE with the subset difference (SD) method were proposed by Libert and Vergnaud [15], Seo and Emura [21], and Lee et al. [13]. Following the model of [5], the first lattice-based R-IBE scheme (without DKER) which satisfies the selective-revocable-identity-time security was constructed by Chen et al. [7], and the first lattice-based constructions with bounded DKER and unbounded DKER were proposed by Takayasu and Watanabe [24] and Katsumata et al. [11], respectively. As it was asserted in [24], there are unavoidable bugs in the security proof of Cheng and Zhang's adaptive-id secure lattice-based R-IBE scheme [8].

The study of OR-IBE was initiated by Li et al. [14], whose scheme introduces cloud computing service into R-IBE to alleviate the offload of PKG. In particular, a semi-trusted key update cloud service provider KU-CSP is adopted to update every user's time key. To overcome the decryption challenges for users only with the limited resources, Qin et al. [19] introduced a new revocation method called server-aided R-IBE, contrary to previous OR-IBE, all workload on users are outsourced to the server. Inspired by these two new models of R-IBE, Nguyen et al. [18] and Dong et al. [9] respectively designed the first lattice-based server-aided R-IBE scheme and the first lattice-based OR-IBE scheme (a serious correctness problem and a security problem in [9] will be shown in this paper). Recently, the generic constructions of R-IBE with CS method, SD method, and server-aided ciphertext evolution were respectively proposed by Ma and Lin [16], Lee [12], and Sun et al. [23].

ORGANIZATION. The organization of the paper is as follows. In Sect. 2, we review the definition and scheme of lattice-based OR-IBE proposed by Dong et al. and some background knowledge on lattices. In Sect. 3, we point out that there is a serious correctness problem and a security problem in Dong et al.'s OR-IBE scheme. In Sect. 4, we propose the measures to solve these problems and a new lattice-based OR-IBE scheme with DKER is described and analyzed. In the final section, we conclude our whole paper.

2   Preliminaries

Table 1 refers to the notations used in this paper.

Table 1. Notations of this paper.

Notation	Definition
$\mathbf{a}, \mathbf{A}$	Vectors, matrices
$\xleftarrow{\$}$	Sampling uniformly at random
$\|\cdot\|, \|\cdot\|_\infty$	Euclidean norm ℓ_2, infinity norm ℓ_∞
$\lceil e \rceil, \lfloor e \rceil$	The smallest integer not less than e, the integer closet to e
$\mathcal{O}, \tilde{\mathcal{O}}, \omega$	Standard asymptotic notations
$\log e$	Logarithm of e with base 2
ppt	Probabilistic polynomial-time

2.1   Review of the OR-IBE Scheme

In this subsection, we review the system model and security definition of OR-IBE. OR-IBE is an extension of R-IBE that supports identity (or key) revocation, and additionally it delegates issuance of time update keys to a semi-trusted KU-CSP. A trusted center (i.e., PKG) first generates two master keys (msk, muk) and the public parameters pp, and then sends the master time update key muk to KU-CSP. The trusted center generates a long-term private key sk_{id} for each user with identity id by using the master secret key msk, meanwhile, it distributes a corresponding identity outsourcing key ok_{id} to KU-CSP and maintains a revocation list (RL) recording the state information with regard to revoked users. KU-CSP will periodically issue a time update key $uk_{id,t}$ for a non-revoked user id with time t by using muk, ok_{id} and RL. To decrypt a ciphertext which specifies an identity id and a time t, the non-revoked recipient combines his long-term private key sk_{id} and time update key $uk_{id,t}$ to derive a short-term decryption key $dk_{id,t}$. The system model of OR-IBE is shown in Fig. 1.

Definition 1. *An* OR-IBE *scheme involves four distinct entities: a private key generator* PKG, *a key update cloud service provider* KU-CSP *and the users (senders and recipients), associated with identity space* $\mathcal{I}$, *time space* $\mathcal{T}$ *(the size of* $\mathcal{T}$ *is polynomial in the security parameter, and time is treated as discrete as opposed to continuous), message space* $\mathcal{M}$, *and ciphertext space* $\mathcal{C}$, *and consists of seven polynomial-time algorithms* Setup, PriKeyGen, KeyUpd, DecKeyGen, Encrypt, Decrypt *and* Revoke, *which are defined as follows:*

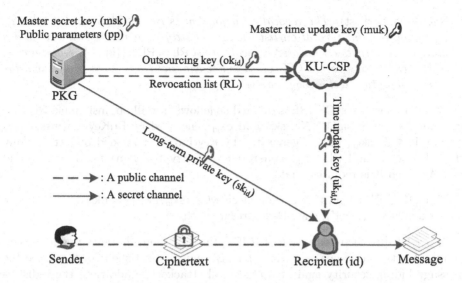

Fig. 1. System model of OR-IBE scheme.

- Setup($1^n, N$): *The setup algorithm is run by* PKG, *and it takes as input a security parameter n and the maximal number of users N. It outputs a master secret key* msk, *a master time update key* muk, *the public parameters* pp, *a user revocation list* RL *(initially empty), and a state* st. *Note:* muk *is sent to* KU-CSP *via a secret channel,* msk *is kept in secret by* PKG, *and* pp *is made public and as an implicit input of all other algorithms.*
- PriKeyGen(msk, id, st): *The key generation algorithm is run by* PKG, *and it takes as input an identity* id $\in \mathcal{I}$, *the master secret key* msk, *and a state* st. *It outputs a long-term private key* sk$_{id}$, *an identity outsourcing key* ok$_{id}$, *and an updated state* st. *Note:* sk$_{id}$ *is sent to the recipient and* ok$_{id}$ *is sent to* KU-CSP *both via a secret channel.*
- KeyUpd(RL, t, muk, id, ok$_{id}$, st): *The key update algorithm is run by* KU-CSP, *and it takes as input current revocation list* RL, *a time* t $\in \mathcal{T}$, *the master time update key* muk, *an outsourcing key* ok$_{id}$ *for the recipient* id, *and a state* st. *It outputs a time update key* uk$_{id,t}$, *or a special symbol* $\perp$ *to indicate that* id $\in$ RL. *Note:* uk$_{id,t}$ *(or* $\perp$*) is sent to user* id *via a public channel.*
- DecKeyGen(sk$_{id}$, uk$_{id,t}$): *The decryption key derivation algorithm is run by the recipient* id, *and it takes as input a long-term private key* sk$_{id}$ *and a corresponding time update key* uk$_{id,t}$ *(or* $\perp$*). It outputs a short-term decryption key* dk$_{id,t}$ *(or* $\perp$ *indicating that the recipient* id *was revoked).*
- Encrypt(id, t, m): *The encryption algorithm is run by the sender, and it takes as input a recipient's identity* id, *an encryption time* t, *and a message* m $\in \mathcal{M}$. *It outputs a ciphertext* ct$_{id,t}$ $\in \mathcal{C}$.
- Decrypt(dk$_{id',t'}$, ct$_{id,t}$): *The decryption algorithm is run by the recipient, and it takes as input a ciphertext* ct$_{id,t}$ $\in \mathcal{C}$ *and a decryption key* dk$_{id',t'}$. *It outputs a message* m $\in \mathcal{M}$, *or a symbol* $\perp$.

– Revoke(id, t, RL, st): *The revocation algorithm is run by* PKG, *and it takes as input the current revocation list* RL, *an identity* id, *a revoked time* t, *and a state* st. *It outputs an updated revocation list* RL = RL ∪ {(id, t)}. *Note: a copy of* RL *will be sent to* KU-CSP *via a public channel (to prevent tampering, the digital signature technology may be adopted).*

The correctness of OR-IBE is defined as follows: for all pp, msk, muk, RL, and st generated by Setup($1^n, N$), sk_{id} and ok_{id} generated by PriKeyGen(msk, id, st) for any id $\in \mathcal{I}$, $uk_{id,t}$ (or $\bot$) generated by KeyUpd(RL, t, muk, id, ok_{id}, st) for any id $\in \mathcal{I}$, t $\in \mathcal{T}$ and RL, $ct_{id,t}$ generated by Encrypt(id, t, m) for any id, t and m $\in \mathcal{M}$, then it is required that:

– If (id, t') $\notin$ RL for all t' $\leq$ t, then DecKeyGen($sk_{id}, uk_{id,t}$) = $dk_{id,t}$.
– If (id = id') $\wedge$ (t = t'), then Decrypt($dk_{id',t'}, ct_{id,t}$) = m.

Since OR-IBE is an extension of R-IBE, the indistinguishability under chosen-plaintext attack (ind-cpa) security of R-IBE must be satisfied to guarantee the message hiding security against an external attacker. In addition, the indistin-guishability under time update key attack (ind-uka) security should be satisfied to guarantee the message hiding security once KU-CSP that owns the master time update key muk became an attacker. In the above two security definitions, we will only consider selective-revocable-identity-time security (a weaker secu-rity notion initially was suggested in R-IBE by Boldyreva et al. [5], subsequently by Chen et al. [7] and Katsumata et al. [11], in which adversary $\mathcal{A}$ sends the challenge identity and time pair (id*, t*) $\in \mathcal{I} \times \mathcal{T}$ to the challenger $\hat{\mathcal{C}}$ before the execution of Setup($1^n, N$)). A slight difference is that we formalize the ind-cpa (and ind-uka) security of OR-IBE adopting a game capturing a stronger privacy property called *indistinguishable from random* as defined in [1,8].

The ind-cpa security model of OR-IBE is the same as that of R-IBE [5,7,11], which considers an external attacker who cannot access msk and muk. In this security model, an attacker can request long-term private key, time update key, revocation, and decryption key queries. One of the most restrictions of this model is that if the attacker has requested a long-term private key for the challenge identity id*, then id* must be revoked before (or at) the time update key query of challenge time t*. Finally, the goal of the attacker is to determine that the challenge ciphertext is completely random or correctly encrypted on the challenge m* corresponding to (id*, t*). A detailed definition of the ind-cpa security model is described as follows:

Definition 2. *The* ind-cpa *security of* OR-IBE *is described as the following game between the challenger* $\hat{\mathcal{C}}_1$ *and adversary* $\mathcal{A}_1$:

– *Initial:* $\mathcal{A}_1$ *first declares a challenge identity and time pair* (id*, t*).
– *Setup:* $\hat{\mathcal{C}}_1$ *runs* Setup($1^n, N$) *to obtain* (msk, muk, pp, RL, st). *Note:* RL *is ini-tially empty.* $\hat{\mathcal{C}}_1$ *keeps* (msk, muk) *in secret by himself and provides* pp *to* $\mathcal{A}_1$.
– *Query phase 1:* $\mathcal{A}_1$ *adaptively makes a polynomially bounded number of queries on the following oracles (Note: all oracles can share the state* st *and the queries should be with some restrictions defined later):*

- PriKenGen($\cdot$): *For the private key query on an identity* id $\in \mathcal{I}$, *it returns a long-term private key* $\mathsf{sk}_{\mathsf{id}}$ *by running* PriKeyGen(msk, id, st). *Note: an outsourcing key* $\mathsf{ok}_{\mathsf{id}}$ *is also generated but not returned.*
- KeyUpd($\cdot$): *For the key update query on* (id, t) $\in \mathcal{I} \times \mathcal{T}$, *it returns a time update key* $\mathsf{uk}_{\mathsf{id},\mathsf{t}}$ *by running* KeyUpd(RL, t, muk, id, $\mathsf{ok}_{\mathsf{id}}$, st).
- Revoke($\cdot$): *For the revocation query on* (id, t) $\in \mathcal{I} \times \mathcal{T}$, *it returns an updated* RL *by running* Revoke(id, t, RL, st).
- DecKeyGen($\cdot$): *For the decryption key query on* (id, t) $\in \mathcal{I} \times \mathcal{T}$, *it returns a short-term decryption key* $\mathsf{dk}_{\mathsf{id},\mathsf{t}}$ *by running* DecKeyGen($\mathsf{sk}_{\mathsf{id}}$, $\mathsf{uk}_{\mathsf{id},\mathsf{t}}$) *(run* PriKeyGen(msk, id, st), KeyUpd(RL, t, muk, id, $\mathsf{ok}_{\mathsf{id}}$, st) *to get* $\mathsf{sk}_{\mathsf{id}}$, $\mathsf{uk}_{\mathsf{id},\mathsf{t}}$*). Note: this oracle is used to define* DKER, *which is not provided by Dong et al.*
- *Challenge:* $\mathcal{A}_1$ *submits a message* $\mathsf{m}^* \in \mathcal{M}$. $\hat{\mathcal{C}}_1$ *samples a bit* $b \xleftarrow{\$} \{0,1\}$. *If* $b = 0$, $\hat{\mathcal{C}}_1$ *returns a challenge ciphertext* $\mathsf{ct}^*_{\mathsf{id}^*,\mathsf{t}^*}$ *by running* Encrypt($\mathsf{id}^*, \mathsf{t}^*, \mathsf{m}^*$), *otherwise, a random* $\mathsf{ct}^*_{\mathsf{id}^*,\mathsf{t}^*} \xleftarrow{\$} \mathcal{C}$.
- *Query phase 2:* $\mathcal{A}_1$ *makes queries as before with the same restrictions.*
- *Guess:* $\mathcal{A}_1$ *outputs a bit* $b^* \in \{0,1\}$, *and wins if* $b^* = b$.

In the above game, the following restrictions must hold:

- KeyUpd($\cdot$) and Revoke($\cdot$) can only be queried in a non-decreasing order of time (i.e., at time that is greater than or equal to the time of all previous queries).
- Revoke($\cdot$) can not be queried at t if KeyUpd($\cdot$) has already been queried at t.
- Revoke($\cdot$) must be queried on (id^*, t) for t $\le \mathsf{t}^*$ if PriKenGen($\cdot$) has already been queried on id^*.
- DecKeyGen($\cdot$) can not be queried at t if KeyUpd($\cdot$) has not been queried at t.
- DecKeyGen($\cdot$) can not be queried on ($\mathsf{id}^*, \mathsf{t}^*$).

The advantage of $\mathcal{A}_1$ in the above game is defined as $\mathsf{Adv}^{\mathsf{ind\text{-}cpa}}_{\mathsf{OR\text{-}IBE},\mathcal{A}_1}(n) = |\Pr[b^* = b] - 1/2|$. An OR-IBE scheme is ind-cpa secure if for all ppt adversary $\mathcal{A}_1$, $\mathsf{Adv}^{\mathsf{ind\text{-}cpa}}_{\mathsf{OR\text{-}IBE},\mathcal{A}_1}(n)$ is negligible in the security parameter n.

The ind-uka security model of OR-IBE is provided in Appendix A.

2.2 Integer Lattices

Definition 3. *For integers* n, m, $q \ge 2$, *a random* $\mathbf{A} \in \mathbb{Z}^{n \times m}_q$, *the* m-*dimensional* q-*ary lattice* $\Lambda^\perp_q(\mathbf{A})$ *is defined as* $\Lambda^\perp_q(\mathbf{A}) = \{\mathbf{e} \in \mathbb{Z}^m \mid \mathbf{A} \cdot \mathbf{e} = \mathbf{0} \bmod q\}$.

Lemma 1 ([10]). *For* n, $q \ge 2$, $m \ge 2n\lceil \log q \rceil$, *assume that the columns of* $\mathbf{A}$ *generate* $\mathbb{Z}^n_q$, *let* $\epsilon \in (0, 1/2)$ *and* $s \ge \eta_\epsilon(\Lambda^\perp(\mathbf{A}))$, *the followings are satisfied:*

1. *For* $\mathbf{e} \xleftarrow{\$} \mathcal{D}_{\mathbb{Z}^m,s}$, *the statistical distance between* $\mathbf{u} = \mathbf{A} \cdot \mathbf{e} \bmod q$ *and an uniform distribution over* $\mathbb{Z}^n_q$ *is at most* 2ϵ.

2. *For* $\mathbf{e} \xleftarrow{\$} \mathcal{D}_{\mathbb{Z}^m,s}$, *then* $\Pr[\|\mathbf{e}\|_\infty \le \lceil s \cdot \log m \rceil]$ *holds with a larger probability.*

A key component in lattice-based cryptography is a ppt trapdoor generation algorithm that returns a statistically close to uniform matrix $\mathbf{A} \in \mathbb{Z}_q^{n \times m}$ together with a low Gram-Schmidt norm basis for $\Lambda_q^{\perp}(\mathbf{A})$.

Lemma 2 ([2,3,17]). *Let $n \geq 1$, $q \geq 2$, $m = 2n\lceil \log q \rceil$, there is a ppt algorithm* TrapGen(q, n, m) *that returns* $\mathbf{A} \in \mathbb{Z}_q^{n \times m}$ *statistically close to an uniform matrix in* $\mathbb{Z}_q^{n \times m}$ *and a trapdoor* $\mathbf{R_A}$ *for* $\Lambda_q^{\perp}(\mathbf{A})$.

Given a trapdoor for $\Lambda_q^{\perp}(\mathbf{A})$, Gentry et al. [10] first showed a creative algorithm to sample shorter vectors (or matrices) from a discrete Gaussian distribution, and an improved algorithm was introduced in [17]. Meanwhile, to delegate a short trapdoor with equal length (e.g., $\| \cdot \|$) for some super-lattice was also introduced by Cash et al. [6].

Lemma 3 ([10,17]). *Let $n \geq 1$, $q \geq 2$, $m = 2n\lceil \log q \rceil$, given $\mathbf{A} \in \mathbb{Z}_q^{n \times m}$, a trapdoor $\mathbf{R_A}$ for $\Lambda_q^{\perp}(\mathbf{A})$, a parameter $s = \omega(\sqrt{n \log q \log n})$, and a vector $\mathbf{u} \in \mathbb{Z}_q^n$, there is a ppt algorithm* SamplePre$(\mathbf{A}, \mathbf{R_A}, \mathbf{u}, s)$ *returning a shorter vector $\mathbf{e} \in \Lambda_q^{\mathbf{u}}(\mathbf{A})$ sampled from a distribution statistically close to $\mathcal{D}_{\Lambda_q^{\mathbf{u}}(\mathbf{A}), s}$.*

Lemma 4 ([6]). *Let $n \geq 1$, $q \geq 2$, $m = 2n\lceil \log q \rceil$, given $\mathbf{A} \in \mathbb{Z}_q^{n \times m}$ whose columns can generate $\mathbb{Z}_q^n$, an arbitrary basis matrix $\mathbf{R_A} \in \mathbb{Z}^{m \times m}$ for $\Lambda_q^{\perp}(\mathbf{A})$, a random $\hat{\mathbf{A}} \in \mathbb{Z}_q^{n \times m'}$, there is a deterministic pt algorithm* ExtBasis$(\mathbf{R_A}, \mathbf{A'} = \mathbf{A}|\hat{\mathbf{A}})$ *that returns a basis matrix $\mathbf{R_{A'}} \in \mathbb{Z}^{(m+m') \times (m+m')}$ for $\Lambda_q^{\perp}(\mathbf{A'})$, and $\mathbf{R_A}$ and $\mathbf{R_{A'}}$ with equal Gram-Schmidt norm. In particular, it holds even for any given permutation of all columns of $\mathbf{A'}$.*

Lemma 5 ([6]). *Let $n \geq 1$, $q \geq 2$, $m = 2n\lceil \log q \rceil$, $s \geq \|\widetilde{\mathbf{R_A}}\| \cdot \omega(\sqrt{\log n})$, $\mathbf{R_A} \in \mathbb{Z}^{m \times m}$ is an arbitrary basis for $\Lambda_q^{\perp}(\mathbf{A})$, there is a ppt algorithm* RandBasis$(\mathbf{R_A}, s)$ *that returns a new basis $\mathbf{R'_A} \in \mathbb{Z}^{m \times m}$ for $\Lambda_q^{\perp}(\mathbf{A})$ and $\|\mathbf{R'_A}\| \leq s \cdot \sqrt{m}$. In particular, for any two basis matrices $\mathbf{R_A^{(1)}}$, $\mathbf{R_A^{(2)}}$ for $\Lambda_q^{\perp}(\mathbf{A})$, and $s \geq \max\{\|\widetilde{\mathbf{R_A^{(1)}}}\|, \|\widetilde{\mathbf{R_A^{(2)}}}\|\} \cdot \omega(\sqrt{\log n})$,* RandBasis$(\mathbf{R_A^{(1)}}, s)$ *is statistically close to* RandBasis$(\mathbf{R_A^{(2)}}, s)$. *This property is useful for securely delegating, because the resulting basis matrix is still short, meanwhile, it is statistically independent to the original one.*

Lemma 6 ([1]). *Let $q > 2$, $m > n$, $\mathbf{A} \in \mathbb{Z}_q^{n \times m}$, $\mathbf{A'} \in \mathbb{Z}_q^{n \times m'}$, and $s > \|\widetilde{\mathbf{R_A}}\| \cdot \omega(\sqrt{\log(m + m')})$, given a trapdoor $\mathbf{R_A}$ for $\Lambda_q^{\perp}(\mathbf{A})$ and $\mathbf{u} \in \mathbb{Z}_q^n$, there is a ppt algorithm* SampleLeft$(\mathbf{A}|\mathbf{A'}, \mathbf{R_A}, \mathbf{u}, s)$ *that returns a shorter $\mathbf{e} \in \mathbb{Z}^{2m}$ sampled from a distribution statistically close to $\mathcal{D}_{\Lambda_q^{\mathbf{u}}(\mathbf{A}|\mathbf{A'}), s}$.*

Lemma 7 ([1]). *Let $q > 2$, $m > n$, $\mathbf{A}$, $\mathbf{B} \in \mathbb{Z}_q^{n \times m}$, $s > \|\widetilde{\mathbf{R_B}}\| \cdot \mathcal{O}(\sqrt{m}) \cdot \omega(\sqrt{\log m})$, given a trapdoor $\mathbf{R_B}$, a low-norm $\mathbf{R} \in \{-1, 1\}^{m \times m}$, and $\mathbf{u} \in \mathbb{Z}_q^n$, there is a ppt algorithm* SampleRight$(\mathbf{A}, \mathbf{B}, \mathbf{R}, \mathbf{R_B}, \mathbf{u}, s)$ *that returns a shorter $\mathbf{e} \in \mathbb{Z}^{2m}$ distributed statistically close to $\mathcal{D}_{\Lambda_q^{\mathbf{u}}(\mathbf{F}), s}$, where $\mathbf{F} = [\mathbf{A}|\mathbf{AR} + \mathbf{B}]$.*

Definition 4. *The* $\mathsf{LWE}_{n,q,\chi}$ *problem is defined as follows: given a random vector* $\mathbf{s} \xleftarrow{\$} \mathbb{Z}_q^n$, *a probability distribution* χ *over* $\mathbb{Z}$, *let* $\mathcal{A}_{\mathbf{s},\chi}$ *be a distribution obtained by sampling* $\mathbf{A} \in \mathbb{Z}_q^{n \times m}$, $\mathbf{e} \xleftarrow{\$} \chi^m$, *and return* $(\mathbf{A}, \mathbf{A}^\top \mathbf{s} + \mathbf{e} \bmod q)$, *and make a distinguish between* $\mathcal{A}_{\mathbf{s},\chi}$ *and an uniform distribution* $\mathcal{U} \xleftarrow{\$} \mathbb{Z}_q^{n \times m} \times \mathbb{Z}_q^m$. *Let* $\beta \geq \sqrt{n} \cdot \omega(\log n)$, *for a prime power* q, *given a* β-*bounded distribution* χ, *the* $\mathsf{LWE}_{n,q,\chi}$ *problem is as least as hard as the shortest independent vectors problem* $\mathsf{SIVP}_{\tilde{\mathcal{O}}(nq/\beta)}$.

Lemma 8 ([1]). *Let* $n \geq 1$, $q > 2$, $m > (n+1)\log q + \omega(\log n)$, $\mathbf{A} \xleftarrow{\$} \mathbb{Z}_q^{n \times m}$, $\mathbf{B} \xleftarrow{\$} \mathbb{Z}_q^{n \times k}$, *and* $\mathbf{R}$ *is chosen uniformly in* $\{-1, 1\}^{m \times k} \bmod q$, *and* $k = poly(n)$. *Then, for all* $\mathbf{w} \in \mathbb{Z}_q^m$, $(\mathbf{A}, \mathbf{AR}, \mathbf{R}^\top \mathbf{w})$ *is statistically close to* $(\mathbf{A}, \mathbf{B}, \mathbf{R}^\top \mathbf{w})$.

Lemma 9 ([1]). *Let* $\mathbf{R}$ *be a* $m \times m$-*matrix chosen uniformly in* $\{-1, 1\}^{m \times m}$ $\bmod q$, *and for any* $\mathbf{w} \in \mathbb{R}^m$, $\Pr[\|\mathbf{R} \cdot \mathbf{w}\|_\infty > \|\mathbf{w}\|_\infty \cdot \sqrt{m} \cdot \omega(\sqrt{\log m})] < negl(m)$.

An injective encoding function $\mathcal{H} : \mathbb{Z}_q^n \to \mathbb{Z}_q^{n \times n}$ is adopted for our modified OR-IBE. An explicit design called encoding with full-rank differences (FRD) was proposed by Agrawal et al. [1].

Definition 5. *Let* $n > 1$, *prime* $q \geq 2$, *an injective encoding function* $\mathcal{H} : \mathbb{Z}_q^n \to \mathbb{Z}_q^{n \times n}$ *is called* FRD *if:*

1. *For* $\forall \mathbf{e}_1, \mathbf{e}_2 \in \mathbb{Z}_q^n$, $\mathbf{e}_1 \neq \mathbf{e}_2$, $\mathcal{H}(\mathbf{e}_1) - \mathcal{H}(\mathbf{e}_2) \in \mathbb{Z}_q^{n \times n}$ *is full-rank.*

2. $\mathcal{H}$ *can be computed in a polynomial time of* $\mathcal{O}(n \log q)$.

2.3 Dong et al.'s Lattice-Based OR-IBE Construction

To alleviate the offload of PKG by adopting cloud computing service, the lattice-based OR-IBE of Dong et al. [9] follows the outsourcing computation method with a semi-trusted KU-CSP proposed by Li et al. [14] for time keys update and the CS revocation scheme of Chen et al. [7] for lattice-based private keys revocation. The PKG maintains a binary tree (BT) to handle revocation (by using the master secret key msk) for a user identity id randomly assigned to a leaf node v_{id} in BT (and its root node is denoted by root), and a long-term private key $\mathsf{sk}_{\mathsf{id}}$ is issued for id associated with the set of nodes defined by $\mathsf{path}(v_{\mathsf{id}})$ denoting the set of nodes on the path from v_{id} to root (both v_{id} and root are included). In order to update a time key for id at time t with the flexible assistance of KU-CSP, an identity outsourcing key $\mathsf{ok}_{\mathsf{id}}$ and the master time update key muk must be sent by PKG, and KU-CSP honestly executes $\mathsf{KUNodes}(\mathsf{BT}, \mathsf{RL}, \mathsf{t})$ algorithm with an updated revocation list RL (also sent by PKG) to return all the non-revoked children of revoked nodes and $\mathsf{KeyUpd}(\mathsf{RL}, \mathsf{t}, \mathsf{muk}, \mathsf{id}, \mathsf{ok}_{\mathsf{id}}, \mathsf{st})$ algorithm to return a time update key $\mathsf{uk}_{\mathsf{id},\mathsf{t}}$ to non-revoked id with time t. The detailed description of $\mathsf{KeyUpd}(\mathsf{RL}, \mathsf{t}, \mathsf{muk}, \mathsf{id}, \mathsf{ok}_{\mathsf{id}}, \mathsf{st})$ will be given later, while $\mathsf{KUNodes}(\mathsf{BT}, \mathsf{RL}, \mathsf{t})$ is omitted here and any interested readers please refer to [5,7,9,18,19,21].

The lattice-based OR-IBE scheme of Dong et al. [9] is described as follows:

- Setup($1^n, N$): On input a security parameter n and the maximal number of system users $N = 2^n$, set the parameters q, s, m valid for scheme. PKG specifies the following steps:
  1. Let the identity space $\mathcal{I} = \mathbb{Z}_q^n$, the time space $\mathcal{T} \subset \mathbb{Z}_q^n$, and the message space $\mathcal{M} = \{0,1\}^n$.
  2. Run TrapGen(q, n, m) to get $\mathbf{A} \in \mathbb{Z}_q^{n \times m}$ with a trapdoor $\mathbf{R_A}$, and $\mathbf{B} \in \mathbb{Z}_q^{n \times m}$ with a trapdoor $\mathbf{R_B}$.
  3. Sample $\mathbf{A}_0, \mathbf{A}_1, \mathbf{B}_0, \mathbf{B}_1 \xleftarrow{\$} \mathbb{Z}_q^{n \times m}$, $\mathbf{U} \xleftarrow{\$} \mathbb{Z}_q^{n \times n}$, and select an FRD function $\mathcal{H} : \mathbb{Z}_q^n \to \mathbb{Z}_q^{n \times n}$.
  4. Set the sate st $= \mathsf{BT}$ that BT is with at least N leaf nodes, and the initial revocation list RL $= \emptyset$.
  5. Set the public parameters pp $= (\mathbf{A}, \mathbf{A}_0, \mathbf{A}_1, \mathbf{B}, \mathbf{B}_0, \mathbf{B}_1, \mathbf{U}, \mathcal{H})$, the master secret key msk $= \mathbf{R_A}$, and the master time update key muk $= \mathbf{R_B}$.
  6. Output (pp, msk, muk, RL, st) where muk is sent to KU-CSP via a *secret* channel, msk is kept in secret by PKG, and pp is made public and as an implicit input of all other algorithms.
- PriKeyGen(msk, id, st): On input an identity id $\in \mathcal{I}$, the master secret key msk, and the state st. PKG specifies the following steps:
  1. Assign id to an unassigned leaf node v_{id} in BT.
  2. For each $\theta \in \mathsf{path}(v_{id})$, if $\mathbf{U}_{1,\theta}, \mathbf{U}_{2,\theta}$ are undefined, sample $\mathbf{U}_{1,\theta} \xleftarrow{\$} \mathbb{Z}_q^{n \times n}$, define $\mathbf{U}_{2,\theta} = \mathbf{U} - \mathbf{U}_{1,\theta}$, and store $(\mathbf{U}_{1,\theta}, \mathbf{U}_{2,\theta})$ in node θ.
  3. Let $\mathbf{A}_{id} = [\mathbf{A} | \mathbf{A}_0 + \mathcal{H}(id)\mathbf{A}_1] \in \mathbb{Z}_q^{n \times 2m}$, and for each $\theta \in \mathsf{path}(v_{id})$, run SampleLeft($\mathbf{A}_{id}, \mathbf{R_A}, \mathbf{U}_{1,\theta}, s$) to generate $\mathbf{E}_{1,\theta} \in \mathbb{Z}^{2m \times n}$ satisfying $\mathbf{A}_{id} \cdot \mathbf{E}_{1,\theta} = \mathbf{U}_{1,\theta} \bmod q$.
  4. For each $\theta \in \mathsf{path}(v_{id})$, let outsourcing key ok$_{id} = \mathbf{U}_{2,\theta} + \mathcal{H}(id) \bmod q$.
  5. Output an updated state st, sk$_{id} = (\theta, \mathbf{E}_{1,\theta})_{\theta \in \mathsf{path}(v_{id})}$, and ok$_{id}$. *Note:* ok$_{id}$ is sent to KU-CSP via a *secret* channel.
- KeyUpd(RL, t, muk, id, ok$_{id}$, st): On input an identity id, time t $\in \mathcal{T}$, the master time update key muk, a revocation list RL, an outsourcing key ok$_{id}$, and the state st. KU-CSP specifies the following steps:
  1. If id $\in$ RL, return $\perp$ and abort, otherwise, store (id, t, ok$_{id}$) to user map.
  2. Let $\mathbf{B}_t = [\mathbf{B} | \mathbf{B}_0 + \mathcal{H}(t)\mathbf{B}_1] \in \mathbb{Z}_q^{n \times 2m}$, for each $\theta \in \mathsf{KUNodes}(\mathsf{BT}, \mathsf{RL}, t)$, run SampleLeft($\mathbf{B}_t, \mathbf{R_B}, \mathsf{ok}_{id} - \mathcal{H}(id), s$) to generate $\mathbf{E}_{2,\theta} \in \mathbb{Z}^{2m \times n}$ satisfying $\mathbf{B}_t \cdot \mathbf{E}_{2,\theta} = \mathsf{ok}_{id} - \mathcal{H}(id) = \mathbf{U}_{2,\theta} \bmod q$.
  3. Output uk$_{id,t} = (\theta, \mathbf{E}_{2,\theta})_{\theta \in \mathsf{KUNodes}(\mathsf{BT}, \mathsf{RL}, t)}$.
- DecKeyGen(sk$_{id}$, uk$_{id,t}$): On input a long-term private key sk$_{id}$ $= (\theta, \mathbf{E}_{1,\theta})_{\theta \in \mathsf{path}(v_{id})}$ and a corresponding time update key uk$_{id,t}$ $= (\theta, \mathbf{E}_{2,\theta})_{\theta \in \mathsf{KUNodes}(\mathsf{BT}, \mathsf{RL}, t)}$. The recipient id specifies the following steps:
  1. If uk$_{id,t} = \perp$, return $\perp$ and abort.
  2. If $\mathsf{path}(v_{id}) \cap \mathsf{KUNodes}(\mathsf{BT}, \mathsf{RL}, t) = \emptyset$, return $\perp$ and abort.
  3. Otherwise, select $\theta \in (\mathsf{path}(v_{id}) \cap \mathsf{KUNodes}(\mathsf{BT}, \mathsf{RL}, t))$ (only one such node θ exists) and return dk$_{id,t} = (\mathbf{E}_{1,\theta}, \mathbf{E}_{2,\theta})$. *Note:* it is easy to draw a conclusion that $\mathbf{A}_{id} \cdot \mathbf{E}_{1,\theta} + \mathbf{B}_t \cdot \mathbf{E}_{2,\theta} = \mathbf{U} \bmod q$.
- Encrypt(id, t, m): On input an identity id $\in \mathcal{I}$, a time t $\in \mathcal{T}$, and a message m $\in \{0,1\}^n$. The sender specifies the following steps:

1. Let $\mathsf{F}_{\mathsf{id},\mathsf{t}} = [\mathbf{A}|\mathbf{A}_0 + \mathcal{H}(\mathsf{id})\mathbf{A}_1|\mathbf{B}_0 + \mathcal{H}(\mathsf{t})\mathbf{B}_1] \in \mathbb{Z}_q^{n \times 3m}$.

2. Sample $\mathbf{s} \xleftarrow{\$} \mathbb{Z}_q^n$, $\mathbf{e} \xleftarrow{\$} \chi^m$, $\mathbf{e}' \xleftarrow{\$} \chi^n$, and $\mathbf{R}_0, \mathbf{R}_1 \xleftarrow{\$} \{1, -1\}^{m \times m}$.

3. Let $\mathbf{c}_0 = \mathbf{U}^T\mathbf{s} + \mathbf{e}' + \mathsf{m}\lfloor \frac{q}{2} \rfloor \bmod q \in \mathbb{Z}_q^n$, and $\mathbf{c}_1 = \mathsf{F}_{\mathsf{id},\mathsf{t}}^T\mathbf{s} + \begin{pmatrix} \mathbf{e} \\ \mathbf{R}_0^T\mathbf{e} \\ \mathbf{R}_1^T\mathbf{e} \end{pmatrix} \in \mathbb{Z}_q^{3m}$.

4. Output $\mathsf{ct}_{\mathsf{id},\mathsf{t}} = (\mathbf{c}_0, \mathbf{c}_1) \in \mathbb{Z}_q^n \times \mathbb{Z}_q^{3m}$.

- Decrypt($\mathsf{dk}_{\mathsf{id}',\mathsf{t}'}, \mathsf{ct}_{\mathsf{id},\mathsf{t}}$): On input a ciphertext $\mathsf{ct}_{\mathsf{id},\mathsf{t}} = (\mathbf{c}_0, \mathbf{c}_1)$ and a decryption key $\mathsf{dk}_{\mathsf{id}',\mathsf{t}'}$. The recipient id' specifies the following steps:
  1. If $(\mathsf{id} \neq \mathsf{id}') \vee (\mathsf{t} \neq \mathsf{t}')$, return $\perp$ and abort.
  2. Otherwise, parse $\mathbf{c}_1 = \begin{pmatrix} \mathbf{c}_{1,0} \\ \mathbf{c}_{1,1} \\ \mathbf{c}_{1,2} \end{pmatrix}$ where $\mathbf{c}_{1,i} \in \mathbb{Z}_q^m$ for $i = 0, 1, 2$.
  3. Compute $\mathbf{w} = \mathbf{c}_0 - \mathbf{E}_{1,\theta}^T \begin{pmatrix} \mathbf{c}_{1,0} \\ \mathbf{c}_{1,1} \end{pmatrix} - \mathbf{E}_{2,\theta}^T \begin{pmatrix} \mathbf{c}_{1,0} \\ \mathbf{c}_{1,2} \end{pmatrix} \bmod q \in \mathbb{Z}_q^n$.
  4. Output $\lfloor \frac{2}{q}\mathbf{w} \rceil \in \{0, 1\}^n$.

- Revoke($\mathsf{id}, \mathsf{t}, \mathsf{RL}, \mathsf{st}$): On input current revocation list RL, an identity id, a time t, and a state $\mathsf{st} = \mathsf{BT}$. PKG specifies the following steps:
  1. Add $(\mathsf{id}, \mathsf{t})$ to RL for all nodes associated with id.
  2. Output an updated RL.

Dong et al. [9] claimed that the above lattice-based OR-IBE scheme is correct and secure if the LWE assumption holds.

3   Analysis of the Lattice-Based OR-IBE Scheme

In this section, we show that Dong et al.'s lattice-based OR-IBE scheme is *not* correct since the decryption fails if the second part of ciphertext $\mathsf{ct}_{\mathsf{id},\mathsf{t}}$ (i.e., $\mathbf{c}_1$) follows the construction with a matrix $\mathsf{F}_{\mathsf{id},\mathsf{t}} \in \mathbb{Z}_q^{n \times 3m}$. In addition, we also show that Dong et al.'s scheme is *not* DKER, a default security requirement since it was introduced into R-IBE by Seo and Emura, since once the short-term decryption key $\mathsf{dk}_{\mathsf{id},\mathsf{t}} = (\mathbf{E}_{1,\theta}, \mathbf{E}_{2,\theta})$ of a non-revoked user id is exposed, anyone obtaining a new time update key $\mathbf{E}'_{2,\theta}$ of id with time $\mathsf{t}' > \mathsf{t}$ can derive a valid short-term decryption key $\mathsf{dk}_{\mathsf{id},\mathsf{t}'} = (\mathbf{E}_{1,\theta}, \mathbf{E}'_{2,\theta})$ of id at time t'.

Theorem 1. *Let* $\mathsf{ct}_{id,t} = (\mathbf{c}_0, \mathbf{c}_1)$ *be a ciphertext sent to a recipient* $\mathsf{id} \in \mathcal{I}$ *associated with a time* $\mathsf{t} \in \mathcal{T}$, *and* $\mathsf{dk}_{\mathsf{id}',\mathsf{t}'} = (\mathbf{E}_{1,\theta}, \mathbf{E}_{2,\theta})$ *be a valid decryption key for a non-revoked* $\mathsf{id}' \in \mathcal{I}$ *at time* $\mathsf{t}' \in \mathcal{T}$. *If* $(\mathsf{id} = \mathsf{id}') \wedge (\mathsf{t} = \mathsf{t}')$, *then* $\mathsf{ct}_{\mathsf{id},\mathsf{t}}$ *cannot be decrypted correctly by using* $\mathsf{dk}_{\mathsf{id}',\mathsf{t}'}$ *in the decryption algorithm.*

Proof. To prove this theorem, we first analyze nodes in BT which are associated with a long-term private key used in PriKeyGen and a time update key used in KeyUpd, and show how the random shorter matrices are generated, meanwhile, satisfying some specific relation. After that, we analyze the construction of a ciphertext and argue that the decryption algorithm will fail due to an incorrect design of the matrix $\mathsf{F}_{\mathsf{id},\mathsf{t}}$ used to construct the second part of ciphertext $\mathsf{ct}_{\mathsf{id},\mathsf{t}}$, that is, the vector $\mathbf{c}_1 \in \mathbb{Z}_q^{3m}$.

By assigning id to an unassigned leaf node v_{id} in BT, and running algorithm SampleLeft($\mathbf{A}_{\mathsf{id}}, \mathbf{R_A}, \mathbf{U}_{1,\theta}, s$), PKG stores two random matrices $\mathbf{U}_{1,\theta}$, $\mathbf{U}_{2,\theta} \in \mathbb{Z}_q^{n \times n}$ in node $\theta \in \mathsf{path}(v_{\mathsf{id}})$ and returns a long-term private key $\mathbf{E}_{1,\theta} \in \mathbb{Z}^{2m \times n}$ to id and an outsourcing key $\mathsf{ok}_{\mathsf{id}} \in \mathbb{Z}_q^{n \times n}$ to KU-CSP. In these constructions, $\mathbf{U}_{1,\theta} + \mathbf{U}_{2,\theta} = \mathbf{U}$, $\mathbf{A}_{\mathsf{id}} \cdot \mathbf{E}_{1,\theta} = \mathbf{U}_{1,\theta} \bmod q$, and $\mathsf{ok}_{\mathsf{id}} = \mathbf{U}_{2,\theta} + \mathcal{H}(\mathsf{id}) \bmod q$.

Once obtaining an outsourcing key $\mathsf{ok}_{\mathsf{id}}$, an identity id, a time $\mathsf{t} \in \mathcal{T}$, and a revocation list RL, KU-CSP runs SampleLeft($\mathbf{B}_{\mathsf{t}}, \mathbf{R_B}, \mathsf{ok}_{\mathsf{id}} - \mathcal{H}(\mathsf{id}), s$) and returns a time update key $\mathbf{E}_{2,\theta} \in \mathbb{Z}^{2m \times n}$ to the non-revoked id (i.e., id $\notin$ RL). In these constructions, $\theta \in \mathsf{KUNodes}(\mathsf{BT}, \mathsf{RL}, \mathsf{t})$ and $\mathbf{B}_{\mathsf{t}} \cdot \mathbf{E}_{2,\theta} = \mathsf{ok}_{\mathsf{id}} - \mathcal{H}(\mathsf{id}) = \mathbf{U}_{2,\theta} \bmod q$.

Obviously, in the decryption key generation algorithm DecKeyGen, for a non-revoked identity id with time t, he can derive a valid decryption key $\mathsf{dk}_{\mathsf{id},\mathsf{t}} = (\mathbf{E}_{1,\theta}, \mathbf{E}_{2,\theta})$, $\theta \in (\mathsf{path}(v_{\mathsf{id}}) \cap \mathsf{KUNodes}(\mathsf{BT}, \mathsf{RL}, \mathsf{t}))$. In particular, the following relation can be checked, $\mathbf{A}_{\mathsf{id}} \cdot \mathbf{E}_{1,\theta} + \mathbf{B}_{\mathsf{t}} \cdot \mathbf{E}_{2,\theta} = \mathbf{U} \bmod q$.

Now, we analyze the constructions of matrix $\mathsf{F}_{\mathsf{id},\mathsf{t}} \in \mathbb{Z}_q^{n \times 3m}$ and a vector $\mathbf{c}_1 \in \mathbb{Z}_q^{3m}$ in ciphertext $\mathsf{ct}_{\mathsf{id},\mathsf{t}}$. It is known, $\mathbf{c}_1$ is constructed by using $\mathsf{F}_{\mathsf{id},\mathsf{t}}$ and its detailed structure is as follows:

$$
\mathbf{c}_1 = \mathsf{F}_{\mathsf{id},\mathsf{t}}^{\mathrm{T}} \mathbf{s} + \begin{pmatrix} \mathbf{e} \\ \mathbf{R}_0^{\mathrm{T}} \mathbf{e} \\ \mathbf{R}_1^{\mathrm{T}} \mathbf{e} \end{pmatrix} = [\mathbf{A} | \mathbf{A}_0 + \mathcal{H}(\mathsf{id}) \mathbf{A}_1 | \mathbf{B}_0 + \mathcal{H}(\mathsf{t}) \mathbf{B}_1]^{\mathrm{T}} \mathbf{s} + \begin{pmatrix} \mathbf{e} \\ \mathbf{R}_0^{\mathrm{T}} \mathbf{e} \\ \mathbf{R}_1^{\mathrm{T}} \mathbf{e} \end{pmatrix}
$$

$$
= \begin{pmatrix} \mathbf{c}_{1,0} \\ \mathbf{c}_{1,1} \\ \mathbf{c}_{1,2} \end{pmatrix} = \begin{pmatrix} \mathbf{A}^{\mathrm{T}} \mathbf{s} + \mathbf{e} \\ (\mathbf{A}_0 + \mathcal{H}(\mathsf{id}) \mathbf{A}_1)^{\mathrm{T}} \mathbf{s} + \mathbf{R}_0^{\mathrm{T}} \mathbf{e} \\ (\mathbf{B}_0 + \mathcal{H}(\mathsf{t}) \mathbf{B}_1)^{\mathrm{T}} \mathbf{s} + \mathbf{R}_1^{\mathrm{T}} \mathbf{e} \end{pmatrix} \bmod q.
$$

The decryption algorithm finally computes the following equation by using $\mathsf{ct}_{\mathsf{id},\mathsf{t}} = (\mathbf{c}_0, \mathbf{c}_1) \in \mathbb{Z}_q^n \times \mathbb{Z}_q^{3m}$ and $\mathsf{dk}_{\mathsf{id},\mathsf{t}} = (\mathbf{E}_{1,\theta}, \mathbf{E}_{2,\theta}) \in \mathbb{Z}^{2m \times n} \times \mathbb{Z}^{2m \times n}$.

$$
\mathbf{w} = \mathbf{c}_0 - \mathbf{E}_{1,\theta}^{\mathrm{T}} \begin{pmatrix} \mathbf{c}_{1,0} \\ \mathbf{c}_{1,1} \end{pmatrix} - \mathbf{E}_{2,\theta}^{\mathrm{T}} \begin{pmatrix} \mathbf{c}_{1,0} \\ \mathbf{c}_{1,2} \end{pmatrix} = \mathbf{U}^{\mathrm{T}} \mathbf{s} + e' + \mathsf{m} \lfloor \tfrac{q}{2} \rfloor
$$

$$
- \mathbf{E}_{1,\theta}^{\mathrm{T}} \begin{pmatrix} \mathbf{A}^{\mathrm{T}} \mathbf{s} + \mathbf{e} \\ (\mathbf{A}_0 + \mathcal{H}(\mathsf{id}) \mathbf{A}_1)^{\mathrm{T}} \mathbf{s} + \mathbf{R}_0^{\mathrm{T}} \mathbf{e} \end{pmatrix} - \mathbf{E}_{2,\theta}^{\mathrm{T}} \begin{pmatrix} \mathbf{A}^{\mathrm{T}} \mathbf{s} + \mathbf{e} \\ (\mathbf{B}_0 + \mathcal{H}(\mathsf{t}) \mathbf{B}_1)^{\mathrm{T}} \mathbf{s} + \mathbf{R}_1^{\mathrm{T}} \mathbf{e} \end{pmatrix} = \mathbf{U}^{\mathrm{T}} \mathbf{s} + e' + \mathsf{m} \lfloor \tfrac{q}{2} \rfloor
$$

$$
- \underbrace{([\mathbf{A} | \mathbf{A}_0 + \mathcal{H}(\mathsf{id}) \mathbf{A}_1] \mathbf{E}_{1,\theta})^{\mathrm{T}} \mathbf{s}}_{= \mathbf{U}_{1,\theta}^{\mathrm{T}} \mathbf{s}} - \mathbf{E}_{1,\theta}^{\mathrm{T}} \begin{pmatrix} \mathbf{e} \\ \mathbf{R}_0^{\mathrm{T}} \mathbf{e} \end{pmatrix} - \underbrace{([\mathbf{A} | \mathbf{B}_0 + \mathcal{H}(\mathsf{t}) \mathbf{B}_1] \mathbf{E}_{2,\theta})^{\mathrm{T}} \mathbf{s}}_{\neq \mathbf{U}_{2,\theta}^{\mathrm{T}} \mathbf{s} = ([\mathbf{B} | \mathbf{B}_0 + \mathcal{H}(\mathsf{t}) \mathbf{B}_1] \mathbf{E}_{2,\theta})^{\mathrm{T}} \mathbf{s}} - \mathbf{E}_{2,\theta}^{\mathrm{T}} \begin{pmatrix} \mathbf{e} \\ \mathbf{R}_1^{\mathrm{T}} \mathbf{e} \end{pmatrix}
$$

$$
= \mathsf{m} \lfloor \tfrac{q}{2} \rfloor + \underbrace{\mathbf{U}_{2,\theta}^{\mathrm{T}} \mathbf{s} - ([\mathbf{A} | \mathbf{B}_0 + \mathcal{H}(\mathsf{t}) \mathbf{B}_1] \mathbf{E}_{2,\theta})^{\mathrm{T}} \mathbf{s}}_{\mathsf{error}_0} + \underbrace{e' - \mathbf{E}_{1,\theta}^{\mathrm{T}} \begin{pmatrix} \mathbf{e} \\ \mathbf{R}_0^{\mathrm{T}} \mathbf{e} \end{pmatrix} - \mathbf{E}_{2,\theta}^{\mathrm{T}} \begin{pmatrix} \mathbf{e} \\ \mathbf{R}_1^{\mathrm{T}} \mathbf{e} \end{pmatrix}}_{\mathsf{error}_1}
$$

According to all parameters settings in Dong et al. [9], it can be checked that the error term error_1 is bounded by $q/5$ (i.e., $\|\mathsf{error}_1\|_\infty < q/5$), while error_0 is uniform and independent over $\mathbb{Z}_q^n$, thus $\mathsf{error}_0 + \mathsf{error}_1$ is also uniform over $\mathbb{Z}_q^n$, and we have the following conclusion:

$$
\lfloor \tfrac{2}{q} \mathbf{w} \rceil = \mathsf{m} + \lfloor \tfrac{2}{q} (\mathsf{error}_0 + \mathsf{error}_1) \rceil = \begin{cases} \mathsf{m} & 0 \le \|\mathsf{error}_0 + \mathsf{error}_1\|_\infty < q/4, \\ \mathsf{m} \oplus i & q/4 \le \|\mathsf{error}_0 + \mathsf{error}_1\|_\infty \le q/2. \end{cases}
$$

where i is an n-dimensional vector whose each component is 1 (i.e., $i = (1, \cdots, 1)$), and $\oplus$ denotes the bitwise XOR.

Thus, the decryption can only be successful if $0 \leq \|\text{error}_0 + \text{error}_1\|_\infty < q/4$, but the decryption always fails if $q/4 \leq \|\text{error}_0 + \text{error}_1\|_\infty \leq q/2$. Thus, $\lfloor \frac{2}{q}\mathbf{w} \rceil = $ m is not always true (and $\lfloor \frac{2}{q}\mathbf{w} \rceil \neq$ m holds with a larger probability about 75%), so the lattice-based OR-IBE scheme of Dong et al. [9] does not satisfy the correctness property of OR-IBE.

Theorem 2. *Let* $\mathsf{dk}_{\mathsf{id},\mathsf{t}} = (\mathbf{E}_{1,\theta}, \mathbf{E}_{2,\theta})$ *be a valid short-term decryption key of a non-revoked identity* id *with time* $\mathsf{t} \in \mathcal{T}$*. If* id *is not revoked at time* $\mathsf{t}' > \mathsf{t}$ *(i.e.,* id $\notin$ RL*), then anyone obtains* $\mathsf{dk}_{\mathsf{id},\mathsf{t}}$ *and a new time update key* $\mathsf{uk}_{\mathsf{id},\mathsf{t}'} = (\theta', \mathbf{E}'_{2,\theta'})_{\theta' \in \mathsf{KUNodes}(\mathsf{BT},\mathsf{RL},\mathsf{t}')}$ *for* id *with* t' *can compute a valid decryption key* $\mathsf{dk}_{\mathsf{id},\mathsf{t}'} = (\mathbf{E}_{1,\theta}, \mathbf{E}'_{2,\theta})$ *for non-revoked* id *with time* t' *to decrypt a ciphertext sent to* id *with time* t'*.*

Proof. To prove this theorem, we first analyze the short-term decryption key generation of an identity id with time t in Dong et al.'s scheme. The lattice-based OR-IBE scheme of Dong et al. adopts the KUNodes algorithm for long-term private keys assignment and time keys update, that is, a long-term private key $\mathsf{sk}_{\mathsf{id}} = (\theta, \mathbf{E}_{1,\theta})_{\theta \in \mathsf{path}(v_{\mathsf{id}})}$ is issued for id associated with the set of nodes defined by $\mathsf{path}(v_{\mathsf{id}})$ denoting the set of nodes on the path from v_{id} to root. The $\mathsf{KUNodes}(\mathsf{BT}, \mathsf{RL}, \mathsf{t})$ algorithm honestly executed by KU-CSP outputs all the non-revoked children of revoked leaf nodes (corresponding to the revoked identities) and $\mathsf{KeyUpd}(\mathsf{RL}, \mathsf{t}, \mathsf{muk}, \mathsf{id}, \mathsf{ok}_{\mathsf{id}}, \mathsf{st})$ algorithm returns a time update key $\mathsf{uk}_{\mathsf{id},\mathsf{t}} = (\theta', \mathbf{E}_{2,\theta'})_{\theta' \in \mathsf{KUNodes}(\mathsf{BT},\mathsf{RL},\mathsf{t})}$ to non-revoked id with time t. Then, the short-term decryption key of the non-revoked id with time t is just $\mathsf{dk}_{\mathsf{id},\mathsf{t}} = (\mathbf{E}_{1,\theta}, \mathbf{E}_{2,\theta})$ where θ is the only one node satisfying $\theta \in (\mathsf{path}(v_{\mathsf{id}}) \cap \mathsf{KUNodes}(\mathsf{BT}, \mathsf{RL}, \mathsf{t}))$.

Since a short-term decryption key $\mathsf{dk}_{\mathsf{id},\mathsf{t}}$ is just putting a long-term private key $\mathsf{sk}_{\mathsf{id}}$ and a time update key $\mathsf{uk}_{\mathsf{id},\mathsf{t}}$ of a non-revoked id with time t together, it is easy to extract some secret information associated with $\mathsf{sk}_{\mathsf{id}}$ (i.e., $\mathbf{E}_{1,\theta}$ in $\mathsf{dk}_{\mathsf{id},\mathsf{t}}$). If id is not revoked at a future time $\mathsf{t}' > \mathsf{t}$ and anyone can extract $\mathbf{E}'_{2,\theta'}$ from the public information $\mathsf{uk}'_{\mathsf{id},\mathsf{t}'} = (\theta', \mathbf{E}'_{2,\theta'})_{\theta' \in \mathsf{KUNodes}(\mathsf{BT},\mathsf{RL},\mathsf{t}')}$. In particular, if no identity with a leaf node on the left of id between t and t' is revoked, $\mathsf{uk}_{\mathsf{id},\mathsf{t}}$ must have a node $\theta' = \theta$, thus anyone can compute a valid short-term decryption key $\mathsf{dk}'_{\mathsf{id},\mathsf{t}'} = (\mathbf{E}_{1,\theta}, \mathbf{E}'_{2,\theta})$ for non-revoked id with time t'. After receiving a ciphertext $\mathsf{ct}_{\mathsf{id},\mathsf{t}'}$ sent to id with time t', anyone can decrypt it successfully by using pre-computed $\mathsf{dk}'_{\mathsf{id},\mathsf{t}'}$, and returns the resulting message. Thus, the lattice-based OR-IBE scheme of Dong et al. is not DKER.

The above attack idea has been discussed by Seo and Eurma, and in a series of subsequent papers the DKER property is treated as a default security requirement for R-IBE.

4 Our Modification to the Lattice-Based OR-IBE Scheme

In previous section, we have shown that the lattice-based OR-IBE scheme of Dong et al. dose not satisfy the correctness, which is the minimum requirement that each cryptographic scheme should satisfy, due to the problem of imperfect construction of matrix $F_{id,t}$ for a ciphertext generation. In addition, we have shown that Dong et al.'s scheme is not DKER, which is a default security requirement for R-IBE, due to the problem of unsafe combined generation of a short-term decryption key. In this section, we propose a modification of the OR-IBE scheme of Dong et al. to guarantee the correctness and the DKER security.

4.1 Description of the Modified Scheme

Our modified lattice-based OR-IBE scheme also consists of seven pt algorithms: Setup, PriKeyGen, KeyUpd, DecKeyGen, Encrypt, Decrypt and Revoke, among which KeyUpd and Revoke are the same as those in Dong et al.'s scheme, so we will not repeat them and only show the new designs in our modified scheme. The main modifications are described as follows:

- Setup($1^n, N$): On input a security parameter n and the maximal number of users $N = 2^n$, set a prime modulus $q = \widetilde{\mathcal{O}}(n^3)$, dimension $m = 2n\lceil \log q \rceil$, a Gaussian parameter $s = \widetilde{\mathcal{O}}(m)$, and a norm bound $\beta = \widetilde{\mathcal{O}}(\sqrt{n})$ for a distribution χ. PKG specifies the following steps:
  1. Let the identity space $\mathcal{I} = \mathbb{Z}_q^n$, the time space $\mathcal{T} \subset \mathbb{Z}_q^n$, and the message space $\mathcal{M} = \{0,1\}^n$.
  2. Run TrapGen(q, n, m) to get $\mathbf{A} \in \mathbb{Z}_q^{n \times m}$ with a trapdoor $\mathbf{R_A}$, $\mathbf{B} \in \mathbb{Z}_q^{n \times m}$ with a trapdoor $\mathbf{R_B}$, and $\mathbf{A}' \in \mathbb{Z}_q^{n \times m}$ with a trapdoor $\mathbf{R_{A'}}$.
  3. Sample $\mathbf{A_0}, \mathbf{A_1}, \mathbf{A_0'}, \mathbf{A_1'}, \mathbf{B_0}, \mathbf{B_1}, \mathbf{B_0'} \xleftarrow{\$} \mathbb{Z}_q^{n \times m}$, $\mathbf{U} \xleftarrow{\$} \mathbb{Z}_q^{n \times n}$, and an FRD function $\mathcal{H} : \mathbb{Z}_q^n \to \mathbb{Z}_q^{n \times n}$.
  4. Set the sate st $=$ BT that BT is with at least N leaf nodes, and the initial revocation list RL $= \emptyset$.
  5. Set pp $= (\mathbf{A}, \mathbf{A}', \mathbf{A_0}, \mathbf{A_1}, \mathbf{A_0'}, \mathbf{A_1'}, \mathbf{B}, \mathbf{B_0}, \mathbf{B_1}, \mathbf{B_0'}, \mathbf{U}, \mathcal{H})$, the master secret key msk $= (\mathbf{R_A}, \mathbf{R_{A'}})$, and the master time update key muk $= \mathbf{R_B}$.
  6. Output (pp, msk, muk, RL, st) where muk is sent to KU-CSP via a *secret* channel, msk is kept in secret by PKG, and pp is made public and as an implicit input of all other algorithms.
- PriKeyGen(msk, id, st): On input an identity id $\in \mathcal{I}$, the master secret key msk, and the state st. PKG specifies the following steps:
  1. Assign id to an unassigned leaf node v_{id} in BT.
  2. Let $\mathbf{A_{id}'} = [\mathbf{A}'|\mathbf{A_0'} + \mathcal{H}(\text{id})\mathbf{A_1'}] \in \mathbb{Z}_q^{n \times 2m}$, run RandBasis(ExtBasis($\mathbf{R_{A'}}, \mathbf{A_{id}'}$), s) to generate a trapdoor $\mathbf{R_{A_{id}'}} \in \mathbb{Z}^{2m \times 2m}$ for $\Lambda_q^\perp(\mathbf{A_{id}'})$.
  3. For each $\theta \in \text{path}(v_{id})$, if $\mathbf{U_{1,\theta}}, \mathbf{U_{2,\theta}}$ are undefined, sample $\mathbf{U_{1,\theta}} \xleftarrow{\$} \mathbb{Z}_q^{n \times n}$, define $\mathbf{U_{2,\theta}} = \mathbf{U} - \mathbf{U_{1,\theta}}$, and store $(\mathbf{U_{1,\theta}}, \mathbf{U_{2,\theta}})$ in node θ.
  4. Let $\mathbf{A_{id}} = [\mathbf{A}|\mathbf{A_0} + \mathcal{H}(\text{id})\mathbf{A_1}] \in \mathbb{Z}_q^{n \times 2m}$, and for each $\theta \in \text{path}(v_{id})$, run SampleLeft($\mathbf{A_{id}}, \mathbf{R_A}, \mathbf{U_{1,\theta}}, s$) to generate $\mathbf{E_{1,\theta}} \in \mathbb{Z}^{2m \times n}$ satisfying $\mathbf{A_{id}} \cdot \mathbf{E_{1,\theta}} = \mathbf{U_{1,\theta}} \bmod q$.
  5. For each $\theta \in \text{path}(v_{id})$, let outsourcing key ok$_{id} = \mathbf{U_{2,\theta}} + \mathcal{H}(\text{id}) \bmod q$.

6. Output an updated state st, $\mathsf{sk_{id}} = (\mathbf{R}_{\mathbf{A}'_{id}}, (\theta, \mathbf{E}_{1,\theta})_{\theta \in \mathsf{path}(v_{id})})$, and $\mathsf{ok_{id}}$.
   Note: $\mathsf{ok_{id}}$ is sent to KU-CSP via a *secret* channel.

- DecKeyGen($\mathsf{sk_{id}}, \mathsf{uk_{id,t}}$):
  On input a long-term private key $\mathsf{sk_{id}} = (\mathbf{R}_{\mathbf{A}'_{id}}, (\theta, \mathbf{E}_{1,\theta})_{\theta \in \mathsf{path}(v_{id})})$, and the
  time update key $\mathsf{uk_{id,t}} = (\theta, \mathbf{E}_{2,\theta})_{\theta \in \mathsf{KUNodes(BT,RL,t)}}$. The recipient id specifies
  the following steps:
  1. If $\mathsf{uk_{id,t}} = \perp$, return $\perp$ and abort.
  2. If $\mathsf{path}(v_{id}) \cap \mathsf{KUNodes(BT, RL, t)} = \emptyset$, return $\perp$ and abort.
  3. Otherwise, define $\mathbf{A}'_{id,t} = [\mathbf{A}'_{id}|\mathbf{B}'_0 + \mathcal{H}(t)\mathbf{A}'_1] \in \mathbb{Z}_q^{n \times 3m}$, run
     SampleLeft($\mathbf{A}'_{id,t}, \mathbf{R}_{\mathbf{A}'_{id}}, \mathbf{U}, s$) to generate $\mathbf{E}_0 \in \mathbb{Z}^{3m \times n}$ satisfying $\mathbf{A}'_{id,t} \cdot \mathbf{E}_0 = \mathbf{U} \bmod q$.
  4. Select $\theta \in (\mathsf{path}(v_{id}) \cap \mathsf{KUNodes(BT, RL, t)})$ (only one such node θ), and
     return $\mathsf{dk_{id,t}} = (\mathbf{E}_0, \mathbf{E}_{1,\theta}, \mathbf{E}_{2,\theta})$.

- Encrypt(id, t, m): On input an identity $\mathsf{id} \in \mathcal{I}$, a time $\mathsf{t} \in \mathcal{T}$, and a message
  $\mathsf{m} \in \{0, 1\}^n$. The sender specifies the following steps:
  1. Let $\mathsf{F_{id,t}} = [\mathbf{A}|\mathbf{A}_0 + \mathcal{H}(\mathsf{id})\mathbf{A}_1|\mathbf{B}|\mathbf{B}_0 + \mathcal{H}(t)\mathbf{B}_1] \in \mathbb{Z}_q^{n \times 4m}$.
  2. Let $\mathsf{F'_{id,t}} = [\mathbf{A}'|\mathbf{A}'_0 + \mathcal{H}(\mathsf{id})\mathbf{A}'_1|\mathbf{B}'_0 + \mathcal{H}(t)\mathbf{A}'_1] \in \mathbb{Z}_q^{n \times 3m}$.
  3. Sample $\mathbf{s}_0, \mathbf{s}_1 \xleftarrow{\$} \mathbb{Z}_q^n$, $\mathbf{e}_0, \mathbf{e}_1, \mathbf{e}_2 \xleftarrow{\$} \chi^m$, $\mathbf{e}'_0, \mathbf{e}'_1 \xleftarrow{\$} \chi^n$,
     $\mathbf{R}_0, \mathbf{R}_1, \mathbf{R}_2, \mathbf{R}_3 \xleftarrow{\$} \{1, -1\}^{m \times m}$.
  4. Sample $\mathsf{m}_0 \xleftarrow{\$} \{0, 1\}^n$ and define $\mathsf{m}_1 = \mathsf{m} \oplus \mathsf{m}_0$.

  5. Let $\mathbf{c}_0 = \mathbf{U}^{\mathrm{T}}\mathbf{s}_0 + \mathbf{e}'_0 + \mathsf{m}_0 \lfloor \frac{q}{2} \rfloor \bmod q \in \mathbb{Z}_q^n$, $\mathbf{c}_1 = \mathsf{F}_{id,t}^{\mathrm{T}}\mathbf{s}_0 + \begin{pmatrix} \mathbf{e}_0 \\ \mathbf{R}_0^{\mathrm{T}}\mathbf{e}_0 \\ \mathbf{e}_1 \\ \mathbf{R}_1^{\mathrm{T}}\mathbf{e}_1 \end{pmatrix} \in \mathbb{Z}_q^{4m}$.

  6. Let $\mathbf{c}_2 = \mathbf{U}^{\mathrm{T}}\mathbf{s}_1 + \mathbf{e}'_1 + \mathsf{m}_1 \lfloor \frac{q}{2} \rfloor \bmod q \in \mathbb{Z}_q^n$, $\mathbf{c}_3 = \mathsf{F}'^{\mathrm{T}}_{id,t}\mathbf{s}_1 + \begin{pmatrix} \mathbf{e}_2 \\ \mathbf{R}_2^{\mathrm{T}}\mathbf{e}_2 \\ \mathbf{R}_3^{\mathrm{T}}\mathbf{e}_2 \end{pmatrix} \in \mathbb{Z}_q^{3m}$.

  7. Output $\mathsf{ct_{id,t}} = (\mathbf{c}_0, \mathbf{c}_1, \mathbf{c}_2, \mathbf{c}_3) \in \mathbb{Z}_q^n \times \mathbb{Z}_q^{4m} \times \mathbb{Z}_q^n \times \mathbb{Z}_q^{3m}$.

- Decrypt($\mathsf{dk_{id',t'}}, \mathsf{ct_{id,t}}$): On input a ciphertext $\mathsf{ct_{id,t}} = (\mathbf{c}_0, \mathbf{c}_1, \mathbf{c}_2, \mathbf{c}_3)$ and a
  decryption key $\mathsf{dk_{id',t'}}$. The recipient id' specifies the following steps:
  1. If $(\mathsf{id} \neq \mathsf{id}') \vee (\mathsf{t} \neq \mathsf{t}')$, return $\perp$ and abort.

  2. Otherwise, parse $\mathbf{c}_1 = \begin{pmatrix} \mathbf{c}_{1,0} \\ \mathbf{c}_{1,1} \\ \mathbf{c}_{1,2} \\ \mathbf{c}_{1,3} \end{pmatrix}$ where $\mathbf{c}_{1,i} \in \mathbb{Z}_q^m$ for $i = 0, 1, 2, 3$.

  3. Compute $\mathbf{w}_0 = \mathbf{c}_0 - \mathbf{E}_{1,\theta}^{\mathrm{T}} \begin{pmatrix} \mathbf{c}_{1,0} \\ \mathbf{c}_{1,1} \end{pmatrix} - \mathbf{E}_{2,\theta}^{\mathrm{T}} \begin{pmatrix} \mathbf{c}_{1,2} \\ \mathbf{c}_{1,3} \end{pmatrix} \bmod q \in \mathbb{Z}_q^n$ and $\mathbf{w}_1 = \mathbf{c}_2 - \mathbf{E}_0^{\mathrm{T}}\mathbf{c}_3 \bmod q \in \mathbb{Z}_q^n$.
  4. Output $\lfloor \frac{2}{q}\mathbf{w}_0 \rceil \oplus \lfloor \frac{2}{q}\mathbf{w}_1 \rceil \in \{0, 1\}^n$.

4.2   Analysis of the Modified Scheme

Efficiency: The efficiency aspect of our modified OR-IBE scheme is as follows:

- The bit-size of public parameters pp is $(10nm + n^2 + n) \log q = \tilde{\mathcal{O}}(n^2)$.

- The long-term private key sk_{id} has a trapdoor and $|\theta \in path(v_{id})|$ matrices, of bit-size $\widetilde{\mathcal{O}}(n^3)$.
- The outsourcing key ok_{id} has bit-size $\widetilde{\mathcal{O}}(n^2)$.
- The time update key $uk_{id,t}$ has bit-size $\mathcal{O}(r \log \frac{N}{r}) \cdot \widetilde{\mathcal{O}}(n^2)$ where r is the number of revoked users.
- The ciphertext $ct_{id,t}$ has bit-size $\widetilde{\mathcal{O}}(n)$.
- The short-term decryption key $dk_{id,t}$ has bit-size $\widetilde{\mathcal{O}}(n^2)$.

Thus, our modified lattice-based OR-IBE scheme enjoys the same asymptotic efficiency as the scheme of Dong et al. [9]. A detailed comparison between our OR-IBE scheme and Dong et al.'s scheme is given in Table 2 (n is security parameter and $N = 2^n$; $|pp|$ denotes the bit-size of public parameters, $|sk_{id}|$ denotes the bit-size of a long-term private key, $|ok_{id}|$ denotes the bit-size of an outsourcing key, $|uk_{id,t}|$ denotes the bit-size of a time update key, $|dk_{id,t}|$ denotes the bit-size of a short-term decryption key, and $|ct_{id,t}|$ denotes the bit-size of a ciphertext.)

Table 2. Comparison of lattice-based OR-IBE schemes ($N = 2^n$)

Schemes	$|pp|$	$|sk_{id}|$	$|ok_{id}|$	$|uk_{id,t}|$	$|dk_{id,t}|$	$|ct_{id,t}|$	Correct	DKER
Dong et al. [9]	$\widetilde{\mathcal{O}}(n^2)$	$\widetilde{\mathcal{O}}(n^3)$	$\widetilde{\mathcal{O}}(n^2)$	$\mathcal{O}(r \log \frac{N}{r}) \cdot \widetilde{\mathcal{O}}(n^2)$	$\widetilde{\mathcal{O}}(n^2)$	$\widetilde{\mathcal{O}}(n)$	no	no
Ours	$\widetilde{\mathcal{O}}(n^2)$	$\widetilde{\mathcal{O}}(n^3)$	$\widetilde{\mathcal{O}}(n^2)$	$\mathcal{O}(r \log \frac{N}{r}) \cdot \widetilde{\mathcal{O}}(n^2)$	$\widetilde{\mathcal{O}}(n^2)$	$\widetilde{\mathcal{O}}(n)$	yes	yes

The correctness and security analysis are provided in Appendix B.

5   Conclusion

In this paper, we first point out that the lattice-based OR-IBE scheme of Dong et al. does not provide the correctness property. The problem of the lattice-based OR-IBE scheme is that the ciphertext generated for a non-revoked id at time t cannot be decrypted correctly by using a short-term decryption key derived from id's long-term private key and a time update key at time t. The reason of this problem is that the design of ciphertext is not correct in which a public matrix of KU-CSP is missed, and the non-revoked id adopts his short-term decryption key at time t cannot get the original message which is exactly masked by a noise vector with a larger size. In addition, we point out that their lattice-based OR-IBE scheme is not DKER, a default security requirement for R-IBE. By creatively reconstructing the ciphertext and the long-term private key, we modified the lattice-based OR-IBE scheme of Dong et al. to be secure without the decryption failure problem and with DKER, that is, we proposed the first lattice-based OR-IBE scheme with DKER that is quantum-resistance.

Acknowledgments. The authors would like to thank the anonymous reviewers of NSS 2021 for their helpful comments and this research was supported by Guangxi key Laboratory of Cryptography and Information Security (Grant No. GCIS201907) and Natural Science Foundation of Henan Province (Grant No. 202300410508).

A   The ind-uka Security of OR-IBE

The ind-uka security model of OR-IBE considers the case that KU-CSP that can access to the master time update key muk is an attacker. In this security model, KU-CSP can request long-term private key, revocation, and decryption key queries. Since KU-CSP can issue an arbitrary time update key by using muk and ok_{id} (*Note*: KU-CSP owns all users' identity outsourcing keys), there is a direct restriction that KU-CSP cannot request a long-term private key for the challenge identity id^* to prevent a simple attack. Finally, the goal of KU-CSP is the same as that in the ind-cpa security model, that is, to determine that the challenge ciphertext is completely random or correctly encrypted on the challenge m^* corresponding to (id^*, t^*). A detailed definition of the ind-uka security is described as follows:

Definition 6. *The* ind-uka *security of* OR-IBE *is described as the following game between the challenger* $\hat{C}_2$ *and adversary* A_2:

- Initial: A_2 *first declares a challenge identity and time pair* (id^*, t^*).
- Setup: $\hat{C}_2$ *runs* Setup$(1^n, N)$ *to obtain* (msk, muk, pp, RL, st). *Note: RL is initially empty.* $\hat{C}_2$ *keeps* msk *in secret by himself and provides* (pp, muk) *to* A_2.
- Query phase 1: A_2 *adaptively makes a polynomially bounded number of queries on the following oracles (Note: all oracles share the* st *and the queries also should be with some restrictions defined later):*
    - PriKenGen$(\cdot)$: *For the private key query on an identity* id $\in I$, *it returns a long-term private key* sk_{id} *and an outsourcing key* ok_{id} *by running* PriKeyGen(msk, id, st).
    - Revoke$(\cdot)$: *For the revocation query on* (id, t) $\in I \times T$, *it returns an updated* RL' *by running* Revoke(id, t, RL, st).
    - DecKeyGen$(\cdot)$: *For the decryption key query on* (id, t) $\in I \times T$, *it returns a short-term decryption key* $dk_{id,t}$ *by running* DecKeyGen(sk_{id}, $uk_{id,t}$). *Note: similarly, this oracle is also used to define* DKER, *which is not provided by Dong et al.*
  Challenge: A_2 *submits a message* $m^* \in M$. $\hat{C}_1$ *samples a bit* $b \xleftarrow{\$} \{0, 1\}$. *If* $b = 0$, $\hat{C}_1$ *returns a challenge ciphertext* $ct^*_{id^*,t^*}$ *by running* Encrypt(id^*, t^*, m^*), *otherwise, a random* $ct^*_{id^*,t^*} \xleftarrow{\$} C$.
- Query phase 2: A_2 *can continue to make additional queries as before with the same restrictions.*
- Guess: A_2 *outputs a bit* $b^* \in \{0, 1\}$, *and wins if* $b^* = b$.

In the above game, the following restrictions must hold:

- Revoke$(\cdot)$ can only be queried in a non-decreasing order of time (i.e., at time that is greater than or equal to the time of all previous queries).
- PriKenGen$(\cdot)$ can be queried on identity id^* while only the outsourcing key $ok^*_{id^*}$ is returned.
- DecKeyGen$(\cdot)$ can not be queried on (id^*, t^*).

The advantage of A_2 in the above game is defined as $\mathsf{Adv}^{\text{ind-uka}}_{\text{OR-IBE}, A_2}(n) = |\Pr[b^* = b] - 1/2|$. An OR-IBE scheme is ind-uka secure if for all ppt adversary A_2, $\mathsf{Adv}^{\text{ind-uka}}_{\text{OR-IBE}, A_2}(n)$ is negligible in the security parameter n.

B   Correctness and Security

Correctness: If the above scheme is operated correctly as specified, and the recipient $id \in \mathcal{I}$ is not revoked at time $t \in \mathcal{T}$, then $dk_{id,t} = (\mathbf{E}_0, \mathbf{E}_{1,\theta}, \mathbf{E}_{2,\theta})$ satisfies that $\mathbf{A}'_{id} \cdot \mathbf{E}_0 = \mathbf{U} \bmod q$, and $\mathbf{A}_{id} \cdot \mathbf{E}_{1,\theta} + \mathbf{B}_t \cdot \mathbf{E}_{2,\theta} = \mathbf{U} \bmod q$.

In the decryption algorithm, the non-revoked id first tries to derive m_0 by using $(\mathbf{E}_{1,\theta}, \mathbf{E}_{2,\theta})$:

$$
\begin{aligned}
\mathbf{w}_0 &= \mathbf{c}_0 - \mathbf{E}_{1,\theta}^{T} \begin{pmatrix} \mathbf{c}_{1,0} \\ \mathbf{c}_{1,1} \end{pmatrix} - \mathbf{E}_{2,\theta}^{T} \begin{pmatrix} \mathbf{c}_{1,2} \\ \mathbf{c}_{1,3} \end{pmatrix} \\
&= \mathbf{c}_0 - \mathbf{E}_{1,\theta}^{T} \begin{pmatrix} \mathbf{A}^{T}\mathbf{s}_0 + \mathbf{e}_0 \\ (\mathbf{A}_0 + \mathcal{H}(id)\mathbf{A}_1)^{T}\mathbf{s}_0 + \mathbf{R}_0^{T}\mathbf{e}_0 \end{pmatrix} - \mathbf{E}_{2,\theta}^{T} \begin{pmatrix} \mathbf{B}^{T}\mathbf{s}_0 + \mathbf{e}_1 \\ (\mathbf{B}_0 + \mathcal{H}(t)\mathbf{B}_1)^{T}\mathbf{s}_0 + \mathbf{R}_1^{T}\mathbf{e}_1 \end{pmatrix} \\
&= \mathbf{c}_0 - \underbrace{([\mathbf{A}|\mathbf{A}_0 + \mathcal{H}(id)\mathbf{A}_1]\mathbf{E}_{1,\theta})^{T}\mathbf{s}_0}_{=\mathbf{U}_{1,\theta}^{T}\mathbf{s}_0} - \mathbf{E}_{1,\theta}^{T} \begin{pmatrix} \mathbf{e}_0 \\ \mathbf{R}_0^{T}\mathbf{e}_0 \end{pmatrix} - \underbrace{([\mathbf{B}|\mathbf{B}_0 + \mathcal{H}(t)\mathbf{B}_1]\mathbf{E}_{2,\theta})^{T}\mathbf{s}_0}_{=\mathbf{U}_{2,\theta}^{T}\mathbf{s}_0} - \mathbf{E}_{2,\theta}^{T} \begin{pmatrix} \mathbf{e}_1 \\ \mathbf{R}_1^{T}\mathbf{e}_1 \end{pmatrix} \\
&= m_0 \lfloor \tfrac{q}{2} \rfloor + \underbrace{\mathbf{e}'_0 - \mathbf{E}_{1,\theta}^{T} \begin{pmatrix} \mathbf{e}_0 \\ \mathbf{R}_0^{T}\mathbf{e}_0 \end{pmatrix} - \mathbf{E}_{2,\theta}^{T} \begin{pmatrix} \mathbf{e}_1 \\ \mathbf{R}_1^{T}\mathbf{e}_1 \end{pmatrix}}_{error'}
\end{aligned}
$$

According to our parameters settings, it can be checked that the error term error' is bounded by $q/5$ (i.e., $\|error'\|_\infty < q/5$), thus, we have the conclusion $\lfloor \tfrac{2}{q}\mathbf{w}_0 \rceil = m_0$ with overwhelming probability.

The non-revoked id then tries to derive m_1 by using $\mathbf{E}_0$:

$$
\mathbf{w}_1 = \mathbf{c}_2 - \mathbf{E}_0^{T}\mathbf{c}_3 = \mathbf{U}^{T}\mathbf{s}_1 + \mathbf{e}'_1 + m_1\lfloor \tfrac{q}{2} \rfloor - \underbrace{([\mathbf{A}'|\mathbf{A}'_0 + \mathcal{H}(id)\mathbf{A}'_1|\mathbf{B}'_0 + \mathcal{H}(t)\mathbf{A}'_1]\mathbf{E}_0)^{T}\mathbf{s}_1}_{=\mathbf{U}^{T}\mathbf{s}_1}
$$

$$
- \mathbf{E}_0^{T} \begin{pmatrix} \mathbf{e}_2 \\ \mathbf{R}_2^{T}\mathbf{e}_2 \\ \mathbf{R}_3^{T}\mathbf{e}_2 \end{pmatrix} = m_1\lfloor \tfrac{q}{2} \rfloor + \underbrace{\mathbf{e}'_1 - \mathbf{E}_0^{T} \begin{pmatrix} \mathbf{e}_2 \\ \mathbf{R}_2^{T}\mathbf{e}_2 \\ \mathbf{R}_3^{T}\mathbf{e}_2 \end{pmatrix}}_{error''}
$$

Similarly, according to our parameters settings, it can be checked that the error term error'' is bounded by $q/5$ (i.e., $\|error''\|_\infty < q/5$), thus, we have the conclusion $\lfloor \tfrac{2}{q}\mathbf{w}_1 \rceil = m_1$ with overwhelming probability.

Thus, the decryption can be successful and recovers the message $\lfloor \tfrac{2}{q}\mathbf{w}_0 \rceil \oplus \lfloor \tfrac{2}{q}\mathbf{w}_1 \rceil = m_0 \oplus m_1 = m$ with overwhelming probability.

ind-cpa: For the ind-cpa security, we show the following theorem.

Theorem 3. *The modified lattice-based OR-IBE is* ind-cpa *secure if the* $\mathsf{LWE}_{n,q,\chi}$ *assumption holds.*

Proof. To proof this theorem, we define a list of games where the first one is identical to the original ind-cpa game as in Definition 2 and show that a ppt adversary $\mathcal{A}_1$ has advantage zero in the last game. We show that $\mathcal{A}_1$ cannot distinguish between these games, and thus $\mathcal{A}_1$ has negligible advantage in winning the original ind-cpa game.

Let id* be a challenge identity and t* be a challenge time, we consider two types of adversaries:

- Type-0: $\mathcal{A}_1$ requests a long-term private key on the challenge identity id*. In this case, id* must be revoked at time $t \le t^*$.
- Type-1: $\mathcal{A}_1$ only requests a long-term private key on the identity $id \ne id^*$. In this case, $\mathcal{A}_1$ may request a short-term decryption key on (id^*, t) where $t \ne t^*$.

ind-uka: For the ind-uka security, we show the following theorem.

Theorem 4. *The modified lattice-based* OR-IBE *is* ind-uka *secure if the* $\text{LWE}_{n,q,\chi}$ *assumption holds.*

Proof. The proof almost enjoys the same description as that of Theorem 3, and we will show the different details later. To proof this theorem, we also define a list of games where the first one is identical to the original ind-uka game as in Definition 3 and show that a ppt adversary $\mathcal{A}_2$ has advantage zero in the last game. We show that $\mathcal{A}_2$ cannot distinguish between these games, and thus $\mathcal{A}_2$ has a negligible advantage in winning the original ind-uka game.

Because the KU-CSP can issue an arbitrary time update key by using the master update key muk and the outsourcing key ok_{id}, a direct restriction is that KU-CSP cannot request a long-term private key for the challenge identity id*, thus, the Type-0 adversary in the proof of Theorem 3 is not considered and only a Type-1 adversary exists.

Due to the limited space, we omit the detailed proofs of Theorems 3 and 4, if any necessary, please contact the corresponding author for the full version.

References

1. Agrawal, S., Boneh, D., Boyen, X.: Efficient lattice (H)IBE in the standard model. In: Gilbert, H. (ed.) EUROCRYPT 2010. LNCS, vol. 6110, pp. 553–572. Springer, Heidelberg (2010). https://doi.org/10.1007/978-3-642-13190-5_28
2. Ajtai, M.: Generating hard instances of lattice problems (extended abstract). In: STOC, pp. 99–108. ACM (1996). https://doi.org/10.1145/237814.237838
3. Alwen, J., Peikert, C.: Generating shorter bases for hard random lattices. Theor. Comput. Sys. **48**(3), 535–553 (2011). https://doi.org/10.1007/s00224-010-9278-3
4. Boneh, D., Franklin, M.: Identity-based encryption from the Weil pairing. In: Kilian, J. (ed.) CRYPTO 2001. LNCS, vol. 2139, pp. 213–229. Springer, Heidelberg (2001). https://doi.org/10.1007/3-540-44647-8_13
5. Boldyreva, A., Goyal, V., Kumar, V.: Identity-based encryption with efficient revocation. In: CCS, pp. 417–426. ACM (2008). https://doi.org/10.1145/1455770.1455823
6. Cash, D., Hofheinz, D., Kiltz, E., Peikert, C.: Bonsai trees, or how to delegate a lattice basis. In: Gilbert, H. (ed.) EUROCRYPT 2010. LNCS, vol. 6110, pp. 523–552. Springer, Heidelberg (2010). https://doi.org/10.1007/978-3-642-13190-5_27

7. Chen, J., Lim, H.W., Ling, S., Wang, H., Nguyen, K.: Revocable identity-based encryption from lattices. In: Susilo, W., Mu, Y., Seberry, J. (eds.) ACISP 2012. LNCS, vol. 7372, pp. 390–403. Springer, Heidelberg (2012). https://doi.org/10. 1007/978-3-642-31448-3_29

8. Cheng, S., Zhang, J.: Adaptive-ID secure revocable identity-based encryption from lattices via subset difference method. In: Lopez, J., Wu, Y. (eds.) ISPEC 2015. LNCS, vol. 9065, pp. 283–297. Springer, Cham (2015). https://doi.org/10.1007/ 978-3-319-17533-1_20

9. Dong, C., Yang, K., Qiu, J., et al.: Outsourced revocable identity-based encryption from lattices. Trans. Emerging Tel. Tech. **30**, e3529 (2018). https://doi.org/10. 1002/ett.3529

10. Gentry, C., Peikert, C., Vaikuntanathan, V.: Trapdoor for hard lattices and new cryptographic constructions. In: STOC, pp. 197–206. ACM (2008). https://doi. org/10.1145/1374376.1374407

11. Katsumata, S., Matsuda, T., Takayasu, A.: Lattice-based revocable (hierarchical) IBE with decryption key exposure resistance. In: Lin, D., Sako, K. (eds.) PKC 2019. LNCS, vol. 11443, pp. 441–471. Springer, Cham (2019). https://doi.org/10. 1007/978-3-030-17259-6_15

12. Lee, K.: A generic construction for revocable identity-based encryption with subset difference methods. PLoS ONE **15**(9), e0239053 (2020). https://doi.org/10.1371/ journal.pone.o239053

13. Lee, K., Lee, D., Park, J.: Efficient revocable identity-based encryption via subset difference methods. Des. Codes Cryptogr. **85**(1), 39–76 (2017). https://doi.org/10. 1007/s10623-016-0287-3

14. Li, J., Li, J., Chen, X., et al.: Identity-based encryption with outsourced revocation in cloud computing. IEEE Trans. Comput. **64**(2), 426–437 (2015). https://doi.org/ 10.1109/TC.2013.208

15. Libert, B., Vergnaud, D.: Adaptive-ID secure revocable identity-based encryption. In: Fischlin, M. (ed.) CT-RSA 2009. LNCS, vol. 5473, pp. 1–15. Springer, Heidelberg (2009). https://doi.org/10.1007/978-3-642-00862-7_1

16. Ma, X., Lin, D.: Generic constructions of revocable identity-based encryption. In: Liu, Z., Yung, M. (eds.) Inscrypt 2019. LNCS, vol. 12020, pp. 381–396. Springer, Cham (2020). https://doi.org/10.1007/978-3-030-42921-8_22

17. Micciancio, D., Peikert, C.: Trapdoors for lattices: simpler, tighter, faster, smaller. In: Pointcheval, D., Johansson, T. (eds.) EUROCRYPT 2012. LNCS, vol. 7237, pp. 700–718. Springer, Heidelberg (2012). https://doi.org/10.1007/978-3-642-29011-4_41

18. Nguyen, K., Wang, H., Zhang, J.: Server-aided revocable identity-based encryption from lattices. In: Foresti, S., Persiano, G. (eds.) CANS 2016. LNCS, vol. 10052, pp. 107–123. Springer, Cham (2016). https://doi.org/10.1007/978-3-319-48965-0_7

19. Qin, B., Deng, R.H., Li, Y., Liu, S.: Server-aided revocable identity-based encryption. In: Pernul, G., Ryan, P.Y.A., Weippl, E. (eds.) ESORICS 2015. LNCS, vol. 9326, pp. 286–304. Springer, Cham (2015). https://doi.org/10.1007/978-3-319-24174-6_15

20. Regev, O.: On lattices, learning with errors, random linear codes, and cryptography. In: STOC, pp. 84–93. ACM (2005) https://doi.org/10.1145/1060590.1060603

21. Seo, J.H., Emura, K.: Revocable identity-based encryption revisited: security model and construction. In: Kurosawa, K., Hanaoka, G. (eds.) PKC 2013. LNCS, vol. 7778, pp. 216–234. Springer, Heidelberg (2013). https://doi.org/10.1007/978-3-642-36362-7_14

22. Shamir, A.: Identity-based cryptosystems and signature schemes. In: Blakley, G.R., Chaum, D. (eds.) CRYPTO 1984. LNCS, vol. 196, pp. 47–53. Springer, Heidelberg (1985). https://doi.org/10.1007/3-540-39568-7_5

23. Sun, Y., Mu, Y., Susilo, W., et al.: Revocable identity-based encryption with server-aided ciphertext evolution. Theor. Comput. Sci. **2020**(815), 11–24 (2020). https://doi.org/10.1016/j.tcs.2020.02.03

24. Takayasu, A., Watanabe, Y.: Lattice-based revocable identity-based encryption with bounded decryption key exposure resistance. In: Pieprzyk, J., Suriadi, S. (eds.) ACISP 2017. LNCS, vol. 10342, pp. 184–204. Springer, Cham (2017). https://doi.org/10.1007/978-3-319-60055-0_10

Preventing Fake News Propagation in Social Networks Using a Context Trust-Based Security Model

Nadav Voloch[1(✉)], Ehud Gudes[1], and Nurit Gal-Oz[2]

[1] Ben-Gurion University of the Negev, P.O.B. 653, 8410501 Beer-Sheva, Israel
voloch@post.bgu.ac.il
[2] Sapir Academic College, 79165 Sderot, Israel

Abstract. Online Social Networks (OSN) security issues have been extensively researched in the past decade. Information is posted and shared by individuals and organizations in social networks in huge quantities. One of the most important non-resolved topics is the Fake News propagation problem. Fake news propagates because of several reasons, one of which is non-trustworthy users. These users, some with malicious intentions, and some with low social media awareness, are the ones actually spreading misleading information. As this occurs, other users, that are valid reliable users, are exposed to false information. In our previous research we have devised a comprehensive Trust-based model that can handle this problem from the user Trust aspect. The model involves Access Control for the direct circle of friends and Flow Control for the friends' networks. In this paper we use this model as a basis for the purpose of prevention of Fake News. We add context awareness and user profiling by analyzing the user's activity in the network (posts, shares, etc.), and then use Machine Learning to detect these problematic users by analyzing data items that are fake or misleading. This addition creates a much more accurate picture of OSN users and their data and helps revealing the sources of the Fake News propagation and can prevent it. These aspects of the model create a strong reliable OSN data infrastructure.

Keywords: Online social networks security · Fake News detection · Trust-based security models

1 Introduction

Handling Online Social Networks (OSN) security is the subject of many research papers in the past years. The issue of privacy in OSN was handled in early papers such as [1] and [2]. According to [3], there is very little or no actual user-awareness to the spreading of personal data throughout the network and the extent to which the data is spread is seldomly evaluated correctly.

The only definite knowledge users have is that their information instances (e.g., pictures, posts, personal details, etc.) are revealed to their direct OSN friends. An Ego node (or Ego user) is an individual focal node, representing a user whose information flow we aim to control. An Ego node along with its adjacent nodes are denoted Ego

© Springer Nature Switzerland AG 2021
M. Yang et al. (Eds.): NSS 2021, LNCS 13041, pp. 100–115, 2021.
https://doi.org/10.1007/978-3-030-92708-0_6

network. In our previous work, we have created an OSN security model for the Ego network, that is composed of three main phases addressing three of its major aspects: Trust, Role-based Access Control [4, 5] and information flow, by creating an Information Flow-Control model for adversary detection [6], or a trustworthy network [7]. In this paper we use this model as a basis to address the problem of Fake News in OSN.

The detection and propagation-prevention of Fake News is done by extending this model with context-awareness and user profiling trust-wise, and then use Machine Learning to find users that have a high probability of being Fake News propagators. The extension of the basic Trust model is done to make an important distinction for data instances, that differ by their subject. For example, a political post might be more sensitive for its publisher than a simple "Good morning everyone". This extension mainly requires analyzing the user's network. The OSN user's friends are not homogenic by nature and accommodate different perspectives and various viewpoints. Accordingly, a user may find a certain friend more trustworthy in some subjects and less trustworthy in others. After creating a unique Trust value to all the Ego-users' friends for each data category, we can evaluate their data in the sense of facticity used in the model. This paper focuses on preventing low trusted users from spreading sensitive information. Our model uses the technique of blocking these users, thus stopping the propagation of false information. In the following parts of this paper, we will present our extended Trust and Context based model for detecting and preventing Fake News propagation in Social Networks.

The rest of this paper is structured as follows: Sect. 2 discusses the background for our work, with explanations for the related papers it relies on. Section 3 describes and defines our basic Trust based model, and its context-aware extension. Section 4 discusses the Machine Learning method part for the identification of possible Fake news propagation in the Ego network. Section 5 present the results of our experimental evaluation. Section 6 is the discussion and conclusion of the paper, with future prospect on further research on this subject.

2 Background and Related Work

Fake News involve two major concerns which have become subjects for research:

a. Identifying and detection of the news as fake ones. This part is a difficult one and has only partial success. The detection on social media is defined and presented in [8], and in [9] an important typology of Fake News is done in categorizing six different categories of Fake News: Native advertising, News satire, Propaganda, Manipulation, News parody, and Fabrication. The most severe form of Fake News is Fabrication since it has a very high Author's immediate intention to deceive, and a very low Level of facticity. [10] presents an approach that uses psychological estimation of OSN users to detect misinformation spreading in the network, and [11] uses semantic context to detect and analyze different categories of Fake News.
b. Preventing Fake News propagation. [12] deals with the propagation of Fake News and shows that the spreading of Fake News is done in a fast and thorough manner, since its nature is one of an extensive content, that has the potential of extremity.

In [13] different types of data spreading scenarios are described. Most of these vulnerabilities occur from discretionary privacy policies of OSN users. These privacy policies create a misleading knowledge of the number and type of users exposed to this shared data. Most of the solutions suggested demand changes in these specific policies. There are several approaches of handling OSN Security and privacy, among them are Access Control, Information Flow Control, and Trust. [14] gives a survey of most of the OSN Access Control models, elaborating the functionalities of the different types. [15] presents a new model for privacy control based on sharing habits, controlling the information flow by a graph algorithm that prevents potential data leakage. In [16] a relationship-based approach is being handled, giving priority to the users' relationships qualities, on which we have based our initial idea for the model. The social network is usually represented as an undirected graph, where nodes are the OSN users, and edges represent relations between them such as friendship relations. As mentioned above, [3] presents the fact that there is very little or no actual user-awareness to the spreading of personal data throughout the network and the extent to which the data is spread is seldomly evaluated correctly.

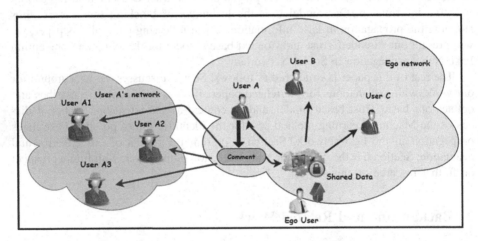

Fig. 1. Data spread, not necessarily intended, in OSN

The only definite knowledge users have is that their information instances (e.g., pictures, posts, personal details, etc.) are revealed to their direct OSN friends.

The problem of data spreading begins when one of these friends acts upon an information instance, e.g., comments on a post, likes or shares a picture, or any other form of OSN action. This action allows any friend of the actor, which is usually not a direct friend of the Ego-node, to see and act, in certain conditions, on this information instance. Figure 1 describes an Ego user's information spreading to friends of friends (Users A1, A2 and A3), triggered by an action (a comment in this example) taken by the ego node's direct friend (User A) on the Ego node's data.

The problem of spammer detection [17] resembles the Fake News propagation problem since both handle the problematic aspect of spreading unwanted data in the network. In [18] this detection is also done on Facebook datasets, where it is shown that spammers usually have noticeable differences in values of certain attributes such as number of friends, tags and mentions. For these linked problems we focus on the suggested approaches and solutions of Access Control, Information Flow Control and Trust.

The main Access Control model used in OSN is Role-Based Access Control (RBAC) that has many versions, as presented in [19], and limits access by creating user-role assignments. The user must have a role that has permission to access that resource.

The most prominent advantage of this method is that permissions are not assigned directly to users but to roles, making it much easier to manage the access control of a single user, since it must only be assigned the right role.

To this model we add the Trust factor [20], and it is based on the network users' interactions history, which could be problematic in assessing relatively unknown new connections. In our model we circumvent this problem by adding independent user attributes to this estimation. An example of using RBAC specifically in Facebook is done in [21], that describes the use of roles in it and the possible breaches that can occur due to the flexible privacy settings of the network. Using Trust in OSN is widely used in different models, and even in relatively early research such as [22], the idea of involving Trust in Access Control for OSN user data is handled, in creating Trust criteria for different subjects (users) and objects (data instances). [23] presents a model named IMPROVE-Identifying Minimal Profile Vectors for similarity-based access control. It elaborates on this specific subject, and gives a 30-item list of attributes, some direct and some derived, that define the user information in an OSN. An important ranking is given to these attributes, based on information gaining from each attribute, assessing their importance in the closeness approximation between users and evaluating their information sharing willingness.

The use of NLP in information security is currently researched and used (e.g. [24, 25]), and the implementation of such techniques is an important feature the is used to evaluate the users' content in different types of action on the OSN. For identifying Fake News with our context model, we need to compute the different Trust values per context for the user's network - different users have will have different Trust values in different context categories. For that, we need to identify the context of a data instance. Such identifications are done in [26] and [27]. Detecting Fake News by different types of learning is the topic of many very recent research papers such as [28], that proposes a linguistic model to find out the properties of content that will generate language-driven features, and [29] that uses geometric deep learning to detect Fake News in OSN. [30] uses supervised learning for this detection, and the work was done specifically on Twitter datasets, that are naturally very accessible due to twitter's publicly open infrastructure. [31] surveys Fake News in a comprehensive manner, in terms of detection, characterization and mitigation of false news that propagate on social media, using a data-driven approach.

The research presented here is based on the papers mentioned above, but the novelty of it the unique combination of Fake News detection with calculating Trust with OSN features and context. This creates an efficient mechanism that handles not just the problematic data, but also the problematic users that propagate it. In the upcoming sections we can see that the extended context-based model portrays an implementation of a strong solution to the security infrastructure of OSN, that helps preventing Fake News propagation in the network.

3   The Trust-Based Model and Its Context Extension

3.1   The Trust Based Model

The model we have presented in previous work [4–7] is composed of three main phases addressing three of its major aspects: trust, role-based access control and information flow.

In the First phase, the Trust phase, we assign trust values on the edges connecting direct friends to the Ego node in their different roles, e.g., Family, Colleagues etc. In the second phase, the Role Based Access Control phase, we remove direct friends that do not have the minimal trust values required to grant a specific permission to their roles. A cascade removal is carried out in their Ego networks as well. After this removal, the remaining user nodes and their edges are also assigned with trust values. In the third and last phase, the Information Flow phase, we remove from the graph edges and nodes that are not directly connected to the Ego-user, and have low trust values, to construct a privacy preserving trusted network. To calculate trust values in the first phase we use a set of OSN parameters carefully selected based on previous research.

We divide these parameters to connection attributes which relate to edges and to user attributes which relate to nodes. In this work we refer to four of these attributes. Two connection attributes: Friendship Duration (FD) and Mutual Friends (MF) and another two user attributes: Total number of Friends (TF) and Age of User Account (AUA). A Trust value ranges between 0 and 1 to reflect the probability of sharing information with a certain user: 0 represents total restriction, and 1 represents definite sharing willingness. The threshold values are denoted here as $T^{property}$ (e.g. for the TF attributes the threshold value is T^{TF}) and their experimental values were achieved in our previous research [4]. In this current research of preventing the propagation of Fake news, we take extra consideration to the attribute of Total number of Friends (TF).

This is because of its importance to the effect of the propagation that users with a big network have-a user that has 1000 friends will have much more effect in propagating Fake news than a user that has only ten friends.

We define the User Trust Value (UTV), as the weighted average of these properties, taking into consideration the different weights (w_i) that were assessed by experimental results in [1] for the significance (weight) of every attribute-factor. The calculation of a certain property value ($p_{property}$) is done by these thresholds and is as follows:

$$p_{property} = \begin{cases} \frac{property}{T^{property}} & (property < T^{property}), \\ 1 & (property \geq T^{property}). \end{cases} \tag{1}$$

The User Trust Value (*UTV*) is calculated as follows, where $|p|$ denotes the number of attributes and $<w>$ denotes the average of their weights:

$$UTV = \langle w_i p_i \rangle = \frac{\sum_{i=1}^{|p|} w_i p_i}{\langle w \rangle |p|}$$ (2)

Fig. 2.The model's phases for creating a trustworthy network.

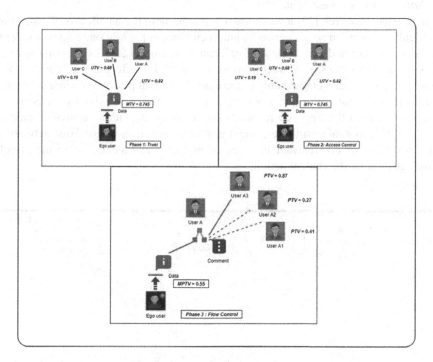

Fig. 2. The model's phases for creating a trustworthy network.

The threshold value for determining whether to give a certain access to a data instance in this model is denoted Minimal Trust Value (*MTV*), and it is administrator dependent, e.g. calculated as the average of *UTV*s within the Ego Network. The attributes' thresholds can be configured per role and per permission according to the OSN administration policy, or according to user-preferences if such exist. The three-phases model described above is presented in Fig. 2. Phase 1 shows the trust values computation. Phase 2 shows the Access Control decisions and their impact on the network- only for the direct friends.

3.2   Context Evaluation Using Sentiment Analysis

A data instance can be characterized by its context (e.g., politics, sports, etc.), and the trust measure must be refined by this context. For context evaluation, we categorize different users in the Ego network by their Trust per context.

We calculate this Trust for the friends in the Ego network: different trust values for every category, meaning that they have a User Trust Value per category denoted here as UTV_κ for each category κ. The calculation is presented in [32]. We can see an example for such a set of UTV_κ's and access granting for certain data instances in Fig. 3, where the Minimum Trust Value of a certain category of a data instance is presented as $MTV\kappa$. Three out of four users hold the necessary trust value ($UTV\kappa$) for $\kappa = Politics$, thus have access to it, while only one user hold the necessary $UTV\kappa$ for $\kappa = Sales$ and has access to it.

In previous research [33] it was shown that Sentiment has an effect on Trust. This is specifically relevant to social networks and their content [34]. In our context model we address this aspect and add an element of Trust according to Sentiment Analysis results of textual data instances we extract from the network. The effect of Sentiment on Trust is relevant in our social context only in the cases of mutual positive sentiment, meaning the Ego user's friend published a post that is recognized as positive by the Sentiment Analysis, and then the Ego user responds positively on it (with a positive comment, a like, etc.). This mutual positive sentiment is a strong confirmation of Trust between the two. This effect is not relevant in cases of negative sentiment, due to the possible disambiguation of the mutual action.

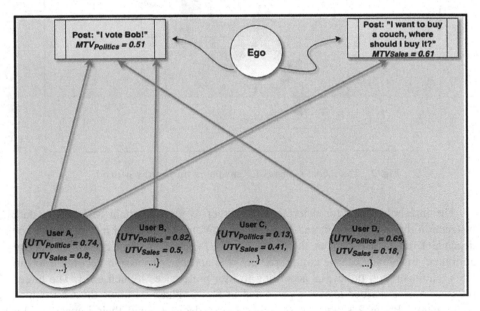

Fig. 3. Access decisions to data in different categories and adapted trust values

For example, a friend can post: "I hate Bob, he is a liar, and I will never vote for him!", and the Ego could then reply: "You are right! I strongly think so too and think it's good that you say that!" which creates a positive sentiment and strengthen the Trust between the two, but he can also respond: "Agreed, Bob is a liar and I hate him too!"

which creates a negative sentiment, but then also strengthen the Trust between the two. (Therefor in our experimental evaluation we consider positive sentiments only and leave negative sentiments for future work).

The Sentiment Analysis in our model is used to estimate the trust of each action. The Sentiment Analysis Factor for an Action i in a κ category, is denoted here as SAF_iA_κ.

This is summed as the total estimation of actions of a user j, and here we define the Sentiment refined value as $STVA_\kappa^j$:

$$STVA_\kappa^j = \langle w_i SAF_i A_\kappa \rangle = \frac{\sum_{i=1}^{|STVA_\kappa^j|}(w_i SAF_i A_\kappa)}{\langle w \rangle |SAF_i A_\kappa|} \tag{3}$$

This value will, of course, also create a refined $UTV\kappa$ denoted here as UTV_κ^j:

$$UTV_\kappa^j = \frac{w_{UTV} UTV + w_{STVA_\kappa^j} STVA_\kappa^j}{\langle w \rangle} \tag{4}$$

These refined parameters give us a good basis for the comparison and analysis of the contextual Trust in the OSN content and connections for the Ego user. Contextual Trust is a trust that is built gradually by the actions of the user in a certain context (topic). In our research we apply the $SAF_i A_\kappa$ for this contextual Trust. The value that is calculated in Eq. 3 - $STVA_\kappa^j$ is the summation of all the $SAF_i A_\kappa$'s of actions i of a user (friend) j in the Ego network that the Ego-user responded positively to them, meaning liked, shared, commented positively, etc. These friend's actioned are evaluated by Sentiment Analysis as explained above. Using context-based trust we can now apply all the algorithms presented in previous work including access control and flow control but applied to a specific context.

4 Prevention of Fake News Propagation

The important use case of these model's extensions is the detection of Fake News and the prevention of their propagation. In this model, users gain or lose trust values in different data categories, and consequently may not be exposed to some data instances. As a result, these users will not be able to spread fake news. This is specifically important in categories, such as Politics, which is one of the main categories for Fake News, especially during election times. The model analyzes the network in a deep and comprehensive manner trust wise. The users and their social content are monitored and users that are not trustworthy, are suspected as potential of speaders of false data, and even as the possible source of this data.

In this part we use the Sentiment Analysis Factor for an Action α in a κ category denoted $SAF_\alpha A_\kappa$ as an important indicator of Fake News. This is because Fake News usually contain polarized emotions (very positive or very negative), as described thoroughly in [35]. The second indicator we use is the user's Trust value UTV_κ^j, that is described in the previous section. The actions that were used to compute the SAF_iA_κ for the UTV_κ^j are different from $SAF_\alpha A_\kappa$-which is a new action that we now examine whether it is considered as Fake News or not.

Q-learning is a reinforcement learning algorithm to learn the value of an action in a particular state, first introduced by [36]. Reinforcement learning involves an agent, a set of states – S, and a set A of actions per state.

By performing an action a, the agent transitions from state to state. Executing an action in a specific state provides the agent with a reward. The goal of the agent is to maximize its total reward. So let us formally define these parameters on our Fake News prevention model, based on Trust and context:

- System – The Ego network.
- Agent – Ego user.
- Action – a user's action in the OSN- e.g., post, share, etc.
- Reward – one point given for accurate prediction of Fake News; a smaller reward can be given for prediction of non-fake ones.
- State- the user's condition after an action – including reward.
- Initial state of the system – All rewards are zero; no actions taken yet; threshold values set for $SAF_\alpha A_\kappa$ and UTV_κ^j.
- Training of the model – comparing the actions and user data to a ground truth of fact checking.

Our basic premise in this part of the model is that actions that have very high, or very low (polar) values of $SAF_\alpha A_\kappa$, done by users that have low UTV_κ^j values, have the potential of being Fake News. For this purpose, we set at the initial state of the system, threshold values for these parameters, that can dynamically change in the process of learning. Although SAF_iA_κ, is used as a part of the calculation of UTV_κ^j, it serves a different purpose here-not as Trust estimator, but as a detector of polarized sentiment of data, thus it must be considered separately. At the end of the learning process, we aim to detect the users that have the most prominent potential of being Fake News propagators. These values can be adapted to another important parameter mentioned above, the Total number of Friends (TF). The higher this number is, the higher is the potential harm of this user. Thus, we can apply stricter thresholds for users that have a large network.

The algorithm for detecting and preventing Fake News propagation with Trust and Reinforcement Learning is as follows:

FakeNewsPrevention(System *Ego_Network*, Fact Checker *FC*, *false_counter=0*)

1. for every user j in *Ego_Network* // initializing users' parameters
    - calculate UTV_κ^j ; calculate $SAF_\alpha A_\kappa$; $reward^j \leftarrow 0$
    - if *FC= False*
        - *false_counter $\leftarrow$ false_counter +1*

//Setting the system initial state (0) with threshold values T^{UTV}, T^{SAF}

2. $T_0^{UTV} \leftarrow AVG$ *of* UTV_κ^j *in Ego_Network*

3. $T_0^{SAF} \leftarrow AVG$ *of* $SAF_\alpha A_\kappa$ *in Ego_Network*

//The training of the model with s States

4. $reward^{MAX} \leftarrow 0$; $max\_index \leftarrow 0$; $T_{MAX}^{SAF} \leftarrow T_0^{SAF}$; $T_{MAX}^{UTV} \leftarrow T_0^{UTV}$

5. for every state $0 \leq s \leq |States|$
    - $reward^s \leftarrow 0$; $UTV\_counter \leftarrow 0$; $SAF\_counter \leftarrow 0$
    - for every user j in *Ego_Network*
        - if $UTV_\kappa^j \leq T_s^{UTV}$ then $UTV\_counter \leftarrow +1$
        - if $SAF_\alpha A_\kappa \geq T_s^{SAF}$ then $SAF\_counter \leftarrow +1$
        - if $UTV_\kappa^j \leq T_s^{UTV}$ and $SAF_\alpha A_\kappa \geq T_s^{SAF}$ and *FC= False*

            $reward^j \leftarrow 1$; $reward^s \leftarrow reward^s + reward^j$
    - *if* $reward^s \geq reward^{MAX}$
        - $reward^{MAX} \leftarrow reward^s$; $max\_index \leftarrow s$
        - $T_{MAX}^{SAF} \leftarrow T_s^{SAF}$; $T_{MAX}^{UTV} \leftarrow T_s^{UTV}$
    - *if* $s < |States|$ // not the last state
        - update T_{s+1}^{UTV} and T_{s+1}^{SAF} using *UTV_counter, SAF_counter, reward^s and false_counter* *

6. return T_{MAX}^{SAF}, T_{MAX}^{UTV}, $reward^{MAX}$, max_index

* The update is done to the thresholds of the next state, and determined by the parameters mentioned, for the purpose of refining these thresholds and giving optimal results in terms of reward and a high probability of prediction of Fake News propagators. For example, if *SAF_counter* is very high relatively to the *reward*^{s}, it means that there were many actions with a $SAF_\alpha A_\kappa$ that were higher than the threshold T_s^{SAF}, we will update T_{s+1}^{SAF} to be higher, and therefore more strict, to get more accurate results.

The purpose of the algorithm is to get the most refined thresholds for $SAF_\alpha A_\kappa$ and UTV_κ^j, that will be able to predict most accurately users that can be Fake News propagators, in comparison with the ground truth of the fact checker.

In stage 1 we make the calculations of the Trust and Sentiment parameters described in the previous section, in stages 2 and 3 we set the system initial state (0) with threshold values that are simple averages of the parameters of the Ego network. Stages 4–6 are the training of the model, that includes the comparison to the fact checker results, and accordingly, updating the parameters and then the thresholds, and finally returning the results of the optimized thresholds.

We can see an exemplification of this part of the model in Fig. 4, where the initial state of the system has two users in state 0, the System initial state is:

If UTV_κ^j is less than 0.3 and $SAF_\alpha A_\kappa$ (simplified in the figure as *SAF*) is higher than 0.6 or lower than −0.6 (relatively very good or very bad), and the action that the user made was proven as Fake News (by the external fact checker) then the reward is received. On the other hand, if a trustworthy user creates an action that is not Fake News, and his UTV_κ^j is more than 0.6 and $SAF_\alpha A_\kappa$ is between −0.6 and 0.6 (moderate sentiment), the reward is also given. This is how the model tries to predict the facticity of the data, and how the learning is done. We can see that User A holds both conditions for Fake News, and it is also verified to be Fake by the fact checker, thus a reward is given. The reward in reinforcement learning is actually given to the agent, which is the Ego user, but we relate it to a certain user, so we can detect our potential Fake News propagators. On the other hand, we can see that no reward was given in relation to User B, since the two terms were not met-the $SAF_\alpha A_\kappa$ was not between −0.6 and 0.6.

These threshold values, and the changes we can do to them, are important in both aspect of prediction-we aim to know, in some level of certainty, in which values we can infer Fake News propagators' actions, and how strict should be the ones with a high *TF* value (highly influencing users).

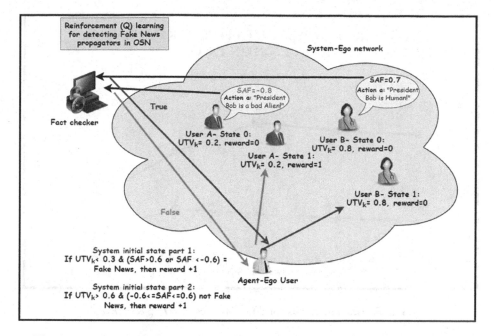

Fig. 4. Learning process of the Ego network for the detection of Fake news spreaders

5 Experimental Results

For the experimental part of this research, we used a dataset of a real Facebook network of 201 users, which are the direct friends of a single Ego user. The Ego user first collected all of the users' data relevant to the basic *UTV* - *pMF, pTF, pAUA,* and *pFD.* We then calculated every *UTV* accordingly. Next, we needed to find the relevant users and data instances for the κ category, the topic selected was *Politics,* since it was the most discussed topic in the Ego network, and usually discussed with strong sentiment. There were 33 relevant users, that had a total of 79 data instances (actions-post, shares, etc.).

At this point we calculated the Sentiment Analysis for each of the actions, for the $SAF_\alpha A_\kappa$ and the summation of $SAF_i A_\kappa$ per user for the calculation of UTV_k^j, as presented in Eqs. 3 and 4. The weights w_i of the factors were 2:1 in favor of the *UTV,* since its *TF* attribute that was discussed above has considerable importance for Fake News propagation. This division can of course be altered in different circumstances or algorithmic decisions.

As mentioned in the previous section, our purpose is to find the most refined thresholds that will give us the highest probability of detecting potential Fake News propagators in comparison with the ground truth of the fact checker. We created a software that will help us analyze the data in the sentiment analysis part. The program was written in Python and used the Vader Sentiment library for sentiment analysis of the Facebook posts, that were scraped manually, due to the Facebook crawling restrictions. Out of 79 actions, 9 were discovered as Fake News. All of them had a

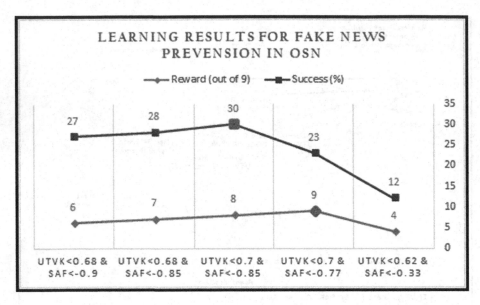

Fig. 5. Learning results for different states of UTV_κ^S & $SAF_\alpha A_\kappa$

relatively strong negative sentiment. Most of the users that spread this data were of relatively lower Trust values than the others. At this point the training of the learning process begun, and the initial state of the system was set to the default averages values: 0.62 for UTV_κ^j and -0.33 for $SAF_\alpha A_\kappa$. Meaning that users that have a Trust value lower than 0.62 and their action has the $SAF_\alpha A_\kappa$ lower than -0.33, it is predicted to be of a false nature.

The reward for such an initial state was of course relatively low: 4 out of 9 Fakes were discovered. Out of the total 34 actions that passed the criteria these 4 indicate a success ratio of just 12%.

We can see the results of the different states after the continuation of the training in Fig. 5. There are two different aspects: the reward aspect, exclusively referring to the proven Fake news indicators, and success ratio aspect, referring also to the ones that pass the criteria and are not proven Fake. If we wish to optimize the system with respect to the actual proven Fake news indicators, most rewards gotten (9 out of 9) are in the state of $UTV_\kappa^j < 0.7$ and $SAF_\alpha A_\kappa < -0.77$. If we wish to refer to success ratios, as explained above, the best ratio (30%) is achieved in the state of $UTV_\kappa^j < 0.7$ and $SAF_\alpha A_\kappa < -0.85$, meaning that users that are in the boundaries of these values, have a 30% chance of being Fake news propagators.

6   Conclusion and Future Work

In this research we presented a Trust-based model that uses context and user evaluation for preventing the propagation of Fake News. These aspects, that include important features of the network data, are very strong in terms of OSN sizes of real user networks. These attributes are hard to fake since they are built on real OSN user presence and real numerical assets. To these aspects we added a reinforcement learning model that helps discover the numeric criteria of users and their actions, that can be focused on Fake news propagators. After applying this model on the OSN, the users that are marked as potential Fake News propagators can be allotted from the Ego Network flow, in a certain category, or in general, depending on the user preference or on other reasons. We showed the results of our experimental evaluation on a real Facebook Ego-network, and exemplified the training of the model, and its results, accordingly. In future work, interesting extensions can be done in several aspects, experimentally and methodically. Other experiments can be done in different OSN-setting such as different categories, other sizes of networks, etc. Methodically the categorizing of Fake News instances, as explained in the beginning of this paper (Fabrication, Satire, propaganda, etc.), could be an interesting development: whether different types of Fake News can be treated differently, and exploring the users that propagate these different types – if they also differ in other Trust attributes.

References

1. Gross, R., Acquisti, A.: Information revelation and privacy in online social networks. In: Proceedings of the 2005 ACM Workshop on Privacy in the Electronic Society, pp. 71–80. ACM (2005)
2. Krishnamurthy, B., Wills, C.E.: Characterizing privacy in online social networks. In: Proceedings of the first Workshop on Online Social Networks, pp. 37–42. ACM, August 2008
3. Misra, G., Such, J.M.: How socially aware are social media privacy controls? Computer **49** (3), 96–99 (2016)
4. Voloch, N., Nissim, P., Elmakies, M., Gudes, E.: A role and trust access control model for preserving privacy and image anonymization in social networks. In: Meng, W., Cofta, P., Jensen, C.D., Grandison, T. (eds.) IFIPTM 2019. IAICT, vol. 563, pp. 19–27. Springer, Cham (2019). https://doi.org/10.1007/978-3-030-33716-2_2
5. Voloch, N., Levy, P., Elmakies, M., Gudes, E.: An access control model for data security in online social networks based on role and user credibility. In: Dolev, S., Hendler, D., Lodha, S., Yung, M. (eds.) CSCML 2019. LNCS, vol. 11527, pp. 156–168. Springer, Cham (2019). https://doi.org/10.1007/978-3-030-20951-3_14
6. Gudes, E., Voloch, N.: An information-flow control model for online social networks based on user-attribute credibility and connection-strength factors. In: Dinur, I., Dolev, S., Lodha, S. (eds.) CSCML 2018. LNCS, vol. 10879, pp. 55–67. Springer, Cham (2018). https://doi.org/10.1007/978-3-319-94147-9_5
7. Voloch, N., Gudes, E.: An MST-based information flow model for security in online social networks. In: The 11th IEEE International Conference on Ubiquitous and Future Networks (2019)

8. Shu, K., Sliva, A., Wang, S., Tang, J., Liu, H.: Fake news detection on social media: a data mining perspective. ACM SIGKDD Explor. Newsl. **19**(1), 22–36 (2017)
9. Tandoc, E.C., Jr., Lim, Z.W., Ling, R.: Defining 'fake news': a typology of scholarly definitions. Digit. Journal. **6**(2), 137–153 (2018)
10. Kumar, K.P.K., Geethakumari, G.: Detecting misinformation in online social networks using cognitive psychology. HCIS **4**(1), 1–22 (2014). https://doi.org/10.1186/s13673-014-0014-x
11. Levi, O., Hosseini, P., Diab, M., Broniatowski, D.A.: Identifying nuances in fake news vs. satire: using semantic and linguistic cues. arXiv preprint arXiv:1910.01160 (2019)
12. Vosoughi, S., Roy, D., Aral, S.: The spread of true and false news online. Science **359** (6380), 1146–1151 (2018)
13. Li, Y., Li, Y., Yan, Q., Deng, R.H.: Privacy leakage analysis in online social networks. Comput. Secur. **49**, 239–254 (2015)
14. Sayaf, R., Clarke, D.: Access control models for online social networks. Soc. Netw. Eng. Secure Web Data Serv. **32**, 32–65 (2012)
15. Levy, S., Gudes, E., Gal-Oz, N.: Sharing-habits based privacy control in social networks. In: Ranise, S., Swarup, V. (eds.) DBSec 2016. LNCS, vol. 9766, pp. 217–232. Springer, Cham (2016). https://doi.org/10.1007/978-3-319-41483-6_16
16. Cheng, Y., Park, J., Sandhu, R.: An access control model for online social networks using user-to-user relationships. IEEE Trans. Dependable Secure Comput. **13**(4), 424–436 (2016)
17. Cohen, Y., Gordon, D., Hendler, D.: Early detection of spamming accounts in large-scale service provider networks. Knowl.-Based Syst. **142**, 241–255 (2017)
18. Zheng, X., Zeng, Z., Chen, Z., Yu, Y., Rong, C.: Detecting spammers on social networks. Neurocomputing **159**, 27–34 (2015)
19. Sandhu, R.S., Coyne, E.J., Feinstein, H.L., Youman, C.E.: Role-based access control models. Computer **29**(2), 38–47 (1996)
20. Lavi, T., Gudes, E.: Trust-based Dynamic RBAC. In: Proceedings of the 2nd International Conference on Information Systems Security and Privacy (ICISSP), pp. 317–324 (2016)
21. Patil, V.T., Shyamasundar, R.K.: Undoing of privacy policies on Facebook. In: Livraga, G., Zhu, S. (eds.) DBSec 2017. LNCS, vol. 10359, pp. 239–255. Springer, Cham (2017). https://doi.org/10.1007/978-3-319-61176-1_13
22. Ali, B., Villegas, W., Maheswaran, M.: A trust based approach for protecting user data in social networks. In: Proceedings of the 2007 Conference of the Center for Advanced Studies on Collaborative Research, pp. 288–293. IBM Corp. (2007)
23. Misra, G., Such, J.M., Balogun, H.: IMPROVE-Identifying Minimal PROfile VEctors for similarity-based access control. In: Trustcom/BigDataSE/ISPA, pp. 868–875. IEEE (2016)
24. Atallah, M.J., McDonough, C.J., Raskin, V., Nirenburg, S.: Natural language processing for information assurance and security: an overview and implementations. In: NSPW, pp. 51–65, September 2000
25. Tsoumas, B., Gritzalis, D.: Towards an ontology-based security management. In: 20th International Conference on Advanced Information Networking and Applications-Volume 1 (AINA'06), vol. 1, pp. 985–992. IEEE, April 2006
26. Wang, X., Tokarchuk, L., Poslad, S.: Identifying relevant event content for real-time event detection. In: 2014 IEEE/ACM International Conference on Advances in Social Networks Analysis and Mining (ASONAM 2014), Beijing, pp. 395–398 (2014)
27. May, C., Ferraro, F., McCree, A., Wintrode, J., Garcia-Romero, D., Van Durme, B.: Topic identification and discovery on text and speech. In: Proceedings of the 2015 Conference on Empirical Methods in Natural Language Processing, pp. 2377–2387, September 2015
28. Choudhary, A., Arora, A.: Linguistic feature based learning model for fake news detection and classification. Expert Syst. Appl. **169**, 114171 (2021)

29. Monti, F., Frasca, F., Eynard, D., Mannion, D., Bronstein, M.M.: Fake news detection on social media using geometric deep learning. arXiv preprint arXiv:1902.06673 (2019)
30. Helmstetter, S., Paulheim, H.: Weakly supervised learning for fake news detection on Twitter. In: 2018 IEEE/ACM International Conference on Advances in Social Networks Analysis and Mining (ASONAM), pp. 274–277. IEEE, August 2018
31. Pierri, F., Ceri, S.: False news on social media: a data-driven survey. ACM SIGMOD Rec. **48**(2), 18–27 (2019)
32. Voloch, N.: Using sentiment analysis and context evaluation for preserving trust-based privacy in social networks (2020). https://www.cs.bgu.ac.il/~voloch/FinalProjectReport.pdf
33. Collomb, A., Costea, C., Joyeux, D., Hasan, O., Brunie, L.: A study and comparison of sentiment analysis methods for reputation evaluation. Rapport de recherche RR-LIRIS-2014-002 (2014)
34. Alahmadi, D.H., Zeng, X.J.: Twitter-based recommender system to address cold-start: a genetic algorithm-based trust modelling and probabilistic sentiment analysis. In: 2015 IEEE 27th International Conference on Tools with Artificial Intelligence (ICTAI), pp. 1045–1052). IEEE, November 2015
35. Cui, L., Wang, S., Lee, D.: SAME: sentiment-aware multi-modal embedding for detecting fake news. In: Proceedings of the 2019 IEEE/ACM International Conference on Advances in Social Networks Analysis and Mining, pp. 41–48, August 2019
36. Watkins, C.J., Dayan, P.: Q-learning. Mach. Learn. **8**(3–4), 279–292 (1992)

A Lightweight Android Malware Detection Framework Based on Knowledge Distillation

Yongbo Zhi, Ning Xi$^{(\boxtimes)}$, Yuanqing Liu, and Honglei Hui

School of Cyber Engineering, Xidian University, Xi'an, China
nxi@xidian.edu.cn, {lyq,hlhui}@stu.xidian.edu.cn

Abstract. Android system is used by a large number of people due to its good operating experience. Following this, the number of malware has risen sharply, and security problems have become more serious. Program analysis technology combined with deep learning to identify malicious applications has become a research central. Most of the existing malware identification frameworks are deployed in the cloud due to the scale and complexity of their models. However, its functions are limited due to network delays, bandwidth, and user privacy information will be leaked. In this paper, we propose a dynamic malware identification framework for mobile terminals. The framework has a customized lightweight deep learning model and we use knowledge distillation to optimize the model. This method effectively avoids the leakage of user privacy due to deployment on mobile devices, and can effectively classify applications.

Keywords: Android malware · Dynamic analysis · Deep learning · Mobile

1 Introduction

According to data from the international company staticta [1] in 2021, the Android operating system is expected to occupy 83.8% in the global mobile operating system market. Android has become the most popular mobile operating system in the world due to its open source and inclusiveness. Following this, there are more and more security issues for Android applications. While some mobile applications provide users with convenience, they also carry advertisements, maliciously charge fees, and disclose privacy, which causes a lot of troubles to users. According to the data provided by the iJiami big data platform [2], the center has collected 3.15 million+ android applications, most of which have high-risk vulnerabilities, 5.46% of the apps have malicious programs, and more than 37% of the apps have unauthorized violations. Malicious applications pose a huge threat to the personal information and property security of mobile users. In order to protect the safety of users, many researchers have made a lot of contributions in the field of malware identification in recent years.

© Springer Nature Switzerland AG 2021
M. Yang et al. (Eds.): NSS 2021, LNCS 13041, pp. 116–130, 2021.
https://doi.org/10.1007/978-3-030-92708-0_7

According to the running state of the program, the analysis method of the application is also divided into static and dynamic analysis. Static analysis technology refers to the analysis of the program without running the application. It has the advantages of fast analysis speed, full code coverage, and no need to rely on the execution environment, so it is widely used in the field of malware identification. Wang et al. [3] use Androguard to analyze the application, which extract permissions, filter intents, and restricted api calls. Luo et al. [4] extract the texture fingerprint information of the malware. They treat Mainfest.xml as a text document and extracts contextual text features through NLP. Su et al. [5] extract app components, intents, requested permissions, code pattern as features, and designs a deep belief network to extract behavior information. Fan et al. [6] construct five features from the subgraph, which are used to identify Android piggybacked apps. In order to improve the classification accuracy and reduce the complexity of the model, Martín et al. [7] propose a new genetic algorithm designed to evolve the parameters, and the architecture, of a Deep Neural Networks. They use malware data sets with static characteristics to test performance.

Static analysis has a high false alarm rate and cannot effectively identify malicious applications that use code obfuscation technology. Dynamic analysis can solve these problems by actually running the application on a sandbox or real device and monitoring the runtime behavior of the application. Faruki et al. [8] use low level device runtime attributes, such as cpu, memory, network, sensors. Yeh et al. [9] introduce a new conversion technology that can convert a series of log information into flat data with two-dimensional features and use convolutional neural networks for training. Feng et al. [10] use dynamic analysis technology to extract information leaks, sms, and dexclass load. They use feature selection algorithm to remove noisy or irrelevant features. Fasano et al. [11] propose a dynamic analysis method that uses battery-related characteristics to identify malware. They use abnormal battery consumption as features, and use four supervised machine learning classification methods. Ferrante [12] et al. propose an automatic analysis method that allows users to identify subsequences of execution traces. They collect dynamic features such as resources usage and system calls during application execution, and use machine learning techniques to analyze the features. Experimental results show that the method can effectively identify suspicious execution traces. Martinelli et al. [13] propose a hybrid tool BRIDEMAID that accurately detects Android malicious applications. BRIDE-MAID uses a static method based on n-grams matching and a dynamic method based on multi-level monitoring of device, app and user behavior. Xiao et al. [14] regard system call sequences as sentences in natural language, and used Long Short-Term Memory to calculate the similarity scores of system call sequences from malware and benign applications. The scores and used to identify malicious applications. Gharib et al. [15] propose a two-layer detection framework DNA-Droid. DNA-Droid uses a dynamic analysis layer as a supplement to the static analysis layer, and uses a deep neural network to achieve detection functions. Moreover, they use Sequence Alignment techniques to profile ransomware families.

Deep learning technology [3] is used in conjunction with application analysis technology to identify malware. Deep learning is a branch of machine learning, which is an algorithm for characterizing and learning data. It has been widely used in the fields of computer vision, speech recognition, and natural language processing. Many excellent deep learning algorithms, such as deep neural networks, convolutional neural networks, recurrent neural networks, are used in the field of Android malware identification. Zhu et al. [16] propose a malware detection model based on fusion convolutional neural networks, which uses different types of features, such as permissions, api, and url. The model has good performance in classification, and the detection time is reduced by 69% compared with traditional detection methods. Li et al. [17] extract the original opcode sequence from the decompiled Android file, and use the optimized deep convolutional neural network for training, which can effectively identify malware. Vasan et al. [18] convert the original malware binary into a color image for fine-tuned CNN training. Nauman et al. [19] use several different deep learning models such as fully connected, convolutional, recurrent neural networks autoencoders and deep belief networks to identify malware. Bayesian machine learning has also been applied to the field of malware identification. Xiao et al. [20] regard the system call sequence as a homogeneous stationary Markov chain and use the backpropagation neural network to identify malicious applications.

Although cloud deployment allows models to benefit from the capabilities of high-performance computing systems, the algorithms are limited due to issues such as latency, bandwidth, and connectivity. A large amount of user privacy is collected during the dynamic analysis of the application, and these contents are handed over to the cloud for detection, which will leak user information. When the model is deployed on Android, the application can be effectively detected without the need for a network. User data, such as sqlite and file system, can be calculated on the local mobile without uploading to the cloud server, and privacy can be effectively protected. This paper proposes a lightweight malware detection framework that can be deployed on mobile. We actually run the application on Android to collect features, including crypto, sqlite, file system, webview and ipc. In order to solve the problem of insufficient performance of the lightweight model, we introduce the teacher network. Knowledge Distillation [21] technology is used to extract the dark information in the teacher network to provide lightweight student network learning.

In summary, our contributions are as follows:

(1) Automated analysis scripts are written so that Inspeckage can analyze applications in batches. We run more than 4000 applications on mobile and extract runtime features such as crypto, sqlite, file system, webview and ipc.
(2) A lightweight malware detection framework based on deep learning and knowledge distillation technology was proposed, and we design the knowledge distillation process. In order to select the appropriate teacher network and student network, we try different deep learning network structures and use accuracy and recall to evaluate the model. A large number of experi-

ments have proved that in the field of malicious application identification, knowledge distillation can better improve the various indicators of student networks.

(3) We deploy the model to the mobile to prove that the framework has lightweight characteristics, and experiments show that the framework can effectively identify malware.

2   Overview

In order to effectively detect malicious applications, this paper proposes a lightweight malware detection framework for mobile terminals. The framework is divided into three parts as shown in Fig. 1. The first part is Feature Extraction. Dynamic analysis is used to extract features. The application is actually run on the Android emulator to obtain the runtime characteristics. The second part is the Deep Learning Training. In order to solve the problem of insufficient accuracy of the lightweight model, we adopt the knowledge distillation. First, we train a teacher network through the training set, and then the lightweight student network is trained to improve accuracy through the guidance of the teacher network. The third part is the Deployment Phase: we transform the trained student network into a torchscript that can be used on the mobile terminal, and deploy it to the mobile through PyTorch Mobile to detect whether the application is benign or malicious.

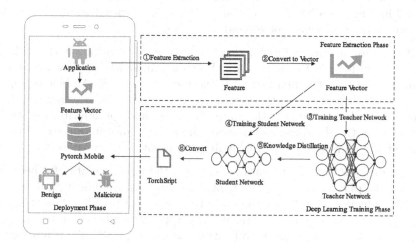

Fig. 1. Lightweight malware detection framework

3   Lightweight Malware Detection Framework

This section is divided into 3 parts: Feature Extraction, Deep Learning Training, and Model Deployment. The Feature Extraction part will introduce in detail why we need to extract these features. The Deep Learning Training part will introduce how to use teacher network and knowledge distillation technology to train a better classifier model. Model Deployment describes how we deploy the model to the mobile.

3.1   Feature Extraction

Since malicious applications implemented using repackaging and obfuscation techniques cannot be identified by static analysis, we use the dynamic analysis method. In the feature extraction stage, the application is actually run in the android emulator. Inspeckage, an Android dynamic analysis tool, is used to monitor the status of the application and obtain the behavior information of the application as features. In order to make Inspeckage run better, we write test scripts using automated testing frameworks such as Selenium and Appium. Each application runs on the simulator for 1 min. The features are extracted, including crypto, sqlite, file system, webview and ipc. This paper gives examples as shown in Table 1.

Crypto. Encryption operations are usually used to hide information and prevent information from being stolen. In finance, more transparent encryption technology (encrypted currency) is usually used as a substitute for legal currency. Malicious applications also use encryption technology to carry out malicious activities, such as ransomware, encryption mining and encryption hijacking. Once a mobile device is infected, its running speed will slow down, and cpu utilization will increase significantly. Malware also uses encryption technology to hide malicious code and bypass some security checks.

SQLite. If a malicious application can operate the sqlite database, the malicious code will be hidden in the sqlite data. When a third-party application accesses the tainted data, it will inadvertently execute hidden code. Malicious applications can also hijack the data in sqlite. For example, the browser saves user information and passwords in the sqlite database, and the information stealing program reads the database and uploads the private information to the remote command and control server, which will cause great distress to users.

File System. Malicious applications will read the file metadata of other applications in the phone, including the name, size, and last modification date of the file, and can brute force the file to obtain the content of the file. Malicious applications can monitor the usage of third-party applications based on two pieces of information, the size and last modification date of a specific file. If a legitimate application chooses to store private data in a file, and the naming of the file name exposes this information, the malicious application will crack the file to obtain the information.

WebView. Webview has the function of prompting the user whether to save the password is enabled by default. When the user chooses to save, the user name and password will be stored in the webview database in plain text, and the malicious application will use privilege escalation or root to obtain the user's

Table 1. Feature set

Features	Examples
Crypto	SecretKeySpec(jjlow59m,DES), Cipher[DES/ECB/PKCS5Padding]
	SecretKeySpec(c4e72f57,DES), Cipher[DES] (DdjFSi+G2xA=, skyid)
	SecretKeySpec(df21a3bf,DES), Cipher[DES] (2igDlFXo8KM=, DES)...
SQLite	SELECT * FROM user
	[Context] getDatabasePath(foo)
	execSQL(PRAGMA user_version = 1)...
File System	R/W [new File(String)]: /system/bin/su
	R/W [new File(String)]: /storage/emulated/0
	R/W [new File(String)]: /system/etc./hztun...
WebView	Load URL: javascript: setLimitState(0)
	addJavascriptInterface(Object, JSInterface)
	Load URL: file:///android_asset/oferta.html...
IPC	registerReceiver: Actions: mj_receive_sms_action_internal
	sendBroadcast: Intent act=com.sdky.jzp.service.CoreService_onCreated
	registerReceiver: Actions: android.provider.Telephony.SMS_RECEIVED

password. The interface functions included in webview can interact with the local java program, and malicious applications will tamper with the URL, which will trigger a series of malicious behaviors such as sending deductible short messages, stealing contacts, and remote control.

IPC. IPC is used for data communication between different processes, and malicious applications will use this feature to perform malicious behaviors. When some low-level processes that are not initiated by the user use the ipc mechanism to communicate with each other to transfer the data in the message, the malicious application will eavesdrop on the transmitted information and save it in a certain register, and it will modify the data without the user's knowledge.

In order to make the features can be trained, we count the frequency of appearance of all features, and sort them according to frequency from high to low. The dictionary file is constructed by selecting features with a frequency greater than 5. During model training, the dictionary file is used to number the features in the training data. For problems with different numbers of features in different samples, we use special characters PAD to fill. For new features that are not in the dictionary file, this paper uses the special character UNK instead. Subsequently, a high-dimensional space whose dimension is the number of all words is embedded into a continuous vector space with a much lower dimension through word embedding, and each feature is mapped to a vector on the real number domain. Each value in the vector is a parameter whose initial value is randomly generated and will changed during the model training process. The embedding matrix composed of vectors is shown in Fig. 2.

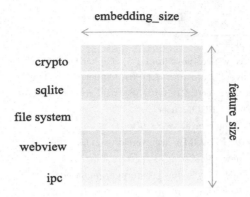

Fig. 2. Feature vector

3.2 Deep Learning Training

The larger model has the characteristics of complex network model and high requirements for deployment resources, so it is not suitable for deployment to the mobile terminal. The lightweight model has low requirements for computing resources but has the problem of insufficient accuracy. We introduce teacher network, which is a large-scale, complex neural network with slow training process but good inference effect. This paper uses this teacher network to guide the training of the student network, which is a neural network with small scale, relatively simple, fast training process but poor inference effect. Knowledge distillation technology is used to extract the knowledge from teacher network to help student network training. A lightweight neural network with small scale and good inference performance will be obtained. The neural network can be deployed at the mobile terminal.

Teacher Network. The teacher network uses the Transformer [22], which is now widely used in the field of natural language processing, and we modify the model to target the field of malicious application identification. Transformer is divided into two main parts: encoder and decoder. In this paper, only the encoder part is used, that is, the process of mapping the feature sequence into the mathematical expression of the hidden layer. As shown in Algorithm 1, first, we use word embedding to convert the input feature X into a vector representation $X_{embedding}$. Since the feature is extracted dynamically, the sequence of feature generation is also very important for model judgment, so we retain the position code PE of the encoder part. PE provides the position information of each feature to the model, and Transformer uses the linear transformation of the sine and cosine functions to provide the position information. Then, the position code is,

$$PE_{(pos,2i)} = sin(pos/10000^{2i/d_{model}})$$

$$PE_{(pos,2i+1)} = cos(pos/10000^{2i/d_{model}})$$

where pos is the position of the feature, and i is the dimension of the word vector. We add $X_{embedding}$ and the PE to get a new vector X.

When the model processes each feature, the self-attention mechanism can help the model view information at other locations in the input sequence. First, X is linearly mapped into three matrices Q, K, and V, and the attention matrix QK^T is obtained. We use the attention matrix to weight V, and use the $\sqrt{d_k}$ to turn the attention matrix into a standard normal distribution. Finally, softmax is used to normalize to get Attention(Q, K, V). This paper further uses 3-head Attention to obtain $X_{attention}$. Then, the Attention(Q, K, V) is,

$$Attention\,(Q, K, V) = softmax\left(\frac{QK^T}{\sqrt{d_k}}\right) V$$

After getting Attention(Q,K,V), we add $X_{attention}$ to the original X, which is the residual. In this way, the problem of network degradation can be solved and the gradient can be directly transmitted back to the initial layer during training. Layer regularization is used to normalize the hidden layer in the neural network to a standard normal distribution, which can speed up training and accelerate convergence. This paper inputs $X_{attention}$ to the feedforward layer to get X_{hidden}. The feedforward consists of two linear layers of activated functions. It is used to make up for the insufficient fitting degree of the attention mechanism to complex processes. We set up two encoder layers and add a linear layer to do linear transformations. In the end, we get two scores, score1 and score2. When score1 is greater than score2, the application is benign, otherwise it is malicious.

Algorithm 1. Teacher Network

INPUT: input feature X
OUTPUT: benign or malicious
1: **for** i=0 to n **do**
2:     $X_{embedding} \leftarrow WE(X)$
3:     $X \leftarrow X_{embedding} + PE$
4:     $Q = Liner(X), K = Liner(X), V = Liner(X)$
5:     $X_{attention} \leftarrow Attention(Q, K, V)$
6:     $X_{attention} \leftarrow X + X_{attention}$
7:     $X_{attention} \leftarrow LayerNorm(X_{attention})$
8:     $X_{hidden} \leftarrow Relu(Linear(Linear(X_{attention})))$
9: **end for**
10: score1,score2 $\leftarrow Linear(X_{hidden})$
11: **if** $score1 > score2$ **then**
12:     benign
13: **else**
14:     malicious
15: **end if**

Student Network. For the selection of the student network, we chose Bi-LSTM [23]. In an ordinary neural network, the transmission of information is one-way. This feature makes the network easier to learn, but it also reduces the ability of the neural network model. For identifying malicious applications, the output of the network is not only related to the current input, but also related to the past output. Recurrent neural networks are suitable for this situation. However, as the distance increases, RNN cannot effectively use historical information. As a special type of RNN, LSTM can learn long-term dependent information. The structure of LSTM has a forget gate, an input gate, and an output gate. The forget gate determines which information will be forgotten through the sigmoid function, the input gate determines which new information will be retained, and the output gate determines what information will be output. We use Bi-directional LSTM so that the model has two-way memory. In order to increase the capabilities of the model, we add linear layers.

Algorithm 2. Knowledge Distillation

INPUT: training data set D_{train}, teacher network N_{tch}, student network N_{stu}
OUTPUT: student network after knowledge distillation N_{stu_kd}
1: **for** $(X, Y) \in D_{train}$ **do**
2:     $gradient \leftarrow 0$
3:     $Out_{stu} \leftarrow N_{stu}(X)$
4:     $Out_{tch} \leftarrow N_{tch}(X)$
5:     Cut off the back propagation of teacher
6:     $loss \leftarrow KD(Out_{stu}, Y, Out_{tch}, temp)$
7:     Calculate the gradient by back propagation
8:     Perform a one-step parameter update through Adam
9: **end for**

Knowledge Distillation. This paper uses knowledge distillation to improve the accuracy of the student network. Algorithm 2 shows the detail of applying knowledge distillation to student network training. First, we select input X and target Y from the training set D_{train} cyclically. The gradient of parameter is set to 0, and X is input to the student network N_{stu} to get the output Out_{stu}. After X is input into N_{tch} to get Out_{tch}, the back propagation of the N_{tch} must be cut off. Next we calculate the total loss, the weighted average of the cross entropy corresponding to the soft label and the hard label, to guide the student network training. The formula is as follows:

$$L_{total} = \alpha * CE\left(Y, S\left(Out_{stu}\right)\right) + \beta * CE\left(ST\left(Out_{tch}\right), ST\left(Out_{stu}\right)\right)$$

where α and β are coefficients, CE() is the cross-entropy loss function, D_{target} is the ground truth label, S() are softmax functions. ST() is the softmax function with temperature:

$$q_i = \frac{exp\left(Out_i/T\right)}{\sum_j exp\left(Out_i/T\right)}$$

where Out_i is the logits value of a certain category, and T is the temperature parameter. When T = 1, it is the standard softmax function, and the probability distribution generated by the softmax function will become softer as T increases, which is dark knowledge. Finally, the Adam algorithm was used for optimization. After the training, we get the student network after knowledge distillation.

3.3 Deployment

This paper use the PyTorch Mobile brought by Facebook in 2019, which supports efficient operation of machine learning on edge devices. We first train the neural network model on the server, and then write a script to convert the trained model into a TorchScript that can run independently of python. It is a method of creating serializable and optimizable models from PyTorch code. TorchScript can be saved from a python process and loaded in a process without python dependencies. We export the model to the Android environment through TorchScript. The transformed model is placed in the assets folder of the android application. It will be packaged as an asset inside the android application and can be used on Android devices.

4 Experiment

This section uses a lot of experiments to prove the following research problems.

- Q1: What is the performance of student network and teacher network in our design method?
- Q2: what is the performance improvement of knowledge distillation for student network?
- Q3: What is the universality of the trained model?
- Q4: What is the effectiveness of the model deployed on the mobile?

The experiment are run on a computer with Intel(R) Core(TM) i5-10400 CPU, 24 GB RAM, and NVIDIA GeForce 1050Ti GPU.

4.1 Data Set

This paper uses the data set named CICMalDroid2020 [24], which contains 1943 benign and 2622 malicious apk, a total of 4565 applications. Malicious are divided into four categories: adware malware, banking malware, mobile riskware and sms malware. In order to ensure the validity of the benign samples, all benign applications are scanned by VirusTotal to ensure that no malicious samples are mixed into them. We run the application on the simulator and use Inspeckage to dynamically analyze the application. Scripts are written to help Inspeckage run better. In order to be able to trigger malicious operations, we use monkey to send a pseudo-random user event stream (such as key input, gesture input, etc.) to the simulator. We set the parameters so that the monkey sends 600 random events to the application at an interval of 100 ms.

4.2   Q1: Performance Evaluation of Student Network and Teacher Network

We use the following indicators: Precision, Recall, Specificity, Accuracy and F1_Score to evaluate the performance of the model.

We divide the features into training data set D_{train} and test data set D_{test}, of which D_{train} accounts for 80%. In order to select the best student network N_{stu}, we test the model performance under different combinations of Bi-LSTM and the number of hidden layers. As shown in Table 2, the network structure with Bi-LSTM of 3 and hidden layer of [256,128] achieves the optimal performance. The Precision, Specificity, F1_score and ACC of this model are 0.960, 0.950, 0.971 and 0.958 respectively, which are significantly better than other networks. Its Recall is only 0.02 lower than the highest model.

Table 2. Performance of different hidden layers

Bi-lstm	Hidden layers	Precision	Recall	Specificity	F1_score	ACC
1	[256]	0.913	**0,942**	0.934	0.927	0.938
1	[256, 128]	0.954	0.921	0.967	0.937	0.948
1	[256, 256, 128]	0.801	0.759	0.860	0.779	0.817
2	[256]	0.913	0.939	0.934	0.926	0.936
2	[256, 128]	0.907	0.924	0.93	0.915	0.927
2	[256, 256, 128]	0.935	0.913	0.954	0.924	0.936
3	[256]	0.956	0.916	0.969	0.936	0.946
3	[256, 128]	**0.960**	0.940	**0.971**	**0.950**	**0.958**
3	[256, 256, 128]	0.894	0.939	0.919	0.916	0.927

We train a teacher network N_{tch} using Transformer. As can be seen from Fig. 3, the performance of N_{tch} surpasses the N_{stu}. The Precision of N_{tch} is 0.969, which is 0.009 larger than N_{stu}. This means that N_{tch}'s prediction accuracy for positive sample results is higher than N_{stu}. Recall is the number of benign apks predicted by the model divided by the number of benign applications. The Recall of N_{tch} is 0.997, which is 0.057 larger than N_{stu}. The specificity of N_{tch} is also greater than N_{stu}. This shows that N_{tch}'s ability to detect malicious apps is stronger than N_{stu}. In order to integrate the performance of Precision and Recall, F1_score is used to measure the performance of the model. The F1_score and ACC of N_{tch} are 0.983 and 0.985 respectively. This is because N_{tch} has a more complex model structure that can better fit the function.

4.3   Q2: Effectiveness of Knowledge Distillation

In the process of knowledge distillation, temperature is a very important parameter. As the temperature increases, the results output by the N_{tch} will become

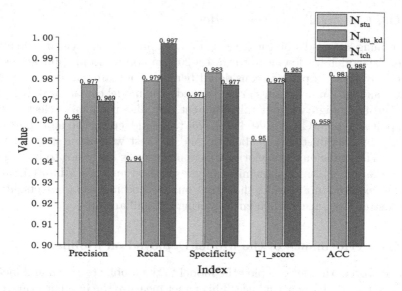

Fig. 3. The performance of N_{stu}, N_{stu_kd} and N_{tch}

smoother, which can provide N_{stu} with dark knowledge. We also measure the effect of different temperature parameters on N_{stu}'s performance improvement. As shown in Fig. 3 and 4, when temperature is 3, the comprehensive performance of the student network after knowledge distillation N_{stu_kd} reach the optimum compared to other temperatures. It surpasses the performance of N_{stu}, where F1_score is increased by 0.028 and ACC is increased by 0.023. The Precision and Specificity of N_{stu_kd} surpasses N_{tch}, and other evaluation index such as Recall, F1_score and Acc are also closer to the N_{tch}. The above experiments prove that N_{stu} has been greatly improved after knowledge distillation.

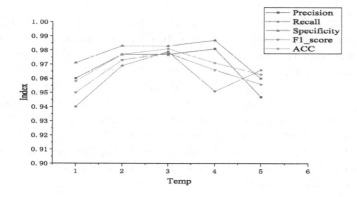

Fig. 4. The performance of N_{stu_kd} under different temperature parameters.

4.4   Q3: Universality of the Model

After training the model on the existing data set, in order to measure the universality of the model, we download the latest 20 common Android applications from Google Play. These apps are considered benign. They are run on the Android emulator and dynamic features are extracted. The model can accurately identify these apps as benign without misjudgment. We also randomly select 20 malicious applications in CICAndMal2017 [25] to be judged by the model, of which only one app was mistaken for benign, and the rest were accurately judged as malware. The malicious behavior of this application is likely not to be triggered because the paper uses a dynamic analysis method and has a limited running time. The experimental results show that our method has good universality and can be better recognized when encountering unfamiliar apps.

4.5   Q4: Performance of the Model Deployed on Mobile

We use PyTorch Mobile to deploy the model to the mobile terminal and measure the cost of the model in actual use. This paper measure the inference time of the model 7 times and take the average as shown in Table 3. The time consumed by the N_{tch} is 492 ms, and N_{stu_kd} is 263 ms. It can be seen that the loss of N_{stu_kd} to mobile devices is relatively small.

Table 3. The time consumed by N_{stu_kd} and N_{tch} (in ms)

N_{stu_kd}	268	273	262	287	243	260	248	Average: 263
N_{tch}	461	483	486	510	509	476	521	Average: 492

5   Conclusion and Future Work

In order to solve the problems caused by model deployment in the cloud, this paper proposes a lightweight malware detection framework, which is deployed on the mobile and can identify malicious applications without connecting to the network. We extract a large number of features of applications through dynamic analysis. Transformer was introduced as a teacher neural network. The knowledge distillation technology is used to improve the performance of the lightweight neural network. We verify the improvement of student network performance under different temperature parameters. Experimental results show that the lightweight model can effectively classify applications. In future work, we will use larger data sets to explore better deep learning network models, and focus on the problem of multi-classification of malware.

References

1. O'Dea, S.: Smartphone OS shipment market share worldwide 2020–2025 [EB/OL]. https://www.idc.com. Accessed 8 July 2021
2. iJiami. National mobile app security situation research report [EB/OL]. https://www.freebuf.com/articles/network/235337.html. Accessed 8 July 2021
3. Wang, W., Zhao, M., Wang, J.: Effective android malware detection with a hybrid model based on deep autoencoder and convolutional neural network. J. Ambient. Intell. Humaniz. Comput. **10**(8), 3035–3043 (2018). https://doi.org/10.1007/s12652-018-0803-6
4. Luo, S., Liu, Z., Ni, B., Wang, H., Sun, H., Yuan, Y.: Android malware analysis and detection based on attention-CNN-LSTM. J. Comput. **14**(1), 31–44 (2019)
5. Xin, S., Shi, W., Xilong, Q., Zheng, Y., Liu, X.: DroidDeep: using deep belief network to characterize and detect android malware. Soft Comput. **24**, 1–14 (2020). https://doi.org/10.1007/s00500-019-04589-w
6. Fan, M., Liu, J., Wang, W., Li, H., Tian, Z., Liu, T.: DAPASA: detecting android piggybacked apps through sensitive subgraph analysis. IEEE Trans. Inf. Forensics Secur. **12**(8), 1772–1785 (2017)
7. Martín, A., Fuentes-Hurtado, F., Naranjo, V., Camacho, D.: Evolving deep neural networks architectures for android malware classification. In: 2017 IEEE Congress on Evolutionary Computation (CEC), pp. 1659–1666. IEEE (2017)
8. Faruki, P., Buddhadev, B., Shah, B., Zemmari, A., Laxmi, V., Gaur, M.S.: Droid-DivesDeep: android malware classification via low level monitorable features with deep neural networks. In: Nandi, S., Jinwala, D., Singh, V., Laxmi, V., Gaur, M.S., Faruki, P. (eds.) ISEA-ISAP 2019. CCIS, vol. 939, pp. 125–139. Springer, Singapore (2019). https://doi.org/10.1007/978-981-13-7561-3_10
9. Yeh, C.W., Yeh, W.T., Hung, S.H., Lin, C.T.: Flattened data in convolutional neural networks: Using malware detection as case study. In: Proceedings of the International Conference on Research in Adaptive and Convergent Systems, pp. 130–135 (2016)
10. Feng, P., Ma, J., Sun, C., Xinpeng, X., Ma, Y.: A novel dynamic android malware detection system with ensemble learning. IEEE Access **6**, 30996–31011 (2018)
11. Fasano, F., Martinelli, F., Mercaldo, F., Santone, A.: Energy consumption metrics for mobile device dynamic malware detection. Procedia Comput. Sci. **159**, 1045–1052 (2019)
12. Ferrante, A., Medvet, E., Mercaldo, F., Milosevic, J., Visaggio, C.A.: Spotting the malicious moment: characterizing malware behavior using dynamic features. In: 2016 11th International Conference on Availability, Reliability and Security (ARES), pp. 372–381. IEEE (2016)
13. Martinelli, F., Mercaldo, F., Saracino, A.: Bridemaid: an hybrid tool for accurate detection of android malware. In: Proceedings of the 2017 ACM on Asia Conference on Computer and Communications Security, pp. 899–901 (2017)
14. Xiao, X., Zhang, S., Mercaldo, F., Hu, G., Sangaiah, A.K.: Android malware detection based on system call sequences and LSTM. Multimed. Tools Appl. **78**(4), 3979–3999 (2019). https://doi.org/10.1007/s11042-017-5104-0
15. Gharib, A., Ghorbani, A.: DNA-Droid: a real-time android ransomware detection framework. In: Yan, Z., Molva, R., Mazurczyk, W., Kantola, R. (eds.) NSS 2017. LNCS, vol. 10394, pp. 184–198. Springer, Cham (2017). https://doi.org/10.1007/978-3-319-64701-2_14

16. Zhu, D., Xi, T., Jing, P., Wu, D., Xia, Q., Zhang, Y.: A transparent and multi-modal malware detection method for android apps. In: Proceedings of the 22nd International ACM Conference on Modeling, Analysis and Simulation of Wireless and Mobile Systems, pp. 51–60 (2019)
17. Li, D., Zhao, L., Cheng, Q., Ning, L., Shi, W.: Opcode sequence analysis of android malware by a convolutional neural network. Concurr. Comput.: Pract. Exp. **32**(18), e5308 (2020)
18. Vasan, D., Alazab, M., Wassan, S., Naeem, H., Safaei, B., Zheng, Q.: IMCFN: image-based malware classification using fine-tuned convolutional neural network architecture. Comput. Netw. **171**, 107138 (2020)
19. Nauman, M., Tanveer, T.A., Khan, S., Syed, T.A.: Deep neural architectures for large scale android malware analysis. Cluster Comput. **21**(1), 569–588 (2018). https://doi.org/10.1007/s10586-017-0944-y
20. Xiao, X., Wang, Z., Li, Q., Xia, S., Jiang, Y.: Back-propagation neural network on Markov chains from system call sequences: a new approach for detecting android malware with system call sequences. IET Inf. Secur. **11**(1), 8–15 (2016)
21. Hinton, G., Vinyals, O., Dean, J.: Distilling the knowledge in a neural network (2015)
22. Vaswani, A., et al.: Attention is all you need (2017)
23. Schuster, M., Paliwal, K.K.: Bidirectional recurrent neural networks. IEEE Trans. Signal Process. **45**(11), 2673–2681 (1997)
24. Mahdavifar, S., Kadir, A.F.A., Fatemi, R., Alhadidi, D., Ghorbani, A.A.: Dynamic android malware category classification using semi-supervised deep learning. In: 2020 IEEE International Conference on Dependable, Autonomic and Secure Computing, International Conference on Pervasive Intelligence and Computing, International Conference on Cloud and Big Data Computing, International Conference on Cyber Science and Technology Congress (DASC/PiCom/CBDCom/CyberSciTech), pp. 515–522. IEEE (2020)
25. Lashkari, A.H., Kadir, A.F.A., Taheri, L., Ghorbani, A.A.: Toward developing a systematic approach to generate benchmark android malware datasets and classification. In: 2018 International Carnahan Conference on Security Technology (ICCST), pp. 1–7. IEEE (2018)

Federated Learning-Based Intrusion Detection in the Context of IIoT Networks: Poisoning Attack and Defense

Nguyen Chi Vy[1,2], Nguyen Huu Quyen[1,2], Phan The Duy[1,2(✉)] (iD),
and Van-Hau Pham[1,2] (iD)

[1] Information Security Laboratory, University of Information Technology,
Ho Chi Minh City, Vietnam
{18521681,18521321}@gm.uit.edu.vn, {duypt,haupv}@uit.edu.vn
[2] Vietnam National University, Ho Chi Minh City, Vietnam

Abstract. The emerging of Federated Learning (FL) paradigm in training has been drawn much attention from research community because of the demand of privacy preservation in widespread machine learning adoption. This is more serious in the context of industrial Internet of Things (IIoT) with the distributed data resources and the sensitive local data in each data owner. FL in IIoT context can help to ensure the sensitive data from being exploited by adversaries while facilitating the acceptable performance by aggregating additional knowledge from distributed collaborators. Sharing the similar trend, Intrusion detection system (IDS) leveraging the FL approach can encourage the cooperation in building an efficient privacy-preserving solution among multiple participants owning the sensitive network data. But a rogue collaborator can manipulate the local dataset and send malicious updates to the model aggregation, aiming to reduce the global model's prediction accuracy rate. The reason for this case is that the collaborator is a compromised participant, or due to the weak defenses of the local training device. This paper introduces a FL-based IDS, named Fed-IDS which facilitates collaborative training between many organizations to enhance their robustness against diverse and unknown attacks in the context of IIoT. Next, we perform the poisoning attack against such an IDS, including label-flipping strategy and Generative Adversarial Networks (GANs). Then, a validation approach is utilized as a countermeasure of rejecting the malicious updates to protect the global model from poisoning attacks. The experiments conducted on Kitsune, a real-world attack dataset, demonstrate the high effectiveness of the validation function in Fed-IDS framework against data poisoning.

Keywords: Intrusion detection · IDS · Federated learning · Poisoning attack · GAN · Generative Adversarial Networks

1 Introduction

Recently, the rapid advances in the communication and internet fields have resulted in a huge increase in the network size and the corresponding data.

© Springer Nature Switzerland AG 2021
M. Yang et al. (Eds.): NSS 2021, LNCS 13041, pp. 131–147, 2021.
https://doi.org/10.1007/978-3-030-92708-0_8

Especially, heterogeneous Internet of Things (IoT) devices in the industrial context have led to a rapid growth in data volume generated during its operation. It leads to more challenges on network orchestration and security risk through data communication, and sharing [10]. Moreover, many IoT weakness and vulnerabilities has been exploiting by a diversity of malwares, adversaries, leading to serious challenges for device and network security in accurately detecting and preventing cyber threats [16]. To this end, the intrusion detection system (IDS) is a crucial component to prevent attack steps in the cyber kill chain, needing to be updated frequently to recognize malicious behaviors in the system or the network. To achieve better performance on unknown malicious traffic, such a system leverages the capability of machine learning (ML) for detecting abnormally action [20]. The benefits from ML in enhancing scalability and improving detection ability are proved in many studies in recent years [7,14]. In fact, these ML models produce results with high accuracy, thanks to the rapid increase in amount of collected network data and the sharing of known indicator of diverse sophisticated threats [8,9]. But the growth of network data is also a major challenge in implementing the centralization of data for training in the large-scale IoT network. In fact, centralized training strategy is often expensive cost for server and system capable of working and training with the huge amounts of data and keeping raw data secure are also a big problem [7]. Furthermore, data privacy is one of the most important problems in all ML applications, especially network traffic data [19]. At the moment, the lack of protection for sensitive and private data has become one of the main issues needing to be resolved while adopting ML in industrial Internet of Things (IIoTs) context [23].

To solve this concern, a novel method of training ML models, named Federated Learning (FL) is advocated in building a better privacy-preserving solution for real-life artificial intelligence adoption [2]. The main target of FL is reducing the pressure on the server, by creating a righteous model on the participant device holding the amount of data from global model fed from the aggregation server [24]. This method not only solves the problem of centralization of data, but also helps ensure data privacy since the training data do not leave the safe perimeter of organizations, or users. In particular, the new types of network attacks and vulnerabilities are increasingly diverse and more difficult to defend. The emergence of FL algorithms marks a step forward in encouraging the collaboration among many network attack data owners to develop an up-to-date detector from others. FL enables local agents to collaboratively learn a shared prediction model while keeping all training data on its premises, decoupling the ability to applying ML from the need to store the training dataset in the cloud or a centralized repository. It helps to release concerns and threats to individual and organizational data privacy. Beside the outstanding benefits that FL method brings, there are still some disadvantages, threats, and vulnerabilities [12,15]. Therein, the training data is heterogeneous and not well validated on different devices can greatly affect the global ML model. Additionally, poisoning attacks can reduce the accuracy performance of a global model if it lacks a verification mechanism of local updates from distributed clients [21].

In general, many studies has been focused on the FL adoption in intrusion detection schemes with high-rate detection accuracy. For instances, Thien Nguyen et al. [18] proposed a FL-based IDS in which a security gateway of each network participates in the collaborative training to automatically detecting threatens to IoT devices. Likewise, Liang Zhao et al. [11] developed FL approach for training DL-based model for IDS in industrial cyber-physical systems (CPSs). Mohamed et al. also proposed Fed-TH [1], a federated deep learning for hunting cyber threats in industrial CPSs. However, recent studies found that the FL-based IDS framework is also suffered poisoning attack. By experiments, they showed that the functionalities of the global model could be damaged through attacker's well-crafted local updates, like the works of Thien et al. [17]. Poisoning attack against FL model can be conducted by flipping labels [4] and Generative Adversarial Networks (GANs)-based data generation [25, 26]. To address these problems, we first give a comprehensive empirical analysis of poisoning attack by flipping labels and Generative Adversarial Networks (GANs)-based strategies to illustrate the differences in predicting attacks of our FL-based IDS model under adversarial environments. Then, to prevent the client model from being poisoned during the training of each client's model, a validation function using Local Outlier Factor (LOF) is integrated into the model aggregation to compare the current model's performance with the accepted models in previous training rounds to further process. Our main contributions are summarized as follows:

- First, our deep learning model, named Fed-IDS is built relying on the structure modification of DeepFed [11] and validated with FL approach on real-world dataset of network intrusions.
- Second, we figure and compare the attack detection model's performance when updating poisoned data from a rogue training collaborator by both strategies of flipping labels and adding fake data generated by Generative Adversarial Networks (GANs).
- Third, a validation function, which is developed and integrated into FL scheme as a verification process before a client's training model is aggregated into the global IDS model.

The remainder of this paper is organized as follows. In Sect. 2, related works on data poisoning attacks, attack detection system for IIoT context are briefly introduced. Also, we discuss the federated learning approach for preserving sensitive data for training ML models and the vulnerabilities of FL. In Sect. 3, we describe the research methodology adopted in this study. The implementation, metrics, and performance evaluation results are presented in Sect. 4. Finally, we conclude the paper in Sect. 5.

2   Related Work

In this section, we briefly review deep learning model, the vulnerabilities and model-poisoning data which are associated with federated learning-based intrusion detection methods.

Initially, N.D. Thien et al. [18] proposed DïoT, an autonomous self-learning distributed system for detecting compromised IoT devices. This system was benchmarked on the dataset collected by several smart homes devices like cameras and routers. Beibei Li et al. proposed DeepFed [11], a federated learning scheme for IDS in industrial cyber-physical systems (CPSs), which conducts collaborative training a deep learning model on each security agents. The model is structured with a combination of convolutional neural networks (CNN) and gated recurrent units (GRUs). This approach helps multiple industrial CPSs to build a comprehensive intrusion detection model and ensure data privacy of involved organizations. Besides that, Fed-TH [1] was proposed by leveraging the characteristics of FL to hunting cyber threats against industrial CPSs.

Despite its ability to protect user privacy-sensitive data, FL still has the vulnerabilities that Nader Bouacida et al. [5] classified adversarial attacks into two categories based on their goals: untargeted attack aiming to reduce the global model accuracy, targeted attack aiming to change model's behavior on a specifically targeted subtask while sustaining good overall accuracy. With the rise of federated learning scenario, many works explore how the poisoning data affects the global model through model updates from a rogue client. The main target of poisoning attack aims to degrade the accuracy of the target model by poisoned data. This data can originate from label flipping strategy or injecting fabricated malicious data when performing local training aiming to misclassify prediction label. Jiale Zhang et al. [26] presented a poison data generation method, named Data_Gen, based on the generative adversarial networks (GAN). The authors also proposed a generative poisoning attack model, named PoisonGAN, against the federated learning-based image classifier on MNIST, F-MNIST, and CIFAR-10 datasets.

Recent studies have shown that FL is vulnerable to poisoning attacks that inject a backdoor into the global model. Sebastien et al. [3] have proposed a novel defense secure FL against backdoor attacks and named it Backdoor detection via Feedback-based Federated Learning (BaFFLe). The diverse datasets from the various clients were used to feedback to the FL process for detecting the poisoning updates from participants. Through empirical evaluation using the CIFAR-10 and FMNIST datasets, BaFFLe also gave the accuracy of 100% and false-positive rate below 5% on detecting poisoning attacks. Likewise, Vale Tolpegin et al. [22] performed poisoning attacks on datasets, which lead the FL-based systems have false-positive. The authors also proposed a method to avoid changing the labels in the datasets by validating the machine learning models before updating into the global models.

In summary, there are several works attempting to adopt FL in many applications, whereas a few studies investigate how poisoning attack can affect the global FL-based model and find the measure to defend. Nevertheless, it lacks the comprehensive study on the performance of FL-based IDS against rogue agents that feed the erroneous data to degrade the efficacy of global model. Recently, I. BeiBei et al. [11] proposed a federated deep learning scheme (DeepFed) for intrusion detection in industrial cyber-physical systems. But they did not consider the security of the FL approach, where malicious users can interfere the training process with poisoned data. Also, Zhang et al. [26] presented a generative poisoning attack against FL (PoisonGAN) which exposes 2 attack methods: labels flipping and generating poisoned data. However, they conduct the poisoning attack on image classification without investigating the effectiveness of defense method on their approach against poisoning attacks.

3   Methodology

This section gives the overview of our FL strategy for making a collaboration between different parties to build a more robust IDS without leaking raw data. After that, we introduce the method of performing poison attack against this FL-based IDS and its countermeasure.

3.1   Federated Learning

In this part, we introduce the FL model for IDS which consist of one global server and many collaborating machines, as shown in Fig. 1

- The server is responsible for aggregating the local models from each machine collaborates to build the global model. Then, the updated global model will be transmitted to the collaborators to continue training and improving the global model. Note that, the server is built on a trust infrastructure to provide the reliability for involved networks.
- The collaborators are responsible for locally training on its raw data and sending the trained parameters up to the global server. These parameters are the weight of the collaborator's training model. A collaborator is a training server representing for IDS builder in each network joined in the FL scheme.

And the workflow of this model can be summarized as follows:

- First, the server sends the weight and gradient of a pre-trained model or a generated model randomly to the collaborators.
- Based on the set of parameters received from the server, the collaborating machines proceeds training based on the amount of data which each machine is holding. In this method, D_i is the dataset at the i-th collaborator and w_i is the set of parameters after training.
- The set of weights w_i and size of the dataset is sent to the server when the collaborator finishes the training process.
- And the new model's set weights will be calculated by Formula 1.
- Finally, the server sends the updated model to collaborating machines for continuous use, evaluation, and train.

To establish the aggregate formula that the server does, we assume that there are N machines participating in collaboration during the training. And we only consider the case that the server must receive enough N models to execute

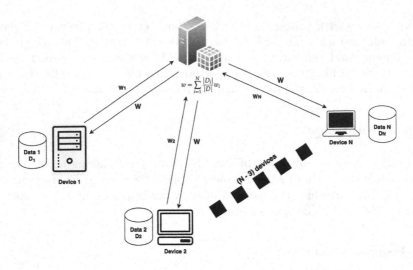

Fig. 1. The architecture of federated learning.

aggregating and updating new model for collaborative machines. Thus, the aggregation formula is calculated as in (1):

$$w = \sum_{i=1}^{N} \frac{|D_i|}{|D|} w_i \tag{1}$$

In the Formula 1, w is the set of weights in new model in the global server. And $|D|$ which is the total size data of N collaborators is calculated as in (2).

$$|D| = \sum_{i=1}^{N} |D_i| \tag{2}$$

3.2   Training on Collaborative Machines

In this study, our training model, Fed-IDS is built based on DeepFed [11] as shown in Fig. 2 which is a combination of deep learning network and federated learning. The Fed-IDS architecture used in this work has been removed Shuffle layer and 1 GRU layer to fit the dataset and minimize calculation overhead while maintain the efficiency. The input x contains features that indicate whether this is an attack or not. x is passed through CNN and GRU model simultaneously. When passing through GRU x will be extracted into the features as consequential information with time and turned into v as in (3).

$$v = GRU(x) \tag{3}$$

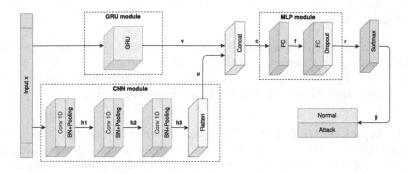

Fig. 2. The architecture of deep learning model - Fed-IDS.

When x comes to CNN module, it goes through 3 convolutional blocks, each includes a Convolutional 1D layer, a Batch Normalization layer, and a Pooling layer. The features are extracted in Convolutional 1D layer using convolution multiplication. Batch Normalize aims to standardize the values which were received from the Convolutional 1D layer at a moderate level, neither too large nor not too small. This is meaningful in retaining the features when going through many layers, many multiplications and avoiding arithmetic overflow. For example, when the number is too large and losing weight, since many small numbers multiplying together will result the zero value. And the last layer in each block is MaxPooling. Three convolutional blocks are denoted as $ConvBlock_1$, $ConvBlock_2$ and $ConvBlock_3$ respectively as in (4).

$$h_1 = ConvBlock_1(x)$$
$$h_2 = ConvBlock_2(h_1) \tag{4}$$
$$h_3 = ConvBlock_3(h_2)$$

The result after passing the 3rd convolution block will be flattened by the Flatten layer as in (5).

$$u = Flatten(h_3) \tag{5}$$

The Concat layer concatenates the result u and v from GRU model and CNN model as in (6).

$$c = Concat(u, v) \tag{6}$$

This result c goes through the MLP module consisting of 2 Fully Connected layers and a Dropout layer to avoid overfitting. 2 Fully Connected layer were denoted as FC_1 and FC_2 respectively as in (7).

$$f = FC_1(c), r = Dropout(FC_2(f)) \tag{7}$$

Finally, the result r passes through the Softmax layer to form the probability $\widetilde{y}$ as in (8).

$$\widetilde{y} = Softmax(r) \tag{8}$$

The objective of this model is to optimize the cross-entropy loss function between the vector ouput $\widetilde{y}$ and vector y which contains the actual label values.

3.3   Poison Attack

Poison Attack is a type of attack that seeks to damage the FL model or reduce its predictability by interfering with the training process. This work performs two strategies of performing poisoning attack, including Label Flipping and Generative Adversarial Networks (GANs)-based Synthetic Data.

Poison Attack with Labels Flipping. Labels Flipping is a type of Data Poisoning Attack where an adversary relabels some samples in a training set to degrade the performance of the resulting classifier. Figure 3 depicts the interfering scheme of a rogue training collaborator.

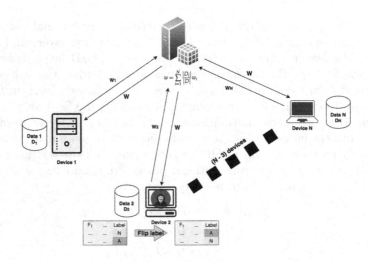

Fig. 3. Poison attack against Fed-IDS using flip-labels.

Poison Attack with Generative Adversarial Networks (GAN). In this strategy, the attacker pretends as a collaborator joining in the FL process and uses fake dataset generated to train the local model, then uploads the generated local parameters to the server. After aggregating from this collaborator, the global model will be poisoned. The overview of poisoning attack using GAN-based poisoned data generation is illustrated on Fig. 4.

To generate lots of artificial data aiming to poison the FL-based IDS, we design a GAN architecture, shown in Fig. 5. It has 2 main networks: Generator and Discriminator. The Discriminator is responsible for distinguishing between the actual data and the data generated by the Generator. Meanwhile, Generator perform the task of crafting new data to bypass the recognition of Discriminator.

The Generator has the same architecture as the CNN module of Fed-IDS scheme, consisting of three convolutional blocks $ConvBlock_1$, $ConvBlock_2$,

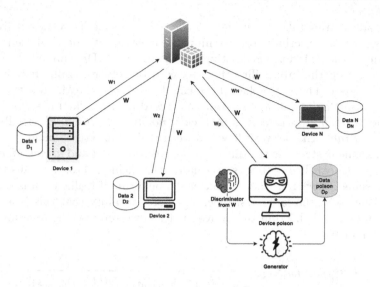

Fig. 4. Poisoning attack against Fed-IDS using GAN.

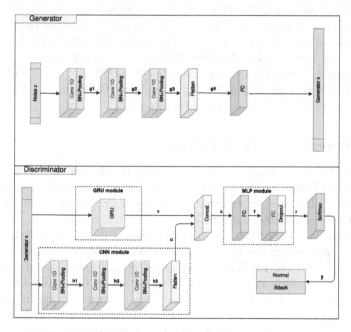

Fig. 5. The GAN-based poisoned data generation structure used in poisoning attack against Fed-IDS.

$ConvBlock_3$ and a Flatten layer. The generator G will take a random noise vector z and generate data x_{gen} as in (9).

$$x_{gen} = G(z) \tag{9}$$

The adversaries take advantage of a predictable model retrieved from the global server as Discriminator to mimic the capability of FL-based IDS in producing attack alerts. The distinguishing result of Discriminator is a vector representing the probability that a record of network traffic flow is attack or normal label. The vector has the form of $[normal, attack]$. And the sum of $normal$ and $attack$ is always 1. And the record of network traffic flow is Normal label if $normal > attack$, is Attack if $normal < attack$. Especially, when $normal = attack$, the network flow data can still be an attack label.

We assume $distance$ is the difference between $normal$ and $attack$ $distance = |normal - attack|$. If $distance$ is gradually approaching zero, it means that the distinguishing function in Discriminator is wondering if traffic data is an attack label. Conversely, the large $distance$, the more certainty that this is an attack label or normal label. From the above analysis, we propose the loss function of GAN as in (10):

$$loss_{generator} = \frac{N}{\sum_{i=1}^{N} \left(D(G(z_i))_{normal} - D(G(z_i))_{attack}\right)^2} \tag{10}$$

D is the Discriminator that will check N generated by generator G, with z_i is the noise vecto i-th and $i = 1, 2, 3, \ldots, N$ $D(G(z_i))_{normal}$ is the probability that $G(z_i)$ is normal and $D(G(z_i))_{attack}$ is the probability that $G(z_i)$ is attacked. Finally, we just optimize loss function $loss_{generator}$ to find the generating function G corresponding to the discriminant function D. Then, we use G to generate the fake dataset for training. Algorithm 1 describes the training scheme of GAN for crafting new poisoning data records.

3.4   Collaborative Model Validation

As mentioned above, protecting FL from Poisoning Attack is a challenging task. To overcome this challenge, we aim to break the connection between the adversaries and the FL model by determining that a trained local model is good and appropriate for global aggregation.

Our defensive method for FL-based intrusion detection is built based on BaFFLe [3], a strategy for backdoor detection in FL-based image classifiers. To keep this defensive method highly effective, we make sure to have l safe models that are aggregated without being attacked to validate local models before updating to the global server. And D is a dataset saved in server which is used in validation process for anti-poisoning attack against FL-based IDS. We assume that S is defined as the global model aggregated on the server. And after l times aggregation, we have a set containing $S_1, S_2, \ldots S_l$. With each S_i in l safe models above, there are two metrics of errors based on data and prediction results. The error based on data with formula $err_D(S_i)^{y \rightarrow X}$ is interpreted as amount of data in D labeled y and misclassified by model S_i. And the error based on predicted results with formula $err_D(S_i)^{X \rightarrow y}$ is interpreted as amount

---

Algorithm 1. Generate fake data using GANs for poisoning attack

Input:
    Global model S;
    List of noise vector $\mathcal{Z}_{noise}$;
    Epochs E
Output: Fake data D_{poison}
  1: $D \Leftarrow S$ ▷ Assign descriminator as global model
  2: $G = Generator()$ ▷ Init generator
  3: $e \Leftarrow 1$
  4: **while** $e \leq E$ **do**   ▷ Training with E epochs
  5:     Calculate $loss_{gen}$
  6:     Optimize G
  7:     $e \Leftarrow e + 1$
  8: **end while**
  9: $\mathcal{X}_{fake} = G(\mathcal{Z}_{noise})$
10: $D_{poison} = []$ ▷ Init fake data
11: **for each** $x \in \mathcal{X}_{fake}$ **do**
12:     $y = D(x)$ ▷ Get label
13:     $D_{poison}.\textbf{add}(data : x, label : y)$ ▷ Add new record
14: **end for**
15: **return** D_{poison}

---

of data in D that model $\mathcal{S}_i$ incorrectly assigns to class y. Then, compute the two differences in errors between model $\mathcal{S}_i$ and $\mathcal{S}_{i+1}$ as in (11):

$$v^s(\mathcal{S}_i, \mathcal{S}_{i+1}, D, y) = err_D(\mathcal{S}_i)^{y \to X} - err_D(\mathcal{S}_{i+1})^{y \to X}$$
$$v^t(\mathcal{S}_i, \mathcal{S}_{i+1}, D, y) = err_D(\mathcal{S}_i)^{X \to y} - err_D(\mathcal{S}_{i+1})^{X \to y} \tag{11}$$

Where Y is the set of labels of data, then we have 2 different vectors respectively as in (12):

$$\vec{v^s} = [v^s(\mathcal{S}_i, \mathcal{S}_{i+1}, D, y)]_{y \in Y}$$
$$\vec{v^t} = [v^t(\mathcal{S}_i, \mathcal{S}_{i+1}, D, y)]_{y \in Y} \tag{12}$$

And $\mathbf{v}_i$ which characterizes the error difference between 2 models $\mathcal{S}_i$ and $\mathcal{S}_{i+1}$ is identified as in (13):

$$\mathbf{v}_i = [\vec{v^s}, \vec{v^t}] \tag{13}$$

With l safe models above, we have $\mathbf{v}$ as the set of the errors difference between 2 models as in (14):

$$\mathbf{v} = [\mathbf{v}_1, \mathbf{v}_2, ... \mathbf{v}_{l-1}] \tag{14}$$

Each subsequent model C from other IDS collaborators is uploaded to server is used to compute $\mathbf{v}_l$ based on $\mathcal{S}_l$. Then, the local model C is evaluated to receive permission to participate in the global model aggregation process by the Local Outlier Factor (LOF) [6] function. The verification process of each local model before aggregated into global models as parameter updates is summarized in Algorithm 2.

Algorithm 2. Verify a local IDS model before aggregation

Input:
    Array **v** are calculated from l safe models;
    Verify model $\mathcal{C}$;
Output:
    0 or 1. 0 is not updated, 1 is updated
1: Calculate $\mathbf{v}_l$
2: **v.add($\mathbf{v}_l$)**   ▷ Add $\mathbf{v}_l$ into **v**
3: **for each** $(v, i) \in \mathbf{v}$ **do**
4:    $lof[i] = LOF_{\lceil \frac{l}{2} \rceil}(v; \mathbf{v}/\{v\})$ ▷ Calculate LOF with $\lceil \frac{l}{2} \rceil$ neighbors
5: **end for**
6: $avg = mean(lof[1], lof[2]...lof[l-1])$
7: **if** $lof[l] < avg$ **then**
8:    **return** 1
9: **else**
10:   **return** 0
11: **end if**

---

4 Experimental Evaluation

In this section, the experiments are conducted to evaluate the performance of Fed-IDS scheme in normal condition, under poisoning attack, and the case of attack with defensive measure. First, we give data resource description and partitioning. Then, we focus on experimental settings, including the environmental settings, baseline studies, and performance metrics. Finally, we carry out a series of experiments to compare the performance of Fed-IDS model in basic case without attack, with attacked case, and with defense case.

4.1 Data Preprocessing

To experimental testing, we utilize Kitsune Network Attack Dataset [13], a collection of 9 network attack datasets captured from an IP-based commercial surveillance system or a network full of IoT devices. Each dataset contains millions of network packets and different cyberattacks. In this data resource, all collected records were labeled by two type states, including: Normal and Attack. And each piece of network data in this data resource contains 115 features and 1 label. And the column chart as in Fig. 6 shows the distribution of the two types of labels of each dataset in Kitsune.

5 Kitsune Dataset

We assess Fed-IDS on Active Wiretap as one of the datasets where the distribution of the two types of labels is quite similar. In our experiments, the Active Wiretap dataset is divided into two major parts, 75% for training and 25% for testing. The training part is divided into equally sized partitions to each collaborator for local model training. Note that all trained models are tested on the same testing data.

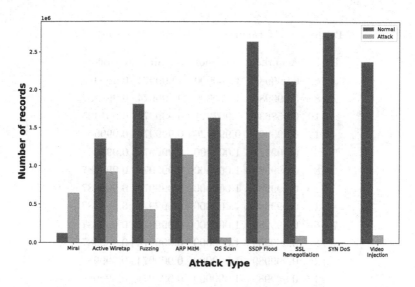

Fig. 6. Kitsune dataset distribution.

5.1 Experimental Settings

Environmental Setup. We implemented Fed-IDS as a federated learning algorithm by using the TensorFlow framework. The designed CNN-GRU model is implemented using Keras. Our experiments are conducted on Google Colab Pro with the Intel Xeon Processor CPU 2 cores 2.3 GHz and the Tesla T4 GPU with 27 GB RAM.

Baseline Studies. In this work, we compare the performance of Fed-IDS model in basic case without attack, with attacked case, and with defended case.

Performance Metrics. We use four metrics as follows: *Accuracy* is the ratio of right classifiers and total; *Precision* is the ratio of right predictions having attack label and total predictions belong to attack class; *Recall* is the right predictions having attack label over the sum of right predictions having attack label and misclassified belong to normal class; *F1-score* is calculated by two times the product of precision and recall over the sum of precision and recall.

5.2 Evaluation Result

In our experiments, we validate Fed-IDS model with above-mentioned baseline studies. We completed a total of 5 experiments, each experiment has the same circumstances with the numbers of agents K = 3, 5, 7 and 9 respectively. The numerical results which are shown in Table 1, Table 2 and Table 3 illustrate the performance of FL models, in terms of the accuracy and F-score, under four

Table 1. Performance of Fed-IDS without attack.

K	R	Accuracy	Precision	Recall	F1-Score
3	6	0.999989	1.000000	0.999974	0.999987
	8	0.999989	1.000000	0.999974	0.999987
	10	0.958631	0.907371	0.999974	0.951425
	12	0.99996	0.999926	0.999974	0.99995
5	6	0.999989	1.000000	0.999974	0.999987
	8	0.999989	1.000000	0.999974	0.999987
	10	0.999989	1.000000	0.999974	0.999987
	12	0.999989	1.000000	0.999974	0.999987
7	6	0.999989	1.000000	0.999974	0.999987
	8	0.999989	1.000000	0.999974	0.999987
	10	0.999989	1.000000	0.999974	0.999987
	12	0.999989	1.000000	0.999974	0.999987
9	6	0.999989	1.000000	0.999974	0.999987
	8	0.999989	1.000000	0.999974	0.999987
	10	0.999989	1.000000	0.999974	0.999987
	12	0.999989	1.000000	0.999974	0.999987

Table 2. The results of Labels Flipping and Counterfeit Data Attack.

K	R	Labels Flipping				Counterfeit Data by GANs			
		Accuracy	Precision	Recall	F1-Score	Accuracy	Precision	Recall	F1-Score
3	6	0.405152	0.405152	1.000000	0.576667	0.407654	0.406166	0.999974	0.577689
	8	0.970938	0.96929	0.95864	0.963936	0.407433	0.406076	0.999974	0.577598
	10	0.405152	0.405152	1.000000	0.576667	0.407308	0.406026	0.999974	0.577547
	12	0.405152	0.405152	1.000000	0.576667	0.405168	0.405159	1.000000	0.576673
5	6	0.405152	0.405152	1.000000	0.576667	0.405152	0.405152	1.000000	0.576667
	8	0.405152	0.405152	1.000000	0.576667	0.594430	0.024000	0.000026	0.000052
	10	0.406913	0.405867	1.000000	0.57739	0.413366	0.408506	0.999974	0.580051
	12	0.405152	0.405152	1.000000	0.576667	0.594188	0.015464	0.000026	0.000052
7	6	0.412162	0.407969	0.999424	0.579417	0.592741	0.00495	0.000026	0.000052
	8	0.405152	0.405152	1.000000	0.576667	0.405653	0.405353	0.999974	0.576866
	10	0.405152	0.405152	1.000000	0.576667	0.405152	0.405152	1.000000	0.576667
	12	0.405152	0.405152	1.000000	0.576667	0.405152	0.405152	1.000000	0.576667
9	6	0.405152	0.405152	1.000000	0.576667	0.405152	0.405152	1.000000	0.576667
	8	0.405152	0.405152	1.000000	0.576667	0.405152	0.405152	1.000000	0.576667
	10	0.432805	0.414464	0.968982	0.580591	0.405152	0.405152	1.000000	0.576667
	12	0.405152	0.405152	1.000000	0.576667	0.405152	0.405152	1.000000	0.576667

Table 3. The results of Labels Flipping and Counterfeit Data Attack with Validation.

K	R	Labels Flipping				Counterfeit Data by GANs			
		Accuracy	Precision	Recall	F1-Score	Accuracy	Precision	Recall	F1-Score
3	6	0.999989	1.000000	0.999974	0.999987	0.999989	1.000000	0.999974	0.999987
	8	0.999989	1.000000	0.999974	0.999987	0.999989	1.000000	0.999974	0.999987
	10	0.999989	1.000000	0.999974	0.999987	0.999989	1.000000	0.999974	0.999987
	12	0.955455	0.900963	0.999974	0.94789	0.999989	1.000000	0.999974	0.999987
5	6	0.999989	1.000000	0.999974	0.999987	0.999989	1.000000	0.999974	0.999987
	8	0.999989	1.000000	0.999974	0.999987	0.999989	1.000000	0.999974	0.999987
	10	0.999989	1.000000	0.999974	0.999987	0.972012	1.000000	0.930920	0.964224
	12	0.999989	1.000000	0.999974	0.999987	0.999989	1.000000	0.999974	0.999987
7	6	0.999988	1.000000	0.99997	0.999985	0.999989	1.000000	0.999974	0.999987
	8	0.970969	0.952534	0.977032	0.964628	0.999989	1.000000	0.999974	0.999987
	10	0.999989	1.000000	0.999974	0.999987	0.999989	1.000000	0.999974	0.999987
	12	0.847266	0.993818	0.626922	0.768842	0.993895	0.985180	0.999974	0.992522
9	6	0.999989	1.000000	0.999974	0.999987	0.982936	0.959607	0.999974	0.979375
	8	0.979997	0.952974	0.999974	0.975909	0.999989	1.000000	0.999974	0.999987
	10	0.910621	0.819278	0.999974	0.900652	0.999989	1.000000	0.999974	0.999987
	12	0.999989	1.000000	0.999974	0.999987	0.999989	1.000000	0.999974	0.999987

different scenarios of agents with the numbers of rounds communication R = 6, 8, 10 and 12, respectively. It can be easily seen that two types of attacks have affected to the performance of Fed-IDS model without defensive measure. And the defense measure has also given the effective to recognize and remove poisoned model before uploading. As the number of communication rounds R increases from 6 to 12, the performance of Fed-IDS model stabilizes when R is sufficiently large. Although, the results of evaluating in FL model without attacked demonstrate predictability with the accuracy and F-score approximately 99.9989% and 99.9987% respectively, the accuracy and F-score dropped sharply at 40.5152% and 40.5152% respectively when model training is attacked with both 2 types: labels flipping and generating counterfeit data by GANs. However, the validated model uploaded to global server can significantly improve the predictability of the aggregated global model. And the validation results in both attack strategies obtain the accuracy and F-score of 99.9989% and 99.9987% respectively. It is clear that Fed-IDS model with validation approach can resolve the problems of Poison Attack against FL-based intrusion detection.

6   Conclusion

In this paper, we have introduced and evaluated Fed-IDS, a federated deep learning model for intrusion detection in the context of IIoT networks. We also evaluated Fed-IDS in the context of being attacked and defending from attacks. First, we built a FL model based on DeepFed [11] for multiple machines participating in local collecting and training to build and aggregate a comprehensive intrusion detection model. Then, we built GAN architecture to generate counterfeit data to attack our FL model. And we also attack our model with labels flipping, which is another data poison attack to compare and evaluate how much data poison affects the accuracy of our model. In addition, we combined a BaFFLe-based method validation [3] with FL model to enhance the performance of our model. The experiments on Kitsune Network Attack Dataset have demonstrated that the FL model is vulnerable and validate function are adoptable for covering and defending the model from attacks. It is worth noting that FL model with validation is very suitable for building a federated intrusion detection system in the context of IIoT networks. Future research directions will focus on encrypt parameters before sending to global model for escaping be divulged information by analyzing uploaded parameters in the context of FL for IDS in IIoT networks.

Acknowledgement. This research is funded by University of Information Technology – Vietnam National University Hochiminh City under grant number D1-2021-28.

Phan The Duy was funded by Vingroup Joint Stock Company and supported by the Domestic Master/ PhD Scholarship Programme of Vingroup Innovation Foundation (VINIF), Vingroup Big Data Institute (VINBIGDATA), code VINIF.2020.TS.138.

References

1. Abdel-Basset, M., Hawash, H., Sallam, K.: Federated threat-hunting approach for microservice-based industrial cyber-physical system. IEEE Trans. Ind. Inform. **18**(3), 1 (2022)
2. Aledhari, M., et al.: Federated learning: a survey on enabling technologies, protocols, and applications. IEEE Access **8**, 140699–140725 (2020)
3. Andreina, S., et al.: BaFFLe: backdoor detection via feedback-based federated learning, November 2020
4. Adversarial label-flipping attack and defense for graph neural networks. In: 2020 IEEE International Conference on Data Mining (ICDM) (2020). IEEE Trans. Ind. Inform
5. Bouacida, N., Mohapatra, P.: Vulnerabilities in federated learning. IEEE Access **9**, 63229–63249 (2021). https://doi.org/10.1109/ACCESS.2021.3075203
6. Breunig, M., et al.: LOF: identifying density-based local outliers, vol. 29, pp. 93–104, June 2000
7. da Costa, K.A.P., et al.: Internet of Things: a survey on machine learning-based intrusion detection approaches. Comput. Netw. **151**, 147–157 (2019). ISSN 1389-1286
8. Hindy, H., et al.: A taxonomy of network threats and the effect of current datasets on intrusion detection systems. IEEE Access **8**, 104650–104675 (2020)
9. Kenyon, A., Deka, L., Elizondo, D.: Are public intrusion datasets fit for purpose characterising the state of the art in intrusion event datasets. Comput. Secur. **99**, 102022 (2020). ISSN 0167-4048
10. Khan, L.U., et al.: Federated learning for Internet of Things: recent advances, taxonomy, and open challenges. IEEE Commun. Surv. Tutor. **23**(3), 1 (2021)
11. Li, B., et al.: DeepFed: federated deep learning for intrusion detection in industrial cyber-physical systems. IEEE Trans. Ind. Inform. **17**(8), 5615–5624 (2021)

12. Lyu, L., Yu, H., Yang, Q.: Threats to federated learning: a survey (2020). arXiv:2003.02133 [cs.CR]
13. Mirsky, Y., et al.: Kitsune: an ensemble of autoencoders for online network intrusion detection. In: The Network and Distributed System Security Symposium (NDSS) 2018 (2018)
14. Mishra, P., et al.: A detailed investigation and analysis of using machine learning techniques for intrusion detection. IEEE Commun. Surv. Tutor. **21**(1), 686–728 (2019)
15. Mothukuri, V., et al.: A survey on security and privacy of federated learning. Future Gener. Comput. Syst. **115**, 619–640 (2021). ISSN 0167-739X
16. Neshenko, N., et al.: Demystifying IoT security: an exhaustive survey on IoT vulnerabilities and a first empirical look on internet-scale IoT exploitations. IEEE Commun. Surv. Tutor. **21**(3), 2702–2733 (2019)
17. Nguyen, T.D., et al.: Poisoning attacks on federated learning-based IoT intrusion detection system. In: Workshop on Decentralized IoT Systems and Security (DISS) @ NDSS Symposium 2020 (2020)
18. Nguyen, T.D., et al.: DÏoT: a federated self-learning anomaly detection system for IoT. In: 2019 IEEE 39th International Conference on Distributed Computing Systems (ICDCS), pp. 756–767 (2019)
19. Rahman, S.A., et al.: Internet of Things intrusion detection: centralized, on-device, or federated learning? IEEE Netw. **34**(6), 310–317 (2020)
20. Sommer, R., Paxson, V.: Outside the closed world: on using machine learning for network intrusion detection. In: 2010 IEEE Symposium on Security and Privacy, pp. 305–316 (2010)
21. Sun, G., et al.: Data poisoning attacks on federated machine learning (2020). arXiv:2004.10020 [cs.CR]
22. Tolpegin, V., et al.: Data poisoning attacks against federated learning systems, July 2020
23. Wang, X., et al.: Towards accurate anomaly detection in industrial Internet-of-Things using hierarchical federated learning. IEEE Internet of Things J. 1 (2021)
24. Yang, Q., et al.: Federated machine learning: concept and applications. ACM Trans. Intell. Syst. Technol. (TIST) **10**, 1–19 (2019). ISSN 2157-6904
25. Zhang, J., et al.: PoisonGAN: generative poisoning attacks against federated learning in edge computing systems. IEEE Internet of Things J. **8**(5), 3310–3322 (2021)
26. Zhang, J., et al.: Poisoning attack in federated learning using generative adversarial nets. In: 2019 18th IEEE International Conference on Trust, Security and Privacy in Computing and Communications/13th IEEE International Conference on Big Data Science and Engineering (TrustCom/BigDataSE), pp. 374–380 (2019)

A Simplified and Effective Solution for Hybrid SDN Network Deployment

Haisheng Yu[1,2]($\boxtimes$) (iD), Wenyong Wang[1,3] (iD), Yan Liu[3], Lihong Cheng[5], and Sai Zou[4] (iD)

[1] University of Electronic Science and Technology of China, Chengdu, China
[2] BII Group Holdings Ltd., Beijing, China
[3] Macau University of Science and Technology, Weilong Road, Taichai, Macao, China
[4] Guizhou University, Guiyang, China
[5] Dalian Jiaotong University, Dalian, China

Abstract. Software-Defined Networking (SDN) is viewed as one of the effective solution for network management, which can provide flexible global control of the network. However, it is difficult to migrating from traditional networks to pure SDN networks in a short term due to many reasons, such as company budget and protocol compatibility. In order to obtain benefits from SDN with a low budget, a hybrid network is proposed, in which only a few SDN switches are needed to achieve flexible control and management. In this hybrid network, one customized server is necessary for obtaining the network information from legacy switches and communicating with SDN controller to manage networks. However, it is difficult to develop and deploy the architecture with custom servers. Therefore, a novel solution is proposed to deploy hybrid SDN network without the customized server. Firstly, a novel method is presented to replace the legacy switches with SDN switches as less as possible to obtain all the link utilizations. Secondly, a new load balancing strategy is proposed to flexibly manage the network and get high performance. Finally, a number of experiments show the effectiveness of the proposed solution.

Keywords: Software-Defined Networking · SDN deployment · Hybrid network · Load balancing

1 Introduction

Many researches have focused on solving this problem, such as the research for reducing the resource consumption of p2p traffics [25], and the research for avoiding the packet accumulation in the networks [15]. However, just like the GMPLS, they are not easy to put into practice due to their high complexity [8].

Software-Defined Networking (SDN) has attracted a lot of attention these years [16] which is a successful solution for managing networks compared to many traditional solutions [8]. SDN is a new network paradigm, which decouples the control plane and forwarding plane. SDN provides the control plane the

M. Yang et al. (Eds.): NSS 2021, LNCS 13041, pp. 148–161, 2021.
https://doi.org/10.1007/978-3-030-92708-0_9

global view of the forwarding plane as well as the open Application Programming Interface (API), shielding the differences among forwarding elements. This seems to the development of personal computers that the computer applications finally run without knowing the details of the exact hardware but only based on the standard Operating Systems (OS). After adding the routing strategy into the SDN controller, administrators can easily know the network state and automatically control the forwarding behaviors of the forwarding plane according to the routing strategy. Due to the great potential, SDN has been one of the most popular research fields both in academia and industry. For example, Google has deployed SDN devices into its network [11], which has improved the average link utilization near to 100%. Besides, many world-famous open source organizations were set up in the past several years to promote the development of SDN, such as ONF [22], Linux Foundation [26], ON.Lab [9] and OpenContrail [19], and each of them has attracted lots of world-famous companies to join in the researches of SDN.

Although SDN has great potential to make it easy to manage the network, there are still many difficulties of putting SDN into practice especially in enterprise networks, including high budget and protocol compatibility. For example, the price of an SDN switch with parameters of 48 * 1000 BASE-T is about $4800, while a legacy switch with the same parameters is about 820. The SDN device is so expensive that many enterprises can't immediately replace all legacy switches with SDN switches. To solve this problem, a hybrid SDN work has been proposed, such as [12, 13, 23, 24]. By controlling the partially deployed SDN switches, we can also easily manage the networks.

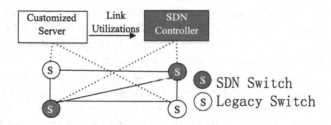

Fig. 1. Hybrid SDN network architecture of current proposals

However, to collect the information related to the legacy switches, current researches usually seek help from another customized server to obtain the network information of legacy switches in the hybrid SDN network, such as [3, 4, 10]. As shown in Fig. 1, to obtain the link utilizations in the whole network, the SDN controller has to communicate with the customized server.

To reduce extra overhead of the customized server, we propose a new solution to deploy hybrid SDN networks. This solution consists of a new replacement method to select proper locations for the SDN switches and a new load balancing strategy for traffic engineering.

On the replacement method, we want to replace the legacy switches with SDN switches as less as possible while guaranteeing there is at least one SDN switch connected by each link. So, we can infer all link utilizations by collected information from the deployed SDN switches.

On the load balancing strategy, we want to increase the traffics that can be adjusted by the deployed SDN switches. So, we can calculate more alternative paths for traffics.

The rest of the paper is organized as follows: Sect. 2 introduces the related work about hybrid SDN network. Section 3 presents the strategy of monitoring network load. Then, Sect. 4 discusses the load balancing strategy. Section 5 shows the effectiveness of our solution according to a large number of experiments. Finally, Sect. 6 concludes this paper.

2 Related Work

Just like our solution, to leverage the advantages of SDN to easily manage the network and improve the network utilization with low budget, a lot of work has been done in the past several years. In this section, we present the related work to our solution. In traditional networks, many researches focus only on the traffic monitoring such as [14] without caring about how to manage the network which is still a complicated problem. On the contrary, in the transitionally deployed SDN networks, some researches focus only on the traffic engineering. The solution proposed in [3] replaces some legacy switches with SDN switches which can adjust the flows to the optimized paths. By both analysis and simulation, the solution shows a big improvement in network utilization. To improve the network utilization, the scheme proposed in [10] firstly calculates an optimized weights of all the links with a greedy algorithm, and then balances the network load via the deployed SDN switches. The scheme that the legacy switches are gradually replaced to SDN switches in several stages was proposed in [25]. During each stage, they choose to replace the node that can enable the most amount of alternative paths, which can be used for network load balancing. In hence they can reduce costs of upgrading the network. The solution in [6] ensures fast failure recovery when only one link is down by designating every switch an SDN switch in the hybrid networks.

Compared to the traditional solutions, our solution can substantially reduce manual interventions. Compared to the current hybrid SDN network solutions, the architecture of them contains a customized server as shown in Fig. 1, while we utilize the deployed SDN switches to both monitor and balance the network load without the help of the customized server. Consequently, the customized server is not necessary in our solution, which can significantly reduce costs and facilitate the hybrid network deployment. More importantly, our proposal has a high load balancing ability by correctly selecting the location of the SDN switch and the routing of network traffic.

3   Monitoring the Network Load

To improve the network utilization, we firstly need to get all the link utilizations and then balance the load based on the knowledge of link utilizations. For this new network architecture, the most important advantage is utilizing SDN switches to obtain all the link utilizations without the help of another customized server. So now we discuss how we can obtain all the link utilizations in this new architecture network.

3.1   Getting the Utilization of a Certain Link

As we all know, to monitor how many bytes have passed through a link, we just need to ask either node of the two nodes that connected by this link. Any one of the two nodes can check out how many bytes it received and transmitted through this link, and the sum of them is the total bytes passed through the link from the startup of the network. This sum minus the sum collected last time leaves the amount of bytes transported by this link during the last period.

3.2   Introduction of Vertex Cover Problem

In hence, to make sure of obtaining all the link utilizations without the help of the customized server, for each link at least one node that connected by it must be replaced to an SDN switch. Besides, to reduce costs of upgrading the network, we should replace the legacy switches to SDN switches as less as possible. In conclusion, there are two factors we should take into consideration:

(1) For each link, replacing at least one of the two nodes it connects to SDN switches.
(2) Replacing the legacy switches with SDN switches as less as possible.

To meet these two conditions, we need to select and replace some nodes in the network, which is a famous Vertex Cover Problem and also a NP-complete problem [13]. Although it's quite difficult to find the optimal solution, it's relatively easy to find the optimized one.

3.3   Solution to Vertex Cover Problem

Vertex Cover Problem is one of the basic NP complete problems [7]. There have been a lot of algorithms proposed for this problem. Some researches focus on parameterized algorithms, that is to decide if there is a k vertices cover of graph G, such as [5,21,27]. Others focus on the optimization algorithms of this problem in the worst case, such as [17,18,20]. Since a lot of researches have focused on the Vertex Cover Problem, it's not difficult to find one that can ensure less SDN switches be deployed.

Since the problem we face here is the first class of problem, we choose a relatively easy but classic approximation algorithm called GE-AVC which was proposed in [5], since it can both obtain all link utilizations and deploy less SDN switches without high complexity. By deploying the nodes calculated by GE-AVC, we can collect all the link utilizations in networks. Consequently, we can perform our load balancing strategy to improve the network utilizations. We'll discuss the load balancing strategy in detail later, and more details about the GE-AVC algorithm are available in [5].

3.4   Timeliness of the Statistics of Network Load

To balance the network load, the SDN controller calculates the balanced paths for the flows referring to the link utilizations of the last period, but not the latest link utilizations in this paper. Although the link utilizations are not up-to-date, the SDN controller collects the traffic load information of the network once in a while to keep the information as latest as possible. As a result, it doesn't make a big difference since traffic load won't change a lot in a short term. Besides, before the sharp change of the traffic load, we have collected the traffic load information once again, which ensures the effectiveness of our load balancing strategy.

4   Load Balancing Strategy

Since we have obtained all the link utilizations, we now discuss how to improve the ability of load balancing and apply the load balancing strategy by controlling the SDN switches. Before introduce them in detail, we declare two definitions first.

Definition 1. We define the packets belongs to a flow if the packets are firstly received by the same switch and also finally received by the same switch. For example, in Fig. 2, all the packets originate from the hosts connected to switch S0 and end at the hosts connected to switch S4 belong to the flow f(S0, S4).

Definition 2. We say that a flow f can be adjusted by an SDN switch s if

(1) Switch s is on the shortest path of f.
(2) There are at least two alternative paths for f.
(3) Switch s can forward f to one of its other alternative paths by itself.

For example, as shown in Fig. 2, path p(S0, S2, S4) is the default shortest path for the flow f(S0, S4). S0 is on the shortest path of f(S0, S4), and it can forward the flow f(S0, S4) to the path p(S0, S1, S4). So we say that f(S0, S4) can be adjusted by S0, and so is S2.

4.1   Improving the Ability of Load Balancing

In the bid to improve the ability of balancing the load, we take three steps to increase the amount of adjustable flows by integrating GE-AVC with considering the new factor of adjusting more flows by choosing proper locations for SDN switches.

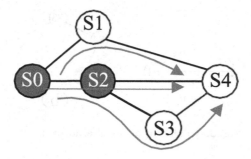

Fig. 2. An example of a flow

Calculating Alternative Paths for All Flows. This is the first step to integrate the algorithm GE-AVC. There're several restraints of alternative paths:

(1) A bit longer alternative path is also acceptable. The alternative paths could be a bit longer but not much longer than the default shortest path to increase the amount of adjustable flows.
(2) Make sure the effectiveness of the alternative paths. Make sure the SDN switch can adjust the flow to the alternative path.
(3) Low time complexity of the algorithm is recommended. For example, to reduce the complexity, we control a flow to traverse a path with the help of only one SDN switch, which can reduce lots of calculation.

Firstly we discuss the validation of a certain alternative path with the restraint of the second factor mentioned above. To clearly illustrate the requirement of the second factor, we give an example below. Both in Fig. 3(a) and Fig. 3(b), S0 is an SDN switch, while others are legacy switches. S0 wants to transmit data to S1. There're two paths to get to the destination, and the shortest path is p(S0, S1). In Fig. 3(a), if we choose p(S0, S2, S1) as an alternative path, after S0 forwards the packets to S2, S2 will forward the packets to S1 since S2 is a legacy switch and the shortest path from S2 to S1 is p(S2, S1). In this way, data is successfully transported to S1 through p(S0, S2, S1). In Fig. 3(b), if we choose p(S0, S4, S3, S2, S1) as an alternative path, then S0 will forward the packets to S4. We hope that S4 to forward the packets to S3, so that the packets can get to its destination gradually. However, because S4 is a legacy switch and the shortest path from S4 to S1 is p(S4, S0, S1), the packets will be sent back to S0, which means the packets can't get to its destination through this path. Therefore, we should not add p(S0, S4, S3, S2, S1) to the alternative paths which means that the path p(S0, S4, S3, S2, S1) failed the validation.

From the validation process above, we can know that this path won't be too long compared to its shortest path if this is really an alternative path of a flow. Therefore, the above validation process can meet both of the first and second condition.

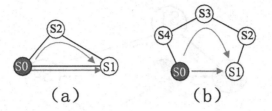

(a)   (b)

Fig. 3. Validation of the alternative paths

Finally, the algorithm of calculating alternative paths of a single flow with low complexity is described as follows:

---

input : Graph G of the given network topology, flow f
output: Alternative paths of the flow f

1 $paths \leftarrow \emptyset$;
2 $shortestPath \leftarrow shortestpath(G, f)$;
3 $addshortestPathtopaths$;
4 **for** $link$ **in** $shortestPath$ **do**
5 | $G = G - link$;
6 | $alternativePath = shortestpath(G, f)$;
7 | $isEffective = validatealternativePath$;
8 | **if** $isEffective = true$ **then**
9 | | add alternativePath to paths;
10 | **end**
11 | $G = G + link$;
12 **end**

Algorithm 1: Calculating the alternative paths of a flow

By Algorithm 1, we can find most of the alternative paths of the flow f. But there may be some questions about step 7 in the above algorithm, which is to validate the alternative path and it has been illustrated through Fig. 3 before.

Calculating the Adjustable Flows of Each Node. As shown in Fig. 2, both S0 and S2 can adjust the flow f. Therefore, we will store the information that flow f can be adjusted by either S0 or S2. After calculating all the flows in the network, we will know how many flows can be adjusted by each node.

Choosing and Replacing the Nodes Can Adjust the Most Amount of Flows. After knowing the amount of adjustable flows of all nodes, we also take into consideration the factor of the amount of adjustable flows when performing the GE-AVC algorithm.

When performing the GE-AVC algorithm, it will choose which node to replace during each stage. If there're several available nodes for the GE-AVC algorithm during a stage, we can consider the factor of the amount of adjustable flows by comparing the amount of adjustable flows of the available nodes, and choosing the node that can adjust the most amount of flows. In this way, not only can we ensure the correctness of the algorithm, but also increase the amount of adjustable flows.

In a large network, it's probable that many nodes are available during each stage for the algorithm GE-AVC, so adding the factor of adjusting more flows is effective to improve the ability of load balancing. Not considering the complexity of the GE-AVC algorithm, the time complexity of calculating the alternative paths of all flows and adjustable flows of all nodes is ($-V-5$). It can be accepted since we only need to perform this algorithm at the step of deploying a hybrid SDN network.

4.2   Route Selecting Strategy

Because the SDN controller knows all the link capacities by asking the SDN switches, the SDN controller can know the remained link bandwidth of all the links after getting the bytes transported in all the links of each period. After knowing all the link utilizations, the SDN controller will take three steps to calculate a balanced alternative path for a flow:

(1) Getting the alternative paths of the flow. These paths have been calculated after the startup of the network.
(2) Choosing the most uncrowded path.
(3) Pushing the flow entry. Pushing a flow entry to the related SDN switches contained in the path, which means selecting a new uncrowded path for the flow by controlling the related SDN switches.

To clearly illustrate the process of choosing an uncrowded path, we now give an example. In Fig. 4, S0 is an SDN switch, and wants to send data to S2. There're two alternative paths for this flow. The controller firstly compares the remained bandwidth of the links that included in each path. Then find the least remained bandwidth link of each path and compares the two least remained bandwidth of the two paths. Then we choose the path that has the most remained bandwidth. From Fig. 4, we can find that the least remained bandwidth of the path p(S0, S4, S3, S2) is 4 Mbps in link l(S0, S4), since 6/10 means 6 Mbps consumed and the capacity is 10 Mbps. Similarly the least remained bandwidth of the path p(S0, S1, S2) is 2 Mbps. Comparing 4 Mbps with 2 Mbps, we finally choose the path p(S0, S4, S3, S2) to forward the flow from S0 to S2 since 4 Mbps is bigger than 2 Mbps. This strategy ensures that the flow not hits a bandwidth bottleneck, which can improve the network utilization significantly.

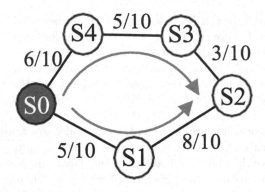

Fig. 4. Strategy of choosing an alternative path

5 Experimental Results

We implement our load balancing strategy on the Floodlight [1] controller, which runs on a server with an Intel CPU (2 * 3.00 GHz, 64 bits) and 2G memory, and it runs Ubuntu Server 12.04 operating system. The testbed consists of 7 computers and a pica8 SDN switch [2].

We build the network topology with the help of the pica8 SDN switch and 7 hosts, which is shown in Fig. 5. There're 6 hosts transmitting packets, 20 Mbytes per round per host, to their common destination host simultaneously with TCP protocol for 10 rounds by using the packets transporting tool IPERF. The source hosts are respectively connected to the source SDN switches that marked in Fig. 5, and the destination host is connected to the SDN switch named S10. In the bid to obviously differentiate the performances, we overlap the links that different flows will pass through as many as possible. During the test, we record the transporting time with the help of IPERF and the time of collecting the network link utilizations of each period by Floodlight. Both in Fig. 6 and Fig. 7, Local represents our solution and Caria represents the solution proposed in [4]. In Fig. 7, the green dashed line doesn't mean different performance of traditional strategy with different amount of deployed SDN switches, since traditional strategy means no switches will be replaced. It only indicates the performance with no switches replaced, and its role is to make the comparisons easier.

Since it's obvious to see the advantages of our simple network architecture can reduce a lot of costs and the workload of administrators, we only perform the experiments related to the deployment strategy and load balancing strategy.

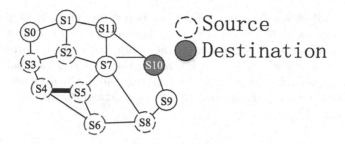

Fig. 5. Polska network topology

5.1 Comparisons of Amount of Adjustable Flows

We firstly take a look at the amount of adjustable flows of Caria and our proposal. From Fig. 6, we can see that the amount of adjustable flows rises with the increase of the amount of deployed SDN switches for both our proposal and Caria. Besides, we can adjust more flows than Caria with the help of the same amount of SDN switches. This is caused by two reasons:

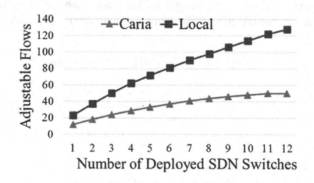

Fig. 6. Adjustable flows of two strategies

(1) Caria does not focus on adjusting more flows. They replace the nodes that have the most amount of alternative paths, while we prefer adjusting the most amount of flows.

(2) Longer alternative paths are not included in Caria. They only choose the paths that have the same hop count with the shortest path, which results in little flows can be adjusted and reduces the ability of adjusting traffics.

5.2 Load Balancing Performance Measurement

Although these experiments were carried out to evaluate the performance of deployment and load balancing strategies, deploying as less as possible SDN switches to collect all the link utilizations is not our main work since it is a famous Vertex Cover Problem and we just chose a relatively better algorithm for this problem. What we concerns here is the performance of our own SDN switch deployment strategy which aims at improving the ability of load balancing.

Instead of precisely recording and comparing the link utilizations, we record and compare the transporting time to give us a straightforward way to see the improvements.

5.3 Comparisons of Different Deployment Strategies

That Caria balances the network load which is not given the traffic matrix beforehand is quite identical to our strategy, which gives us a reason to compare the performance with it. Since Caria does not clearly illustrate a traffic allocation strategy, we implement its traffic allocation strategy the same as ours, which means that we focus on comparing the deployment strategy with it. From Fig. 7 we can see the transporting time of Local strategy is much less than the traditional strategy, which means the network controlled by our proposal can transport more data within the same time. Besides, the transporting time of Local strategy is overall lower than Caria, which also verifies the high ability of adjusting network traffics of our proposal. Therefore, we can conclude that our proposal can highly contribute to the improvement of the network utilization.

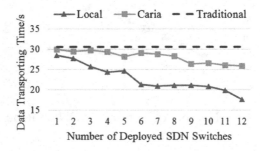

Fig. 7. Data transporting time (Color figure online)

5.4 Comparisons of Different Amount of Deployed SDN Switches

As shown in Fig. 7, the transporting time of both the Local and Caria strategies are lower than the traditional scheme which deploys no SDN switches. Besides, with the increase of the amount of deployed SDN switches, the transporting time of both Local and Caria strategies decreases gradually. Therefore, we can draw the conclusion that the more SDN switches are deployed, the better will be the performance. Also, the performance of deploying several SDN switches is relatively close to the full deployment with the increase of the amount of deployed SDN switches. Therefore, we do not need to replace all the nodes to SDN switches sometimes.

5.5   Statistics Collecting Time Experiments

Now we compare the statistics collecting time of deploying different amount of SDN switches, which shows the necessity of building hybrid SDN networks. While doing the experiment, we record the statistics collecting time every once in a while as shown in Fig. 8. It is obviously that statistics collecting time of partial deployment, which we deploy 7 SDN switches following our deploying strategy here, is lower than the full deployment for most cases. The reason is that collecting the statistics information from all the network devices needs to send more requests and last more time, from which we can know that deploying less SDN switches is also beneficial to accelerate the pace of collecting statistics information.

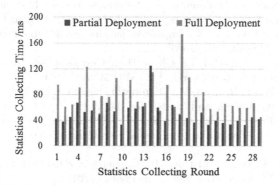

Fig. 8. Statistics collecting time

6   Conclusions

With the increase of the complexity of the traditional network, it requires complex manual intervention during the network monitoring and management. Although some proposals were proposed to solve this problem, there is still a serious problem that the network architecture is too complex for hybrid SDN networks. They usually need a customized server to collect the network information such as link utilizations, which will increase a lot of workload to deploy a hybrid SDN network. To overcome these problems, we proposed a simple but effective solution of hybrid SDN network deployment and load balancing strategy. As a result, not only our proposal reduce the costs and the workload of administrators, but also improve the network utilization significantly. By considering the experimental results, we conclude that there is a promising improvement of network utilization with low budget and deployment difficulty using our proposal analyzed through this paper.

Acknowledgement. This work is supported by Macau Science and Technology Development Fund (Grant No. 0018/2021/A), the National Natural Science Foundation of China (Grant No. U2033212), the National Key Research and Development Project of China (Grant No. 2020YFB1711000) and the Key Research and Development Project of Science and Technology Department of Sichuan Province (Grant No. 2021YFG0014).

References

1. Floodlight project. https://floodlight.atlassian.net/wiki/spaces/floodlight controller
2. Pica8 company. http://www.pica8.org/
3. Agarwal, S., Kodialam, M., Lakshman, T.V.: Traffic engineering in software defined networks. In: IEEE Infocom (2013)
4. Caria, M., Jukan, A., Hoffmann, M.: A performance study of network migration to SDN-enabled traffic engineering. In: Global Communications Conference (2014)
5. Chen, J., Kanj, I.A., Ge, X.: Improved parameterized upper bounds for vertex cover. Theor. Comput. Sci. (2006)
6. Chu, C.Y., Kang, X., Min, L., Chao, H.J.: Congestion-aware single link failure recovery in hybrid SDN networks. In: INFOCOM (2015)
7. Cooper, C., Klasing, R., Zito, M.: Dominating sets in web graphs. In: International Workshop on Algorithms and Models for the Web-Graph (2004)
8. Das, S., Parulkar, G., Mckeown, N.: Why OpenFlow/SDN can succeed where GMPLS failed. In: European Conference Exhibition on Optical Communications (2012)
9. Devlic, A., John, W., Sköldström, P.: Carrier-grade network management extensions to the SDN framework. Skldstrm Pontus (2013)
10. Guo, Y., Wang, Z., Xia, Y., Shi, X., Wu, J.: Traffic engineering in SDN/OSPF hybrid network. In: 2014 IEEE 22nd International Conference on Network Protocols (ICNP) (2014)
11. Jain, S.: B4: experience with a globally-deployed software defined WAN. ACM SIGCOMM Comput. Commun. Rev. **43**(4), 3–14 (2013)
12. Jin, C., Lumezanu, C., Xu, Q., Zhang, Z.L., Jiang, G.: Telekinesis: controlling legacy switch routing with openflow in hybrid networks. ACM (2015)
13. Katiyar, R., Pawar, P., Gupta, A., Kataoka, K.: Auto-configuration of SDN switches in SDN/non-SDN hybrid network. In: ACM, pp. 48–53 (2015)
14. Lee, S., Levanti, K., Kim, H.S.: Network monitoring: present and future. Comput. Netw. **65**(Jun.2), 84–98 (2014)
15. Liu, W., Yi, J., Zhao, D.: Genetic algorithm-based fuzzy controller to avoid network congestion. Intell. Autom. Soft Comput. **15**(2), 237–248 (2009)
16. Mckeown, N., et al.: Dpenflow: enabling innovation in campus networks. Comput. Commun. Rev. **38**(2), 69–74 (2008)
17. Monien, B., Speckenmeyer, E.: Some further approximation algorithms for the vertex cover problem. In: Ausiello, G., Protasi, M. (eds.) CAAP 1983. LNCS, vol. 159, pp. 341–349. Springer, Heidelberg (1983). https://doi.org/10.1007/3-540-12727-5_21
18. Oliveto, P.S., He, J., Xin, Y.: Analysis of population-based evolutionary algorithms for the vertex cover problem. In: IEEE Congress on Evolutionary Computation (2008)
19. Pujolle, G.: Open source software for networks. In: Software Networks: Virtualization, SDN, 5G, and Security

20. Robson, J.M.: Algorithms for maximum independent sets. J. Algorithms **7**(3), 425–440 (1986)
21. Niedermeier, R., Rossmanith, P.: A general method to speed up fixed-parameter-tractable algorithms. Inf. Process. Lett. **73**(3–4), 125–129 (2000)
22. Sachs, G.: Open networking foundation (2015)
23. Salsano, S., et al.: OSHI - open source hybrid IP/SDN networking and Mantoo - a set of management tools for controlling SDN/NFV experiments (2015)
24. Santos, M., Oliveira, B.D., Margi, C., Astuto, B.N., Turletti, T., Obraczka, K.: Software-defined networking based capacity sharing in hybrid networks. In: Third International Conference on Image Information Processing (2016)
25. Shen, W., Lei, H., Zhang, X., Chong, Z.: A new streaming media network architecture based on the fusion of P2P and CDN. In: 2010 International Conference on Multimedia Technology (2010)
26. Wasserman, M., Hartman, S.: Security analysis of the open networking foundation (ONF) openflow switch specification (2013)
27. Yang, J.: Improved greedy-edge approximation algorithm of the optimal vertex-cover. J. Comput. Appl. (2006)

Group Key Exchange Compilers
from Generic Key Exchanges

Hector B. Hougaard[1]([✉]) and Atsuko Miyaji[1,2,3]

[1] Graduate School of Engineering, Osaka University, Suita, Japan
hector@cy2sec.comm.eng.osaka-u.ac.jp
[2] Center for Quantum Information and Quantum Biology, Osaka University,
Suita, Japan
[3] Japan Advanced Institute of Science and Technology (JAIST), Nomi, Japan
https://cy2sec.comm.eng.osaka-u.ac.jp/miyaji-lab/

Abstract. We propose a group key exchange compiler using any two-party key exchange for which the shared key space is the subset of a group and whose security reduces to a decisional hard problem, such that the security of the group key exchange relies on the security of the two-party key exchange and, in turn, the hardness of the underlying decisional problem.

This work is a generalization of the multicast Burmester-Desmedt group key exchange in a modified G-CK$^+$ security model.

For n parties, the group key exchange protocol has constant round complexity and communicational complexity $O(\log_2 n)$. We also present a peer-to-peer version with round complexity $O(\log_2 n)$ and constant communicational complexity.

Keywords: Group key exchange · Compiler · Burmester-desmedt · G-CK$^+$

1 Introduction

In cryptography, the notion of a key exchange is essential. Without secure key exchanges, there can be no secure communication. Diffie and Hellman ushered in a new age of cryptography when they presented their famous Diffie-Hellman key exchange, relying on the hardness of the decisional Diffie-Hellman problem for public key security, which itself relied on the hardness of the discrete logarithm problem (DLP). Ever since, cryptographers have been building on this key exchange and presenting similar key exchanges based on hard problems other than DLP. With the age of quantum computing on the horizon, the quest for quantum secure cryptography has begun. On this quest, quantum secure cryptosystem alternatives to classical cryptosystems are the goal. Due to the breadth and depth of modern cryptography, this is an enormous undertaking and one with a time limit. It also beckons the question, what shall we do when an even more powerful form of computing is discovered?

© Springer Nature Switzerland AG 2021
M. Yang et al. (Eds.): NSS 2021, LNCS 13041, pp. 162–184, 2021.
https://doi.org/10.1007/978-3-030-92708-0_10

Nowadays, with group messaging and group signatures, a two-party key exchange will not suffice. However, group key exchanges can be difficult to prove secure because of the number of parties involved. Several two-party key exchanges already exist in the literature, such as the classic Diffie-Hellman key exchange, so Burmester and Desmedt considered how to create efficient group key exchanges from the Diffie-Hellman key exchange in [4] (BDI) and [5] (BDII).

In this paper, we present a group key exchange compiler that relies on the security of almost any underlying secure two-party key exchange to achieve its security. Our result is essentially a generalization of the multicast Burmester-Desmedt (BDII) group key exchange protocol of Burmester, Lange, and Desmedt [5,7], to relying on a generic and generalized definition of a two-party key exchange as well as a related generic decisional hard problem. We also update the security model to the modern standard, G-CK$^+$ [17] with some modifications to the model.

The paper is organized as follows. In Sect. 2, we define our security model, as well as a generic, two-party "0/1-interactive key exchange" (0/1-IKE) and generic decisional hard (GDH) problem before defining and proving the security of our group key exchange compilers, GKE-C and P2P-GKE-C, in Sect. 3. In Sect. 4, we do a basic complexity analysis of our GKE compilers. Finally, we give our concluding remarks in Sect. 5.

2 Preliminaries

We begin by defining the notation and security model we will use in our treatment of the group key exchange.

On notation, if χ is a probability distribution over a set S, then sampling an element $s \in S$ according to the distribution χ is denoted by $s \xleftarrow{R} \chi$. Choosing an element $s \in S$ uniformly at random from S, we denote $s \xleftarrow{R} S$. If Algo is an algorithm, then $y \leftarrow \text{Algo}(x)$ denotes the algorithm output y given input x. If the algorithm is probabilistic, we may draw attention to this by using the notation $y \xleftarrow{R} \text{Algo}(x)$.

2.1 Security Model

For the security of our GKE protocols, we consider the G-CK$^+$ model of Suzuki and Yoneyama [17]. Although their model is for authenticated GKEs, we use it nonetheless, modifying it to fit the security requirements of GKEs. We reformulate their description to using our notation and note where we add to the definition to fit the specific purposes of this article.

Consider a finite set of parties $\mathbb{P} = \{\mathcal{P}_0, \ldots, \mathcal{P}_\eta\}$ modeled by probabilistic polynomial-time (PPT) Turing machines with security parameter 1^λ. A party $\mathcal{P}_i$ generates its own static secret key SSK_i and static public key SPK_i, where the public key is linked with $\mathcal{P}_i$'s identity in some public system like a Public Key Infrastructure (PKI). For a party $\mathcal{P}_i$, we denote the ephemeral secret (public) key by ESK_i (EPK_i).

The security model requires that we consider static keys, however, our compilers do not use any static keys. This means that we do not need to consider any attacks on static keys, but we include the queries to modify the security model as little as possible.

Session. Any subset $\{\mathcal{P}_{i_1}, \ldots, \mathcal{P}_{i_n}\} \subseteq \mathbb{P}$, where $2 \leq n \leq \eta$, can, at any time, decide to invoke a new GKE protocol. We call such an invocation a *session*, managed by a tuple $(\Pi, \mathcal{P}_{i_l}, \{\mathcal{P}_{i_1}, \ldots, \mathcal{P}_{i_n}\})$, where Π is the protocol identifier and $\mathcal{P}_{i_l}$ is the party identifier.[1] Without loss of generality, we hereafter suppose that $\mathcal{P}_{i_l} = \mathcal{P}_l$. $\mathcal{P}_i$ outputs EPK_i and receives $EPK_{i'}$ from $\mathcal{P}_{i'}$ from all relevant (necessary) parties and outputs the session key.[2]

When $\mathcal{P}_i$ is the i-th party of a session, we may define the *session id* as the tuple $\mathsf{sid} = (\Pi, \mathcal{P}_i, \{\mathcal{P}_1, \ldots, \mathcal{P}_n\}, EPK_i)$. We call $\mathcal{P}_i$ the *owner* of sid, if the second coordinate of sid is $\mathcal{P}_i$, and a *peer* of sid if it is not. A session is said to be *completed* if its owner computes the session key. We say that $(\Pi, \mathcal{P}_{i'}, \{\mathcal{P}_1, \ldots, \mathcal{P}_n\})$ is a *matching session* of $(\Pi, \mathcal{P}_i, \{\mathcal{P}_1, \ldots, \mathcal{P}_n\})$, where $i' \neq i$.

Adversary. We consider an adversary $\mathcal{A}$, modeled as a (not necessarily classical) PPT Turing machine that controls all communication, including session activation and registration of parties. It does so using the following queries:

SEND$(\mathcal{P}_i, m)$: $\mathcal{P}_i$ is the receiver and the message has the form $(\Pi, \mathcal{P}_i, \{\mathcal{P}_1, \ldots, \mathcal{P}_n\}, Init)$ if it is an initializing message for session activation, and includes $(\Pi, \mathcal{P}_{i'}, \{\mathcal{P}_1, \ldots, \mathcal{P}_n\}, EPK_{i'})$ with any other message.

ESTABLISH$(\mathcal{P}_i, SPK_i)$: Adds a new party to $\mathbb{P}$. Note that $\mathcal{A}$ is not required to prove possession of the corresponding SSK_i. If a party is registered by such a query, then the party is called *dishonest*, if not, the party is called *honest*.

As an addition to the G-CK$^+$ model, we differentiate between two different adversary types: *fair* and *manipulating*. Both types of adversary may send an initializing message to a subset of parties to start a GKE protocol between them, but the *fair adversary* may not create, omit, nor manipulate any message between parties, honestly relaying messages between parties as per the protocol. The *manipulating adversary* has no such restrictions. The fair adversary mimics an adversary against GKEs and the manipulating adversary mimics an adversary

---

[1] Suzuki and Yoneyama [17] define their sessions with a 'role' for a party, which may be indexed differently from the party index, as well as a corresponding 'player' definition. In our protocols, the role of a party is determined by the placement in the double-tree (see Sect. 3), which in turn is determined by the index of the party, which can be altered as needed, hence the role is uniquely determined by the party index. We therefore remove this 'role' (and 'player') from our definition of session.

[2] Suzuki and Yoneyama [17] assume that each party receives public keys from all other parties, but this forces a GKE to have at least linear order in n, which we aim to avoid, hence we have altered the model slightly. In the end, parties only need as many keys as are relevant or necessary to compute the session key, which our alteration highlights.

against authenticated GKEs. In this article, we only consider GKEs and therefore only fair adversaries.

The adversary is further given access to the following attack queries.

SESSIONREVEAL(sid)**:** Reveals the session key of a session sid to the adversary, only if the session is completed.

STATEREVEAL(sid)**:** Reveals to the adversary the session state of the owner of the sid if the session is not yet completed, i.e. the session key has yet to be established. The session state contains all ephemeral secret keys and intermediate computation results except for immediately erased information, but it does not contain the static secret key. The protocol specifies what the session state contains.

STATICREVEAL($\mathcal{P}_i$)**:** Reveals the static secret key of party $\mathcal{P}_i$ to $\mathcal{A}$.

EPHEMERALREVEAL(sid)**:** Reveals to the adversary all ephemeral secret keys of the owner of sid if the session is not yet completed. This does not reveal other state information such that an adversary might trivially win.

Definition 1. *Let* $\text{sid}^* = (\Pi, \mathcal{P}_i, \{\mathcal{P}_1, \ldots, \mathcal{P}_n\}, EPK_i)$ *be a completed session between honest parties* $\{\mathcal{P}_1, \ldots, \mathcal{P}_n\}$, *owned by* $\mathcal{P}_i$. *If a matching session exists, then let* $\overline{\text{sid}^*}$ *be a matching session of* sid^*. *We say that* sid^* *is **fresh** if none of the following is true:*

1. *$\mathcal{A}$ queried* SESSIONREVEAL(sid^*), *or* SESSIONREVEAL($\overline{\text{sid}^*}$) *for any* $\overline{\text{sid}^*}$ *if* $\overline{\text{sid}^*}$ *exists; or*
2. *$\overline{\text{sid}^*}$ exists, and $\mathcal{A}$ queried either* STATEREVEAL(sid^*) *or* STATICREVEAL($\overline{\text{sid}^*}$); *or*
3. *$\overline{\text{sid}^*}$ does not exist, and $\mathcal{A}$ queried* STATEREVEAL(sid^*); *or*
4. *$\mathcal{A}$ queried both* STATICREVEAL($\mathcal{P}_i$) *and* EPHEMERALREVEAL(sid^*); *or*
5. *$\overline{\text{sid}^*}$ exists (the owner of $\overline{\text{sid}^*}$ is $\mathcal{P}_{i'}$), and $\mathcal{A}$ queried both* STATICREVEAL($\mathcal{P}_{i'}$) *and the query* EPHEMERALREVEAL($\overline{\text{sid}^*}$); *or*
6. *$\overline{\text{sid}^*}$ does not exist, and $\mathcal{A}$ queried* STATICREVEAL($\mathcal{P}_{i'}$) *for any intended peer $\mathcal{P}_{i'}$ of $\mathcal{P}_i$.*

*Otherwise, we call the session **exposed**.*

Initially, $\mathcal{A}$ is given a set of honest users and makes use of its attack queries as described above. Eventually, $\mathcal{A}$ makes the following query.

TEST(sid^*)**:** Issues the final test. Once the adversary decides that they have enough data, they query the TEST oracle for a challenge. A random bit b is generated; if $b = 1$ then the adversary is given the session key, otherwise they receive a random key from the key space.

Before and after TEST(sid^*) is issued, the adversary is allowed to make adaptive queries, issuing oracle queries with the condition that it cannot expose the test session. By the definition of freshness, the TEST query requires that sid^* is completed. Eventually, $\mathcal{A}$ guesses a bit b'. We let $\mathsf{Succ}_{\mathcal{A}}(\Pi)$ be the event that $\mathcal{A}$ guesses $b' = b$, i.e. guesses the TEST bit b correctly, and define the advantage

$$\mathsf{Adv}(\mathcal{A}) = \left| Pr[\mathsf{Succ}_{\mathcal{A}}(\Pi)] - \frac{1}{2} \right|.$$

In this model, we define GKE security to be the following.

Definition 2. *A group key exchange is said to be a* **secure group key exchange (GKE)** *in the G-CK$^+$ security model if for any fair PPT adversary $\mathcal{A}$,*

1. *If two honest parties complete matching sessions, these sessions produce the same session key as output, except with at most negligible probability;*
2. *$\mathsf{Adv}(\mathcal{A})$ is negligible in security parameter 1^λ for the test session sid^*.*

Note that, for the sake of forward secrecy, the STATICREVEAL query is considered. If a group key exchange is secure in this model, it is said to have *forward security* or be *forward-secure*, i.e. revealing static keys does not expose previous session keys.

We make one more assumption on the security model w.r.t. the freshness of a session, however the specifics can only be stated after our protocol definition. See Note 3, Sect. 3, for the specifics.

2.2   Diffie-Hellman Key Exchange, Hard Problem, and Multicast Burmester-Desmedt GKE

In order to make our work abundantly clear, we give a description of the Diffie-Hellman (DH) key exchange protocol, the corresponding decisional hard problem, as well as the multicast Burmester-Desmedt (BDII) GKE, which our work generalizes and proves secure in a newer security model. Note that we have changed the descriptions slightly to fit our framework, but this does not affect the protocols or problem.

Let $\mathbb{Z}_q$ be the group of integers modulo q, i.e. $\mathbb{Z}_q = \mathbb{Z}/q\mathbb{Z} = \{0, 1, \ldots, q-1\}$. The Diffie-Hellman key exchange protocol is a one round, two-party key exchange protocol that consists of a security parameter 1^λ and a parameter generating algorithm Gen that, on input 1^λ, outputs a description of a cyclic group $\mathbb{G}$, its order q, and a generator $g \in \mathbb{G}$.

Definition 3 (DH key exchange). *For parties $\mathcal{P}_i$, $i = 0, 1$, the DH protocol is as follows:*

Setup: *For the security parameter 1^λ, Gen outputs to both parties the tuple of public parameters: $\mathfrak{P} = (\mathbb{G}, q, g) \leftarrow \mathsf{Gen}(1^\lambda)$.*
Publish: *Each party $\mathcal{P}_i$ chooses a uniform $x_i \xleftarrow{R} \mathbb{Z}_q$ as their secret key and computes $h_i = g^{x_i}$ as their public key, sending it to the other party.*
KeyGen: *Party $\mathcal{P}_i$, upon receiving key h_{1-i}, uses their own secret key to compute the shared key $k_i := h_{1-i}^{x_i}$.*

This protocol satisfies correctness, i.e. $k_0 = k_1 = k$.

It is well-known that the passive adversary (eavesdropper) security of the DH protocol reduces to the following (classically) hard problem, which we therefore state but do not show the reduction for.

Definition 4 (Decisional Diffie-Hellman (DDH) problem). *Given a tuple sampled with probability $1/2$ from one of the following two distributions:*

- *$(\mathfrak{P}, (g^{x_0}, g^{x_1}), k)$, where $\mathfrak{P} = (\mathbb{G}, q, g)$ for $\mathbb{G}$ a cyclic group with order q and generator g, where $x_0, x_1 \overset{R}{\leftarrow} \mathbb{Z}_q$ are sampled uniformly, and $k = g^{x_0 x_1} \in \mathbb{G}$ is the final key of the Diffie-Hellman key exchange protocol (Definition 3),*
- *$(\mathfrak{P}, (g^{x_0}, g^{x_1}), k')$, where $\mathfrak{P} = (\mathbb{G}, q, g)$ for $\mathbb{G}$ a cyclic group with order q and generator g, where $x_0, x_1 \overset{R}{\leftarrow} \mathbb{Z}_q$ are sampled uniformly, and $z \overset{R}{\leftarrow} \mathbb{Z}_q$ is uniformly sampled such that $k' = g^z$ is uniformly distributed in $\mathbb{G}$,*

determine from which distribution the tuple is sampled.

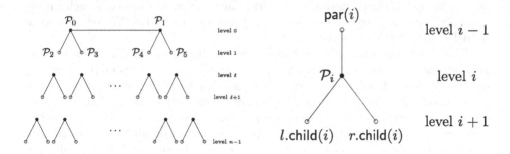

Fig. 1. Binary tree structure

Fig. 2. The neighbours of $\mathcal{P}_i$: Parent and children.

For BDII, the parties are assumed to be arranged in two binary trees, connected at the roots (see Fig. 1). This means that excepting the leaves of the tree, each party $\mathcal{P}_i$ has a parent $par(i)$, left child $l.child(i)$, and right child $r.child(i)$ - the *neighbours* of $\mathcal{P}_i$ (see Fig. 2). We let $ancestors(i)$ be the set of indexes of all ancestors of a party $\mathcal{P}_i$, including i but having removed 0 and 1. $\mathcal{P}_0$ and $\mathcal{P}_1$ are assumed to be parents of each other. Assume that for the protocol, n parties $\mathcal{P}_0, \mathcal{P}_1, \ldots, \mathcal{P}_{n-1}$ wish to generate a shared key.

Protocol 1 (BDII). *We assume there exists a set of n parties arranged in a binary tree. Consider the following protocol.*

Setup: *Takes a security parameter 1^λ and outputs a prime p and generator g for a group of order p.*

Publish₁: *Each $\mathcal{P}_i$ computes $z_i = g^{r_i}$ for a secretly chosen, uniformly random $r_i \xleftarrow{R} \mathbb{Z}_p^*$ and sends it to its neighbours.*

Publish₂: *Each $\mathcal{P}_i$ computes both $x_{l.child(i)} = \left(\frac{z_{par(i)}}{z_{l.child(i)}}\right)^{r_i} = g^{r_i r_{par(i)} - r_i r_{l.child(i)}}$*

and $x_{r.child(i)} = \left(\frac{z_{par(i)}}{z_{r.child(i)}}\right)^{r_i} = g^{r_i r_{par(i)} - r_i r_{r.child(i)}}$, and multicasts these to all its left and right descendants, respectively.

KeyGen: *Each $\mathcal{P}_i$ computes a shared key $K = (z_{par(i)})^{r_i} \cdot \prod_{j \in ancestors(i)} x_j = g^{r_0 r_1}$.*

Theorem 2 (Security of BDII [7]). *Assuming the DDH problem over $\mathbb{G}$ is hard, BDII is a secure GKE protocol.*

2.3 Generic Two-Party 0/1-Interactive Key Exchange and Hard Problem

The following generic key exchange protocol definition is based on the Diffie-Hellman key exchange [8], SIDH key exchange [9], and R-LWE key exchange with Peikert's tweak [14,16]. As the latter two may not be generally well-known, and as we use them as examples, we have included descriptions of each in our appendix, to wit, SIDH exchange in Appendix 1 and R-LWE key exchange with Peikert's tweak in Appendix 2.

Public-key key exchange protocols are usually categorized as either being non-interactive or interactive. Both types begin with some handshaking: agreeing on a set of common and public parameters, which is usually assumed to be output to each party by a parameter generator, before any actual calculation begins. In a non-interactive protocol, parties then randomly choose a secret key and output a public key. They may then retrieve the other party's public key at leisure and calculate the shared key. In an interactive protocol, after an initial public key is published, a round occurs wherein a party calculates a new public key using at least the initial public key of the other party. Yet another interaction round (by the party having the initial public key) may then occur, using this newest public key (if the newest public key is not used, we may consider the public key calculated to be part of the initial round, since all used information was already available). Such rounds may be repeated as necessary, until both parties are able to calculate a shared key.

As non-interactive key exchanges are not general enough for our purposes, and interactive protocols too general, we will need an inchoate concept of interaction. For this purpose, we define an encompassing concept, a "0/1-interactive key exchange" (0/1-IKE). This definition encompasses non-interactive key exchanges (0-IKEs) and once-interactive key exchanges, 1-IKEs (or "one-sided" interactive key exchanges, as only one party is expected to publish a new public key, related to the other party's public key). Our definition can be generalized to arbitrary n, but as our main results only hold for $n = 0, 1$, we restrict our definition to these values. This also significantly simplifies our notation throughout.

In the below protocol, for the security parameter 1^λ, we consider the algorithm Gen that generates the public parameters for the key exchange. Furthermore, we consider the algorithms: secret key generators $\mathsf{Sec}, \mathsf{Sec'}$, public key generators $\mathsf{Pub}, \mathsf{Pub'}$, and Key_I and Key_A, the inactive party and active party final key generators, respectively.

Protocol 3 (0/1-interactive key exchange (0/1-IKE)). *The parties $\mathcal{P}_0$ and $\mathcal{P}_1$, generate a two-party key exchange protocol Π as follows:*

Setup: *For the security parameter 1^λ, Gen outputs to both parties the tuple of public parameters:*

$$\mathfrak{P} = (\mathfrak{P}_0, \mathfrak{P}_1) \xleftarrow{R} \mathsf{Gen}(1^\lambda),$$

where $\mathfrak{P}_0$ and $\mathfrak{P}_1$ are party-specific tuples of public values.

Publish: *Each party chooses a random secret key and uses it to compute a public key:*

$$sk_0 \xleftarrow{R} \mathsf{Sec}(\mathfrak{P}_0), \quad pk_0 \leftarrow \mathsf{Pub}(sk_0, \mathfrak{P}_0),$$

$$sk_1 \xleftarrow{R} \mathsf{Sec}(\mathfrak{P}_1), \quad pk_1 \leftarrow \mathsf{Pub}(sk_1, \mathfrak{P}_1),$$

where $sk_0, sk_1 \in \mathcal{K}_S$ and $pk_0, pk_1 \in \mathcal{K}_P$, i.e. elements of the primary secret key and public key spaces, respectively. Each party then sends their public key to the other party.

Interact: *This round can be activated by either party. Designate the activating party the active party, $\mathcal{P}_A$, and the other the inactive party, $\mathcal{P}_I$ (for example, $\mathcal{P}_A := \mathcal{P}_1$ and $\mathcal{P}_I := \mathcal{P}_0$). Party $\mathcal{P}_A$, upon receiving pk_I, generates a second secret key and computes a second public key:*

$$sk_A' \xleftarrow{R} \mathsf{Sec'}(sk_A, pk_I, \mathfrak{P}_A), \quad pk_A' \leftarrow \mathsf{Pub'}(sk_A, sk_A', pk_I, \mathfrak{P}_A),$$

where $sk_A' \in \mathcal{K}_{S'}$ and $pk_A' \in \mathcal{K}_{P'}$, i.e. elements of the secondary secret key and public key spaces, respectively. $\mathcal{P}_A$ sends pk_A' to $\mathcal{P}_I$ and continues on to the next step.

KeyGen: *After receiving the necessary public keys, the final keys are calculated in the following ways.*

$$\mathcal{P}_I : k_I \leftarrow \mathsf{Key}_I(sk_I, pk_A, pk_A', \mathfrak{P}_I), \qquad \mathcal{P}_A : k_A \leftarrow \mathsf{Key}_A(sk_A, sk_A', pk_I, \mathfrak{P}_A),$$

where k_I and k_A are elements of the final key space $\mathcal{K}$.

If $k_I = k_A$, with non-negligible probability, then we say that the protocol satisfies **correctness**, *i.e. $k = k_I = k_A$ is a shared key.*

Note 1. Notes on the above key exchange protocol.

1. In a non-interactive key exchange, the **Interact** round is simply omitted, such that sk_A' and pk_A' are empty values, resulting in final keys:

$$\mathcal{P}_I : k_I \leftarrow \mathsf{Key}_I(sk_I, pk_A, \mathfrak{P}_I), \qquad \mathcal{P}_A : k_A \leftarrow \mathsf{Key}_A(sk_A, pk_I, \mathfrak{P}_A),$$

as expected.

2. Not all values are necessarily used in each of the algorithms but are present
for the sake of generality. It could also, for example, be the case that only
one party publishes a public key in the **Publish** round, while the other party
acts as the active party in the **Interact** round (leaving pk_A, and possibly
sk_A, as empty values). Some values may also be equal, such as $\mathfrak{P}_0 = \mathfrak{P}_1$ or
$K_S = K_{S'}$, depending on the specific key exchange, but have been indexed
here for the sake of generality. The definition is left as general as possible to
include as many key exchanges as possible, past and future.

Using the above notation, we define the generic decisional hard problem
that we will need for our security reduction later. This definition is inspired to
encompass the decisional problems used to prove the indistinguishability property of KEs and GKEs. It is primarily based on the (decisional) hardness problems for DH, SIDH, and R-LWE with Peikert's tweak, i.e. the decisional Diffie-
Hellman (DDH), supersingular DDH (SSDDH), and DDH-like problems (stated
in Sect. 2.2, Appendix 1, and Appendix 2, respectively).

Definition 5 (Generic decisional hard (GDH) problem). *Consider a*
(group) key exchange protocol Π satisfying correctness. Given a tuple sampled
with probability $1/2$ from one of the following two distributions:

- *$(\mathfrak{P}, \mathbf{pk}, k)$, where $\mathfrak{P}$ and $\mathbf{pk}$ are the party-specific public values and keys in*
  Π, and $k \in \mathcal{K}$ is the corresponding key in the final key space for Π,
- *$(\mathfrak{P}, \mathbf{pk}, k')$, where $\mathfrak{P}$ and $\mathbf{pk}$ are the party-specific public values and keys in*
  Π, and $k' \in \mathcal{K}'$ is a key sampled uniformly at random from $\mathcal{K}' \supseteq \mathcal{K}$,

determine from which distribution the tuple is sampled. If any probabilistic
polynomial-time adversary solves this problem with at most negligible probability,
*we say that the GDH problem is **hard**.*

Remark 1. The problem is considered in regards to the computational ability
of the adversaries such that hardness w.r.t. classical/quantum/etc. adversaries
gives corresponding classical/quantum/etc. hardness.

Note 2. For the 0-IKE, we generally have $(\mathfrak{P}, \mathbf{pk}, k) = (\mathfrak{P}, (pk_0, pk_1), k)$. For the
1-IKE: $\mathfrak{P} = (\mathfrak{P}_0, \mathfrak{P}_1)$ and $\mathbf{pk} = (\mathbf{pk}_I, \mathbf{pk}_A) = (pk_0, (pk_1, pk'_A))$.
    For an n-party GKE, we could potentially have

$$(\mathfrak{P}, \mathbf{pk}, k) = ((\mathfrak{P}_0, \mathfrak{P}_1, \cdots, \mathfrak{P}_{n-1}), (\mathbf{pk}_0, \mathbf{pk}_1, \cdots, \mathbf{pk}_{n-1}), k).$$

To ease the reader into these generic definitions and as an overview, we have
compiled Table 1 below. In the table, we consider the DH, SIDH, and R-LWE
with Peikert's tweak key exchanges, from left to right. In the upper half, we
note whether the KE is 0-interactive or 1-interactive and then list the protocol
specific values for $\mathfrak{P}_0, \mathfrak{P}_1, sk_0, sk_1, pk_0, pk_1, sk'_A, pk'_A, k_I$, and k_A, if applicable. In
the second half, we do the same for the respective hard problems DDH, SSDDH,
and DDH-like. See Sect. 2.2, Appendix 1, and Appendix 2 for the respective
protocol and hard problem details.

Table 1. Examples of key exchanges in the 0/1-IKE notation and their corresponding hard problems.

Key exchanges			
	DH [8]	SIDH [9]	R-LWE w/ Peikert tweak [14,16]
0/1	0	0	1
$\mathfrak{P}_0$	$(\mathbb{G}, q, g)$	$(p, E, \{P_0, Q_0\}, \{P_1, Q_1\})$	(n, R, q, R_q, χ, a)
$\mathfrak{P}_1$	Same as $\mathfrak{P}_0$	$(p, E, \{P_1, Q_1\}, \{P_0, Q_0\})$	Same as $\mathfrak{P}_0$
sk_0	$x_0 \xleftarrow{R} \mathbb{Z}_q$	$r_0 \xleftarrow{R} \mathbb{Z}/\ell_0^{e_0}\mathbb{Z}$	$s_0, e_0 \xleftarrow{R} \chi$
sk_1	$x_1 \xleftarrow{R} \mathbb{Z}_q$	$r_1 \xleftarrow{R} \mathbb{Z}/\ell_1^{e_1}\mathbb{Z}$	$s_1, e_1 \xleftarrow{R} \chi$
pk_0	$h_0 = g^{x_0}$	$(E_0, \phi_0(P_1), \phi_0(Q_1))$	$b_0 = as_0 + e_0$
pk_1	$h_1 = g^{x_1}$	$(E_1, \phi_1(P_0), \phi_1(Q_0))$	$b_1 = as_1 + e_1$
sk'_A	None	None	$e'_1 \xleftarrow{R} \chi$
pk'_A	None	None	$c = \langle \bar{v} \rangle_{2q,2}$
k_I	$h_1^{x_0}$	$j(E_{0,1})$	$\mathbf{rec}(2b_1 s_0, c)$
k_A	$h_0^{x_1}$	$j(E_{1,0})$	$\lceil \bar{v} \rfloor_{2q,2}$
Hard problems			
	DDH [8]	SSDDH [9]	DDH-like [1]
$\mathfrak{P}$	$(\mathbb{G}, q, g)$	$\mathfrak{P}_i = (p, E, \{P_i, Q_i\}, \{P_{i-1}, Q_{i-1}\})$ for $i = 0, 1$	(n, R, q, R_q, χ, a)
pk	(h_0, h_1)	(pk_0, pk_1)	$(b_0, (b_1, c))$
k	$g^{x_0 x_1}$ or g^z for $z \xleftarrow{R} \mathbb{Z}_q$	$E_{0,1} \cong E/\langle P_0 + [r_0]Q_0, P_1 + [r_1]Q_1\rangle$ or $E_x \cong E/\langle P_0 + [r'_0]Q_0, P_1 + [r'_1]Q_1\rangle$ for $r'_i \xleftarrow{R} \mathbb{Z}/\ell_i^{e_i}\mathbb{Z}, i = 0, 1$	$\lceil \bar{v} \rfloor_{2q,2}$ or $k \xleftarrow{R} \{0,1\}^n$

3   Group Key Exchange Compilers

For our group key exchange compiler, it is absolutely crucial that the key space for the final keys, $\mathcal{K}$, is a subset of a group $\mathbb{G} = (\mathcal{G}, \cdot)$, i.e. a group with multiplicative operation,[3] so that we may manipulate final keys by using inverses and the group operation. It could also be a subset of a ring, but we require only the group superset property.

We would now like to define the group key exchange compiler. In order to do so, we introduce the concept of arranging parties in a binary tree. Assume that from a set of parties, $\mathbb{P}$, we have $n \geq 2$ parties $\mathcal{P}_0, \mathcal{P}_1, \ldots, \mathcal{P}_{n-1}$ that wish to generate a shared key. The parties are arranged in a binary tree, indexing the parties in ascending order from the top-leftmost root, going right, and continuing down the tree level-wise, not branch-wise (see Fig. 1). We assume that all parties are unique. Excepting the leaves of the tree, each party $\mathcal{P}_i$ has a parent $\mathsf{par}(i)$, left child $l.\mathsf{child}(i)$, and right child $r.\mathsf{child}(i)$, the *neighbours* of $\mathcal{P}_i$ (see Fig. 2).

---

[3] Note that "$+$" could be used instead, but the notation is pedagogical for our compiler. We also do not assume that the group is abelian. Furthermore, note that any set S can be made into a group, namely the Free Group, or Universal Group, generated by S, so this requirement is trivially satisfied. For computation purposes however, we assume that the group operation is efficient.

We let ancestors(i) be the set of indexes of all the direct ancestors of a party $\mathcal{P}_i$, including i but having removed 0 and 1. $\mathcal{P}_0$ and $\mathcal{P}_1$ are assumed to be parents of each other.

We define **score** recursively as the following: $score(0) := 0$, $score(1) := 1$, and $score(i) = score(\mathsf{par}(i)) + 1$, where $i \geq 2$ is the index of the party $\mathcal{P}_i$. We assume that the score is calculated individually by the parties when the graph is fixed and does not occur as a bandwidth or computational cost in our protocol. Using this score, we define the map $\iota = \iota(i) := score(i) \pmod 2$. Score itself will not be used explicitly, but ι is used in our security proof for Theorem 5 below.

The group key exchange compiler (GKE-C) for n parties, Π_n, given below, takes as input a security parameter 1^λ and a 0/1-IKE protocol, Π, (using the same security parameter) including the algorithms: Gen, Sec, Sec$'$, Pub, Pub$'$, and Key$_I$, Key$_A$, the **public parameters generator**, the **secret key generators**, the **public key generators**, and the **final key generators**. The GKE-C outputs a shared key $k \in \mathcal{K}$ where $\mathcal{K} \subseteq \mathcal{G}$ is the same key space as the final key space of Π and is a subset of a group $(\mathcal{G}, \cdot)$.

The **multi-party parameter generator** algorithm, Gen$_{\mathsf{mp}}$, is used to decide public parameters for the group key exchange protocol. It takes as input the security parameter, 1^λ, the number of parties, n, and an 0/1-IKE protocol, Π, and outputs a tuple consisting of public parameters for each party $\mathcal{P}_i$ and a binary tree for the n parties.

For security reasons to be discussed in Note 3 below, we distinguish a set of *root parties* during the protocol.

Protocol 4 (Group key exchange compiler (GKE-C)). *Parties $\mathcal{P}_i$, for $i = 0, 1, \ldots, n - 1$, generate a group key exchange protocol Π_n as follows:*

Setup: *For the security parameter 1^λ, number of parties n, and two-party 0/1-IKE protocol Π, the algorithm outputs to each party $\mathcal{P}_i$ the tuple:*

$$\mathfrak{P} = ((\mathfrak{P}_0, \mathfrak{P}_1), \Gamma) \leftarrow \mathsf{Gen}_{\mathsf{mp}}(1^\lambda, n, \Pi),$$

where $(\mathfrak{P}_0, \mathfrak{P}_1)$ is as given by $\mathsf{Gen}(1^\lambda)$ in Π and Γ is a binary tree. Set the root parties to be $\mathfrak{R} := \{\mathcal{P}_0, \mathcal{P}_1\}$.

Publish$_1$: *Each $\mathcal{P}_i$ chooses a random secret key $sk_i \xleftarrow{R} \mathsf{Sec}(\mathfrak{P}_\iota)$ and generates a public key $pk_i \leftarrow \mathsf{Pub}(sk_i, \mathfrak{P}_\iota)$. $\mathcal{P}_i$ then multicasts its public key to its neighbours (parent and up to two children).*

If using a $1 - IKE$, each child acts as the active party with its parent acting as the inactive party.[4] Regardless, the parties continue and complete their respective key exchanges, culminating in the shared keys for each i: $k_{\mathsf{par}(i),i}$, $k_{l.\mathsf{child}(i),i}$, and $k_{r.\mathsf{child}(i),i}$, between $\mathcal{P}_i$ and the parent, left child, and right child, respectively.

Publish$_2$: *Each $\mathcal{P}_i$ with children computes $x_{l.\mathsf{child}(i)} = (k_{l.\mathsf{child}(i),i})^{-1} \cdot k_{\mathsf{par}(i),i}$ and $x_{r.\mathsf{child}(i)} = (k_{r.\mathsf{child}(i),i})^{-1} \cdot k_{\mathsf{par}(i),i}$, and multicasts these to all its left and right descendants, respectively.*

---

[4] This means that at most a single secondary key is chosen per party as each party has only a single parent.

KeyGen: *Each P_i computes a shared key $K_i = k_{par(i),i} \cdot \prod_{j \in ancestors(i)} x_j = k_{0,1} = K$.*

Proposition 1 (Correctness). *Each party in the group key exchange compiler (GKE-C) (Protocol 4) computes the same key $K = k_{0,1}$, with non-negligible probability.*

Proof. This can be seen by induction. Obviously, $K = K_0 = K_1 = k_{0,1}$ with non-negligible probability. Assume that $K_{par(i)} = K$, then, as

$$K_{par(i)} = k_{par(par(i)),par(i)} \cdot \prod_{j \in ancestors(par(i))} x_j,$$

we have that

$$K_i = k_{par(i),i} \cdot \prod_{j \in ancestors(i)} x_j = k_{par(i),i} \cdot (k_{i,par(i)})^{-1} \cdot k_{par(par(i)),par(i)} \cdot \prod_{j \in ancestors(par(i))} x_j$$

$$= K_{par(i)} = K,$$

with non-negligible probability.   □

The shared key of the group is simply the shared key of the initial parties P_0 and P_1.

Note 3. The security of the GKE-C protocol relies on a reduction to the GDH problem from Definition 5. For this purpose, we must assume that neither the static secret keys of the root parties (see Setup description in Protocol 4) in all sessions nor the ephemeral secret keys in the test session, are revealed by any attack query done by the adversary. Although this additional assumption means that our security model is slightly weaker than both the MSU model (also called the G-eCK+ model), the Bresson-Manulis model [3], and the model which we consider in this paper, G-CK+, it still allows for strong corruptions of ephemeral secrets such that it remains a strong model, stronger than the security models given by Bresson et al. [2] and Katz and Yung [15], which do not address (strong) corruptions of ephemeral secrets.

This addition would also be needed to prove the security of the original Desmedt-Lange-Burmester [7] GKE and authenticated GKE compiler in the G-CK+ model.

Remark 2. It is possible to define the GKE-C to work with variable children for each node, but for the ease of proof and explanation, we consider all nodes to have the same number of children, excepting the leaves and initial two parties, and we set that number to two children.

In order to prove that our GKE-C is secure, we show a reduction to the GDH problem. We do this by showing that breaking the GDH problem for the GKE-C equates to breaking the GDH problem for the underlying two-party 0/1-IKE. Because of this, be mindful that our GKE-C only has the same security as the underlying 0/1-IKE.

Theorem 5. *Suppose we have an 0/1-IKE protocol, Π, with security parameter 1^λ and algorithms* Gen, Sec, Sec', Pub, Pub', *and* Key_I, Key_A. *If the 0/1-IKE protocol satisfies correctness and reduces to an instance of the GDH problem that is hard, then GKE-C, with security parameter 1^λ and using Π as its underlying 0/1-IKE, is a secure group key exchange.*

Proof. We must show that the protocol in Protocol 4 satisfies the security notion given in Definition 2. For the proof, we consider the more complicated case of using a 1-IKE. The first requirement is satisfied by the correctness shown in Proposition 1.

For the second requirement, assume that there exists a (not necessarily classical) polynomial-time adversary $\mathcal{A}$ with non-negligible advantage $\mathsf{Adv}(\mathcal{A}) = \varepsilon$, distinguishing between the correct final key in a GKE-C instance and a random key in the key space, which is by definition the same as that of the underlying 1-IKE. We build a polynomial-time distinguisher $\mathcal{D}$ for the GDH problem (Definition 5) for an instance of 1-IKE, i.e. the security of GKE-C reduces to the security of 1-IKE. The distinguisher is given in Algorithm 1.

As an analysis of our distinguishing algorithm, we note the following. For the ℓ'th session, using the public value $\mathfrak{P}_0$ for $\mathcal{P}_0$ and $\mathfrak{P}_{\iota(2)} = \mathfrak{P}_1$ for $\mathcal{P}_2$, the algorithm completes a 1-IKE instance with the secret key $\mathbf{sk}_2 = (sk_2, sk_2')$ of party $\mathcal{P}_2$, giving the shared key $k_{0,2} = k_{2,0}$, with non-negligible probability, as we have assumed that the 1-IKE satisfies correctness. Likewise, it finds $k_{0,3} = k_{3,0}$, using $\mathbf{sk}_3 = (sk_3, sk_3')$ and the public values $\mathfrak{P}_{\iota(3)}$ of $\mathcal{P}_3$. Using the public values $\mathfrak{P}_1$ for $\mathcal{P}_1$, and public values $\mathfrak{P}_{\iota(4)}$, it completes a 1-IKE instance with the secret key $\mathbf{sk}_4 = (sk_4, sk_4')$ of party $\mathcal{P}_4$, giving the shared key $k_{1,4} = k_{4,1}$, and likewise $k_{1,5} = k_{5,1}$ using $\mathbf{sk}_5 = (sk_5, sk_5')$ and the public values $\mathfrak{P}_{\iota(5)}$. All other shared keys may be computed as the secret keys for $\mathcal{P}_i$ are known for $i = 2, \ldots, n-1$.

As the $\mathbf{sk}_i$ are chosen uniformly at random for $i \geq 2$, the distribution of the $\mathbf{pk}_i = (pk_i, pk_i')$ and $\mathbf{x}_i' = (x_{l.\mathsf{child}(i)}', x_{r.\mathsf{child}(i)}')$ are identical to that in a GKE-C instance.

The transcript given to $\mathcal{A}$ by $\mathcal{D}$ is $(\mathbf{pk}_0, \ldots, \mathbf{pk}_{n-1}, \mathbf{x}_0', \mathbf{x}_1', \ldots, \mathbf{x}_{n-1}')$, where we assign a blank value for the $\mathbf{x}'$ value when there is no child.

If the ℓ'th session is $\mathcal{A}$'s test session, then $\mathcal{D}$ is issuing $K = k$, as $\mathcal{A}$'s test key. If K is a valid final key for the GKE-C, then $k = K = k_{0,1} = k_{1,0}$, i.e. $(\mathfrak{P} = (\mathfrak{P}_0, \mathfrak{P}_1), \mathbf{pk} = (pk_0, (pk_1, pk_A')), k)$ is indeed a valid GDH tuple for the underlying two-party 1-IKE protocol Π and can be distinguished.

If the test session is *not* the ℓ'th session, then $\mathcal{D}$ outputs a random bit, i.e. it has advantage 0. If the test session *is* the ℓ'th session, which happens with probability $1/\eta$, then $\mathcal{A}$ will succeed with advantage ε. Hence, the final advantage of the GDH distinguisher $\mathcal{D}$ is ε/η, which is non-negligible. $\square$

3.1   Peer-to-Peer Group Key Exchange Compiler

Like Desmedt, Lange, and Burmester [7], we also give a peer-to-peer version of our compiler. Such a peer-to-peer version is sequential and can be used when memory and communication complexity needs to be reduced due to, for example,

Algorithm 1. GDH distinguisher, $\mathcal{D}$.

Input: $\mathfrak{P} = (\mathfrak{P}_0, \mathfrak{P}_1), \mathbf{pk} = (\mathbf{pk}_I, \mathbf{pk}_A) = (pk_0, (pk_1, pk'_A))$, and k

1: $\ell \leftarrow \{1, \ldots, \theta\}$ uniformly chosen, where θ is an upper bound on the number of sessions activated by $\mathcal{A}$ in any interaction.

2: Invoke $\mathcal{A}$ and simulate protocol to $\mathcal{A}$, except for the ℓ'th activated protocol session.

3: For the ℓ'th session:

4:    Set the public parameters as $(\mathfrak{P} = (\mathfrak{P}_0, \mathfrak{P}_1), \Gamma)$, where Γ is an n-party binary graph.

5:    Using $\mathcal{A}$ to relay messages (such as public values), simulate the 0/1-IKE between $\mathcal{P}_0$ and $\mathcal{P}_1$ using $(\mathfrak{P}_0, \mathfrak{P}_1)$, i.e. by setting the inactive party to be $\mathcal{P}_0$ and the active party to be $\mathcal{P}_1$.

   Generate $sk_i \overset{R}{\leftarrow} \mathsf{Sec}(\mathfrak{P}_\iota)$ uniformly at random for $i = 2, \ldots, n-1$, and set $pk_i \leftarrow \mathsf{Pub}(sk_i, \mathfrak{P}_\iota)$. Simulate multicasting using $\mathcal{A}$ and follow protocol Π for each $\mathcal{P}_i$ and neighbour, letting the parent in each pair act as the inactive party and the children act as the active parties, generating secondary secret and public keys as needed.

   Eventually, for each neighbour of $\mathcal{P}_i$, $i = 2, \cdots, n-1$, there exists shared keys available to $\mathcal{P}_i$: $k_{\mathsf{par}(i),i}$, $k_{l.\mathsf{child}(i),i}$, and $k_{r.\mathsf{child}(i),i}$.

6:    Set

$$x'_{l.\mathsf{child}(0)} := (k_{0,2})^{-1} \cdot k, \qquad x'_{r.\mathsf{child}(0)} := (k_{0,3})^{-1} \cdot k,$$

$$x'_{l.\mathsf{child}(1)} := (k_{1,4})^{-1} \cdot k, \qquad x'_{r.\mathsf{child}(1)} := (k_{1,5})^{-1} \cdot k, \text{ and}$$

$$x'_{l.\mathsf{child}(i)} := (k_{l.\mathsf{child}(i),i})^{-1} \cdot k_{\mathsf{par}(i),i},$$

$$x'_{r.\mathsf{child}(i)} := (k_{r.\mathsf{child}(i),i})^{-1} \cdot k_{\mathsf{par}(i),i},$$

   for $i \geq 2$ where $\mathcal{P}_i$ is not a leaf in Γ. Simulate multicasting for each applicable $\mathcal{P}_i$.

7: **if** the ℓ'th session is chosen by $\mathcal{A}$ as the test session **then**

8:    Provide $\mathcal{A}$ as the answer to the test query,

9:    $d \leftarrow \mathcal{A}$'s output

10: **else**

11:    $d \overset{R}{\leftarrow} \{0, 1\}$ uniformly at random.

Output: d

bandwidth restrictions. We call our protocol the peer-to-peer group key exchange compiler, P2P-GKE-C, and note that the number of rounds and the communication complexity switches, the communication complexity becoming constant and the number of rounds becoming logarithmic. The differences between the protocols begins after the **Publish₁** round.

In the below protocol, the peer-to-peer group key exchange compiler (P2P-GKE-C) for n parties, Π_n^{P2P}, takes as input a security parameter 1^λ and a 0/1-IKE protocol, Π, (using the same security parameter) including the algorithms: $\mathsf{Gen}, \mathsf{Sec}, \mathsf{Sec}', \mathsf{Pub}, \mathsf{Pub}'$, and $\mathsf{Key}_I, \mathsf{Key}_A$, the **public parameters generator**, the **secret key generators**, the **public key generators**, and the **final key generators**. The P2P-GKE-C outputs a shared key $k \in \mathcal{K}$ where $\mathcal{K} \subseteq \mathcal{G}$ is the same key space as the final key space of Π and is a subset of a group $(\mathcal{G}, \cdot)$.

The **multi-party parameter generator** algorithm, $\mathsf{Gen}_{\mathsf{mp}}$, is used to decide public parameters for the group key exchange protocol. It takes as input the security parameter, 1^λ, the number of parties, n, and an 0/1-IKE protocol, Π, and outputs a tuple consisting of public parameters for each party $\mathcal{P}_i$ and a binary tree, Γ, for the n parties.

Protocol 6 (P2P-GKE-C). *The parties $\mathcal{P}_i$, for $i = 0, 1, \ldots, n-1$, generate a group key exchange protocol Π_n^{P2P} as follows:*

Setup: *For the security parameter 1^λ, number of parties n, and two-party 0/1-IKE protocol Π, the algorithm outputs to each party $\mathcal{P}_i$ the tuple:*

$$\mathfrak{P} = ((\mathfrak{P}_0, \mathfrak{P}_1), \Gamma, sID) \leftarrow \mathsf{Gen}_{\mathsf{mp}}(1^\lambda, n, \Pi),$$

where $(\mathfrak{P}_0, \mathfrak{P}_1)$ is as given by $\mathsf{Gen}(1^\lambda)$ in Π and Γ is a binary tree. Set the root parties to be $\mathfrak{R} := \{\mathcal{P}_0, \mathcal{P}_1\}$.

Publish$_1$: *Each $\mathcal{P}_i$ chooses a random secret key $sk_i \xleftarrow{R} \mathsf{Sec}(\mathfrak{P}_\iota)$ and generates a public key $pk_i \leftarrow \mathsf{Pub}(sk_i, \mathfrak{P}_\iota)$. $\mathcal{P}_i$ then multicasts its public key to its neighbours (parent and up to two children).*

If using a 1-IKE, each child acts as the active party with its parent acting as the inactive party.[5] Regardless, the parties continue and complete their respective key exchanges, culminating in the shared keys for each i: $k_{\mathsf{par}(i),i}$, $k_{l.\mathsf{child}(i),i}$, and $k_{r.\mathsf{child}(i),i}$, between $\mathcal{P}_i$ and the parent, left child, and right child, respectively.

Publish$_2$: *Parties $\mathcal{P}_0$ and $\mathcal{P}_1$ have already computed the same final key $K = k_{0,1} = K_0 = K_1$ (with non-negligible probability) and send*

$$x_{l.\mathsf{child}(0)} = K \cdot (k_{l.\mathsf{child}(0),0})^{-1}, \text{ respectively, } x_{l.\mathsf{child}(1)} = K \cdot (k_{l.\mathsf{child}(1),1})^{-1}, \text{ and}$$

$$x_{r.\mathsf{child}(0)} = K \cdot (k_{r.\mathsf{child}(0),0})^{-1}, \text{ respectively, } x_{r.\mathsf{child}(1)} = K \cdot (k_{r.\mathsf{child}(1),1})^{-1},$$

to their left, respectively right, children.[6]

KeyGen and Publish$_3$: *Upon receiving $x_{\mathsf{par}(i)}$, $\mathcal{P}_i$ computes the final key*

$$K_i = x_{\mathsf{par}(i)} \cdot k_{\mathsf{par}(i),i}.$$

Each party $\mathcal{P}_i$ with children (this excepts the leaves of Γ), then computes $x_{l.\mathsf{child}(i)} = K_i \cdot (k_{l.\mathsf{child}(i),i})^{-1}$ and $x_{r.\mathsf{child}(i)} = K_i \cdot (k_{r.\mathsf{child}(i),i})^{-1}$ and multicasts this to its left, respectively right, child.

It is easy to see that this protocol satisfies correctness: We have that $K_0 = K_1 = K$ with non-negligible probability. Assume that $\mathcal{P}_{\mathsf{par}(i)}$ obtained the final key $K_{\mathsf{par}(i)} = K$. For party $\mathcal{P}_i$, we have $K_i = x_{\mathsf{par}(i)} \cdot k_{\mathsf{par}(i),i} = K_{\mathsf{par}(i)} \cdot (k_{i,\mathsf{par}(i)})^{-1} \cdot k_{\mathsf{par}(i),i} = K$, with non-negligible probability. Security follows from an analogous argument to that of the proof for Theorem 5.

---

[5] This means that at most a single secondary key is chosen per party as each party has only a single parent.

[6] The products in these x values could also be reversed, as long as the rest of the procedure remains consistent, for example in the **KeyGen and Publish$_3$** round, regardless of the commutativity of the group.

Theorem 7. *Suppose we have an 0/1-IKE protocol, Π, with security parameter 1^λ and algorithms* Gen, Sec, Sec$'$, Pub, Pub$'$, *and* Key$_I$, Key$_A$. *If the 0/1-IKE protocol satisfies correctness and reduces to an instance of the GDH problem, then P2P-GKE-C, with security parameter 1^λ and using Π as its underlying 0/1-IKE, is a secure group key exchange.*

Parties in P2P-GKE-C have the same final key as in GKE-C, namely the shared key of parties $\mathcal{P}_0$ and $\mathcal{P}_1$.

As our compilers require a 0/1-IKE and GDH problem, for the 0/1-IKEs given in this article and their hard problems, Table 2 gives an overview of the (literature of the) GKEs that result from them.

Table 2. Examples of GKE-C compiled GKEs.

	BDII [7]	SIT [11]	Tree-R-LWE-GKE [12]
0/1-IKE	DH [8]	SIDH [9]	R-LWE w/ Peikert's tweak [14,16]
GDH problem	DDH [8]	SSDDH [9]	DDH-like [1]

4 Complexity Analysis

In this section, we consider the computation and communication complexities of our group key exchange compilers.

Our chosen comparison parameters are: the number of rounds, the number of public values, the communication complexity, and the number of values stored until the final key computation, i.e. the memory complexity. The number of rounds is taken to be the maximum number of times any party must wait for information from other parties in order to proceed (this includes sequential rounds that a party may not be directly involved in). The number of public values is taken to be the maximum number of public values (keys, etc.) computed and multicast per party (without multiplicity). The communication complexity considers the maximum number of broadcast/multicast messages received by any party in one call of the protocol.[7] The memory complexity takes into account the maximum number of stored values needed to compute the final key.

In this paper, we have assumed a balanced tree, indeed a binary tree, i.e. where each non-leaf node has two children, in which case both compilers have a maximum complexity $O(\log_2 n)$. Table 3 shows comparable parameters for our two GKE compilers.

---

[7] In doing so, we assume that multicasting a message does not depend on the number of receivers but that receiving l messages means that the receiver incurs a cost of l, even if all messages are received in a single round. The reason for this is that it takes into account that receiving messages requires being online and also storing said messages while multicasting is usually a one-time operation.

Table 3. Comparison of our GKE compilers. $\mathfrak{A}$ denotes a value from the underlying 0/1-IKE while $\mathfrak{G}$ denotes a value from the GKE-C.

Compiler	Rounds	Public	Communications	Memories
GKE-C	$2\mathfrak{A} + \mathfrak{G}$	$2\mathfrak{A} + 2\mathfrak{G}$	$5\mathfrak{A} + (\log_2 n)\mathfrak{G}$	$\mathfrak{A} + (\log_2 n)\mathfrak{G}$
P2P-GKE-C	$2\mathfrak{A} + (\log_2 n)\mathfrak{G}$	$2\mathfrak{A} + 2\mathfrak{G}$	$5\mathfrak{A} + \mathfrak{G}$	$\mathfrak{A} + \mathfrak{G}$

For GKE-C, we have three rounds, as the 0/1-IKE public keys are exchanged in the first and second round, and group element products are multicast in the third round. The public values multicast by each party consist of the 0/1-IKE public key(s) and one group element product per child (or no product, in the case of the leaves). The multicast values received are the one 0/1-IKE public key of the parent and one for each child, as well as one group element product from each ancestor (minus itself, plus either $\mathcal{P}_0$ or $\mathcal{P}_1$), which is maximally $\log_2 n$, for a leaf. The values needed to compute the final key consist of one group element product from each ancestor (minus itself, plus either $\mathcal{P}_0$ or $\mathcal{P}_1$) as well as the 0/1-IKE key shared with the parent.

P2P-GKE-C, more or less, exchanges the number of rounds with the communication and memory complexity.

5   Concluding Remarks

We introduced definitions of generic two-party KEs, with up to one interaction, and generic decisional hard problems for (G)KEs. We then proposed our GKE compiler (GKE-C) based on these generic definitions and showed how the security of our compiler reduces to the security of the underlying two-party KE, which we assumed relied on the hardness of an underlying decisional problem. We also proposed a peer-to-peer GKE compiler (P2P-GKE-C).

We would like to note that both the GKE-C and P2P-GKE-C can be modified to have multiple children per node, e.g. $k > 2$ (giving $O(\log_k(n))$-complexity), but also modified to have a variable number of children per node, e.g. 2 for party $\mathcal{P}_2$ and 3 for party $\mathcal{P}_3$. This means that the tree can be built to take into consideration the computational power and memory capacity of individual nodes. It must be kept in mind that the compilers essentially turn a two-party ephemeral key into a static key for the duration of the GKE and as the security of the GKE relies on the security of the underlying two-party KE, static key vulnerabilities may be transferred to the GKE. However, due to our assumption for the root parties, this is of no concern as the security of the GKEs lie solely on the security of the secret values of the root parties.

We sincerely hope that the generality of our definitions and compilers inspires more research and publications towards generalizing current works and creating a system of cryptographic protocols such that regardless of the computational power paradigm that may come, we have a ready-set system of cryptography, ready to go.

Thanks and Acknowledgment. This work is partially supported by CREST (JPMJCR1404) at Japan Science and Technology Agency, enPiT(Education Network for Practical Information Technologies) at MEXT, and Innovation Platform for Society 5.0 at MEXT.

Appendix 1   SIDH Key Exchange and Hard Problem

We assume knowledge of elliptic curves. An isogeny may be understood as a non-zero rational homomorphism between two elliptic curves, generated by a subgroup of the first curve. Finding the isogeny between them is called the isogeny finding problem. We define the SIDH key exchange by Jao and De Feo [9, 13] in the form of the supersingular isogeny key encapsulation (SIKE[8]) protocol as given by Furukawa et al. in [10].

Consider the SIDH key exchange between parties $\mathcal{P}_0$ and $\mathcal{P}_1$. Given a security parameter 1^λ, Gen outputs $(p, E, \{P_0, Q_0\}, \{P_1, Q_1\})$, where $p = f\ell_0^{e_0}\ell_1^{e_1} \pm 1$ is prime for a small integer $f > 0$ and with $\ell_0^{e_0} \approx \ell_1^{e_1}$ (usually $\ell_0 = 2$ and $\ell_1 = 3$), E is a randomly chosen supersingular elliptic curve over $\mathbb{F}_{p^2}$ such that $\#E(\mathbb{F}_{p^2}) = (p\pm 1)^2$, and $\{P_i, Q_i\}$ is a randomly chosen basis of $E[\ell_i^{e_i}]$ for $i = 0, 1$.

Protocol 8 (Supersingular isogeny Diffie-Hellman (SIDH) key exchange [10]). *For parties $\mathcal{P}_0$ and $\mathcal{P}_1$, the SIDH protocol is as follows:*

Setup: *For the security parameter 1^λ, Gen outputs to both parties the tuple of public parameters:*

$$\mathfrak{P} = (\mathfrak{P}_0, \mathfrak{P}_1) = ((p, E, \{P_0, Q_0\}, \{P_1, Q_1\}), (p, E, \{P_1, Q_1\}, \{P_0, Q_0\})) \leftarrow \mathsf{Gen}(1^\lambda),$$

where $\mathfrak{P}_0, \mathfrak{P}_1$ are party-specific tuples.

Publish: *Each party $\mathcal{P}_i$, for $i = 0, 1$, chooses $r_i \xleftarrow{R} \mathbb{Z}/\ell_i^{e_i}\mathbb{Z}$ uniformly at random and computes $R_i := P_i + [r_i]Q_i$. Then it computes the isogeny $\phi_i : E \to E_i \cong E/\langle R_i \rangle$ having $\ker(\phi_i) = \langle R_i \rangle$, as well as the points $\phi_i(P_{1-i})$ and $\phi_i(Q_{1-i})$. $\mathcal{P}_i$ has secret and public keys*

$$sk_i := r_i \ and \ pk_i := (E_i, \phi_i(P_{1-i}), \phi_i(Q_{1-i})),$$

of which it sends pk_i to $\mathcal{P}_{1-i}$.

KeyGen: *Party $\mathcal{P}_i$ takes pk_{1-i} as input and computes an isogeny $\phi_i' := E_{1-i} \to E_{1-i,i}$ with $\ker(\phi_i') = \langle \phi_{1-i}(R_i) \rangle$ and computes $k_i = j(E_{1-i,i}) \in \mathbb{F}_{p^2}$ (see Fig. 3).*

It holds that $E_{1,0} = \phi_0'(\phi_1(E)) \cong \phi_1'(\phi_0(E)) = E_{0,1}$, i.e. $k_0 = j(E_{1,0}) = j(E_{0,1}) = k_1$, such that $\mathcal{P}_0$ and $\mathcal{P}_1$ have the shared key $k = k_0 = k_1$.

The following definition is taken from De Feo et al. [9] with minor changes to fit our notation.

---

[8] https://sike.org/.

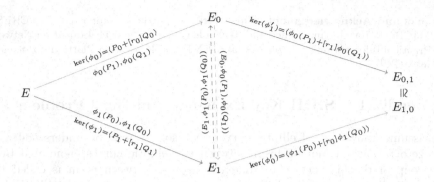

Fig. 3. SIDH key exchange. Quantities only known by $\mathcal{P}_0$, respectively $\mathcal{P}_1$, are drawn in red, respectively blue. The dotted lines signify public keys being exchanged. (Original TikZ code courtesy of De Feo via GitHub [6].)

Definition 6 (Supersingular decisional Diffie-Hellman (SSDDH) problem). *Given a tuple sampled with probability* $1/2$ *from one of the following two distributions:*

- $(\mathfrak{P}, (pk_0, pk_1), k)$, *where* $\mathfrak{P}, pk_0 = (E_0, \phi_0(P_1), \phi_0(Q_1))$, *and* $pk_1 = (E_1, \phi_1(P_0), \phi_1(Q_0))$ *are as in the SIDH protocol (Definition 8) and* $k = E_{0,1} \cong E/\langle P_0 + [r_0]Q_0, P_1 + [r_1]Q_1\rangle$,
- $(\mathfrak{P}, (pk_0, pk_1), k')$, *where* $\mathfrak{P}, pk_0 = (E_0, \phi_0(P_1), \phi_0(Q_1))$, *and* $pk_1 = (E_1, \phi_1(P_0), \phi_1(Q_0))$ *are as in the SIDH protocol (Definition 8) and* $k' = E_x \cong E/\langle P_0 + [r'_0]Q_0, P_1 + [r'_1]Q_1\rangle$, *where* r'_0 *(respectively* r'_1) *is chosen at random from* $\mathbb{Z}/\ell_0^{e_0}\mathbb{Z}$ *(respectively* $\mathbb{Z}/\ell_1^{e_1}\mathbb{Z}$),

determine from which distribution the tuple is sampled.

Theorem 9 (Security of SIDH [9]). *Under the SSDDH assumption, the key-agreement protocol of Definition 8 is session-key secure in the authenticated-links adversarial model of Canetti and Krawczyk.*

Appendix 2   R-LWE Key Exchange and Hard Problem

Although R-LWE protocols are usually expected to reduce to the R-LWE problem, Bos et al. [1] give a Diffie-Hellman-like definition of indistinguishability that takes Peikert's key reconciliation into consideration and show how it reduces to the hardness of the R-LWE problem. All definitions are taken from Bos et al. [1].

Let $\mathbb{Z}$ be the ring of integers and denote $[N] = \{0, 1, \ldots, N-1\}$. In this article, we set $R = \mathbb{Z}[X]/(f(X))$ where $f(X) = X^n + 1$ for $n = 2^l, l > 0$ for some l. We let q be a modulus defining the quotient ring $R_q = R/qR \cong \mathbb{Z}_q[X]/(f[X])$, where $\mathbb{Z}_q = \mathbb{Z}/q\mathbb{Z}$.

Definition 7 (Decisional R-LWE (D-R-LWE) problem). *Let the values* n, R, q *and* R_q *be as above. Let* χ *be a distribution over* R *and let* $s \xleftarrow{R} \chi$. *Define* $O_{\chi,s}$ *as an oracle that does the following:*

1. *Sample* $a \xleftarrow{R} R_q$ *and* $e \xleftarrow{R} \chi$,
2. *Return* $(a, as + e) \in R_q \times R_q$.

*The **decisional R-LWE problem** for* n, q, χ *is to distinguish* $O_{\chi,s}$ *from an oracle that returns uniformly random samples from* $R_q \times R_q$.

Let $\lceil \cdot \rfloor$ denote the rounding function: $\lceil x \rfloor = z$ for $z \in \mathbb{Z}$ and $x \in [z - 1/2, z + 1/2)$.

Definition 8 ([1], Definition 2). *Let* q *be a positive integer. Define the **modular rounding** function* $\lceil \cdot \rfloor_{q,2} : \mathbb{Z}_q \rightarrow \mathbb{Z}_2, x \mapsto \lceil x \rfloor_{q,2} = \lceil \frac{2}{q} x \rfloor \mod 2$, *and the **cross-rounding** function* $\langle \cdot \rangle_{q,2} : \mathbb{Z}_q \rightarrow \mathbb{Z}_2, x \mapsto \langle x \rangle_{q,2} = \lfloor \frac{4}{q} x \rfloor \mod 2$. *Both functions are extended to elements of* R_q *coefficient-wise: for* $f = f_{n-1} X^{n-1} + \cdots + f_1 X + f_0 \in R_q$, *define*

$$\lceil f \rfloor_{q,2} = \left(\lceil f_{n-1} \rfloor_{q,2}, \lceil f_{n-2} \rfloor_{q,2}, \ldots, \lceil f_0 \rfloor_{q,2} \right),$$
$$\langle f \rangle_{q,2} = \left(\langle f_{n-1} \rangle_{q,2}, \langle f_{n-2} \rangle_{q,2}, \ldots, \langle f_0 \rangle_{q,2} \right).$$

*We also define the **randomized doubling** function* dbl $: \mathbb{Z}_q \rightarrow \mathbb{Z}_{2q}, x \mapsto$ dbl$(x) = 2x - e$, *where* e *is sampled from* $\{-1, 0, 1\}$ *with probabilities* $p_{-1} = p_1 = \frac{1}{4}$ *and* $p_0 = \frac{1}{2}$.

The doubling function may be applied to elements in R_q by applying it on each of the coefficients, as done with the rounding functions. Such an application of the doubling function results in a polynomial in R_{2q}. The reason for considering such a doubling function is that this allows for odd q.

The rounding of the doubling function on a uniformly random element in $\mathbb{Z}_q$ results in a uniformly random element in $\mathbb{Z}_{2q}$.

Lemma 1 ([1], Lemma 1). *For odd* q, *if* $v \in \mathbb{Z}_q$ *is uniformly random and* $\overline{v} \xleftarrow{R}$ dbl$(v) \in \mathbb{Z}_{2q}$, *then* $\lceil \overline{v} \rfloor_{2q,2}$ *is uniformly random, given* $\langle \overline{v} \rangle_{2q,2}$.

We may now define Peikert's reconciliation function, rec$(\cdot)$, which recovers $\lceil v \rfloor_{q,2}$ from an element $w \in \mathbb{Z}_q$ that is "close" to the original $v \in \mathbb{Z}_q$, given only w and the cross-rounding of v.

Definition 9. *Define sets* $I_0 = \{0, 1, \ldots, \lceil \frac{q}{2} \rceil - 1\}$ *and* $I_1 = \{-\lceil \frac{q}{2} \rceil, \ldots, -1\}$. *Let* $E = [-\frac{q}{4}, \frac{q}{4})$, *then define the map* rec $: \mathbb{Z}_{2q} \times \mathbb{Z}_2 \rightarrow \mathbb{Z}_2$,

$$(w, b) \mapsto \begin{cases} 0, & \text{if } w \in I_b + E \mod 2q, \\ 1, & \text{otherwise}. \end{cases}$$

Reconciliation of a polynomial in R_q is done coefficient-wise so the following lemma allows us to reconcile two polynomials in R_q that are close to each other.

Lemma 2 ([1], **Lemma 2**). *For odd q, let $v = w + e \in \mathbb{Z}_q$ for $w, e \in \mathbb{Z}_q$ such that $2e \pm 1 \in E \pmod q$. Let $\bar{v} = \mathtt{dbl}(v)$, then $\mathtt{rec}(2w, \langle \bar{v} \rangle_{2q,2}) = \lceil \bar{v} \rfloor_{2q,2}$.*

We may finally define the R-LWE key exchange below. Given a security parameter 1^λ, Gen outputs $\mathfrak{I} = (n, R, q, R_q)$ as in the D-R-LWE problem (Definition 7), a distribution χ on R_q (usually the Discrete Gaussian distribution), and a uniformly random $a \xleftarrow{R} R_q$.

Protocol 10 (R-LWE key exchange w/ Peikert's tweak [14,16]). *Parties $\mathcal{P}_0$ and $\mathcal{P}_1$ generate an R-LWE key exchange w/ Peikert's tweak protocol as follows:*

Setup: *For the security parameter 1^λ, Gen outputs to both parties the tuple of public parameters: $\mathfrak{P} = (\mathfrak{I}, \chi, a) \leftarrow \mathsf{Gen}(1^\lambda)$.*

Publish$_1$: *Each party $\mathcal{P}_i$ chooses $s_i, e_i \xleftarrow{R} \chi$ as their secret key and error key,[9] respectively, computes their public key $b_i = as_i + e_i \in R_q$, and sends their public key b_i to party $\mathcal{P}_{1-i}$.*

Publish$_2$: *Party $\mathcal{P}_1$, upon receiving b_0 from P_0, chooses a new error key $e_1' \xleftarrow{R} \chi$, computes $v = b_0 s_1 + e_1' \in R_q$, and uses the randomized doubling function on v to receive $\bar{v} \xleftarrow{R} \mathtt{dbl}(v) \in R_{2q}$. Using the cross-rounding function, $\mathcal{P}_1$ computes $c = \langle \bar{v} \rangle_{2q,2} \in \{0,1\}^n$ and sends c to $\mathcal{P}_0$*

KeyGen: *In order to generate the final key, party $\mathcal{P}_0$ uses the reconciliation function to output $k_0 \leftarrow \mathtt{rec}(2b_1 s_0, c) \in \{0,1\}^n$. Party $\mathcal{P}_1$ simply computes $k_1 = \lceil \bar{v} \rfloor_{2q,2} \in \{0,1\}^n$.*

Except with negligible probability $k_0 = k_1 = k$, i.e. this protocol satisfies correctness.

The protocol reduces to a decisional hardness problem that Bos et al. [1] dub the decision Diffie-Hellman-like (DDH-like) problem. We give a reformulation, which is equivalent, but fits the other security definitions in this paper.

Definition 10 (Decision Diffie-Hellman-like (DDH-like) problem). *Let n, R, q, χ be R-LWE key exchange parameters. Given a tuple sampled with probability $1/2$ from one of the following two distributions:*

- *$(\mathfrak{P}, (b_0, (b_1, c)), k)$, where $\mathfrak{P} = (\mathfrak{I}, \chi, a)$ for a $\xleftarrow{R} R_q$, $s_0, s_1, e_0, e_1, e_1' \xleftarrow{R} \chi$, $b_i = as_i + e_i$ for $i = 0, 1$, $v = b_0 s_1 + e_1'$, $\bar{v} \xleftarrow{R} \mathtt{dbl}(v)$, $c = \langle \bar{v} \rangle_{2q,2}$, and $k = \lceil \bar{v} \rfloor_{2q,2}$,*

---

[9] Both must remain secret, so essentially, this is a single secret key in the form of a pair.

- $(\mathfrak{P}, (b_0, (b_1, c)), k')$, where $\mathfrak{P} = (\mathfrak{I}, \chi, a)$ for a $\xleftarrow{R} R_q$, $s_0, s_1, e_0, e_1, e_1' \xleftarrow{R} \chi$, $b_i = as_i + e_i$ for $i = 0, 1$, $v = b_0 s_1 + e_1'$, $\overline{v} \xleftarrow{R} \mathtt{dbl}(v)$, $c = \langle \overline{v} \rangle_{2q,2}$, and $k' \xleftarrow{R} \{0,1\}^n$,

determine from which distribution the tuple is sampled.

Theorem 11 (Hardness of DDH-like problem; [1], Theorem 1). *Let q be an odd integer, let n a parameter, R a polynomial ring, and χ a distribution on R_q. If the decision R-LWE problem for q, n, χ is hard, then the DDH-like problem for q, n, χ is also hard.*

References

1. Bos, J.W., Costello, C., Naehrig, M., Stebila, D.: Post-quantum key exchange for the TLS protocol from the ring learning with errors problem. In: IEEE Symposium on Security and Privacy, pp. 553–570. IEEE Computer Society (2015). http://dblp. uni-trier.de/db/conf/sp/sp2015.html#BosCNS15
2. Bresson, E., Chevassut, O., Pointcheval, D., Quisquater, J.J.: Provably authenticated group Diffie-Hellman key exchange. In: Proceedings of the 8th ACM Conference on Computer and Communications Security, CCS 2001, pp. 255–264. Association for Computing Machinery, New York (2001). https://doi.org/10.1145/501983. 502018
3. Bresson, E., Manulis, M.: Securing group key exchange against strong corruptions. In: Proceedings of the 2008 ACM Symposium on Information, Computer and Communications Security, ASIACCS 2008, pp. 249–260. Association for Computing Machinery, New York (2008)
4. Burmester, M., Desmedt, Y.: A secure and efficient conference key distribution system. In: De Santis, A. (ed.) EUROCRYPT 1994. LNCS, vol. 950, pp. 275–286. Springer, Heidelberg (1995). https://doi.org/10.1007/BFb0053443
5. Burmester, M., Desmedt, Y.G.: Efficient and secure conference-key distribution. In: Lomas, M. (ed.) Security Protocols 1996. LNCS, vol. 1189, pp. 119–129. Springer, Heidelberg (1997). https://doi.org/10.1007/3-540-62494-5_12
6. De Feo, L., Jao, D.: defeo/sidh-paper. https://github.com/defeo/sidh-paper/blob/ master/eprint.tex
7. Desmedt, Y., Lange, T., Burmester, M.: Scalable authenticated tree based group key exchange for ad-hoc groups. In: Dietrich, S., Dhamija, R. (eds.) FC 2007. LNCS, vol. 4886, pp. 104–118. Springer, Heidelberg (2007). https://doi.org/10. 1007/978-3-540-77366-5_12
8. Diffie, W., Hellman, M.: New directions in cryptography. IEEE Trans. Inf. Theor. **22**(6), 644–654 (2006). https://doi.org/10.1109/TIT.1976.1055638
9. Feo, L.D., Jao, D., Plût, J.: Towards quantum-resistant cryptosystems from supersingular elliptic curve isogenies. J. Math. Cryptol. **8**(3), 209–247 (2014). https:// doi.org/10.1515/jmc-2012-0015
10. Furukawa, S., Kunihiro, N., Takashima, K.: Multi-party key exchange protocols from supersingular isogenies. In: 2018 International Symposium on Information Theory and Its Applications (ISITA), pp. 208–212 (2018)
11. Hougaard, H.B., Miyaji, A.: SIT: supersingular isogeny tree-based group key exchange. In: 15th Asia Joint Conference on Information Security, AsiaJCIS 2020, Taipei, Taiwan, 20–21 August 2020, pp. 46–53. IEEE (2020). https://doi.org/10. 1109/AsiaJCIS50894.2020.00019

12. Hougaard, H.B., Miyaji, A.: Tree-based ring-LWE group key exchanges with logarithmic complexity. In: Meng, W., Gollmann, D., Jensen, C.D., Zhou, J. (eds.) ICICS 2020. LNCS, vol. 12282, pp. 91–106. Springer, Cham (2020). https://doi.org/10.1007/978-3-030-61078-4_6
13. Jao, D., De Feo, L.: Towards quantum-resistant cryptosystems from supersingular elliptic curve isogenies. In: Yang, B.-Y. (ed.) PQCrypto 2011. LNCS, vol. 7071, pp. 19–34. Springer, Heidelberg (2011). https://doi.org/10.1007/978-3-642-25405-5_2
14. Ding, J., Xie, X., Lin, X.: A simple provably secure key exchange scheme based on the learning with errors problem. Cryptology ePrint Archive, Report 2012/688 (2012). https://eprint.iacr.org/2012/688
15. Katz, J., Yung, M.: Scalable protocols for authenticated group key exchange. J. Cryptol. **20**(1), 85–113 (2007)
16. Peikert, C.: Lattice cryptography for the internet. In: Mosca, M. (ed.) PQCrypto 2014. LNCS, vol. 8772, pp. 197–219. Springer, Cham (2014). https://doi.org/10.1007/978-3-319-11659-4_12
17. Suzuki, K., Yoneyama, K.: Exposure-resilient one-round tripartite key exchange without random oracles. IEICE Trans. **97-A**(6), 1345–1355 (2014). https://doi.org/10.1587/transfun.E97.A.1345

An Architecture for Processing a Dynamic Heterogeneous Information Network of Security Intelligence

Marios Anagnostopoulos[1]([envelope]) [iD], Egon Kidmose[2] [iD], Amine Laghaout[3] [iD],
Rasmus L. Olsen[2] [iD], Sajad Homayoun[4] [iD], Christian D. Jensen[4] [iD],
and Jens M. Pedersen[1] [iD]

[1] Department of Electronic Systems, Aalborg University, Copenhagen, Denmark
{mariosa,jens}@es.aau.dk
[2] Department of Electronic Systems, Aalborg University, Aalborg, Denmark
{egk,rlo}@es.aau.dk
[3] CSIS Security Group A/S, Vestergade 2B, 4. sal, Copenhagen K, Denmark
[4] Department of Applied Mathematics and Computer Science, Technical University of Denmark, Kongens Lyngby, Denmark
{sajho,cdje}@dtu.dk

Abstract. Security intelligence is widely used to solve cyber security issues in computer and network systems, such as incident prevention, detection, and response, by applying machine learning (ML) and other data-driven methods. To this end, there is a large body of prior research works aiming to solve security issues in specific scenarios, using specific types of data or applying specific algorithms. However, by being specific it has the drawback of becoming cumbersome to adjust existing solutions to new use cases, data, or problems. Furthermore, all prior research, that strives to be more generic, is either able to operate with complex relations (graph-based), or to work with time varying intelligence (time series), but rarely with both. In this paper, we present the reference architecture of the SecDNS framework for representing the collected intelligence data with a model based on a graph structure, which simultaneously encompasses the time variance of these data and providing a modular architecture for both the data model and the algorithms. In addition, we leverage on the concept of belief propagation to infer the maliciousness of an entity based on its relations with other malicious or benign entities or events. This way, we offer a generic platform for processing dynamic and heterogeneous security intelligence with an evolving collection of sources and algorithms. Finally, to demonstrate the modus operandi of our proposal, we implement a proof of concept of the platform, and we deploy it in the use case of phishing email attack scenario.

Keywords: Security intelligence · Belief propagation · System architecture · Graph network · Design matrices

This research is carried out in the SecDNS project, funded by Innovation Fund Denmark.

M. Yang et al. (Eds.): NSS 2021, LNCS 13041, pp. 185–201, 2021.
https://doi.org/10.1007/978-3-030-92708-0_11

1   Introduction

As a rule of thumb, security intelligence deals with the collection, analysis and presentation of data within a computational or network system with the purpose to improve the security of that system [2]. There exists a plethora of information and networking resources exposed to potential threats and involved in security incidents, thus data from these sources can reveal the perpetrators' modes of operation and their intentions. Furthermore, the compilation and standardisation of the intelligence data can contribute to cross-organisation intelligence sharing and hence enhance the collaborative actions against the evildoers [19].

However, the diversity of intelligence sources, along with the variations of the analysing methods, as well as the evolution of the cyber threats and the emergence of new ones, renders the development of a universal solution challenging [10]. Usually, the related research focuses on specific application domains or sources of data. On the contrary, the works aspiring to provide a more universal approach, typically they operate by expressing the relationships of the data through complex graph structures, or they function with time varying data, but they are usually ineffective to combine both approaches.

Although, there exist solutions to spatio-temporal problems in graph machine learning (GML), they do not satisfy the requirements of 1) the heterogeneity of nodes that are attributed, 2) the time-dependence of these nodes and their attributes, 3) the time-dependence of their relationships, 4) scoring of the nodes, and 5) expressing arbitrary interactions other than bipartite, like these of hyperedges. All these conditions are however required in the cybersecurity domain. Attempts to combine graph and time-based approaches, such as spatio-temporal graphs [20], take into account the space-time aspects of a problem but cannot accommodate the heterogeneity of the graph. On the other hand, solutions, such as GraphSAGE [7], that consider the heterogeneity of the nodes, they cannot model the time-evolution of the node attributes or the edges. Furthermore, the main shortcoming of GML lies in the fact that interactions between entities are limited to bipartite relationships. This renders GML unsuitable for problems where an interaction involves an arbitrary number of vertices with no particular directionality.

In our work, we present the architecture of a novel security intelligence framework based on a graph model for representing the intelligence data along with their time variance. The main novelty of our proposal is that it capitalizes on the belief propagation concept to deduce the maliciousness or trustworthiness of the monitored entities as their status changes over time or are involved in new emerging events. Furthermore, the framework is domain agnostic, namely the structure of the graph does not depend on the specifics of the application domain, but rather provides the generic relationships between events or, as we call it, the formation of the *entity-relationship diagram* (ERD). In addition, it consists of a modular architecture enabling the incorporation of both the data model and the algorithms applied to these data. Finally, as a proof of concept, we demonstrate the handling of the interactions between the various components by applying the model to the use case scenario of the phishing email attack.

Bear in mind, that the framework defines the components of the model in an abstract layer, while the actual designation of the entities is based on the expert's knowledge of the specific domain.

Our contribution is to offer a framework that advances the state of the art for managing security intelligence by:

- Providing a graph-based model for representing the intelligence data. This model is also capable of capturing the evolution of the intelligence data over time,
- Utilizing the belief propagation to spread the impact of an observation to the related instances,
- Enabling modular changes to the data model, this way it is straightforward to extend the entity and relationship types or add new ones on the fly, and
- Enabling modular changes to the intelligence processing routines, namely it is trivial to remove, add, or update functionalities on the fly.

The rest of the paper is structured as follows: Sect. 2 introduces the related work. Section 3 details the architecture of the proposed framework and explains its components. Section 4 describes the application of the framework to the use case scenario of the phishing campaigns. Finally, Sect. 5 concludes the paper with a discussion and draws possible future directions.

2 Related Work

Graph-based methods have been applied to cyber security intelligence, e.g., to infer new appearing malicious domain from known malicious domains in a bipartite client-domain graph [16]. Similar problems have been addressed with homogeneous graphs of domains and bipartite host-domain graphs [8,11]. For example, ATIS is a generic framework for processing cyber threat intelligence similar to our proposal, offering modularity and a heterogeneous graph as the data model, but without the notion of time offered by our framework [12]. HinCTI applies ML methods, namely Graph Convolutional Network (GCN), on a heterogeneous graph, or Heterogeneous Information Network (HIN) as they refer it [4]. Moreover, Sun et al. [17] proposed to apply a spatial HIN model for domain names and five related entity types. A GCN variant is applied, namely *meta-path guided short random walk* (with six specified meta-paths), having intrinsic features for domains, but not for entities in general. In addition to the graph-based methods, there are also research works that rely on time-based analysis, e.g., to detect botnet infected clients [3] or malicious domain names [13]. On the other hand, Tran et al. [18] proposed a graph mechanism that capitalizes on the belief propagation to infer a domain's reputation score based on the relationship between domain names and IP addresses.

Overall, there are ample of examples applying graph-based or time-based methods, demonstrating how they can be used independently to solve security problems. At the same time, there exist works that combine graph-based and time-based methods, however, they deal with specific use case of threat intelligence. For instance, Garcia-Lebron et al. [5], although, considered both the graph-based and time-based aspects of the relations, their proposed framework is tailored to the use case of detecting reconnaissance behaviour of cyber attacks and may not be applicable to other scenarios. To the best of our knowledge, no other work has explored the combination of graph-based and time-based methods in a generic framework that also prioritises modularity and the ability to support general ML techniques. Put it differently, the novelty of the proposed framework lies in its modularity and ability to generalize to virtually any use case that consists of attributed entities with a score of maliciousness.

3   Method

In this section, we detail our framework by providing initially the preliminaries that are essential for understanding the general overview of our proposal. Then, we present the theoretical framework with a formal representation of the entities and processes, while afterwards we describe and explain the system architecture, before concluding with some considerations on implementation suggestions.

3.1   Preliminaries

Cyber security intelligence data, or simply *intelligence*, is any collection of data useful for preventing, detecting, or responding to security incidents [15]. To be suitable, intelligence must be related to the security of the use case of interest, as in our paradigm to phishing. Namely, intelligence should contain one or more specific instances of some entity types, and it must describe the entity (or entities), either through attribute(s) or by their relationship. For example, it can describe the knowledge that a client resides on the network of interest (identification of an instance, e.g., by an IP address), that the client is powered on (an attribute characterising the state of the client), and that the client used the Domain Name System (DNS) to resolve a domain name (interaction between the client and DNS servers).

The complete corpus of all security intelligence is not practically available and processable, however significant fragments of it can be monitored and analysed. The types of intelligence incorporate also enriched observations, such as the relation between a host's IP address and the hostname obtained via reverse DNS lookup on the IP. Either way, monitoring of data is one approach to collect intelligence. Another option is to gather intelligence from third parties, via public or private feeds, which are provided for free or under some commercial agreement.

Whether intelligence originates from controlled monitoring systems, third parties, or other sources, the observation of new intelligence is expected to occur at specific points in time, because monitoring reveals events from observed data, or as new data arrive from a feed. To capture this, we define an *event* as a timestamped observation of intelligence data, where an observation may for example be either a first time observation, an intermediate since last modification or an affirmation that the previous intelligence data are still current. For instance, a DNS query from a client is an event which encompass several pieces of intelligence; there is a client on the network that has a certain IP address, it is active, and it aims to connect to the domain name in question.

Intelligence may also be obtained from ML, heuristics, manual processing and so forth. The common characteristic for all these processes is that they receive some intelligence as input and generate some new or updated intelligence as output. This type of process is referred hereafter as a *Map* process. Essentially, a map encapsulates the knowledge of a variety of domain experts into an automated framework that enriches the intelligence. The mapping process is the fundamental aspect of our proposed approach for providing security intelligence, and is formalised in Sect. 3.2.

3.2 Theoretical Framework

Problem Domain. We shall first present a data-centred—as opposed to system-centred—overview of the components that are the building blocks of our scheme for the generation and storage of intelligence. Our starting point is to acknowledge that the cyberspace can be represented by an *entity-relationship diagram* (ERD) that links a heterogeneous set of entity types, such as domain names, IP addresses, e-mail addresses, executables, physical devices and so on. Each entity is characterised by a set of *intrinsic* features. As an example, the entity representing the domain `example.com` has as features the length of its string with value 11 and its top-level domain, which is `com`. Such features are deemed intrinsic as they are independent of any other entity or event. Cyberspace, however, is not simply build up from disjoint entities, but rather it is the scene of all sorts of well-defined *relationships* between them. For example, sending an email forms a relationship between the sender and one or more recipients, along with one or more attached files. Likewise, a DNS request establishes a relationship between the querying IP address of the end-user, the queried domain name, the resolving IP address, and one or more name servers involved in the resolution. These relationships, called *hyperedges* in the ERD, play an important role into the feature space of the involved entities. The features resulting from interactions shall be called *extrinsic*, since they depend on neighbouring entities. For example, in the case of a domain, extrinsic features could be considered the registrant or the IP addresses hosting the domain and their respective geolocation. A partial representation of the ERD for cyberspace is illustrated in Fig. 1, where the nodes (notated as ε) represent possible entities and the edges (notated as ρ) constitute a subset of relationships among these entities. An exhaustive diagram is heavily reliant on domain expertise and beyond the scope of this work.

The last component is the *belief* that an entity is involved in a given cyber threat. These beliefs, which shall be quantified as probabilities, are the end products of the intelligence generation pipeline in the sense that they are readily actionable. For example, access to a given domain can be blocked if it is believed that it hosts a certain malware with a probability of say 60%.

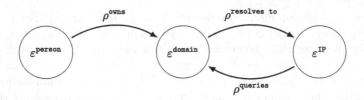

Fig. 1. Subset of the ERD spanning cyberspace. The nodes are entities, whereas the edges are relationships or part of them.

The name of the game in intelligence generation is therefore to infer the beliefs of out-of-sample entities with the best possible accuracy compared to the (presumed) ground truth. Intuitively, this is achieved by monitoring *events* and updating accordingly the beliefs of the involved entities using well-defined computational modules, namely the *maps* as introduced in Sect. 3.1. Features and beliefs shall be jointly referred to as *intelligence* throughout our research.[1]

Notation. We shall denote each entity instance by $\varepsilon_k^{(j)}$ where k is the unique instance label and

$$j \in \mathcal{E} = \{\texttt{domain}, \texttt{IP address}, \texttt{registrant}, \texttt{ASN}, \cdots\} \tag{1}$$

is the entity type among the overall set of types $\mathcal{E}$. To each entity, we shall indicate its intrinsic features by $\boldsymbol{f}_k^{(j)}$, its extrinsic features as per a relationship type i by $\boldsymbol{r}_k^{(j,i)}$, and its beliefs by $\boldsymbol{b}_k^{(j)}$. Note that the elements of the belief vector $\boldsymbol{b}$ are probabilities that span an ordered tuple of cyber threats[2]

$$\mathcal{B} = (\texttt{benign}, \texttt{botnet}, \texttt{phishing}, \cdots). \tag{2}$$

The concatenation[3]

$$\boldsymbol{d}_k^{(j)}(t) = \boldsymbol{b}_k^{(j)}(t) \oplus \boldsymbol{f}_k^{(j)}(t) \oplus \left[\bigoplus_i \boldsymbol{r}_k^{(j,i)}(t)\right] \tag{3}$$

of these three vectors shall be called the *data vector* of the entity $\varepsilon_k^{(j)}$ and encodes all the known information about that entity at the time t. Note that the extrinsic

---

[1] A rough, qualitative distinction can be made between features and beliefs in that the former represent raw intelligence whereas the latter represent "business-grade"—i.e., actionable—intelligence.

[2] Note that $\boldsymbol{b}$ need not add up to unity since the threats may overlap. Indeed, the threats to be predicted fall into a taxonomy which is eminently domain-specific and beyond the scope of this article.

[3] The concatenation of vectors shall be represented by the symbol $\oplus$ for the direct sum.

features are themselves concatenated over all the relationship types i that an entity of type j can be involved in, i.e., i is drawn from the overall set

$$\mathcal{R} = \{ \text{ DNS queried, e-mail sent,}$$
$$\text{domain registered, packet received,}$$
$$\text{file opened, } \cdots \} \tag{4}$$

of possible relationship types. For example, a domain can be involved in a DNS query (as the queried domain), or in an e-mail being sent (as the sender's or recipient's domain), but cannot be involved in the opening of a file—at least not directly.

Design Matrices. The cornerstone of the data storage architecture proposed herein is the *design matrix*. The matrices are indexed in time, and express the features and beliefs of all entity instances of a given type j.

$$\mathcal{D}^{(j)}(t) = \begin{bmatrix} \vdots \\ d_k^{(j)}(t) \\ \vdots \end{bmatrix}, \tag{5}$$

Thus, they encode a snapshot of the captured intelligence up to time t of all entities of that given type j.

Maps. While the design matrices are the passive repositories of the intelligence, the *maps* are the active operations on that intelligence. Namely, they ensure that the design matrices are updated to reflect the latest events observed "in the wild", i.e., a map $\mathcal{M}$ is any read or write operation on the design matrices. Even more, a map can run on historical data, i.e., on older snapshots of the design matrices. More specifically, in addition to merely reading design matrices, a map is able to perform updates to:

1. The intrinsic features,
2. The extrinsic features upon the instantiation of a relationship,
3. The beliefs.

In the most general sense, the maps can thus be formalised as an update of the data vectors over a time increment δt between successive events, i.e.,

$$\mathcal{M} : \bigcup_{\varepsilon_k^{(j)}} \left\{ d_k^{(j)}(t-\delta t) \right\} \rightarrow \bigcup_{\varepsilon_{k'}^{(j')}} \left\{ d_{k'}^{(j')}(t) \right\}, \tag{6}$$

where the sets of input and output entities, $\varepsilon_k^{(j)}$ and $\varepsilon_{k'}^{(j')}$, may or may not overlap. Paradigms of maps could be:

- A DNS lookup of some domain instance k

$$\mathcal{M}^{\texttt{dig}} : d_k^{(\texttt{domain})}(t-\delta t) \rightarrow r_{k'}^{(\texttt{IP address, DNS query})}(t), \tag{7}$$

- A blacklisting of malicious domains k

$$\mathcal{M}^{\texttt{blacklist}} : b_k^{(\texttt{domain})}(t-\delta t) \rightarrow b_k^{(\texttt{domain})}(t) \tag{8}$$

- A detector of algorithmically-generated domains based on ML classifier

$$\mathcal{M}^{\texttt{ML-DGA}} : f_k^{(\texttt{domain})}(t-\delta t) \rightarrow b_k^{(\texttt{domain})}(t), \tag{9}$$

which would perform lexical analysis on the domain string $f_k^{(\texttt{domain})}$.

Maps are therefore attuned to any change in the environment—e.g., instantiations of relationships, or inputs from third-party intelligence—and thus govern the appropriate data enrichment logic on the design matrices. This requires an algorithm which can aggregate intelligence both in time (as per the history of updates) and space (as per the topology of the ERD, see Fig. 1). A generic architecture that deals with such aggregation is proposed in [9].

3.3   System Architecture

Figure 2 illustrates the architecture of our framework, accompanied by the components and data flows. In its conceptual essence, we propose a system comprised of:

- A mechanism as a generic concept for distributing the occurring events, that is the Data Platform,
- A storage mechanism that directly conceives the concept of design matrices, that is the Intelligence Database,
- The concept of Maps that outline the subsystems responsible for querying the intelligence database, consuming and producing events from the external "world" and from internal events regarding data processing, and updating the intelligence database, and finally
- The Graphical User Interface (GUI) that is connected to the data stream and is in charge of visualising the statistics and other relevant information.

The core requirement of the system is to provide an architecture that supports execution of potentially large number of Maps. These Maps need access to the historical data, i.e., on the older snapshots of the design matrices, hence a database is required to efficiently preserve these historical data. We call this database the Intelligence Database and, while in practice could be instantiated by several distributed databases, conceptually operates as a single. To support these two key components, we introduce the Data Platform that connects and facilitates the data exchange between the Maps and the Intelligence Database. The data exchange requires also data normalisation and the handling of time properties. Finally, the GUI component is linked to the Data Platform to visualize the important events, and to accommodate the user's interactions to the Intelligence Database and organisation of the Maps.

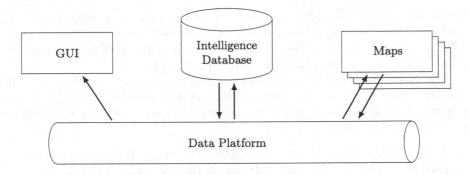

Fig. 2. System architecture

3.4 Maps

To retrieve, enrich, refine, and expand the intelligence, some form of processing is required. This capability is formally defined with Eq. (6), where the Maps process a set of instances and produce new intelligence. By supporting the instances to have historical data as property, we enable the processing of time-series data with the Maps, and by recording their relations we enable graph-based processing. The capability to maintain the Maps independently (including operations such as adding, removing, updating, re-training, etc., of the Maps) is accomplished by considering each Map as a component on its own designated by the corresponding domain expert.

At a high level, a map is essentially a "subsystem" with access to lookup/ query the intelligence database, as well as with the capability to monitor the flow of "things happening". Thus, each map is able to store data in the intelligence database by triggering updates that allow the map to be responsible for dedicated areas of the design matrices, namely a set of features (columns) of these matrices. In other words, a Map can be considered as an API providing an answer to the question "How likely is this entity involved in a (specific) malicious action". This process is expressed as a lookup to the intelligence database where specific belief(s) generated by (an) other map(s) are resolving this query and returned as response.

The flexibility, modularity, and scalability requirements adhere that multiple Maps may produce intelligence data for their own feature/column in the design matrix, while running in parallel. This will introduce typical consistency challenges for distributed data processing. One approach to resolve this issue could be to let the collection of Maps maintain their own data, but this conflicts with the goal of each Map being a simple and modular component. Therefore, the task of managing and storing the data is delegated to the Intelligence Database as discussed below. However, a Map may still store internally the state between calculations, and may cache intelligence data whenever required.

The body of intelligence data is expected to be of significant size, as many instances and long-term historical data are anticipated. This implies that the volume of data transferred from the Intelligence Database to the Maps can cause stability issues. To mitigate this, the data transfers should be limited to include only the design matrices for the relevant entity types, and sliced to the instances (rows), features (columns) and time spans of relevance.

The Maps may have different implementations and functionalities, but the general characteristics for generating intelligence are common across all of them. However, throughout our research, we recognize two types of Maps according to the input source they use:

- External Maps: these Maps receive intelligence feeds from external sources. They rely on frameworks and tools outside the system, such as `dig`, and they usually monitor for events and are invoked whenever new ones are raised.
- Internal Maps: these Maps are based on the aforementioned mathematical framework for belief calculation. They are fed from the Intelligence Database or from the output of other Maps. In essence, these Maps implement variations of Eq. (6) for specific use case entities.

3.5   Intelligence Database

Essentially, the Intelligence Database provides intelligence data to the Maps, and in return receives events with new intelligence. Although that the Intelligence Database seems as a static graph database at any given instant, it is actually evolving through time and thus the intelligence data is treated as time-dependent by our framework, as indicated by Eq. (6).

As already explained, the Intelligence Database is responsible for storing the intelligence data. This scheme is illustrated by a set of entity types $\mathcal{E}$ having attributes features $f^{(\varepsilon_k)}$, a set of relationships $\mathcal{R}$ determining relationship features $r^{(\varepsilon_k)}$, and beliefs $\mathcal{B}$ declaring the contents of the belief vector $b^{(\varepsilon_k)}$. As motivated from the aforementioned description of Maps, the data provided by the Intelligence Database should be slice-able (i.e., the range of instances, features, and time span can be chosen).

Being the single component that preserves the complete view of data in the system, the Intelligence Database is also the central point in the architecture where all changes in data, i.e., events, are observed. This makes it feasible, given adequate knowledge on which Maps rely on what data, to determine the appropriate Maps to invoke. Therefore, the Intelligence Database also has an active role in triggering the Maps when required, and thus it is not simply a passive storage component. Section 3.8 delves into more details of the implementation considerations, however we expect that an event-driven approach is promising. Even more, an event-driven approach can possibly include timers that periodically schedule execution of Maps, when needed. This is appropriate for Maps that rely on dynamic resources as input which however do not notify about the changes, like in the case of DNS data or blacklisting of online resources. Nevertheless, the discussion of how to dispatch events to maps, e.g., by broadcasting or by a publish-subscribe pattern, is deferred to future work.

3.6   Data Platform

The role of the Data Platform is decisive as it facilitates the data exchange among the Intelligence Database, Maps and GUI. Key requirements, such as data normalisation and time synchronisation across components, are also handled by the Data Platform. A subscription/notification and request interaction pattern that is flexible to support a high variety of information types and amount is required as well.

The Intelligence Database is not limited to run on a single machine, but rather may be composed of a distributed set of machines hosting different databases, which in conjunction operate as the Intelligence Database. Therefore, it is critical that the Data Platform also supports load balancing of not only the processing capabilities, but also the storage and network resources to ensure that the individual machines do not become bottlenecks.

3.7   Graphical User Interface (GUI)

Finally, the GUI component has the role of the Front-End of the framework. This component is responsible for providing the interface to the external consumers, i.e., systems and users, allowing them to retrieve the intelligence. In the simplest form, the Front-End relays queries to the Intelligence Database. However, an event-driven interface, e.g., using subscriptions, can also be supported.

Examples of relevant Front-End functionalities include:

- Functionality for users/domain experts to manually evaluate entities or their beliefs.
- Functionality to retrieve real time updates, for example like a heat map overlaid over an atlas of sinkhole activity.
- An API for specific domain's data retrieval.

3.8   Implementation Considerations

In this section, we elaborate into some practical issues regarding the distribution of the events in the system. The execution of Maps requires some form of time scheduling of the Map's invocation, and this can be addressed by two different approaches, viz. event-driven (Fig. 3) and periodic scheduling (Fig. 4).

Event Driven. In an event-driven scheduling setup, events will be triggered sporadically from maps with external interface, and whenever internal maps have produced new results. In both cases the events, are forwarded to the Intelligence Database, as outlined in Sect. 3.5. In addition, the events are re-transmitted to relevant Maps, i.e., to those that use the updated intelligence as input, and therefore they need to be informed about the changes. After completing execution, each Map sends the results to the Intelligence Database, for storage and re-transmission of this new relevant event.

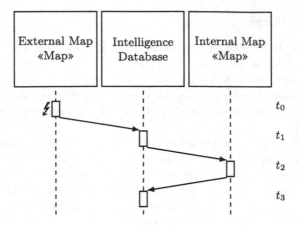

Fig. 3. Interaction diagram with events transmitted under an event-driven scheduling approach. ⚡ indicates external events triggering interactions in the system.

This is the quickest possible path from the producing Map through the Intelligence Database to the consuming Map/GUI, as events are transmitted and map execution is completed with the minimum delay from the inception of the event to the propagation of its results. However, special care must be paid of what triggers a message, i.e., if the intelligence changes constantly, then the data platform will be flooded with event notifications. The event driven approach also ensures that maps are only executed when their input, as aware by the Intelligence Database, is modified, which is the least likely to introduce delays in the overall process. However, an evident drawback of the event-driven scheduling approach combined with the feedback loop between the Intelligence Database and the Maps (Fig. 2), is that it might lead to indefinitely propagation of events. For instance, if the belief of an IP address is used as input, together with other intelligence, to derive the belief of an email address being used for phishing, and the belief of this email address is afterwards used to calculate a belief for the same IP address, then this event would in turn be used to generate a belief for the email address and so forth. This situation will potentially lead to an infinite loop. To avoid such infinite loops, we can adopt for instance a *Max Hop Counter*, in such way that an event may be forwarder a fixed number of loops before it is ceased propagation.

Periodic Scheduling. Periodic scheduling is an alternative approach where Maps are executed at fixed time, so they produce events periodically. This approach has the benefit that the Intelligence Database does not need to trace to which Maps a given event needs to be re-transmitted, and thus the aforementioned issue with the possible infinite loops is avoided. After the execution of the periodic Maps, the events are stored in the Intelligence Database without any further requirement for re-transmission. On the contrary, one apparent drawback is that occasional events might appear just after a period commenced. In

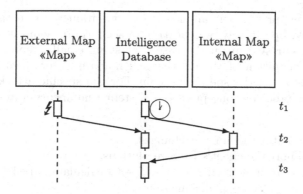

Fig. 4. Interaction diagram with events transmitted under a periodic scheduling app-roach. ⚡ indicates external events triggering interactions in the system. ⏱ indicates internal periodic timers triggering interactions in the system.

that case, the new intelligence is passed to the relevant maps only after the next period, i.e., making this approach sensitive to the selection of the time interval of the period. Furthermore, the propagation of intelligence can only happen for one map per period, so if for instance three maps are chained one depending on the other, it will take three periods for the propagation to complete and that is the best - quickest - case, where the map execution completes within a period. Another drawback is that without tracking by the Intelligence Database of data changes and which Maps rely on that data, all maps have to be re-executed on all the data on every period.

Lastly, recall that maps can use any part of the design matrices, including historical data. Consequently, the periodic scheduling implies that all data have to be transferred to all Maps, and all Maps have to be evaluated for each period. This is expected to be cumbersome, given the anticipated amount of intelligence data, let alone complicated to perform frequently enough in order to achieve propagation that approaches near real-time.

4 Use Case Scenario: Phishing Attack

In a nutshell, phishing email attack is a well known cyber crime that seeks to trick a victim into revealing personal data, credit cards, passwords and other sensitive information [14]. Phishing can be performed in various ways, but typi-cally evolves around deceiving an unsuspecting user to access a malicious website under the control of the attacker. However, this website aims to mimic a trust-worthy one. One main approach for detecting phishing campaigns is the analysis of domain names contained in potential phishing emails [6]. Since the resolu-tion of a domain name to IP address takes place before the browser connects to the phishing site, such an approach can protect a victim before they access the website.

Following, we present the application of our framework to the use case of phishing attack. Specifically, we construct a scenario to demonstrate the interactions within our system, in the case a phishing email is spreading over the Internet. The definition of the entities and maps is determined based on the expert's knowledge of the specific domain. For the specific attack scenario, we implemented a proof of concept of our system that incorporates in total five Maps:

- A Map to monitor the email exchanges.
- A Map to report the client's DNS resolutions.
- A Map using an undefined ML classifier to calculate a belief of whether a DNS request is about a malicious domain.
- A Map implementing the heuristic if a *URL* is hosting malicious content, such as a phishing page or a malicious script.
- Finally, a Map inferring if an email is part of a phishing attack.

The interactions of the involved system components are depicted in Fig. 5 and constitute three major phases:

1. At the beginning, the *Email Monitoring* Agent reports an email containing a URL. This event is transmitted to the *Intelligence Database* and propagated to the *Email is Phishing* Map, which applies the heuristic whether a given email is malicious. Then, the *Email is Phishing* Map triggers the *URL is Malicious* Map, which derives a maliciousness score according to its internal heuristic. The *Email is Phishing* then outputs a phishing score to the *Intelligence Database*. If the URL is not considered malicious then the email does not contain phishing contents. The relevant belief is thus set to 0.0.
2. Following, the *DNS Resolver* Agent reports that the client, which had previously received the email, resolves afterwards the domain `evil.com`. This event is forwarded to the *Domain is Malicious* Map, where the domain is determined as malicious, and the result is stored in the database.
3. After a while the *Email Monitoring* Agent reports a new email containing a URL similar to the previous. The *Intelligence Database* triggers the *Email is Phishing* Map. In turn, this Map hands over the URL to *URL is Malicious* and receives the maliciousness score of 1.0 for the URL. The *Email is Phishing* Map then outputs *Phishing Email*:1.0 to the *Intelligence Database*. Since, the user resolved a malicious domain (`evil.com`) right after receiving an email containing this malicious URL, the heuristics of *Email is Phishing* Map predicts that the email is phishing attack, and thus set the value of that belief to 1.0.

This example scenario follows a belief propagation approach to spread the impact of an event/interaction to the involved instances. In this case, the data related to instances involved in the event would be updated to reflect the dynamic behaviour of that instance. In our use case scenario, the query for the domain *evil.com* by the recipient of the email affects the maliciousness score of the email and the URL of the subsequent events.

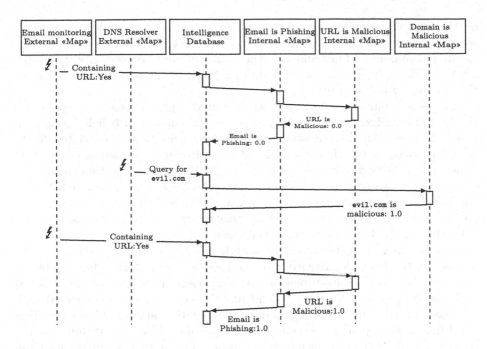

Fig. 5. Events propagation during the phishing email scenario. ⚡ indicates external events triggering interactions in the system. Arrows signify event transmission, with labels informally summarising the new or updated intelligence (New rows for, or updates to, the design matrices). The Maps rely on pulling additional data from the Intelligence Database, but this is omitted here for brevity and simplicity.

5   Conclusion

As the sophisticated techniques from the side of the evildoers are evolving with the purpose to disguise their actions and deceive the end-users, more advanced methodologies are also required for distinguishing between benign and malicious resources and activities. The perpetrators behind malicious actions are constantly in move, thus, making a static counteraction against the involved entities unsuitable for such a dynamic environment. What can be considered benign one day, it can turn malicious the next day, and vice versa on a later day. By statically blacklisting and blocking the malicious sources of today's cannot provide protection in the long run. In this context, security intelligence aims to uncover threats and threat actors, in order to prevent and mitigate their impact. However, traversing through all available intelligence requires automated processes, making the belief propagation approach a necessity to meet requirements and expectations of end-users who anticipate a safer Internet.

To this end, we present the reference architecture of a framework that allows the use of intelligence to provide beliefs in which degree specific entities or resources may be involved in malicious activities. The framework is designed on the basis to accommodate intelligence from various topics and applications, so it will be generic, domain agnostic, and capable to incorporate a non-limited number of sources and information types. Furthermore, to exemplify the framework's mode of operation, we provide as a proof of concept its deployment to the use case of phishing attacks.

In essence, our framework is centred around a graph structure representation of the intelligence data and leverages on the concept of belief propagation in accordance with the trustworthiness of the events that it is related to. In addition, based on functionality of the Maps and their invocation as new threats appear, the intelligence knowledge is updated and evolved. Over time, new types of intelligence sources will be discovered or relation will be formulated. Hence, the framework supports extensions to new maps, both for external and internal interactions. Furthermore, the design matrix approach enables a flexible and extensible method to achieve this requirement.

The formulation of the data types and the operations on the intelligence data depend on the expert's knowledge of the specific domain. Therefore, as future work, we plan to enhance our platform with a variety of use case scenarios related with the domain of DNS security and how domain names are correlated with malicious actions, like botnets, malware propagation and phishing campaigns [1]. Finally, we intend to investigate the appropriate ML algorithms for the accurate and timely calculation of the belief propagation in an event-driven implementation of the proposed platform.

References

1. Anagnostopoulos, M., Kambourakis, G., Gritzalis, S.: New facets of mobile botnet: architecture and evaluation. Int. J. Inf. Sec. **15**(5), 455–473 (2016)
2. Barnum, S.: Standardizing cyber threat intelligence information with the structured threat information expression (stix). Mitre Corporation **11**, 1–22 (2012)
3. Choi, H., Lee, H.: Identifying botnets by capturing group activities in DNS traffic. Comput. Netw. **56**(1), 20–33 (2012)
4. Gao, Y., Xiaoyong, L., Hao, P., Fang, B., Yu, P.: Hincti: A cyber threat intelligence modeling and identification system based on heterogeneous information network. IEEE Trans. Knowl. Data Eng., 1–1 (2020). https://doi.org/10.1109/TKDE.2020.2987019
5. Garcia-Lebron, R.B., Schweitzer, K.M., Bateman, R.M., Xu, S.: A framework for characterizing the evolution of cyber attacker-victim relation graphs. In: MILCOM 2018–2018 IEEE Military Communications Conference (MILCOM), pp. 70–75. IEEE (2018)
6. Hageman, K., Kidmose, E., Hansen, R.R., Pedersen, J.M.: Can a TLS Certificate Be Phishy? In: 18th International Conference on Security and Cryptography, SECRYPT 2021, pp. 38–49 (2021)
7. Hamilton, W.L., Ying, R., Leskovec, J.: Inductive representation learning on large graphs. In: Proceedings of the 31st International Conference on Neural Information Processing Systems, pp. 1025–1035 (2017)
8. Khalil, I., Yu, T., Guan, B.: Discovering malicious domains through passive DNS data graph analysis. In: Proceedings of the 11th ACM ASIACCS, pp. 663–674. ACM (2016)

9. Laghaout, A.: Supervised learning on heterogeneous, attributed entities interacting over time. arXiv preprint arXiv:2007.11455 (2020)
10. Li, V.G., Dunn, M., Pearce, P., McCoy, D., Voelker, G.M., Savage, S.: Reading the tea leaves: a comparative analysis of threat intelligence. In: 28th USENIX Security Symposium, pp. 851–867 (2019)
11. Manadhata, P.K., Yadav, S., Rao, P., Horne, W.: Detecting malicious domains via graph inference. In: Kutyłowski, M., Vaidya, J. (eds.) ESORICS 2014. LNCS, vol. 8712, pp. 1–18. Springer, Cham (2014). https://doi.org/10.1007/978-3-319-11203-9_1
12. Modi, A., et al.: Towards automated threat intelligence fusion. In: 2nd IEEE CIC, pp. 408–416. IEEE (2016)
13. Moura, G.C., Müller, M., Wullink, M., Hesselman, C.: ndews: a new domains early warning system for TLDS. In: NOMS 2016, pp. 1061–1066. IEEE (2016)
14. Panum, T.K., Hageman, K., Hansen, R.R., Pedersen, J.M.: Towards adversarial phishing detection. In: 13th USENIX Workshop on CSET20 (2020)
15. Qamar, S., Anwar, Z., Rahman, M.A., Al-Shaer, E., Chu, B.T.: Data-driven analytics for cyber-threat intelligence and information sharing. COSE **67**, 35–58 (2017)
16. Rahbarinia, B., Perdisci, R., Antonakakis, M.: Segugio: efficient behavior-based tracking of malware-control domains in large ISP networks. In: 45th Annual IEEE/IFIP DSN, pp. 403–414. IEEE (2015)
17. Sun, X., Wang, Z., Yang, J., Liu, X.: Deepdom: malicious domain detection with scalable and heterogeneous graph convolutional networks. COSE **99**, 102057 (2020)
18. Tran, H., Nguyen, A., Vo, P., Vu, T.: Dns graph mining for malicious domain detection. In: 2017 IEEE International Conference on Big Data (Big Data), pp. 4680–4685. IEEE (2017)
19. Wagner, T.D., Mahbub, K., Palomar, E., Abdallah, A.E.: Cyber threat intelligence sharing: survey and research directions. COSE **87**, 101589 (2019)
20. Zhang, J., Shi, X., Xie, J., Ma, H., King, I., Yeung, D.Y.: GaAN: gated attention networks for learning on large and spatiotemporal graphs. arXiv preprint arXiv:1803.07294 (2018)

The Complexity of Testing Cryptographic Devices on Input Faults

Alisher Ikramov[✉] and Gayrat Juraev

National University of Uzbekistan, Tashkent, Uzbekistan
a.ikramov@mathinst.uz

Abstract. The production of logic devices faces the occurrence of faults during production. We analyze the complexity of testing a special type of logic device on inverse, adhesion, and constant input faults. The focus of this work is on devices that implement cryptographic functions. The aim is to demonstrate the effect of bijection of the function on the complexity of its testing. We find and prove the complexity values not only of the main faults but also of some frequently occurring subsets. The work shows that for a special case of the length of the text block is equal to the length of the key the complexity of testing cryptographic devices is asymptotically half the complexity of testing logic devices on the same types of input faults.

Keywords: Complexity · Cryptographic devices · Input faults · Testing

1 Introduction

We have a logic device with some inputs and outputs. The number of inputs and outputs for each given device is fixed. It is assumed that this device in good condition implements a Boolean function f with n variables. If we know a function, but we want to know if the device is implemented correctly, then we can use the testing method. The main aim is to reduce the time consumed by the testing of each device. Statistical methods do not allow to have a 100% certainty in the absence of the faults of the given type and require a lot of time. The testing approach constructs the exact test set for each type of faults and allows us to have a certainty in the absence of these faults if the testing is successful.

Using Shannon's function to measure the complexity of testing we can determine the upper boundary of the length of each test and limit the time required for the testing.

1.1 Objective

The aim of the work is to demonstrate the change in complexity of testing cryptographic devices on the selected types of input faults in contrast with the complexity of testing Boolean function with the same total number of inputs on the same types of input faults. Cryptographic devices are often tested on the Control Example, however, not all input faults can be tested using such Examples. The study of the complexity of testing of cryptographic devices on input faults is a new direction in the field.

© Springer Nature Switzerland AG 2021
M. Yang et al. (Eds.): NSS 2021, LNCS 13041, pp. 202–209, 2021.
https://doi.org/10.1007/978-3-030-92708-0_12

1.2 Definitions

We will use definitions similar to [1].

A fault is a mapping $\varphi: E_2^n \rightarrow Q$, where $Q \subseteq E_2^n$.

A checking test for a set of faults $\Phi = \{\varphi$ is a fault$\}$ and a function f is a $T \subseteq E_2^n$ such that for any fault $\varphi \in \Phi$ the fact that $f(\varphi) \neq f$ implies the existence of an $\alpha \in T$ such that $f(\varphi(\alpha)) \neq f(\alpha)$. So, for any fault that affects the current function there is at least one vector in T on which the initial function and the function affected by the fault have different values.

Faults of the conjunctive adhesion type split the set of variables X^n into non-empty subsets $Z_1(\varphi), \ldots, Z_{q_\varphi}(\varphi)$, $q_\varphi \in N_{n-1}$ so that for any $\alpha \in E_2^n$, $\alpha = (\alpha_1, \ldots, \alpha_n)$ we put $\varphi(\alpha) = \beta = (\beta_1, \ldots, \beta_n)$, where $\beta_i = \min\{\alpha_j : x_j \in Z_l(\varphi)\}$, if $x_i \in Z_l(\varphi)$, $l \in N_{q_\varphi}$, $i = \overline{1, n}$. The notation is $S_{\&}^2$. These types of faults are determined by the subset of inputs. All inputs in this subset are made to be equal the same value, which is the minimum value in the initial values of inputs in this subset. So, they all will be 0 by this fault if at least one input is assigned 0, and they all will be 1 by this fault if and only if they all are assigned 1.

Faults of disjunctive adhesion type split the set of variables X^n into non-empty subsets $Z_1(\varphi), \ldots, Z_{q_\varphi}(\varphi)$, $q_\varphi \in N_{n-1}$ so that for any $\alpha \in E_2^n$, $\alpha = (\alpha_1, \ldots, \alpha_n)$ we put $\varphi(\alpha) = \beta = (\beta_1, \ldots, \beta_n)$, where $\beta_i = \max\{\alpha_j : x_j \in Z_l(\varphi)\}$, if $x_i \in Z_l(\varphi)$, $l \in N_{q_\varphi}$, $i = \overline{1, n}$. The notation is $S_\vee^2$. These types of faults are determined by the subset of inputs. All inputs in this subset are made to be equal the same value, which is the maximum value in the initial values of inputs in this subset. So, they all will be 1 by this fault if at least one input is assigned 1, and they all will be 0 by this fault if and only if they all are assigned 0.

Let $\oplus$ be addition modulo 2 and $\alpha \oplus \beta = \gamma$, where $\alpha_i \oplus \beta_i = \gamma_i$. We put In = $\{\varphi_\sigma : \sigma \in E_2^n \ (\varphi_\sigma(\alpha) = \alpha \oplus \sigma)\}$. We denote $\tilde{0} = (0, 0, \ldots, 0) \in E_2^n$. The set $F_{in}^2 =$ In $\setminus \{\varphi_{\tilde{0}}\}$ is called the class of inverse faults. An inverse fault affects a selected subset of inputs changing their initial values to the opposite values. The subset of inputs that is affected by the fault φ_σ is defined by those positions that are equal 1 in σ.

We denote (1) $F_{in}^2 = \{\varphi_\sigma \in$ In: $\sigma \in E_2^n, \|\sigma\| = 1\}$. These faults change only one input to the opposite value.

The complexity of testing a function $\{f\}$ for a fault class K is called the minimum $|T|$ (where $|T|$ is the number of elements in the set T), where T is a checking test. The notation is $L(f, K)$.

The complexity of testing a set of functions N for a class of faults K is L (N, K) = $\max_{f \in N} L(f, K)$.

Constant faults identify some subset of variables as some fixed values. The notation is C^2. These faults change values of some inputs to the constant values regardless of the initial assignment of the inputs of the device.

A transformation $F : E_2^{n+m} \rightarrow E_2^n$ is called a cryptographic function if for all k in E_2^m the function $F(\cdot, k)$ is a bijective mapping onto E_2^n. The class of all such functions will be denoted by Cr (n, m).

1.3   Related Work

D.S. Romanov [2] studied the issue of the complexity of testing devices with faults on inputs such as permutation of inputs and gave an upper bound $n \log_2 n$. The result was based on a modification of G.R. Poghosyan (Lemma 24 from Chapter 3 in [1]). G.V. Antyufeev and D.S. Romanov in [3] determined the complexity of testing logic devices with faults on inputs such as a simple shift equal to 2. In simple shifts, the fault function shifts the variables to the left, and sets the freed values of the last variables to constant values (these values and the shift value determine this fault). It is worth noting that this work also studied the complexity of diagnosing a fault (determining a specific type of malfunction), the order of which is $2^{n/2}$.

D.S. Romanov and G.V. Antyufeev studied the issue of the complexity of testing for local constant faults in [4]. In local constant faults, only a certain number of consecutive variables are set to constant values. While in [1] the linear complexity of checking tests for all constant faults was shown, the authors demonstrated the exponential (on the number of variables that are set to constants) complexity of the diagnostic test.

E.V. Morozov and D.S. Romanov studied the complexity of testing for linear adhesions in [5], in addition, K.A. Popkov studied certain types of circuits, for example, built only from functional elements with exactly two inputs in [6].

2   Results

Here we expand further results from the achieved in [7] and [8]. The linear and cyclic faults are not covered as they were already presented in [9].

2.1   Inverse Faults

Both the complexity of checking for the presence of single inversions at the inputs (a common fault) and checking for the entire class of inverse malfunctions are interesting issues for engineers. The following statement is true:

Theorem 1. $L(Cr(n, m), F_{in}^2(1)) = m - t$, where $2^{t-1} + t \leq m \leq 2^t + t$.

Proof. Since a fault can occur only on one input and any cryptographic function $F(\cdot, k)$ is bijective, any set of one vector tests the presence of an inversion of one input in the first n variables. Hence, the complexity of testing cannot exceed the complexity of testing a function with m inputs (since any test also checks the first n inputs). We get the upper boundary of $L(Cr(n, m), F_{in}^2(1)) \leq m - t$.

We construct function $F = (f_1, \ldots, f_n)$ as follows:

$$f_i(x_1, \ldots x_{n+m}) = x_i \oplus f_c(x_{n+1}, \ldots, x_{n+m})$$

$$f_c(x_1, \ldots, x_m) = \bigvee_{i=t+1}^{m} x_i j_{\alpha_1^i}(x_1) \ldots j_{\alpha_t^i}(x_t),$$

where vector α^i is equal to binary representation of the number i. The function $j_\beta(x)$ is equal 1 when $\beta = x$, otherwise it equals 0. According to Sentence 12 in Chapter 3 of [1] the complexity of testing function f_c for single inversion is $m - t$. Then we get the bottom boundary of $L(F, F_{in}^2(1)) \geq m - t$. Combining two boundaries we get $L(Cr(n, m), F_{in}^2(1)) = m - t$. $\square$

Next, we consider the complexity of testing cryptographic functions on all inverse faults.

Theorem 2. $2[(m-1)/2] + 1 \leq L(Cr(n, m), F_{in}^2) \leq m + 1$.

Proof. Let us consider an arbitrary vector α and a cryptographic function F. The function $F(\cdot, k)$ is bijective when k is fixed. The number of vectors $\beta = (\beta_1,\ldots, \beta_n, k_1, \ldots, k_m)$ such that $F(\beta) \neq F(\alpha)$ is equal to $2^n - 1$ (the function can have similar value only on one vector among all vectors with the same key value). Therefore, the number of faults $\phi_\sigma \in F_{in}^2$ that can be checked using the vector α is equal to $2^m(2^n - 1) = 2^{n+m} - 2^m$. Hence, the number of unchecked faults is equal to $2^m - 1$. Using Lemma 24 from Chapter 3 in [1] the number of vectors in the smallest checking test cannot exceed $m + 1$.

We get the bottom boundary from Theorem 7 in [1] if we choose the function $F = (f_1,\ldots, f_n)$ as

$$f_i(x_1,\ldots x_{n+m}) = x_i \oplus f_{in}(x_{n+1}, \ldots, x_{n+m}).$$

where $f_{in}(x_1, \ldots, x_{2t+1}) = x_{2t+1} \oplus \sum_{i=1}^t x_{2i-1} \& x_{2i}$. We have $2t + 1 = m$ for odd values of m, and $2t + 2 = m$ for even values of m. $\square$

2.2   Adhesion Faults

As two types of faults $S_\vee^2$ and $S_\&^2$ are ambivalent, their complexity of testing must be the same.

Theorem 3. $m - 1 \leq L(Cr(n, m), S_\vee^2) \leq m +]\log_2 n[$.

Proof. We choose a vector α in which the first n components are equal to 0, and the remaining components are equal to 1. This vector is called "separating", since by the definition of a cryptographic function it will allow us to determine whether any adhesion of any of the first n variables with any of the rest m variables occurs.

A logarithmic system is a system of$]\log_2 n[$ vectors whose weight in the first n components is equal to $n/2$ (in the case of odd n it is equal to $[n/2$ or$]n/2[$), as well as the weight of the first n values of the component sum modulo 2 of any of two vectors from this system is equal to $n/2$ (that is, in the place of half of the units of one vector, the second vector has ones, in the place of the remaining units of the first vector, the second vector has zeros, similarly to half of the zeros of the first vector, the second vector corresponds to ones, the remaining zeros of the first vector to zeros of the second vector).

Using any logarithmic system with components from $n + 1$ to $n + m$ being equal to 1, we can determine any adhesion of the first n variables.

The logarithmic system makes it possible at each step to reduce the number of unverified adhesion faults of the first n variables by half. Due to bijectivity with respect to the first n variables, any change in the vector will lead to a change in the value of the function. Using Lemma 20 from [1], we construct a test for checking m key variables (knowing from previous testing vectors that there are certainly no other adhesions in the device under study). This requires no more than $m - 1$ vectors in the test set (according to Proposition 6 in [1]). Therefore, the constructed set of vectors is a checking test with $m +]\log_2 n[$ vectors.

The bottom boundary can be achieved using $F(x_1,\ldots, x_n, x_{n+1},\ldots, x_{n+m}) = (f_1,\ldots, f_n)$ with

$$f_i(x_1, x_2, \ldots, x_n, \ldots x_{n+m}) = x_1 \oplus (x_2 \& \ldots \& x_{n+m})$$

$$f_i(x_1, \ldots, x_{n+m}) = x_i \text{ for } 2 \leq i \leq n.$$

The adhesion of m last variables can be checked with not less than $m - 1$ vectors in the test set according to Theorem 5 in [1]. □

Corollary 1. $m - 1 \leq L(Cr(n, m), S_\&^2) \leq m +]\log_2 n[$

Theorem 4. The following is true for all $m, n \geq 2$:

$$2(m - 1) \leq L(Cr(n,m), S_V^2 \cup S_\&^2) \leq 2m +] \log_2 n[.$$

Proof. At first, we use two separating vectors (the second one is the inverse of the separating vector in Theorem 3). As $S_V^2 \cup S_\&^2$ means that only one type of fault can be on inputs, not of both types mixed, these two separating vectors allow us to consider text and key variables separately. To check adhesion of the first n variables it is enough to use one logarithmic system where all input variables from $n + 1$ to $n + m$ are either all zeros or all ones in order to exclude the adhesion of those variables from interference. Then, we add vectors to check both types of adhesion of variables $x_{n+1}, \ldots, x_{n+m}$. According to Theorem 8 in [1] we get the test set. Thus, $L(Cr(n,m), S_V^2 \cup S_\&^2) \leq 2 +] \log_2 n[+ 2(m - 1) = 2m +] \log_2 n[.$

For the bottom boundary we use cryptographic function $F(x_1, \ldots, x_n, x_{n+1}, \ldots, x_{n+m}) = (f_1, \ldots, f_n)$ with

$$f_i(x_1, \ldots, x_{n+m}) = x_1 \oplus x_2 \& \ldots \& x_{n+m} \oplus \overline{x_2} \& \ldots \& \overline{x_{n+m}}$$

$$f_i(x_1, \ldots, x_{n+m}) = x_i \text{ for } 2 \leq i \leq n.$$

As F changes its behavior only when keys are $(0, \ldots, 0)$ and $(1, \ldots, 1)$, and when components from 2 to n being equal to key values, then the checking test of adhesion of $x_{n+1}, \ldots, x_{n+m}$ must be a union of checking tests for conjunctive and disjunctive adhesions, or $L(F, S_V^2 \cup S_\&^2) \geq 2(m - 1)$. □

2.3   Constant Faults

We will consider only constant faults with the same constant value. The constant faults that identify some variables with only value 1 are denoted as C_1^2. Similarly, the constant faults that identify some variables with only value 0 are denoted as C_0^2.

Theorem 5. $L(Cr(n, m), C_v^2) = m + 1$, where $v \in \{0, 1\}$

Proof. Let us choose vector α as $\alpha_i = \overline{v}$ for $i = \overline{1, n}$, and $\alpha_j = v$ for $j = \overline{n+1, n+m}$. Using the bijectivity of a cryptographic function with the fixed key components, we can see that any constant fault changing value of any one of first n variables will be checked by α. Thus, we only need to check for the constant faults on the rest of the variables. According to Theorem 3 in [1] the complexity of the smallest test on m variables does not exceed m. Adding vector α we get the full checking test for the function F, so, the complexity is $L(Cr(n, m), C_v^2) \leq m + 1$.

Let us consider $F \in Cr(n, m)$ as $F = (f_1, ..., f_n)$, where $f_i = x_i$ for $i = \overline{1, n-1}, f_n = x_n \oplus g(x_{n+1}, ..., x_{n+m})$, and $g(x_{n+1}, ..., x_{n+m}) = j_v(x_{n+1}) \& ... \& j_v(x_{n+m})$. The function $j_v(x)$ is equal to 1 only when x is equal to v. According to Theorem 3 in [1] the complexity of testing g on constant faults is not less than m. The smallest test set consists of vectors β^i with $\beta_{n+i}^i = \overline{v}$, $\beta_j^i = v$, $j \in \{n + 1, ..., n + m\}$ \ $\{i + n\}$. All these vectors can contain arbitrary values of the first $n - 1$ variables. However, if any of these vectors has x_n not equal to v, we can find the fault from C_v^2, that is not checked by this set: for vector β^k the fault of identifying both variables x_n and x_{n+k} as v. If there are several such vectors, then the fault assigns all corresponding variables and x_n to v. Hence, we do not have any vector that checks x_n being solely identified as v. Therefore, it is not enough to have m vectors in the checking test. So, we have the complexity $L(Cr(n, m), C_v^2) \geq m + 1$. $\square$

We have a specific subset of constant faults where only one variable can be set to constant. The set of all these faults is denoted as C_v^2 (1).

Corollary 2. $L(Cr(n, m), C_v^2 (1)) = m + 1$, $v \in \{0, 1\}$

2.4   Special Case

According to Shannon [10], a necessary condition for an ideal cipher is the following condition: the cardinality of the key space must not be less than the cardinality of the text space. Therefore, in symmetric block data encryption algorithms, the minimum key size is equal to the text block size. Therefore, the question of assessing the complexity of testing for $m = n$ is of interest. Due to partial bijectivity, these assessments take on a specific form.

Corollary 3. $L(Cr(n, n), F_{in}^2(1)) \sim \frac{1}{2} L(2n, F_{in}^2(1))$

Proof. According to Theorem 1 we have $L(Cr(n, n), F_{in}^2(1)) = n - t$, where $2t - 1 + t \leq n \leq 2t + t$. Dividing the complexity of testing on single inverse faults by this result we get:

$$\frac{L\big(2n, F_{in}^2(1)\big)}{L\big(Cr(n,n), F_{in}^2(1)\big)} \sim \frac{2n-]\log_2 2n[}{n-]\log_2 n[} \sim \frac{2n}{n} = 2 \qquad\qquad \square$$

Corollary 4. $L(Cr(n,\ n),\ F_{in}^2) \sim \frac{1}{2} L(2n, F_{in}^2))$

Proof. Using Theorem 2 from $n - 1 \le L(Cr(n,\ n), F_{in}^2)) \le n + 1$ we get:
  $L(2n, F_{in}^2)) \div L(Cr(n,\ n), F_{in}^2)) \sim 2n \div n = 2$
  For adhesion faults we have:

Corollary 5. $L(Cr(n,\ n),\ S_t^2) \sim \frac{1}{2} L(2n, S_t^2)$, where $t \in \{\vee,\ \&\}$
Proof. Using Theorem 3 and Sentence 6 in [1] we get:
  $L(Cr(n,\ n), S_t^2) : L(2n, S_t^2) = (n +] \log_2 n[) : (2n - 1) \sim n : (2n) = \frac{1}{2} \square$

Corollary 6. $L(Cr(n,\ n),\ C_t^2) \sim \frac{1}{2} L(2n, C_t^2)$, where $t \in \{0,\ 1\}$
Proof. Using Theorem 5 and Theorem 3 in [1] we get:
  $L(Cr(n,\ n), C_t^2) : L(2n, C_t^2) = (n + 1) : (2n - 2]\log_2 n[) \sim n : (2n) = \frac{1}{2} \square$

3 Conclusion and Discussion

Using the bijectivity of a cryptographic function on any fixed key value we achieved asymptotically half of the complexity for all main types of input faults with the same length of text block as the length of the key value. It helps to test produced cryptographic devices almost twice faster in comparison with the other devices with the same number of inputs. This process not only reduces the testing time but also increases certainty in the absence of the input faults in the case of the successful test.

Funding. The research was fulfilled under project UZB-Ind-2021-98 – "Research and development of stream encryption algorithm".

Conflict of Interests Authors declare no conflict of interests.

References

1. Kudryavtsev, V.B., Gasanov, E.E., Dolotova, O.A., Pogosyan, G.R.: Theory of Testing Logical Devices. Fizmatlit, Moscow (2006)
2. Romanov, D.S.: Proc. XVI International Conf. Problems of Theoretical Cybernetics (N. Novgorod) 396 (2011)
3. Romanov, D.S., Antyufeev, G.V.: 2012 Proc. XI International Seminar Discrete Mathematics and Its Applications (Moscow: MSU) 163–5 (2012)
4. Antyufeev, G.V., Romanov, D.S.: J. Iss. Radio Electron. **7**, 49–51 (2016)
5. Morozov, E.V., Romanov, D.S.: J. Appl. Ind. Math. **9**(2), 263–270 (2015)
6. Popkov, K.A.: J. Disc. Anal. Oper. Res. **26**(1), 89–113 (2019)
7. Ikramov, A.A.: On complexity of testing cryptographic devices on inverse input faults. In: Proc. Lomonosov-2013, MSU, Moscow (2013)

8. Ikramov, A.A.: On complexity of testing cryptographic devices on adhesion input faults. In: Proc. Lomonosov-2014, MSU, Moscow (2014)
9. Ikramov, A.: Complexity of testing cryptographic functions on linear and cyclic input faults. In: Proc. Computational Models and Technologies: Abstracts of the Uzbekistan-Malaysia International Online Conference, pp. 102–4 (2020)
10. Shannon, C.E.: Communication theory of secrecy systems. Bell Syst. Tech. J. **28**(4), 656–715 (1949)

A Malware Family Classification Method Based on the Point Cloud Model DGCNN

Yuxin Ding[✉], Zihan Zhou, and Wen Qian

Harbin Institute of Technology, Shenzhen, China
yxding@hit.edu.cn

Abstract. Currently the number and types of malware increase rapidly, and traditional malware family classification technologies become more and more difficult to deal with them. With the rise of deep learning technology, various malware family classification methods based on deep learning technologies have been proposed, and these methods have achieved excellent results. One problem of most deep learning based models is that they need the input data should have a fixed data relationship. However, no prior knowledge shows that there existed such fixed data relationships. Another problem is that in present the characteristics of malware are often be expressed as binary sequences, API call sequences, Opcode sequences etc. These features are low-level features, and are not easy to be understood. To solve these issues, we propose a method based on the point cloud model to detect malware families. In the point cloud model each malware behavior is mapped to a point in the high-dimensional space. The point cloud model can learn the relationships among these behaviors. The method avoids predetermining the relationships among data, which is more reasonable for malware detection. In addition, we use the behavior report to describe malware behavior features, which can be easily understand by people. We apply this method to classify malware families. The experimental results show that the average precision and recall for family classification reach 96.67%, 96.58%, surpassing traditional deep learning models such as LSTM, CNN, and LSTM with attention mechanism.

Keywords: Malware · Machine learning · Point cloud · Deep learning

1 Introduction

In present Internet has become an important communication tool in people's daily life. When enjoying the convenience brought by Internet, we are also facing severe security challenges from the Internet. The wide application of Internet has led to the rapid growth of malware. Malware not only invades company servers or spreads ransom ware, but also invades personal computers, steals privacy information, and even invades into IoT devices to achieve various illegal purposes. Characterizing the malware families can improve the detection process and understand the malware patterns. Therefore, malware family classification has received more and more attentions in recent years. Malware can constantly evolve and change. Hackers can generate a malware by only a slight modification on an original malware. The rapid growth in the

© Springer Nature Switzerland AG 2021
M. Yang et al. (Eds.): NSS 2021, LNCS 13041, pp. 210–221, 2021.
https://doi.org/10.1007/978-3-030-92708-0_13

number and types of the malware have gradually made traditional malware classification methods very difficult to deal with it.

With the rise of deep learning technology, various malware family classification methods based on deep learning technologies have been proposed to detect malware, and these methods have achieved excellent results. Most deep learning based models need the input data should have a fixed data relationship, such as the input data for LSTM and RNN based models are sequences, while CNN requires the data can be constructed as a matrix. To satisfy the requirements of these models, a malware has to be divided into sequences with a certain length to form a picture, then CNN is used to extract features. The API calls of malware are organized as a sequence in chronological order and submitted to LSTM for processing.

Although malware behaviors occur sequentially, the time dependency relationship between these behaviors is often very weak. Sometimes the order of different behaviors can be random, and sometimes one behavior must precede other behaviors. To evade detection, malware writers often introduces many useless behaviors to hide malware. These behaviors are often independent with each other. Therefore, aforementioned deep learning models may not be well-suitable for learning the characteristics of malware. In addition, the input data used by deep learning are low-level malware behaviors, such as API sequence, Opcode sequences, etc. It is difficult for people to understand the meaning of these data.

To solve these issues, we propose to use point cloud model to detect malware families. Point cloud is a data set of points in a certain coordinate system, which has the characteristics of rigid transformations, varying sampling density, anti-density interference, and noise robustness. Deep learning models for point cloud need to meet these characteristics of point clouds. Point cloud models need not assume a predetermined relationships in data, and they can learn the relationships in data from training samples. The point model we use is DGCNN model proposed by Wang et al. [1]. We represent each behavior as a point in the high-dimensional space, and each malware as an object in the high-dimensional space. We use DGCNN to find the relationships among these data points. In our work, DGCNN is applied to classify different malware families. In addition, we use system behaviors to represent malware. Compare with the low level behaviors such as API sequences and opcode sequences, system behaviors, such as opening and deleting files, modifying the registry, have clear and concrete semantics, and can be easily understand.

2 Related Work

Malware detection methods can be divided into two categories: static detection and dynamic detection according to the extracted behaviors. In our work we use dynamic method to detect malware. Here, we only focus on the dynamic detection methods in this fields. Dynamic methods extract program behaviors by running malware. Some works in this field are described as follows.

Karbabet al. [2] obtained program behaviors by running programs in a sandbox, and used natural language processing methods such as BoW and n-gram to extract the features of behaviors. Then they used machine learning models such as SVM and KNN for classification. Jindal et al. [3] also used the similar method to obtain program behaviors, but they classified malware through a deep learning model, changing the malware classification problem into a text classification problem. Due to the use of the CNN network, feature engineering becomes simpler and can be easily generalized to other data.

Chistyakov et al. [4] used the various operations of programs on files as training data, and they represented each malware as a bipartite graph. There are two types of nodes in this bipartite graph, one representing event and the other representing parameters. The corresponding events and parameters are connected by edges. They used the autoencoder to train this sparse vector, and use the intermediate representation of the neural network as the embedding vector.

San et al. [5] proposed a static-based detection method. When signature detection cannot correctly classify malware into various families, they run the malware in a sandbox, and used the API sequence called by a malware as feature data, and then used random forest to classify malware families. Mohaisen et al. [6] also put programs into a sandbox for execution, and used the file system, memory, and network information in the report generated by the sandbox as features, then used traditional machine learning models, SVM and KNN for family classification.

Elkhawas et al. [7] used opcode as features, used n-gram to construct a vector representation of an individual, the PE header of the program also be used as auxiliary features. Manavi et al. [8] converted opcode into grayscale image, then constructed GIST vector from the grayscale image, and finally used GIST as features for classification. Lu et al. [9] regarded Opcode sequence as a kind of language, uses word2vec training to get word vectors, uses ELMO to get new word vectors, and finally used average pooling layer to get individual vector representation. Hardy et al. [10] expressed the appearance of a system API as 1, and no appearance as 0. The embedding vector representation of individuals are learned, and the neural network is used to classify malware families. Agrawal et al. [11] divided the original API sequence into sub-sequences, used the CNN model to extract the features of the sub-sequences, and then used the extracted vectors as features to classify malicious samples and benign samples.

Azmoodeh et al. [12] used the Opcodes of malware as features to establish a directed acyclic graph. The weight of an edge on this graph is the frequency of the two nodes appearing together. The convolutional neural network is used to classify the malware. Vikas et al. [13] proposed BLADE based on Opcode segments. Experiments show that BLADE is effective for recognizing different obfuscated malware.

Yang Pin et al. [14] used the system API sequence recorded by the cuckoo sandbox to construct a data flow graph of a malware. The weight of an edge in this data flow graph is the number of data flows and the amount of data. The graph embedding algorithm is used to learn the representation of nodes. They used individual graph embedding for malware classification.

Zhu et al. [15] marked the taint of APIs, and obtained API call graph by tracking API calls. They found that the same subgraph pattern tends to be in the same family. Wang et al. [16] extracted individual features through a multilayer neural network with attention mechanism. The multilayer attention mechanism provides different levels of information. They only used benign samples as the training data, and classify malware according to the distance between samples in the test set and training set.

Sun et al. [17] proposed an architecture of a malware intelligent detection model based on behavior graphs, which achieved high classification accuracy while reducing the high cost of graph matching. Pedro et al. [18] tried to combine multiple algorithms to improve model performance. They analyzed the benefits and disadvantages of using multiple algorithms to detect malware under different configurations. Akshara [19] proposed a CNN-based model to extract visual features from malware images. This model outperforms existing methods on benchmark datasets such as MalImg. Yang et al. [20] used the control flow graph (CFG) of the program as the source graph, and used graph convolution to learn embedding features of the control flow graph for family classification.

3 Our Approach

3.1 Embedded Representation of Behavioral Features

Malware can be represented using their behaviors. Different behaviors can be extracted from malware, such as API sequences and opcode sequences. In our work, we use system behaviors to describe a malware sample. Some samples of system behaviors of malware samples are shown in Table 1. Compared with the low level behaviors, such as API sequences and opcode sequences, system behaviors have clear and concrete semantics, and can be easily understand by people.

To get system behaviors of malware, we build a cuckoo sandbox on the Virtual Box, give enough permissions to programs in the sandbox, turn off the windows firewall, and modify the contents of the registry, so that malware cannot discover the existence of a sandbox. Our goal is to prevent a malware finds itself in a sandbox, otherwise, it will hide its malicious behaviors. We set a restore point. Every time a new malware is executed, the sandbox returns to the restore point. The sandbox monitors the running of a program and outputs its system behaviors into a behavior report. We extract the behaviors of each program from behavior reports and use them to represent malware samples.

Table 1. Examples of behaviors of malware

Individual malware	Behavior
7877d3f98d11	dll_load,C:\Windows\system32\pnrpnsp.dll
fa5ead3aa8c0	dll_load,C:\Windows\system32\pnrpnsp.dll
fa5ead3aa8c0	file_recreated,\Device\KsecDD

We extract 6,187 different behaviors, and identify each behavior with a unique number. We only take the first 300 behaviors from each malware, so that a malware sample can be represented as a 300 dimensional vector, such as [2351, 256, 874,..., 0], and each element in the vector is a ID of a system behavior. If a malware sample has less than 300 behaviors, we add the number 0 to the end of the vector. At this time, the behavior feature vector of a malware is a discrete vector. We use the embedding learning algorithm to learn the semantic representation of each behavior. We represent each behavior with a 100-dimensional embedding vector, and the embedding of each behavior is initialized randomly according to the normal distribution. In our work, we add an embedding layer before DGCNN to learn the embedding of each behavior.

3.2   Malware Detection Model

DGCNN [1] is a kind of dynamic graph convolution network inspired by PointNet and convolution operations. Instead of working on a single point like PointNet, it obtains the local geometric structure by constructing a local neighborhood graph and applies edge convolution operations on the local geometric structure to learn the embedded representation of graph nodes. Unlike traditional graph convolutional network, the graph structure in DGCNN is not fixed, which can be dynamically updated by each convolution layer of the network. That is, the set of k nearest neighbors of a point varies from one layer to another layer of the network, and is calculated according to the embedding order. Each convolution layer calculates the embedding of graph nodes by convoluting the node with its nearest k neighbors.

We denote the behavioral features of each malware as

$$X = \{x_1, x_2, \ldots, x_n\} \tag{1}$$

Each x_i is a behavior represented as a point on a high-dimensional coordinate, so that each malware is transformed into an object in a high-dimensional space, and e_{ij} is defined as the edge between x_i and x_j.

DGCNN model uses multiple convolution layers to learn the embedding of x_i. Each convolution layer transforms x_i into a new x_i'. The new x_i' not only contains the information of x_i itself, but also contains the information transferred from the nearest k neighbors of x_i. In order to obtain the local relationships between points, DGCNN uses the k-nearest neighbor algorithm to find the nearest k points for every point x_i, which is represented as (2). Therefore, DGCNN can use the local neighborhood information and global information to learn the embedding of x_i.

$$x\_neighbor\_k = \{x_{j1}, x_{j2}, \ldots, x_{jk}\} \tag{2}$$

Let x_j belong to x_neighbor_k, if the model has a disturbance T, then we have:

$$x_j + T - (x_i + T) = x_j - x_i \tag{3}$$

From (3) the corresponding local relationships can be obtained by $(x_j$-$x_i)$, and the translational interference is reduced. In order to keep the global information, x_i is also added, so we get an updated representation of edge e_{ij}', which is shown as (4).

$$e'_{ij} = ReLU\left(\theta x_i + \mu\left(x_j - x_i\right)\right) \tag{4}$$

Where θ and μ are the parameters of the adaptive learning model. We can get k updated edges for x_i, and choose the maximum value in each dimension among them as the new x_i', which is shown as (5).

$$x'_i = max\left(e'_{ij}\right) \tag{5}$$

The structure of DGCNN used in our work is shown in Fig. 1.

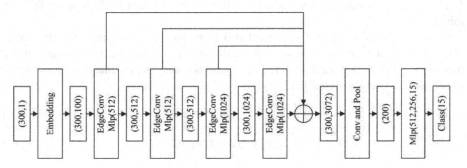

Fig. 1. Structure of DGCNN

Table 2. Values of hyperparameters

Hyperparameters	Value
Epoch	1000
Lr	0.01
Batch size	16
Random seed	1
Factor	0.1
Patience	50

The hyperparameters of DGCNN are shown in Table 2. We use the Adam optimizer to optimize the training algorithm and adjust the learning rate adaptively. When the loss does not decrease for a long time, the learning rate is reduced.

In our work, we use DGCNN to recognize malware families. We need to label the family of each malware. Each malware sample is sent to different anti-virus tools for analyzing its behaviors. Each anti-virus tool generates a behavior report for a malware, then we extract the behavior information from a report, and use AVCLASS to mark its families. We analyze 9568 malware samples and get their behavior reports. We delete some behavior reports only including a small number of behaviors, and finally get 8159 reports which can be used for experiments.

4   Experiments

4.1   Dataset and Evaluation Criteria

The number of malware samples is 8159, and these samples belong to 15 malware families. We choose four-fifths of samples from each family as the training set and the remaining samples as the test data. The task is to recognize the family a sample belongs to.

Because this is a multi-classification problem, we use accuracy, overall precision and overall recall to evaluate model performance. For each family F, we define TP as the number of samples in F correctly classified as F, TN as the number of samples in F misclassified as other families, and FP is the number of samples from other families misclassified as F.

The precision for family F is defined as (6), and the recall for family F is defined as (7). The overall precision and overall recall for all families are the average of the precision and recall for each family. The overall accuracy is percentage of the samples in all families correctly classified.

$$Precision = TP/(TP + FP) \tag{6}$$

$$Recall = TP/(TP + FN) \tag{7}$$

$$Accuracy = samples\ correctly\ classified/testing\ samples\ in\ all\ families \tag{8}$$

4.2   Experimental Results

In DGCNN, the number of neighbors k is also a hyperparameter. The value of k should not be as large as possible. If the value of k is too large, each point will be connected to too many surrounding points, which will produce a lot of redundant information. If the value of k is too small, the model will degenerate into a CNN model. We try different values of k to train the model. The experimental results are shown in Table 3.

Table 3. Experimental results for different values of k

K	Overall precision	Overall precision recall	Accuracy
5	0.9706	0.9475	0.9565
10	0.9720	0.9647	0.9657
20	0.9732	0.9582	0.9631

It can be seen that when k is greater than 10, the model performance become stable, and does not increase with the increase of neighbors. In our experiments, we set k as 10. When k = 10, the performance of DGCNN for each family is shown in Table 4. We can see DGCNN achieves good performance for recognizing members of each malware family. The overall precision, overall recall and accuracy of DGCNN are greater than 96%.

We also evaluate the influence of embedding size on the performance of the model. We still set k = 10, and make comparative experiments when the length of embedding vectors is set to different values. The experimental results are shown in Table 5.

In the experiment, we found that if the size of embedding vectors is too large (greater than 100 in our cases), the performance of DGCNN begins to decrease. The reason is that we cannot provide enough training samples to learn the complex embedding representations, and the model cannot fit training samples very well, on the other hand, the cost for model training significantly increase. If the embedding size is too small (smaller than 100 in our cases), the model cannot learn embedding vectors which can fully represent malware behaviors, so the model cannot accurately recognize malware families.

Table 4. Performance of DGCNN as k = 10

Family	Precision	Recall	Count
Scrinject	0.9833	0.9076	65
Blacole	0.9130	1.0	21
Gafgyt	1.0	1.0	52
Faceliker	0.9533	0.9825	229
Infected	0.96	1.0	48
Benign	1.0	1.0	110
Refresh	1.0	0.9545	44
Redir	0.9873	0.9285	84
Coinhive	0.9895	0.9310	203
Fareit	1.0	1.0	79
Playtech	1.0	1.0	35
Ramnit	0.9303	0.9962	268
Fakejquery	0.9463	0.9527	148
Expkit	0.9454	0.8965	58
Hidelink	0.9722	0.9210	76

Table 5. Experimental results for embedding vectors with different lengths

Embedding	Precision	Recall	Accuracy
50	0.9692	0.9562	0.9598
100	0.9720	0.9647	0.9657
300	0.9542	0.9330	0.9447

To intuitively observe the behavior distributions of malware families in the embedding space, we use TSNE to reduce the dimension of the embedding vector of each malware behavior to 3 dimensions. After removing the duplicate behaviors shared by all families, we can see the difference between families in Fig. 2.

In Fig. 2 we select four malware families, and each graph shows the behavior distributions of each family. Each behavior is a point in the coordinate system, and the behaviors belonging to different families appear different shapes and positions in the space, so DGCNN can learn the characteristics of each family well.

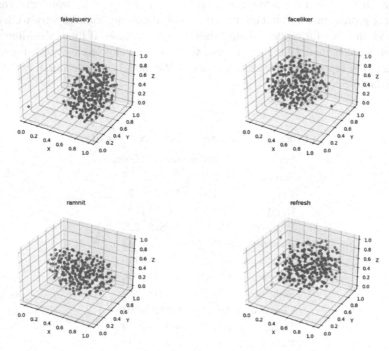

Fig. 2. The shapes and distributions of behaviors in different families

4.3   Comparative Experiments

We also train the LSTM, CNN, and MLP models on the same dataset to classify malware families. These models also have embedding and the embedding size of them is set to 100. At the beginning, the training accuracy of these deep models is very low. After we increase the batch size, the model accuracy increases significantly. The performance of these models is shown in Table 6.

Table 6. Experimental results of traditional deep learning model

Model	Batch size	Precision	Recall	Accuracy
RNN	512	0.7970	0.8098	0.8072
LSTM	512	0.8224	0.8153	0.8723
CNN	512	0.9399	0.9341	0.9429
MLP	512	0.9356	0.9400	0.9361

We found that the RNN has the worst performance, and LSTM also performs poorly. The input data of RNN and LSTM are behavior sequences. This shows that the temporal relationships between behaviors are weak, and temporal sequences cannot accurately represent the characteristics of malware behaviors. In order to learn the global relationships between behaviors, we tried the LSTM model with attention mechanism. The model can calculate an attention weight for each intermediate state of the LSTM network, and get the final result by weighting the attention weights. The experimental result is shown in Table 7.

It can be seen that compared with the original LSTM model, the performance of the LSTM model increases significantly, but it is still slightly lower than that of the DGCNN model. From the analysis of the results, we can see that the DGCNN can learn the relationships between malware samples. It uses the global information and local information to represent embedding of malware behaviors, which can better describe the characteristics of malware, therefore DGCNN achieves the best performance.

Table 7. Experimental result of LSTM with attention mechanism

Batch size	Precision	Recall	Accuracy
64	0.9724	0.9575	0.9612

Our data set is obtained by ourselves from the sandbox, which is not the same as other researchers' dataset. Here we only show some similar work for reference. The comparison results are shown in Table 8.

Table 8. Comparison with other methods

Model	Precision	Recall	Accuracy
Paper [14]	0.9074	0.9044	0.9048
Paper [20]	0.9381	0.9391	0.9379
Our	0.9720	0.9647	0.9657

Because the data sets are different, the results may not be accurate, but we can see that our method has higher performance than the comparison method, which shows that our method is effective for malware detection.

5 Conclusion

In our work, we use DGCNN to classify malware families. The contributions of this paper are as follows.

1. We use high-level features, system behaviors extracted from behavior reports to represent malware. Compared with traditional behavioral representation methods, system behavior can allow people to better understand malware.
2. Due to the similarity between point cloud and malware behavior, we apply a point cloud model, DGCNN to classify malware families. Compared with other deep models, DGCNN can learn the relations in data, which is well-suitable for malware detection.

The experimental results show that compared with other models, DGCNN achieves higher performance, which shows that DGCNN is suitable for learning the characteristics of malware. This study is supported by the National Natural Science Foundation of China (Grant No. 61872107), and we are very grateful for the support.

References

1. Wang, Y., Sun, Y., Liu, Z.: Dynamic graph CNN for learning on point clouds. ACM Trans. Graph. (TOG) **38**(5), 1–12 (2019)
2. Karbab, E.M.B., Debbabi, M.: Portable, data-driven malware detection using natural language processing and machine learning techniques on behavioral analysis reports. Dig. Invest. **28**, 77–87 (2019)
3. Jindal, C., Salls, C., Aghakhani, H.: Neurlux: dynamic malware analysis without feature engineering. In: Proceedings of the 35th Annual Computer Security Applications Conference, pp. 444–455 (2019)
4. Chistyakov, A., Lobacheva, E., Kuznetsov, A.: Semantic Embeddings for Program Behavior Patterns. arXiv preprint arXiv:1804.03635 (2018)
5. San, C.C., Thwin, M.M.S., Htun, N.L.: Malicious software family classification using machine learning multi-class classifiers. In: Proceedings of the Sixth International Conference on Computational Science and Technology, pp. 423–433 (2019)
6. Mohaisen, A., Alrawi, O., Mohaisen, M.: Amal: high-fidelity, behavior-based automated malware analysis and classification. Comput. Secur. **52**, 251–266 (2015)
7. Elkhawas, A.I., Abdelbaki, N.: Malware detection using opcode trigram sequence with SVM. In: The 26th International Conference on Software, Telecommunications and Computer Networks (SoftCOM), pp. 1–6 (2018)
8. Manavi, F., Hamzeh, A.: A new method for malware detection using opcode visualization. In: Artificial Intelligence and Signal Processing Conference, pp. 96–102 (2017)
9. Lu, R.: Malware Detection with LSTM Using Opcode Language. arXiv preprint arXiv:1906.04593 (2019)
10. Hardy, W., Chen, L., Hou, S.: DL4MD: a deep learning framework for intelligent malware detection. In: Proceedings of the International Conference on Data Mining, p. 61 (2016)
11. Agrawal, R., Stokes, J.W., Marinescu, M.: Robust neural malware detection models for emulation sequence learning. In: IEEE Military Communications Conference, pp. 1–8 (2018)
12. Azmoodeh, A., Dehghantanha, A., Choo, K.K.R.: Robust malware detection for internet of (Battlefield) things devices using deep eigenspace learning. IEEE Trans. Sustain. Comput. **4**(1), 88–95 (2018)
13. Vikas, S., Manu, V., Pradeep, S.: BLADE: robust malware detection against obfuscation in android. For. Sci. Int. Dig. Invest. **38**, 30116 (2018)

14. Yang, P., Zhu, Y., Zhang, L.: Malicious code family classification based on attribute data flow graph. Inf. Secur. Res. **6**(3), 226–234 (2020)
15. Zhu, X.B., Zhou, A.M., Zuo, Z.: Malicious code detection based on frequent subgraph mining of family behavior. Inf. Secur. Res. **5**(2), 105–113 (2019)
16. Wang, S., Chen, Z., Yu, X.: Heterogeneous graph matching networks for unknown malware detection. In: International Joint Conferences on Artificial Intelligence, pp. 3762–3770 (2019)
17. Yi, S., Kashif, A., Usman, T.: Effective malware detection scheme based on classified behavior graph in IIoT. Ad Hoc Netw. **102**, 102588 (2021)
18. Pedro, M., Matilda, R., Ilir, G.: Waste not: using diverse neural networks from hyperparameter search for improved malware detection. Comput. Secur. **108**, 102339 (2021)
19. Akshara, P., Rudra, B.: Study of a hybrid approach towards malware detection in executable files. SN Comput. Sci. **2**(4), 1–7 (2021). https://doi.org/10.1007/s42979-021-00672-y
20. Yan, J., Yan, G., Jin, D.: Classifying malware represented as control flow graphs using deep graph convolutional neural network. In: The 49th Annual IEEE/IFIP International Conference on Dependable Systems and Networks, pp. 52–63 (2019)

Collection of the Main Anti-Virus Detection and Bypass Techniques

Jérémy Donadio[1], Guillaume Guerard[1(✉)], and Soufian Ben Amor[2]

[1] Léonard de Vinci Pôle Universitaire, Research Center,
92 916 Paris La Défense, France
{jeremy.donadio,guillaume.guerard}@devinci.fr
[2] LI-PARAD Laboratory EA 7432, Versailles University, 55 Avenue de Paris,
78035 Versailles, France
soufianben.amor@uvsq.fr

Abstract. A large amount a new threats, technologies and business models have emerged in the cybersecurity area through the COVID-19 pandemic. The remote work involved unplanned cloud migrations and swift procurement of IT products and services the remote landscape. In this context, the role of anti-viruses is crucial for the private life and work. In this paper, we study the workings of anti-viruses as to understand how to avoid them. We created a collection of the main bypass techniques whilst analyzing their respective advantages and drawbacks. We show that it is possible to avoid both static and emulation analyses, while enunciating the techniques and approaches being used.

Keywords: Malware bypass · Anti virus · Static analysis · Dynamic analysis

1 Introduction

More than ever, the Covid-19 pandemic revealed that both our public and private computerized systems were vulnerable to computer attacks [8,19,26]. Anyone inclusing hospitals [1], private companies [3] or an individual for example as energy consumers [25] are the victims of such attacks like the well-know WannaCry malware.

The sole fact that 90% of all data breaches were initiated by a human error showcases the urgency to detect them. The objective of the black hats[1] is to achieve monetary gain through stealing or destroying data. It is worthwhile to note that the most common ransomwares are: Lockergoga, Katyusha, WannaCry, Jigsaw, Pewcrypt, Ryuk, Dharma, Gandcrab, Revil, Samsam [6]. We recommend

---

[1] The term *black hat* designates a hacker who breaches into a computerized system or network with malevolent intentions. Such motives usually are a monetary gain.

J. Donadio—Research Student.

M. Yang et al. (Eds.): NSS 2021, LNCS 13041, pp. 222–237, 2021.
https://doi.org/10.1007/978-3-030-92708-0_14

the following books for a deep understanding of cybersecurity, noting attacks and issues [30, 31].

Cybercrime statistics estimate the economic impact of the ransomware phenomenon to be of around 600 billion dollars which is more profitable than the drug market, estimated to a 400 billion dollars value[2].

To introduce the problem of cybercrime, we refer to the following statistics from ENISA[3], and specifically cite the following:

- 10.1 billion euros were paid in ransom in 2019 (compared to 3.3 billion in 2018).
- 66% of health organizations were victim of at least one ransomware attack[4] in 2019.
- 45% of targets pay the ransom.
- 28% of security incidents within businesses have been attributed to malwares.
- Ransomware detection within businesses augmented by 365% in 2019.

According to the same source, 88% of companies that have more than one million folders unknowingly have more than 100,000 folders that are publicly accessible. Furthermore, according to Varonis Systems' reports[5], 30% of companies have more than 1,000 sensitive folders accessible publicly. Additionally, 57% of companies have more than 1,000 folders with inadequate access permissions.

We therefore formulate the following hypothesis: the existence of a business implies the existence of a risk; the more this business is important, the higher the risk is. This paper will explore the workings of Anti-Virus software, as well as means to avoid them. It will provide a global yet detailed view of the working and possible bypass techniques of said software.

Strengthening anti-virus implementations is therefore a critical subject for our society, Kaspersky provides a real time map showing the cyberattacks[6]. The aim of this paper is to focus on breaches in these software, as to diminish the risk faced by the stakeholders making up our society. We will first study the workings of anti-viruses, then we will list the ways in which one can avoid them. This will shed light onto some of the flaws of anti-malware software, which developers can then patch.

In the second section, we define the terms of malware and anti-virus, as well as detailing the ways in which malwares are detected. The third section will showcase bypass techniques to the previously listed detection methods. The last section will enumerate the results from the experiments that we conducted.

---

[2] Nick Galov. *40 Worrisome Hacking Statistics that Concern Us All in 2020.* In february 18, 2021.

[3] The European Union Agency for Cybersecurity. https://www.enisa.europa.eu/publications/ransomware.

[4] Ransomware: program that first encrypts all a computer's data, then asks for a ransom in return of the data being decrypted.

[5] Varonis. *2018 Global Data Risk Report From The Varonis Data Lab.* In 2019.

[6] https://cybermap.kaspersky.com/stats.

2   Definition and Categorization of Malwares and Anti-Malwares

There exist multiple types of malevolent programs such as viruses, rootkits, key-loggers, stealers, ransomwares, trojans, Remote Access Tools (R.A.T.), worms and spywares [32].

To keep the discussion simple, we will use the general appellation of *malware* to designate any malevolent program whose purpose is to spy on or corrupt a computer. This encompasses all programs aiming to control one or more periph-erals (keyboard, mouse, camera, ...), but also the overarching system (visualiza-tion, copy, alteration, or deletion of files), or encrypt folders (ransomware).

Simplifying the term malware is important as this study focuses on their modes of action, detection, and bypass. As to protect the computers of busi-nesses and individuals, some cyber-protection parties started to develop software dedicated to detecting and protect against malwares. Such softwares are known as anti-malwares, commonly referred to as anti-viruses.

We can identify two main functionalities of anti-virus softwares, being the detection and neutralization of threats. Focusing on the detection step, we can see that it is usually broken-down into the following three steps:

1. Static analysis: analysis without executing the program.
2. Virtual Machine (VM) analysis: analyzing program execution within a virtual machine.
3. Real time (proactive) analysis: executing the program natively and analyzing it in real time.

2.1   Static Analysis

Static analysis aims to analyze the code of a program without executing it, which is comparable to analyzing *inert code*. By this method, one can detect a malware without executing it and therefore corrupt the computer system. In practice, the anti-virus software analyzes the binary code of the program to determine its degree of malevolence. We will then describe some of the commonly used detection methods: the signature, pattern analysis, spectral analysis, by machine learning, by checksum, by using additional data.

The Signature – Every anti-virus possesses what is referred to as a dictionary. Such dictionaries are large databases composed of short byte sequences, or sig-natures[7] from malevolent programs. When analyzing a program, the anti-virus cross-checks the database with the program's binary code, looking for instances of known signatures. If such a match is found, then the program is classified as potentially dangerous as shown in Fig. 1.

---

[7] Joxean Koret and Elias Bachaalany. The Antivirus Hacker's Handbook. September 28, 2015.

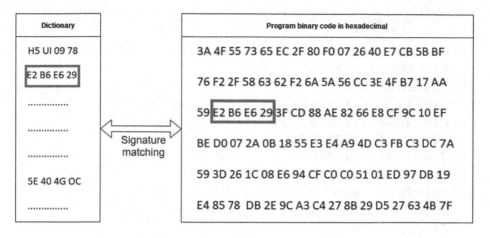

Fig. 1. Example of detection by signature.

It is also possible to apply this method with program hashes[8]. In this instance, the anti-virus possesses a dictionary of known malevolent program hashes. Therefore, when analyzing a new program, the anti-virus computes its hash and cross-checks it with its dictionary, looking for a match indicating the program is potentially malevolent.

This malware detection method is one of the first approaches ever invented and remains one of the most commonly used. Its weak point is that one needs to already know a malware to detect it. This method is therefore less and less efficient due to the creation of new types of malwares as polymorphic malwares and because the overall number of malwares ever created augments exponentially.

Pattern Analysis and Disassembly – It is possible to deduct a program's behavior from analyzing its instruction sequences. Looking at a program's behavioral pattern, one can infer whether or not it is malevolent as shown in Fig. 2. There are numerous ways to identify and understand such patterns [17]. One can analyze the PE (.EXE) format of the program, disassemble it, and possibly apply machine learning methods [5].

To summarize, the aim is to understand the behavior of some of the program's functions, rather than search for a "precise byte sequence" within the program's binary code.

Spectral Analysis – Spectral analysis entails analyzing the number of occurrences of all instructions within the program. The number of instructions or possible states attainable by the processor (CPU) being determined, one can

---

[8] Hash: a sequence of numbers and letters generated by a cryptographic hashing function.

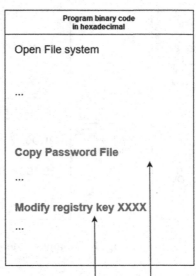

Program binary code in hexadecimal	Program binary code in hexadecimal
74 65 72 6E 65 74 20 70 65 75 20 63 6F 6E 6E 75 29 20 0D 0A 20 20 70 65 72 6D 65 74 20 64 65 20 70 61 73 73 65 72 20 C3 A0 20 74 72 61 76 65 72 73 20 6C 27 41 56 20 73 74 61 74 69 71 75 65 20 20 0D 0A 0D 0A 41 6E 61 6C 79 73 65 20 64 79 6E 61 6D 69 71 75 65 3A 0D 0A 31 29 4D 65 74 74 72 65 20 75 6E 20 74 69 6D 65 72 20 64 ...	Open File system ... **Copy Password File** ... **Modify registry key XXXX** ...

Potential dangerous instructions, potential malware detected

Fig. 2. Simplified example of a behavioral analysis.

compute the number of times, the frequency, the CPU is in each of these states. A program spectrum corresponds to a graph of the all the possible CPU instructions, against the frequency of each instruction.

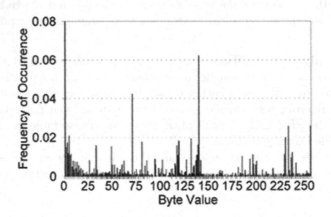

Fig. 3. Example of a normal program spectrum [18].

This spectrum in Fig. 3 depicts a simplified representation of reality, where there are 255 possible byte values with their corresponding frequency. For this analysis to be useful, on needs to analyze the actual instruction rather than the byte values. We now show the spectrum of an encrypted program in Fig. 4.

This spectrum reveals that all the instructions associated to the program's binary code are biased due to the program being encrypted. It is also possible to use spectral analysis to detect polymorphic malwares[9], by computing a similarity index based on the programs' instructions, for which we will observe that their specters are identical.

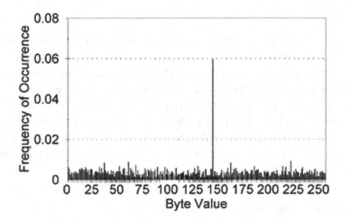

Fig. 4. Example of a secured program spectrum [18].

Using Machine Learning in Static Analysis – It is possible to use machine learning techniques to achieve a more accurate program analysis, thus augmenting the odds of detecting malevolant programs. Shijo et al. [29] presents a method consisting in integrating a large number of known malwares and inoffensive programs in the training set. Features are then obtained by extracting Printable String Information [11,12] contained within the program's binary code. This data is then used as inputs for different classification algorithms.

Integrity Checksum Analysis – Checksum analysis consists in gathering multiple pieces of information regarding a file, such as its name, size, last-modified date, hash, as well as other parameters as presented in Fig. 5. Once the data has been acquired, the anti-virus will attempt to sum them as to obtain a unique value. Any attempt from the malware to duplicate itself within the file will result in an automatic change in file size, hash, last-modified date, and other variables. The resulting checksum will then change, and if the value is deemed too different from the original one, then it is possible that the program

---

[9] Malware having the capacity to modify its signature every time it is generated.

is a malware. On the other hand, if one manually modifies or uses the file, then the checksum will not change drastically, and no alert will be raised. This technique therefore creates an important number of false positives, which is why it is important to use it alongside other analysis methods.

Fig. 5. Analysis by integrity checksum.

Using Additional Data – It is possible to use other data elements to gauge how dangerous is a program [15]. For instance, one can verify the libraries or Application Programming Interfaces (API) being used to determine whether they are documented [24]. One can also verify interrupt vectors, analyze the file format, etc. It is also important to note that there exists a large number of other static analysis techniques such as integrity verification [7], and that a lot of them now use machine learning techniques [9]. Further discussion of such statistical analysis techniques has been omitted due to their large similarity to the aforementioned techniques.

2.2   Emulation Analysis

VM analysis is used to detect a malware in the case where it succeeds in going through static analysis undetected. As previously stated, static analysis has for aim to analyze the code without running it. However, it is possible for this analysis to not yield any results, making executing the code a necessary step. Because this kind of testing can cause damage to the computer system, one usually runs it in an insulated *sandbox*. Such an environment is comprised of a virtual machine separated from the main system in which the program is executed. This way, any harm that is caused by the malware is contained to within the virtual machine, thus not affecting the main system's integrity.

Fig. 6. Analysis of a program by emulation.

The different steps carried during VM analysis are (also see Fig. 6):

1. Creating the virtual machine.
2. Save the VM (in the event when we want to go back to the save point to execute the program once again).
3. Run the program.
4. Second save (in the event when one wants to re scan the program's execution result - the saves are there to gain time in the event when one wants to jump to a specific step in the analysis).
5. Gathering and analysis of the data.
6. Restoration of the virtual machine.

The objective is therefore to execute the program in a secure environment and analyze its behavior to determine whether or not it is malevolent. Such an analysis is based upon many axes, some of the main ones being:

- Registry.
- File system.
- Network analysis.

We will detail each of these axes below.

The Registry – The registry is used to determine which programs are launched upon starting up the system. The registry also manages these program's access permissions and configurations. A malware will be forced to interact with the registry if it attempts to present itself to the system as a legitimate program or tried to become persistent (be present upon restarting the computer). Therefore, registry analysis is a primordial step in guaranteeing the system's security.

The File System – Analyzing the file system is essential as the malware will likely attempt to modify a file or a process, warranting particular attention.

The Network Analysis – In the event where the malware succeeds in finding the targeted information, it will likely create a network connection with a third party like a hacker as to send over the stolen data. Network analysis is therefore a major step in guaranteeing system reliability.

There exist other axes that are being monitored, and the list provided in this paper is not exhaustive.

2.3 Real-Time Analysis (Dynamic/Proactive)

In the event where previously mentioned analysis techniques fail, one can use proactive analysis [10]. Proactive analysis consists in a real-time analysis of the system where each anti-virus uses multiple *agents* to protect the system. An agent is a program whose purpose is to guard against a specific type of intrusion. Such intrusions include deletion of files from another program, transfer of packets between the user and the outside world through a network, mail, web, etc. Each agent is therefore tasked with analyzing a specific part of the main system.

3   Anti-Virus Bypass and Tests

We will detail the different methods that can be used to bypass each type of analysis. In order to put into practice the theoretical methods discussed in this paper, we have developed a keylogger as well as a ransomware, while testing most of the aforementioned bypassing methods.

Here are the complementary information about the operating system and the installed anti-virus:

- Operating system used: Windows 10 family on version 19042.928.
- Anti-Virus tested: Avast premium 21.2.2455 with 1.0.644 interface.
- Viral database: Avast premium 210609-10.

3.1   Bypassing Static Analysis

In this section, we will detail the main static analysis bypassing techniques.

Writing Your Own Malware – Static analysis' main pitfall is that it requires the anti-virus to have encountered the malware at least once in order to detect it. This implies that if one writes their own malware, the chances of it being detected by an anti-virus are negligible.

Changing Signatures – Another way to make it through static analysis is to change a malware's signature . If the malware's signature is known from the anti-virus, it is possible to change it manually by cutting the program in small pieces using a tool such as *UK splitter*, then analyze such pieces to locate which ones are being flagged as malevolent, then change them using a hexadecimal editor [28]. It is also possible to create a program that has the ability to change its signature at each instantiated code. Such malevolent programs are called *polymorphic malwares*.

Malware Encryption – We previously mentioned that static analysis was based upon comprehension of the program's binary code. It is therefore sufficient to encrypt the program's content, thus its instruction, to make it illegible and undecryptable by the anti-virus. The program is thus fully encrypted, bypassing all static analysis methods. Once the program is executed, it can decrypt itself and execute its code. Such *crypters* are downloadable on the internet and enable encryption of one's program as to bypass anti-viruses.

```
Int main()
    {
      DecryptCode();
      ExecuteShellCode();
      Return 0;
    }
```

Packers – The primary function of a *packer* is to compress a program without altering its function. Packers are used by software/game developers to make the produced executable illegible as to prevent attempts at reverse-engineering or piracy. Packers have the ability to package, compress and encrypt the executable. Such abilities are very useful to conceal a malware. There exist multiple popular packers such as UPX [23] or Themida [16].

Supplementary Techniques – As stated in the *malware encryption* part, it is possible to carry out multiple actions to bypass the analysis of a program [21]. Such actions include disabling the Firewall, the Task Manager, the Command Prompt, the User Account Control, etc. This list is non-exhaustive and there exist multiple methods to bypass static analysis [4], such as the use of concealers [2]. However, the techniques remain the same:

1. Encrypt the program.
2. Make it unreadable.
3. Write the malware from scratch so that its signature is unknown.

3.2 Static Analysis Bypass Tests

Changing signatures manually works. We have been able to make a malware undetectable from anti-viruses by modifying its signature. It is important to note than this method can be time consuming, and that the malware may become dysfunctional. However, after changing the signature, our malware remained undetectable and functional. You will find two screenshots in the annex, showing the detection of the malware before and after execution of this method.

Changing signatures using a polymorphic malware works as well. It is important to note than this method will only work if the polymorphic malware is well programmed, and that it drastically changes signatures frequently enough. Otherwise, it may be detected by various machine learning or spectral analysis methods.

We also wrote a keylogger and a ransomware, none of which were detected by statistical analysis despite their potential dangerousity.

Using free packers did not yield successful results. However, we believe that the creation of a complex packer unknown to the anti-virus would work. We were not able to test paid packers but it would be logical that they yield a higher success rate compared to the free ones. Nevertheless, we think that they may not work against all anti-viruses.

The testing of malware encryption is currently in progress. We have set the objective of writing our own program capable of encrypting code. We have not been able to test already existing implementations, but we think that this method should work in light of our previous test cases.

3.3 Emulation Analysis Bypass

The main issue with emulation analysis is the time it takes to analyze the program, which is easily detectable. Indeed, VM analysis starts when a program is executed, and it is only once a program has been analyzed that it is truly run for the user. This signifies that the longest the analysis lasts, the longer the user will wait. In order to provide an enjoyable user experience, it is important that the analysis time remains short. The second problem is that the VM requires a certain number of resources to run (RAM, CPU), making the VM startup detectable by the malware. The primary methods to bypass emulation analysis are the following:

– Wait for a certain lapse of time before executing the malware.
– Detect the VM and remain inactive while it is analyzing.
– Prevent the VM from starting.

We now showcase an illustration of some of the aforementioned methods with some results. There exist other methods allowing to bypass emulation analysis. In order to learn more, Nasi et al.'s article [22] is oftentimes used in this section. The other techniques being used are all analogous to those already discussed (wasting time, detect or block the VM) which is why we omitted further discussion of said methods.

Excessive Increment – The aim is to make the program stall for a certain lapse of time before executing it. This effect is achieved by using a for loop that is tasked with waiting for an excessive amount of time before executing the remainder of the program. The idea is that the program does not start during the analysis. The VM analysis only observes a useless increment and will rule the program as benevolent. Here is a working code example:

```
Void LoopFud()
    {
    ShowWindow(GetConsoleWindow(), SW\_HIDE);
    for (int i = 0; i < 4000; i++) {Sleep(1);}
    }
```

Timer – Similar to the previous function, except that one uses a timer rather than a for loop.

```
Void Timer()
    {
    ShowWindow(GetConsoleWindow(), SW_HIDE);
    int total_time = 60;
    time_t current_time = time(0);
    while(time(0) - current_time < total_time){Sleep(1);}
    }
```

VM Detection – As previously stated, setting up a VM necessitates a certain quantity of resources (RAM, CPU). It is therefore possible to detect the VM by monitoring program memory allocations as well as running processes. Once detected, the program should be paused while the VM is running on the system. The bypassing method is summarized with the following pseudo-code:

1. If a lot of memory is allocated or a process asks for a certain quantity of resources, then the malware is most likely contained within a VM.
2. While the malware is contained within the VM: do not execute the program.

It is also possible to detect the VM with respect to its process name.

Too Much Memory – It is also possible to prevent the emulation analysis from starting entirely. Indeed, a VM needs to allocate memory to run the program when starting up. However, the program will not be able to run if the program requests too much memory.

Say My Name – When the code is emulated within the VM, no other process bearing the same name can be started. The program can then conclude that as long as its name does not appear in another process, then it is contained within a VM. It can therefore choose to execute if and only if its name appears in another process.

3.4   Emulation Analysis Bypass Tests

The Excessive Increment method (for loop) proved successful. The code used in the description of this method is the code that has been used to successfully bypass the emulation analysis.

The Timer method also proved successful using the code in the description.

The Say My Name method seems to be working. We do have access to the programs' process name, and we can verify whether it is within a VM. However, we do not have access to other processes' names. This detail is irrelevant for this part but is a potential source for issues in the Dynamic Analysis Bypass part.

3.5   Dynamic or Real-Time Analysis Bypass

The dynamic analysis is the most complex one to bypass due to its technicity. There exist two main methods to bypass this analysis:

1. Make the anti-virus believe that we have the credentials to perform an admin task (erase a file, modify a file, etc.).
2. Insert oneself within or impersonate a known legitimate program to carry out the desired task.

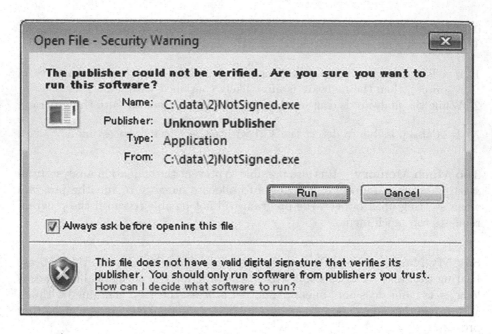

Fig. 7. Example of a window displaying the code signature certificate.

Legitimacy Gain – The most commonly used method to gain legitimacy is to use a code signature certificate as shown in Fig. 7. When you execute a program on your computer, it will display a window mentioning the type of file being executed, the name of the publisher, and the file location. Here is an example of a window appearing when executing a program.

Here, we can see that the program is unsigned because the publisher's name is unknown. However, if you install trustworthy software such as Word, you will have a publisher name like Microsoft, indicating that the file is safe. One can purchase such a certificate for prices between 200 and 1000 euros in many websites, allowing malwares to bypass dynamic analysis.

Insertion Within a Legitimate Program – In this instance, the malware attempts to impersonate a legitimate program already existing on the computer. It will therefore try to insert itself in a running process. Such an endeavor is called an injection [27], which happen at the memory or DLL level most of the time. Other injection methods include Shellcode Injections, Inline Hooking and others [20].

3.6   Targeting the Core of the Operating System

The methods that have been discussed above work at the application layer of the operating system. However, it is possible to create malwares acting upon the kernel or bios layers, making them undetectable. Such malwares operating on low level layers are also referred to as rootkits, and their main specificity is that they are undetectable from anti-viruses. Among all the methods used to bypass anti-viruses, the *Blue Pills* method [14], developed by Joanna Rutkowska, will never be able to be stopped or detected on consumer operating systems (windows, linux, unix, etc.), making it one of the most powerful yet elegant methods to date.

The malware will download an operating system on one of the computer's storage devices (flash drive, hard dirk, etc.). Once downloaded, the operating system will behave like a VM in which the native operating system will run. In other words, launching Windows will result in it executing within another operating system [13]. This other operating system will be able to spy on your computer and render all anti-viruses inefficient as they are limited by the bounds of the native operating system and therefore will be oblivious to the other operating system's existence. The process of the Blue Pills' attack is shown in Fig. 8.

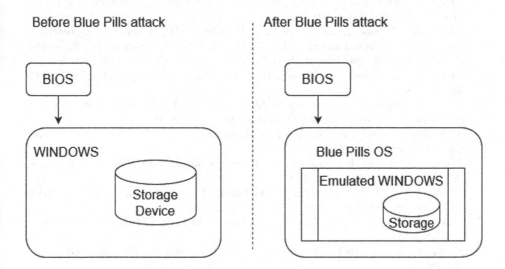

Fig. 8. Blue pills' attack.

You now understand that the name Blue Pills is a reference to The movie "The Matrix" because it illustrates a machine running within another machine. It is also important to note that the researcher who created the Blue PILLS attack also created an operating system known as *Qube OS*, which is able to prevent Blue Pills attacks.

4   Conclusion

To conclude, we underline in this paper that static analysis is based on a program's binary, without running it. However, this method can be insufficient in case where the program is eligible or if the anti-virus never encountered the malware.

With respect to emulation analysis (VM) which aims at studying the behavior of a program by making it run within a sandbox, we can consider that it will become obsolete because it is easy to detect or block the VM, as well as make our program inactive during the analysis timeframe.

The most efficient and hard to bypass analysis is the dynamic one. There exist however multiple ways to pass through, and multiple of these methods, such as by injection, will be tested in future work.

In the future, our work and research will focus on the functioning and bypassing of dynamic analysis, especially methods by injection.

References

1. Akselrod, H.: Crisis standards of care: cyber attack during a pandemic. Ann. Intern. Med. **174**(5), 713–714 (2021)
2. Alazab, M., Venkatraman, S., Watters, P., Alazab, M., Alazab, A.: Cybercrime: the case of obfuscated malware. In: Georgiadis, C.K., Jahankhani, H., Pimenidis, E., Bashroush, R., Al-Nemrat, A. (eds.) e-Democracy/ICGS3 -2011. LNICST, vol. 99, pp. 204–211. Springer, Heidelberg (2012). https://doi.org/10.1007/978-3-642-33448-1_28
3. Alladi, T., Chamola, V., Zeadally, S.: Industrial control systems: cyberattack trends and countermeasures. Comput. Commun. **155**, 1–8 (2020)
4. Anderson, H.S., Kharkar, A., Filar, B., Roth, P.: Evading Machine Learning Malware Detection. Black Hat (2017)
5. Aslan, Ö.A., Samet, R.: A comprehensive review on malware detection approaches. IEEE Access **8**, 6249–6271 (2020)
6. Aurangzeb, S., Aleem, M., Iqbal, M.A., Islam, M.A., et al.: Ransomware: a survey and trends. J. Inf. Assur. Secur. **6**(2), 48–58 (2017)
7. Calderon, P., Miavril, V., Présent, P.: Contournement d'analyse dynamique de code viral
8. Fontanilla, M.V.: Cybercrime pandemic. Eubios J. Asian Int. Bioethics **30**(4), 161–165 (2020)
9. Gandotra, E., Bansal, D., Sofat, S.: Malware analysis and classification: a survey. J. Inf. Secur. **2014** (2014)
10. Idika, N., Mathur, A.P.: A survey of malware detection techniques. Purdue Univ. **48**, 2007-2 (2007)
11. Islam, R., Tian, R., Batten, L., Versteeg, S.: Classification of malware based on string and function feature selection. In: 2010 Second Cybercrime and Trustworthy Computing Workshop, pp. 9–17. IEEE (2010)
12. Islam, R., Tian, R., Batten, L.M., Versteeg, S.: Classification of malware based on integrated static and dynamic features. J. Netw. Comput. Appl. **36**(2), 646–656 (2013)
13. King, S.T., Chen, P.M.: SubVirt: implementing malware with virtual machines. In: 2006 IEEE Symposium on Security and Privacy (S&P 2006), 14-pp. IEEE (2006)
14. King, S., Chen, P.: SubVirt: implementing malware with virtual machines. In: 2006 IEEE Symposium on Security and Privacy (S&P 2006), p. 14 pp.-327 (2006). https://doi.org/10.1109/SP.2006.38

15. Lagadec, P.: Dynamic malware analysis for dummies. In: Symposium Sur la Sécurité des Technologies de l'information et des Communications, SSTIC (2008)
16. Lee, J.H., Han, J., Lee, M.W., Choi, J.M., Baek, H., Lee, S.J.: A study on API wrapping in Themida and unpacking technique. J. Korea Inst. Inf. Secur. Cryptol. **27**(1), 67–77 (2017)
17. Liu, W., Ren, P., Liu, K., Duan, H.X.: Behavior-based malware analysis and detection. In: 2011 First International Workshop on Complexity and Data Mining, pp. 39–42. IEEE (2011)
18. Ludwig, M.A.: The Giant Black Book of Computer Viruses. American Eagle Publications, Show Low (1998)
19. Macdonald, S., Jarvis, L., Lavis, S.M.: Cyberterrorism today? Findings from a follow-on survey of researchers. Stud. Confl. Terror., 1–26 (2019)
20. Mohanta, A., Saldanha, A.: Code injection, process hollowing, and API hooking. In: Malware Analysis and Detection Engineering, pp. 267–329. Apress, Berkeley (2020). https://doi.org/10.1007/978-1-4842-6193-4_10
21. Moser, A., Kruegel, C., Kirda, E.: Limits of static analysis for malware detection. In: Twenty-Third Annual Computer Security Applications Conference (ACSAC 2007), pp. 421–430. IEEE (2007)
22. Nasi, E.: Bypass antivirus dynamic analysis. Limitations of the AV model and how to exploit them (2014)
23. Oberhumer, M.F.: UPX the ultimate packer for executables (2004). http://upx. sourceforge.net/
24. Osorio, F.C.C., Qiu, H., Arrott, A.: Segmented sandboxing-a novel approach to malware polymorphism detection. In: 2015 10th International Conference on Malicious and Unwanted Software (MALWARE), pp. 59–68. IEEE (2015)
25. Plėta, T., Tvaronavičienė, M., Casa, S.D., Agafonov, K.: Cyber-attacks to critical energy infrastructure and management issues: overview of selected cases (2020)
26. Ramadan, R.A., Aboshosha, B.W., Alshudukhi, J.S., Alzahrani, A.J., El-Sayed, A., Dessouky, M.M.: Cybersecurity and countermeasures at the time of pandemic. J. Adv. Transp. **2021** (2021)
27. Ray, D., Ligatti, J.: Defining code-injection attacks. ACM SIGPLAN Not. **47**(1), 179–190 (2012)
28. Scott, J.: Signature based malware detection is dead. Institute for Critical Infrastructure Technology (2017)
29. Shijo, P., Salim, A.: Integrated static and dynamic analysis for malware detection. Procedia Comput. Sci. **46**, 804–811 (2015)
30. Sikorski, M., Honig, A.: Practical Malware Analysis: The Hands-On Guide to Dissecting Malicious Software. No Starch Press, San Francisco (2012)
31. Singer, P.W., Friedman, A.: Cybersecurity: What Everyone Needs to Know. OUP, New York (2014)
32. Tahir, R.: A study on malware and malware detection techniques. Int. J. Educ. Manage. Eng. **8**(2), 20 (2018)

Profiled Attacks Against the Elliptic Curve Scalar Point Multiplication Using Neural Networks

Alessandro Barenghi[1]📵, Diego Carrera[2], Silvia Mella[2,3]📵, Andrea Pace[2],
Gerardo Pelosi[1(✉)]📵, and Ruggero Susella[2]

[1] Politecnico di Milano, Milan, Italy
{alessandro.barenghi,gerardo.pelosi}@polimi.it
[2] STMicroelectronics, Agrate Brianza, Italy
{diego.carrera,silvia.mella,andrea.pace,ruggero.susella}@st.com
[3] RadBoud University, Nijmegen, The Netherlands

Abstract. In recent years, machine learning techniques have been successfully applied to improve side-channel attacks against different cryptographic algorithms. In this work, we deal with the use of neural networks to attack elliptic curve-based cryptosystems. In particular, we propose a deep learning based strategy to retrieve the scalar from a double-and-add scalar-point multiplication. As a proof of concept, we conduct an effective attack against the scalar-point multiplication on NIST standard curve P-256 implemented in BearSSL, a timing side-channel hardened public library. The experimental results show that our attack strategy allows to recover the secret scalar value with a single trace from the attacked device and an exhaustive search over a set containing a few hundreds of the sought secret.

Keywords: Computer security · Applied cryptography · Profiled side channel attacks · Neural networks · Elliptic curve cryptography

1 Introduction

Side channel attacks (SCAs) aim at deriving the data being processed during a computation, by modeling the data-dependent behavior of the computing device itself. So called passive side channel attacks exploit the physical behaviors that can be measured without disrupting the computation, such as computation time [6,19], power consumption [20,24], or radiated electromagnetic emissions [1,13,29]. The time series obtained by the measurement of such quantities are also known as *traces*. To retrieve a secret value used during a computation, an attacker tries to map the collected traces onto multiple instances of a key-dependent model of the behavior of the device under attack. By observing which key-dependent model is most fitting, the actual value of the secret is inferred.

A powerful class of SCA is the class of profiled side channel attacks. In this scenario, the attacker has full control of a copy of the device under attack (e.g.,

M. Yang et al. (Eds.): NSS 2021, LNCS 13041, pp. 238–257, 2021.
https://doi.org/10.1007/978-3-030-92708-0_15

a sample of a microcontroller similar to the target one). She first builds a good leakage model of the duplicate and then uses this leakage model to exploit the actual leakage of the target device and retrieve the secret information. One of the most used approach in profiled SCA is the one of *template attacks* [9], where a set of multivariate Gaussian models are built to describe the measurements recorded under fixed value of (a portion of) the secret data. The attacker may derive which value is used during the target computation, by applying a maximum likelihood estimation approach on the built models. In the best case, a single trace from the device under attack can be sufficient to mount the attack. Other approaches, that received significant attention in recent years, are those based on machine learning techniques [22,25,37]. In particular, attacks based on neural networks proved to be effective against both symmetric and asymmetric cryptosystems, also in defeating some side-channel countermeasures [7,8,16,23,26,33,34,36].

Given the nature of the cryptographic algorithm under attack, the amount of secret-dependent data points contained in a measurement may be small with respect to the total amount of collected information. For this reason, it is common practice to process the traces to extract the time instants where most of the secret key-related information is expected to be present. Such instants are known as *Points-of-Interest* (PoI). Effective PoI selection algorithms include the selection of trace samples exhibiting maximum variance, or the selection of trace samples corresponding to time instants when the processing of data is highly correlated with the hypothetical model for the sensitive operation (e.g., the Hamming weight of an operation result or the Hamming distance between a result and an operand) [24].

Contributions. In this work, we present a profiled attack against the double-and-add-always algorithm employed in Elliptic Curve Cryptography (ECC). We use machine learning techniques to model the power consumption behavior of the device under attack. Specifically, we aim at identifying when some arithmetic operations underlying the double-and-add-always algorithm share a common operand. We then use such information to distinguish the portion of the secret scalar value related to such operations. To this end, we build and train a set of Multilayer Perceptrons (MLPs) to extract information on the processed operands (specifically on the Hamming weight (HW) of their words), and propose a simple metric to decide on the equality of the operands themselves based on such information. This approach is similar to the one presented in [8], where information on specific bits of some operands is extracted to infer the secret exponent used in a RSA implementation. As our testbed, we attack a 2-bit windowing-based double-and-add-always implementation of the elliptic curve scalar-point multiplication. The implementation is one of those contained in the open-source BearSSL software library, which is hardened against timing side channel attacks [27]. On this experimental testbed, we are able to correctly guess all-but-two bits of the secret scalar on average, with a single trace from the attacked device.

Paper Organization. In Sect. 2, we summarize related works and the difference with our study. In Sect. 3, we first provide background information on profiled SCA using neural networks and then detail the BearSSL windowing-based implementation of the elliptic curve scalar-point multiplication algorithm optimized for the NIST curve P-256. In Sect. 4 we describe our attack methodology, while in Sect. 5 we report the results of our experimental validation. Finally, Sect. 6 reports our concluding remarks.

2   Related Work

Attacks based on *collision technique* rely on the capability of distinguishing whether two distinct operations share a common input operand or not. They were applied to extract secret key values from a single execution trace of RSA [35] and ECC [17,31] algorithms, as well as from their implementations exhibiting some SCA countermeasures [4,10]. In these works, the authors employ either Euclidean distance or statistical correlation as quantitative metrics to detect whether two operations share a common input or not.

In [8] the authors describe a profiled strategy based on neural network classifiers to detect such property in an RSA implementation. They take advantage of a peculiar architectural property of the device under attack. In particular, they exploit the fact that the target chip leaks significant information on the value of the twelfth bit of each limb of a multiple-precision arithmetic operation. They use such information to understand whether two operands in subsequent iterations of the main loop of the algorithm have the same value. From this information they can then distinguish the secret exponent bits used in such iterations.

In this work, we use a similar approach and extract information on the HW of each limb, instead of a specific bit, and exploit it to attack ECC implementations. Moving to the HW leakage model is justified by the fact that the HW model carries more information about the whole operand than single bits. Moreover, the HW leakage model, together with the Hamming distance model, has been proven to be the most effective in different SCA scenarios. To manage this new leakage model, we employ neural networks as regressors, instead of (binary) classifiers as in [8].

In [34], the authors present a successful attack on a windowing-based implementation of the Edwards-curve Digital Signature Algorithm (EdDSA) in the WolfSSL software library [2]. They exploit the presence of table-lookup operations in the windowing based implementation and profile their power consumption. They then use the built models to infer which ones of the precomputed values are used during the target execution. In our work, we also try to understand the precomputed values used during the computation, but we profile the multiple-precision multiplication operation instead of table-lookup operations. The reason behind this choice is that our attack may in principle be applied also to non windowing-based implementations, which do not rely on table-lookup but only on multiple-precision arithmetic operations.

Other interesting applications of machine learning applied to profiled attacks against ECC implementations exploit different attack paths. In [36], the authors target an ECDSA implementation where the first four bits of the scalar are recovered via profiled SCA and employed to derive the private key via a computational lattice based attack, improving the effectiveness of the horizontal attack introduced in [28]. In [33] the authors attack two implementations of EdDSA with Curve25519. The first is the implementation provided by the WolfSSL library [2], where the full scalar is profiled by nibbles in a horizontal fashion. The second one is the protected implementation provided by the Libsodium library [11], based on the Montgomery Ladder scalar multiplication. The authors exploit the presence of an arithmetic-based conditional swap to profile each iteration of the main loop. In this work, the authors do not consider only neural network-based attacks, but compare the effectiveness of other profiling techniques, such as Template Attacks, Random Forests, and Support Vector Machines. In [26], the authors propose a deep learning-based method to incrementally correct secret keys recovered via horizontal attack. This is especially helpful in the presence of randomized scalars or exponents.

3   Background

In this section we first provide an overview on profiled attacks and neural networks. We then describe the double-and-add algorithm which will be the target of our attacks, detailing the implementation of the open source library BearSSL that we will use in our experimental validation.

3.1   Profiling Techniques

Profiled side channel attacks are performed in two stages. The first stage is known as *profiling stage* and consists in building a statistical model of the side channel behavior of a copy of the device under attack, for each possible value of a chosen portion of the secret key to be recovered. To build an accurate model, an appropriate leakage model for the device must be chosen. Common choices are the Hamming weight (HW) and the Hamming distance (HD) of a sensitive intermediate value that is computed by the algorithm and depends on the target secret key portion.

The second stage is known as *key-extraction stage*. In this phase, the attacker aims at classifying one (or a few) measurement(s) obtained from the target device by computing the probability that it matches (they match) each of the models built in the profiling phase. Since each model is associated with a guess on the sensitive variable value, the highest probability indicates the most likely one.

Deep Learning Attacks. A class of machine learning algorithms frequently used in profiled SCA is deep learning. In this scenario, the profiling stage maps onto the *learning* phase, where one or more neural networks are trained, while the key-extraction stage is mapped onto the *prediction* phase, where the networks are used to guess the target data. A neural network can be represented through a graph, where the nodes represent the neurons (i.e. the elementary processing elements), and the arcs represent the dataflow across the neurons. The neurons are organized in *layers*, where each layer groups together all the neurons acting in parallel on the same set of inputs. The neurons acting on the input values provided to the network compose the *input layer* of the network, while neurons acting on the outputs of other neurons compose the *hidden layers*. The neurons computing the outputs of the neural network belong to the *output layer*.

In this work, we employ a neural network architecture known as Multilayer Perceptron (MLP). In an MLP, also known as *feed-forward neural network* [5], each layer is fully connected to the next layer. Each node of an MLP computes a weighted sum of its inputs $(x_0, \ldots, x_{m-1})$ and applies to the result a nonlinear *activation function* $\phi(\cdot)$, yielding as output a value $z = \phi\left(\sum_{i=0}^{m-1} w_i x_i\right)$. The choice of the activation function depends on the features of the multivariate function to be approximated (learned) by the MLP. Common choices for the activation function include the *sigmoid* or a *softmax* function, when a real valued output in the $[0, 1]$ range is desired (e.g., to model a probability); the hyperbolic tangent, a *Rectified Linear Unit* (ReLU), or a *LeakyReLU function*, otherwise. The weights of the inputs, $w_0, \ldots, w_{m-1}$ are specific to each neuron and they are computed during the learning phase of the MLP, starting from an initial random choice.

The learning phase of an MLP is split in three sub-phases: training, validation and test. During the training phase, a set of inputs for which the desired output is known, is fed to the network. The weights of the neurons are updated in order to steer the results of the network towards the desired outputs. This is done by minimizing the difference between the outputs of the neural network and the expected results, according to a chosen error function (e.g., least squares), which is known as *loss function* [12,18]. Since the learning process of the MLP requires the values for the desired outputs, this is known as *supervised learning*, as opposed to *unsupervised learning* that does not require the desired output values. In the validation phase, a first assessment of the quality of the prediction capability of the neural network is measured. This is done by feeding to the network a fresh set of inputs, known as validation inputs, for which also the desired output is known. The difference between the expected and actual output of the network is known as validation error. Training and validation sub-phases are combined in what is known as *epoch*.

While in principle the learning phase may include an unbounded number of epochs, training over a very large amount of epochs may cause a phenomenon known as *overfitting*. In this case, the neural network is remarkably accurate in producing the desired results on the sets of inputs employed during the training, but poorly tolerates small variations on the said input sets which results in bad performance on unseen data [30]. To preserve the desirable *generalization* property of the network (i.e. tolerance to input changes), the learning phase should be stopped whenever the prediction error on the validation inputs (which are different from the training inputs) has a minimum. In fact, the validation error exhibits a concave trend, with a steep descent in the initial phase, followed by a slow increase due to the start of the overfitting phenomenon. The number of epochs to be computed is thus chosen minimizing the validation error of the network. To mitigate the overfitting phenomenon, a special neuron layer, known as *dropout layer*, can be used. In such layer, each neuron takes as input the output of exactly one neuron from the previous layer, not shared with anyone else, and it outputs either the input received or zero with a chosen probability. Such probability is known as *dropout rate* [32]. Finally, the final sub-phase of the network learning, i.e., the testing sub-phase, is performed. During the testing sub-phase, a further independent set of inputs is fed to the network to assess the performance of the fully trained network. The role of the testing phase is to assess whether the minimum in the validation error that was achieved in the training and validation sub-phases is indeed a satisfactory result for the application scenario at hand.

Feature Selection. When neural networks are employed in a machine learning based SCA, the inputs to the network are the data point composing the side channel trace. Since the operations involving sensitive data are typically few and far apart in a trace, providing all the trace samples acquired as inputs to the network may provide more noise than actual information to the network itself. Consequentially, it is commonplace to adopt a *feature selection procedure* to improve the efficiency and effectiveness of the network learning phase as well as the effectiveness of the network as a classifier/regressor. This procedure allows either to select a subset of the trace samples based on their sensitive leakage information content or to filter out redundant and uncorrelated information, by combining the trace samples to obtain a smaller set of features. Different methods may be applied for feature selection. Some effective techniques are *Difference Of Means* (DOM) [9], *Sum Of Squared Differences* (SOSD) [15], *Sum Of Squared pairwise T-differences* (SOST) [15], *Signal-to-Noise Ratios* (SNR) [24], *Mutual Information Analysis* (MIA) [14], and *Principal Component Analysis* [3].

3.2 Elliptic Curve Scalar-Point Multiplication in BearSSL

We now describe a generic double-and-add-always algorithm and provide details of the version which will be used as our case study, i.e., the optimized implementation for P-256 provided in the BearSSL software library [27]. BearSSL is commonly used to implement TLS connectivity on inexpensive embedded systems. One of the main goals of BearSSL is the immunity to timing attacks, achieved through constant-time implementation of cryptographic primitives.

In the following, we denote the binary representation of a value in $\mathbb{F}_p$ stored in a variable v as $(v_{n-1}, \ldots, v_0)_2$, while we highlight the physical storage of the same value as a sequence of W-bit architectural words/limbs as $(\mathsf{v}_{m-1}, \ldots, \mathsf{v}_0)_{2^W}$. We denote the j-th bit $0 \leq j < W$ of the i-th word as $\mathsf{v}_{i,j}$, whist $v^{(t)}$ denotes the value of the variable v during the t-th iteration of the main loop of a double-and-add(-always) algorithm. We denote with capital letters, e.g., P, the points of an elliptic curve with coordinates over the finite field $\mathbb{F}_p$.

Algorithm 1 reports the general structure of a double-and-add-always algorithm to perform scalar point multiplication. A naive double-and-add (non-always) algorithm scans the natural binary representation of the scalar (e.g., from left to right), performing a doubling at each scanned bit and an addition at each set bit of the scalar. While this approach produces a correct result, it is

Algorithm 1: Left-to-right double-and-add-always	**Algorithm 2:** Schoolbook multi-precision multiplication
Input: $P \in \mathbb{E}(\mathbb{F}_p)$: generator of a large subgroup of $\mathbb{E}$, $k = (k_{t-1}k_{t-2} \ldots k_0)_2$: scalar value **Output:** $Q = [k]P$: scalar-point multiplication result	**Input:** $x = (X_{m-1}X_{m-2} \ldots X_0)_{2^W}$ $y = (Y_{n-1}Y_{n-2} \ldots Y_0)_{2^W}$ **Output:** $z = x \cdot y$ **Data:** $c = (C_1C_0)_{2^W}$: double precision temporary value
1 $Q \leftarrow \mathcal{O}, D \leftarrow \mathcal{O}$ 2 **for** $i \leftarrow t-1$ **to** 0 **do** 3 $Q \leftarrow [2]Q$ 4 **if** $k_i = 1$ **then** 5 $Q \leftarrow P + Q$ 6 **else** 7 $D \leftarrow P + Q$ 8 **return** Q	1 $z \leftarrow 0$ 2 **for** $i \leftarrow 0$ **to** $m-1$ **do** 3 **for** $j \leftarrow 0$ **to** $n-1$ **do** 4 $(C_1C_0) \leftarrow z_{i+j} + X_i \cdot Y_j + C_1$ 5 $z_{i+j} \leftarrow C_0$ 6 $z_{i+n+1} \leftarrow C_1$ 7 **return** z

also vulnerable to timing attacks and simple power analysis, as it performs an operation (the addition) only if a condition on the secret scalar is met. To avoid this information leakage, the double-and-add-always variant employs a *dummy* accumulator variable (curve point D, line 7), which stores the result of a dummy addition operation that is performed when the scalar bit being scanned is not set. The double-and-add-always algorithm thus always computes both a doubling and an addition for each scalar bit, however the additions performed when the scalar bit is not set do not contribute to the final result.

In the BearSSL optimized implementation for the NIST standard curve P-256, the field operations are realized computing integer addition or multiplication followed by a modulo reduction. We note that for other curves, an alternative approach relying on the Montgomery multiplication is applied in the library, although it does not hinder the nature of our attack. In the multiply and reduce approach applied in BearSSL, multiple precision multiplications and squarings are executed applying the schoolbook approach reported in Algorithm 2, as it is the optimal one given the size of the operands and the fact that the modulo operation can be performed quite efficiently making use of the special binary form of the field characteristic recommended for the NIST standard curve P-256.

A notable detail in the word-by-word processing described in Algorithm 2 is the use of a single-word multiplier (line 4) that is able to compute the multiplication of two W-bit words yielding the corresponding $2W$-bit result. Finally, a notable implementation choice for curve P-256 in the BearSSL library, concerns the encoding of multi-precision integer values as a sequence of $W = 30$ bit words (each one fit into the least significant positions of a 32-bit architecture word) to manage the propagation of carries during additions and multiplications more efficiently.

Algorithm 3: BearSSL Scalar-point Multiplication for $\mathbb{E}(\mathbb{F}_p)$ NIST Standard Elliptic Curves

---

Input: $P \in \mathbb{E}(\mathbb{F}_p)$: generator of a large subgroup of $\mathbb{E}(\mathbb{F}_p)$,
$\quad\quad k = (k_{t-1} k_{t-2} \ldots k_0)_2$: scalar value
Output: $Q = [k]P$: scalar-point multiplication result
Data: CMOVE(BooleanExpression, SecondParam, ThirdParam): a *conditional move* copies the value of the third parameter into the second one, when the Boolean condition specified as the first parameter is true

---

1 $Q \leftarrow \mathcal{O}$
2 $P_2 \leftarrow 2P$
3 $P_3 \leftarrow P_2 + P$
4 **for** $i \leftarrow t - 1$ **to** 1 **by** -2 **do**
5 $\quad$ $w \leftarrow (k_i k_{i-1})_2$ $\quad\quad\quad\quad$ // extract a 2-bit window from the scalar
6 $\quad$ $Q \leftarrow [2]Q$
7 $\quad$ $Q \leftarrow [2]Q$
8 $\quad$ $T \leftarrow P, U \leftarrow Q$
9 $\quad$ CMOVE($w = (10)_2, T, P_2$)
10 $\quad$ CMOVE($w = (11)_2, T, P_3$)
11 $\quad$ $U \leftarrow U + T$
12 $\quad$ CMOVE($w \neq (00)_2 \wedge Q = \mathcal{O}, Q, T$)
13 $\quad$ CMOVE($w \neq (00)_2 \wedge Q \neq \mathcal{O}, Q, U$)
14 **return** Q

Algorithm 3 describes the actual scalar-point multiplication algorithm adopted in the BearSSL cryptographic implementation of ECC based on the NIST standard elliptic curves with prime characteristic, $\mathbb{E}(\mathbb{F}_p)$, in Jacobian coordinates. It shows a left-to-right double-and-add-always approach with the left-to-right scanning of the binary representation of the secret scalar that considers two bits for each iteration of the main loop of the algorithm. The algorithm starts by setting the accumulator variable Q to the point at infinity (line 1), and precomputes the values of the double and triple of the base point P (lines 2–3). The main loop of the Algorithm (lines 4–13) scans the scalar k from left to right, considering two bits of the scalar, $(k_i k_{i-1})_2$ per iteration (line 5), and computes the quadruple of the accumulator Q via two doubling operations (lines 6–7). The remainder of the loop body performs a sequence of conditional assignments with the purpose of adding to Q one out of: nothing, P, $[2]P$, or $[3]P$, depending on whether the values of $(k_i k_{i-1})_2$ are $(00)_2$, $(01)_2$, $(10)_2$, or $(11)_2$, respectively. This is accomplished saving the quadruple of Q in a temporary variable, U, and performing a sequence of conditional assignments employing a constant time conditional move function (CMOVE), which overwrites its destination operand (fed into the second parameter) with the source one (fed into the third parameter) only if the Boolean condition provided as the first parameter of the CMOVE function is true. The first two conditional assignments, (lines 9 and 10) change

Table 1. Summary of the pairs of variables, employed as operands in the point doubling and addition operations, of which the value collision are exploited, together with the corresponding value of the two scalar bits being revealed

First value	Line in Algorithm 3	Second value	Line in Algorithm 3	Values	Inferred (k_i, k_{i-1}) with i from $t-1$ downto 1
$P^{(0)}$	2	$T^{(i)}$	11	$=$	$(0,0)$
$Q^{(i)}$	11	$Q^{(i-2)}$	6	$=$	
$P^{(0)}$	2	$T^{(i)}$	11	$=$	$(0,1)$
$Q^{(i)}$	11	$Q^{(i-2)}$	6	$\neq$	
$P_2^{(0)}$	2	$T^{(i)}$	11	$=$	$(1,0)$
$P_3^{(0)}$	2	$T^{(i)}$	11	$=$	$(1,1)$

the value of the point to be added, T, from the P value taken in the assignment in line 8 to [2]P or [3]P, depending on whether the pair of scalar bits is equal to $(10)_2$ or $(11)_2$. The value T is then added to the copy of the quadrupled point value Q (line 11). Finally, the last two conditional assignments (line 12 and line 13) take care of replacing the value of the quadrupled point Q with its sum with one out of P, [2]P or [3]P, which is stored in T. This action needs to be performed only if the two scalar bits are not null (as this in turn implies that an addition is needed in this iteration). The reason for having two conditional assignments is to handle the fact that the accumulator curve point Q is set to the point at infinity at the beginning of the algorithm. This in turn would cause the point addition at line 11 to mis-compute the result of the sum of the accumulator with a multiple of the base point. As a consequence, a simple copy of the base point multiple is made if $Q = \mathcal{O}$.

4   Proposed Attack Workflow

In the following, we describe our attack strategy against Algorithm 3. We start by describing which algorithmic feature is exploited in our attack, and how we determine a criterion to deduce the value of the scalar bits from the information leaked by the side channel measurements. Subsequently, we detail what is the workflow of the power trace processing in the learning and prediction phase of a neural network based classifier which will allow us to detect the value collisions in the algorithm.

4.1   Inferring the Secret Scalar Value via Collisions

Our attack exploits the fact that, in each iteration of the main loop of Algorithm 3, the conditional assignments driven by the values of the scalar bits will change the value of the accumulator Q only if the scalar bits are not equal to $(0,0)$, and will select different values to be added to the temporary curve point

U. Exploiting the side channel leakage of the device to detect whenever operands of the base field arithmetic operations match among the operations will allow us to deduce the value of the scalar bit pair.

A summary of the values for which we test the equality via side channel attack, and the corresponding inferred values for the scalar bits are reported in Table 1. The two bottom rows in Table 1 describe the two straightforward cases when the derivation of $(k_i, k_{i-1}) = (1, 0)$ or $(k_i, k_{i-1}) = (1, 1)$, is performed by testing whether the value of the addend T in the point addition at line 11, during the current i-th iteration, equals two or three times the base point, respectively. The values of the double and triple of the base point, $P_2^{(0)}$ and $P_3^{(0)}$, are computed outside the loop body (conventionally, at the zero-th iteration), and are denoted at lines 2–3 of Algorithm 3 as P_2 and P_3. The remaining cases when the value of the operand T of the point addition at line 11 matches the base point itself needs additional information to infer whether $(k_i, k_{i-1}) = (0, 1)$ or $(k_i, k_{i-1}) = (0, 0)$, i.e., if the point addition result is being actually used or not in this iteration. We derive this additional information from the fact that, if $(k_i, k_{i-1}) = (0, 0)$ nothing should be added to the accumulator value Q during the iteration where the loop index equals i. Indeed, in case $(k_i, k_{i-1}) = (0, 0)$ the conditional move operations at lines 12–13 do not change the value of the accumulator point $Q^{(i)}$. As a consequence, we will have that, on the next loop body iteration (i.e., the one with loop index equal to $i - 2$), the value of $Q^{(i-2)}$ employed as operand to the point doubling at line 6 of Algorithm 3 will match the value of $Q^{(i)}$ (i.e., the value at the previous iteration) as first operand in the point addition operation at line 11.

Through the collision analysis of the values in Table 1 we are thus able to distinguish the value of the two bits of the scalar for each loop iteration in all the cases but the single corner case of them being either $(0, 0)$ or $(0, 1)$ in the last iteration of the double-and-add algorithm. Indeed, since we would need information from a subsequent loop iteration to tell these case apart, and there is no further iteration, the last bit of the scalar must be guessed in this case.

Our approach to distinguishing whether the values taken by two curve point variables are the same or different relies on a leakage of the Hamming weight of the multiple precision arithmetic operands, i.e., the curve point coordinates, which we experimentally verified to be present. Under the assumption of this leakage being present, we analyzed the point doubling and point addition formulas, reported in Algorithm 4 and Algorithm 5 in the Appendix. Both algorithms report the formulas considering the points as expressed in Jacobian coordinates, as per the BearSSL implementation. We highlighted in blue all the multiple precision arithmetic operations involving as operands the coordinates of any of the operand points (the addends for the addition, the point to be doubled for the doubling). We note that, save for two instructions in the point doubling (lines 2 and 3, Algorithm 5), all the sensitive multiple precision operations are either multiplications or squares.

4.2   Testing for Equality via Side Channel Data Extraction

We now describe how we employed a neural-network based regressor to detect whenever two curve point variables have the same values. In particular, we describe our preprocessing of the traces, aimed at reducing their number of samples, keeping only the ones which are expected to contain relevant information. Subsequently, we describe how we trained our neural network based regressors, and how their results are combined to yield the value match estimation.

For the sake of clarity, we will consider the power trace of the entire double-and-add algorithm as split into a sequence of slices of contiguous samples, corresponding to an iteration of the loop body in Algorithm 3, and denote them *single-iteration sub-traces*. Each single-iteration sub-trace contains two sequences of samples which correspond to the execution of the point doubling at line 6 of Algorithm 3 and to the execution of the point addition at line 11. These two sequences are the ones containing the samples of interest for our attack, and will be denoted as *addition sub-trace* and *doubling sub-trace*.

Since the addition and doubling sub-traces are composed by a number of samples in the tens of thousands, we decided to perform a selection of the *points of interest*, i.e., derive a set of time instants corresponding to the samples most relevant for our analysis. To this end, we collected a set of traces where all the operands were known, and computed the sample Pearson correlation coefficient between the Hamming weight of each operand word and the power consumption itself. We determined a first set of points of interest, S_{PoI}^1 considering all the time intervals where the correlation with the Hamming weight of any of the operand words exceeded a given threshold h, and adding a sample preceding and a sample following each time interval. A second set of points of interest S_{PoI}^2 was determined as the sequence of time instants between the first and last time instants in which the Pearson correlation coefficient exceeds the threshold h. The threshold is selected to be above the value of the non significant correlation for a given number of traces n_{traces}, i.e., $\frac{4}{\sqrt{n_{traces}}}$ [24].

Once the sets of points of interest were determined, only the projection of the traces on the time instants contained in the said sets were employed as input to our regressor learning, validation and testing phases. We employed as a regressor, an MLP neural network, which was trained with the projected traces labelled with the sequence of Hamming weights of the multiple precision arithmetic operand, therefore learning to regress the sequence of the Hamming weights of the operand words. The PoI selection and learning (training) procedure was repeated for each multiple precision operand which is involved in curve point variable comparison, obtaining a dedicated MLP for each one of them, i.e., for each coordinate of the points reported in Table 1. Our choice employing a set of MLP neural networks for each multiple precision operand (i.e., each coordinate of a curve point) is motivated by the manipulations of the said operands taking place in different time instants during the addition and doubling steps.

In order to exploit the results of our trained classifiers on a power trace sampled from a device with an unknown scalar value, we partition the power trace at hand in the two addition and doubling sub-traces, apply the projection on the PoIs and feed the resulting decimated sub-traces onto the 9 regressors (one for each Jacobian coordinate X, Y, Z of the three elliptic curve point variable Q, T, U). Since a regressor outputs a sequence of values corresponding to its best estimate of the Hamming weights of the operand at hand, we need to compare two sequence of values to infer if the operands match or not. We note that, in the case of the comparison between the three precomputed window points, i.e., $P = P^{(0)}$, $P_2 = [2]P^{(0)}$, $P_3^{(0)} = [3]P^{(0)}$ and the runtime value taken by T, only the Hamming weights of T are unknown, while the others are fixed and known. This, in turn, allows us to compare the regressed estimate of the Hamming weight of the words of the coordinates of T with the known values of the Hamming weight of the words of the coordinates of P, P_2, P_3.

The comparison between two curve points is performed taking the three vectors of 9 estimates of the Hamming weights for each coordinate of the points (e.g., Q, T) on the curve P-256, concatenating the vectors to obtain a 27 element vector for each point, and computing the Manhattan distance between the two 27 elements vectors. We recall that the Manhattan distance is defined as the sum of the absolute values of the coordinate-wise differences of two vectors, which are in our case the two sequences of Hamming weights. We deem two curve points equal if the Manhattan distance is below a given threshold. We employed traces from the learning (training) set to determine the threshold on the Manhattan distance allowing the best success rate in comparisons.

5   Experimental Evaluation

The device under test was a 32-bit ARM® Cortex®-M4 microcontroller with 256 kiB of Flash memory, 40 KiB of SRAM, supporting a maximum frequency of 72 MHz, while the recording of the power consumption traces was performed via a ChipWhisperer 1200 Pro digital sampling kit. The sampling is performed synchronously with the target microcontroller clock signal, providing one sample per clock cycle. This clock-locking approach removes artifacts coming from eventual clock jitter, and was possible with the Chipwhisperer Pro acquisition board locking the microcontroller clock to an external crystal oscillating at 7.37 MHz. To focus our analysis on the learning aspects of the profiled phase of attack, we employed triggers signals to single out point addition and doubling subtraces out of the entire execution of the elliptic curve scalar-point multiplication.

Our experiments were done running the BearSSL ver. 0.6 library [27], compiled with gcc ver. 9.2.1, and compilation options -Os. We recall that BearSSL encodes the multiple precision integer operands employing 30-bit limbs, which are embedded in the least significant bits of 32-bit architectural words. As a consequence, the binary values of curve point coordinates are represented employing a number of 32-bit machine words which is not a power of two; e.g., point coordinates of the NIST standard curve P-256 are defined over a prime finite field, where each element is encoded as a sequence of 256 bits which in turn corresponds to 9, 32-bit machine words.

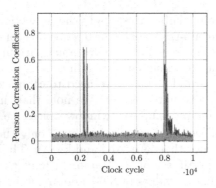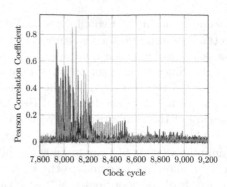

Fig. 1. Pearson correlation coefficient between the values of the Hamming weight of each one of the nine words of the x-coordinate of Q (the point being doubled in a point doubling operation) and the power consumption measurements from the device, as a function of time. Each one of the nine colours represents the correlation of a given coordinate word. (Left) Time interval corresponding to the leading part of a point doubling sub-trace – no significant correlation is observed outside the shown samples; (Right) zoom on the second set of peaks reported also in the left sub-figure, highlighting the different time instants where the coordinate words are being processed

The MLPs were generated and tested using TensorFlow v1.12.0 and Keras v2.1.6-tf. Experimental tests have been run on an Intel(R) Xeon(R) Gold 6254 processor running at 3.1 GHz. Training all the required MLPs (i.e., nine neural networks, three for each curve point), requires a total time of seven hours. Extracting the key values once the models are available takes a couple of seconds.

As a first step, we tested if the assumption of Hamming weight leakage on the curve operands was practically verified. To this end, we collected 3,000 traces of the curve point doubling and addition with known random input and computed the Pearson correlation coefficient among the sampled values and the Hamming weight of the words composing the coordinates of the operands.

Figure 1 reports the result of the computation of the Pearson correlation coefficient between the Hamming weight of each one of the nine words of the x-coordinate of Q during a point doubling operation and the power consumption trace (line 6 or line 7 in Algorithm 3). Each correlation with a given word out of nine is represented with a different colour. As it can be seen, there are time instants where a non-negligible correlation is present for each one of the nine coordinate words. Similar results are obtained with the words of the remaining coordinates, and with the words of the curve addition operands, and are omitted for space reasons. Given the obtained results, we set our threshold h for the Pearson correlation coefficient to build the sets of PoIs to 0.3, as there is at least one time instant where a significant correlation is present for each word of each one of the curve coordinates.

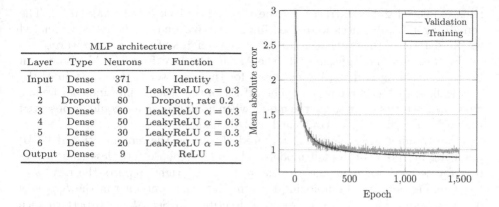

Fig. 2. (Left) Architecture of the MLP employed to regress the value of the Hamming weights of the multiple precision coordinates of curve points. (Right) Training and validation accuracy of the MLP for the prediction of the x-coordinate of the point Q. Each epoch employs 24k traces

We built nine regressors, one for each coordinate of the three points Q, U, and T, using the same MLP model. To choose our MLP regressor, we tested different neural network architectures and compared their performance with respect to their topology and hyper-parameters, using the accuracy and loss metrics. The number of layers and the number of neurons per layers were determined by subsequent refinement passes which reduced them until the accuracy results started worsening. We tested different number of epochs and batch sizes. As optimizer algorithms, we tested the ADAM optimizer and the RmsProp optimizer, with different learning rates.

We eventually designed our MLP regressor as an 8-layer MLP; a description of the complete architecture is reported in the left part of Fig. 2. We employed 7 dense neuron layers, and 1 random dropout layer (the third) with dropout rate 0.2 to prevent overfitting. We chose to employ the Leaky Rectified Linear Unit (LeakyReLU) [21] activation function, which is defined as

$$f(x) = \begin{cases} \alpha x, & \text{if } x \le 0 \\ x, & \text{if } x > 0 \end{cases}$$

employing a leaking parameter $\alpha = 0.3$, for all the dense layers of the MLP save for the last. The choice of the LeakyReLU activation function was empirically substantiated by the fact that the LeakyReLU performed better than the original ReLU counterpart (i.e., LeakyReLU with $\alpha = 0$). We employed the mean squared error loss function and employed the Root Mean Square propagation (RMSprop) learning algorithm, with a batch size of 32.

For the learning phase of our attack, we collected a set of 75k sub-traces with known inputs. We used 30k of such sub-traces for the training/validation phase, with an 80/20 split between training and validation sets. Each epoch thus employed 24k sub-traces for the training and 6k for the validation. The remaining 45k sub-traces were used for the testing phase. The label associated to the dataset is the sequence of 9 Hamming weights of the operand words.

Figure 2, on the right, reports the Mean Absolute Error (MAE) trends in both the training and validation phase, for the regressor that tries to infer the x-coordinate of the curve point Q. The MLPs for the other points and coordinates gave similar results. We saved the model when no improvement could be observed in the MAE. The test set confirmed a MAE under 1.

The training for each model required 45 min on the aforementioned CPU, resulting in about 7 h for all models. The testing phase took less than a second for each of the nine models. Figure 2, on the right, reports the results of the training performed employing the time instants contained in the S^1_{PoI} sets of PoIs, determined with the criterion described in Sect. 4.2. No performance improvement have been observed using S^2_{PoI} in our setup, in turn showing that enlarging the set of PoIs (we recall that $S^2_{\mathrm{PoI}} \supseteq S^1_{\mathrm{PoI}}$) introduces no advantage.

Moving to the prediction phase, we employed the aforementioned nine models to extract information from a fresh set of 15k sub-traces to perform an attack. We were able to correctly match the value of T against the possible matching values, i.e., P, [2]P, and [3]P with perfect accuracy. We were therefore able to classify correctly all the occurrence of the scalar bit pairs where $w = (10)_2$ (i.e., T = [2]P) or $w = (11)_2$ (i.e., T = [2]P). Distinguishing the case where $w = (00)_2$ from $w = (01)_2$, i.e., distinguishing when the accumulator point Q has the same value was not possible with perfect accuracy.

To maximize the accuracy of the comparison of the values of the doubled point Q, we optimized the threshold above which the Manhattan distance between the two vectors of Hamming weight estimates are deemed to represent the Hamming weights of two different values. Figure 3 reports the number of misclassified bits of the secret scalar (256-bit wide), averaged over 50 scalar multiplications, as a function of the Manhattan distance threshold employed to decide if a pair of regressed Hamming weight sets correspond to the same value. We note that, for a rather large interval of possible thresholds, our approach misclassifies less than a single bit out of the entire scalar, on average. Finally, we note that, in case the least significant bit pair in the scalar is either $(0, 1)$ or $(0, 0)$, we are not able to recover the value of the least significant bit. Indeed, telling the aforementioned cases apart requires to extract the information on the doubled point Q, which should retain its value between the last iteration and the (non-existing) following one of the scalar-point multiplication. We therefore need to guess its value in the aforementioned case, which can be detected as the next-to-least significant bit is extracted to be 0.

Summing up, we are able to retrieve the entire value of the scalar of a scalar-point multiplication on the P-256 curve with a single power trace and an exhaustive search over at most 128 possible values for the scalar, since we misclassify on average less than a single bit, which can appear only in 64 out of the 256 possible positions, and we may need to guess the value of the least significant bit of the scalar 1 out of 2 times on average.

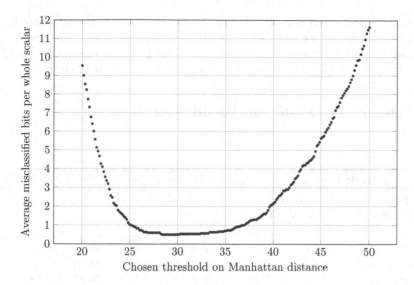

Fig. 3. Average number of mis-classified bits for an entire scalar, as a function of the chosen threshold on the Manhattan distance between the two sequences of regressed Hamming weights (all mis-classifications are caused by the point doubling operand matching)

6 Concluding Remarks

We presented a profiled side channel attack based on neural network against the elliptic curve scalar-point multiplication. We validated our attack technique on the elliptic curve scalar-point multiplication implemented in BearSSL, running on a Cortex-M4 microcontroller. Our attack strategy achieves a perfect success rate with an extremely small exhaustive search (128 possible scalar values for the P-256 curve), employing a single power trace from the attacked device, and a learning phase with 75k traces. The attack requires seven hours to perform the neural network training on an Intel(R) Xeon(R) Gold 6254 processor running at 3.1 GHz, while the actual key extraction and exhaustive search phase takes a couple of seconds.

We note that our attack can in principle be applied to non-windowing-based implementations, too. For instance, by looking at Algorithm 1 we can observe that $k_i = 0$ implies that the addition (line 7) at iteration i and the double (line 3) at iteration $i + 1$ share the same operand Q, similarly to what is exploited to attack Algorithm 3. We also note that the scalar blinding countermeasure becomes ineffective in a scenario where the attacker has full control of another instance of the device under attack, and she can perform the profiling phase disabling the countermeasures. In fact, our attack path relies on the knowledge of the precomputed values and the presence of internal collisions through subsequent iterations, which are not removed by scalar blinding. The well known countermeasures of *coordinates randomization* and *re-randomization*, would remove such requirements and thus block our attack. However, if the attacker has no access to a clone device without countermeasures, then she would not be able to mount the attack neither in the presence of scalar blinding, as she would not know the information needed to label the dataset for the profiling phase.

A   Details of Double-and-Add Algorithm

Algorithm 4: Elliptic Curve Point Addition in the BearSSL library [27]

Input: $U = (x_1, y_1, z_1) \in \mathbb{E}(\mathbb{F}_p); T = (x_2, y_2, z_2) \in \mathbb{E}(\mathbb{F}_p)$
Output: $(x_1, y_1, z_1) = U + T$

1 $t_3 = z_2^2$
2 $t_1 = x_1 \cdot t_3$
3 $t_4 = z_2 \cdot t_3$
4 $t_3 = y_1 \cdot t_4$
5 $t_4 = z_1^2$
6 $t_2 = x_2 \cdot t_4$
7 $t_5 = z_1 \cdot t_4$

8 $t_4 = y_2 \cdot t_5$
9 $t_2 = t_2 - t_1$
10 $t_4 = t_4 - t_3$
11 $t_4 = t_4 \bmod p$
12 $t_7 = t_2^2$
13 $t_6 = t_1 \cdot t_7$
14 $t_5 = t_7 \cdot t_2$

15 $x_1 = t_4^4$
16 $x_1 = x_1 - t_5$
17 $x_1 = x_1 - t_6$
18 $x_1 = x_1 - t_6$
19 $t_6 = t_6 - x_1$
20 $y_1 = t_4 \cdot t_6$
21 $t_1 = t_5 \cdot t_3$

22 $y_1 = y_1 - t_1$
23 $t_1 = z_1 \cdot z_2$
24 $z_1 = t_1 \cdot t_2$
25 **return** (x_1, y_1, z_1)

Algorithm 5: Elliptic Curve Point Doubling in the BearSSL library [27]

Input: $Q = (x_1, y_1, z_1) \in \mathbb{E}(\mathbb{F}_p)$
Output: $(x_1, y_1, z_1) = [2]Q$

1 $t_1 = z^2$
2 $t_2 = x_1 + t_1$
3 $t_1 = x_1 - t_1$
4 $t_3 = t_1 \cdot t_2$
5 $t_1 = t_3 + t_3$
6 $t_1 = t_3 + t_1$

7 $t_3 = y_1^2$
8 $t_3 = t_3 + t_3$
9 $t_2 = x_1 \cdot t_3$
10 $t_2 = t_2 + t_2$
11 $x_1 = t_1^2$
12 $x_1 = x_1 - t_2$

13 $x_1 = x_1 - t_2$
14 $t_4 = y_1 \cdot z_1$
15 $z_1 = t_4 + t_4$
16 $t_2 = t_2 - x_1$
17 $y_1 = t_1 \cdot t_2$
18 $t_4 = t_3^2$

19 $t_4 = t_4 + t_4$
20 $y_1 = y_1 - t_4$
21 **return** (x_1, y_1, z_1)

References

1. Agrawal, D., Archambeault, B., Rao, J.R., Rohatgi, P.: The EM side—channel(s). In: Kaliski, B.S., Koç, K., Paar, C. (eds.) CHES 2002. LNCS, vol. 2523, pp. 29–45. Springer, Heidelberg (2003). https://doi.org/10.1007/3-540-36400-5_4
2. Barthelmeh, J.: WolfSSL (formerly cyassl) library: a small, fast, portable implementation of TLS/SSL for embedded devices (2016). https://github.com/wolfSSL/wolfssl

3. Batina, L., Hogenboom, J., van Woudenberg, J.G.J.: Getting more from PCA: first results of using principal component analysis for extensive power analysis. In: Dunkelman, O. (ed.) CT-RSA 2012. LNCS, vol. 7178, pp. 383–397. Springer, Heidelberg (2012). https://doi.org/10.1007/978-3-642-27954-6_24

4. Bauer, A., Jaulmes, E., Prouff, E., Wild, J.: Horizontal collision correlation attack on elliptic curves. In: Lange, T., Lauter, K., Lisoněk, P. (eds.) SAC 2013. LNCS, vol. 8282, pp. 553–570. Springer, Heidelberg (2014). https://doi.org/10.1007/978-3-662-43414-7_28

5. Bishop, C.: Pattern Recognition and Machine Learning. Information Science and Statistics, Springer, New York (2006)

6. Brumley, D., Boneh, D.: Remote timing attacks are practical. In: Proceedings of the 12th USENIX Security Symposium, Washington, D.C., USA, 4–8 August 2003, pp. 1–13. USENIX Association (2003). https://www.usenix.org/conference/12th-usenix-security-symposium/remote-timing-attacks-are-practical

7. Cagli, E., Dumas, C., Prouff, E.: Convolutional neural networks with data augmentation against jitter-based countermeasures. In: Fischer, W., Homma, N. (eds.) CHES 2017. LNCS, vol. 10529, pp. 45–68. Springer, Cham (2017). https://doi.org/10.1007/978-3-319-66787-4_3

8. Carbone, M., et al.: Deep learning to evaluate secure RSA implementations. IACR Trans. Cryptogr. Hardw. Embed. Syst. **2019**(2), 132–161 (2019). https://doi.org/10.13154/tches.v2019.i2.132-161

9. Charl, S., Rao, J.R., Rohatgi, P.: Template attacks. In: Kaliski, B.S., Koç, K., Paar, C. (eds.) CHES 2002. LNCS, vol. 2523, pp. 13–28. Springer, Heidelberg (2003). https://doi.org/10.1007/3-540-36400-5_3

10. Danger, J.-L., Guilley, S., Hoogvorst, P., Murdica, C., Naccache, D.: Improving the big mac attack on elliptic curve cryptography. In: Ryan, P.Y.A., Naccache, D., Quisquater, J.-J. (eds.) The New Codebreakers. LNCS, vol. 9100, pp. 374–386. Springer, Heidelberg (2016). https://doi.org/10.1007/978-3-662-49301-4_23

11. Denis, F.: The Sodium cryptography library. Libsodium (2013). https://doc.libsodium.org/

12. Duchi, J.C., Hazan, E., Singer, Y.: Adaptive subgradient methods for online learning and stochastic optimization. In: Kalai, A.T., Mohri, M. (eds.) COLT 2010 - The 23rd Conference on Learning Theory, Haifa, Israel, 27–29 June 2010, pp. 257–269. Omnipress (2010). http://colt2010.haifa.il.ibm.com/papers/COLT2010proceedings.pdf#page=265

13. Gandolfi, K., Mourtel, C., Olivier, F.: Electromagnetic analysis: concrete results. In: Koç, Ç.K., Naccache, D., Paar, C. (eds.) CHES 2001. LNCS, vol. 2162, pp. 251–261. Springer, Heidelberg (2001). https://doi.org/10.1007/3-540-44709-1_21

14. Gierlichs, B., Batina, L., Tuyls, P., Preneel, B.: Mutual information analysis. In: Oswald, E., Rohatgi, P. (eds.) CHES 2008. LNCS, vol. 5154, pp. 426–442. Springer, Heidelberg (2008). https://doi.org/10.1007/978-3-540-85053-3_27

15. Gierlichs, B., Lemke-Rust, K., Paar, C.: Templates vs. stochastic methods. In: Goubin, L., Matsui, M. (eds.) CHES 2006. LNCS, vol. 4249, pp. 15–29. Springer, Heidelberg (2006). https://doi.org/10.1007/11894063_2

16. Gilmore, R., Hanley, N., O'Neill, M.: Neural network based attack on a masked implementation of AES. In: IEEE International Symposium on Hardware Oriented Security and Trust, HOST 2015, Washington, DC, USA, 5–7 May 2015, pp. 106–111. IEEE Computer Society (2015). https://doi.org/10.1109/HST.2015.7140247

17. Hanley, N., Kim, H.S., Tunstall, M.: Exploiting collisions in addition chain-based exponentiation algorithms using a single trace. In: Nyberg, K. (ed.) CT-RSA 2015. LNCS, vol. 9048, pp. 431–448. Springer, Cham (2015). https://doi.org/10.1007/978-3-319-16715-2_23
18. Kingma, D.P., Ba, J.: Adam: a method for stochastic optimization. In: Bengio, Y., LeCun, Y. (eds.) 3rd International Conference on Learning Representations, ICLR 2015, Conference Track Proceedings, San Diego, CA, USA, 7–9 May 2015 (2015). http://arxiv.org/abs/1412.6980
19. Kocher, P.C.: Timing attacks on implementations of Diffie-Hellman, RSA, DSS, and other systems. In: Koblitz, N. (ed.) CRYPTO 1996. LNCS, vol. 1109, pp. 104–113. Springer, Heidelberg (1996). https://doi.org/10.1007/3-540-68697-5_9
20. Kocher, P., Jaffe, J., Jun, B.: Differential power analysis. In: Wiener, M. (ed.) CRYPTO 1999. LNCS, vol. 1666, pp. 388–397. Springer, Heidelberg (1999). https://doi.org/10.1007/3-540-48405-1_25
21. Maas, A.L., Hannun, A.Y., Ng, A.Y.: Rectifier nonlinearities improve neural network acoustic models. In: ICML Workshop on Deep Learning for Audio, Speech and Language Processing (2013)
22. Maghrebi, H.: Assessment of common side channel countermeasures with respect to deep learning based profiled attacks. In: 31st International Conference on Microelectronics, ICM 2019, Cairo, Egypt, 15–18 December 2019, pp. 126–129. IEEE (2019). https://doi.org/10.1109/ICM48031.2019.9021728
23. Maghrebi, H., Portigliatti, T., Prouff, E.: Breaking cryptographic implementations using deep learning techniques. In: Carlet, C., Hasan, M.A., Saraswat, V. (eds.) SPACE 2016. LNCS, vol. 10076, pp. 3–26. Springer, Cham (2016). https://doi.org/10.1007/978-3-319-49445-6_1
24. Mangard, S., Oswald, E., Popp, T.: Power Analysis Attacks - Revealing the Secrets of Smart Cards. Springer, Boston (2007). https://doi.org/10.1007/978-0-387-38162-6
25. Masure, L., Dumas, C., Prouff, E.: A comprehensive study of deep learning for side-channel analysis. IACR Cryptology ePrint Archive 2019/439 (2019). https://eprint.iacr.org/2019/439
26. Perin, G., Chmielewski, L., Batina, L., Picek, S.: Keep it unsupervised: horizontal attacks meet deep learning. IACR Trans. Cryptogr. Hardw. Embed. Syst. **2021**(1), 343–372 (2021). https://doi.org/10.46586/tches.v2021.i1.343-372
27. Pornin, T.: BearSSL, a smaller SSL/TLS library (2016). https://bearssl.org/index.html
28. Poussier, R., Zhou, Y., Standaert, F.-X.: A systematic approach to the side-channel analysis of ECC implementations with worst-case horizontal attacks. In: Fischer, W., Homma, N. (eds.) CHES 2017. LNCS, vol. 10529, pp. 534–554. Springer, Cham (2017). https://doi.org/10.1007/978-3-319-66787-4_26
29. Quisquater, J.J., Samyde, D.: Eddy current for magnetic analysis with active sensor. In: Proceedings of Esmart 2002, Nice, France, pp. 185–194, September 2002
30. Reed, R.D., Marks, R.J.: Neural Smithing: Supervised Learning in Feedforward Artificial Neural Networks. MIT Press, Cambridge (1998)
31. Roelofs, N., Samwel, N., Batina, L., Daemen, J.: Online template attack on ECDSA: extracting keys via the other side. In: Nitaj, A., Youssef, A. (eds.) AFRICACRYPT 2020. LNCS, vol. 12174, pp. 323–336. Springer, Cham (2020). https://doi.org/10.1007/978-3-030-51938-4_16
32. Srivastava, N., Hinton, G.E., Krizhevsky, A., Sutskever, I., Salakhutdinov, R.: Dropout: a simple way to prevent neural networks from overfitting. J. Mach. Learn. Res. **15**(1), 1929–1958 (2014)

33. Weissbart, L., Chmielewski, Ł, Picek, S., Batina, L.: Systematic side-channel analysis of Curve25519 with machine learning. J. Hardw. Syst. Secur. **4**(4), 314–328 (2020). https://doi.org/10.1007/s41635-020-00106-w

34. Weissbart, L., Picek, S., Batina, L.: One trace is all it takes: machine learning-based side-channel attack on EdDSA. In: Bhasin, S., Mendelson, A., Nandi, M. (eds.) SPACE 2019. LNCS, vol. 11947, pp. 86–105. Springer, Cham (2019). https://doi.org/10.1007/978-3-030-35869-3_8

35. Witteman, M.F., van Woudenberg, J.G.J., Menarini, F.: Defeating RSA multiply-always and message blinding countermeasures. In: Kiayias, A. (ed.) CT-RSA 2011. LNCS, vol. 6558, pp. 77–88. Springer, Heidelberg (2011). https://doi.org/10.1007/978-3-642-19074-2_6

36. Zhou, Y., Standaert, F.X.: Simplified single-trace side-channel attacks on elliptic curve scalar multiplication using fully convolutional networks. In: 40th WIC Symposium on Information Theory in the Benelux (2019). https://dial.uclouvain.be/pr/boreal/object/boreal:226275

37. Zotkin, Y., Olivier, F., Bourbao, E.: Deep learning vs template attacks in front of fundamental targets: experimental study. IACR Cryptology ePrint Archive 2018/1213 (2018). https://eprint.iacr.org/2018/1213

Deep Cross-Modal Supervised Hashing Based on Joint Semantic Matrix

Na Chen, Yuan Cao$^{(\boxtimes)}$, and Chao Liu

Ocean University of China, Qingdao 266000, ShanDong, China
cy8661@ouc.edu.cn

Abstract. Cross-modal hashing is to project sample data of different modalities into a common binary space, where the correlation between different modalities can be effectively measured. The purpose of cross-modal retrieval is to realize flexible search between different modalities. This paper proposes a novel cross-modal retrieval model, called the Deep Cross-modal Supervised Hashing based on Joint Semantic Matrix (DCSJM). We utilize the joint semantic matrix as the uniform similarity metrics, which meticulously integrates the original domain information of different modalities and can capture the potential inherent semantic similarity between different modalities. Furthermore, by combing the label information and the joint semantic similarity information as the supervision information, we can get more comprehensive and accurate search results. A large number of experiments show that the proposed DCSJM model achieves significant improvements in various cross-modal retrieval tasks.

Keywords: Cross-modal · Hashing · Retrieval

1 Introduction

Due to the development of science and technology and the rapid development of the era of big data, Approximate Nearest Neighbor (ANN) methods play an important role in machine learning and image retrieval applications. Hashing has been extensively studied by researchers due to its high efficiency and low storage characteristics to solve ANN search problems. The main principle of hashing is that the data is mapped from the original space to the Hamming space, preserving the similarity between the original space and the Hamming space as much as possible. The binary codes can be used for large-scale retrieval or other applications, which can not only greatly reduce the storage space but also increase the search speed. In most of the current application fields, data tends to be multi-modal (image, text, audio, etc.). As for large-scale multi-modal retrieval problems, hashing has also been widely used. The basic framework of the cross-modal hash method is shown in Fig. 1, and the process from left to right shows the basic process of the cross-modal hash method. The specific process is to input the original data of different modalities into the network set for different modalities to extract the features and obtain the sub-optimal hash code, and then the

© Springer Nature Switzerland AG 2021
M. Yang et al. (Eds.): NSS 2021, LNCS 13041, pp. 258–274, 2021.
https://doi.org/10.1007/978-3-030-92708-0_16

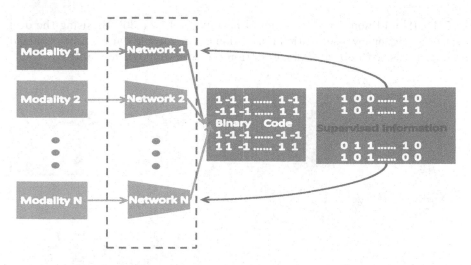

Fig. 1. The basic framework of the cross-modal approach.

sub-optimal hash code obtained by the network and the supervision information are distanced in a suitable way. To continuously train the network until the desired result is reached. Multi-modal hashing is generally divided into two categories depending on whether all data points have common multiple modalities. One is called multi-source hashing that requires all data points having common multiple modalities. The other is called cross-modal hashing. In cross-modal hashing, it is allowed if some of the data points do not have all multiple modalities. Since it is more difficult to require all objects to have common modalities in real applications, cross-modal hashing is more widely used. Multi-modal hashing can be also divided into supervised cross-modal hashing and unsupervised cross-modal hashing depending on whether the label information is used in the training process. For example, in DSCMR [1], the label information is used as the supervision information for training the deep network, making the network parameters more accurate under the supervision of the label information. However, in DJSRH [2], the authors do not use the label information as the supervision information. A novel joint semantic matrix is constructed as the supervision information of the subsequent training network. The matrix integrates the original domain relationship among the data samples. Multi-modal hashing methods are also different in consideration of the hash codes learning process. One kind maps different modalities of the same object into similar binary codes in the Hamming space [1,5]. The other kind maps different modalities of the same object into the same binary code [3,4] in the Hamming space to preserve similarity among different modalities of the same object. From another point of view, cross-modal hashing can be divided into deep cross-modal hashing

[3–5,11–18] and non-deep cross-modal hashing [6–10,24–30]. By using the deep networks, higher-level semantic information of the sample data can be obtained, making it easier to obtain the correlation between different modalities.

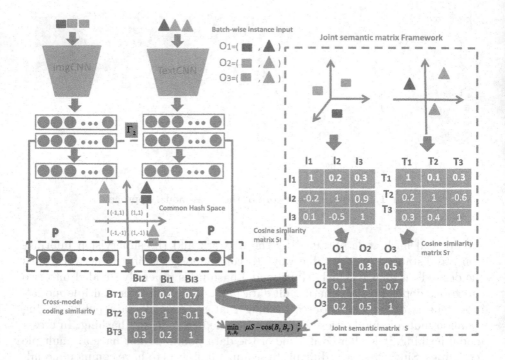

Fig. 2. The Framework of DCSJM. The right part represents joint semantic matrix generation, the left part represents image text pair training in the network. The purple network layer in the picture represents the label prediction layer P. The optimization of the network parameters mainly uses the joint semantic matrix on the left as supervision information. (Color figure online)

In this paper, we propose a new cross-modal retrieval method called Cross-modal Supervised Hashing based on Joint Semantic Matrix (DCSJM). In our model, the label information is used to form a linear classifier as the supervision information to optimize the network parameters. In order to make full use of the potential relevance of the training data, a joint semantic information is also used as the supervision information of the training data. Since the joint semantic matrix can obtain the original information of a large amount of the training data, it can make the network parameters more precise.

1) This paper proposes a model that combines joint semantic matrix and label information as a model of supervised information training network parameters. The model explores the correlation between different modalities in the public space by using label information and the original neighborhood relationship, and generates accurate and compact hash codes for different modalities.

2) This paper presents a novel form of supervision information to train deep networks by combining the label supervision information with the unsupervised joint semantic matrix. On the one hand, the label can obtain superior network parameters. On the other hand, the joint semantic matrix can obtain the latent semantic information of the features. Our model can achieve a better learning effect by using the two different weights as the supervision information.

3) The test results on the widely used data set Pascal Sentence show that DCSJM is superior to other cross-modal hashing algorithms.

2 Related Work

In this chapter, we will briefly review related work from the following four aspects: non-deep cross-modal methods, deep cross-modal hashing methods, supervised cross-modal hashing methods, and unsupervised cross-modal hashing methods.

2.1 Non-Deep Cross-Modal Hashing

When the deep neural network has not yet developed vigorously, the most primitive cross-modal hashing method evolved from the single-modal hashing method. Take the Cross-View Hashing (CVH) [6] method as an example. It is an extension of spectral hashing. Its idea is to learn the hash function by minimizing the weighted average Hamming distance of different modalities, and use the generalized special diagnosis method to obtain the minimum value. Then to the later Linear Cross-Modal Hashing (LCMH) [24], this method inherits some of the ideas of AGH as a representative of the linear method. This method uses the scalable K-Means algorithm to calculate the distance between the data point and the center point to maintain the modal Internal similarity. By minimizing the distance between different modalities in the public space and the same object, the similarity between modalities is ensured.

Then to the later Collective Matrix Factorization Hashing (CMFH) [28] method and Latent Semantic Sparse Hashing (LSSH) [29]. The collective matrix factorization method uses collective matrix factorization to help build a hash function model. The latent semantic sparse hash method uses sparse coding to obtain high-dimensional salient features, and uses matrix factorization to learn latent semantics.

2.2   Deep Cross-Modal Hashing

In recent years, deep learning has developed rapidly. The reason is that the deep features extracted by deep learning methods include richer semantic information, and the ability to express raw data is stronger. The combination of deep learning and hashing methods applied to multi-modal retrieval can significantly improve retrieval efficiency.

For example, the Deep Cross-Modal Hashing (DCMH) [5], which integrates feature learning and hash learning into an end-to-end framework. This learning model means that each part can provide feedback to the other part during the learning process. DCMH [5] uses negative log-likelihood function to maintain the similarity of image and text features. Although DCMH [5] is a breakthrough deep hashing method, it does not deal with the correlation within data modalities and the further correlation between hash codes and different modal features. Therefore, some researchers later proposed the shortcomings of Pairwise Relationship Deep Hashing (PRDH) [4] to improve DCMH [5]. The main innovation of PRDH [4] is to integrate different types of paired constraints to better reflect the hash code similarity of data between and within modalities. PRDH [4] also introduces additional decorrelation constraints to enhance the independence between hash code bits. Later, with the development of deep networks, more and more researchers started to use deep networks to train and obtain research results. There are also many excellent research results worthy of our study. The method we propose is to use deep network training to get the hash function.

2.3   Supervised Cross-Modal Hashing

Data dependence methods can be roughly divided into unsupervised and supervised according to the use of data supervision information. The supervised learning method generally needs to use the label information of the data to train to obtain the result.

Taking Discrete Robust Supervised Hashing for Cross-Modal Retrieval (DRSH) [12] as an example, the method first merges class labels and features from different modalities, and learns a robust similarity matrix through low-rank constraints, which can explain its structure and capture the noise in it.

2.4   Unsupervised Cross-Modal Hashing

The unsupervised cross-modal hashing method does not use the artificial label information of the data, but only uses the original feature distribution information of the data as the supervised information to train the model. Because the unsupervised cross-modal hash algorithm does not use artificial label information, the retrieval results are relatively poor compared to the supervised cross-modal hash method.

Unsupervised method, for example, DJSRH [2], the author proposes a new type of joint semantic reconstruction matrix, which uses the original feature information of the sample to construct a joint semantic matrix to maintain the original domain relationship between the data. Then we use the joint semantic matrix as the supervision information to train the network parameters, and finally get good retrieval results.

3 Method

In this part, we first introduce some definitions and symbols used in the interpretation method. Then, we explain the theoretical part of the cross-modal semantic joint method proposed in the article in detail. Finally, we describe the specific implementation steps of the related methods.

3.1 Problem Formulation

Without losing generality, we still use image and text pairs for training. We use n to indicate that there are n instances of image text pairs used in the experiment, denoted as $\phi = \left\{ (x_i^I, x_i^T)_{i=1}^n \right\}$, where x_i^I represents the i-th instance in the image instance and x_i^T indicates the i-th instance in the text instance. Each image text pair (x_i^I, x_i^T) is assigned a category vector $T_i = [t_{1i}, t_{2i}, ..., t_{ci}]$, where c represents the number of categories, If the i-th instance is in the j-th category, then $t_{ij} = 1$, otherwise, $t_{ij} = 0$.

Cross-modal hashing is to learn different functions for different modalities, and this article only uses two modal training of picture and text to learn two functions: $m_i = f(x_i^I; \Theta_I) \in \mathbb{R}^n$ is for Image modal and $n_i = g(x_i^T; \Theta_T) \in \mathbb{R}^n$ is for Text modal, Where n represents the number of dimensions of the public space representation, x^I represents the image training sample data, and Θ_I represents the network parameters learned by the image network training. Similarly, x^T represents the text training sample data, and Θ_T represents the network parameters learned by the text network training. In the following, the image representation matrix in the training sample, the text representation matrix and the label representation matrix are respectively denoted as $M = [m_1, m_2, ..., m_n]$, $N = [n_1, n_2, ..., n_n]$, $T = [T_1, T_2, ..., T_n]$, Where m_i represents the image of the i-th instance in the common representation space, and n_j represents the text of the j-th instance.

3.2 Framework of DCSJM

The method proposed in this paper includes three parts as shown in Fig. 2 the calculation of the joint semantic matrix, the picture subnet and the text subnet.

We first calculate the aforementioned joint semantic matrix based on the training data of different modalities.

The two subnets include a deep network for training images shown in Table 1 and a deep network for training text shown in Table 2. Both networks are trained in an end-to-end manner. The deep neural network used for image modalities is a 19-layer VGGNet pre-trained on ImageNet. We use the 4096-dimensional features generated from the fc7 layer as the original high-level semantic representation of the image, denoted as F_i^I, fc8 learns the public representation of the picture, denoted by m_i, and the last layer generates a d-dimensional binary code to represent the hash code, denoted as b_i^I. Without loss of generality, we use the Word2Vec model for text modal training, which has been pre-trained for one billion words in Google News. First, each network is represented as a k-dimensional feature vector, and then the text is fed to the convolutional layer in the same configuration as the sentence CNN [22] in the form of a matrix to learn the public representation of the text, denoted as n_i, and the last layer generates a d-dimensional binary code to represent the hash code, denoted as b_i^T. In order to ensure that the image subnet and the text subnet learn a common representation, we force the weights of the last fully connected layer to be shared. Empirically speaking, this can make images and texts of the same category of two characters generate as similar representations as possible.

Finally, a linear classifier with a parameter matrix P is connected to two subnets to use label information to supervise the training of network parameters. Therefore, the cross-modal correlation can be well understood, and at the same time, the discriminative features can be distinguished.

3.3 Joint Semantic Matrix

We first introduce some definitions used in constructing the joint semantic matrix. We use l to represent the batch size. The specific description is as follows, we use $\mathcal{O} = O_1, O_2, ..., O_l$ to represent l instances of each batch. Each instance is represented by a pair of images and text like $O_k = [x_k^I, x_k^T]$. For the sample $O_k = [x_k^I, x_k^T]_{k=1}^l$ of the random training batch, we use $R_I \in \mathbb{R}^{l \times d}$ and $R_T \in \mathbb{R}^{l \times d}$ to represent the original data features of the image data and text data, respectively. In the same way, $B_I \in \{-1, +1\}^{l \times d}$ and $B_T \in \{-1, +1\}^{l \times d}$ respectively represent the binary code obtained from the image network and the text network, where d represents the length of the binary code.

Next, we carefully describe the construction method of the joint semantic matrix. Firstly, we normalize the original features R_I and R_T obtained by different modalities to obtain $\hat{R}_I$ and $\hat{R}_T$, and then calculate the respective cosine similarities to obtain the image modal similarity matrix $S_I = \hat{R}_I \hat{R}_I^T \in [-1, +1]^{l \times l}$ and text similarity matrix $S_T = \hat{R}_T \hat{R}_T^T \in [-1, +1]^{l \times l}$. We use the aforementioned cosine similarity matrix to represent the original domain relationship of different modal input data. Similarly, for the Hamming space, the similarity matrix between binary codes generated by the deep network can also be obtained by using the cosine similarity.

Compared with the previous hash method that retains the original domain structure, the joint semantic matrix does not simply retain the two affinity matrices in a separate manner, but makes full use of the complementary information of the two affinity matrices, and integrates the more accurate Field description. The joint semantic matrix is represented as $S = \psi(S_I, S_T) \in [-1, +1]^{l \times l}$, where S_I represents the image similarity matrix, S_T represents the text similarity matrix, and $\psi()$ represents the fusion relationship of the two matrices. We use $S_{ij} \in [-1, +1]$ to represent the latent semantic correlation between instances O_i and O_j. In order to better explain the combination function ψ, we first fuse S_I and S_T in the weighted summation method as follows,

$$\tilde{S} = \xi S_I + (1 - \xi)S_T, \xi \in [0, 1]. \tag{1}$$

Then, we use each row in the resulting $\tilde{S} \in [-1, +1]^{l \times l}$ matrix as a new feature of each instance, expressing the similarity relationship between this instance and other instances. We will then calculate $\tilde{S}\tilde{S}^T$ to obtain high-level domain descriptions between instances. This method is based on the principle that two semantically related instances should share similarity relationships with other instances. Therefore, the final representation is as follows,

$$
\begin{aligned}
S &= \psi(S_I, S_T) \\
&= \delta \frac{\tilde{S}\tilde{S}^T}{l} + (1 - \delta)\tilde{S} \\
&= (1 - \delta)[\xi S_I + (1 - \xi)S_T] + \frac{\delta}{l}[\xi^2 S_I S_I^T \\
&\quad + \xi(1 - \xi)S_I S_T^T + \xi(1 - \xi)S_T S_I^T + (1 - \xi)^2 S_T S_T^T].
\end{aligned}
\tag{2}
$$

Among them, δ is a trade-off parameter, used to adjust the importance of high-order neighborhood description.

Compared with the label information, the joint semantic information matrix in Eq. 2 can obtain more potential relevance information, and can also obtain more semantic information. More scientifically speaking, the joint semantic matrix used in the article also conforms to the diffusion theorem [23], which proves the usability of joint semantics from the side.

3.4   Objective Function

The purpose of this method is to learn the semantic relevance of different modal data, that is, in a common space, even if the data comes from different modalities, the samples from the same semantic category should be similar. Therefore, it is also necessary to use the joint semantic matrix as the training of the supervised network parameters. In order to learn the discriminative features of multimodal data, we propose to minimize the discriminative loss in the label space and the public representation space.

At the same time, we also minimize the distance between the representation of each image-text pair to reduce the difference between cross-modalities. Furthermore, we minimize the distance between the joint semantic matrix and the linear classifier to fully utilize the potential correlations obtained by the label information and the joint matrix. Below, we will introduce the DCSJM objective function in detail.

Table 1. Image model network configuration.

Layer	Configuration
conv1_1	$224 \times 224 \times 3$, relu
conv1_2	$224 \times 224 \times 64$, relu
pooling	2×2, maxpooling
conv2_1	$112 \times 112 \times 128$, relu
conv2_2	$112 \times 112 \times 128$, relu
pooling	2×2, maxpooling
conv3_1	$56 \times 56 \times 256$, relu
conv3_2	$56 \times 56 \times 256$, relu
conv3_3	$56 \times 56 \times 256$, relu
pooling	2×2, maxpooling
conv4_1	$28 \times 28 \times 512$, relu
conv4_2	$28 \times 28 \times 512$, relu
conv4_3	$28 \times 28 \times 512$, relu
pooling	2×2, maxpooling
conv4_1	$14 \times 14 \times 512$, relu
conv4_2	$14 \times 14 \times 512$, relu
conv4_3	$14 \times 14 \times 512$, relu
full6	4096, relu
full7	4096, relu
full8	Hash code length c

Table 2. Text model network configuation.

Layer	Configuration
full1	4096, relu
full2	4096, relu
full3	Hash code length c

First, we first minimize the discrimination loss of sample in the two modalities in the public representation space,

$$\Gamma_1 = \frac{1}{l^2} \sum_{i,j=1}^{l} \left(\log(1 + e^{\varrho_{ij}}) + A_{ij}^{IT} \varrho_{ij} \right)$$

$$+ \frac{1}{l^2} \sum_{i,j=1}^{l} \left(\log(1 + e^{\varpi_{ij}}) + A_{ij}^{II} \varpi_{ij} \right) \qquad (3)$$

$$+ \frac{1}{l^2} \sum_{i,j=1}^{l} \left(\log(1 + e^{\vartheta_{ij}}) + A_{ij}^{TT} \vartheta_{ij} \right),$$

where $\varrho_{ij} = \frac{1}{2}\cos(m_i, n_j)$, $\varpi_{ij} = \frac{1}{2}\cos(m_i, m_j)$, $\vartheta_{ij} = \frac{1}{2}\cos(n_i, n_j)$, $A_{ij}^{IT} = \mathbf{1}\{m_i, n_j\}$, $A_{ij}^{II} = \mathbf{1}\{m_i, m_j\}$, $A_{ij}^{TT} = \mathbf{1}\{n_i, n_j\}$, $\cos()$ is the cosine function used to calculate the similarity between two vectors, and $\mathbf{1}$ is an indicator function, whose value is 1 when two elements are in same class, otherwise 0. The negative log likelihood function used in the above Eq. 3 is defined as follows,

$$p(A_{ij}^{IT}|m_i, n_j) = \begin{cases} \upsilon(\varrho_{ij}), & if A_{ij}^{IT} = 1; \\ 1 - \upsilon(\varrho_{ij}), & otherwise. \end{cases} \qquad (4)$$

In order to eliminate cross-modal differences, we first minimize the distance between feature representations between image-text pairs learned by the network. More specifically, we express the modal invariance loss function of the feature representation space as follows,

$$\Gamma_2 = \frac{1}{l}\|M - N\|_F. \qquad (5)$$

Then we want to preserve the distinction of samples from different categories after projection. We use a linear classifier to predict the semantic labels of the projected samples in the public representation space. Therefore, we use the following objective function to measure the discrimination loss in the label space,

$$\Gamma_3 = \frac{1}{l}\|P^I M - T\|_F + \frac{1}{l}\|P^T N - T\|_F. \qquad (6)$$

Regarding the joint semantic matrix part, we calculated the joint semantic matrix S to explore the latent semantic relations of the input examples. Therefore, we can use the following objective function to minimize the error between the domain matrix S and the hash code Cosine similarity that needs to be learned to learn semantically related binary codes:

$$\begin{aligned} \Gamma_4 = &\, k_1 \|\gamma S - \cos(B_I, B_T)_F^2\|_F \\ &+ k_2 \|\gamma S - \cos(B_I, B_I)_F^2\|_F \\ &+ k_3 \|\gamma S - \cos(B_T, B_T)_F^2\|_F, \end{aligned} \qquad (7)$$

where γ is the hyper-parameter which makes our joint semantic matrix framework more flexible and S is joint semantic matrix.

According to Eqs. 3, 5, 6 and 7, we can get the objective function of our DCSJM as follows,

$$\Gamma = \Gamma_1 + j_1\Gamma_2 + j_2\Gamma_3 + j_3\Gamma_4, \qquad (8)$$

where j_1, j_2 and j_3 are hyper-parameters. The details of proposed DCSJM optimisation procedure are summarised in Algorithm 1.

Algorithm 1. The learning algorithm of DCSJM.

Require:

The training data set of different batches $O_k = [x_k^I, x_k^T]$ and their corresponding original feature R_I and R_T, the label matrix T, the hash code length l, the batch size b_s, the learning rate l_r, the number of epoches n_e, and the hyper parameters $J_1, J_2, J_3, k_1, k_2, k_3$.

Ensure:

The optimised parameters for Image and Text network Θ_I, Θ_T;

1: Randomly initialize the parameters Θ_I, Θ_T of the two subnets of pictures and text and the parameters of the linear classifier P;

2: **for** $i = 1, 2, ..., n_e$ **do**

3:     **for** $j = 1, 2, ..., b_s$;

4: Calculate the representations M_I and M_T for the samples in the batch by forward-propagation;

5: Calculate the normalized $\tilde{R}_I$ and $\tilde{R}_T$ and compute the cosine matrices $S_I = \tilde{R}_I \tilde{R}_I, S_T = \tilde{R}_T \tilde{R}_T$ to generate joint semantic matrix S with Eq. (2) ;

6: Calculate the result of loss function in Eq. (8);

7: Update the parameters of the linear classifier P by minimising Γ in Eq. (8);

8: Update the parameters of the Image and Text network by minimising Γ in Eq. (8) with descending their stochastic gradient;

9:     **end for**;

10: **end for** ;

---

4   Experiment

In order to verify the feasibility of our proposed method DCSJM, we conducted experiments on Pascal Sentence [19], a widely used benchmark data set.

4.1   Datasets and Features

Pascal Sentence: This data set, which is a subset of Pascal VOC, contains 1000 pairs of image and text description from 20 categories. In our experiments, we follow the data set division and feature correction strategies in [20, 21]. We use 19-layer VGGNet to learn the data representation, and use the 4096-dimensional features learned by the fc7 layer as the image representation vector. To represent text samples. We use sentence CNN [22] to learn a 300-dimensional representation vector for each text.

4.2   Baseline Methods and Evaluation Metrics

The comparison baseline methods we used are SCM_orth [26], SCM_seq [26], LSSH [29], CMFH [28], SMFH [32], LCMFH [33], LCSMFH [31].

SCM_orth [26]: The purpose of semantic correlation maximization hash (SCM) is to make the distance of the hash code equal to the similarity of the tag vector; SCM_orth indicates the use of orthogonal projection to learn the hash code.

SCM_seq [26]: The purpose of Semantic Relevance Maximization Hashing (SCM) is to make the distance of the hash code equal to the similarity of the tag vector; SCM_seq indicates the sequential learning method used to learn the hash code.

LSSH [29]: Latent semantic sparse hashing uses sparse coding and matrix factorization of images and texts to learn hash codes, respectively.

CMFH [28]: Collective Matrix Factorization hash method learns the hash code of a single modality through collective matrix factorization, and maps the data of different modalities to the same space for evaluation.

SMFH [32]: The supervised matrix factorization hash method increases the constraints of matrix factorization by modeling label consistency and local geometric similarity.

LCMFH [33]: This method uses the label consistent matrix decomposition hash to directly use the label information as a constraint on the data representation in the public space to complete the solution of the objective function.

LCSMFH [31]: This method improves the supervised information based on matrix factorization by keeping the similarity between the modalities and the modalities in the original space and making full use of the label information to obtain the objective function.

Among them, SCM algorithm is a more basic cross-modal hash retrieval method; LSSH and CMFH are unsupervised hash methods. This method is compared with LSSH and CMFH because they are based on matrix factorization and the results are superior at the time of publication. Finally, compare it with some of the most advanced supervised cross-modal hash retrieval methods SMFH, LCMFH and LCSMFH.

We use a commonly used retrieval evaluation index: mean Average Accuracy (mAP) to evaluate the retrieval performance of all methods. mAP is one of the most commonly used indicators to jointly evaluate search accuracy and ranking. Given a query and a list of L retrieval results, the average precision(AP) of query is defined as $AP = \frac{1}{n} \sum_{l=1}^{L} P(l)\xi(l)$, where l is the number of ground-truth similar instances of the query in the database, and $P(l)$ indicates the precision of top r retrieved instances. $\xi(l) = 1$ when the l-th retrieval instance is similar to the query, otherwise $\xi(l) = 0$. mAP is defined as the average of APs for all queries.

Table 3. Parameters at different bits.

Bits	J1	J2	J3	k_1	k_2	k_3
16 bits	0.001	0.1	0.001	0.8	0.1	0.1
32 bits	0.002	0.1	0.001	0.8	0.1	0.1
64 bits	0.002	0.1	0.002	0.9	0.1	0.1
128 bits	0.005	0.1	0.005	1.0	0.1	0.1

4.3   Implementation Details

The experimental result is to calculate the two parts of the cross-modal retrieval mAP separately. One part is to use text query data to retrieve picture data. As shown in Fig. 5, we use text keywords to retrieve related pictures in the database. The other part is to use picture data to retrieve text data.

We experimented many times and finally set the hyper-parameters as shown in Table 3, and obtained relatively superior results. As shown in the Table 3, in the 16-bits experiment, we set parameters to $J_1 = 0.0001$, $J_2 = 0.1$, $J_3 = 0.0001$, $k_1 = 0.8$, $k_2 = 0.1$ and $k_3 = 0.1$. In the 32-bits experiment, we set parameters to $J_1 = 0.002$, $J_2 = 0.1$, $J_3 = 0.001$, $k_1 = 0.8$, $k_2 = 0.1$ and $k_3 = 0.1$. In the 64-bits experiment, we set parameters to $J_1 = 0.002$, $J_2 = 0.1$, $J_3 = 0.002$, $k_1 = 0.9$, $k_2 = 0.1$ and $k_3 = 0.1$. In the 128-bits experiment, we set parameters to $J_1 = 0.005$, $J_2 = 0.1$, $J_3 = 0.005$, $k_1 = 1.0$, $k_2 = 0.1$ and $k_3 = 0.1$. The reason why these hyper-parameters are set in this way is because we have found that such parameters account for the best effect in the experiment. The hyper-parameters in other loss functions are adjusted in the experiment according to the actual situation.

Table 4 shows the mAP value of the method we proposed more on the Pascal Sentence dataset and the other 7 baseline methods. We can see from Table 4. The experimental results of using images to query text are better than other baseline methods at all search lengths. However, the search results with longer query length in the text query method are not superior to LCSMFH [31], but they are not much different. In summary, the method we propose is desirable to a certain extent.

4.4   Results

Figure 3 and Fig. 4 shows the comparison of the proposed method and the other 7 baseline methods using mAP diagrams with multiple texts in pictures. Figure 3 shows the mAP results of the image search text. The results show that the method proposed in the article is better than the retrieval results of the baseline task at each search length. Taking 16-bits as an example, the proposed method has 2% higher accuracy than the best baseline method. Figure 4 shows the mAP result of the text search picture part. The 16-bit length of the method proposed in this paper is superior to other baseline tasks. Although the search results of other lengths are not very superior, it is also worth learning.

Table 4. Results on the Pascal sentence dataset.

Task	Method	16 bits	32 bits	64 bits	128 bits
Image To Text	SCM_seq	0.2536	0.2570	0.2522	0.2490
	SCM_orth	0.1469	0.1380	0.1352	0.1456
	LSSH	0.3677	0.3779	0.3914	0.4064
	CMFH	0.4872	0.5298	0.5556	0.5665
	SMFH	0.5761	0.6005	0.6147	0.6251
	LCMFH	0.5802	0.6583	0.6708	0.6814
	LCSMFH	0.5786	0.6552	0.6902	0.7089
	DCSJM	**0.6032**	**0.6563**	**0.7016**	**0.7124**
Text To Image	SCM_seq	0.2984	0.2985	0.2861	0.2895
	SCM_orth	0.1749	0.1719	0.1659	0.1637
	LSSH	0.3598	0.3824	0.3926	0.4053
	CMFH	0.4462	0.4840	0.5110	0.5249
	SMFH	0.6187	0.6590	0.6635	0.6827
	LMFH	0.6443	0.69344	0.6981	0.6973
	LCSMFH	0.6557	**0.7322**	**0.7525**	**0.7608**
	DCSJM	**0.6723**	0.7032	0.7117	0.7324

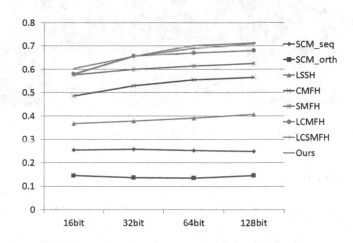

Fig. 3. The comparison result of image to text.

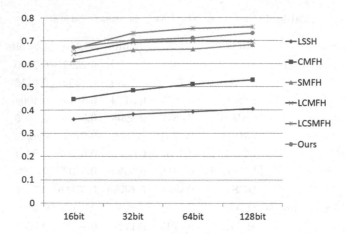

Fig. 4. The comparison result of text to image.

Fig. 5. The example of Text search Image.

5   Conclusion

This paper proposes a novel and effective cross-modal hashing retrieval method called DCSJM. This method uses supervised labeling and unsupervised joint semantic proof as the supervised information. Tags can effectively train network parameters so that different modalities can achieve the same standard evaluation operation in the same Hamming space. The joint semantic matrix can obtain the potential high-level semantic relevance of the feature space. Therefore, our model not only uses the semantic information of the label, but also uses the latent semantic information that exists in the feature space. The experimental results show that the proposed model performs better than other baseline methods.

Acknowledgment. This work is supported by the Natural Science Foundation of Shandong Province Grant No. ZR2020QF041; the 69th batch of China Postdoctoral

Science Foundation Grant No. 862105020017; the Postdoctoral Applied Research Program of Qingdao Grant No. 862005040007; the Fundamental Research Funds for the Central Universities under Grant 842113037.

References

1. Zhen, L., Hu, P., Wang, X., Peng, D.: Deep supervised cross-modal retrieval. In: 2019 IEEE/CVF Conference on Computer Vision and Pattern Recognition (CVPR) (2020)
2. Su, S., Zhong, Z., Zhang, C.: Deep joint-semantics reconstructing hashing for large-scale unsupervised cross-modal retrieval. In: 2019 IEEE/CVF International Conference on Computer Vision (ICCV) (2019)
3. Ji, Z., Yao, W., Wei, W., Song, H., Pi, H.: Deep multi-level semantic hashing for cross-modal retrieval. IEEE Access 7, 23667–23674 (2019)
4. Yang, E., Deng, C., Liu, W., Liu, X., Tao, D., Gao, X.: Pairwise relationship guided deep hashing for cross-modal retrieval (2017). https://aaai.org/ocs/index.php/AAAI/AAAI17/paper/view/14326
5. Jiang, Q.Y., Li, W.J.: Deep cross-modal hashing, pp. 3270–3278 (2017)
6. Kumar, S., Udupa, R.: Learning hash functions for cross-view similarity search. In: International Joint Conference on Artificial Intelligence (2011)
7. Song, J., Yang, Y., Yang, Y., Huang, Z., Shen, H.T.: Inter-media hashing for large-scale retrieval from heterogeneous data sources, p. 785 (2013)
8. Bronstein, M.M., Bronstein, A.M., Michel, F., Paragios, N.: Data fusion through cross-modality metric learning using similarity-sensitive hashing. In: Computer Vision and Pattern Recognition (2010)
9. Lin, Z., Ding, G., Hu, M., Wang, J.: Semantics-preserving hashing for cross-view retrieval (2015)
10. Cheng, J., Leng, C., Li, P., Wang, M., Lu, H.: Semi-supervised multi-graph hashing for scalable similarity search. Comput. Vis. Image Underst. 124, 12–21 (2014)
11. Li, C., Deng, C., Li, N., Liu, W., Gao, X., Tao, D.: Self-supervised adversarial hashing networks for cross-modal retrieval (2018)
12. Yao, T., Zhang, Z., Yan, L., Yue, J., Tian, Q.: Discrete robust supervised hashing for cross-modal retrieval. IEEE Access 7, 39806–39814 (2019)
13. Hu, D., Nie, F., Li, X.: Deep binary reconstruction for cross-modal hashing. IEEE Trans. Multimedia 21(4), 973–985 (2018)
14. Zhang, X., et al.: HashGAN: attention-aware deep adversarial hashing for cross modal retrieval (2017)
15. Chen, Z., Zhong, F., Min, G., Leng, Y., Ying, Y.: Supervised intra- and inter-modality similarity preserving hashing for cross-modal retrieval. IEEE Access 6, 27796–27808 (2018)
16. Gu, W., Gu, X., Gu, J., Li, B., Wang, W.: Adversary guided asymmetric hashing for cross-modal retrieval (2019)
17. Cao, W., Lin, Q., He, Z., He, Z.: Hybrid representation learning for cross-modal retrieval. Neurocomputing 345, 45–57 (2019)
18. Ding, K., Fan, B., Huo, C., Xiang, S., Pan, C.: Cross-modal hashing via rank-order preserving. IEEE Trans. Multimedia 19(3), 571–585 (2017)
19. Rashtchian, C., Young, P., Hodosh, M., Hockenmaier, J.: Collecting image annotations using amazon's mechanical turk, pp. 139–147 (2010)
20. Peng, Y., Qi, J., Yuan, Y.: CM-GANs: cross-modal generative adversarial networks for common representation learning (2018)

21. Qi, J., Peng, Y.: Cross-modal bidirectional translation via reinforcement learning. In: Twenty-Seventh International Joint Conference on Artificial Intelligence IJCAI-18 (2018)
22. Kim, Y.: Convolutional neural networks for sentence classification. Eprint Arxiv (2014)
23. Donoser, M., Bischof, H.: Diffusion processes for retrieval revisited. In: CVPR (2013)
24. Zhu, X., Huang, Z., Shen, H.T., Zhao, X.: Linear cross-modal hashing for efficient multimedia search. In: Proceedings of the 21st ACM International Conference on Multimedia, Series MM 2013, pp. 143–152. Association for Computing Machinery, New York, NY, USA (2013). https://doi.org/10.1145/2502081.2502107
25. Zhen, Y., Yeung, D.-Y.: Co-regularized hashing for multimodal data. In: Pereira, F., Burges, C.J.C., Bottou, L., Weinberger, K.Q. (eds.) Advances in Neural Information Processing Systems, vol. 25. Curran Associates Inc. (2012). https://proceedings.neurips.cc/paper/2012/file/5c04925674920eb58467fb52ce4ef728-Paper.pdf
26. Zhang, D., Li, W.-J.: Large-scale supervised multimodal hashing with semantic correlation maximization (2014). https://www.aaai.org/ocs/index.php/AAAI/AAAI14/paper/view/8382
27. Wang, D., Gao, X., Wang, X., He, L.: Semantic topic multimodal hashing for cross-media retrieval (2015). https://aaai.org/ocs/index.php/IJCAI/IJCAI15/paper/view/10682
28. Ding, G., Guo, Y., Zhou, J.: Collective matrix factorization hashing for multimodal data. In: IEEE Conference on Computer Vision and Pattern Recognition, pp. 2083–2090 (2014)
29. Zhou, J., Ding, G., Guo, Y.: Latent semantic sparse hashing for cross-modal similarity search. ACM (2014)
30. Wang, J., Li, G., Pan, P., Zhao, X.: Semi-supervised semantic factorization hashing for fast cross-modal retrieval. Multimedia Tools Appl. **76**(19), 20197–20215 (2017). https://doi.org/10.1007/s11042-017-4567-3
31. Xue, F., Wang, W., Zhou, W., Zeng, T., Yang, T.: Cross-modal retrieval via label category supervised matrix factorization hashing. Pattern Recogn. Lett. **138**(2), 469–475 (2020)
32. Tang, J., Wang, K., Shao, L.: Supervised matrix factorization hashing for cross-modal retrieval. IEEE Trans. Image Process. **25**(7), 3157–3166 (2016)
33. Wang, D., Gao, X.-B., Wang, X., He, L.: Label consistent matrix factorization hashing for large-scale cross-modal similarity search. IEEE Trans. Pattern Anal. Mach. Intell. **41**(10), 2466–2479 (2018)

Short Papers

Accurate Polar Harmonic Transform-Based Watermarking Using Blind Statistical Detector

Yu Sang[1(✉)], Yilin Bei[2], Zhiyang Yang[1], and Chen Zhao[1]

[1] School of Electronic and Information Engineering,
Liaoning Technical University, Huludao 125105, China
sangyu2008bj@sina.com
[2] School of Information Science and Technology, Taishan University,
Taian 271000, China

Abstract. Digital image watermarking is an effective image copyright protection technology, which embeds the copyright information into the image to be protected, therefore achieving the purpose of image copyright protection. The recently proposed Polar harmonic transforms (PHTs) have provided a set of powerful tools for image representation. However, the accuracy of PHTs suffers from various errors, such as the geometric and numerical integration errors. In this paper, we propose an accurate computational framework of PHTs based on wavelet integration approach and present a novel accurate PHT-based multiplicative watermarking algorithm. We embed watermark data into selected blocks of the host image by modifying the PHT magnitudes due to strong robustness against various attacks. At the receiver, the distribution of watermarked noisy PHT magnitudes is analytically calculated; closed form expressions are obtained for extracting the watermark bits. Compared with other decoders, the proposed decoder has better performance in terms of watermark robustness. In addition, the proposed watermarking algorithm can effectively resist geometrical attacks and common image processing attacks.

Keywords: Digital image watermarking · Polar harmonic transform (PHT) · Numerical stability · Blind statistical detector

1 Introduction

Easy access to the Internet has enabled easy distribution and sharing of digital media. However, such easy access also makes illegal distribution of digital media easier and poses challenges to intellectual property protection of digital content. Digital image watermarking technology includes 2 main steps: watermark embedding and watermark detection. Watermark detection is used to judge whether there is a watermark in an image, and it can be accomplished by 1 of 2 methods: a correlation-based detection method or a statistical-based detection method. The Correlation-based detection method is a linear correlation between the extracted watermark and the original watermark signal to ascertain whether the watermark is in the data [1, 2]. Signal detection theory finds that the correlation-based detection method is optimal when the watermark carrier is subject to Gaussian distribution. However, research shows that

© Springer Nature Switzerland AG 2021
M. Yang et al. (Eds.): NSS 2021, LNCS 13041, pp. 277–288, 2021.
https://doi.org/10.1007/978-3-030-92708-0_17

both the spatial domain and the transform domain do not obey a Gaussian distribution, so correlation-based detection is not the optimal detection. The statistical-based detection method can be used to solve this problem [3].

A good image watermarking method should have some important traits such as imperceptibility and robustness. In addition, blind watermarking methods are preferred because they can extract the embedded watermarks from the watermarked signal without using the host image. The above 2 constraints, robustness and imperceptibility, are very important for a watermarking scheme but the major problem for researchers is the non-orthogonality of these constraints [4, 5]. Typically, the trade-off between robustness and imperceptibility can be achieved by taking into account the properties of the human visual system during the embedding process [6]. Generally, watermark embedding approaches can be categorized as either the additive embedding methods [7–9].

Although various image multiplicative watermarking algorithms based on optimum detectors have been developed, their purpose is to detect whether there is hidden information in the host image, and they cannot extract watermark information. In their study, Akhaee et al. [10] proposed a semi-blind scaling-based image watermarking algorithm in wavelet domain using an ML decoder with an optimum strength factor. On that basis, they designed an improved multiplicative image watermarking system in Contourlet transform domain with GG distribution in a subsequent study [11], in which watermark is embedded into the directional sub-band with the highest energy. Hamghalam et al. [12] proposed an image watermarking scheme using an optimum detector, in which geometric tools are used to achieve the trade-off between the watermark robustness and imperceptibility. An ML decoder is used to detect the watermark.

As known, watermarking algorithms can be categorized into two classes: spatial domain algorithms [13, 14] and transform domain algorithms [12, 15–17]. Although spatial domain algorithms are easy to apply, transform domain algorithms provide better performance in terms of imperceptibility and robustness. Typical transforms include DFT [15], DCT [16], DWT [17], Contourlet transform [12]. Because image transform coefficients have poor robustness against image attacks, especially geometric attacks, image moments are introduced into image processing. As highly condensed image features, image moments can be used to represent images, and have a strong ability to resist noise and geometric attacks. Therefore, various image moments have been widely exploited in image watermarking in recent years, including Zernike moments (ZMs) [18], Exponent moments (EMs) [19], and polar harmonic transforms (PHTs) [20, 21]. Due to its good image description ability, the PHT has been widely used in image processing. However, the accuracy of the PHT suffers from various errors, such as the geometric error and numerical integration error, in which the high-order moments are vulnerable to numerical instability [22]. In this paper, an accurate calculation method of PHTs based on wavelet integration is presented, which not only removes the geometric and numerical integration errors, but also provides high orders of numerical stability to the PHT.

By using the accurate PHT as a watermark carrier, this paper proposes a blind multiplicative watermarking algorithm. In watermark embedding, the original image is divided into non-overlapping blocks, and the accurate PHTs of the highest entropy blocks are computed. Then the watermark is embedded into the PHT magnitudes using multiplicative embedding. In watermark detection, the algorithm uses the ML decision rule based on the BKF distribution. Experimental results show BKF-based decoder has the best performance in terms of watermark robustness. It is also demonstrated that the proposed watermarking algorithm can resist geometric and common image processing attacks effectively.

The rest of the paper is structured as follows. Sections 2 introduce the accurate computational framework of the PHT. The proposed watermarking algorithm is described in Sect. 3. In Sect. 4, the performance of the proposed watermarking algorithm is provided. Section 5 concludes the paper.

2 Polar Harmonic Moments

2.1 Definition of Polar Harmonic Moments

PHTs consist of 3 transforms [22], namely polar complex exponential transform (PCET), polar cosine transform (PCT) and polar sine transform (PST). The PHT of order m and repetition n with $m > 0$ and $|n| \geq 0$ for a continuous function $f(r, \theta)$ over a unit disk is defined as

$$M_{m,n} = \frac{1}{\pi} \int_0^{2\pi} \int_0^1 [H_{mn}(r, \theta)]^* f(r, \theta) r dr d\theta. \tag{1}$$

The operator $[\bullet]^*$ refers to the complex conjugate. The function $H_{mn}(r, \theta)$ is the radial basis function (RBF):

$$H_{m,n}(r, \theta) = R_m(r)e^{-in\theta} = e^{-i2\pi mr^2}e^{-in\theta}. \tag{2}$$

These basis functions satisfy the orthogonality condition:

$$\int_0^{2\pi} \int_0^1 H_{m,n}(r, \theta) [H_{m',n'}(r, \theta)]^* r dr d\theta = \pi \delta_{mm'} \delta_{nn'}, \tag{3}$$

where the symbol $\delta_{mm'}$ refers to the Kronecker function and $\hat{i} = \sqrt{-1}$.

2.2 Accurate Computation of PHTs

It is important to note that the zeroth-order approximation of double integration leads to the numerical integration error. The magnitude of the numerical integration error is not known. However, it is expected to be high for high orders of m. When m is high, the rate of change of function in the intervals $r \in [0, 1]$ will be proportionally high, which is shown in Fig. 1. This demonstrates the variation of $R_m(r)$ for various values of m. Another important characteristic of the radial kernel function is its singular behavior at

$m = 0$. This trend will result in the numerical instability of high-order moments; hence, the reconstruction performance of the image center is very poor.

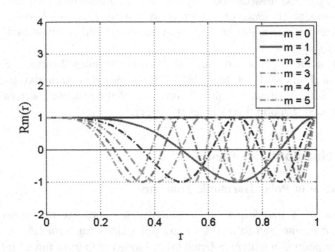

Fig. 1. RBF $R_m(r)$ of RHT with $m = 0, 1, \ldots, 5$.

In this section, we provide a computational framework for the calculation of PHTs, which reduces geometric error and numerical integration errors. In the proposed method, we use the wavelet integration method [23] to compute the basis function of PHTs.

If $f(x)$ is a 1-D function, then its wavelet numerical integration in the interval $[a, b]$ is given by:

$$\int_a^b f(x)dx \cong \frac{(b-a)}{2W} \sum_t^{2W} f\left(a + \frac{(b-a)(t-0.5)}{2W}\right), \quad (4)$$

where $W = 2^j$ and $j = 1, 2, \ldots, J$. The integer j indicates the level of the wavelet, and the maximum level of resolution is the integer J. In the proposed method, we use $j = 2$, $j = 3$ for computational efficiency.

The 2-D formulation of the numerical integration of $f(x, y)$ is expressed as:

$$\int_a^b \int_c^d f(x, y)dxdy \cong \frac{(b-a)(d-c)}{4W^2}$$
$$\times \sum_{t=1}^{2W} \sum_{h=1}^{2W} f\left(a + \frac{(b-a)(t-0.5)}{2W}, c + \frac{(d-c)(h-0.5)}{2W}\right). \quad (5)$$

We now accurately compute the PCET by resorting to wavelet numerical integration of the double integration.

$$M_{m,n} = \frac{1}{\pi W^2 N^2} \sum_{i=0}^{N-1} \sum_{k=0}^{N-1} f(x_i, y_k) \sum_{t=0}^{2W} \sum_{h=0}^{2W} H^*_{mn}\left(\frac{2iW-NW+t-0.5}{WN}, \frac{2kW-NW+h-0.5}{WN}\right),$$ (6)

$$\left(\frac{2iW-NW+t-0.5}{WN}\right)^2 + \left(\frac{2iW-NW+h-0.5}{WN}\right)^2 \leq 1.$$

Image reconstruction capability is one of the major characteristics of orthogonal moments. The improvements in the accuracy of PHTs can be observed though the quality of the reconstructed images.

3 Proposed Algorithm

3.1 Watermark Embedding

Let $I = \{f(m, n), 0 \leq m < M, 0 \leq n < N\}$ be the original host image. The binary watermark $W = \{w_i, 0 \leq i < L\}$ is generated using a pseudo-random sequence generator with a secret key as its initial value. The watermark embedding procedure is described as follows.

Step 1: The original image I is divided into $N_{block}(N_{block} \geq L)$ non-overlapping blocks and their entropy are computed. Entropy is used because the human eye is less sensitive to high-entropy blocks [11], which will improve the imperceptibility of the watermark.

Step 2: The PHTs of the L highest entropy blocks are computed, and any 1 moment $M_{m,n}$ from accurate moment set S is selected as the accurate moment for 1 block. Hence, accurate moments for L can be obtained, and the magnitudes $x_i(i = 1, 2, \cdots L)$ arc used to embed the watermark W.

It is known that multiplicative watermarks are image content dependent and thus provide more robustness and greater imperceptibility than additive ones. Hence, multiplicative embedding is used in this paper with:

$$x'_i = \begin{cases} x_i \cdot f_1(x_i), w_i = 1 \\ x_i \cdot f_0(x_i), w_i = 0 \end{cases},$$ (7)

where x'_i is the watermarked PHT magnitude.

As a nonlinear increasing function, the exponential function gives us a large change in larger magnitudes and small changes in smaller magnitudes [11]. Watermark strength functions $f_1(x)$ and $f_0(x)$ are chosen to be monotonous exponential functions. To achieve the best performance, we define them as follows

$$f_1(x) = a_1 e^{a_2|x|} + a_3,$$ (8)

$$f_0(x) = b_1 e^{b_2|x|} + b_3,$$ (9)

where $f_1(x)$ is the exponentially ascending function for $x > 0$ which is larger than 1, and $f_0(x)$ is the exponentially descending function for $x > 0$ which is smaller than 1. These functions are chosen exponentially in order that larger NSST coefficients change more than smaller ones during the watermarking process, because the larger NSST coefficients are related to the strong edges in the supposed directional sub-band. In this paper, we choose $a_1 = -0.5$, $b_1 = 0.15$, $a_2 = b_2 = -0.05$, $a_3 = 2.2$, and $b_3 = 0.6$.

It should be noted that the PHTs are conjugated with repetition $m = 0$, or, in other words, $M^*_{m,n} = M_{m,-n}$. To ensure the watermarked image can be reconstructed accurately, the PHT $M_{m,-n}$ should be modified when the watermark is embedded into the PHT $M_{m,n}$.

Step 3: Where $f_r(m, n)$ is the reconstructed image block using the originally selected PHT and $f_{r'}(m, n)$ is the reconstructed image block using the watermarked PHT, the watermarked image block $f_w(m, n)$ can be obtained as follows:

$$f_w(m, n) = f_o(m, n) - f_r(m, n) + f_{r'}(m, n), \tag{10}$$

where $f_o(m, n)$ is the original image block.

Next, the watermarked image I^* can be obtained by combining the L watermarked image blocks and $N_{block} - L$ original image blocks.

3.2   Watermark Detection

Watermark detection can be considered the detection of a known signal in a noisy environment, where the PHT magnitudes represent the noisy environment and the watermark is the signal to be detected. To detect the watermark in the PHT magnitudes of watermarked image $I^* = \{f(m, n), 0 \leq m < M, 0 \leq n < N\}$, a blind statistical watermark detector using the ML decision rule based on the Weibull distribution is developed.

The watermarked image I^* is divided into $N_{block}(N_{block} \geq L)$ non-overlapping blocks and the entropies of these blocks are computed. The PHT of the highest entropy blocks for L are computed, and the same moment $M_{m,n}$ in watermark embedding from accurate moment set S is selected as the accurate moment. Hence, accurate moments for L can be obtained and their magnitudes $y_i (i = 1, 2, \ldots, L)$ are used to detect the watermark $W^* = \{w_i^*, 0 \leq i < L\}$.

A basic assumption is that the statistical distribution of the PHT magnitudes is not altered after embedding the watermark. The watermark bits are assumed to be equally probable and the PHT magnitudes are assumed to be independent and identically distributed by the BKF distribution. To detect the hidden watermark in the PHT magnitudes, we develop a blind statistical watermark detector using the ML decision rule based on the BKF distribution. At the receiver, we receive the PHT magnitudes attacked by noise or other kinds of attacks. We assume that the attacked noise is zero mean AWGN with the distribution of $N(0, \sigma_n^2)$. Thus, the received PHT magnitudes are $y = x' + n$. Since the PHT magnitudes are considered to be independent of the noise term, we have $P(y) = P(x') * P(n)$, where $*$ denotes the convolution operator. Thus, considering the BKF distribution of PHT magnitudes x, we have:

$$P(y) = \int_{-\infty}^{\infty} \frac{\left(\frac{c}{2}\right)^{-\frac{p}{2}-\frac{1}{4}} \left|\frac{g(z)}{2}\right|^{p-\frac{1}{2}} K_{p-\frac{1}{2}}\left(\sqrt{\frac{2}{c}}|g(z)|\right)}{\sqrt{\pi}\Gamma(p)(g(z)f'(g(z))+f(g(z)))} \cdot \frac{1}{\sqrt{2\pi\sigma_n^2}} e^{-\frac{(y-z)^2}{2\sigma_n^2}} dz, \qquad (11)$$

where $g(x)$ is the inverse function of the $x' = xf(x)$ in the practical range of x; that is, $g(x') = x$.

To find a closed-form answer for $P(y)$, we estimate the Gaussian PDF using the three-sigma rule [11], as follows:

$$\Lambda_G(x) = \begin{cases} \frac{-x+3\sigma_n}{9\sigma_n^2}, & 0 < x \le 3\sigma_n \\ 0, & |x| > 3\sigma_n \\ \frac{x-3\sigma_n}{9\sigma_n^2}, & -3\sigma_n \le x < 0 \end{cases} \qquad (12)$$

Then, substituting the above function in Eq. (12), and using the Simpsons integration approximation rule [6], we have:

$$P(y) = \frac{3\sigma_n}{2} \cdot \left[\frac{H\left(y+\frac{3\sigma_n}{2}\right)\Lambda_G\left(-\frac{3\sigma_n}{2}\right) + H\left(y+3\sigma_n\right)\Lambda_G(-3\sigma_n)}{2} + \frac{H(y)\Lambda_G(0) + H\left(y+\frac{3\sigma_n}{2}\right)\Lambda_G\left(-\frac{3\sigma_n}{2}\right)}{2} \right.$$
$$\left. + \frac{H(y)\Lambda_G(0) + H\left(y-\frac{3\sigma_n}{2}\right)\Lambda_G\left(\frac{3\sigma_n}{2}\right)}{2} + \frac{H\left(y-\frac{3\sigma_n}{2}\right)\Lambda_G\left(\frac{3\sigma_n}{2}\right) + H\left(y-3\sigma_n\right)\Lambda_G(3\sigma_n)}{2} \right].$$
$$\qquad (13)$$

where

$$H(y) = \frac{\left(\frac{c}{2}\right)^{-\frac{p}{2}-\frac{1}{4}} \left|\frac{g(y)}{2}\right|^{p-\frac{1}{2}} K_{p-\frac{1}{2}}\left(\sqrt{\frac{2}{c}}|g(y)|\right)}{\sqrt{\pi}\Gamma(p)(g(y)f'(g(y))+f(g(y)))}. \qquad (14)$$

After some manipulations, Eq. (13) can be converted to:

$$P(y) \approx \frac{1}{2} \left[\frac{H\left(y-\frac{3\sigma_n}{2}\right)}{2} + H(y) + \frac{H\left(y+\frac{3\sigma_n}{2}\right)}{2} \right]. \qquad (15)$$

By considering that the received PHT magnitudes $y_i(i = 1, 2, \cdots, m)$ is an iid (independent identical distribution) distribution [11], we have

$$P(y_1, y_2, ..., y_L|1) = \prod_{i=1}^{L} \frac{H_1\left(y_i - \frac{3\sigma_n}{2}\right) + 2H_1(y_i) + H_1\left(y_i + \frac{3\sigma_n}{2}\right)}{4} \qquad (16)$$

$$P(y_1, y_2, ..., y_L|0) = \prod_{i=1}^{m} \frac{H_0\left(y_i - \frac{3\sigma_n}{2}\right) + 2H_0(y_i) + H_0\left(y_i + \frac{3\sigma_n}{2}\right)}{4} \qquad (17)$$

where $H_1(y)$ and $H_0(y)$ are computed using Eq. (14) by the strength functions $f_1(x)$ and $f_0(x)$, respectively.

Finally, we can obtain the optimal watermark detector by using ML decision

$$w_i^* = \frac{H_1\left(y_i - \frac{3\sigma_n}{2}\right) + 2H_1(y_i) + H_1\left(y_i + \frac{3\sigma_n}{2}\right)}{H_0\left(y_i - \frac{3\sigma_n}{2}\right) + 2H_0(y_i) + H_0\left(y_i + \frac{3\sigma_n}{2}\right)} \begin{array}{c} 1 \\ > \\ < \\ 0 \end{array} T_i \tag{18}$$

where

$$T_i = \sum_{i=1}^{L} \ln \frac{g_1(y_i)f_1'(g_1(y_i)) + f_1(g_1(y_i))}{g_0(y_i)f_0'(g_0(y_i)) + f_0(g_0(y_i))} \tag{19}$$

where y_i represents the watermarked PHT magnitudes. As we can see, the best decision depends on the noise standard deviation σ_n. In this paper, we use the famous Monte-Carlo method to estimate the parameter. After constructing the ML detector, the scale parameter c and shape parameter p should be estimated from the watermarked PHT magnitudes. We use the moment-based statistical parameter estimation method in [24], which is as follows

$$\hat{p} = \frac{3(n-2)(n-3)m_2^2}{(n-1)\left[(n+1)m_4 - 3(n-1)m_2^2\right]}$$

$$\hat{c} = \frac{nm_2}{(n-1)\hat{p}} \tag{20}$$

where n indicates the number of samples used in the estimate, m_2 and m_4 are the second and fourth-order sample central moments, respectively.

4   Experimental Results

In our experiments, 20 grayscale images with 512×512 pixels are used as the original images. The number of non-overlapping blocks is set to $N_{block} = 64 \times 64$, hence, the size of block is 8×8 pixels. Moment M_{22} is used as the accurate moment. The watermark information is a binary pseudorandom sequence. The parameters of watermark embedding strength function are $a_1 = -0.5$, $b_1 = 0.15$, $a_2 = b_2 = -0.05$, $a_3 = 2.2$, and $b_3 = 0.6$. The performance of the proposed algorithm is measured in terms of watermark imperceptibility and watermark robustness.

4.1   Watermark Imperceptibility

Figure 2 is the result of applying different watermarking approach for data embedding in the test images. Figure 2 (a)–(c) show the watermarked image Lena, Barbara, and Couple using different approach. Figure 2 (d)–(f) are the absolute difference between

Fig. 2. The watermark embedding examples by using different watermarking schemes: (a) The watermarked image (using method [11]). (b) The watermarked image (using scheme [12]), (c) The watermarked image (using the proposed method), (d) The absolute difference between original image and watermarked image (using method [11]), (e) The absolute difference between original image and watermarked image (using method [12]), (f) The absolute difference between original image and watermarked image (using the proposed method).

origin image and watermarked images for different approach respectively, multiplied by 20 for display. Table 1 gives the PSNR of different watermarking schemes. From the Fig. 2 and Table 1, we know that the proposed scheme is better than methods [11, 12] in terms of the transparency.

Table 1. The PSNRs for various watermarking methods (dB)

	Lena	Barbara	Mandrill	Peppers
The method [11]	40.01	36.71	40.10	42.37
The method [12]	41.65	38.02	41.46	42.56
Proposed method	44.32	41.85	44.57	46.37

4.2   Watermark Robustness

Watermark robustness is evaluated by the bit error rate (BER) of the detected watermark. The performance of the proposed BKF-based decoder is compared with the Weibull, Cauchy, and GG-based decoders. To obtain accuracy, the results are obtained by averaging over 100 runs with 100 watermark sequences. Table 2 gives the detected BERs between the BKF-based decoder and Weibull, Cauchy, and GG-based decoders for Barbara, Lena, and Couple. The watermark length is 512 bits. It can be seen from Table 2 that the BKF-based decoder provides a lower BER than the Weibull, Cauchy, and GG-based decoders. Similar results are also obtained for the other test images.

Table 2. Comparison of the detected BERs between BKF-based decoder and Weibull, Cauchy, and GG-based decoders.

Attack	Barbara				Lena			
	BKF	Cauchy	Weibull	GG	BKF	Cauchy	Weibull	GG
Non-attack	0.59	1.56	4.49	8.59	0.41	1.86	7.03	9.57
AWGN 15	0.97	3.51	5.27	11.60	0.95	1.92	8.48	11.44
JPEG compression 10	5.27	10.55	21.48	36.37	6.66	18.41	23.34	38.30
Salt & Pepper noise 0.05	2.92	4.55	12.36	18.16	2.60	5.33	14.90	23.38
Median filtering 3 × 3	2.53	4.77	16.21	23.71	2.87	5.67	20.18	25.68
Gaussian filtering 3 × 3	0.78	2.34	8.07	11.48	0.61	1.86	9.79	12.87
Scaling 256 × 256	4.88	12.75	19.55	25.37	3.36	14.33	22.23	27.64
Rotation 90°	0.59	1.56	4.49	8.59	0.41	1.86	7.03	9.57
Vertical flipping	0.59	1.56	4.49	8.59	0.41	1.86	7.03	9.57

For the obtained results, one can conclude the following. The number of non-overlapping blocks is known in this paper, to be 64×64. For scaling attacks, assuming that the size of an image after scaling attack is $N_s \times N_s$, the size of the image block is $\frac{N_s}{64} \times \frac{N_s}{64}$. When $\frac{N_s}{64} = k, k \in Z$, the algorithm can extract the watermark information accurately, which is due to the scaling invariance of PHT magnitudes. When $\frac{N_i}{64}$ is not an integer, we will change the size of the image to $64k \times 64k, k \in Z$. Therefore, the proposed algorithm can resist image scaling. Because the number of non-overlapping blocks is known in this paper, the algorithm is still a blind detection.

For image flipping and rotation, when an image is flipped or rotated by 90°, the image blocks undergoes the same transform. The content of the transformed image blocks is the same as the original ones; hence, their entropies are unchanged. The PHT magnitudes are invariant to image flipping and rotation. Therefore, the proposed algorithm can resist image flipping and image rotation by 90°.

For other attacks, such as AWGN, JPEG compression attacks, salt and pepper noise, and image filtering, the proposed algorithm has excellent performance.

5 Conclusion

In this paper, a new blind multiplicative watermarking algorithm based on PHT and BKF distribution has been proposed. The proposed watermark decoder using the ML decision rule has been developed based on the BKF PDF. Experimental results have shown that the performance of the proposed BKF-based decoder is superior to that of Weibull, Cauchy, and GG-based decoders in terms of watermark robustness. It has also been shown that the proposed watermarking algorithm can resist geometric attacks effectively.

Acknowledgement. This work was supported in part by the National Science Foundation of China (NSFC) under Grant No. 61602226; in part by the PhD Startup Foundation of Liaoning Technical University of China under Grant No. 18-1021; in part by Science and Technology Development Plan Project of Taian City under Grant No. 2019GX027.

References

1. Bao, P., Ma, X.H.: Image adaptive watermarking using wavelet domain singular value decomposition. IEEE Trans. Circuits Syst. Video Technol. **15**(1), 96–102 (2005)
2. Liu, X.L., Han, G.N.: Fractional Krawtchouk transform with an application to image watermarking. IEEE Trans. Signal Process. **65**(7), 1894–1908 (2017)
3. Dong, L., Yan, Q., Lv, Y., Deng, S.: Full band watermarking in DCT domain with Weibull model. Multimedia Tools Appl. **76**(2), 1983–2000 (2016). https://doi.org/10.1007/s11042-015-3115-2
4. Qin, C., Chang, C.C.: A novel joint data-hiding and compression scheme based on SMVQ and image inpainting. IEEE Trans. Image Process. **23**(3), 969–978 (2014)
5. Qin, C., Zhang, X.Z.: Effective reversible data hiding in encrypted image with privacy protection for image content. J. Vis. Commun. Image Represent. **31**(C), 154–164 (2015)
6. Makbol, N.M., Khoo, B.E., Rassem, T.H.: Block-based discrete wavelet transform-singular value decomposition image watermarking scheme using human visual system characteristics. IET Image Process. **10**(1), 34–52 (2016)

7. Rahman, S.M.M., Ahmad, M.O., Swamy, M.N.S.: A new statistical detector for DWT-based additive image watermarking using the Gauss-Hermite expansion. IEEE Trans. Image Process. **18**(8), 1782–1796 (2009)

8. Cheng, Q., Huang, T.S.: An additive approach to transform-domain information hiding and optimum detection structure. IEEE Trans. Multimedia **3**(3), 273–284 (2001)

9. Briassouli, A., Tsakalides, P., Stouraitis, A.: Hidden messages in heavy-tails: DCT-domain watermark detection using alpha-stable models. IEEE Trans. Multimedia **7**(4), 700–715 (2005)

10. Akhaee, M.A., Sahraeian, S.M.E.: Robust scaling-based image watermarking using maximum-likelihood decoder with optimum strength factor. IEEE Trans. Multimedia **11** (5), 822–833 (2009)

11. Akhaee, M.A., Sahraeian, S.M.E., Marvasti, F.: Contourlet-based image watermarking using optimum detector in a noisy environment. IEEE Trans. Image Process. **19**(4), 967–980 (2010)

12. Hamghalam, M., Mirzakuchaki, S., Akhaee, M.A.: Geometric modelling of the wavelet coefficients for image watermarking using optimum detector. IET Image Process. **8**(3), 162–172 (2014)

13. Coatrieux, G., Pan, W., Cuppens-Boulahia, N.: Reversible watermarking based on invariant image classification and dynamic histogram shifting. IEEE Trans. Inf. Forensic Secur. **8**(1), 111–120 (2013)

14. Zong, T.R., Xiang, Y., Natgunanathan, I.: Robust histogram shape-based method for image watermarking. IEEE Trans. Circuits Syst. Video Technol. **25**(5), 717–729 (2015)

15. Barni, M., Bartolini, F., De Rosa, A.: Optimum decoding and detection of multiplicative watermarks. IEEE Trans. Signal Process. **51**(4), 1118–1123 (2003)

16. Briassouli, A., Strintzis, M.G.: Locally optimum nonlinearities for DCT watermark detection. IEEE Trans. Image Process. **13**(12), 1604–1617 (2004)

17. Wang, J.W., Liu, G.J.: Locally optimum detection for Barni's multiplicative watermarking in DWT domain. Signal Process. **88**(1), 117–130 (2008)

18. Kim, H.S., Lee, H.K.: Invariant image watermark using Zernike moments. IEEE Trans. Circuits Syst. Video Technol. **13**(8), 766–775 (2003)

19. Wang, X.Y., Shi, Q.L., Wang, S.M.: A blind robust digital watermarking using invariant exponent moments. AEU-Int. J. Electron. Commun. **70**(4), 416–426 (2016)

20. Li, L.D., Li, S.S., Abraham, A., Pan, J.S.: Geometrically invariant image watermarking using Polar Harmonic Transforms. Inf. Sci. **199**(16), 1–19 (2012)

21. Qi, M., Li, B.Z., Sun, H.F.: Image watermarking using polar harmonic transform with parameters in SL (2, R). Signal Process. Image Commun. **31**, 161–173 (2015)

22. Singh, C., Upneja, R.: Accuracy and numerical stability of high-order polar harmonic transforms. IET Image process. **6**(6), 617–626 (2012)

23. Aziz, I., Haq, F.: A comparative study of numerical integration based on Haar wavelets and hybrid functions. Comput. Math. with Appl. **59**(6), 2026–2036 (2010)

24. Bian, Y., Liang, S.: Image watermark detection in the wavelet domain using Bessel K densities. IET Image Process. **7**(4), 281–289 (2013)

Cloud Key Management Based on Verifiable Secret Sharing

Mustapha Hedabou[✉]

School of Computer Science, UM6P-CS University Mohammed VI Polytechnic,
Benguerir, Morocco
Mustapha.hedabou@um6p.ma

Abstract. Managing encryption keys in cloud computing is a very challenging task, especially where the model is shared and entirely controlled by the cloud providers. Hardware Security Module (HSM) solutions turned out to be an efficient approach for delivering cloud key management services. Unfortunately, the HSM approach has shown some shortcomings related to key migration when it comes to widespread cloud deployment. Recent systems based on homomorphic encryption and multiparty computation suffer from security issues or heavy overhead costs inherent to underlying cryptographic techniques. In this paper, we introduce a new software cloud key management system based on a dedicated (t, n) verifiable secret sharing protocol that tolerates up to t byzantine adversaries. The proposed design meets the requirements of BYOK (Bring Your Own Keys) model and multi-clouds deployment that are gaining more attraction among the biggest cloud industry players. Taking advantage of our verifiable secret sharing protocol, that reduces by a factor t the opening phase of the VSS protocols known in the literature, the proposed design offers promising performances. We also provide a formal model of our construction and proof of security. Finally, we implement a prototype of our design and give some experimental results about its performance along with some optimizations that make it efficient enough to be deployed in real-world applications.

Keywords: Cloud computing · Key Management System · Verifiable Secret Sharing · Commitment scheme

1 Introduction

Key management encompasses operations like key generation, storage, archiving, distribution, and destruction at the end of every life-cycle [3, 9, 13]. Due to their sensitivity, encryption keys must be handled with care. They must be generated in a random way, stored in a safe place, and exchanged via secure protocols [6, 7]. Typically, this is done by the use of hardware facilities. For some users, smart cards or Trusted Platform Module (TPM) can be applied, whereas Hardware Security Module (HSM) fits more to the needs of companies and government agencies.

© Springer Nature Switzerland AG 2021
M. Yang et al. (Eds.): NSS 2021, LNCS 13041, pp. 289–303, 2021.
https://doi.org/10.1007/978-3-030-92708-0_18

To alleviate cloud users from directly managing keys, which is their main goal when embracing cloud services, cloud providers offer HSM as a service. With AWS CloudHSM, Amazon provides HSM appliances in data centers to be used as a service to users [2]. Undoubtedly, the physical HSM limitations related to lack of elasticity and operability have been addressed by HSM as-a-service. Yet, there is a need for software infrastructure, owned and procured by cloud services providers to operate HSM as-a-service. In a nutshell, HSM as-a-service has brought some desired security and easy management properties, but since the HSM technology was not originally developed for the cloud settings, it still posses some limitations, especially from the cloud user's perspective.

Another approach for delivering cloud key management services can be provided by software-based systems, where the on-premise system is running in the cloud provider platform. The key management vendor provides either a server or a docker container for hosting the software. The configuration and deployment of the key management system are left to cloud users. Software-based key management may fit the need of users who do not leverage HMSs services. This approach is only appropriate for IaaS as users should be able to perform the full installation and configuration on their server in order to run the key management system. Offering the same functions as HSMs, tighten implementation of Software-based key management can provide nearly the same security level for a significantly lower cost. The downside is its non-compliance with FIPS-certified hardware, the incoming charge of handling fail-over and replication to cloud users.

Recently an effective attempt for achieving software cloud key management based on the use of homomorphic encryption has also gained wide recognition [19]. It is dedicated expressly to cloud services and was designed in such a way to meet the five characteristics of the cloud computing paradigm including elasticity, on-demand self-service, and availability. The solution is already integrated with Amazon Web Services (AWS) and RedHat, but it can work with any cloud platform. The security of this approach can only be proved in the semi-honest model with weaker adversaries. Therefore, the Porticor solution provider must be trusted to implement the protocol as specified. Also, the cloud provider's platform executing the implementation needs to have a neutral behavior.

This paper introduces a new software-based cloud key management fully controlled by cloud clients that can be proved secure in strong adversarial models. The design, based on a new (t, n) verifiable secret sharing mechanism (VSS), splits up the master key among n servers hosted on cloud providers platforms that communicate on asynchronous private and authenticated channels. The security model can be realized in the presence of passive or active adversaries. In the passive model, the corrupted servers are supposed to behave in the expected way whereas in the active model the dishonest servers can not follow the prescribed protocol. Thanks to the (t, n) verifiable secret sharing security, the confidentiality and the integrity of exported keys are still guaranteed as long as no more than t servers are compromised.

Our design assumes that secure enclaves are leveraged to conduct sensitive computation in the cloud computing side in such a way to prevent cloud providers from observing the computation taking place in their platforms. The design is fully synchronized with the key management system on-premise to ensure an easy integration within clients applications. Taking advantage of the (t, n) verifiable secret sharing protocol designed specifically for that purpose combined with some optimization on the threshold t of faulty servers the performance of the proposed design turned out to be enough efficient to be implemented in real-world applications.

Our Contributions. The main contribution of this paper is an efficient yet secure software-based cloud key management system based on a new (t, n) verifiable secret sharing protocol developed for that specific purpose. The design distributes the keys storage in cloud computing providers side so that no key will be located in one location under any circumstances. The challenge that consists of achieving the security regarding the confidentiality and the integrity of exported keys in the presence of passive and active adversaries was addressed through the combination of keys refreshing and (t, n) verifiable secret sharing techniques.

The other major contribution of this paper is the improvement of conventional (t, n) verifiable secret sharing schemes performances that suffer from heavy costs related to the amount of broadcast messages and number of shares verification. For this purpose, we develop a new (t, n) verifiable secret sharing scheme based on commitment that brings broadcast required by conventional schemes to $\mathcal{O}(1)$ instead of $\mathcal{O}(n)$. The scheme divides the number required verifications by a factor t, where t is the tolerated Byzantine adversaries. These enhancements are the result of a generalization of Kate's et al. [17] work in such a way to commit multiple evaluations to a single element of fixed size, allowing the verification of t shares in only one go.

Our last contribution is a formal model of our design with a security and efficiency study. A discussion on optimal choices for t and n along with a prototype of implementation showing that the proposed cloud key management system is practical enough to be used in real-world applications are also given.

Outline. This paper is organized as follows: Sect. 2 introduces the model of our design with some assumptions whereas Sect. 3 covers an overview of Kate et al.'s polynomial commitment scheme. A generalization of this scheme is introduced in Sect. 4 and in Sect. 5, we introduce our verifiable secret sharing scheme based on the generalized commitment. The final section is devoted to our cloud key management system along with security and efficiency studies.

Related Work. For many cloud end users, HSM-based cloud key management systems are not affordable because they come with an expensive cost and do not scale well into a multi-cloud architecture. In another line of work, there have been attempts to implement a secure cloud key management by leveraging advanced cryptographic techniques of Homomorphic encryption and multi-party computation. The Porticor Homomorphic Key Management (HKM) [19] is mainly built on top of an existing partially homomorphic encryption algorithm to split up cloud user's master keys into two parts. One part is under the full control of the cloud user whereas the other is under control of the Porticor Virtual Appliance, which resides in the cloud provider platform. Taken advantage of homomorphic encryption, the master key is processed in encrypted form and is never exposed in plain text. However, if the HKM's provider and the cloud provider hosting the appliance collude, it may be possible for an attacker to learn sensitive information including the master key.

More recently, two cloud key management systems based on multi-party computation have also been proposed [1], namely Unbound vHSM by Unbound Tech company and Sepior KMaaS by Danish Sepior ApS company. Sensitive information including keys is stored and handled in a shared way. The keys can not be stored or reconstructed on a single server under any circumstances. The computations are conducted by using MPC capabilities. Despite their security, MPC computations including light-weight MPC protocols that assume less powerful adversaries are still far from being efficient for real-world applications. Furthermore, as for the Porticor solution, the lack of detailed technical information about the system and the span of its adoption undermines the final cloud user's confidence in their security and efficiency.

To overcome this limitation related to existing models for delivering cloud key management services, we propose a new software-based cloud key management system. Our design built on top of a new verifiable secret sharing protocol is intended to provide secure, distributed storage of keys on the cloud providers sides. It aims to extend the security of the existing work on cryptographic storage systems such as windows EFS, Tahoe-LAFS and NCryptfs [10,23,24] that achieve end-to-end security on untrusted storage servers. Unlike cryptographic storage systems, where end users are required to securely manage their keys, our design addresses the settings where servers are expected to operate autonomously in the cloud providers platforms. Verifiable secret sharing is leveraged to achieve availability and confidentiality of keys in presence of a corrupted majority of servers that can not be provided by secret sharing alone.

2   Model and Assumptions

Our main goal is to design a software-based cloud secure key management system as an ad-on facility to an existing on-premise key management system. The design must be secure under strong models and enough efficient to meet the requirements of real-world deployments. For this purpose, our design must meet two specific requirements, namely security, in particular regarding the confidentiality and integrity of exported keys and easy integration with the already available applications. The design must enforce the key-and-lock-separation principle, called BYOK, which stipulates that encryption keys and encrypted data should be stored in separate locations. In other words, for cloud computing settings the encryption keys should not stored in the cloud provider platform that hosts the encrypted data.

Assuming that an on-premise software key management system following the best practices is already available. Keys are exported, stored, and handled on the cloud providers sides securely. While they are in transit, conventional and well-established techniques, including SSL, SSH, and DH key exchange are leveraged to achieve security. On the cloud providers side, keys are stored in a distributed way through n servers $S_1, S_2, \cdots, S_n$. Later, keys are reconstructed and their integrity is verified by using verifiable secret sharing. All sensitive operations involving keys in cloud computing sides are supposed to be performed in a secure enclave in such a way to benefit from the secure computation facilities.

More formally, the proposed design conducts the cryptographic tasks following the above essential operations:

Key Generation. Key s is generated in clients side using the KMS on-premise.

Client-side Encryption. Files in cleartext are encrypted before to be upload to cloud computing side under the key s generated by the KMS on-premise.

Key Exportation. Key shares $s[i]$ obeying to a (n, t) verifiable secret sharing model $((n, t)$-VSS) are computed by the KMS on-premise and are sent to the servers trough secure channels.

Key Storage. Each server S_i splits-up its share following the (n, t) verifiable secret sharing model and sends the new shares $s[i, j]$ to servers S_j where $j \neq i$.

Cloud-side Decryption. The individual key shares $s[i]$ are reconstructed by each server S_i and exported to others servers. The key recovery process following the (n, t)-VSS is launched by each server to recover the key s. The ciphertext is decrypted by the reconstructed key s.

The proposed protocol can be modeled as follows:

- Secure computation. The n servers $S_1, S_2, \cdots, S_n$ are involved in secure computation online phases taking place on the cloud providers side. Hardware enclaves can be leveraged for this purpose.

- Online and Offline phases. The protocol goes through periods where servers are active and sometimes idle. In the active periods, the servers are requested to send back their shares and additional information (witnesses) to a dealer who conducts the secure computation for reconstructing and checking the validity of recovered keys. These periods, called on online phases, alternate with other where the servers are inactive. The latter is called Offline periods. The Online and Offline phases must be synchronized in order to switch between active and idle status.

As for on-premise settings, the proposed key management system is implemented as a stand-alone application. The servers in the cloud computing sides are fully autonomous, that is they can switch between Offline and Online phases without any interactions with the outside cloud instances. The servers can only communicate with each other to conduct the whole process. In other words, the only players involved are the servers themselves. This model comes with a limited level of confidentiality and availability that can be provided. This level is tightly related to the number of servers required for restoring the secret key without revealing any information about it.

The confidentiality threshold can be defined as the minimum number of servers an adversary can break into to learn the secret key, whereas the availability threshold is defined as the minimal number of the uncorrupted server that should be available for restoring the key. In the fully autonomous scenario, the number of malicious servers must be at most t for ensuring confidentiality and availability of the protocol. This limitation is mainly due to the requirement that servers are not allowed to communicate with any instance from outside the cloud. The requirement about the number of malicious servers can be relaxed by allowing limited interaction with an on-premise key management system.

We make standard assumptions about the well-established cryptographic techniques regarding the ability of an adversary to undermine their security. The techniques used for establishing secure and private channels or for authenticating parties, including SSL, SSH, DH key exchange are assumed secure in standard models.

3   Preliminaries

Like conventional schemes [11,12,15,18], polynomial commitment is a very attractive area of research motivated by its application in verifiable secret sharing. A fundamental result in reducing the size of a commitment to a constant was proposed by Kate et al., [17]. Their main contribution is to commit to polynomial $p(x) \in Z_x[x]$ over the bilinear group in such a way to provide a single element commitment with a constant size. An element called the witness is created to allow efficient opening of the commitment to any correct value $p(i)$ giving a verifier the ability to confirm $p(i)$ as the evaluation of the polynomial $p(x)$ at i. The idea behind the construction lies in an algebraic property of polynomials, that is $(x - i)$ is a divisor of $p(x) - p(i)$ for any $i \in Z_p$.

The hiding and binding properties are based on well-studied assumptions such as the discrete logarithm (DL) problem and the Strong Diffie-Hellman assumption [5]. Let $\epsilon(k)$ be a negligible function.

Definition 1. *Discrete Logarithm (DL) assumption. Given a generator g of multiplicative group G and $a \in_R Z_p^*$, for an adversary A_{DL}, $Pr[A_{DL}(g, g^a) = a] = \epsilon(k)$*

Definition 2. *t-Strong Diffie-Hellman (t-SDH) assumption. Let $\alpha \in Z_p^*$. Given as input $(t + 1)-tuples < g, g^\alpha, \cdots, g^{\alpha^t} > \in G^{t+1}$, for an adversary A_{t-SDH}, the probability $Pr[A_{t-SDH}(< g, g^\alpha, \cdots, g^{\alpha^t}) = < c, g^{\frac{1}{\alpha+c}} >] \leq \epsilon(k)$ for $c \in Z_p \backslash \{-\alpha\}$.*

According to the formal definition, their polynomial commitment scheme can be described as follows:

Setup(1^k; t). Let G and G_T be two groups of prime order p and let g be a random generator of G. We assume that p, providing k-bit security, is chosen in such a way that there exists a symmetric bilinear $e : G \times G \to G_T$ for which the t-SDH assumption is verified. Let $\alpha \in_R Z_p^*$ a secret parameter. The Setup algorithm outputs public parameters $PK = (g, G, G_T)$ and $(t+1)-$tuples $(g, g^\alpha, \cdots, g^{\alpha^t})$. Note that the parameter α stands for a secret key that is generated by a trusted authority and is not requested for the rest of the construction.

Commit$(PK, \mathbf{p(x)})$. For a polynomial $p(x) = \sum_{j=0}^{deg(p)} p_j x^j \in Z_p[x]$ computes the commitment $C = g^{p(\alpha)}$ and outputs $C = \prod_{j=0}^{deg(p)} (g^{\alpha^j})^{p_i}$ as a commitment to $p(x)$.

Open$(PK, C, p(x))$. Outputs the polynomial $p(x)$ for which the commitment C was created.

VerifyPoly$(PK, C, p(x))$. Outputs 1 if $C \overset{?}{=} \prod_{j=0}^{deg(p)} (g^{\alpha^j})^{p_i}$ and 0 otherwise. This works only when $deg(p) \leq t$.

CreateWitness$(PK, p(x), i)$. Outputs $< i, p(i), w_i >$ where $w_i = g^{\psi_i(\alpha)}$ and $\psi_i(x) = \frac{p(x)-p(i)}{x-i}$. Note that w_i is computed with the same manner as for C.

VerifyEval$(PK, i, p(i), w_i)$. Checks whether or not $p(i)$ is obtained as an evaluation of i by the polynomial committed to C. It outputs 1 if $e(C, g) \overset{?}{=} e(w_i, g^\alpha/g^i)e(g, g)^{p(i)}$ and 0 otherwise.
  Unlike the conventional commitment schemes that require $t+1$ commitments of the form g_i^p where $j = 0, \cdots, t$ for a polynomial $p(x) = \sum_{i=0}^{i=t} p_i x^i$, Kate et al., scheme provides only one commitment, namely $g^{p(\alpha)}$. In addition to evaluation $p(i)$ of $p(x)$ at index i, their scheme broadcasts a witness w_i which leads to a reduction of broadcasts to $\mathcal{O}(1)$ instead of $\mathcal{O}(n)$.

4   Generalized Commitment to a Polynomial

Proving an evaluation of a polynomial at a value with only one group element of constant size as a commitment is a powerful result. Now, we introduce an improvement allowing the evaluation of a polynomial in any number of values while still using a single group element as a commitment. It turned out that this improvement fits the requirement of (t, n)-secret sharing schemes where we need to check the validity of at least $t+1$ shares before starting to recover the shared secret. The security of the proposed commitment scheme is based on t-BSDH assumption [16].

Definition 3. *t-strong Diffie-Hellman (t-BSDH) assumption. Let $\alpha \in Z_p^*$. Given as input a $(t+1)-$tuples $< g, g^\alpha, \cdots, g^{\alpha^t} > \in G^{t+1}$, for an adversary A_{t-BSDH} the probability $Pr[A_{t-BSDH}(< g, g^\alpha, \cdots, g^{\alpha^t}) = < c, e(g, g)^{\frac{1}{\alpha+c}} >] \leq \epsilon(k)$ for $c \in Z_p\backslash\{-\alpha\}$.*

Let $A \in \mathbb{N}$ a set with size k, where $k > 1$ and let $\{y_j\}_{i\in A}$ be a list of k polynomial evaluations of group elements $\{z_j\}_{i\in A}$, i.e. $y_j = p(z_j)$ for $j \in A$. Let $I(x)$ be the polynomial that goes through all the points $\{(z_i, y_i)\}_{j \in A}$ obtained by Lagrange interpolation shown in Eq. 1.

$$I(x) = \sum_{i \in A} y_i \prod_{j \in A, j \neq i} \frac{x - z_j}{z_i - z_j} \tag{1}$$

Obviously, the polynomial $I(x)$ has the same roots as any k degree polynomial $p(x)$ that goes through the points (z_i, y_i) for $i \in A$. As for Kate's et al. scheme, our construction is based on the following algebraic property: $\prod_{j \in A}(x - z_i)$ divides perfectly $p(x) - I(x)$. Thus we can define only one function ψ for creating a single witness for all evaluations of $p(x)$ at group of elements $z_0, \cdots, z_k$, as shown by Eq. 2.

$$\psi(x) = \frac{p(x) - I(x)}{\prod_{j \in A}(x - z_j)} \tag{2}$$

If we set the witness $w_A = g^{\psi(\alpha)}$, and $q(x) = \prod_{j \in A}(x - z_i)$ the validity check of a polynomial $p(x)$ evaluation at a group of values $\{z_j\}_{i \in A}$ is done by Eq. 3.

$$e(w_A, g^{q(\alpha)})e(g^{I(\alpha)}, g) \stackrel{?}{=} e(C, g) \tag{3}$$

The construction of a generalized commitment scheme is slightly different from Kate et al. The sub-protocols **Setup()**, **Commit( )**, **Open( )** and **Verify-Poly()** are the same, only **CreateWitness()** and **VerifyEval()** are different. Let A be a finite set of integers.

GenCreateWitness$(PK, p(x), A)$ outputs $\{< i, p(i), w_A >\}_{i \in A}$ where $w_A = g^{\psi(\alpha)}$ and $\psi(x) = \frac{p(x) - I(x)}{\prod_{j \in A}(x - z_j)}$. The witness w_A is computed in the same manner as for C.

GenVerifyEval$(PK, A, \{< i, p(i), w_A >\}_{i \in A})$ check whether or not the set $\{p(i)\}_{i \in A}$ is obtained as evaluations of $\{i \in A\}$ by the polynomial committed to C. It outputs 1 if

$$e(w, g^{q(\alpha)})e(g^{I(\alpha)}, g) \stackrel{?}{=} e(C, g)$$

and 0 otherwise.

The correctness of **VerifyEval()** is straightforward as shown below:

$$e(w_A, g^{q(\alpha)})e(g^{I(\alpha)}, g) = e(g, g)^{\frac{p(\alpha) - I(\alpha)}{q(\alpha)}} e(g, g)^{q(\alpha)} e(g, g)^{I(\alpha)}$$

$$= e(g, g)^{p(\alpha)} = e(C, g)$$

Theorem 1. *Given the assumptions above, the proposed construction is a secure polynomial commitment scheme under the the DL and t-BSDH assumptions.*

Proof. Let's suppose that an adversary provides a commitment C and two valid openings $< w_A, A >$ and $< w'_A, A >$ for a set $A \in \{1, \cdots, n\}$ such as $w_A \neq w'_A$. This means that there exist at least one index $i \in A$ such $p(i) \neq I(i)$. If we set w_i as the witness of $p(i)$, created by using Kate's et al. scheme, we get the following equation:

$$e(w, g^{q(\alpha)})e(g^{I(\alpha)}, g) = e(C, g) = e(w_i, g^\alpha/g^i)e(g, g)^{p(i)}.$$

Let $I'(x) = \frac{I(x) - I(i)}{x - i}$ and $p'(x) = \frac{p(x)}{x - i}$, by taking the logarithm of the both side of the equation we have:

$$\frac{1}{\alpha - i} = \frac{p'(\alpha)\phi(\alpha) - \psi_i(\alpha) + I'(\alpha)}{p(i) - I(i)},$$

Therefore the adversary solves the t-BSDH problem as follows

$$e(g, g)^{\frac{1}{\alpha - i}} = e(g^{p'(\alpha)}, w_A) e(g^{I'(\alpha)} / w_A, g)^{\frac{1}{p(i) - I(i)}}$$

5 Verifiable Secret Sharing Based on Commitment

Secret sharing has many applications, multiparty computation is by far the most relevant one [4,8,9,20,22]. We focus in this paper on Shamir-based secret sharing scheme [20]. We assume that a dealer wants to share a secret s amongst n parties so that no fewer than $t+1$ parties can recover the secret, whereas it can easily be recovered by any $t+1$ or more parties. This is referred to as (t, n) secret sharing. Shamir-based secret sharing scheme is built upon polynomials over finite field F, with $|F| > n$. For the sake of correctness and simplicity, we suppose that $F = F_p$ with $p > n$.

Shamir's early idea of distributing shares of a secret as evaluations of a polynomial has become a standard building block in threshold cryptography. The scheme is based on polynomial interpolation. Given $t + 1$ couples (x_i, y_i), with distinct x_i s, there is one and only one polynomial $p(x)$ of degree t such that $p(x_i) = y_i$ for all i. This basic statement can be proved by using Lagrange interpolation. Without loss of generality, we can assume that the secret s is a number. To divide it into pieces $[s]_i$, we pick a random $t + 1$ degree polynomial $p(x) = p_0 + p_l x + \cdots + p_t x^t$ in which $p(0) = s$, and evaluate $[s]_1 = p(1), \cdots [s]_i = p(i) \cdots, [s]_n = p(n)$.

Given any subset of $t + 1$ of these $[s]_i$ values together with their identifying indices, we can find the coefficients L_i of $p(x)$ by interpolation, and then evaluating Eq. 4 below

$$s = p(0) = \sum_{i=1}^{i=t+1} L_i[s]_i, \text{ where } L_i - \prod_{j \neq i} (\frac{x_j}{x_j - x_i}) \tag{4}$$

The basic secret sharing scheme will have flaws if some participants are dishonest [14]. For withstanding malicious participants, a new type of secret sharing scheme was proposed by Fieldman [14], called the verifiable secret sharing (VSS) scheme. The coefficients of this polynomial are hidden in the exponent of the generator of a group in which the discrete-log assumption holds, before been published. This allows that the participants can validate correctness only for their shares received from the dealer in the distribution phase. In [21], Stadler introduced the Publicly Verifiable Secret Sharing (PVSS) scheme that allows that anyone can verify the validity of shares without revealing any secret information.

In Fig. 1, we present our secure (t, n) verifiable secret sharing scheme based on the generalized polynomial commitment protocol that satisfies the secrecy and correctness properties. Let t be the number of tolerated byzantine adversaries and $\{A_j\}_{j \in J} \subset \{0, \cdots, n\}$ the subsets of size $t + 1$. We write $[s]_i$ to denote a share of a secret s and S_i to denote a server involved in the protocol.

Protocol Set UP $VSSSet_{up}(t, 1^k)$
The dealer runs Setup() algorithm of Kate's commitment scheme and generates public parameters PK
Protocol Share: $VSS\text{-}Share(s, 1^k)$
To share a secret s, the dealer samples random number $a_1, \cdots, a_n \in Z_p^*$
Sets $a_0 = s$ and $p(x) = \sum_{i=0}^{i=t} a_i x^i$
Computes $[s]_i = p(i)$ for $i = 1, \cdots, n$
Protocol Commit: $VSS\text{-}Commit(PK, p(x), \{A_j\}_{j \in J})$
For each group of shares $\{[s]_i\}_{i \in A_j}$, the dealer runs $GenCreateWitness()$
then broadcasts $C_i = <i, [s]_i, w_{A_j}>$ to each server S_i where $i \in A_j$.
Protocol VerifyCommit $VSS\text{-}VerifyCommit(PK, \{C_i\}_{i \in \{1, \cdots, n\}}, \{A_j\}_{j \in J})$
For each group witness w_{A_j}, a random server S_i, where $i \in A_j$, runs GenVerifyEval()
If GenVerifyEval() outputs 1 then accepts share $[s]_i$, otherwise broadcasts a failure warning message
If more than t failure messages are broadcast, abort the protocol
Protocol Recover $VSS\text{-}Recover(PK, \{C_i\}_{i \in \{1, \cdots, n\}}, \{A_j\}_{j \in J})$
At any $t + 1$ response of accepted group shares $\{<i, p(i), w_{A_j}>\}_{i \in A_j}$
Each server samples a group share $\{<i, p(i), w_{A_j}>\}_{i \in A_j}$ and runs $GenVerifyEval()$.
If the group share is valid then interpolate the pairs $\{<i, p(i)>\}_{i \in A_j}$ and reconstruct the secret s
Otherwise, send a failure message and sample another group of shares
If there are $t + 1$ failure messages abort the protocol.

Fig. 1. VSS based on generalized polynomial commitment

We should notice that the number of set $A_j \subset \{1, \cdots, n\}$ where $|A_j| = t + 1$ is $C_n^{t+1} >> n$. This requires to significantly create more witnesses and run more function evaluations than with the original commitment scheme of Kate et al. An optimal way to take advantage of the improvements brought by our generalized commitment scheme is to exploit the fact that all subsets $\{A_j\} \subset \{0, \cdots, n\}$ of size $t + 1$ are not needed to conducted the protocol VSS-Recover. Only $t + 1$ subsets $\{A_i\}_{j \in J}$ of disjoint sets of size $t + 1$ (i.e. $|J| = t + 1$), such that $\cup \{A_i\}_{j \in J} = \{1, \cdots, n\}$ are sufficient to reconstruct the secret or to conclude that there is more then t byzantine adversaries. Indeed, if all $t + 1$ groups of shares are invalid this means that there is at leat one corrupted share in each group and consequently there is more $t + 1$ corrupted servers. On the other hand, if only one group of shares is valid this implies that all its $t + 1$ shares are valid allowing to recover the secret s. The simplest way to achieve this purpose is to choose $A_i = \{it, it + 1, \cdots, (i + 1)(t + 1)\}$ for $i = 0, \cdots, \lfloor \frac{n}{t} \rfloor$. One set may have size less than $t + 1$, it can be completed by element redundancy.

6   Cloud Key Management Design

Our protocol for managing keys in cloud computing consists of two main components, namely the key management system on-premise and n servers

$S_1, S_2, \cdots, S_n$ located on cloud providers sides. For sake of simplicity, we designate a server S_i as the main appliance acting as the dealer, but in real settings, any server that first gets the KMS request can act as a dealer. The servers are assumed to benefit from secure computation environments available on the cloud providers side.

As mentioned before, our protocol $cloud_{KMS}$ assumes that a key management system is already active on the cloud user on-premise. The latter is responsible for generating the keys that will be used on the cloud computing side following the model BYOK. For the sake of simplicity, we assume that we are dealing with a single key, namely the master key s. The protocol $cloud_{KMS}$ can be conducted in three sub-protocols. A **Setup** Setup protocol generating the public parameters and additional information that will be used for creating the commitments. A **Share** protocol that computes shares, the corresponding commitments and that broadcasts them to the servers. Finally, a **SecretReconstruction** protocol checking the validity of the received shares and reconstructing the master key. This design is not secure against offline attacks since an attacker breaking into less than $t + 1$ idle servers can combine the information collected from several attempts for getting access to more than $t + 1$ shares and hence to recover the secret key. To prevent this kind of attack, the shares must be refreshed each time the servers go from the online to the offline phase. For this purpose, two more protocols, namely **ReShare** and **ReShareReconstruction** , are integrated to $cloud_{KMS}$ design.

We now introduce the formal model of our protocol $cloud_{KMS}$ that consists of five sub-protocols.

Setup(1^k): this protocol is executed by the KMS on premise. It takes a security parameter k and outputs the same public parameters $PK = (g, G, G_T)$ and $(t + 1)$−tuples $(g, g^\alpha, \cdots, g^{\alpha^t})$ of the generalized commitment scheme.

Share(PK, s): executed by the key management system, it takes the public parameters PK and the secret key s. The protocol samples $t + 1$ disjoint sets $\{A_j\}_{j=1,\cdots,t+1}$, where $|A_j| = t + 1$ and $\cup A_j = \{1, \cdots, n\}$ and executes the sub-protocols **VSS − Share(s, 1^k)**,

and **VSS − Commit(PK, p(x), A_j)** for $j = 1, \cdots, t+1$. For each set A_j, the sub-protocol broadcasts share $\{< i, [s]_i, w_{A_j} >\}$ to each server S_i where $i \in A_j$.

ReShare([s]_i, 1^k): executed by each server S_i, the protocol runs the sub-protocol **Share(PK, [s]_i)** and broadcast shares $[s]_{i,j}$ for $j = 0, \cdots, n$ where $j \neq i$ to all n servers.

ReShareReconstruction(i, $\{[s]_{i,j}\}_{j=1,\cdots,n,j\neq i}$): executed by each server S_i, the protocol interpolate the $t + 1$ samples $(i, [s]_{i,j})$ and computes $[s]_i$. The sub protocol broadcasts the reconstructed shares $[s]_i$ to all servers S_j where $j \neq i$.

SerectReconstruction(PK, $\{< i, [s]_i, w_{A_j} >\}_{j=1,\cdots,t+1,i\in A_j}$: executed by each server S_i, it takes as inputs public parameters, shares $[s]_i$ and witnesses w_{A_j}. The protocol runs

VSS − Recover() and outputs the shared secret s or aborts the protocol.

Security Study. The security of the protocol $cloud_{KMS}$ relies on its capacity to guarantee the confidentiality and integrity of the master key on the cloud computing providers side. Another security aspect of our protocol is its resistance to attacks against binding and hiding properties, that is the capacity of an attack on commitment scheme to drive any information about $p(j)$ for any $j \notin A$ from the knowledge of $< PK, A, \{p(i)\}_{i \in A} >$ or to provide a witness $< Pk, p(i), i >$ such that $VerifyPoly(PK, A, p(i), i) = 1$ from the knowledge of a valid witness $\{< j, p(j), w_A >\}_{j \in A}$. This latter security property of the protocol $cloud_{KMS}$ is inherited from the generalized commitment scheme. The following theorem proves that protocol $cloud_{KMS}$ provides confidentiality and integrity of the shares and hence of the master key

Theorem 2. *Given the assumptions above, the confidentiality and integrity of a share stored and retrieved by each server S_i using the $cloud_{KMS}$ protocol is guaranteed as long as not more than t servers are corrupted.*

Proof. In addition to assumptions introduced in Sect. 4, we assume that servers S_i have access to a secure source of randomness and deletion. By secure deletion, we mean that the data erased on the online phase by a server can not be recovered by an adversary on the offline phase. Considering the underlying assumptions, an adversary can corrupt up to t servers at each round. Since the $cloud_{KMS}$ encrypts shares $[s]_i$ at shutdown phase by using the mechanism of *Resharing*, the adversary **A** can only recovers shares $[s]_{j,i}$ for $i \in A$ where $|A| < t + 1$ and $j = 1, \cdots, n$. Thus for any share $[s]_i$, the adversary will have only access to at most t shares $[s]_{j,i}$.

Let $< \pi(), \mu >$ be a distribution scheme, where μ is a uniform probability distribution on $\mathbb{Z}_p$. By the interpolation theorem, for every set of random integers $T = \{[s]_{j,i}\}$ where $j \in A$, $|A| = t$ and for every $a \in \mathbb{Z}_p$ we have

$$Pr\left[\pi(a, u)_T = \{[s]_{j, i_{(j \in A, |A|=t)}}\}\right] < \frac{1}{p^t}$$

Therefore the probability for a polynomial bounded adversary **A** corrupting up to t servers to get access to any share $[s]_i$ is bounded by a negligible function. From the hiding property of the generalized commitment scheme shown in Sect. 4, the adversary can not learn anything about shares which proves the confidentiality property. The proof of integrity can be derived easily from the biding property. Indeed, the adversary can provide the dealer with valid shares $[s]'_i$, $i \in A$ where $|A| > t$ can only occur by breaking the binding property of the commitment scheme or by creating a polynomial $p'(x)$ of degree at least $t + 1$ providing the same evaluations as the secret polynomial $p(x)$. This latter probability is bounded by $\frac{1}{p^{t+1}}$ which conclude the proof of theorem 2.

Efficiency Study. Here, we discuss the efficiency of our design. Since there no other available software-based cloud key management system in the literature, we restrict ourselves to benchmark the performances of the prototype of implementation. As the system is built on top of a (n, t) verifiable secret sharing based on commitment, its complexity depends heavily on the efficiency of the underlying cryptographic technique, namely the commitment scheme. Thus, the complexity improvement brought by the proposed design will be expressed as the gains resulting from our commitment scheme whereas the cost of other operations related to communication broadcast will be expressed in terms of latency.

The use of the generalized version of Kate et al.'s commitment allows reducing the number of $VerifyEval()$ by a factor of t. It requires only $\mathcal{O}(1)$ broadcast instead of $\mathcal{O}(n)$ needed by all other known verifiable secret sharing schemes. Since in our protocol the KMS on-premise acts as a trusted authority, the computation of $SK = \alpha$ and PK can be done in a very efficient way rather than using the costly distributed computation protocols over $\mathbb{Z}_p$. Furthermore, the phases requiring heavy computation, namely Set_Up, $Commit$, $VSS - Commit$, $CreateWitness$, and $GenCreateWitness$ are performed only once and are executed by the KMS on-premise supposed to have huge computation resources.

The verification of witnesses, performed in $GenVerifyEval$ phase, involves the computation of $g^{q(\alpha)}$ and $g^{I(\alpha)}$ where $q(\alpha) = \prod_{i=0}^{k-1}(\alpha - z_i)$ and $I(\alpha) = \sum_{i=0}^{k-1} y_i \prod_{i=1}^{t+1} \frac{\alpha - z_j}{z_i - z_j}$ by any server S_i. The parameter α is only known by the KMS, the computation of $g^{q(\alpha)}$ and $g^{I(\alpha)}$ can be done by expressing $\prod_{i=0}^{k-1}(\alpha - z_i)$ and each $\prod_{i=0}^{k-1} \frac{\alpha - z_j}{z_i - z_j}$ as polynomials $\phi(\alpha) = \sum_{i=0}^{deg(\phi)} a_i \alpha^i$, $a_i \in \mathbb{Z}_p$ where $deg(\phi) \leq t$ and calculating $g^{q(\alpha)} = \prod_{i=0}^{k-1} (g^{\alpha^i})^{a_i}$ and $g^{I(\alpha)} = \prod_{i=0}^{k-1} (g^{\alpha^i a_i})^{p(i)}$ by using the public parameters $< g, g^\alpha, \cdots, g^{\alpha^t} >$.

As our design assumes the presence of a trusted authority, namely the KMS on-premise, we can get better performance by computing and broadcasting $g^{\prod_{i=0}^{k-1}(\alpha - z_i)}$ and $g^{\frac{\alpha - z_j}{z_i - z_j}}$ for every set used in $GenCreateWitness$. This does not undermine the security of the proposed design since the published information can be derived from the public parameters $< g, g^\alpha, \cdots, g^{\alpha^t} >$.

For some choices of t, namely $t \leq \lfloor \frac{n}{t+1} \rfloor$, the performance of the proposed design can be significantly optimized. Indeed, if we have $t \leq \lfloor \frac{n}{t+1} \rfloor$, we can split up the n secret shares to a more than t sets of size $t + 1$. Thus we can recover the exact shared secret if only one witness of set elements of size $t + 1$ is valid. If more than t witnesses are going wrong, then we can conclude that more than t parties are corrupted, and the protocol aborts. The current optimization reduces the amount of broadcast and verification by a factor of t. This optimization is optimal for the settings where the number of servers is about 10 which is very appropriate for any real-world application such as cloud key management systems.

We implemented our protocol $cloud_{KMS}$ using a 64 bits Windows operating system with i7-8565 (1.8 GHz) processor and 16Go installed RAM. JCraft library is leveraged for establishing private channels between servers and dealers. All experimental have been conducted with some servers deployed on-premise with Proxmox solution. The remaining servers are hosted on virtual machines and located on the cloud providers platforms (OVH and Scaleway). We consider real-world keys AES-192 and RSA-2048, generated by Openssl library.

Table 1. Cost of running $cloud_{KMS}$ protocol in seconds. Timings do not include virtual machines (VMs) deployment and start-up times. The VMs hosting the servers are running Linux OS with 1.5 GiB RAM and 1.2 GHz processor.

Key size		AES-256		RSA-2048
Servers	$cloud_{KMS}$	Latency	$cloud_{KMS}$	Latency
5 servers ($t = 2$)	19,34	± 1,35	18,35	± 1,19
7 servers ($t = 3$)	21,17	± 1,71	22,56	± 1,34
9 servers ($t = 4$)	24,29	± 1,93	23,81	± 1,54

The benchmark in Table 1 shows that the timing cost of running the prototype of our software-based cloud key management system for optimized setting is indeed practical for real-world application deployment. Furthermore, the results analysis emphasis that the timing cost grows slowly with the number of servers which proves that our system can meet the requirement of very critical application such as cryptocurrency wallets.

7   Conclusion and Future Work

We extended the recent result by Kate et al., which commits to a polynomial $p(x) \in Z_x[x]$ over bilinear group in such a way that it provides a single element commitment with a constant size. We generalized kate's et al. scheme to the evaluation of a set $\{(i, p(i))\}$ that can be opened only once, while still creating a single element commitment with a constant size. We provided an efficient algorithm for implementing the scheme with pre-computation phase that can be performed by trust authority. This result is exploited to build a software-based cloud key management system fully controlled by cloud clients with an amount of commitment exchanged reduced by a factor t, where t is the number of faulty parties. We constructed a formal model and prove its security under some well-known assumptions. In the future, we plan to explore other vector commitment approaches to avoid the costly pairing evaluation operations.

References

1. Archer, W., et al.: From Keys to databases real-world applications of secure multi-party computation. In cryptology ePrint Archive, Report 450 (2018)
2. Amazon, A. W. S. CloudHSM (2015)
3. Azougaghe, A., Ait Oualhaj, O., Hedabou, M., Belkasmi, M., Kobbane, A.: Many-to-one matching game towards secure virtual machines migration in cloud computing. In: 2016 International Conference on Advanced Communication Systems and Information Security (ACOSIS), IEEE (2017)
4. Blakley, G. R.: Safeguarding cryptographic keys. In: Proceedings of the 1979 AFIPS National Computer Conference, pp. 313–317 (1979)

5. Boneh, D., Boyen, X.: Short signatures without random oracles. In: Cachin, C., Camenisch, J.L. (eds.) EUROCRYPT 2004. LNCS, vol. 3027, pp. 56–73. Springer, Heidelberg (2004). https://doi.org/10.1007/978-3-540-24676-3_4

6. Bentajer, A., Hedabou, M., Abouelmehdi, K., Elfezazi, S.: CS-IBE: a data confidentiality system in public cloud storage system. Proc. Comput. Sci. **141**, 559–564 (2018)

7. Bentajer, A., Hedabou, M.: Cryptographic key management issues in cloud computing. Adv. Eng. Res. **34**, 78–112 (2020)

8. Benaloh, J., Leichter, J.: Generalized secret sharing and monotone functions. In: Goldwasser, S. (ed.) CRYPTO 1988. LNCS, vol. 403, pp. 27–35. Springer, New York (1990). https://doi.org/10.1007/0-387-34799-2_3

9. Barker, E., Roginsky, A.: Recommendation for cryptographic key generation. US Department of Commerce, National Institute of Standards and Technology (2012). https://doi.org/10.6028/NIST.SP.800-133

10. The Encrypting File System (EFS). http://technet.microsoft.com/en-us/library/cc700811.aspx. A white paper from Microsoft Corporation

11. Haitner, I., Reingold, O.: Statistically-hiding commitment from any one-way function. In: Proceedings of the Thirty-Ninth Annual ACM Symposium on Theory of Computing, pp. 1–10 (2007)

12. Hedabou, M., Bénéteau, L., Pinel, P.: Some ways to secure elliptic curve cryptosystems. Adv. Appl. Clifford Algebras **48**, 677–688 (2008)

13. ChandramoulI, R., Iorga, M., Chokhani, S.: Cryptographic Key management issues and challenges in cloud services. In: Secure Cloud Computing, pp. 1–30. Springer, New York, NY (2014). https://doi.org/10.6028/NIST.IR.7956

14. Feldman, P.: A practical scheme for non-interactive verifiable secret sharing. In: Proceedings of FOCS 1987, pp. 427–437 (1987)

15. Damgard, I.: Commitment schemes and zero-knowledge protocols. In: Lectures on Data Security, pp. 63–86. Springer (1999)

16. Goyal, V.: Reducing trust in the PKG in identity based cryptosystems. In: Menezes, A. (ed.) CRYPTO 2007. LNCS, vol. 4622, pp. 430–447. Springer, Heidelberg (2007). https://doi.org/10.1007/978-3-540-74143-5_24

17. Kate, A., Zaverucha, G.M., Goldberg, I.: Constant-size commitments to polynomials and their applications. In: Abe, M. (ed.) ASIACRYPT 2010. LNCS, vol. 6477, pp. 177–194. Springer, Heidelberg (2010). https://doi.org/10.1007/978-3-642-17373-8_11

18. Naor, M.: Bit commitment using pseudorandomness. J. Cryptol. **4**(2), 151–158 (1991). https://doi.org/10.1007/BF00196774

19. Rosen, A.: Analysis of the porticor homomorphic key management protocol. Available at: https://wulujia.com/attachments/porticor/Porticor

20. Shamir, A.: How to share a secret. Commun. ACM **22**(11), 612–613 (1979)

21. Stadler, M.: Public verifiable secret sharing. EUROCRYPT LNCS **1996**(1070), 190–199 (1996)

22. Simmons, G.J., Jackson, W., Martin, K.M.: The geometry of shared secret schemes. Bull. ICA **1**, 71–88 (1991)

23. Wilcox-O'Hearn, Z., Warner, B.: Tahoe: the least-authority file system. In: Proceedings of the 4th ACM International Workshop on Storage Security and Survivability, StorageSS 2008, pp. 21–26, New York, NY, USA. ACM (2008)

24. Wright, C., Martino, M., Zadok, E.: NCryptfs: a secure and convenient cryptographic file system. In: Proceedings of the Annual USENIX Technical Conference, pp. 197–210. USENIX Association (2003)

A Scheme for Sensor Data Reconstruction in Smart Home

Yegang Du[✉]

Dalian Maritime University, 1 Linghai Road, Dalian, China
`yg.du@dlmu.edu.cn`

Abstract. Today, a large number of sensors are spatially deployed to monitor the environment in smart home. Through sensed data, home automation systems can perceive the surroundings and further provide corresponding services. However, such systems rely on highly available data which cannot be guaranteed by sensors. If some sensors report unavailable data to home automation systems without verification, the systems might malfunction and even affect the safety of residents. In this paper, a generalized highly available data interpolation (HADI) scheme is proposed to serve as a guarantor for sensed data in smart home. HADI takes advantage of the relationship between the faulty sensor and the other heterogeneous sensors to reconstruct the highly available data. Experiments reveal that our proposed scheme can achieve high data availability with less computation cost.

Keywords: Smart home · Data restoration · Data availability · Data interpolation · Home sensor

1 Introduction

Nowadays, numerous advanced Internet of Things (IoT) technologies and devices have been implemented in the smart home environment. Due to the remarkable sensing, communication, processing technologies and devices, the interconnection be-tween physical and virtual things is successfully achieved. In IoT-enabled applications, sensor networks are the most important component. Critical information from both external surroundings and inner systems is sampled by networked sensors [1]. As a typical research field in IoT, the smart home makes full use of sensor networks to sense the ambient physical information and even detect human activities [2]. With the information collected from sensor networks, several home automation systems such as home energy management systems (HEMS) or heating, ventilation, and air conditioning (HVAC) systems have been achieved. Therefore, sensors are playing a significant role in smart home.

However, according to [3], experiments revealed that sensors in smart home environment are facing various problems which result in sensor faults or even failures. Fault sensors will generate unavailable data, and these data will be imported into home automation systems. Unavailable data may cause undesired

© Springer Nature Switzerland AG 2021
M. Yang et al. (Eds.): NSS 2021, LNCS 13041, pp. 304–313, 2021.
https://doi.org/10.1007/978-3-030-92708-0_19

control, which not only cost additional energy consumption but also carry risk to normal operation of actuators. For example, in the home energy control system [4], faulty sensors transfer unavailable data to the controller, which may trigger temporary invalidation. Furthermore, actuators that receive continual unavailable data probably result in system failure. Consequently, the efficiency of the control system is challenged.

In this paper, a novel data interpolation scheme HADI is proposed to restore accurate and available data to maintain the regular operation of home automation systems. Temperature, relative humidity, solar irradiance, and wind speed are detected through the data obtained from our experiment platform. This paper mainly focuses on restoring highly available solar irradiance data. The novelty is mainly reflected in taking advantage of spatiotemporal heterogeneous data. Hence processing time and training samples are reduced dramatically, which differs from the general approaches.

Three main contributions are achieved by HADI. First, this paper summarizes the format and pattern of unavailable data and illustrates the definition of data availability in smart home. Then HADI algorithm is proposed, and analysis in theory is given to explain the effectiveness of our algorithm. Moreover, several experiments have been done to compare the performance of our HADI with the state-of-the-art method. Experiments show that high availability of data is guaranteed, meanwhile, the processing time and training samples are reduced dramatically.

The rest of the paper is structured as follows. Section 2 shows the background and related works on data restoration. Section 3 illustrates the definition and categories of data availability in smart home. Section 4 details the HADI models and mathematical expressions. Section 5 demonstrates solar irradiance data restoration using HADI, and shows the evaluation of the HADI scheme. The paper is concluded in Sect. 6.

2   Related Work

Research related with data restoration have been carried out in the last 20 years. Related works are mainly divided into three kinds of mechanisms: Principle component analysis, Linear regression, Artificial Neural Network.

In [5], PCA first achieves data recovery for HVAC system, however, this approach merely considers the temporal data of target data, which results in a weak response by data variation. Given by the progress of Yu et al. [1], a recursive principal component analysis (R-PCA) is proposed. R-PCA represents a remarkable efficiency on data fault detection, data aggregation, and recovery accuracy, whereas recursion increases the burden on processing units. Meanwhile, R-PCA costs a longer processing time due to the high complexity.

Linear regression is a widely-used approach in data analysis. Efficient temporal and spatial data recovery (ETSDR) [6] integrate Auto Regressive Integrated Moving Average (ARIMA) model with spatiotemporal data, furthermore, realized the dynamic model identification and accurate intermittent data recovery.

But the performance of dealing with continual unavailable data by using ETSDR is a great challenge. Since the ETSDR update the linear model for every single data for each sensor, the processing time and burden on the processor are doubted as well.

In addition, Artificial Neural Network (ANN) [7] has been applied on temperature recovery for HVAC systems in 1996. And neural network-based model is optimized by Z. Liu et al. [8] by deep multimodal encoder (DME) framework, which has excel-lent performance on high unavailability. However, either ANN or DME requires the reliable data as training sample s, besides, the iterative process of the neural network is time-consuming for dynamic systems. Therefore, an approach is expected to reduce processing time and achieve accurate data restoration will be presented in this paper.

3   Data Availability in Smart Home

3.1   Definition of Data Availability

In [9], availability is general purposed as the following equation:

$$\lim_{t \to \infty} = A = \frac{MTTF}{MTTF + MTTR} \tag{1}$$

where t denotes the time of item, moreover, $MTTF$, $MTTR$ is the mean time to failure and to repair, respectively. Therefore, for sensor x, we have the sensor availability A_x defined by faults in this scheme:

$$\lim_{t \to T} A_x(t) = A_x = \frac{IAD}{(IUD + AD)} \tag{2}$$

where T is the operation time. Similarly, IAD, IUD is the interval of available and unavailable data, respectively.

3.2   Unavailable Data Description

Fig. 1. Process of unavailable data investigation.

In this paper, we investigated availability of the temperature, relative humidity, solar irradiance and wind speed data. Note that, we don't consider the data loss and data delay in our model as shown in Fig. 1. In addition, we classify the unavailable for-mat for single data as shown in Table 1 according to [10].

Table 1. Unavailable format and description.

Format	Description
Outlier	Isolated data point or sensor unexpectedly distant from models
"Stuck-at"	Multiple data points with a much greater than expected rate of change
Calibration	Sensor reports values that are offset from the ground truth

Table 2. Pattern of unavailable data and description.

Duration	Description
Intermittent	Data act as unavailable in one or several seconds. Most intermittent unavailable data are mainly caused by outlier or spike
Continual	Unavailable data last for a long period, a few minutes, even hours. Most continual unavailable data are related with "Stuck-at" and calibration

In Table 2, we define the pattern of unavailable data as intermittent and continual. It will help us to recognize the unavailable data and figure out the interpolation method.

Through the investigation, we define threshold $[0,1360]$ (W/m^2) as the range of available solar irradiance values. Through availability investigation in the year 2016, we find unavailable data in the daytime last 574.2 h. It means that the pyranometer is unavailable for nearly 1.6 h every single day. Meanwhile, most of the unavailable data reveals a continual pattern. Hence, this paper will focus on solar irradiance interpolation.

4   Models of HADI Scheme

4.1   HADI Structure

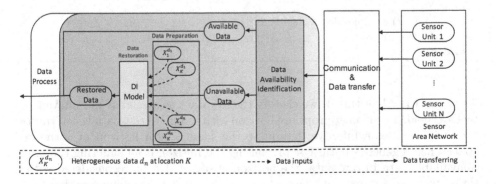

Fig. 2. Structure of HADI scheme.

Figure 2 shows the structure of the HADI scheme, we suppose HADI is located in the data process module. Raw data from each sensor unit is identified as available or unavailable data in the availability detection stage. Available data will continue the data process. However, Unavailable data are supposed to be restored by Data Interpolation (DI) model with spatiotemporal heterogeneous data. Therefore, due to the HADI scheme, high availability is guaranteed.

4.2 HADI Algorithm

Algorithm 1. Highly available data interpolation (HADI) scheme.

---

if $Y_i(n,t) > \theta_y$ then // $Y_i(n,t)$ is unavailable.
$\quad \check{Y}_i(n,t) \leftarrow Y_i(n,t)$
$\quad$ // Determine spatial and temporal horizon as:
$\quad H_{Y_i} = Y_i(n-h) : Y_i(n-1)$
$\quad H_{X_{1:K}} = X_{1:K}(n-h) : X_{1:K}(n-1)$
$\quad$ if $A_{H_{Y_i}} < 50\%$ then
$\quad\quad$ // Available data are rare, reconsider horizon with restored data
$\quad\quad H_{Y_i} = \left\{ \check{Y}_i \bigcup \tilde{Y}_i \right\}(n-h) : \left\{ \check{Y}_i \bigcup \tilde{Y}_i \right\}(n-1)$
$\quad$ end if
$\quad$ // Aggregate the available data set in horizon $H_{Y_{(i)}}$
$\quad \hat{Y}_i(C(1:m)) = \left[\hat{Y}_i(C(1)), \cdots, \hat{Y}_i(C(m)) \right]$
$\quad$ for each $u = 1 : K$ do
$\quad\quad X_u(C(1:m)) = [X_u(C(1)), \cdots, X_u(C(m))]$
$\quad\quad$ // Substitute $X_u(C(1:m))$ for Data Interpolation(DI) model
$\quad\quad \tilde{Y}_u(C(1:m)) = \left[\tilde{Y}_u(C(1)), \cdots, \tilde{Y}_u(C(m)) \right]$
$\quad\quad$ // Calculate the Root Mean Square Error
$\quad\quad \varphi(u) = \sqrt{\dfrac{\left(\tilde{Y}_u(C(1)) - \hat{Y}_u(C(1))\right)^2 + \cdots + \left(\tilde{Y}_u(C(m)) - \hat{Y}_u(C(m))\right)}{m}}$
$\quad$ end for
$\quad \varphi(p) = min(\varphi(1:K))$
$\quad$ // Calculate current time $\tilde{Y}_i(n,t)$
$\quad \check{Y}_i(n,t) = f(X_p(n,t))$
else
$\quad$ // $Y_t(n,t)$ is available.
$\quad \check{Y}_t(n,t) \leftarrow Y_t(n,t)$
end if

As shown the Algorithm 1, we classify the raw data as available and unavailable by threshold. Then, an appropriate horizon with temporal raw data is determined for training. Meanwhile, we determine the same length horizon of correlated spatial heterogeneous data. For preventing the horizon from suffering too much unavailable data in raw data, the horizon of target data is reconsidered with a set of available and restored data when unavailable data occupy more than 50%.

As all horizons are completed, the positions of available data in the target data horizon compose the set $C(1:m)$. Besides, to keep time synchronization, we need to find the corresponding data $X_{1:K}(C(1:m))$ in a heterogeneous horizon. DI model contains the correlations between X and Y, these correlations can be described as $Y = f(X)$, hypothetically. With spatial heterogeneous data as inputs, K groups of simulated data are generated. Through calculating RMSE between K groups simulated data and available data in target data horizon, we can find sensors at locations p determine the minimum RMSE. Finally, with current heterogeneous data input, interpolation of target data is accomplished by inputting correlated heterogeneous data at location p into the DI model.

5   Di Model for Hourly Solar Irradiance

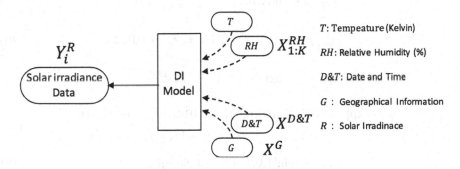

Fig. 3. DI model for solar irradiance interpolation.

In this section, we will apply our HADI scheme to solve the low availability of solar irradiance. As shown in Fig. 3, heterogeneous data inputs include the time information, geographical information, temperature, and relative humidity data from sensors distributed in 11 spots of the experiment platform.

5.1   Hourly Solar Irradiance

In this paper, we apply an improved hourly solar irradiance method for conversion. According to [11], the equations are described as follows:

Solar irradiance R (W/m^2) and global solar irradiance R_{clear} (W/m^2) can be expressed as:

$$R = \tau_c R_{clear} \tag{3}$$

where τ_c denotes a radiative transmittance coefficient, which is supposed to be an empirical function of relative sunshine duration:

$$\tau_c = a + bn/N + c(n/N)^2 \tag{4}$$

where a, b, c are the model parameters. n/N represents relative sunshine duration. Moreover, R_{clear} (W/m^2) consists of surface beam irradiance $R_{b,clear}$ (W/m^2) and solar diffuse irradiance $R_{d,clear}$ (W/m^2):

$$R_{clear} = R_{b,clear} + R_{d,clear} \tag{5}$$

$$R_{b,clear} = R_0 \bar{\tau}_{b,clear} \tag{6}$$

$$R_{d,clear} = R_0 \bar{\tau}_{d,clear} \tag{7}$$

where R_0 (W/m^2) is the solar irradiance on a horizontal surface at the extraterrestrial level [11]. The broadband solar beam radiative transmittance $\bar{\tau}_{(b,clear)}$ and radiative transmittance $\bar{\tau}_{(d,clear)}$) are able to be described as:

$$\bar{\tau}_{b,clear} \approx \max(0, \bar{\tau}_{oz}\bar{\tau}_w\bar{\tau}_g\bar{\tau}_r\bar{\tau}_a - 0.013) \tag{8}$$

$$\bar{\tau}_{d,clear} \approx 0.5[\bar{\tau}_{oz}\bar{\tau}_g\bar{\tau}_w(1 - \bar{\tau}_a\bar{\tau}_r) + 0.013] \tag{9}$$

$$\bar{\tau}_g = \exp(-0.0117(m')^{0.3139}) \tag{10}$$

$$\bar{\tau}_r = \exp[-0.008735(m')(0.547 + 0.014(m') - 0.00038(m')^2 \\ +4.6 \times 10^{-6}(m')^3)^{-4.08}] \tag{11}$$

$$\bar{\tau}_w = \min[1.0, 0.909 - 0.036 ln(mv)] \tag{12}$$

$$\bar{\tau}_{oz} = \exp[-0.0365(ml)^{0.7136}] \tag{13}$$

$$\bar{\tau}_a = \exp\{-m\beta[0.6777 + 0.1464(m\beta)^2]^{-1.3}\} \tag{14}$$

$$m = 1/[\sin h + 0.15(57.296h + 3.885)^{-1.253}] \tag{15}$$

$$m' = mp/p_0 \tag{16}$$

$$p = p_0 \exp(-z/H_T) \tag{17}$$

where $\bar{\tau}_{oz}, \bar{\tau}_w, \bar{\tau}_g, \bar{\tau}_r, \bar{\tau}_a$ are the radiative transmittance due to ozone absorption, water vapor absorption, permanent gas absorption, Rayleigh scattering, and aerosol extinction, respectively. In addition, h (rad) denotes the solar elevation, m refers to relative air mass, m' is the pressure-corrected air mass, p_0 (Pa) is the standard atmospheric pressure, p (Pa) is the surface pressure. l is the thickness of ozone and β in Eq. 14 is the Ångström turbidity coefficient. z is surface elevation from the mean sea level, H_T is the scale height of an isothermal atmosphere, and H_T is 8430.

5.2   Evaluation of HADI Scheme

In this section, we evaluate the efficiency of HADI. To evaluate the performance, we use the RMSE and mean absolute error (MAE). RMSE reveals the accuracy of simulation results, then, for data series with a length of N, RMSE can be written as:

$$RMSE = \sqrt{\frac{\sum_{n=1}^{N}\left(d(n) - \widetilde{d}(n)\right)^2}{N}} \qquad (18)$$

Moreover, MAE is used to measure how close the simulated values are to the original measured value:

$$MAE = \frac{1}{N}\sum_{n=1}^{N}\left|d(n) - \widetilde{d}(n)\right| \qquad (19)$$

In Eq. 18 and Eq. 19, $d(n)$ denotes the original measured data, and $\widetilde{d}(n)$ is the simulated data.

To show the performance of HADI better, we compare HADI with the ETSDR scheme. Simulation results consist of intermittent and continual unavailable data restoration by HADI and ETSDR, respectively.

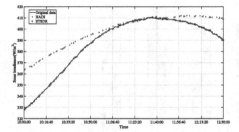

Fig. 4. Intermittent unavailable data interpolation.

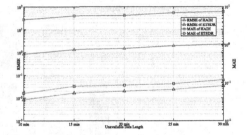

Fig. 5. Performance of intermittent unavailable data interpolation.

Intermittent Unavailable Data Interpolation. Figure 4 shows an example of intermittent unavailable data interpolation. In 100 min' dataset, we interpolate 10 minutes' unavailable data at a random time. Although ETSDR performs a higher accuracy, however, high availability is guaranteed with HADI as well as ETSDR.

In addition, we increase the percentage of unavailable data from 10% to 30% as shown in Fig. 5, and results reveal that ETSDR shows extremely high accuracy with-out the influence of unavailable data increase.

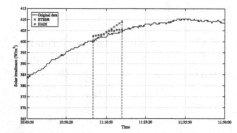 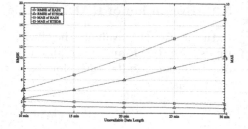

Fig. 6. Continual unavailable data interpolation.

Fig. 7. Performance of continual unavailable data interpolation.

Continual Unavailable Data Interpolation. On the other hand, we consider the circumstance of continual unavailable. Figure 6 shows continual unavailable interpolation of same length unavailable data in Fig. 4. Results reveal that HADI performs better than ETSDR on dealing with continual unavailable data. Without real-time data to update the ARIMA model in ETSDR, the interpolation data regress to straight line rapidly, and consequent enormous error gradually.

However, as shown in Fig. 7, HADI shows a steady performance on accuracy whose RMSE and MAE vary at a low value despite the percentage of unavailable data growth.

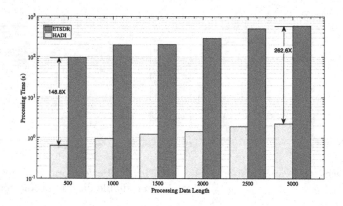

Fig. 8. Performance of processing time.

Processing Time Comparison. Processing time is a significant feature for real-time home automation systems as well, therefore we compare the processing time between two schemes. In each processing data length, we keep the percentage of unavailable data as 10%, and Fig. 8 shows that on a logarithmic scale, it is obvious that ETSDR costs much more processing time than HADI. Hence, we can conclude that HADI achieves a dramatic efficiency on continual unavailable data problems.

6   Conclusion and Future Work

In this paper, we purposed a new data interpolation scheme based on spatiotemporal heterogeneous data to solve continual unavailable issues. HADI is able to maintain relatively high accuracy and absolutely available. Furthermore, HADI shows amazing efficiency in processing time. HADI is a generalized scheme that can be widely used not only in smart home but also in other crowded sensor networks. Our future work will focus on attempting to introduce more models and correlations into HADI so that home automation systems will be isolated from unavailable data.

References

1. Yu, T., Wang, X., Shami, A.: Recursive principal component analysis-based data outlier detection and sensor data aggregation in IoT systems. IEEE Internet Things J. **4**(6), 2207–2216 (2017)
2. Du, Y., Lim, Y., Tan, Y.: Rf-arp: Rfid-based activity recognition and prediction in smart home. In: 2019 IEEE 25th International Conference on Parallel and Distributed Systems (ICPADS), pp. 618–624. IEEE (2019)
3. Choi, J., Jeoung, H., Kim, J., Ko, Y., Jung, W., Kim, H., Kim, J.: Detecting and identifying faulty IoT devices in smart home with context extraction. In: 2018 48th Annual IEEE/IFIP International Conference on Dependable Systems and Networks (DSN), pp. 610–621. IEEE (2018)
4. Radja, M., Hungilo, G., Emmanuel, G., Suyoto, S.: IoT: Improved home energy control system based on consumer. In: IOP Conference Series: Materials Science and Engineering, vol. 1098, p. 042028. IOP Publishing (2021)
5. Hao, X., Zhang, G., Chen, Y.: Fault-tolerant control and data recovery in HVAC monitoring system. Energy Build. **37**(2), 175–180 (2005)
6. Nower, N., Tan, Y., Lim, A.O.: Efficient temporal and spatial data recovery scheme for stochastic and incomplete feedback data of cyber-physical systems. In: 2014 IEEE 8th International Symposium on Service Oriented System Engineering, pp. 192–197. IEEE (2014)
7. Lee, W.Y., Shin, D., House, J.: Fault diagnosis and temperature sensor recovery for an air-handling unit. Technical report, American Society of Heating, Refrigerating and Air-Conditioning Engineers (1997)
8. Liu, Z., Zhang, W., Quek, T.Q., Lin, S.: Deep fusion of heterogeneous sensor data. In: 2017 IEEE International Conference on Acoustics, Speech and Signal Processing (ICASSP), pp. 5965–5969. IEEE (2017)
9. Rausand, M., Hoyland, A.: System reliability theory: models, statistical methods, and applications, vol. 396. John Wiley & Sons (2003)
10. Ni, K., et al.: Sensor network data fault types. ACM Trans. Sensor Networks (TOSN) **5**(3), 1–29 (2009)
11. Yang, K., Koike, T.: A general model to estimate hourly and daily solar radiation for hydrological studies. Water Resour. Res. **41**(10) (2005)

Privacy-Preserving and Auditable Federated Deep Reinforcement Learning for Robotic Manipulation

Xudong Zhu[1(✉)] and Hui Li[2]

[1] Xi'an University of Architecture and Technology, Xi'an 710055, China
zhudongxu@vip.sina.com
[2] Xidian University, Xi'an 710071, China
lihui@mail.xidian.edu.cn

Abstract. DRL (Deep Reinforcement Learning) has been widely used in the field of robotic manipulation. The accuracy of DRL depends on large amounts of data for training. However, training data is distributed among different organizations and is difficult to share due to information security and privacy concerns. In order to solve the security problem of robotic manipulation and improve the accuracy of robotic manipulation, a new privacy-protecting federated reinforcement learning scheme, called PFRL, was proposed. Through PFRL, the robot learns the global reinforcement model safely through the local reinforcement model with the help of the cloud, and well protects the sensitive data of each robot. Specifically, with a secure multi-party vector aggregation algorithm, all local models are encrypted by their owners before being sent to the cloud, and can be directly operated without decryption. And in order to prevent malicious cloud servers or robots to damage the correctness of training, we have integrated non-interactive zero-knowledge proof tools to provide the auditability of collaborative training processes. Detailed security analysis shows that PFRL can resist various known security threats. Moreover, PFRL has been tested in Mujoco simulation environment, and a large number of simulations show that PFRL is feasible.

Keywords: Robotic manipulation · Federated deep reinforcement learning · Privacy-preserving

1 Introduction

In recent years, deep reinforcement learning has achieved unprecedented accuracy in the field of autonomous robots, such as manipulation [1], locomotion [2] and automatic driving [3]. In order to achieve higher accuracy, a large amount of training data is needed to input into the deep enhancement model. However,

Supported by National Key Research and Development Program of China (2019YFD1100901), Natural Science Foundation of Shaanxi (Grant No. 2013JM8022).

M. Yang et al. (Eds.): NSS 2021, LNCS 13041, pp. 314–325, 2021.
https://doi.org/10.1007/978-3-030-92708-0_20

the training data are scattered among various robot manufacturers or users, and a single manufacturer or user can only collect a small amount of training data, which cannot produce a sufficiently accurate deep enhancement model. To overcome these difficulties, Google first introduced the FL (Federated Learning) approach [4], in which the global model is updated by federated distributed participants while maintaining their local data. Unfortunately, distributed federated deep reinforcement learning has more privacy issues than traditional independent deep reinforcement learning.

First, the federated deep reinforcement learning does not protect the confidentiality of participants' training data, even the training data is divided and stored separately. For example, [5,6] inferred the important information of participants' training data through the intermediate gradient. And [7] points out that even if the differential privacy technology is adopted to protect the intermediate gradient [8], the curious parameter server can still infer the important information of participants' training data through GAN (Generative Adversarial Network).

Furthermore, federated deep reinforcement learning does not consider the security threats of malicious parameter servers and participants' dishonest behaviors to the deep reinforcement model. For example, the parameter server might deliberately remove the gradient of some participants or update the parameters incorrectly. Recently, [9] demonstrated the existence of this problem that dishonest parties can poison the collaborative model by replacing the updating model with its exquisitely designed one. Therefore, federated deep learning guarantee not only confidentiality of gradients, but auditability of the correctness of gradient collecting and parameter update.

In this paper, we propose PFRL, a secure federated deep reinforcement learning scheme based on cryptographic primitives, which can provide data confidentiality, and computation auditability for robots to participate in federated learning. With PFRL, multiple robots learn the global reinforcement model through their local reinforcement model with the help of the cloud, while well protecting the private local data and model of the robot. Meanwhile, the learned global model is also kept confidential from the cloud. And non-interactive zero-knowledge proof technology is used to ensure the auditability of federated learning process. To summarize, in this paper we made the following contributions:

- First, PFRL solves the privacy and data security issues of federated deep reinforcement learning. With PFRL, the private local model of the robot is encrypted using the Paillier encryption system, and are operated without decryption. Therefore, the privacy data of the robot can be well protected and the confidentiality of the global model can be ensured.
- Second, PFRL implements accurately federated deep reinforcement learning. A secure multi-party vector aggregation algorithm based on paillier cryptosystem with threshold decryption is proposed. The algorithm supports lossless federated reinforcement learning while protecting robot privacy.
- Third, PFRL guarantees that any robot can audit the correctness of federated reinforcement learning processes. In PFRL, we introduce non-interactive zero-

knowledge proof for the federated reinforcement learning processes, according to the UVCDN (Universally Verifiable CDN) protocol [10].

– Fourth, we implemented a PFRL prototype and tested the effectiveness of the PFRL in a Mojoco simulation environment. Extensive results show that PFRL is efficient and can be implemented with real datasets.

The remainder of this paper is organized as follows. In Sect. 2, we formalize the system model, security requirements, and identify our design goals. Then, we presented our PFRL in Sect. 3, followed by a safety analysis and a performance evaluation in Sect. 4 and Sect. 5, respectively. Finally, we draw the conclusion in Sect. 6.

2   Models and Security Requirement

In this section, we formalize the system model and security requirements, as well as the security goals that PFRL can achieve to meet these requirements.

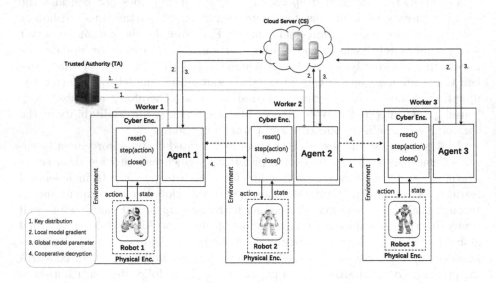

Fig. 1. System model under considered.

2.1   System Model

In our system model, we mainly focus on how to provide privacy-preserving federated deep reinforcement learning for robotic manipulation. Each robot is connected to its local edge device which can connect to other edge devices and the cloud. Specifically, the system consists of four parts: 1) **TA** (Trusted Authority), 2) **ROs** (Robots), 3) **EDs** (Edge Devices) and 4) **CS** (Cloud Server). This is shown in Fig. 1.

- **TA** is a trusted authority which bootstraps the system initialization through generating the system parameters, and distributing keys for edge devices.
- **ED**$s = \{ED_1, \cdots, ED_n\}$ is a set of n edge devices. In our system, $ED_i \in$ **ED**s independently controls its local robot RO_i (i.e., local environment), and trains its actor and critic models to control RO_i optimally through its reinforcement algorithm. Meanwhile, in order to obtain a more precise global actor-critic model, ED_i shares its encrypted local model via cooperative computing with other **ED**s and **CS**.
- **CS** is a cloud server which assists edge devices to generate global model. **CS** is responsible for aggregating the encrypted local models, and generating the final global model via cooperative computing with **ED**s. In our system, **CS** undertakes the most calculations during the federated model learning process.

2.2 Threat Model and Security Goals

In this section, we discuss threats to federated deep reinforcement learning, and security goals that PFRL can achieve to tackle those threats. In our threaten model, we consider that **CS** and **AG**s may be malicious. Specifically,

Threat 1: Disclosure of local data and model. Although in federated training each AG_i only uploads its local gradients to **CS**, still **CS** can infer through those gradients important information about its local data and model by launching an inference attack or membership attack [18,19].

Threat 2: Participants with malicious behaviors. Participants may have malicious behaviors during federal training. For example, they can randomly select their inputs and thus generate incorrect gradients, aiming to mislead the federated training process. In addition, dishonest participants may terminate their local training process prematurely to save on training costs.

Considering above security issues, the following security goals should be satisfied.

Goal 1: Privacy. Protects the privacy of each AG_i local model. Specifically, the local model of each AG_i must not be leaked to **CS** and other **AG**s during federated learning.

Goal 2: Confidentiality. Protects the learned global model from **CS**. Specifically, after the federated learning process, the global model can only be retrieved by **AG**s.

Goal 3: Auditability. Provides auditability for gradient collection and parameter updates. During the gradient collecting, participants provides encrypted gradients and correctness proofs, allowing a third party to audit whether a participant gives a correctly encrypted construction of gradients. After parameters are updated, participants download and collaboratively decrypt the parameters by providing their decryption shares and corresponding proofs for correctness verification.

3   Proposed Privacy-Preserving Scheme

In this section, we present our PFRL scheme, which mainly includes four phases: 1) system initialization; 2) local model training and gradient encryption; 3) federated learning based on encrypted gradient; 4) collaborative decryption and model parameter update. The overview of PFRL is described in Fig. 2. At first, **TA** generates system parameters, calculates the public key PK and corresponding private key SK of the paillier crypto-system, and splits the private key SK into several parts for multiple **ED**s to achieve threshold decryption. Then, by interacting with local RO_i, ED_i executes reinforcement learning algorithm to train the local Actor-Critic model and encrypts the local model gradient, which will be submitted to the CS later. And then CS executes aggregate computing based on encrypted gradients from **ED**s to obtain the encrypted global model, and send the encrypted global model to **ED**s. Finally, the global model is obtained by collaborative decryption of encrypted global model.

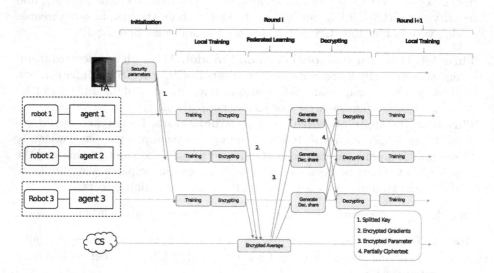

Fig. 2. Privacy-protecting federated reinforcement learning scheme.

3.1   System Initialization

During the system initialization phase, **TA** generates the system parameters, and splits the secret key SK of paillier crypto-system for **ED**s.

   TA first generates a modulus $N = pq$ where p and q are two large safe prime numbers. That is, $p = 2p' + 1$, and $q = 2q' + 1$ where p' and q' are also prime, and $gcd(N, \varphi(N)) = 1$. Then, **TA** picks up $\beta \in \mathbb{Z}_N^*$ at random, and computes the values, $m = p'q'$, $\theta = m\beta \bmod N$, $\triangle = n!$. Because $\lambda(N^2) = lcm(\varphi(p^2), \varphi(q^2)) = 2Nm$, note that $x \in \mathbb{Z}_{N^2}^*$, $x^{2Nm} \equiv 1 \bmod N^2$.

Furthermore, the public key PK and the secret key SK are $PK = (N, g, \theta)$ and $SK = \beta m$ where $g = -a^{2N}$ and $a \in \mathbb{Z}^*_{N^2}$. The cipher text c of a message M is defined as $c = g^M r^N \ mod \ N^2$ where $r \in \mathbb{Z}$ is random.

Finally, in order to share the decryption key $SK = \beta m$, **TA** generates a polynomial f with a_i chosen at random from $\{0, 1, ..., Nm - 1\}$, $f(x) = \beta m + a_1 x + a_2 x^2 + \cdots + a_t x^t \ mod \ Nm$. **TA** can split SK into $M + 1$ parts through computing $f(i)$. Also, **TA** chooses a random value $r \in \mathbb{Z}^*_{N^2}$ and publishes the verification key vk as $vk = v = r^2 \ mod \ N^2$, and $vk_i = v^{\triangle f(i)} \ mod \ N^2$ for ED_i. These verification keys are necessary for **ED**s to prove that the decryption procedure is done correctly.

TA publishes the system parameters $<PK, vk, \{vk_i\}_{i \in [1,...,M]}>$. Each $ED_i \in$ **ED**s requests **TA** for its distributed secret key $SK_{ED_i} = f(i)$.

3.2   Local Training and Gradient Encryption

Local Model Training. Each edge device ED_j starts a sequential interaction with its local robot RO_j at the time step $t = 0$, and finishes at the time step T when the end condition is met. At every time step t, ED_j receives a representation s_t of RO_j's state and selects an action a_t that is executed in RO_j which in turn provides a reward signal r_{t+1} and a representation s_{t+1} of the successor state. For every time step t, ED_j stores the tuple $<s_t, a_t, r_{t+1}, s_{t+1}>$ as its experience into its trajectory memory. And each ED_j's reinforcement learning algorithm calculates the gradients for the optimization of actor and critic models by using the tuples stored in the trajectory memory. For the deep learning models of ED_j, the gradients are the vectors of partial derivatives with respect to the parameters of the models and they are used to find the optimal models to control RO_j.

Local Model Gradient Encryption. Training gradients are vectors with multiple elements, i.e., $\triangle \mathbf{W}_{ij} = (w^1_{ij}, w^2_{ij}, ..., w^l_{ij})$, where l is the length of $\triangle \mathbf{W}_{ij}$, i is the index of current training iteration, and j is the ID of ED_j, $j = 1, 2, \cdots, M$. Then ED_j chooses random number $r^k_{ij} \in \mathbb{Z}_N$, executes the following operation to encrypt each element in $\triangle \mathbf{W}_{ij}$ with the public key $PK = N$,

$$C(w^k_{ij}) = g^{w^k_{ij}} (r^k_{ij})^N \ mod \ N^2 \tag{1}$$

and forms $C(\triangle \mathbf{W}_{ij}) = (C(w^1_{ij}), C(w^2_{ij}), ..., C(w^l_{ij}))$. And to guarantee encryption correctness, ED_j computes the following publicly auditable proof.

$$Proof_{PK_{i,j}} = fsprove(\Sigma_{PK}; C(\triangle \mathbf{W}_{ij}); \triangle \mathbf{W}_{ij}; \mathbf{r}_{ij}) \tag{2}$$

Finally, ED_j submit $<C(\triangle \mathbf{W}_{ij}), Proof_{PK_{i,j}}>$ to CS.

3.3   Federated Model Training

In the federated training phase, CS collects the encrypted local gradients produced by the learning process of **ED**s. After receiving total m encrypted local gradient packet $<C(\triangle\mathbf{W}_{ij}), Proof_{PK_{i,j}}>$, for $j = 1,\cdots,m$, CS firstly verifies correctness of the encrypted gradients $C(\triangle\mathbf{W}_{ij})$ via function

$$fsver(\Sigma_{PK}; C(\triangle\mathbf{W}_{ij}); Proof_{PK_{i,j}}) \tag{3}$$

Specifically, it verifies whether $C(\triangle\mathbf{W}_{ij})$ is indeed the encryption of $\triangle\mathbf{W}_{ij}$ with random number $\mathbf{r}_{ij}$. If correct, CS executes update operations by

$$C(\mathbf{W}_{i+1}) = C(\mathbf{W}_i) \cdot \frac{1}{m} \cdot (C(\triangle\mathbf{W}_{i,1}) \cdot C(\triangle\mathbf{W}_{i,2}) \cdot\cdots\cdot C(\triangle\mathbf{W}_{i,m})) \tag{4}$$

Finally, CS sends $C(\mathbf{W}_{i+1})$ to all **EDs**.

3.4   Collaborative Decryption and Parameter Updating

Collaborative Decryption. After receiving the encrypted global model packet $C(\mathbf{W}_{i+1})$, named C_{i+1} for brevity, ED_j cooperatively decrypts C_{i+1} to obtain the global model $\mathbf{W}_{i+1}$. Concretely, for every element in C_{i+1}, ED_j computes

$$C(w_{i+1}^k)^{(ED_j)} = C(w_{i+1}^k)^{SK_{(ED_j)}} \tag{5}$$

with its distributed secret SK_{ED_j} obtain $C_{i+1}^{(ED_j)}$, and the corresponding proofs for correct shares $Proof_{CD_{ij}}$, as follows.

$$Proof_{CD_{i,j}} = fsprove(\Sigma_{CD}; (C_{i+1}, C_{i+1}^{(ED_j)}), VK, VK_j); SK_{(ED_j)}) \tag{6}$$

Then ED_j shares its $<C_{i+1}^{ED_j}, Proof_{CD_{i,j}}>$ to other **EDs** through a secure channel. Furthermore, the global model $\mathbf{W}_{i+1}$ can be retrieved by ED_j with the follow steps.

STEP 1. Decryption Group Generation. ED_i maps $\{ED_1, ED_2, \cdots, ED_M)\}$ to $\{1, 2, \cdots, M\}$, and $\{C_{i+1}^{(ED_1)}, C_{i+1}^{(ED_2)}, \cdots, C_{i+1}^{(ED_M)}\}$ to $\{C_{i+1}^{(1)}, C_{i+1}^{(2)} \cdots, C_{i+1}^{(M)}\}$. Once the number of **EDs**, which have shared their $C_{i+1}^{(j)}$, is greater than $u - 1$, ED_j can select v ($v \le u$) numbers from $\{1, 2, \cdots, M\}$ to construct the global model decryption set GDS.

STEP 2. Collaborative Global Model Decryption. ED_i verifies $Proof_{CD_{i,j}}$ validity of the decryption shares, i.e., $\triangle SK_{(ED_j)} = log_{C_i^4}C_{ij}^2 = log_{vk}vk_j$, through function $fsver(\Sigma_{CD}; (C_{i+1}, C_{i+1}^{(ED_j)}); Proof_{CD_{i,j}})$. Then ED_j executes the following calculations to obtain w_{i+1}^k, which is the plaintext of each element in C_{i+1}.

$$\begin{cases} \triangle_{l,GDS}(x) = \varepsilon \cdot \prod_{l' \in GDS, l' \neq l} \frac{x - \alpha_{l'}}{\alpha_l - \alpha_{l'}} \\ (w_{i+1}^k)' = \prod_{l \in GPS} C(w_{i+1}^k)^{\triangle_{l,GDS}(0)} \bmod N^2 \\ w_{i+1}^k = L((w_{i+1}^k)')/\varepsilon \bmod N \end{cases} \tag{7}$$

Finally, through decrypting each elements in C_{i+1} with executing the above steps, all **ED** can achieve the global model $\mathbf{W}_{i+1}$ which is presented as

$$\mathbf{W}_{i+1} = (w_{i+1}^1, w_{i+1}^2, \cdots, w_{i+1}^l) \tag{8}$$

Parameter Updating. Each ED_j optimize the current local model once more using the global model $\mathbf{W}_{i+1}$ received from CS.

4   Security Analysis

In this section, we analyze the security of the proposed PFRL. Specifically, following the security requirements discussed earlier, our analysis focuses on how to protect privacy data during federated deep reinforcement learning.

Theorem 1. PFRL achieves the privacy of ED_j's local gradients $\triangle \mathbf{W}_j$ and the confidentiality of global federated model parameters $\mathbf{W}$ against honest-but-curious model (i.e., CS want to obtain the underlying plaintext of $C(\triangle \mathbf{W}_j)$ and $C(\mathbf{W})$ for stealing ED_j's local gradients $\triangle \mathbf{W}_j$ and the global federated model parameters $\mathbf{W}$, meanwhile, $\mathbf{ED}$s expect to achieve each other's local gradients).

Proof. We illustrate that both $\triangle \mathbf{W}_i$ and $\mathbf{W}$ can be well protected during different phases of PFRL.

- In the local gradients encryption phase, all elements are encrypted with the public key $PK = N$, and a local gradient $\triangle \mathbf{W}_j$ is transformed to $C(\triangle \mathbf{W}_j)$ by its owner via computing $C(w_{ij}^k) = g^{w_{ij}^k}(r_{ij}^k)^N \bmod N^2$, where $j = 1, \cdots, m$ and $k = 1, \cdots, t$. Note that N is the public key of paillier cryptosystem with threshold decryption, and the corresponding secret key SK is splitted into n distributed secret keys $sk_{ED_1}, \ldots, sk_{ED_n}$ for parties. Since a sole distributed key sk cannot retrieve the ciphertext $C(w_{ij}^k)$, therefore, it is impossible for a individual ED_j to decrypt the $C(\triangle \mathbf{W}_j)$. Thus, the privacy of $\triangle \mathbf{W}_i$ can be well protected in this phase.
- In the federated training phase, CS aggregates the encrypted gradients of $\{\triangle \mathbf{W}_j\}_{j \in [1, \cdots, m]}$ with the homomorphic characteristic of paillier cryptosystem to obtain the encrypted global model parameters. In this process, only all EDs partially decrypt the $C(\triangle \mathbf{W}_j)$, thus, it is impossible for the ED' to obtain the original data of $\triangle \mathbf{W}_j$. In addition, due to all operations in CS are over ciphertext, CS finally obtain the encrypted global model parameters $C(\mathbf{W})$, which can only be decrypted by EDs. Therefore, the confidentiality of $\mathbf{W}$ is guaranteed.
- In the parameter updating phase, all EDs decrypt the $C(\mathbf{W})$ distributedly, and each ED_j shares its partially decryption result $C(\mathbf{W})^{ED_j}$. Meanwhile, $C(\mathbf{W})$ can only be retrieved while the number of EDs participating in the decryption is greater the threshold, thus, it is impossible for an individual $ED_j \in \mathbf{ED}$s to decrypt the final global model than other EDs, which guarantees that all EDs can obtain the final global model.

5   Performance Evaluation

In this section, we implement PFRL and apply it to robot control, and evaluate its integration performance.

5.1   Evaluation Environment

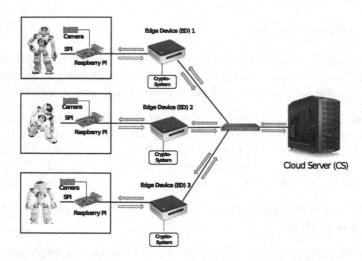

Fig. 3. Our experiment configuration with multiple robots, multiple edge devices, and one *CS* (Cloud Server).

In order to verify the effectiveness of the system, we set up an experimental system for controlling real robots as shown in Fig. 3. In the system, there are three *EDs* (Edge Devices) and one *CS* (Cloud Server), and each *ED* is connected with its robot. Each robot is installed with an external camera that provides status information about the robot. The Raspberry Pi 3 Model B connects to robot and a *ED* through a SPI (Serial Peripheral Interface). Raspberry Pi gets the actions that need to be performed from the reinforcement learning agent in *ED* and eventually sends it to the robot. Also, it takes observed robot's status through a camera, and sends them to the reinforcement learning agent in *ED*. Each *ED* contains an crypto-system that implements the threshold Paillier algorithm in JAVA. There is also a switch for the connection between the *EDs* and *CS*. For the communication among the *EDs*, and the *CS*, the MQTT protocol is used.

CS and *EDs* are powered by 2.2 GHz six-core processor, 8 GB RAM and Ubuntu 16.04 LTS, and are connected via an 802.11G WLAN. In Paillier Cryptosystem, the bit-length of public key N is set to 1024. The reinforcement learning agent in *ED* implements the Actor-Critic PPO algorithm using Python 3.6 and PyTorch 1.2. The actor and critic models use a multi-layer perceptron with three hidden layers and two separate output layers. The two models share three hidden layers, each containing 128 neurons. For the actor model, the first output layer produces nine values (i.e., nine action types) that add up to 1. For the critic model, the second output layer produces a single value that evaluates the action chosen by the actor model. Also, we use the hyper-parameters of the Actor-Critic PPO which Clipping parameter is 0.9, model optimization is Adam optimizer, GAE parameter is 0.99, Actor and Critic model's learning rates are 0.001, trajectory memory size is 400 and batch size is 128.

5.2 Effect Evaluation

In order to verify the effectiveness of PFRL, we used three OpenAI Gym's MoJoCo robot simulators simultaneously to simulate three completely independent robots. Each MoJoCo's 2-D simulator is actually a video game that controls a three-jointed robotic arm to a specific location. The robotic arm consists of four links and three joints, whose configurations are consistent to the specifications of a Baxter arm, including joints constraints. The game player observes the arm through an external camera placed directly aside it with a horizontal point of view, and sends specific commands to the individual joints "S1", "E1" and "W1" to control the robotic arm. So the simulator outputs the raw pixel image representing the state of the arm and has nine options for action, i.e., three actions for each joint: joint angle increasing, decreasing and hold. The joint angle increasing/decreasing step is constant at 0.02 rad. At the beginning of each round, joints "S1", "E1" and "W1" will be set to a certain initial pose, such as $[0.0, 0.0, 0.0]$ rad; and the target will be randomly selected. In the game, the player is rewarded every time they perform an action. The reward of each action is determined according to the distance change between the end-effector and the target. If the distance gets closer, the reward function returns 1; if gets further, returns -1; otherwise returns 0. If the sum of the latest three rewards is smaller than -1, the game terminates.

Figure 4 shows the effectiveness of the proposed PFRL for the experimental system. For each of the three EDs (Edge Devices), the blue line in Fig. 4 shows the change of the weighted moving average scores from the last 10 rounds when each ED performs the learning process individually, while the golden line in Fig. 4 shows the change of the ones when the proposed scheme is applied. As known in the figure, at about 300 episodes, the learning process of all EDs is completed when the proposed scheme is applied. However, without the proposed scheme, the learning process of ED_1 and ED_2 are completed at about 820 episodes and the one of ED_3 is completed at 570 episodes. From the figure, it can be seen that the learning speed becomes much higher and the variation in learning time for each robot is also reduced when the proposed scheme is applied. While we also found that the performance increases as the number of EDs increases from 1 to 8 in the experimental system. Therefore, with PFRL, the quality of online robotic manipulation can be greatly improved.

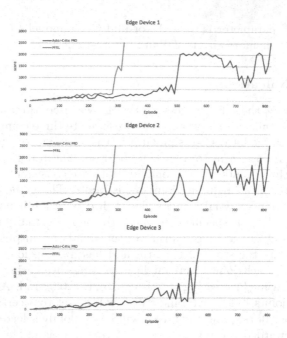

Fig. 4. Effectiveness of the proposed federated reinforcement learning scheme.

6   Conclusion

In this paper, we proposed a novel privacy-preserving federated deep reinforcement learning scheme, called PFRL. Based on paillier cryptosystem with threshold decryption, multiple edge devices can securely learn a more accurate global model with their local model gradients in the assistance of cloud, meanwhile, the confidentiality of the final global model parameters can be ensured. Specifically, before being sent to the cloud, all of the local model gradients are encrypted by their owner, and calculated without decryption during the federated learning process. Therefore, edge devices cannot obtain each other's private data, and cloud servers cannot achieve any private information of edge devices, as well as the final global model. In addition to confidentiality, we provide auditability by addressing the issue that malicious edge devices may disrupt the federated training process. In particular, we integrate the tool of non-interactive zero-knowledge proof to provide auditability of the federated training process. Detailed security analysis shows its security strength and privacy-preserving ability, and extensive experiments were conducted to demonstrate its efficiency.

References

1. Kober, J., Bagnell, J.A., Peters, J.: Reinforcement learning in robotics: a survey. Int. J. Robot. Res. **32**(11), 1238–1274 (2013)

2. Deisenroth, M.P., Neumann, G., Peters, J.: A survey on policy search for robotics. Found. Trends Robot. **2**(1–2), 1–142 (2013)
3. Kober, J., Peters, J.R.: Policy search for motor primitives in robotics. Mach. Learn. **84**, 171–203 (2009)
4. McMahan, H.B., Moore, E., Ramage, D., Hampson, S., Arcas, B.A.: Communication-efficient learning of deep networks from decentralized data. In Proceedings of the 20th International Conference on Artificial Intelligence and Statistics, pp. 1273–1282. AISTATS (2017)
5. Son, C., Ristenpart, T., Shmatikov, V.: Machine learning models that remember too much. In Proceedings of the 2017 ACM SIGSAC Conference on Computer and Communications Security, pp. 587–601, ACM (2017)
6. Melis, L., Song, C., De Cristofaro, E., and Shmatikov, V.: Inference attacks against collaborative learning. arXiv preprint arXiv:1805.04049 (2018)
7. Hitaj, B., Ateniese, G., Perez-Cruz, F.: Deep models under the gan: information leakage from collaborative deep learning. In: Proceedings of the 2017 ACM SIGSAC Conference on Computer and Communications Security, pp. 603–618. ACM (2017)
8. Shokri, R., Shmatikov, V.: Privacy-preserving deep learning. In: Allerton Conference on Communication, Control, and Computing, pp. 909–910 (2015)
9. Bagdasaryan, E., Veit, A., Hua, Y., Estrin, D., Shmatikov, V.: How to backdoor federated learning. arXiv preprint arXiv:1807.00459 (2018)
10. Schoenmakers, B., Veeningen, M.: Universally verifiable multiparty computation from threshold homomorphic crypto-systems. In: International Conference on Applied Cryptography and Network Security, pp. 3–22. Springer (2015)
11. Paillier, P.: Public-key crypto-systems based on composite degree residuosity classes. In: Advances in Cryptology - EUROCRYPT 1999, International Conference on the Theory and Application of Cryptographic Techniques, pp. 223–238 (1999)
12. Mnih, V., et al.: Human-level control through deep reinforcement learning. Nature **518**(7540), 529–533 (2015)
13. Lillicrap, T.P., et al.: Continuous control with deep reinforcement learning. arXiv preprint arXiv:1509.02971 (2015)

HALNet: A Hybrid Deep Learning Model for Encrypted C&C Malware Traffic Detection

Ruiyuan Li[1]🆔, Zehui Song[1], Wei Xie[1], Chengwei Zhang[1,2](✉)🆔,
Guohui Zhong[1], and Xiaobing Pei[1]

[1] Huazhong University of Science and Technology, Wuhan, China
{ruiyuanli,zehuisong,weixie,zhangcw,zhonggh,xiaobingp}@hust.edu.cn
[2] Hubei Key Laboratory of Smart Internet Technology,
Huazhong University of Science and Technology, Wuhan, China

Abstract. Command and Control (C&C) malwares are particularly difficult to be detected with traditional technologies due to their explorations of multi-stage attack and encryption technology. Though Artificial Intelligence (AI) methods have shown great potential in malicious attack detection, it is difficult for C&C malwares to collect network traffic covering whole attack commands. The AI model trained with partial attack traffic needs excellent generalizability to detect the uncovered traffic. Our paper firstly analyzes the attacking progress of C&C malwares and finds a suitable way to learn the representation of C&C malicious traffic. Then we propose a hybrid Deep Learning (DL) model named HALNet with better generalizability. HALNet adopts the multi-head attention mechanism and a skip-LSTM structure to learn the two-level representation of byte feature and multi-temporal feature. Experiments show that HALNet can achieve good performance as the previous works on the public traffic dataset CICIDS2017. To better evaluate the generalizability of different models, we collect the real traffic generated by C&C malwares and construct a new malicious traffic dataset named CCE2021. With further experiments on CCE2021, HALNet can result the highest 97.95% detection accuracy on CCE-II among all the models. The overall results prove that, under approximate detection performance, HALNet has the better generalizability than the other models.

Keywords: HALNet · Deep learning · Intrusion detection · Multi-temporal feature · Encrypted C&C Malware traffic

1   Introduction

Network devices keep increasing at present and a growing number of information for individuals, companies and governments is spreading around the world.

R. Li and Z. Song—contributed equally to this work. This work was supported by the National Key Research and Development Program of China (No. 2018YFB0805004).

M. Yang et al. (Eds.): NSS 2021, LNCS 13041, pp. 326–339, 2021.
https://doi.org/10.1007/978-3-030-92708-0_21

The economic value in Internet information expanded rapidly. Meanwhile, the hacking activities occurred more frequently. The malware intrusion, attempting to access the unauthorized resources in the network [9], has threatened people's information privacy seriously and caused huge economic losses. For example, the ASEAN (Association of Southeast Asian Nations) region lost up to 19 billion dollars in a hypothetical global ransomware attack according to the report of Malwarebytes LABS in 2020.

Compared with the detection methods based on host logs, traditional malware traffic detection methods rely on the analysis of traffic packet message. However, the encryption technology has been widely used gradually, which makes the matching characters implicit and brings great difficulties to matching rules designing. Reporting from Watchguard, more than 32 million malware variants and 1.7 million cyber attacks were detected by about 44,000 vendor security devices throughout the world in the first quarter of 2020.

The Command and Control (C&C) malwares, which adopt not only encryption technology but also the multi-stage attack approach, are much harder to be detected by traditional analysis methods due to the fact that they mainly design matching rules for one single packet. Due to the tremendous breakthroughs of Deep Learning in the field of Computer Vision (CV) and Natural Language Process (NLP), lots of researchers ignore the specific characteristics of traffic and intuitively convert traffic into images [16] or texts to treat the malicious traffic detection as common classification tasks. Though it can obtain excellent performances in some datasets, it doesn't consider the applicability of the model. The high redundancy of public datasets have difficulties in dividing training sets and test sets. The generalizability of models is hard to be evaluated because of the high correlation between the training data and testing data.

In this paper, we analyze the structure of the C&C traffic and summarize the potential feature representations. We try to extract features from two levels of bytes and packets. The byte feature extractor and multi-temporal feature extractor are integrated in the proposed model HALNet. We use t-SNE to visualize the representation of different stages of HALNet in Fig. 1. The main contributions of our paper are listed as follows:

- We design an end-to-end DL model named HALNet on raw data of network traffic, which learns representations in both bytes and packets levels. HALNet has precise classification ability and desirable generalizability.
- To evaluate the generalizability of HALNet, we build a malicious traffic dataset named CCE2021 containing the training set CCE-I and the test set CCE-II with reasonable methods of data division.
- A series of comparative experiments have been conducted to evaluate the performance of HALNet, other relative DL models and the traditional intrusion detection system (IDS, e.g., Suricata).

The remainder of this paper is organized as follows: Sect. 2 introduces the related work on anomaly detection. Section 3 analyzes the features extracted from the malicious network traffic. Section 4 presents the hybrid model HALNet and explains the components in detail. Section 5 illustrates the experiment results compared with the DL models and traditional methods. Finally, conclusions are drawn in Sect. 6.

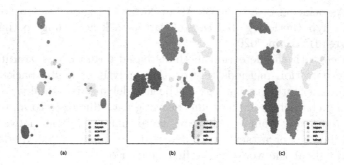

Fig. 1. The Visualization results of traffic distribution in CCE2021 during the inference process through t-SNE. (a) Illustration of the distribution for original bytes. (b) Illustration of the distribution of the Byte Feature Extractor's output in HALNet. (c) Illustration of the distribution of the output after the Multi-temporal Feature Extractor in HALNet.

2   Related Work

Some well-known intrusion detection systems, such as Zeek, Suricata, can report the malware attacks accurately while their rules are strictly designed or configured. The methods based on rules designing are effective on the traditional traffic detection and protection. Whereas for the growing encrypted attacking traffic, these methods perform poorly and unpredictably [10].

DL algorithms can accelerate the detection of new malwares and save the costs for time and professional resources. DL algorithms for CV or NLP were exploited to transform the network traffic to pictures or statements, then the classic models were used to detect and categorize the malicious network traffic. Wang [16] processed the traffic bytes into a 28 * 28 grayscale image and used a CNN2D architecture similar to LeNet-5. They achieved 98.52% accuracy for the traffic classifications with their proposed dataset USTC-TFC2016. GAN [3] has been used to visualize the traffic and achieved around 95.74% average accuracy in the traffic classification. Torres and his colleagues in [11] transformed the network traffic into a time-series sequence and used the RNN model to detect the botnet behavior.

Fig. 2. The hierarchical structure with two levels of bytes and packets.

The network traffic is a hierarchical structure and it has two levels of bytes and packets as shown in Fig. 2. Inspired by two-stage hierarchical structures, the hybrid models began to use the unspecific structure for the network intrusion. Manuel Lopez-martin et al. [5] presented the first application of the RNN and CNN models to a Network Traffic Classifier (NTC) problem with six features extracted from the packet heads. HAST-II [15] used CNN1D and LSTM to extract the byte features and temporal features separately. The auto-encoder has been introduced in [14] for feature expression and extraction. An attention-based Bi-LSTM model, proposed by Yuqi et al. [17], has presented a better way for the anomalous http traffic detection.

For the C&C malwares traffic detection assignment, we expect to learn a distinct representation of the single packet and utilize the temporal relationships among the regular interactive packets in the C&C malwares attack progress. We choose the hybrid structure to extract features from two levels of bytes and packets.

3   Analysis of C&C Malware Traffic Feature

3.1   Introduction of C&C Malware

Table 1. The cyber kill chain

Stage	Category	Description
1	Reconnaissance	Research targets and attempts to identify vulnerabilities
2	Weaponization	Create remote access and tailore to vulnerabilities
3	Delivery	Transmit weapon to target via e-mail attachments, etc
4	Exploitation	Take action on target network to exploit vulnerability
5	Installation	Malware weapon installs access point usable
6	Command and Control (C& C)	Enable intruders to have "hands on the keyboard" persistent access to targets
7	Actions on objective	Take action to achieve goals, such as data exfiltration, data destruction

Malwares can be divided into seven categories according to the attack stage in Cyber Kill Chain [2] shown in Table 1. The C&C malwares locate at the back end of the attack chain with powerful attack tools. The attacking process has complicated multi-stage interactions between the client and server, which is a huge challenge for the rule-based detection methods, E.g., Suricata rule sets.

These traditional methods mainly design the specific match-character rules of the single packet thus they perform poorly for the attacks composed by a series of related malicious packets. Whereas the DL models learn the latent representation of the C&C malwares' attack traffic and classify traffic based on extracted features. We analyze of some C&C malwares, such as Dewdrop and Nopen, to support our design of HALNet and record our analysis of multi-temporal feature and byte feature of C&C malware traffic in the following sections.

3.2 Analysis of Multi-temporal Feature

Different protocols provide distinct network communication modes and we find that most C&C malwares utilize Transmission Control Protocol (TCP) to conduct attacks. The link is established through sending packets alternately by hosts. Similarly, the attack process of C&C malwares has the similar stage. We divide the attack of C&C malwares into the attack establishment process and the attack execution process int Fig. 3.

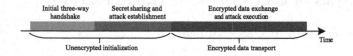

Fig. 3. A scheme of encrypted attack process.

We visualize the specific behaviours of C&C malware in Fig. 4(a). The interacting behaviours can be viewed as a kind of temporal sequence [13]. Two adjacent packets constitute an information exchange between the client and server. Several groups like this compose the global temporal sequence described as 4(b). Two packets separated by the middle one are from the same host and they form a regular pattern. The upstream and downstream traffic in this stage respectively stand for the information pattern of the client and server. They are another kind of temporal relationship and described as 4(c) and (d). Multiple combinations of the packets constitute the multi-temporal feature and benefit to learning the full temporal representation.

Once the attack has been established, the C&C malwares control and damage the target hosts through sending attack commands hidden in the normal packets' payload. Due to the encryption technology, the message payload is incomprehensible. This stage is unconspicuous and less valuable. Therefore, we retain more packets of the attack establishment process and discard the packets in the attack execution process.

3.3 Analysis of Byte Feature

The distinct feature of bytes makes the multi-temporal feature more effective. A packet is composed of the packet header and payload. The encryption communication uses encryption algorithms to protect the message in payload and causes the character implicit. However, the message in packet header is closely related to the the design of the malware and is the presentation of the communication protocol.

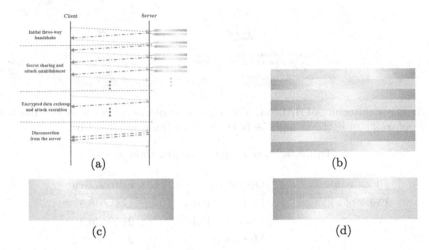

Fig. 4. (a) The specific behaviors of the client and server in the C&C attack process. (b) The description of global temporal sequence of whole traffic. (c) The description of temporal sequence of upstream traffic. (d) The description of temporal sequence of downstream traffic.

The C&C malwares use their own private protocols or tamper with the Internet Protocol to execute their attacks. In the packet header, every frame symbolizes the specific information. The protocol controls the behaviours in the communication through setting the specific bytes. Therefore, the relationship among bytes can symbolize the used protocol and the communication software. In addition, the temporal feature relies on the pattern among byte representation of single packet. We are eager to learn a distinct representation of bytes by adjusting the distribution of attention. Paying more attention into the valuable and generic features and reducing the weight of specific command-related features contribute to the improvement of generalizability.

4 Design of HALNet

Through the analysis of C&C malware traffic feature, we have designed HALNet, an end-to-end hybrid model, which can extract the byte feature and multi-temporal feature adequately. HALNet contains a byte feature extractor and a multi-temporal feature extractor sequentially. The 1D convolution operation and the multi-head attention mechanism are used in the byte feature extractor and the multi-temporal feature extractor including parallel Bi-LSTM and Skip-LSTM structures. The hybrid HALNet architecture is shown in Fig. 5 and the specific parameters are summarized in Table 2.

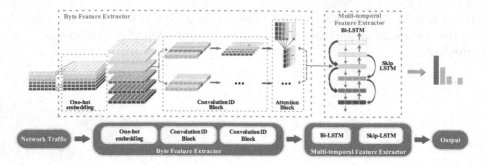

Fig. 5. The architecture of HALNet. The upper part of this figure shows the dimension change of traffic in HALNet and the bottom shows the basic structures.

Table 2. Basic structures and parameters

Block name	Operation	Filters/Neurons
Conv block	Conv1D+ReLU	$128 \times [8,6]$
	Conv1D+ReLU	$256 \times [6,4]$
	Maxpool1D	2
	FC	384
Attention block	Multi-head attention	/
	FC+ReLU	512
	Globalmaxpool1D	/
Multi-temporal block	Bi-LSTM+skip-LSTM	$128 + 2 \times 128$
Classify Block	FC+Softmax	6

4.1 Byte Feature Extractor

We first convert bytes into word vectors as the word embedding approaches by NLP. We choose the one-hot embedding method after comparing with the trainable encoding methods. The one-hot encoding performs better because the bytes in packets are relatively independent in semantics and there are fewer parameters to be trained. Then a 1D convolution block is used to capture the dependency between neighbor bytes similar like Raff et al. [8]. These bytes are treated as the same in the preliminary feature extraction, which means no tendency to concentrate on the more valuable features for model. The attention mechanism [12] is applied to our model to adjust the weight of features. The essence of the attention mechanism can be described as a mapping from a *query* (Q) to a series of *key* (K)-*value* (V) pairs, which formulated as follows:

$$attention(Q_i, K, V) = \sum_j \frac{\exp(\text{score}(Q_i, K_j))}{\sum_j \exp(\text{score}(Q_i, K_j))} V_j. \tag{1}$$

The *score* function here has different types and we describe some forms used commonly in following:

$$\text{score}(Q_i, K_j) = \begin{cases} Q_i^T K_j, & \text{dot}, \\ Q_i^T W_a K_j, & \text{general}, \\ v_a^T \tanh(W_a[Q_i; K_j]), & \text{concat}, \end{cases} \quad (2)$$

where the corner mark i and j symbolize the position in the feature vector sequence. W_a and v_a are the linear weight matrices. In numerous variants of attention structures, the self attention mechanism is more popular due to its simple structure and great improvement on the basis. It uses the same feature matrix to get Q, K, V through performing different linear transformations.

The multi-head attention conducts multiple attention calculations with unshared parameters and concatenate them together. It has a simple architecture and it contributes to the classification of categories with high similarities.

$$head_m = attention(Q^m, K^m, V^m), \quad (3)$$

$$multihead = concat(head_1, head_2, ..., head_h)W^O, \quad (4)$$

where m is the order of the number of heads. Though the attention mechanism improves the performance, it inevitably loses the original relative position information. To use the sequence's order, we must inject some position information to the input of attention architecture by adding position encodings. In our work, we use sine and cosine functions of different frequencies:

$$PE_{(pos,2i)} = sin(pos/10000^{2i/d_f}), \quad (5)$$

$$PE_{(pos,2i+1)} = cos(pos/10000^{2i/d_f}). \quad (6)$$

Here *pos* presents the position in the sequence and i is the place in the feature vector. d_f means the dimension of the feature vector.

We design an extractor to represent the byte feature with the advantages of the attention mechanism. It first embeds the byte as one-hot. Then the extractor uses two convolutional blocks to learn the dependency between the neighbor bytes. The attention block follows each convolutional block to adjust the feature distribution. Finally, the output is concatenated and send into multi-temporal blocks.

4.2 Multi-temporal Feature Extractor

For the temporal sequence classification, the recurrent neural layer, such as LSTM [1], is commonly used and can mitigate the problem of long-term dependence by three gate structures. Moreover, this structure has the ability to memorize the valuable information in past. The Bi-LSTM variants can not only keep contact with the previous information but also be able to perceive the future message.

The recurrent-skip component [4], based on the traditional LSTM units, is designed to extend the time span and simplify the optimization process simultaneously. It inherits the advantage of memorizing dependencies and performs better than the original form. It also has the acute discernment of the periodic pattern due to its specific structure, which adds skip-links to the current hidden cells and those in the same phase in adjacent periods. The updating process can be formulated as

$$f_t = \sigma(W_f \cdot [h_{t-p}, x_t] + b_f), \tag{7}$$

$$i_t = \tanh(W_i \cdot [h_{t-p}, x_t] + b_i), \tag{8}$$

$$c_t = \tanh(W_c \cdot [h_{t-p}, x_t] + b_c), \tag{9}$$

$$o_t = \sigma(W_o[h_{t-p}, x_t] + b_o), \tag{10}$$

$$h_t = o_t \cdot \tanh(C_t). \tag{11}$$

In detail, the forget gate determines the ratio of retaining the unit state c_{t-p} at the previous step as the current time c_t. The input gate controls the relationship between input x_t and unit state c_t at present and the output gate has the ability to adjust the influence of unit state c_t on output h_t. Here W is the weight matrix in each internal structure and b is the bias value. h_{t-p} stands for the hidden layer from previous p time steps and x_t is the current input of units.

For the temporal features of C&C malware traffic, we propose the upstream and downstream temporal sequence. They are composed by the neighboring packets sending by one host. We set p to 2 and then the skip-links are added to a series of packets separated by the middle one. It is equivalent to use the upstream or downstream traffic as input sequentially. The skip-LSTM structure can focus on only upstream or downstream traffic in a certain period. We utilize this skip structure to learn the partial temporal features to simplify the behaviors of C&C malware attack. A Bi-LSTM is used to extract the global temporal features and the whole structure is compatible with different protocols and malwares.

In all, we make use of the parallel blocks containing the Bi-LSTM and skip-LSTM structure to extract the complex multi-temporal feature. Finally, a simple linear classifier is used at the end of the model.

4.3   The Architecture of HALNet

In this section, we describe the whole architecture of our proposed hybrid DL model HALNet. We first embed the byte as one-hot to map a single value to a feature vector. Two parallel convolutional blocks are set to extract bytes relations preliminarily because the Conv1D has the ability to learn the dependencies between bytes. The Attention block with the multi-head attention mechanism follows each convolutional block to adjust the attention distribution. The output of attention blocks is concatenated and then sends into the multi-temporal block, which contains Bi-LSTM to learn the global temporal features and skip-LSTM to extract the partial temporal feature. Finally, simple Dense layers and the softmax operation are used to classify the traffic. The diversity of feature representation improves HALNet's generalizability.

5   Experiments

5.1   Dataset and Data Preprocessing

The datasets selection and the approach of preprocessing have great influence on the models' performance. Public datasets, such as KDD and CICIDS2017 [7], are often used to train models and evaluate the performance of them. However, they can't satisfy all the needs for the following drawbacks:

1. Redundant. Similar traffic are collected into dataset. They are generated by executing scripts with repeated commands in a fixed environment, which makes models overfit easily and have an unreal excellent performance.
2. Incomplete. On one hand, the traffic in datasets always couldn't cover all attack types. On the other hand, for a particular malware, it couldn't contain its whole attack methods and commands.
3. Unavailable. Due to the high coupling of traffic characteristics and network environment, it is difficult for public datasets to be used in solving reality.

To better evaluate the desirable generalizability for the proposed DL model, we built our own dataset, named CCE2021, to overcome the drawbacks of public datasets. We selected two C&C malwares, dewdrop and nopen, which are used internally by the NSA organization to conduct intrusion. Both of them involve multiple stages with encrypted traffic. Their execution processes are extremely similar to two normal services, ssh and telnet. Therefore these malwares could successfully cheat the rule-based IDS. We also found that nopen is similar with another encrypted intrusion tool scanner, so their traffic detection would be confused and detected falsely. CCE2021 dataset is constructed with traffic generated by this five tools (dewdrop, nopen, ssh, telnet and scanner) to evaluate the performance with HALNet and other models.

We built two totally different commands sets, one of which is executed to collect the training set called CCE-I and the other is used to constitute the testing set CCE-II. This classification method can reduce the data similarity between the training and testing sets and evaluate the performance of the model on the testing set can effectively demonstrate the generalizability. We also captured the real communication traffic on gateway as the benign part. We recorded the number and percentage of each category of traffic in the Table 3.

For the preprocessing operation detail, we divided the traffic into sessions according to five-tuple information first and then eliminate some deviations, such as the IP address, port numbers, which may lead to overfitting. Each session is processed into a $m \times n$ matrix: m represents m packets intercepted from per session and n stands for n bytes in each packet. We also use sliding windows to cut off longer sessions for data enhancement.

Table 3. The number of each category in CCE-I and CCE-II

Category	CCE-I		CCE-II	
	Number	Percentage	Number	Percentage
Normal	10000	21.83%	1500	13.70%
Dewdrop	10242	22.35%	3161	28.87%
Nopen	6813	14.87%	1971	18.00%
Scanner	10719	23.39%	2269	20.72%
SSH	3546	7.74%	1011	9.23%
Telnet	4500	9.82%	1038	9.48%
Total	45820	100%	10950	100%

5.2 Performance Evaluation

Suricata, the traditional IDS, was used to detect the malicious traffic in CCE2021 first. We visually summarized the results in Fig. 6. Suricata results are extremely terrible and only half of the dewdrop traffic triggers the alert. The proportion of scanner detected is just 21%. The worst is nopen and it can't be detected at all. But the normal types, ssh and telnet, have not been misdetected as malwares. In all, the traditional methods don't perform well in C&C malware traffic detection, even for the normal encrypted malware scanner.

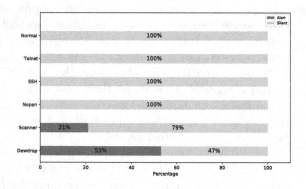

Fig. 6. The performance of Suricata. For each category, the bars indicate the proportion of traffic that triggered alarms and not respectively.

We conducted comparative experiments on the CICIDS2017 dataset with different models to compare the performance on general traffic classification tasks and record the results in the Table 4.

We can find that HALNet has the best performance with 99.95% in accuracy, 98.96% in recall, 99.96% in precision and 99.45% in f1-score. The HAST-II also has similar good results on CICIDS2017. Though Wang's has a precision of

Table 4. Results between HALNet and other models on CICIDS2017

Model	Accuracy (%)	Recall (%)	Precision (%)	F1-score (%)
G.Marín's [6]	96.93	69.99	92.37	79.64
Wang's [16]	99.69	92.65	99.78	95.68
HAST-II [15]	99.39	99.02	99.56	99.28
HALNet	**99.95**	**98.96**	**99.96**	**99.45**

99.69%, it has only 92.65% in recall. The G. Marín's scores worst in the comparitive models. For an insightful analysis, the hybrid models are generally superior to CNN and RNN models.

The experimental results has verified the superiority of HALNet in common traffic classification assignments. Furthermore, we conducted experiments on CCE2021 to prove the existence and validity of the multi-temporal feature. We fixed the structure of byte feature extractor and conducted comparative experiments on different temporal feature extractors. The line chart in Fig. 7 illustrates our multi-temporal feature extractor has the obvious advantage. The order of performance from good to bad is our extractor, LSTM, Bi-LSTM and FC.

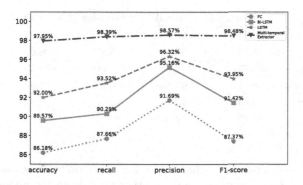

Fig. 7. The results of different temporal feature extracting approaches on CCE-II

Finally, we compared HALNet with other models on CCE2021 and record the results in Table 5. HALNet has excellent scores on all evaluate indexes at around 99.4% in CCE-I and 98.0% in CCE-II. Though the HAST-II has pretty good results on CCE-I, it drops significantly on CCE-II. This means that HAST-II only fits the training set while it doesn't have enough generalizability for the data distribution slightly different from training data. The performances of Wang's on CCE-I and CCE-II are almost the same while they only have scores around 90%. The G.Marín's model is really far behind. We can conclude that HALNet shows the best classification ability and generalizability among all the models.

Table 5. Results between HALNet and others on CCE2021

Model	Dataset	Accuracy (%)	Recall (%)	Precision (%)	F1-score (%)
G.Marín's	CCE-I	72.92	80.39	82.18	70.54
	CCE-II	67.38	65.51	54.94	55.12
Wang's	CCE-I	89.37	90.30	92.37	90.80
	CCE-II	89.89	91.64	91.05	90.38
HAST-IDS	CCE-I	99.92	99.89	99.91	99.90
	CCE-II	89.89	90.62	95.38	91.68
HALNet	**CCE-I**	**99.41**	**99.36**	**99.57**	**99.47**
	CCE-II	**97.95**	**98.39**	**98.57**	**98.48**

We summerized the statistical results of each category in Table 6. Though the tools covered in CCE2021, except telnet, are all using encrypted communications and some of them have high similarities, HALNet has excellent detection effect in all categories with over 98% in accuracy. The other scores are also higher than 95%. This means HALNet can classify the traffic accurately, which is generated by commands different from the training set.

Table 6. The each category results of HALNet on CCE-II

Category	Accuracy (%)	Recall (%)	Precision (%)	F1-score (%)
Normal	99.95	99.93	99.73	99.83
Dewdrop	98.03	97.43	95.83	96.62
Nopen	99.73	98.52	100.00	99.25
Scanner	98.31	95.46	96.39	95.92
SSH	99.89	99.70	99.10	99.40
Telnet	99.97	99.90	99.80	99.85

In all, HALNet is not only effective for the common traffic classification tasks on CICIDS2017, but also superior than other models on the generalizability for the C&C encrypted traffic detection.

6   Conclusion

In this paper, we made an intensive study on the C&C malware attacks and proposed the multi-temporal feature of traffic. We designed HALNet based on our analysis. The multi-head attention mechanism is used to extract the byte feature and we used the skip-LSTM structure to extract the multi-temporal feature among packets for classification. In addition, we summarized the drawbacks of the existing public datasets and then built a C&C malicious traffic dataset CCE2021. We also conducted a series of experiments to evaluate the generalizability of HALNet and the experimental results demonstrate that HALNet is effective in the traffic detection and shows better performance in model generalization than the other methods.

References

1. Hochreiter, S., Schmidhuber, J.: Long short-term memory. Neural Comput. **9**(8), 1735–1780 (1997)
2. Hutchins, E.M., Cloppert, M.J., Amin, R.M., et al.: Intelligence-driven computer network defense informed by analysis of adversary campaigns and intrusion kill chains. Lead. Issues Inf. Warf. Secur. Res. **1**(1), 80 (2011)
3. Kim, J.Y., Bu, S.J., Cho, S.B.: Zero-day malware detection using transferred generative adversarial networks based on deep autoencoders. Inf. Sci. **460**, 83–102 (2018)
4. Lai, G., Chang, W.C., Yang, Y., Liu, H.: Modeling long-and short-term temporal patterns with deep neural networks. In: The 41st International ACM SIGIR Conference on Research and Development in Information Retrieval. pp. 95–104 (2018)
5. Lopez-Martin, M., Carro, B., Sanchez-Esguevillas, A., Lloret, J.: Network traffic classifier with convolutional and recurrent neural networks for internet of things. IEEE Access **5**, 18042–18050 (2017)
6. Marín, G., Casas, P., Capdehourat, G.: Deep in the dark-deep learning-based malware traffic detection without expert knowledge. In: 2019 IEEE Security and Privacy Workshops (SPW), pp. 36–42. IEEE (2019)
7. Panigrahi, R., Borah, S.: A detailed analysis of CICIDS2017 dataset for designing intrusion detection systems. Int. J. Eng. Technol. **7**(3.24), 479–482 (2018)
8. Raff, E., Barker, J., Sylvester, J., Brandon, R., Catanzaro, B., Nicholas, C.: Malware detection by eating a whole exe. arXiv preprint arXiv:1710.09435 (2017)
9. Selvakumar, B., Muneeswaran, K.: Firefly algorithm based feature selection for network intrusion detection. Comput. Secur. **81**, 148–155 (2019)
10. Sherry, J., Lan, C., Popa, R.A., Ratnasamy, S.: BlindBox: deep packet inspection over encrypted traffic. In: Proceedings of the 2015 ACM Conference on Special Interest Group on Data Communication, pp. 213–226 (2015)
11. Torres, P., Catania, C., Garcia, S., Garino, C.G.: An analysis of recurrent neural networks for botnet detection behavior. In: 2016 IEEE Biennial Congress of Argentina (ARGENCON), pp. 1–6 (2016)
12. Vaswani, A., et al.: Attention is all you need. In: Advances in Neural Information Processing Systems, pp. 5998–6008 (2017)
13. Velan, P., Čermák, M., Čeleda, P., Drašar, M.: A survey of methods for encrypted traffic classification and analysis. Int. J. Netw. Manage. **25**(5), 355–374 (2015)
14. Wang, Q., et al.: Adversary resistant deep neural networks with an application to malware detection. In: Proceedings of the 23rd ACM SIGKDD International Conference on Knowledge Discovery and Data Mining, pp. 1145–1153 (2017)
15. Wang, W., et al.: Hast-ids: Learning hierarchical spatial-temporal features using deep neural networks to improve intrusion detection. IEEE Access **6**, 1792–1806 (2017)
16. Wang, W., Zhu, M., Zeng, X., Ye, X., Sheng, Y.: Malware traffic classification using convolutional neural network for representation learning. In: 2017 International Conference on Information Networking (ICOIN), pp. 712–717 (2017)
17. Yu, Y., Liu, G., Yan, H., Li, H., Guan, H.: Attention-based Bi-LSTM model for anomalous http traffic detection. In: 2018 15th International Conference on Service Systems and Service Management (ICSSSM), pp. 1–6. IEEE (2018)

Tracing Software Exploitation

Ayman Youssef[✉], Mohamed Abdelrazek, Chandan Karmakar,
and Zubair Baig

Deakin University, Geelong, Australia
ayman.youssef@research.deakin.edu.au,
{mohamed.abdelrazek,karmakar,zubair.baig}@deakin.edu.au

Abstract. Current exploit detection techniques are designed based on expert observations, manual analysis, and heuristic-like techniques. Because of the manual process for creating such defences, they are usually limited in the number of exploit techniques that can be detected. Machine Learning-based techniques offer greater promise to detect zero-day exploits. Current research in the use of machine learning for unknown attack detection is limited to intrusion detection and malware analysis, limited research is available for the detection of exploits targeting zero-day vulnerabilities using machine learning methods. These limitations stem from the lack of extensive datasets that are tailored for the problem of software exploitation. In this paper, we introduce a method and toolset for creating exploit traces datasets. Our approach allows capturing full traces of benign software under exploitation and recording of the vulnerable threads within an application, providing a comprehensive view of program execution. We evaluated our method and tools on 13 unique and distinct applications and recorded their traces while they were under attack. Our approach was able to successfully trace 53% of the applications and was able to detect the exploit payloads in 71% of the applications that were successfully traced.

Keywords: Exploit · Trace collection · Zero-day · Dataset · Machine learning

1 Introduction

A recent report published by security firm FireEye™ [1], identified that during the period from 2018 to 2019, almost 58% of announced vulnerabilities were exploited as zero-day vulnerabilities. Furthermore, 42% of the announced vulnerabilities were exploited after a patch was issued. From that 42%, 12% were exploited within one week of patch issuance while 15% were exploited after one week of patch issuance but within one month of the issuance date. As per FireEye™, these are conservative estimates since they are based on the first recorded exploitation and not necessarily the actual first exploitation to occur.

As shown by the above reports, even with the presence of software patches, it takes time for the security operations engineers to patch vulnerable applications, and a need for an effective anti-exploitation solution is needed that does not rely on a signature-based approach but a more generic approach capable to detect zero-day exploits. Signature-based approaches require that an attack already occurred, was discovered,

© Springer Nature Switzerland AG 2021
M. Yang et al. (Eds.): NSS 2021, LNCS 13041, pp. 340–352, 2021.
https://doi.org/10.1007/978-3-030-92708-0_22

and analysed. Furthermore, talented experts are needed to scrutinize attack traces to identify the vulnerability and create a signature, a laborious and costly approach.

Most of the research focused on exploit detection currently present is based on observations noted by security and software experts [2, 3]. Different hypotheses are implemented to identify specific features of exploits, such as spatial characteristics of heap memory [4], or stack invariants [5]. However, these approaches are limited in scope and are relatively easy to circumvent [6].

Research that is based on machine learning (ML) is limited by the quality of available datasets. To expand on the topic of using ML for zero-day exploit detection there is a need for a large exploit-specific dataset. This paper introduces a method and toolset that thoroughly captures traces of software under exploitation. The proposed method for dataset creation will enable researchers to launch exploits against vulnerable software whilst simultaneously collecting traces of the vulnerable application under test (AUT) being exploited. Our approach of complete trace recording aims at providing a large variety of possible feature combinations to be used for experimentation with different ML algorithms. A sample trace is shown in Fig. 3.

The rest of this paper is organized as follows; Sect. 2 gives an overview of related work. Section 3 discusses the proposed method, Sect. 4 bpAnalyzer, and Sect. 5 dive into VAET. Section 6 discusses the evaluation experiments. Finally, Sect. 7 provides a conclusion and future work.

2 Related Work

Related work can be segmented into two sections. The first section is the IDS datasets. IDS datasets are considered the closest type of datasets to exploits, hence an overview of why they do not fully address exploit datasets problem is presented. The second section is previous ML techniques used to detect software exploits. To the best of our knowledge, no currently published research presents a method and/or tool for creating exploit traces datasets.

2.1 IDS Datasets

ADFA, short for Australian Defence Force Academy, present in [7] by Waqas et al. Presented two subsets of datasets. The first is the ADFA windows dataset (ADFA-WD) and the second is ADFA Stealth Attacks Addendum (ADFA-WD: SAA). Both are aimed at provided training datasets for training host intrusion detection systems that use ML-based techniques.

ADFA-WD contained traces that were created based on audit data recorded by the Windows OS from a group of 9 system DLLs. The traces were collected while exploiting 12 known vulnerabilities which covered several attack vectors including browser attacks, web-based vectors, and malware-based attachments. ADFA-Linux Dataset 12 (ADFA-LD12) [8] was built using Ubuntu Linux version 11.04. A vulnerability was present in two applications (TikiWiki and the PHP component of the Apache server). Traces were generated using Unix program audited and were filtered based on size, where any events outside the size range of 300 Bytes to 6 kB were rejected.

The DARPA dataset is composed of several datasets, DARPA 98 [9] and DARPA 99 [10]. The training subset was created throughout 7 weeks of network-based attacks along with background traffic. The list of attacks in DARPA 98 contains malware attacks, software exploits, and OS exploits targeting design vulnerabilities. The attacks used in the DARPA 99 included denial of service attacks, user-to-root attacks, remote-to-local attacks, probes, and data leakage attacks [11].

Other network-based datasets include the datasets produced by the Canadian Institute for Cybersecurity which are titled CSE-CIC-IDS2018 [12]. In CSE-CIC-IDS2018, 5 attack types were emulated (email delivered exploit, HTTP DoS, web service attacks, Heartbleed vulnerability attack). In [13], researchers focused on insider attacks through scenarios that did not trace memory related errors.

As shown in the above examples, the datasets contain a broad range of attacks, covering OS design flaws, denial of service attacks, and malware. However, software exploits were limited and do not provide a large enough dataset for applying ML techniques.

2.2   ML Approaches for Exploit Detection

In Elsabagh et al. [14], a framework called EigenROP was created to detect ROP attacks using anomaly detection. The evaluation was performed on 12 Linux applications. EigenROP achieved an overall accuracy of 81%. The best performance across all applications reached an 80% true positive rate (TPR) and 0.8% false-positive rate (FPR).

Differences between EigenROP and our work include, first, Elsabagh et al. captured intervals of the program, i.e., samples. We do not claim to know which microarchitecture (independent) features are of strong relevance beforehand, hence, we captured all traces within the vulnerable execution path of the AUT. Second, Elsabagh et al. assumed that control flow subversion had already occurred and focuses only on return-oriented ROP chains. In our work, we provide complete traces of the overflow attack as well as the ROP chain regardless of the type of ROP attack.

The second research was presented by Li et al. [15]. Lie et al. created ROPNN. ROPNN is a tool aimed at detecting ROP exploits using deep neural networks. ROPNN is deployed in the network in a fashion similar to Snort IDS [16]. ROPNN was trained on 5 Linux applications. The testing results provided detection rates between 98.1% to 99.3% and false-positive error rates between 0.01% to 0.05%.

Our work is different from the one presented in [15] in several aspects. First, our approach includes the complete exploit and not just the ROP gadgets, including the buffer overflow. Second, our approach will present a more holistic picture of the program context execution, including register values, memory regions, and opcodes. This is in contrast to [15] where only the opcodes were used for the evaluation. Third, our approach relies on the traces extracted directly from the memory and CPU, unlike in [15] which inspects network packets to identify ROP gadgets.

Guillermo et al. [17] used anomaly detection techniques to detect exploits against Android's mediaserver component. Guillermo et al.'s approach is focused only on one vulnerability, using multiple exploits to attack. In our approach, we focus on a specific category of exploits, buffer overflows, and ROP-based attacks (although the technique is expandable to include other techniques). Hence, we can generate traces for different vulnerabilities.

3 Method Overview

Our focus is on Windows-based exploits running on x86 based processors. Windows OS is the most prevalent OS with a global desktop market share greater than 70% [18]. While the x86-based Intel and AMD x86-based processors accounted for almost 100% of all desktop CPUs worldwide [19].

We focus on user space vulnerable applications only, excluding any kernel modules. OS kernel security has been enhanced during the past few years with increased research in vulnerability detection [20], new exploitation methods [21], and new defences [22]. The framework is composed of the AUT/exploit pair, a debugger, debugger extensions (bpAnalyzer and VAET), exploits, and the validation scripts.

The steps of our approach can be divided across the following phases:

1) Trace initialization: This phase includes downloading the AUT/exploit pair, installation of the AUT, validating the exploit, and finally identifying the payload consumption vector. For downloading of the AUT/exploit pair, we relied on exploit-db.com (EDB).

The next step we install the AUT and run the exploit. Finally, the payload consumption vector is identified to determine the type of breakpoint to be used. We categorize exploits as local and remote. We further categorize local exploits based on payload consumption vector, whether "bad user input" or "bad file" input or "bad configuration" file input.

2) Trace execution: We relied on well-defined breakpoints for starting the debugging process to enable the experiments to be repeated and verified by other researchers. The breakpoints are identified using the tool bpAnalyzer.

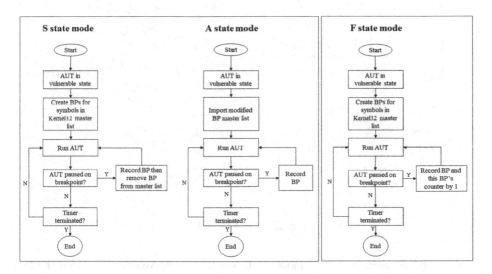

Fig. 1. bpAnalyzer workflow

Next step we execute the trace. First, the AUT is launched and put in a vulnerable position. For example, if a PDF reader is exploited by malicious PDFs, then the vulnerable position would be launching the PDF reader, clicking on the open file button, and selecting the malicious file (without opening it). Then the debugger is attached and VAET script is launched. After launching VAET, the exploit is launched. In our PDF reader example, the open file button is clicked.

3) Trace validation: This is the final stage. After the trace ends two trace files are created, one representing the control flow and the other changes in the memory content. These are then examined to verify if traces are successfully detected.

4 bpAnalyzer

The tool bpAnalyzer has three modes of operations as shown in Fig. 1. First is the "s" mode, bpAnalyzer attempts at eliminating all kernel32 symbols that could be triggered before the exploit is launched. The output of this mode is a text file that contains all kernel32 symbols that get triggered prior to the launch of the exploit.

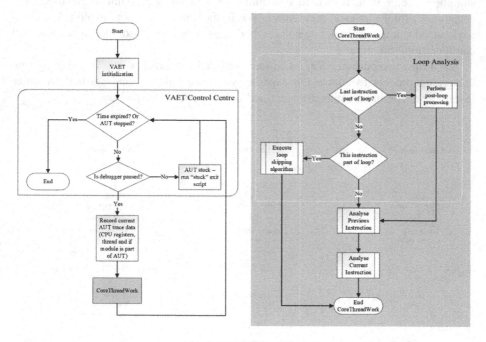

Fig. 2. VAET workflow

The second mode is the "a" mode. In this mode, the bpAnalyzer identifies the first kernel32 symbol that gets called after launching the exploit. The bpAnalyzer in this mode takes as input the list of breakpoints that were triggered during the "s" mode. The third and last mode is the "f" mode. In this mode, the bpAnalyzer's objective is to identify within normal AUT operation, which are the most frequent kernel32 symbols being used. The objective of this mode is to generate the top three symbols used from kernel32 to use them to get out of stuck "run states". Stuck "run states" is a situation that occurs when threads require synchronization and cannot do it because of the single-threaded nature of debuggers.

5   VAET

VAET is the main tool for gathering traces and creation of the dataset. VAET passes through 4 main phases, as shown in Fig. 2, these are the initialization, control centre, recording and finally the CoreThreadWork. Through these phases VAET accomplishes three main functions, first is the recording of the traces, second is data enrichment by categorizing instruction and modules, and third is adaptive control of the AUT flow. Below is an explanation of the functions performed throughout the different phases.

5.1   VAET Functions

The following subsections elaborate on the different functions performed by VAET.

Recording. Recording of features such as CPU registers information, memory contents, opcodes of instructions along with their assembly translation. The recording is done in JSON format to facilitate the consumption of the traces in other tools and the validation process.

Data Enrichment. This happens on multiple levels to provide information about the state of the AUT. The first level is on the module level, each instruction is labelled to be part of an "AUT module" or a "non-AUT module". The second is on the thread level, where the thread id of each instruction is recorded in the same trace line as that instruction. The third is the instruction level, which includes multiple labels that are assigned to instructions depending on their type. Instructions are first labelled based on their functional category, i.e., is it a control flow altering instruction or a general instruction. Then they are categorized based on their impact on memory (do they change memory locations).

Adaptive Control: VAET controls the execution of the program to ensure that the most complete traces are acquired in the most time-effective manner possible. Hence, VAET assigns a label to each instruction titled "action". Actions are the commands issued to the debugger based on the context of the instruction. If an instruction for example is a call instruction, and the target of the call is a "non-AUT module", VAET deems this as out of scope and issues a "step over" command to the debugger. Similarly, if an instruction is a call instruction with a target within an "AUT module" then VAET deems this is a relevant piece of code to be traced and issues a command of "step in" to the debugger.

Furthermore, to control the time of the execution, VAET performs a loop skipping algorithm. If the analysis results in a verdict that the AUT is currently going through a loop, then VAET skips this loop and lands on the first instruction to be executed after the loop. More on the loop skipping algorithm is detailed in Sect. 5.2. Finally, VAET limits the number of threads that are traced. VAET operates under the assumption that not all threads contain the vulnerable AUT code, and that the vulnerability is contained in a single thread within locally exploited AUTs and within two threads within the remotely exploited AUTs. Instructions detected on other threads are neglected.

5.2   VAET Phases

As stated above there are several phases for the VAET. Below is an illustration of each phase.

Initialization. VAET identifies the AUT name, path, and loaded modules. In this phase, VAET also validates the supplied arguments which include an identification if the current AUT is exploited in "local" or "remote" modes. Custom breakpoints that were detected during bpAnalyzer's execution are used among other inputs to tune the data enrichment process (eg: names of AUT modules that are dynamically loaded mid-execution as discovered by the validation scripts).

Control Centre. This phase is recurring after each instruction execution. This phase evaluates whether the tracing should continue or be terminated. The decision-making is done based on a timer and the state of the AUT/debugger. If the AUT has closed or the debugging process has been halted, then VAET terminates the tracing process.

Recording. In this phase, the main components of the data collection occur. The recording commences for the CPU registers, thread ID, classification of the current module, and opcodes of the current instruction along with the translation of the opcode into assembly language format.

CoreThreadWork. This is the largest phase and contains the bulk of the adaptive control and data enrichment functions of VAET. It is composed of the following:

Loop Analysis. A single loop that processes the payload by performing string copy operation from one memory location to another can take up to 24 h of the debugging time. To resolve this issue without compromising the integrity of the trace, a loop skipping algorithm is employed.

The algorithm works by recording all instructions along with their EIP address and a counter for the number of times that instruction was executed. After an instruction of the type "jump" is executed three times, the program is deemed to be currently in a loop. Loop skipping is performed by scanning the history of the instructions executed until the same current jump instruction is reached. The scan result will be the list of instructions residing in the loop body. Each instruction within the loop is evaluated if it is a call/jump. The target of the call/jump is identified and checked if it lands within the loop body or not. If it does not land within the loop, then a breakpoint is created for that address. The jump instruction that triggered the loop analysis is also investigated. If based on the history of executing that instruction the jump address was triggered each time, then the following address after the jump will not be part of the loop and would be set as the last breakpoint. While if the jump instruction was a conditional jump and the condition was never materialized, then the jump target is set as a final breakpoint.

After all potential breakpoints have been set, the program is put in a run state instead of single stepping. The debugger will execute the rest of the loop then will stop at the first instruction to be executed outside of the loop. As soon as the debugger pauses after the loop, a memory dump is created, to ensure that any memory changes created are recorded.

Analysis of Previous Instruction: The analysis of previous instructions aims at identifying if the previous instruction mandates that a memory dump or content update is needed. If the previous instruction was categorized as "memory impacting" instruction, then if there was a memory address referenced in the destination, the contents of that memory address will be recorded in this phase. Instructions are identified as "memory impacting" by comparing the instruction against a list of instructions created by manually scanning the intel developer guide [23], and manually picking all instructions that perform data movements/arithmetic/logical operations while accepting the destination to be a memory location. Furthermore, if there was an increment in the ESP, then the newly created stack space is recorded.

Analysis of Current Instruction: This phase performs data enrichment by categorizing the current instructions. Instructions are categorized as either call/jump/general, with special categorization for the call/jump depending on the target of these instructions. Each call/jump is further categorized based on the target, whether it is within or outside of AUT modules. Based on the categorization, VAET performs dynamic decision-making regarding the AUT flow. VAET avoids stepping into modules that are not part of the AUT code (i.e., system DLLs) and only steps in call instructions that have targets within the AUT.

6 Evaluation

The evaluations targets measuring if the proposed method and toolset can accurately record the AUT traces before and during the exploitation. The correct recording of the AUT execution is reflected in sound control flow and memory recording. To ensure completeness of the tracing, investigation of unknown modules and modules that were mistakenly classified as "non-AUT" is also executed on the trace files. Moreover, to verify if this method is suitable for the problem of software exploitation, exploit payload presence is verified within the traces. Finally, measuring the number of instructions traced and the time it took VAET to generate the traces demonstrates the practicality of the approach and toolset. A tool that takes minutes to generate traces is more likely to be used for practical applications and more likely to be used by exploit analysts to assist in their work.

6.1 Evaluation Approach

The evaluation is performed by analysing the two trace files generated by VAET. These files are in JSON format, hence are easily consumed in python scripts. However, unlike VAET and bpAnalyzer, these scripts are launched from outside the debugger.

{ "opCode_type": "callOutAUT", "edi": "0", "ebp": "1615432", "target_module": "ether.dll", "edx": "9746776",
 "ebx": "1616740", "true_target_module": "", "esp": "1614556", "jmp_target": "", "Debugged_path": "",
 "breakpoints": [], "thread_id": "2328", "debug_messages": [], "call_target_module": "excepted_module",
 "target_aut": "False", "esi": "9568256", "status": "1", "eax": "1614584", "Debugged_Name": "",
 "AUT_modules": [], "ecx": "1614576", "count": 182, "eip": "9572584", "opCode": "E8 A3130000",
 "current_status": "", "current_module": "ether.dll", "target_verification": "", "current_aut": "False",
 "action": "stepIn", "command": "CALL ether.00922490" }

(a)

{"eip": "1980570585",
 "stack_change": {"newESP": "1614604", "new_content": "[0x64][0xab][0x18][0x00]", "oldESP": "1614608"},
 "count": 12,
 "mem_dump": []}

{"eip": "1980570584",
 "stack_change": {},
 "count": 11,
 "mem_dump": [{"current_thread_stackBottom": "1593344", "current_thread_stackSize": "45056",
 "current_thread_stackTop": "1638400"}, {"heap_addresses": "[2949120, 9699328, 35127296, 36765696,
 36044800, 45088768, 47185920]"}, {"2130563072": {"access": "4", "end_address": "2130567168", "section":
 "", "content": "[0x6c][0xa7][0x18][0x00][0x00][0x00][0x19][0x00]...}}

(b)

Fig. 3. Samples of log traces. (a) control flow trace log (b) memory capture log

Evaluating Control Flow Sanity. Based on the labelling process that is applied on the instructions, it is possible from the traces to evaluate if the program flow is correct or not. For example, if an instruction is labelled as "callOutAUT" and the action "step Over", then the next traced instruction should be the one below the "callOutAUT" instruction within the AUT module. Other forms of checking include checking the proper categorization of modules and ach instruction.

Evaluating Unknown Modules. The validation script scans through all the log lines. Reading the module name in each line. If a module is not part of the AUT modules that were loaded at load time and not part of system DLLs, then it is evaluated as a potential runtime loaded AUT module. This module can be inserted as part of the argument in a second iteration of the script to ensure that it is traced as an AUT module.

Evaluating Memory Recording Sanity. This validation approach ensures that instructions that are marked as memory impacting invoke an actual update of the memory contents.

Evaluating for the Presence of a Payload. For each AUT a validation "reference" file is manually created by the researcher. This file contains the exploit payload and is used during the validation process.

6.2 Dataset

Each trace consists of two main text files. One file for the control flow and another for the memory operations. Each line represents a single instruction with all trace information recorded within the single JSON object. Each control flow JSON object contains a total of 29 fields. Please refer to Fig. 3 (a) for a sample of a line of output within the control flow trace.

The memory content file JSON object contains 4 fields. Whenever values are pushed on the stack, or memory impacting instructions or loop skipping occurs, this file is updated either with a complete memory dump or dump of specific memory addresses. Figure 3 (b) contains an example of two lines of memory content records.

Table 1. Overview of AUTs tested

AUT N°	AUT Name	Trace success	Payload detected	Inst. trace size (KB)	Mem dump size (MB)	N° of inst	Trace time (min)
1	Easy WMV/ASF/ASX to DVD Burner 2.3.11	Yes	Yes	178	18.5	282	5.0
2	Easy Video to PSP Converter 1.6.20	Yes	Yes	374	33.9	607	11.25
3	MP3 WAV to CD Burner 1.4.24	Yes	Yes	673	67.3	1041	20.1
4	My Video Converter 1.5.24	Yes	Yes	645	44.6	810	14.5
5	Easy Video to iPod/MP4/PSP/3GP Converter 1.5.20	Yes	Yes	305	46	485	9.5
6	Disk Pulse Enterprise 9.9.16	Yes	No	141	69	225	5.0
7	Disk Sorter Enterprise 9.5.12	Yes	No	500	251	805	20.1
8	VUPlayer 2.49	No	No	N/A	N/A	N/A	N/A
9	Free MP3 CD Ripper 2.6	No	No	N/A	N/A	N/A	N/A
10	Publish-It 3.6d	No	No	N/A	N/A	N/A	N/A
11	T-Mobile Internet Manager	No	No	N/A	N/A	N/A	N/A
12	i-FTP 2.20	No	No	N/A	N/A	N/A	N/A
13	Calavera UpLoader 3.5	No	No	N/A	N/A	N/A	N/A

6.3 Evaluation Results

We evaluated 13 local-based AUTs suffering from buffer-overflow vulnerabilities. The submissions for those exploits dated between 2014 and 2017. Out of the 13, 7 (53% of 13) successfully produced program traces. Out of those 7, 2 (28% of 7) did not include payload traces, while the other 5 (71% of 7) included them.

As for the 6 (46% of 13) applications that failed, 5 out of the 6 applications failed because the application crashed as the bpAnalyzer stepped through them to evaluate which breakpoints to be used. While 1 crashed because of a unique assembly instruction that VAET could not evaluate.

For the AUTs that were traced, the average trace time was 12 min, with the maximum trace time being 20 min and the minimum trace time 5 min. The average number of executed instructions is 607 instructions. The maximum number of instructions traced was 1041 and the minimum was 225. The average size of instruction tracing files is 402 KB, with a maximum file size of 673 KB and a minimum of 141 KB. Finally, the average size for the memory dumps is 75.5 MB, with a maximum of 251 MB and a minimum of 18.5 MB. All successful traces included sound control flow and memory recording. Moreover, AUT modules were not traced in the first run for AUTs 1, 2 and 3. These were detected by the validation script and were included in a second iteration.

A review of AUTs tested is presented in Table 1. Different breakpoints were selected based on the automated script. AUTs no. 1 to 5 congested the payload via "bad user input" and Kernel32.LoadLibraryA symbol was used as the starting breakpoint. AUT no. 6 ingested the payload via importing a configuration file, and Kernel32.CreateMutexW was used as the starting breakpoint. While AUT no. 7, although same technique for ingesting the payload, Kernel32.GetThreadLocale was the first symbol to be detected after the exploit launch. Interesting to note that the application failures are only considered in the situation where bpAnalyzer and VAET are being used. It is possible to investigate those applications using the Immunity Debugger manually without crashing the applications. However, we aim to automate and pave the way to reach to the same level of efficacy of manual investigations using ML.

6.4   Toolset Limitations

First limitation is the multi-threading nature of some applications. Traces for applications that have vulnerable code available across more than two threads will not have complete traces. Second, the Immunity Debugger only supports 32-bit applications, hence 64-bit based traces are not currently possible. Finally, AUTs may employ anti-debugging features to protect intellectual property, although this was not observed within the dataset found on EDB.

7   Conclusion and Future Work

We presented a method and toolset for exploit trace collection. It enables researchers to create a trace of an execution of an exploit against a vulnerable application capturing hundreds of assembly instructions along with their relevant memory regions in minutes. Our work enables exploit analysts to develop datasets for training ML models that would detect/analyse exploit activity. Our evaluation included testing traces for control flow conformity as well as the presence of payload traces. Future work might expand to address applications that utilize more than 2 threads and 64-bit based applications. Finally, we aim to include different types of vulnerabilities/exploits, such as use-after-free, and provide a more detailed analysis of the logs generated.

References

1. Mandiant-Threat-Intelligence-Research: Think fast: time between disclosure, patch release and vulnerability exploitation — intelligence for vulnerability management, Part Two|FireEye Inc. https://www.fireeye.com/blog/threat-research/2020/04/time-between-disclosure-patch-release-and-vulnerability-exploitation.html. Accessed 13 Jan 2021
2. Gupta, S., Pratap, P., Saran, H.: Dynamic code instrumentation to detect and recover from instrumentation, pp. 65–71 (2006)

3. Snow, K.Z., Monrose, F., Davi, L., Dmitrienko, A., Liebchen, C., Sadeghi, A.R.: Just-in-time code reuse: on the effectiveness of fine-grained address space layout randomization. In: Proceedings of IEEE Symposium on Security and Privacy, pp. 574–588 (2013). https://doi.org/10.1109/SP.2013.45

4. Jia, X., Zhang, C., Su, P., Yang, Y., Huang, H., Feng, D.: Towards efficient heap overflow discovery. In: Proceedings of 26th USENIX Conference on Security Symposium, pp. 989–1006 (2017)

5. Monrose, F., Dacier, M., Blanc, G., Garcia-Alfaro, J. (eds.): RAID 2016. LNCS, vol. 9854. Springer, Cham (2016). https://doi.org/10.1007/978-3-319-45719-2

6. Carlini, N., Wagner, D.: ROP is still dangerous: breaking modern defenses. In: Proceedings of the 23rd USENIX conference on Security Symposium, p. 256 (2014)

7. Haider, W., Creech, G., Xie, Y., Hu, J.: Windows based data sets for evaluation of robustness of Host based Intrusion Detection Systems (IDS) to zero-day and stealth attacks. Future Internet **8**, 29 (2016). https://doi.org/10.3390/fi8030029

8. Creech, G., Hu, J.: A semantic approach to host-based intrusion detection systems using contiguous and discontiguous system call patterns. IEEE Trans. Comput. **63**, 807–819 (2014). https://doi.org/10.1109/TC.2013.13

9. 1998 DARPA Intrusion Detection Evaluation Dataset|MIT Lincoln Laboratory. https://www.ll.mit.edu/r-d/datasets/1998-darpa-intrusion-detection-evaluation-dataset. Accessed 1 Feb 2021

10. 1999 DARPA Intrusion Detection Evaluation Dataset|MIT Lincoln Laboratory. https://www.ll.mit.edu/r-d/datasets/1999-darpa-intrusion-detection-evaluation-dataset. Accessed 1 Feb 2021

11. (MIT), Massachusetts Institute of Technology: MIT Lincoln Laboratory: DARPA Intrusion Detection Evaluation. https://archive.ll.mit.edu/ideval/docs/attackDB.html#secret. Accessed 1 Feb 2021

12. IDS 2018|Datasets|Research|Canadian Institute for Cybersecurity|UNB. https://www.unb.ca/cic/datasets/ids-2018.html. Accessed 1 Feb 2021

13. Glasser, J., Lindauer, B.: Bridging the gap: a pragmatic approach to generating insider threat data. In: Proceedings of IEEE CS Security and Privacy Workshops, SPW 2013, pp. 98–104 (2013). https://doi.org/10.1109/SPW.2013.37

14. Elsabagh, M., Barbara, D., Fleck, D., Stavrou, A.: Detecting ROP with statistical learning of program characteristics. In: Proceedings of the Seventh ACM on Conference on Data and Application Security and Privacy, pp. 219–226. ACM, New York, NY, USA (2017). https://doi.org/10.1145/3029806.3029812

15. Li, X., Hu, Z., Fu, Y., Chen, P., Zhu, M., Liu, P.: ROPNN: detection of ROP payloads using deep neural networks (2018)

16. Snort - Network Intrusion Detection & Prevention System, https://www.snort.org/. Accessed 1 Feb 2021

17. Suárez-Tangil, G., Dash, S.K., García-Teodoro, P., Camacho, J., Cavallaro, L.: Anomaly-based exploratory analysis and detection of exploits in android mediaserver. IET Inf. Secur. **12**, 1 (2018). https://doi.org/10.1049/iet-ifs.2017.0460

18. Desktop Operating System Market Share Worldwide|StatCounter Global Stats. https://gs.statcounter.com/os-market-share/desktop/worldwide. Accessed 5 Apr 2021

19. PassMark CPU Benchmarks - AMD vs Intel Market Share. https://www.cpubenchmark.net/market_share.html. Accessed 5 Apr 2021

20. Project Zero: About Project Zero. https://googleprojectzero.blogspot.com/p/about-project-zero.html. Accessed 6 Apr 2021

21. Chen, Y., Lin, Z., Xing, X.: A systematic study of elastic objects in Kernel exploitation. In: Proceedings of ACM Conference on Computer and Communications Security, pp. 1165–1184 (2020). https://doi.org/10.1145/3372297.3423353
22. Introducing Kernel Data Protection, a new platform security technology for preventing data corruption - Microsoft Security. https://www.microsoft.com/security/blog/2020/07/08/introducing-kernel-data-protection-a-new-platform-security-technology-for-preventing-data-corruption/. Accessed 6 Apr 2021
23. Intel® 64 and IA-32 Architectures Software Developer Manuals. https://software.intel.com/content/www/us/en/develop/articles/intel-sdm.html. Accessed 6 Apr 2021

A Secure and Privacy Preserving Federated Learning Approach for IoT Intrusion Detection System

Phan The Duy[1,2](✉) [ID], Huynh Nhat Hao[1,2], Huynh Minh Chu[1,2], and Van-Hau Pham[1,2] [ID]

[1] Information Security Laboratory, University of Information Technology, Ho Chi Minh City, Vietnam
{duypt,haupv}@uit.edu.vn, {17520444,17520293}@gm.uit.edu.vn
[2] Vietnam National University, Ho Chi Minh City, Vietnam

Abstract. Recently, machine learning (ML) has been shown as a powerful method for outstanding capability of resolving intelligent tasks across many fields. Nevertheless, such ML-based systems require to centralize a large amount of data in the training phase that causes privacy leaks from user data. This is also true with the ML-based intrusion detection system (IDS) due to containing sensitive user and network data, especially in the context of Internet of Things (IoT) intrusion detection. To promote the collaboration between multiple parties in building an efficient IDS model to detect more attack types and cope with the privacy preservation issues, federated learning (FL) is considered as a potential approach for localized training scheme without sharing any data collection between organizations or data silos. In this paper, we investigate the feasibility of adopting FL for anomaly behavior detection in the context of large-scale IoT networks while facilitating the secure and privacy preserving aggregation using homomorphic encryption and differential privacy.

Keywords: Intrusion detection · Federated learning · Privacy preservation · Secure aggregation · Differential privacy · Homomorphic encryption

1 Introduction

With the constant growth of the Internet of Things (IoT), the increases in the number of cyberattacks against IoT devices have emphasized the need for a cyber threat protection [19]. To mitigate this problem, an efficient Intrusion Detection System (IDS) be of help. Such detection systems are designed to protect its target against potential attack through a continuous monitoring of all data streams generated from diverse sources and analyzing it to detect possible attacks. Current IDSs can be classified as either signature-based or anomaly based. In terms of signature-based IDS, the traffic data monitored by the IDS is compared to the known pattern of attacks (as known as signatures), hence can quickly detect the attacks. But this method can only detect known attacks that have already

© Springer Nature Switzerland AG 2021
M. Yang et al. (Eds.): NSS 2021, LNCS 13041, pp. 353–368, 2021.
https://doi.org/10.1007/978-3-030-92708-0_23

been described in the database. In contrast to signature-based IDS, anomaly-based IDS does not require signatures to detect intrusion, instead it identifies anomalies in the monitored data thanks to machine learning techniques [28]. This method thus can detect the unknown attacks, therefore during the past years most IDS-related research have focused on anomaly-based IDS [11].

Although machine learning (ML) has been considered to be one of the most effective techniques in anomaly detection, building high quality IDS-ML models require a huge amount of training data from diverse sources. However, in most organizations this data cannot be share between multiple organizations due to the concerns about data privacy and confidentiality. This concern is getting more serious in the context of Internet of Things (IoTs) or industrial IoTs (IIoTs) since the sensitive data is located in each local network and right on devices [10]. The collection of all such this information in a central entity for training ML model will violate the privacy preservation for data owners [20].

Federated Learning (FL) is a machine learning technique that train a model across multiple decentralized edge devices or servers holding local data samples without accessing training sets of other parties. There is no raw data exchange during training phase, since FL scheme trains a model by only sharing gradients. [17]. This approach enables multiple participants to build a common, robust ML-IDS model without sharing data, thus allowing to address critical issues such as data privacy, data security. To resolve security and privacy threats to the IoT applications, FL has drawn much attention from academia and industry [7,35]. Anomalies of IoT/IIoT devices might expose sensitive data about users of high authenticity and validity in the network, most of the privacy-preserving solutions in building anomaly detector in IoT/IIoT context prefer to choose FL approach as a universal anomaly detection model from various agents, like the work of Wang et al. [29], DeepFed [12], or Fed-TH [1].

However, the privacy of FL may suffer from reverse engineering since it is trained on sensitive user data [4,25]. Specifically, existing works reveal that the shared gradient still retains the sensitive information about the training set from the training collaborator. Even worse, an adversary may capture and forge exchanged gradients if there is no encryption in the aggregation process. To overcome this problem, many approaches have been proposed [2,4,13,30]. Among them, *homomorphic encryption* (HE) and *differential privacy* (DP) are one of the most potential solutions. HE is a form of encryption with an additional evaluation capability for computing over encrypted data without decrypting it first. In addition, the result of the homomorphic operation after decryption is equivalent to the operation on the plaintext data [32]. Since the operation is performed on encrypted data, the security of privacy data can be guaranteed. DP is a widely used privacy-preserving technique in industry, it can be used by adding noises to personal sensitive attributes, thus each user's privacy is protected.

In this paper, we focus on ensuring the reliability and privacy preservation for FL in IDS by taking advantage of HE. In summary, the main contribution of this work as follows:

- We design an IDS architecture leveraging FL strategy with LSTM and VGG models, then adopt homomorphic encryption and differential privacy in such these models to secure the parameter updates during model aggregation.
- We then carry out simulations using the real-world dataset (CICIDS2017) to benchmark our detection model under centralized and FL approach.

2   Related Work

2.1   Privacy in Federated Learning

Federated Learning can be considered as privacy-preserving decentralized collaborative machine learning; therefore, it is tightly related to multi-party privacy-preserving machine learning. As mentioned above, researchers have proposed various solutions to preserve privacy in federated learning.

Secure Multi-party Computation (SMC) and Homomorphic Encryption (HE): SMC allows multiple parties to compute a joint function of their private inputs while revealing nothing but the output. In SMC, communication is secured and protected with cryptographic methods and currently homomorphic encryption is by far the most prominent solution in SMC. Homomorphic encryption (HE) is one type of cryptography that allows computation on encrypted data without decrypting them first. It is helpful to mask local gradient updates before clients sends them out for parameter updates aggregation. Recently, there have been many works that uses the HE scheme, notably Paillier cryptosystem [23] in FL such as [5,14,15]. In addition, to improve performance of partial HE in FL, Zhang [33] proposed a technique called *batch encryption* which significantly reduces the encryption overhead and data transfer amount.

Differential Privacy (DP) enables organizations or companies to utilize sensitive data from other sources without compromising the privacy of an individual. In FL, DP is introduced to add noise to participant's uploaded parameters to avoid inverse data retrieval. DP-FedAVGGAN framework proposed in [31] utilizes DP to make GAN-based attacks inefficient in inferencing training data of other participants in FL. Geyer [6] proposed an implementation of DP in FL, which increases privacy in FL at the cost of severely reduced model performance. In addition, both works in [8,27] combines both HE and DP to achieve a secured FL model with high accuracy.

2.2   Federated Learning in Intrusion Detection System

Recently, FL has also been adopted tremendously in Intrusion Detection problem. To start with, Preuveneers [24] described a permissioned blockchain-based federated learning method to develop an anomaly detection ML model in IDS. Also, Nguyen [21], designed a distributed self-learning system to detect compromised IoT devices based on FL approach. In addition, Zhao [34] also proposed an IDS-FL model using LSTM, achieving a high accuracy model. Besides that, Viraaji Mothukuri et al. [18] also used FL approach on Gated Recurrent Units

(GRUs) in building anomaly detection system in IoT networks. Yi Liu et al. [16] proposed a FL-based anomaly detection with the combination of CNN and LSTM units for time-series data in IIoT to prevent edge device failures. In the context of industrial Cyber-physical systems (CPSs), there are several works such as DeepFed [12], or Fed-TH [1] creating a collaborative training scheme between multiple agents, i.e., CPSs, to build a comprehensive IDS model without sharing training data. Although most related works do not apply any solution to enhance privacy in FL-based IDS, the researchers in [12] proposed DeepFed framework to build a comprehensive intrusion detection model in a privacy-preserving way by implementing Paillier cryptosystem. Howerver, as shown in [33], additive HE such as Paillier can create significant overhead to computation and communication.

3   Methodology

In this section, we describe the details of our FL-based IDS architecture, including the machine learning model's parameters, the strategy of protecting privacy in updates aggregation from each client to the IDS server.

3.1   LSTM, FCN and VGG for Intrusion Detection Model

LSTM for Intrusion Detection Model. LSTM is an extension of RNN, capable of learning long-term dependencies. Our LSTM model utilizes an input with 78 neurals (which equals to the number of features), number of features in the hidden state is 32, follow by a linear layer with 2 outputs.

Fully Connected Network for Intrusion Detection Model. Fully connected networks model (FCN) is a type of artificial neural network which consists of multiple hidden layers with nodes and ways of interconnecting nodes. Our Fully connected network consists of 6 layers: an input layer, four hidden layers (that contain 1024, 512, 256 and 128 nodes, respectively) and an ouput layer.

VGG for Intrusion Detection Model. VGG is a convolutional neural network with a specific architecture that was proposed in the paper [26] by a group of researchers (visual geometry group) from the University of Oxford. In this paper, we utilize transfer learning to train the VGG-11 and VGG-16 model. In detail, we apply pretrained models VGG-11 and VGG-16 with feature extraction in our experiments. General VGG has two parts: feature extraction and classifier. We freeze the first part, feature extraction, in both models and pass its output into a max pooling layer to reduce the number of parameters. Finally, we modify the second part (classifier) in VGG by some fully connected layers with ReLu activation. The Fig. 1 shows our modified VGG's architecture.

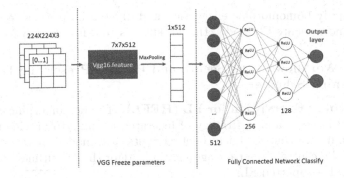

Fig. 1. VGG-based model architecture by adding fully connected network

3.2 Federated Learning Architecture for IoT-IDS

To implement the intrusion detection using FL approach, we first construct a general FL architecture as shown in Fig. 2. The proposed architecture is mainly made up of two components: participants and aggregator.

- **Aggregator**: the aggregator is generally a cloud server that is responsible for receiving the model weights from participants, aggregating and sending them back to the participants. This work also assume that this aggregator will be *honest-but-curious*, a common setting used in FL privacy such as in [4].
- **Participants**: the participants are generally selected edge devices with strong enough computing power and rich computing resources. Each edge device uses local data resources (receiving from IIoT nodes) to train the IDS models and upload model weights to the aggregator. Once the training is done, the IDS models are obtained and deployed right in the edge devices.

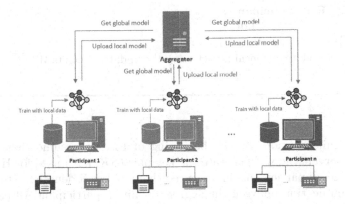

Fig. 2. FL-IDS

Then we apply homomorphic encryption and differential privacy techniques to provide a more secure FL model, the workflow is shown in Sect. 3.3.

3.3 The Workflow of the Secure and Privacy-Preserving Federated Learning Scheme

Homomorphic Encryption for FL (HEFL). The homomorphic encryption is combined in the training strategy of federated learning to provide the secure aggregation in IDS context. Each client encrypts their model's parameters before sending to the central server for aggregation. Algorithm 1 outlines the training process of HE-supported FL.

Algorithm 1: HEFL

Input: Participants set $\mathcal{P}$, data resources of N participants
$\{\mathcal{D}_k | k \in (1, 2, 3...N)\}$, number of communication rounds R
Output: Aggregated IDS Model
Init: $\forall k \in (1, 2, 3...N)$ $\mathcal{P}_k$ splits their $\mathcal{D}_k$ into R parts $\{d_k^1, d_k^2, ...d_k^R\}$.
  A trusted server generates key pair (SK,PK).
  The aggregator randomly select a participant as a leader to initialize
  weights W_0.

1 **for** $r \leq R$ **do**
2 | **(I). For participants:**
   | **for** $\forall k \in (1, 2, 3...N)$ **do**
3 | | $\mathcal{P}_k$ trains and computes the r-th round local model weights W_k^r using d_k^r.
4 | | $\mathcal{P}_k$ encrypt the weights: $E(W_k^r) = Encrypt(W_k^r, PK)$
5 | | $\mathcal{P}_k$ sends the encrypted weights $E(W_k^r)$, and size of d_k^r, denoted by α_k^r
   | | to the aggregator.
6 | **(II). For aggregator:**
   | $C = Aggregate(W_1^r, ..., W_N^r, \alpha_1^r, ..., \alpha_N^r)$.
   | The aggregator then distributes the aggregated ciphertext C to all
   | $\mathcal{P}_k(k \in (1, 2, 3...N))$
7 | **(III). For participants:**
   | **for** $\forall k \in (1, 2, 3...N)$ **do**
8 | | $\tilde{W}_k^r = Decrypt(C, SK)$
9 | | $\mathcal{P}_k$ updates its local model using the updated weights $\tilde{W}_k^r$.
10 | $r \leftarrow r + 1$

---

1. System Initialization: At the beginning of FL, we assume that there is a trusted server who will generate the key pair (SK, PK) used for HE and distributes to all participants in a secured channel. Let R denote the total rounds of communication between the aggregator and a participant. All participants should split their data $\mathcal{D}_k$ into R parts $\{d_k^1, d_k^2, ...d_k^R\}$. Then, the aggregator will select a participant as a leader to initialize weights W_0. Again, W_0 are then also synchronized with the other participants.

2. Local model training: After receiving the initial weights W_0, each participant trains a deep learning-based IDS model locally using their data resources $\mathcal{D}_k$. The detailed training is summarized in Algorithm 1. When a model is trained, each participant $\mathcal{P}_k$ encrypts the model weights W_k^r using $Encrypt(W_k^r, PK)$. Then this encrypted weights, along with size of training data, are uploaded to the aggregator by each participant.

3. Model weights aggregation: Given the size of training data and the encrypted weights from all participants, the aggregator starts to aggregate them by $Aggregate(...)$ - an implementation of FedAvg algorithm. Then, the aggregated ciphertexts C are sent back to participants.

4. Local model updating: by decrypting the ciphertexts C using $Decrypt(C, SK)$, each participant can obtain the updated model weights $\tilde{W}_k^r$ and use them to update the local model.

After R rounds of interactions between the aggregator and participants, we can finally obtain a deep learning-based IDS model.

Differential Privacy for FL (DPFL). Differential Privacy increases the privacy in FL by injecting a controlled amount of statistical noise to obscure the data contributions from individuals in the dataset. The use of differential privacy is a careful trade off between privacy preservation and model utility.

1. System Initialization: let R denote the total rounds of communication between the aggregator and a participant. All participants should split their data $\mathcal{D}_k$ into R parts $\{d_k^1, d_k^2, ...d_k^R\}$. Then, the aggregator will select a participant as a leader to initialize weights W_0 and send them to the other participants.

2. Local model training: After receiving the initial weights W_0, each participant trains a deep learning-based IDS model locally using their data resources $\mathcal{D}_k$. The detailed training is summarized in Algorithm 2. When a model is trained, each participant $\mathcal{P}_k$ adds noise to the model weights W_k^r using $AddNoise(W_k^r)$. Then this noised weights, along with size of training data, are uploaded to the aggregator by each participant.

3. Model weights aggregation: Given the size of training data and the weights from all participants, the aggregator starts to aggregate them by the FedAvg algorithm. Then, the aggregated weights W_{global} are sent back to participants.

4. Local model updating: the participants obtain the global model weights W_{global} and use them to update the local model.

After R rounds of interactions between the aggregator and participants, we can finally obtain a deep learning-based IDS model.

Algorithm 2: DPFL

Input: Participants set $\mathcal{P}$, data resources of N participants
$\{\mathcal{D}_k | k \in (1, 2, 3...N)\}$, number of communication rounds R
Output: Aggregated IDS Model
Init: $\forall k \in (1, 2, 3...N)$ $\mathcal{P}_k$ splits their $\mathcal{D}_k$ into R parts $\{d_k^1, d_k^2, ...d_k^R\}$.
The aggregator randomly select a participant as a leader to initialize weights W_0.

1   **for** $r \leq R$ **do**
2   **(I). For participants:**
       for $\forall k \in (1, 2, 3...N)$ **do**
3          $\mathcal{P}_k$ trains and computes the r-th round local model weights W_k^r using d_k^r.
4          $\mathcal{P}_k$ adds noise to the weights: $\tilde{W}_k^r = AddNoise(W_k^r)$
5          $\mathcal{P}_k$ sends the noised weights $\tilde{W}_k^r$, and size of d_k^r, denoted by α_k^r to the aggregator.
6   **(II). For aggregator:**
       $W_{global} = Aggregate(\tilde{W}_1^r, ..., \tilde{W}_N^r, \alpha_1^r, ..., \alpha_N^r)$.
       The aggregator then distributes the global weights W_{global} to all $\mathcal{P}_k(k \in (1, 2, 3...N))$
7   **(III). For participants:**
       for $\forall k \in (1, 2, 3...N)$ **do**
8          $\mathcal{P}_k$ receives model W_{global} from the aggregator and update the local model.
9       $r \leftarrow r + 1$

---

4 Experiments

4.1 Dataset and Data Preprocessing

In this work, we use the CICIDS2017 dataset [9] for benchmarking the performance of FL approach. Each row in the dataset consists of 78 flow features. First, we remove all NaN and InF values from the dataset. For LSTM and FCN, we applied the standard scaler to standardized features by removing the mean and scaling to unit variance. The standard score of a sample x is calculated as Eq. 1.

$$z = \frac{x - u}{s} \tag{1}$$

where u is the training samples or zero, and s is the standard deviation of the training samples or one.

For VGG-16 model, we first apply the min-max normalization technique to scale the data to a fixed range of 0 and 1 using the following equation:

$$x_{scale} = \frac{x - min(X)}{max(X) - min(X)} \tag{2}$$

We extend the number of features from 78 to 81, then convert them to an 2D array of 9×9 (9×9 grayscale images). Next, we convert to 224×224 and transformed to RBG color images, as shown in Fig. 5. Subsequently, we assign all BENIGN labels to 0, the remaining labels are assigned to 1. Then, we balance the dataset by apply undersampling technique, which remove examples from the dataset that belong to the majority class (BENIGN class). We will apply LSTM and Fully connected network on the entire balanced dataset, while the VGG16 and VGG11 models apply on 10% of the balanced dataset.

4.2 Implementation and Experiment Settings

Environmental Setup. Our experiments are conducted on an Ubuntu 18.04.5 LTS platform with an Intel Xeon E5-2660 v4 (16 cores) and 64 GB RAM.

TenSEAL. TenSEAL [3] is a library for doing homomorphic encryption operations on tensors, built on top of Microsoft SEAL. It supports CKKS scheme which allows additions and multiplications on encrypted real or complex numbers, but yields only approximate results.

Opacus. Opacus [22] is a library that enables training PyTorch models with differential privacy. Here, we used it to implement differential privacy in our federated learning model.

Federated Learning System. In this work, we use a combination of Pytorch framework, Flask framework to build a simple federated learning system. Then we also made use of TenSEAL and Opacus to implement homomorphic encryption and differential privacy in our FL system.

We use Adam optimizer with learning rate of $1e-3$ and Cross Entropy loss function in experiments. Number of epoch for every round is 10 for LSTM and FCN, and only one for two VGG models, the batch size for every mini-batch is 64.

4.3 Result Analysis

We use many metrics including Accuracy, Precision, Recall, F-score to evaluate the performance of experimental ML models. To show the comparison of three ML-based approaches, i.e., our federated learning model, the centralized IDS model is also built by only one authority on all data, as well as the local IDS constructed by each agent on its private data.

Performance Under Homomorphic Encryption. Three groups of experiments are conducted, where different numbers of participants $K = 2, 4, 6$ are respectively considered.

Table 1 shows the numerical results about the performance of LSTM federated intrusion detection models with HE, in terms of the accuracy, precision, recall, and F-score under three different scenarios with number of rounds of communication $R = 3, 5, 7$ respectively. As the number of communication rounds R

Table 1. Results of the LSTM-HEFL models

K	Round	Accuracy	Precision	Recall	F1
2	3	0,9824	0,9773	0,9877	0,9825
	5	0,98	0,9829	0,9768	0,9799
	7	**0,9842**	**0,9818**	**0,9866**	**0,9842**
4	3	0,9817	0,9796	0,9838	0,9817
	5	0,9815	0,9718	0,9918	0,9817
	7	0,9828	0,9787	0,987	0,9828
6	3	0,9801	0,9695	0,9913	0,9803
	5	0,9798	0,9667	0,9937	0,98
	7	0,9802	0,9688	0,9924	0,98

increases from 3 to 7, the performance of each IDS model generally improves, while the number of participants generally does not affect the performance.

In addition, the size of communication data between each client and aggregation server is measured to compare the bandwidth consumption in Homomorphic Encryption adoption in our proposed FL-based IDS framework. The size of ML models transmitted for each round is illustrated in Table 2.

Performance Under Differential Privacy. Similarly, Table 3 shows the numerical results about the performance of LSTM federated intrusion detection models with DP. As we can see, the performance also improves when the number of rounds R increases, but gradually drops when the number of participants increases. This is understandable because the more number of participants, the more noises are added to model weights.

Table 2. The performance of HE-based models on the communication data size

Model	The number of parameters	Plaintext size	Ciphertext size	Time to encrypt
LSTM	14402	254.76 KB	57.68 MB	~2 s
FCN	204930	1.76 MB	219.5 MB	~5 s
VGG11	9384962	96.21 MB	4.62 GB	~84 s
VGG16	14879170	152.69 MB	7.5 GB	~211 s

Performance Comparison Between Proposed Methods. For LSTM, FCN, and VGG models, we use five different scenarios to evaluate:

1. Local: participants train local model with their local data resources.
2. Ideal: all participants share data resources to train a global model.
3. HEFL: using a FL approach with HE.
4. DPFL: using a FL approach with DP.
5. Hybrid: using a FL approach with a combination of HE and DP.

Table 3. Results of the LSTM-DPFL models

K	R	Accuracy	Precision	Recall	F1
2	3	0.9565	0.9437	0.9707	0.957
	5	0.9595	0.9437	0.9772	0.9602
	7	**0.9601**	**0.944**	**0.978**	**0.9607**
4	3	0.951	0.9392	0.9642	0.9515
	5	0.9517	0.9383	0.9667	0.9523
	7	0.9532	0.9413	0.9666	0.9538
6	3	0.9489	0.9364	0.963	0.9495
	5	0.9489	0.9369	0.9625	0.9496
	7	0.9495	0.9377	0.9628	0.9501

Here, we also specifically use K = 2, R = 7 due to its potentiality as we can see in the previous experiments. As shown in Fig. 3, we observe that the HEFL model has good results when compared with the IDEAL model, the DPFL model gives lower accuracy results, and the hybrid model has the same results as the DPFL because the model is lost accuracy due to the addition of noise with DP, while HE has almost no loss of accuracy.

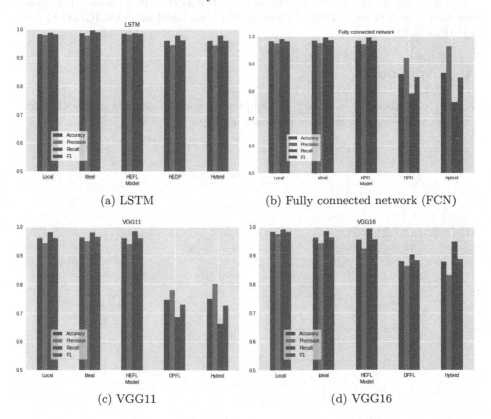

(a) LSTM

(b) Fully connected network (FCN)

(c) VGG11

(d) VGG16

Fig. 3. All model result with K = 2 and R = 7

5   Conclusion

The concern of privacy leaks on sensitive data on ML-based system promotes the adopting of federated learning recently. Sharing the similar trend, advocates in network security begin to explore the feasibility of local training ML-based IDS right on the involved parties without exposing their data. This paper introduces an architecture and workflow of federated learning approach for collaboratively building the efficient IDS in the context of multiple IoT network. Therein, we adopt Homomorphic Encryption and Differential Privacy to facilitate the privacy preserving and secure aggregation for preventing privacy concerns in federated learning-based IDS. Through experiments on various number of parties and aggregation rounds on CICIDS2017 dataset, this approach shows the potential in the context of Industrial IoT where a huge number of heterogeneous devices locating in many organizations communicate and share sensitive data under the various cyber risk and attacks. Specifically, each distributed IDS model is a representative for a security gateway in the local network, and their network traffic is used itself without leaking out during the training operation.

Acknowledgement. Phan The Duy was funded by Vingroup Joint Stock Company and supported by the Domestic Master/PhD Scholarship Programme of Vingroup Innovation Foundation (VINIF), Vingroup Big Data Institute (VINBIGDATA), code VINIF.2020.TS.138.

A   Appendix

Table 4 describes the number of samples of each label in the CICIDS-2017 dataset, while its scatter chart is shown as Fig. 4.

Table 4. CICIDS-2017 dataset summary

File (CSV)	Type of traffic	Number of record
Monday-WorkingHours	Benign	529,918
Tuesday-WorkingHours	Benign	432,074
	SSH-Patator	5,897
	FTP-Patator	7,938
Wednesday-WorkingHours	Benign	440,031
	DoS Hulk	231,073
	DoS GoldenEye	10,293
	DoS Slowloris	5,796
	DoS Slowhttptest	5,499
	Heartbleed	11
Thursday-WorkingHours-Morning-WebAttacks	Benign	168,186
	Web Attack-Brute Force	1,507
	Web Attack-Sql Injection	21
	Web Attack-XSS	652
Thursday-WorkingHours-Afternoon-Infilteration	Benign	288,566
	Infiltration	36
Friday-WorkingHours-Morning	Benign	189,067
	Bot	1,966
Friday-WorkingHours-Afternoon-PortScan	Benign	127,537
	Portscan	158,930
Friday-WorkingHours-Afternoon-DDos	Benign	97,718
	DdoS	128,027
Total		**2,830,743**

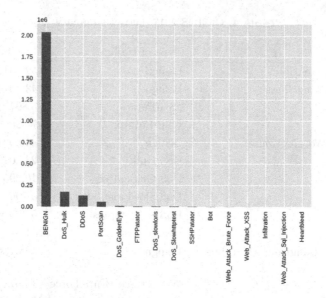

Fig. 4. Distribution of data on the CICIDS2017 dataset by label

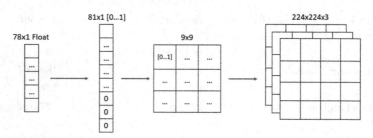

Fig. 5. Image conversion from network flow features for training VGG models.

References

1. Abdel-Basset, M., Hawash, H., Sallam, K.: Federated threat-hunting approach for microservice-based industrial cyber-physical system. IEEE Trans. Ind. Inf. **18**(3), 1905–1917 (2022)
2. Aono, Y., Hayashi, T., Wang, L., Moriai, S., et al.: Privacy-preserving deep learning via additively homomorphic encryption. IEEE Trans. Inf. Forensics Secur. **13**(5), 1333–1345 (2017)
3. Benaissa, A., Retiat, B., Cebere, B., Belfedhal, A.E.: TenSEAL: a library for encrypted tensor operations using homomorphic encryption (2021)
4. Bonawitz, K., et al.: Practical secure aggregation for privacy-preserving machine learning. In: Proceedings of the 2017 ACM SIGSAC Conference on Computer and Communications Security, pp. 1175–1191 (2017)
5. Cheng, K., et al.: SecureBoost: a lossless federated learning framework. IEEE Intell. Syst., (01), 1, 5555 (2021)

6. Geyer, R.C., Klein, T., Nabi, M.: Differentially private federated learning: A client level perspective. arXiv preprint arXiv:1712.07557 (2017)

7. Guo, Y., Zhao, Z., He, K., Lai, S., Xia, J., Fan, L.: Efficient and flexible management for industrial internet of things: a federated learning approach. Comput. Netw. **192**, 108122 (2021)

8. Hao, M., Li, H., Xu, G., Liu, S., Yang, H.: Towards efficient and privacy-preserving federated deep learning. In: ICC 2019–2019 IEEE International Conference on Communications (ICC), pp. 1–6. IEEE (2019)

9. Iman Sharafaldin, A.H.L., Ghorbani, A.A.: Toward generating a new intrusion detection dataset and intrusion traffic characterization. In: 4th International Conference on Information Systems Security and Privacy (ICISSP) (2018)

10. Khan, L.U., Saad, W., Han, Z., Hossain, E., Hong, C.S.: Federated learning for internet of things: Recent advances, taxonomy, and open challenges. IEEE Commun. Surv. Tutor. **23**(3), 1759–1799 (2021)

11. Kilincer, I.F., Ertam, F., Sengur, A.: Machine learning methods for cyber security intrusion detection: datasets and comparative study. Comput. Netw. **188**, 107840 (2021)

12. Li, B., Wu, Y., Song, J., Lu, R., Li, T., Zhao, L.: DeepFed: federated deep learning for intrusion detection in industrial cyber-physical systems. IEEE Trans. Ind. Inf. **17**, 5615–5624 (2020)

13. Li, T., Sahu, A.K., Talwalkar, A., Smith, V.: Federated learning: challenges, methods, and future directions. IEEE Signal Process. Mag. **37**(3), 50–60 (2020)

14. Liu, C., Chakraborty, S., Verma, D.: Secure model fusion for distributed learning using partial homomorphic encryption. In: Calo, S., Bertino, E., Verma, D. (eds.) Policy-Based Autonomic Data Governance. LNCS, vol. 11550, pp. 154–179. Springer, Cham (2019). https://doi.org/10.1007/978-3-030-17277-0_9

15. Liu, Y., Kang, Y., Xing, C., Chen, T., Yang, Q.: A secure federated transfer learning framework. IEEE Intell. Syst. **35**(4), 70–82 (2020)

16. Liu, Y., Garg, S., Nie, J., Zhang, Y., Xiong, Z., Kang, J., Hossain, M.S.: Deep anomaly detection for time-series data in industrial Iot: a communication-efficient on-device federated learning approach. IEEE IoT J. **8**(8), 6348–6358 (2021)

17. McMahan, B., Moore, E., Ramage, D., Hampson, S., y Arcas, B.A.: Communication-efficient learning of deep networks from decentralized data. In: Artificial Intelligence and Statistics, pp. 1273–1282. PMLR (2017)

18. Mothukuri, V., Khare, P., Parizi, R.M., Pouriyeh, S., Dehghantanha, A., Srivastava, G.: Federated learning-based anomaly detection for IoT security attacks. IEEE IoT J., 1 (2021)

19. Neshenko, N., Bou-Harb, E., Crichigno, J., Kaddoum, G., Ghani, N.: Demystifying IoT security: an exhaustive survey on IoT vulnerabilities and a first empirical look on internet-scale IoT exploitations. IEEE Commun. Surv. Tutor. **21**(3), 2702–2733 (2019)

20. Nguyen, D.C., Ding, M., Pathirana, P.N., Seneviratne, A., Li, J., Poor, H.V.: Federated learning for internet of things: A comprehensive survey. IEEE Commun. Surv. Tutor. (2021)

21. Nguyen, T.D., Marchal, S., Miettinen, M., Fereidooni, H., Asokan, N., Sadeghi, A.R.: Dïot: a federated self-learning anomaly detection system for IoT. In: 2019 IEEE 39th International Conference on Distributed Computing Systems (ICDCS), pp. 756–767. IEEE (2019)

22. Opacus PyTorch library. opacus.ai

23. Paillier, P.: Public-key cryptosystems based on composite degree residuosity classes. In: Stern, J. (ed.) EUROCRYPT 1999. LNCS, vol. 1592, pp. 223–238. Springer, Heidelberg (1999). https://doi.org/10.1007/3-540-48910-X_16
24. Preuveneers, D., Rimmer, V., Tsingenopoulos, I., Spooren, J., Joosen, W., Ilie-Zudor, E.: Chained anomaly detection models for federated learning: an intrusion detection case study. Appl. Sci. 8(12), 2663 (2018)
25. Shokri, R., Stronati, M., Song, C., Shmatikov, V.: Membership inference attacks against machine learning models. In: 2017 IEEE Symposium on Security and Privacy (SP), pp. 3–18. IEEE (2017)
26. Simonyan, K., Zisserman, A.: Very deep convolutional networks for large-scale image recognition (2015)
27. Truex, S., et al.: A hybrid approach to privacy-preserving federated learning. In: Proceedings of the 12th ACM Workshop on Artificial Intelligence and Security, pp. 1–11 (2019)
28. Tsai, C.F., Hsu, Y.F., Lin, C.Y., Lin, W.Y.: Intrusion detection by machine learning: a review. Expert Syst. Appl. 36(10), 11994–12000 (2009)
29. Wang, X., et al.: Towards accurate anomaly detection in industrial internet-of-things using hierarchical federated learning. IEEE IoT J., 1 (2021)
30. Wei, K., et al.: Federated learning with differential privacy: algorithms and performance analysis. IEEE Trans. Inf. Forensics Secur. 15, 3454–3469 (2020)
31. Xie, L., Lin, K., Wang, S., Wang, F., Zhou, J.: Differentially private generative adversarial network. arXiv preprint arXiv:1802.06739 (2018)
32. Yi, X., Paulet, R., Bertino, E.: Homomorphic encryption. In: Homomorphic Encryption and Applications. SCS, pp. 27–46. Springer, Cham (2014). https://doi.org/10.1007/978-3-319-12229-8_2
33. Zhang, C., Li, S., Xia, J., Wang, W., Yan, F., Liu, Y.: BatchCrypt: efficient homomorphic encryption for cross-silo federated learning. In: 2020 {USENIX} Annual Technical Conference ({USENIX}{ATC} 20), pp. 493–506 (2020)
34. Zhao, R., Yin, Y., Shi, Y., Xue, Z.: Intelligent intrusion detection based on federated learning aided long short-term memory. Phys. Commun. 42, 101157 (2020)
35. Zhou, J., et al.: A survey on federated learning and its applications for accelerating industrial internet of things (2021)

Cryptanalysis of a Fully Anonymous Group Signature with Verifier-Local Revocation from ICICS 2018

Yanhua Zhang[1(✉)], Ximeng Liu[2], Yupu Hu[3], and Huiwen Jia[4]

[1] Zhengzhou University of Light Industry, Zhengzhou 450001, China
yhzhang@email.zzuli.edu.cn
[2] Fuzhou University, Fuzhou 350108, China
[3] Xidian University, Xi'an 710071, China
yphu@mail.xidian.edu.cn
[4] Guangzhou University, Guangzhou 510006, China
hwjia@gzhu.edu.cn

Abstract. For group signatures with verifier-local revocation (GS-VLR), selfless-anonymity (SA), which only ensures the anonymity of a signature against an adversary not possessing the signing secret-keys for members who were involved in the generation of the challenge signature, is strictly weaker than the de facto standard anonymity notion, full-anonymity, where the adversary is allowed to corrupt all members. At ICICS 2018, Hou et al. delivered a lattice-based fully anonymous GS-VLR scheme (as one core building block for their semi-generic construction of hierarchical GS-VLR) based on the first lattice-based GS scheme introduced by Gordon et al. at ASIACRYPT 2010. In this paper, we demonstrate that their scheme does not consider the anonymity for revoked members (no matter the misbehaving members or the honest ones who voluntarily leave), an implicit requirement for GS-VLR in a real-life application. Subsequently, we provide a modification of their construction to fix the mentioned weakness.

Keywords: Group signature · Lattices · Verifier-local revocation · Selfless-anonymity · Full-anonymity

1 Introduction

One desirable functionality of many multi-member signature systems (and group signatures (GS) [7], in particular) is the support of membership revocation (disabling the signing ability of the misbehaving members or honest ones who voluntarily leave). Additionally, the revocation not affecting the remaining unrevoked members (i.e., the valid members) is also a non-trivial problem. For group signatures with membership revocation, the verifier-local revocation (VLR) mechanism seems to be the most flexible choice (compared with re-initialized whole systems or accumulators) when considering some large group (e.g., group of

© Springer Nature Switzerland AG 2021
M. Yang et al. (Eds.): NSS 2021, LNCS 13041, pp. 369–382, 2021.
https://doi.org/10.1007/978-3-030-92708-0_24

all employees of a big company, such as Huawei and Alibaba), because it only requires verifiers to download up-to-date revocation information, and signers are not involved and free from this concern. Furthermore, VLR is practical and more suitable for a mobile environment where the signers (i.e., members) are often off-line (in addition, in most of real-life scenarios, the number of verifiers is much less than that of signers) or some computationally weak devices are pervasively adopted (e.g., smart cards).

The concept of group signatures with verifier-local revocation (GS-VLR) was formalized by Boneh and Shacham [5] at CCS 2004, and subsequently investigated and extended in [4,6,12,13,16,17]. However, all of these constructions are operating in a bilinear map setting, and vulnerable to be resistance against quantum computers for a future post-quantum cryptography era. As the old saying goes, not putting all your eggs in one basket, thus it is encouraging to consider some alternative instantiations, post-quantum constructions, e.g., based on the lattice-based cryptosystem.

LATTICE-BASED GS-VLR. Lattice-based GS-VLR scheme was first proposed by Roux-Langlois et al. [21] at PKC 2014, and thus, the first such quantum-resistant construction supporting membership revocation. Subsequently several improved schemes achieving different levels of efficiency and security notions were proposed [8,14,18,20,22–25]. But almost of them only achieve selfless-anonymity (SA), which only ensures the anonymity of a signature against an adversary not possessing the signing secret-keys for members who were involved in the generation of challenge signature, is strictly weaker than the de facto standard anonymity notion, full-anonymity (FA)[1], where adversary is allowed to corrupt all members.

For a conventional lattice-based GS-VLR, an additional argument called revocation list (RL) is provided for signature verification, which contains a list of revocation tokens (RT) for the revoked members. Once some member is revoked (by adding his RT to RL, no matter a misbehaving member or a voluntary one), the issued signatures after the member's revocation can be detected and cannot be accepted by signature verification algorithm any more (although the real identity information may not be disclosed). Further, anyone, including manager, verifiers

---

[1] At SCN 2018, Ishida et al. [12] proposed the basic framework of fully anonymous GS-VLR builded on ideas from creative work of Bellare et al. [3]. Concretely, a fully anonymous GS-VLR is obtained from a digital signature scheme, a key-private public-key encryption scheme, and a non-interactive zero-knowledge proof system. However, no any specific cryptographic scheme was given by Ishida et al., and we do not know how to adopt algorithms over lattices to substitute all the operations efficiently and safely, and we cannot simply follow the steps of [12] to design a lattice-based FA-GS-VLR scheme. At ICICS 2018, Perera and Koshiba [19] claimed that the first lattice-based GS-VLR scheme achieving full security (i.e., FA and full-traceability) was successfully constructed by them. However, in fact, their construction does not satisfy FA and we explain this in detail in our another paper which was just accepted by ACNS 2021 workshops. Therefore, we have to tailor a new construction so that it can rely on some new and creatively techniques for lattice-based cryptography.

and even an adversary, who has all members' RTs (the corresponding relationship between the member's identity and his RT) can determine the member's real identity using the implicit-tracing algorithm (by successively executing the signature verification algorithm which returns Invalid). Thus, in the anonymity definition of a conventional lattice-based GS-VLR, the RTs of two distinct members id_0 and id_1 selected by an adversary in the generation of the challenge signature cannot be given. Particularly, to eliminate a need for a trusted revocation authority and not disclosure the real identity of revoked members, RT is directly dependent on member's signing secret-key (e.g., RT is just a half of signing secret-key [5] or a modular multiplication of some public matrix and the part of signing secret-key vector [8, 14, 18, 20–25]). Thus, the signing secret-keys of these two selected members (i.e., id_0 and id_1) also cannot be provided to the adversary, which is exactly the definition of SA introduced by Boneh and Shacham [5] at CCS 2004.

As it was first asserted by Ishida et al. [12] at SCN 2018, a GS-VLR scheme (including lattice-based constructions) with the conventional design method for RT (i.e., the RT is directly dependent on signing secret-key) can *never* achieve a stronger anonymity, the FA security, and we have to look for other creative ways to construct, or even from scratch. Additionally, although it was not explicitly introduced in the anonymity definition for SA-GS-VLR, the anonymity (i.e., not disclosing the real identity information) for the revoked members (e.g., the misbehaving members) should also be guaranteed in a real-life application, especially for a non-misbehaving member who inadvertently loses his signing secret-key or an honest member who voluntarily leaves for some reason, such as a promotion. After all, no member is willing to expose his real identity information to others under any circumstance (except the manager in the implicit-tracing). Thus, in all present literature for the SA-GS-VLR constructions, where RT is directly and exactly dependent on the member's signing secret-key (even in a pioneering work for GS-VLR [5], whose RT is directly the left half of signing secret-key), given a RT in RL, the real identity information for the corresponding revoked member is not disclosed for all verifiers (an exception is the group manager owning all the corresponding relationships between the members' identities and their RTs). Therefore, in the design of FA-GS-VLR schemes (including lattice-based ones), besides the classical two security definitions, FA and full-traceability, the above anonymity requirement should also be automatically inherited. Encouragingly, a basic framework of FA-GS-VLR construction given by Ishida et al. [12] satisfies the anonymity for revoked members.

At ICICS 2018, Hou et al. [11] delivered a lattice-based FA-GS-VLR, one core building block for their semi-generic construction of hierarchical GS-VLR, based on the first lattice-based GS introduced by Gordon et al. [10] at ASIACRYPT 2010. Then main innovations of Hou et al. are to set the tracing secret-keys $\mathbf{R}_{B_0}, \mathbf{R}_{B_1}, \cdots, \mathbf{R}_{B_{N-1}}$ for manager in [10] as the members' RTs and incorporate original signature verification algorithm and signature open algorithm into their new signature verification algorithm. For other steps (mainly including the key generation algorithm (KeyGen) and signature algorithm (Sign)), they are almost entirely following the same operations in [10]. Because the RT of a member is completely independent of his signing secret-key, the adversary is allowed to corrupt all members and sign a message by himself arbitrarily. That is exactly based on the independence of RT, Hou et al. concluded that the FA security of their construction is achieved, and thus a lattice-based FA-GS-VLR scheme was constructed successfully (although with a relatively low efficiency).

OUR RESULTS. In this paper, we demonstrate that the scheme of Hou et al. [11] does not consider the anonymity for revoked members (what we discussed earlier), and thus cannot satisfy this implicit security requirement in most of real-life scenarios. Subsequently, we provide a modification of Hou et al.'s construction to fix this weakness so that it achieves this security notion which was implicit in [5,8,14,18,20–25]. To avoid our cryptanalysis (i.e., an attack) presented in this paper, we exploit a key permutation operation for the group public-keys (Gpk) and let Gpk of the new GS-VLR system is rearranged the original order in [11]. Moreover, we also regenerate the signature corresponding to the rearranged Gpk despite the signer does not know this permutation. As a result, we obtain an effective modification thanks to the randomness and zero-knowledge of the exploited permutation, and a well-known hardness assumption of learning with errors (LWE) problem in the random oracle model. The detailed cryptanalysis and scheme description are given latter in Sects. 4 and 5.

ORGANIZATION. After establishing some preliminaries (e.g., the syntax and security model of GS-VLR and the background on lattices) in Sect. 2. Then Sect. 3 turns to review the lattice-based FA-GS-VLR proposed by Hou et al. at ICICS 2018. In Sect. 4, we give a detailed cryptanalysis to show that their construction does not consider the anonymity for revoked members, and anyone possessing the up-to-date RTs can compute the real identity of revoked members. Our modification, which simply exploits an extra permutation, is proposed in Sect. 5. In the final section, we conclude our whole paper.

2   Preliminaries

NOTATIONS. All vectors are in the column form and denoted in bold-faced, lowercase letters (e.g., $\mathbf{a}$, $\mathbf{b}$), and matrices are denoted in bold-faced, upper-case letters (e.g., $\mathbf{A}$, $\mathbf{B}$). We use $\mathcal{S}_k$ to denote the set of all permutations of k elements, and $h \xleftarrow{\$} \mathcal{S}$ to denote that the variable h is uniformly sampled from a finite set $\mathcal{S}$. $\|\cdot\|$ (and $\|\cdot\|_\infty$) is used to denote the Euclidean norm ℓ_2 (and the infinity norm ℓ_∞) of a vector. The standard notations $\widetilde{\mathcal{O}}$, ω are used to classify the growth of functions, without specification, $\log e$ denotes the logarithm of e with base 2, and PPT stands for "probabilistic polynomial-time".

2.1   Group Signatures with Verifier-Local Revocation

In this subsection, we recall the syntax and security model of GS-VLR, which was formalized by Boneh and Shacham [5] and further studied in [8,16,17,22–25].

Definition 1. *A* GS-VLR *scheme consists of three following algorithms:*

- KeyGen($1^n, N$): *A* PPT *algorithm takes as input the security parameter n and the group size N (i.e., N is the maximum number of members), and it outputs the group public-key* Gpk, *a set of members' signing secret-keys* Gsk $= (\text{gsk}_0, \text{gsk}_1, \cdots, \text{gsk}_{N-1})$, *a set of members'* RT*s,* Grt $= (\text{grt}_0, \text{grt}_1, \cdots, \text{grt}_{N-1})$, *where* gsk_i *(and* grt_i*) denotes signing secret-key (and* RT*) for member id with index* $i \in \{0, 1, \cdots, N-1\}$.
- Sign(Gpk, gsk_i, m): *A* PPT *algorithm takes as input* Gpk, *a signing secret-key* gsk_i *for id with index i, a message* m $\in \{0,1\}^*$, *and it outputs a signature σ.*
- Verify(Gpk, RL, σ, m): *A deterministic algorithm takes as input* Gpk, *a set of* RT*s,* RL $\subseteq$ Grt *and a signature σ on a message* m $\in \{0,1\}^*$, *and it returns either* Invalid *or* Valid. *The* Valid *indicates that σ is a valid signature on* m *and the real signer (i.e., a member) has not been revoked.*

Remark: Any valid GS-VLR scheme enjoys an implicit-tracing algorithm: given (m, σ), the party owning Grt (i.e., a corresponding relationship between the member's real identity and his RT) can determine the signer of σ by successively executing Verify(Gpk, RL $= \{\text{grt}_i\}, \sigma, \text{m}$) for $i = 0, 1, \cdots$ and outputting the first identity index $i^* \in \{0, 1, \cdots, N-1\}$ for which Verify returns Invalid.

A FA-GS-VLR scheme should satisfies the following three properties: correctness, FA, and full-traceability.

Definition 2. *A* GS-VLR *scheme is* correct *if for all* (Gpk, Gsk, Grt) $\leftarrow$ KeyGen, *any member $i \in \{0, 1, \cdots, N-1\}$, all* $\text{gsk}_i \subseteq$ Gsk, *all* RL $\subseteq$ Grt *and* m $\in \{0,1\}^*$, *we have that*

$$\text{Verify}(\text{Gpk}, \text{RL}, \text{Sign}(\text{Gpk}, \text{gsk}_i, \text{m}), \text{m}) = \text{Valid} \Leftrightarrow \text{grt}_i \notin \text{RL}.$$

Definition 3. *A* GS-VLR *scheme is* fully anonymous *if no* PPT *adversary has a non-negligible advantage* $\text{Adv}_{\mathcal{A}}^{\text{Full-anon}}$ *in the following game (between a challenger $\mathcal{C}$ and an adversary $\mathcal{A}$).*

a. Initialization: $\mathcal{C}$ *obtains* (Gpk, Gsk, Grt) $\leftarrow$ KeyGen *and sends* (Gpk, Gsk) *to $\mathcal{A}$.*
b. Query phase: *Before outputting two challenge identities, $\mathcal{A}$ adaptively makes a polynomially bounded number of revoking queries:*

- Revoking: *Request for a revocation token* RT *for id with i, $\mathcal{C}$ returns* grt_i.

c. Challenge: $\mathcal{A}$ *outputs a message* m$^* \in \{0,1\}^*$, *two distinct members* id_0 *and* id_1, *with indices i_0 and i_1, respectively. $\mathcal{A}$ did not make revoking query at either member, i.e., id_0 and id_1 have not been revoked. $\mathcal{C}$ chooses a bit $b \xleftarrow{\$} \{0, 1\}$, and returns $\sigma^* \leftarrow$ Sign(Gpk, gsk_{i_b}, m*) as a challenge on* m* *by* id_b.
d. Restricted query: *After obtaining a challenge signature σ^*, $\mathcal{A}$ can still make queries as before, but with the restriction not allowed to make query for* id_0 *or* id_1.
e. Guessing: $\mathcal{A}$ *outputs a bit $b^* \in \{0, 1\}$, and wins if $b^* = b$.*

The advantage of $\mathcal{A}$ in the above Full-Anonymity game is defined as

$$\mathsf{Adv}_{\mathcal{A}}^{\mathsf{Full\text{-}anon}} = |\Pr[b^* = b] - 1/2|.$$

Definition 4. *A GS-VLR scheme is* fully traceable *if no* PPT *adversary has a non-negligible advantage* $\mathsf{Adv}_{\mathcal{A}}^{\mathsf{Full\text{-}trace}}$ *in the following game.*

a. *Initialization:* $\mathcal{C}$ *obtains* $(\mathsf{Gpk}, \mathsf{Gsk}, \mathsf{Grt}) \leftarrow \mathsf{KeyGen}$ *and provides* $(\mathsf{Gpk}, \mathsf{Grt})$ *to* $\mathcal{A}$. *It also defines a initial corruption set* $\mathsf{Corr} = \varnothing$.
b. *Query phase: Before outputting a valid forgery,* $\mathcal{A}$ *adaptively makes a polynomially bounded number of queries:*

- *Signing: Request for a signature on* $\mathsf{m} \in \{0,1\}^*$ *for* id *with index* i, $\mathcal{C}$ *returns* $\sigma \leftarrow \mathsf{Sign}(\mathsf{Gpk}, \mathsf{gsk}_i, \mathsf{m})$.
- *Corrupting: Request for a signing secret-key for* id *with index* i, $\mathcal{C}$ *returns* gsk_i *and then sets* $\mathsf{Corr} = \mathsf{Corr} \cup (\mathsf{id}, i)$.

c. *Forgery:* $\mathcal{A}$ *outputs a message-signature pair* (m^*, σ^*), *a set of members' revocation tokens* $\mathsf{RL}^* \subseteq \mathsf{Grt}$. $\mathcal{A}$ *wins the game if:*

- $\mathsf{Verify}(\mathsf{Gpk}, \mathsf{RL}^*, \sigma^*, \mathsf{m}^*) = \mathsf{Valid}$.
- *The* implicit-tracing *algorithm fails, or traces to a member outside of the coalition* $\mathsf{Corr} \backslash \mathsf{RL}^*$ *(Because* σ^* *cannot be traced to a member* $i^* \in (\mathsf{Corr} \cap \mathsf{RL}^*)$, *thus* $\mathsf{Corr} \backslash \mathsf{RL}^*$ *can also be modified to* Corr).
- *The signature* σ^* *is non-trivial, i.e.,* $\mathcal{A}$ *has not obtained* σ^* *by making a signing query on* m^*.

The advantage of $\mathcal{A}$ in the above Full-Traceability game is defined as its probability in wining as $\mathsf{SuccPT}_{\mathcal{A}}$, and denoted by $\mathsf{Adv}_{\mathcal{A}}^{\mathsf{Full\text{-}Trace}} = \mathsf{SuccPT}_{\mathcal{A}}$.

2.2 Cryptographic Tools from Lattices

In this subsection, we recall several useful cryptographic tools from lattices (for our cryptanalysis and modifications).

Definition 5. *For integers* n, m, $q \geq 2$, *a random matrix* $\mathsf{A} \in \mathbb{Z}_q^{n \times m}$, *the* m-*dimensional* q-*ary orthogonal lattice* $\Lambda_q^{\perp}(\mathsf{A})$ *is defined as:*

$$\Lambda_q^{\perp}(\mathsf{A}) = \{\mathbf{e} \in \mathbb{Z}^m \mid \mathsf{A} \cdot \mathbf{e} = 0 \bmod q\}.$$

For $s > 0$, the Gaussian function on $\mathbb{R}^m$ with center $\mathbf{c}$ is defined as:

$$\forall \mathbf{e} \in \mathbb{R}^m, \ \rho_{s,\mathbf{c}}(\mathbf{e}) = \exp(-\pi \|\mathbf{e} - \mathbf{c}\|^2 / s^2).$$

For $\mathbf{c} \in \mathbb{R}^m$, the discrete Gaussian distribution over Λ is defined as:

$$\forall \mathbf{e} \in \mathbb{Z}^m, \ \mathcal{D}_{\Lambda,s,\mathbf{c}} = \rho_{s,\mathbf{c}}(\mathbf{e}) / \textstyle\sum_{\mathbf{e} \in \Lambda} \rho_{s,\mathbf{c}}(\mathbf{e}),$$

where $\mathcal{D}_{\Lambda,s,\mathbf{c}}$ is denoted as $\mathcal{D}_{\Lambda,s}$ if $\mathbf{c} = \mathbf{0}$.

Lemma 1 ([9]). *For integers n, $q \geq 2$, $m \geq 2n \log q$, let a positive real number $s \geq \omega(\sqrt{\log m})$, then the following properties are satisfied:*

1. *For all but a $2q^{-n}$ fraction of all $\mathbf{A} \in \mathbb{Z}_q^{n \times m}$, and $\mathbf{e} \xleftarrow{\$} \mathcal{D}_{\mathbb{Z}^m, s}$, the distribution of $\mathbf{A} \cdot \mathbf{e} \bmod q$ is statistical close to uniform distribution over $\mathbb{Z}_q^n$.*

2. *For $\mathbf{e} \xleftarrow{\$} \mathcal{D}_{\mathbb{Z}^m, s}$ and $\beta = \lceil s \cdot \log m \rceil$, $\Pr[\|\mathbf{e}\|_\infty \leq \beta]$ is overwhelming.*
3. *The min-entropy of $\mathcal{D}_{\mathbb{Z}^m, s}$ is at least $m - 1$ (i.e., for any $\mathbf{e} \in \mathcal{D}_{\mathbb{Z}^m, s}$, we have $\mathcal{D}_{\mathbb{Z}^m, s}(\mathbf{e}) \leq 2^{1-m}$).*

We recall three PPT algorithms from previous works that will be used in our work (mainly in the design of modifications). The TrapGen algorithm is adopted to return a statistically close to uniform $\mathbf{A} \in \mathbb{Z}_q^{n \times m}$ together with a trapdoor (with a low *Gram-Schmidt* norm) for a q-ary $\Lambda_q^\perp(\mathbf{A})$; The SamplePre algorithm is adopted to return some short Gaussian vectors over $\Lambda_q^u(\mathbf{A})$, which is a coset of $\Lambda_q^\perp(\mathbf{A})$. The OrthoSamp algorithm is a variant of TrapGen, and it returns a matrix $\mathbf{A} \in \mathbb{Z}_q^{n \times m}$ with an associated trapdoor $\mathbf{R_A}$ with the requirement that the rows of $\mathbf{A}$ are orthogonal to the row of a given matrix $\mathbf{B} \in \mathbb{Z}_q^{n \times m}$.

Lemma 2 ([1,2,15]). *Let $n \geq 1$, $q \geq 2$, and $m \geq 2n\lceil \log q \rceil$, there exists a PPT algorithm TrapGen(q, n, m) outputting $\mathbf{A} \in \mathbb{Z}_q^{n \times m}$ and $\mathbf{R_A}$, such that $\mathbf{A}$ is statistically close to uniform in $\mathbb{Z}_q^{n \times m}$ and $\mathbf{R_A}$ is a trapdoor for $\Lambda_q^\perp(\mathbf{A})$.*

Lemma 3 ([9,15]). *Let $n \geq 1$, $q \geq 2$, and $m \geq 2n\lceil \log q \rceil$, given $\mathbf{A} \in \mathbb{Z}_q^{n \times m}$, a trapdoor $\mathbf{R_A}$ for $\Lambda_q^\perp(\mathbf{A})$, a Gaussian parameter $s = \omega(\sqrt{n \log q \log n})$, $\mathbf{u} \in \mathbb{Z}_q^n$, there exists a PPT algorithm SamplePre$(\mathbf{A}, \mathbf{R_A}, \mathbf{u}, s)$ returning a Gaussian vector $\mathbf{e} \in \Lambda_q^u(\mathbf{A})$ sampled from a distribution statistically close to $\mathcal{D}_{\Lambda_q^u(\mathbf{A}), s}$.*

Lemma 4 ([10]). *Let $n \geq 1$, $q \geq 2$, and $m \geq n + 8n\lceil \log q \rceil$, given $\mathbf{B} \in \mathbb{Z}_q^{n \times m}$, whose columns span $\mathbb{Z}_q^n$, there is a PPT algorithm OrthoSamp$(\mathbf{B}, q, n, m)$ returning $\mathbf{A} \in \mathbb{Z}_q^{n \times m}$ and $\mathbf{R_A}$, such that $\mathbf{A}$ is statistically close to uniform over $\mathbb{Z}_q^{n \times m}$ and $\mathbf{R_A}$ is a trapdoor for $\Lambda_q^\perp(\mathbf{A})$, and $\mathbf{A} \cdot \mathbf{B}^\top = 0 \bmod q$, in particular.*

We review the learning with errors (LWE) problem, together with its hardness result.

Definition 6. *The $\mathsf{LWE}_{n, q, \chi}$ problem is defined as follows: given a random vector $\mathbf{s} \xleftarrow{\$} \mathbb{Z}_q^n$, a probability distribution χ over $\mathbb{Z}$, let $\mathcal{A}_{\mathbf{s}, \chi}$ be a distribution obtained by sampling $\mathbf{A} \in \mathbb{Z}_q^{n \times m}$, $\mathbf{e} \xleftarrow{\$} \chi^m$, and output $(\mathbf{A}, \mathbf{A}^\top \mathbf{s} + \mathbf{e})$, and make distinguish between $\mathcal{A}_{\mathbf{s}, \chi}$ and uniform distribution $\mathcal{U} \xleftarrow{\$} \mathbb{Z}_q^{n \times m} \times \mathbb{Z}_q^m$.*

Let $\beta \geq \sqrt{n} \cdot \omega(\log n)$, for a prime power q, given a β-bounded distribution χ, the $\mathsf{LWE}_{n, q, \chi}$ problem is at least as hard as the shortest independent vectors problem $\mathsf{SIVP}_{\widetilde{\mathcal{O}}(nq/\beta)}$.

3   Hou et al.'s FA-GS-VLR Scheme

In this section, we review Hou et al.'s FA-GS-VLR scheme [11]. The description is as follows.

- KeyGen($1^n, 1^N$): On input the security parameter n and the group size $N = poly(n)$. Let the dimension $m = 8n\lceil \log q \rceil$, the modulus $q = poly(n)$ and a parameter $s = c\sqrt{n \log q} \cdot \omega(\sqrt{\log m})$, where the absolute constant $c < 40$. This algorithm works as follows:
  1. For $i \in \{0, 1, \cdots, N-1\}$, run TrapGen($q, n, m$) to generate $\mathbf{B}_i \in \mathbb{Z}_q^{n \times m}$ and a trapdoor $\mathbf{R}_{\mathbf{B}_i}$.
  2. For $i \in \{0, 1, \cdots, N-1\}$, run OrthoSamp($\mathbf{B}_i, q, n, m$) to generate $\mathbf{A}_i \in \mathbb{Z}_q^{n \times m}$ and $\mathbf{R}_{\mathbf{A}_i}$.
  3. Let the member i's signing secret-key be $\mathsf{gsk}_i = \mathbf{R}_{\mathbf{A}_i}$ and its revocation token be $\mathsf{grt}_i = \mathbf{R}_{\mathbf{B}_i}$.
  4. Output the group public-key $\mathsf{Gpk} = ((\mathbf{B}_0, \mathbf{A}_0), (\mathbf{B}_1, \mathbf{A}_1), \cdots, (\mathbf{B}_{N-1}, \mathbf{A}_{N-1}))$, the members' signing secret-keys $\mathsf{Gsk} = (\mathsf{gsk}_0, \mathsf{gsk}_1, \cdots, \mathsf{gsk}_{N-1})$ and the revocation tokens $\mathsf{Grt} = (\mathsf{grt}_0, \mathsf{grt}_1, \cdots, \mathsf{grt}_{N-1})$.
- Sign($\mathsf{Gpk}, \mathsf{gsk}_i, \mathsf{m}$): Let $\mathcal{H} : \{0, 1\}^* \to \mathbb{Z}_q^n$ be a hash function, modeled as a random oracle. On input Gpk and a message $\mathsf{m} \in \{0, 1\}^*$, the member i with a signing secret-key $\mathsf{gsk}_i = \mathbf{R}_{\mathbf{A}_i}$ does as in [10], i.e., specifying the following steps:
  1. Sample $\mathbf{v} \xleftarrow{\$} \{0, 1\}^n$.
  2. For $j \in \{0, 1, \cdots, N-1\}$, define $\mathbf{h}_j = \mathcal{H}(\mathsf{m}, \mathbf{v}, j) \in \mathbb{Z}_q^n$.
  3. For $j = i$, run SamplePre($\mathbf{A}_i, \mathbf{R}_{\mathbf{A}_i}, \mathbf{h}_i, s$) to obtain $\mathbf{e}_i \in \mathbb{Z}^m$.
  4. For $j \neq i$, sample $\mathbf{e}_j \in \mathbb{Z}_q^m$ satisfying the condition that $\mathbf{A}_j \cdot \mathbf{e}_j = \mathbf{h}_j \bmod q$.
  5. For $j \in \{0, 1, \cdots, N-1\}$, sample $\mathbf{s}_j \xleftarrow{\$} \mathbb{Z}_q^n$ and compute $\mathbf{z}_j = \mathbf{B}_j^\top \cdot \mathbf{s}_j + \mathbf{e}_j \bmod q$.
  6. Compute a non-interactive witness-indistinguishable (NIWI) proof δ for the gap language $L_{s,\gamma}$ as discussed in [10].
  7. Output a signature $\sigma = (\mathbf{v}, \mathbf{z}_0, \mathbf{z}_1, \cdots, \mathbf{z}_{N-1}, \delta)$.
- Verify($\mathsf{Gpk}, \mathsf{RL}, \mathsf{m}, \sigma$): On input Gpk, a signature σ on a message $\mathsf{m} \in \{0, 1\}^*$, and a set of revocation tokens $\mathsf{RL} = \{\{\mathbf{R}_{\mathbf{B}_{j_\ell}}\}_{j_\ell}\} \subseteq \mathsf{Grt}$, the verifier specifies the following steps:
  1. Parse the signature $\sigma = (\mathbf{v}, \mathbf{z}_0, \mathbf{z}_1, \cdots, \mathbf{z}_{N-1}, \delta)$.
  2. If δ is not correct, then return Invalid.
  3. For $j \in \{0, 1, \cdots, N-1\}$, compute $\mathbf{h}_j = \mathcal{H}(\mathsf{m}, \mathbf{v}, j)$.
  4. For $j \in \{0, 1, \cdots, N-1\}$, if $\mathbf{A}_j \cdot \mathbf{z}_j = \mathbf{h}_j \bmod q$ does not hold, then return Invalid.
  5. For $\mathbf{R}_{\mathbf{B}_{j_\ell}} \in \mathsf{RL}$, $\ell = 1, 2, \cdots, |\mathsf{RL}|$, compute $\mathbf{e}'_{j_\ell} = \mathbf{R}_{\mathbf{B}_{j_\ell}}^\top \cdot \mathbf{z}_{j_\ell} \bmod q$ and $\mathbf{e}_{j_\ell} = (\mathbf{R}_{\mathbf{B}_{j_\ell}}^\top)^{-1} \cdot \mathbf{e}'_{j_\ell}$. If $\mathbf{e}_{j_\ell} \leq s\sqrt{m}$, then return Invalid.
  6. Return Valid.

4   Our Cryptanalysis of Hou et al.'s Scheme

By our analysis carefully, technically, the FA-GS-VLR scheme of Hou et al. [11] is mainly built from the first lattice-based GS scheme introduced by Gordon et al. [10]. The central work of Hou et al. is setting the tracing secret-keys $\mathbf{R}_{\mathbf{B}_0}$, $\mathbf{R}_{\mathbf{B}_1}, \cdots, \mathbf{R}_{\mathbf{B}_{N-1}}$ for manager in [10] as the member's RT and incorporate original verification algorithm and open algorithm into a new verification algorithm.

Because the RT of any group member is completely independent of his signing secret-key, the adversary is allowed to corrupt all members and sign a message by himself. It is exactly based on the independence of RT, Hou et al. concluded that their lattice-based GS-VLR scheme achieved the FA security, and took it for granted that their new construction also inherits all the security of the existing SA-GS-VLR schemes. As we have discussed in Introduction, no members (including the misbehaving members, non-misbehaving members and honest members) are willing to expose their real identity information to others under any circumstance (except a manager in the implicit-tracing operation), thus the anonymity (i.e., not disclosing the real identity information) for the revoked members should also be guaranteed in a real-life application, and this anonymity requirement is satisfied by all present literature for the SA-GS-VLR constructions and a basic FA-GS-VLR framework introduced by Ishida et al. [12]. Since the RTs of Hou et al. are completely related to the public matrices in Gpk, which imply a certain corresponding relationship with the members' identities information, any verifiers (even including the adversary) may achieve some other confidential information other than those in the standard anonymity definition (SA and FA). Based on this observed fact, we describe a cryptanalysis (i.e., an attack) for the FA-GS-VLR construction of Hou et al. [11].

Description of Our Cryptanalysis. Our cryptanalysis is as follows.

1. Once some member (e.g., the member with an identity index $i \in \{0, \cdots, N - 1\}$) is revoked, his RT, the matrix $\mathbf{R}_{\mathbf{B}_i} \in \mathbb{Z}^{m \times m}$, will be added into RL.
2. Once obtaining Gpk $= ((\mathbf{B}_0, \mathbf{A}_0), (\mathbf{B}_1, \mathbf{A}_1), \cdots, (\mathbf{B}_{N-1}, \mathbf{A}_{N-1}))$ and RL $\subseteq$ Grt, the verifier $\mathcal{V}$ uniformly samples an element from RL, without loss of generality, we assume that the matrix is $\mathbf{R}_{\mathbf{B}_i} \in \mathbb{Z}^{m \times m}$.
3. Since $\mathbf{R}_{\mathbf{B}_i}$ is the trapdoor basis of orthogonal lattice $\Lambda_q^{\perp}(\mathbf{B}_i)$ (according to Lemma 2, thus $\mathbf{B}_i \cdot \mathbf{R}_{\mathbf{B}_i} = \mathbf{0} \bmod q$. By successively executing $\mathbf{B}_j \cdot \mathbf{R}_{\mathbf{B}_i} \bmod q$ for $j = 0, 1, \cdots, \mathcal{V}$ outputs the first matrix $\mathbf{B}_i$ for which the matrix product returns $\mathbf{0}$.
4. Further, $\mathcal{V}$ checks that $\mathbf{A}_i \cdot \mathbf{B}_i^{\top} \stackrel{?}{=} \mathbf{0} \bmod q$ (here, $\mathbf{A}_i$ is the matrix behind $\mathbf{B}_i$), if it holds, then returns the sequence number i^* of $\mathbf{A}_i$ in Gpk (*Remark:* the sequence number of Gpk starts with 0 and ends with $2N - 1$).
5. Let $i = (i^* - 1)/2$, which is just the identity index of a revoked member whose RT is $\mathbf{R}_{\mathbf{B}_i}$.
6. For other RTs in RL, $\mathcal{V}$ re-executes the steps 3, 4 and 5, and returns all indices.

Correctness of Our Cryptanalysis. The correctness of our cryptanalysis is straightforward. First, the steps 1–4 are the basic facts according to the KeyGen algorithm in [11] and [10]. Second, because the group size $N = poly(n)$, the steps 5 and 6 can be done in a polynomial time, and for every valid RT $\in$ RL, there must be an index returned, thus the real identity information of revoked member is disclosed, and so our cryptanalysis algorithm outputs the correct answer with probability 1.

5 Our Modification

Now, we present the modification of Hou et al.'s lattice-based FA-GS-VLR scheme. As it was discussed in Sect. 4, the reason for their failure on achieving the anonymity requirement for the revoked members is that the RT of a member is related to some public matrix, whose sequence number in Gpk just implies the member's identity information (i.e., the identity index). We attempt to break the tight correspondence between sequence numbers and public matrices in Gpk and disorganize the order of some public matrices with a key permutation operation.

5.1 Description of the Scheme

The main steps are described as follows:

- KeyGen($1^n, 1^N$): On input the security parameter n and the group size $N = poly(n)$. All other parameters and the first three steps are the same as in Hou et al.'s scheme, and the subsequent PPT algorithms are as follows:
    4. Sample a permutation $\varphi \xleftarrow{\$} \mathcal{S}_N$ (Remark: $\mathcal{S}_N$ denotes the set of all permutations of the elements $0, 1, \cdots, N - 1$, and thus the number of φ is $|\mathcal{S}_N| = N!$.
    5. For $i \in \{0, 1, \cdots, N - 1\}$, define $\mathbf{C}_i = (\mathbf{C}_{i,0}, \mathbf{C}_{i,1}) = (\mathbf{B}_i, \mathbf{A}_i)$.
    6. Output Gpk $= (\mathbf{C}_{\varphi(0)}, \mathbf{C}_{\varphi(1)}, \cdots, \mathbf{C}_{\varphi(N-1)})$, Gsk $= (\mathrm{gsk}_0, \cdots, \mathrm{gsk}_{N-1})$, and Grt $= (\mathrm{grt}_0, \cdots, \mathrm{grt}_{N-1})$.
- Sign(Gpk, gsk_i, m): As in Hou et al.'s scheme, let $\mathcal{H} : \{0, 1\}^* \to \mathbb{Z}_q^n$ be a hash function and modeled as a random oracle. On input Gpk and a message m $\in \{0, 1\}^*$, the member i with $\mathrm{gsk}_i = \mathbf{R}_{\mathbf{A}_i}$ does as follows:
    1. Sample $\mathbf{v} \xleftarrow{\$} \{0, 1\}^n$.
    2. For $j \in \{0, 1, \cdots, N - 1\}$, define $\mathbf{h}_j = \mathcal{H}(\mathsf{m}, \mathbf{v}, j) \in \mathbb{Z}_q^n$.
    3. Compute the sequence number of $\mathbf{C}_{j,1}$ such that $\mathbf{C}_{j,1} \cdot \mathbf{R}_{\mathbf{A}_i} = \mathbf{0} \bmod q$ (Since $\mathbf{R}_{\mathbf{A}_i}$ is the trapdoor basis of $\Lambda_q^\perp(\mathbf{A}_i)$, thus $\mathbf{A}_i \cdot \mathbf{R}_{\mathbf{A}_i} = \mathbf{0} \bmod q$, by successively executing $\mathbf{C}_{j,1} \cdot \mathbf{R}_{\mathbf{A}_i} \bmod q$ for $j = 0, 1, \cdots$, output the first matrix $\mathbf{C}_{j,1}$ for which the matrix product returns $\mathbf{0}$), we assume that the sequence number is k.
    4. For $j = k$, run SamplePre($\mathbf{C}_{k,1}, \mathbf{R}_{\mathbf{A}_i}, \mathbf{h}_i, s$) to obtain $\mathbf{e}_k \in \mathbb{Z}^m$.
    5. For $j \neq k$, sample $\mathbf{e}_j \in \mathbb{Z}_q^m$ satisfying $\mathbf{C}_{j,1} \cdot \mathbf{e}_j = \mathbf{h}_j \bmod q$.
    6. For $j \in \{0, 1, \cdots, N - 1\}$, sample $\mathbf{s}_j \xleftarrow{\$} \mathbb{Z}_q^n$ and compute $\mathbf{z}_j = \mathbf{C}_{j,0}^\top \cdot \mathbf{s}_j + \mathbf{e}_j \bmod q$.
    7. Compute an NIWI proof δ for the gap language $L_{s,\gamma}$ as in Hou et al.'s scheme and [10].

8. Output the signature $\sigma = (\mathbf{v}, \mathbf{z}_0, \mathbf{z}_1, \cdots, \mathbf{z}_{N-1}, \delta)$.

- Verify(Gpk, RL, m, σ): On input Gpk, a signature σ on a message $\mathsf{m} \in \{0, 1\}^*$, and a set of revocation tokens RL $= \{\{\mathbf{R}_{\mathbf{B}_{j_\ell}}\}_{j_\ell}\} \subseteq$ Grt, the verifier does almost the same first four steps as in Hou et al.'s scheme except replacing $\mathbf{A}_j$ with $\mathbf{C}_{j,1}$. For the subsequent two algorithms, they do as follows:

    5. For $j \in \{0, 1, \cdots, N-1\}$ and $\mathbf{R}_{\mathbf{B}_{j_\ell}} \in$ RL, compute $\mathbf{e}'_{j_\ell, j} = \mathbf{R}^\top_{\mathbf{B}_{j_\ell}} \cdot \mathbf{z}_j \bmod q$ and $\mathbf{e}_{j_\ell, j} = (\mathbf{R}^\top_{\mathbf{B}_{j_\ell}})^{-1} \cdot \mathbf{e}'_{j_\ell, j}$. If $\mathbf{e}_{j_\ell, j} \leq s\sqrt{m}$, then return Invalid.

    6. Return Valid.

5.2   Analysis of the Scheme

Correctness: Technically, our modification creatively exploits a permutation φ of integers $0, 1, \cdots, N-1$, and the number of φ is $N! \approx \sqrt{2\pi N} \cdot (\frac{N}{\exp})^N > \widetilde{\mathcal{O}}(2^n)$ (the group size $N = poly(n)$). For any adversary (including the members) except the manager can correctly guess φ with a probability at most $1/N!$, which is negligible. For the signer (i.e., the member), although he also does not know this permutation φ, he generates a signature by correctly computing the sequence number of a public matrix in Gpk, which is corresponding to his signing secret-key. For our other steps, they are the same as in Hou et al.'s scheme, and thus, our modification, a lattice-based FA-GS-VLR scheme that achieves the anonymity for revoked members, is correct.

FA and Full-Traceability: For the FA and full-traceability, we show the theorem:

Theorem 1. *Let parameters q, m, s be defined as in Sect. 5.1, if* $\mathsf{LWE}_{n,q,\chi=\Psi_\alpha^m}$ *problem is hard for $\alpha = s/(q\sqrt{2})$, GapSVP_γ problem is hard for $\gamma = \widetilde{\mathcal{O}}(n)$ and the whole proof system adopted is witness indistinguishable, then our lattice-based $\mathsf{GS-VLR}$ scheme is FA and full-traceable, meanwhile, achieving the anonymity for revoked members.*

Proof. The details of our proof are exactly the same as in Hou et al.'s scheme, and it is omitted here.

Efficiency: For our lattice-based FA-GS-VLR scheme, it enjoys the same parameters (except permutation φ), matrices and vectors as in Hou et al. [11]. The Gpk has bit-size $N \cdot \widetilde{\mathcal{O}}(n^2)$, gsk has bit-size $\widetilde{\mathcal{O}}(n^2)$ and grt has bit-size $\widetilde{\mathcal{O}}(n^2)$, meanwhile, the signature σ has bit-size $N \cdot \widetilde{\mathcal{O}}(n^2)$. Thus, our construction is also with a low efficiency as [11].

A detailed comparison between our modification and previous lattice-based GS-VLR works, in terms of asymptotic efficiency, functionality and security, is given in Table 1 (security parameter is n, $N = 2^\ell = poly(n)$; |Gpk| denotes the bit-size of group public-key, |gsk| denotes the bit-size of signing secret-key, |σ| denotes the bit-size of signature; "$-$" means that the item does not exist in the corresponding scheme).

Table 1. Comparison of known lattice-based GS schemes ($N = 2^{\ell}$).

Schemes	$|Gpk|$	$|gsk|$	$|\sigma|$	Functionality	FA-security	Anonymity for revoked members
LLNW [21]	$\ell \cdot \widetilde{\mathcal{O}}(n^2)$	$\ell \cdot \widetilde{\mathcal{O}}(n)$	$\ell \cdot \widetilde{\mathcal{O}}(n)$	VLR	No	Yes
ZHGJ [22]	$\widetilde{\mathcal{O}}(n^2)$	$\widetilde{\mathcal{O}}(n)$	$\widetilde{\mathcal{O}}(n+\ell)$	VLR	No	Yes
GHZW [8]	$\widetilde{\mathcal{O}}(n^2)$	$\widetilde{\mathcal{O}}(n)$	$\widetilde{\mathcal{O}}(n+\ell)$	VLR	No	Yes
LNLW [14]	$\ell \cdot \widetilde{\mathcal{O}}(n^2)$	$\ell \cdot \widetilde{\mathcal{O}}(n)$	$\ell \cdot \widetilde{\mathcal{O}}(n)$	VLR	No	Yes
KP [18]	$\ell \cdot \widetilde{\mathcal{O}}(n^2)$	$\ell \cdot \widetilde{\mathcal{O}}(n)$	$\ell \cdot \widetilde{\mathcal{O}}(n)$	Fully dynamic	No	Yes
KP [19]	$\ell \cdot \widetilde{\mathcal{O}}(n^2)$	$\ell \cdot \widetilde{\mathcal{O}}(n)$	$\ell \cdot \widetilde{\mathcal{O}}(n)$	VLR	No	Yes
KP [20]	$\ell \cdot \widetilde{\mathcal{O}}(n^2)$	$\widetilde{\mathcal{O}}(n)$	$\ell \cdot \widetilde{\mathcal{O}}(n)$	Fully dynamic	No	Yes
HLQL [11]	$N \cdot \widetilde{\mathcal{O}}(n^2)$	$\widetilde{\mathcal{O}}(n^2)$	$N \cdot \widetilde{\mathcal{O}}(n^2)$	VLR	Yes	No
ZHZJ [23]	$\widetilde{\mathcal{O}}(n^2)$	$\widetilde{\mathcal{O}}(n)$	$-$	VLR	No	Yes
ZLHZJ [24]	$\widetilde{\mathcal{O}}(n^2)$	$\widetilde{\mathcal{O}}(n)$	$\ell \cdot \widetilde{\mathcal{O}}(n)$	VLR	No	Yes
ZLYZJ [25]	$\widetilde{\mathcal{O}}(n^2)$	$\widetilde{\mathcal{O}}(n)$	$-$	VLR	Yes	Yes
Ours	$N \cdot \widetilde{\mathcal{O}}(n^2)$	$\widetilde{\mathcal{O}}(n^2)$	$N \cdot \widetilde{\mathcal{O}}(n^2)$	VLR	Yes	Yes

6   Conclusion

In this paper, we propose a cryptanalysis of the lattice-based FA-GS-VLR scheme proposed by Hou et al. [11] at ICICS 2018, and draw a negative conclusion on their construction for the anonymity of revoked members. Then, we provided a modification of their scheme to satisfy the implicit anonymity requirement for all existing lattice-based GS-VLR constructions, but the new FA-GS-VLR scheme is also less efficient as original scheme.

Acknowledgments. The authors would like to thank the anonymous reviewers of NSS 2021 for their helpful comments and this research was supported by National Natural Science Foundation of China (Grant No. 61802075), Guangxi key Laboratory of Cryptography and Information Security (Grant No. GCIS201907) and Natural Science Foundation of Henan Province (Grant No. 202300410508).

References

1. Ajtai, M.: Generating hard instances of lattice problems (extended abstract). In: STOC, pp. 99–108. ACM (1996). https://doi.org/10.1145/237814.237838
2. Alwen, J., Peikert, C.: Generating shorter bases for hard random lattices. Theor. Comput. Sys. **48**(3), 535–553 (2011). https://doi.org/10.1007/s00224-010-9278-3
3. Bellare, M., Micciancio, D., Warinschi, B.: Foundations of group signatures: formal definitions, simplified requirements, and a construction based on general assumptions. In: Biham, E. (ed.) EUROCRYPT 2003. LNCS, vol. 2656, pp. 614–629. Springer, Heidelberg (2003). https://doi.org/10.1007/3-540-39200-9_38

4. Bichsel, P., Camenisch, J., Neven, G., Smart, N.P., Warinschi, B.: Get shorty via group signatures without encryption. In: Garay, J.A., De Prisco, R. (eds.) SCN 2010. LNCS, vol. 6280, pp. 381–398. Springer, Heidelberg (2010). https://doi.org/10.1007/978-3-642-15317-4_24
5. Boneh, D., Shacham, H.: Group signatures with verifier-local revocation. In: CCS, pp. 168–177. ACM (2004). https://doi.org/10.1145/1030083.1030106
6. Bringer, J., Patey, A.: VLR group signatures: how to achieve both backward unlinkability and efficient revocation checks. In: Pierangela, S., (eds.) SECRYPT 2012, pp. 215–220. (2012). https://doi.org/10.1007/3-540-46416-6_22
7. Chaum, D., van Heyst, E.: Group signatures. In: Davies, D.W. (ed.) EUROCRYPT 1991. LNCS, vol. 547, pp. 257–265. Springer, Heidelberg (1991). https://doi.org/10.1007/3-540-46416-6_22
8. Gao, W., Hu, Y., Zhang, Y., et al.: Lattice-based group signature with verifier-local revocation. J. Shanghai JiaoTong Univ. (Sci.) **22**(3), 313–321 (2017). https://doi.org/10.1007/s12204-017-1837-1
9. Gentry, C., Peikert, C., Vaikuntanathan, V.: Trapdoor for hard lattices and new cryptographic constructions. In: STOC, pp. 197–206. ACM (2008) https://doi.org/10.1145/1374376.1374407
10. Gordon, S.D., Katz, J., Vaikuntanathan, V.: A group signature scheme from lattice assumptions. In: Abe, M. (ed.) ASIACRYPT 2010. LNCS, vol. 6477, pp. 395–412. Springer, Heidelberg (2010). https://doi.org/10.1007/978-3-642-17373-8_23
11. Hou, L., Liu, R., Qiu, T., Lin, D.: Hierarchical group signatures with verifier-local revocation. In: Naccache, D., et al. (eds.) ICICS 2018. LNCS, vol. 11149, pp. 271–286. Springer, Cham (2018). https://doi.org/10.1007/978-3-030-01950-1_16
12. Ishida, A., Sakai, Y., Emura, K., Hanaoka, G., Tanaka, K.: Fully anonymous group signature with verifier-local revocation. In: Catalano, D., De Prisco, R. (eds.) SCN 2018. LNCS, vol. 11035, pp. 23–42. Springer, Cham (2018). https://doi.org/10.1007/978-3-319-98113-0_2
13. Libert, B., Vergnaud, D.: Group signatures with verifier-local revocation and backward unlinkability in the standard model. In: Garay, J.A., Miyaji, A., Otsuka, A. (eds.) CANS 2009. LNCS, vol. 5888, pp. 498–517. Springer, Heidelberg (2009). https://doi.org/10.1007/978-3-642-10433-6_34
14. Ling, S., Nguyen, K., Langlois, A., et al.: A lattice-based group signature scheme with verifier-local revocation. Theor. Comput. Sci. **730**, 1–20 (2018). https://doi.org/10.1016/j.tcs.2018.03.027
15. Micciancio, D., Peikert, C.: Trapdoors for lattices: simpler, tighter, faster, smaller. In: Pointcheval, D., Johansson, T. (eds.) EUROCRYPT 2012. LNCS, vol. 7237, pp. 700–718. Springer, Heidelberg (2012). https://doi.org/10.1007/978-3-642-29011-4_41
16. Nakanishi, T., Funabiki, N.: Verifier-local revocation group signature schemes with backward unlinkability from bilinear maps. In: Roy, B. (ed.) ASIACRYPT 2005. LNCS, vol. 3788, pp. 533–548. Springer, Heidelberg (2005). https://doi.org/10.1007/11593447_29
17. Nakanishi, T., Funabiki, N.: A short verifier-local revocation group signature scheme with backward unlinkability. In: Yoshiura, H., Sakurai, K., Rannenberg, K., Murayama, Y., Kawamura, S. (eds.) IWSEC 2006. LNCS, vol. 4266, pp. 17–32. Springer, Heidelberg (2006). https://doi.org/10.1007/11908739_2
18. Perera, M.N.S., Koshiba, T.: Achieving almost-full security for lattice-based fully dynamic group signatures with verifier-local revocation. In: Su, C., Kikuchi, H. (eds.) ISPEC 2018. LNCS, vol. 11125, pp. 229–247. Springer, Cham (2018). https://doi.org/10.1007/978-3-319-99807-7_14

19. Perera, M.N.S., Koshiba, T.: Achieving full security for lattice-based group signatures with verifier-local revocation. In: Naccache, D., et al. (eds.) ICICS 2018. LNCS, vol. 11149, pp. 287–302. Springer, Cham (2018). https://doi.org/10.1007/978-3-030-01950-1_17

20. Perera, M.N.S., Koshiba, T.: Achieving strong security and verifier-local revocation for dynamic group signatures from lattice assumptions. In: Katsikas, S.K., Alcaraz, C. (eds.) STM 2018. LNCS, vol. 11091, pp. 3–19. Springer, Cham (2018). https://doi.org/10.1007/978-3-030-01141-3_1

21. Langlois, A., Ling, S., Nguyen, K., Wang, H.: Lattice-based group signature scheme with verifier-local revocation. In: Krawczyk, H. (ed.) PKC 2014. LNCS, vol. 8383, pp. 345–361. Springer, Heidelberg (2014). https://doi.org/10.1007/978-3-642-54631-0_20

22. Zhang, Y., Hu, Y., Gao, W., et al.: Simpler efficient group signature scheme with verifier-local revocation from lattices. KSII Trans. Internet Inf. Syst. **10**(1), 414–430 (2016). https://doi.org/10.3837/tiis.2016.01.024

23. Zhang, Y., Hu, Y., Zhang, Q., Jia, H.: On new zero-knowledge proofs for lattice-based group signatures with verifier-local revocation. In: Lin, Z., Papamanthou, C., Polychronakis, M. (eds.) ISC 2019. LNCS, vol. 11723, pp. 190–208. Springer, Cham (2019). https://doi.org/10.1007/978-3-030-30215-3_10

24. Zhang, Y., Liu, X., Hu, Y., Zhang, Q., Jia, H.: Lattice-based group signatures with verifier-local revocation: achieving shorter key-sizes and explicit traceability with ease. In: Mu, Y., Deng, R.H., Huang, X. (eds.) CANS 2019. LNCS, vol. 11829, pp. 120–140. Springer, Cham (2019). https://doi.org/10.1007/978-3-030-31578-8_7

25. Zhang, Y., Liu, X., Yin, Y., Zhang, Q., Jia, H.: On new zero-knowledge proofs for fully anonymous lattice-based group signature scheme with verifier-local revocation. In: Zhou, J., et al. (eds.) ACNS 2020. LNCS, vol. 12418, pp. 381–399. Springer, Cham (2020). https://doi.org/10.1007/978-3-030-61638-0_21

Author Index